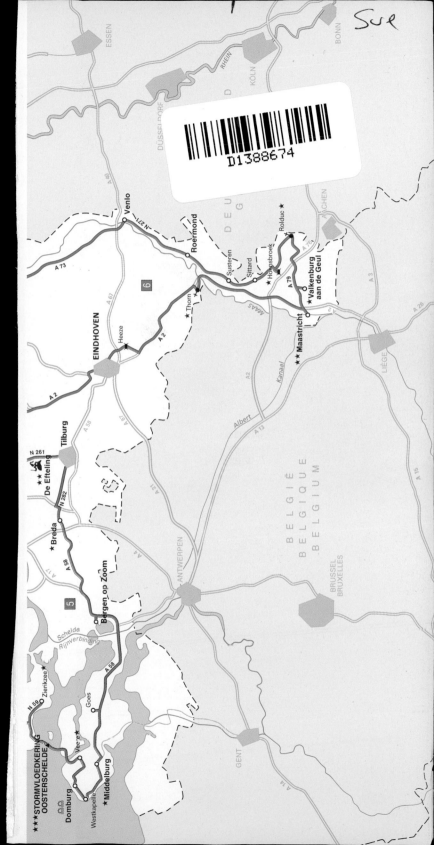

NETHERLANDS

Editorial Director   Cynthia Clayton Ochterbeck

THE GREEN GUIDE NETHERLANDS

Editor   Alison Coupe
Principal Writer   Sean Sheehan
Production Manager   Natasha G. George
Cartography   Alain Baldet, Michèle Cana, Peter Wrenn
Photo Editor   Yoshimi Kanazawa
Proofreader   Jonathan P. Gilbert, Rachel Mills
Layout & Design   Natasha George, John Higginbottom
Cover Design   Ute Weber, Laurent Muller

Contact Us: The Green Guide
                             Michelin Maps and Guides
                             One Parkway South
                             Greenville, SC 29615
                             USA
                             www.michelintravel.com
                             michelin.guides@us.michelin.com

                             Michelin Maps and Guides
                             Hannay House
                             39 Clarendon Road
                             Watford, Herts WD17 1JA
                             UK
                             ☎(01923) 205 240
                             www.ViaMichelin.com
                             travelpubsales@uk.michelin.com

Special Sales: For information regarding bulk sales,
                             customized editions and premium sales,
                             please contact our Customer Service
                             Departments:
                             USA   1-800-432-6277
                             UK   (01923) 205 240
                             Canada 1-800-361-8236

One Team...
A Commitment to Quality

There's just one reason our team is dedicated to producing quality travel publications—you, our reader.

Throughout our guides we offer **practical information**, **touring tips** and **suggestions** for finding the best places for a break.

Michelin driving tours help you hit the highlights and quickly absorb the best of the region. Our descriptive **walking tours** make you your own guide, armed with directions, maps and expert information.

We scout out the attractions, classify them with **star ratings**, and describe in detail what you will find when you visit them.

Michelin maps featured throughout the guide offer vibrant, detailed and easy-to-follow outlines of everything from close-up museum plans to international maps.

Places to stay and eat are always a big part of travel, so we research **hotels and restaurants** that we think convey the essence of the destination and arrange them by geographic area and price. We walk you through the best shopping districts and point you towards the host of entertainment and recreation possibilities available.

We **test**, **retest**, **check and recheck** to make sure that our guidebooks are truly just that: a personalized guide to help you make the most of your visit. And if you still want a speaking guide, we list local tour guides who will lead you on all the boat, bus, guided, historical, culinary, and other tours you shouldn't miss.

In short, we remove the guesswork involved with travel. After all, we want you to enjoy exploring with Michelin as much as we do.

The Michelin Green Guide Team

PLANNING YOUR TRIP

INTRODUCTION TO THE NETHERLANDS

Mattes/ MICHELIN

CONTENTS

DISCOVERING THE NETHERLANDS

HOW TO USE THIS GUIDE

PLANNING YOUR TRIP

The blue-tabbed PLANNING YOUR TRIP section at the front of the guide gives you **ideas for your trip** and **practical information** to help you organize it. You'll find tours, a host of breaks in the great outdoors, a calendar of events, information on shopping, sightseeing, kids' activities and more.

INTRODUCTION

The orange-tabbed INTRODUCTION section explores **Nature** and the Sea. The **History** section spans early human settlement in the Netherlands through today. The **Art and Culture** section covers architecture, art, literature, language, traditions and folklore, while

Sidebars

Throughout the guide you will find peach-colored text boxes (like this one), with lively anecdotes, detailed history and background information.

the **Country Today** delves into modern Netherlands.

DISCOVERING

The green-tabbed DISCOVERING section is an **A–Z** of the Netherlands' Principal Sights worth a visit, featuring the most interesting local **Sights**, **Walking Tours**, nearby **Excursions**, and detailed **DrivingTours**.

Contact information, admission charges, hours of operation, and a host of other **visitor information** is given wherever possible. Admission prices shown are normally for a single adult.

STAR RATINGS★★★

Michelin has given star ratings for more than 100 years. If you're pressed for time, we recommend you visit the ★★★, or ★★ sights first:

★★★   Highly recommended
★★   Recommended
★   Interesting

Address Books - Where to Stay, Eat and more...

WHERE TO STAY

We've made a selection of hotels and arranged them within the cities by price category to fit all budgets (see the Legend on the cover flap for an explanation of the price categories). For the most part, we've selected accommodations based on their unique regional quality, their regional feel, as it were. So, unless the individual hotel embodies local ambience, it's rare that we include chain properties, which typically have their own imprint. If you want a more comprehensive selection of accommodations, see the **red-cover Michelin Guide** Benelux.

WHERE TO EAT

We thought you'd like to know the popular eating spots in the Netherlands. So, we selected restaurants that capture the regional experience—those that have a unique regional flavor. We're not rating the quality of the food per se; as we did with the hotels, we selected restaurants for many towns and villages, categorized by price to appeal to all wallets (see the Legend on the cover flap for an explanation of the price categories). If you want a more comprehensive selection of dining recommendations, see the **red-cover** Michelin Guide Benelux.

MAPS

- Regional **Driving Tours** map on the cover flap with color-coded routes.
- Netherlands map with the **Principal Sights** highlighted.
- Maps for major **cities** and **villages**.
- **Local tour** maps.

All maps in this guide are oriented north, unless otherwise indicated by a directional arrow. The term "Local Map" refers to a map within the chapter or Tourism Region. A complete list of the maps

found in the guide appears at the back of this book, as well as a comprehensive index and list of restaurants and accommodations.
See the map Legend at the back of the guide for an explanation of map symbols.

> ### A Bit of Advice
> Green advice boxes found in this guide contain practical tips and handy information relevant to the sight in the Discovering section.

ORIENT PANELS

Vital statistics are given for each principal sight in the DISCOVERING section:

- **Information**: Tourist Office/Sight contact details.
- ▶ **Orient Yourself:** Geographic location of the sight with reference to surrounding boroughs, towns, and roads.
- **Parking:** Where to park.
- **Don't Miss:** Unmissable things to do.
- **Organizing Your Time:** Tips on organizing your stay; what to see first, how long to spend, crowd avoidance, market days and more.
- **Especially for Kids:** Sights of particular interest to children.
- **Also See:** Nearby PRINCIPAL SIGHTS featured elsewhere in the guide.

SYMBOLS

Spa **Spa Facilities**	**Tours**
Kids **Interesting for Children**	**On-site Parking**
Also See	▶ **Directions**
Tourist Information	**On-site eating Facilities**
Hours of Operation	**Swimming Pool**
Periods of Closure	**Camping Facilities**
Closed to the Public	**Beaches**
Entry Fees	**Breakfast Included**
Credit Cards not Accepted	**A Bit of Advice**
Wheelchair Accessible	**Warning**

Contact - Addresses, phone numbers, opening hours and prices published in this guide are accurate at the time of press. We welcome corrections and suggestions that may assist us in preparing the next edition. Please send your comments to:

UK
Michelin Maps and Guides
Hannay House
39 Clarendon Road
Watford, Herts WD17 1JA
travelpubsales@uk.michelin.com
www.michelin.co.uk

USA
Michelin Maps and Guides
Editorial Department
P.O. Box 19001
Greenville, SC 29602-9001
michelin.guides@us.michelin.com
www.michelintravel.com

Festival of flags on Terschelling Island
Bludzin/ MICHELIN

MICHELIN DRIVING TOURS

Regional Drives

Use the Driving Tours Map on the cover flap to plan a sightseeing trip to:

- **The IJsselmeer**
  (350km/217.4mi – 5 days)
- **The Grand North**
  (300km/186.4mi – 3 days)
- **Gelderland**
  (200km/124mi – 4 days)
- **The great towns**
  (200km/124mi – 8 days, incl. 2 days in Amsterdam)
- **The river and Delta region**
  (400km/248.5mi in 5 days)
- **The Meuse region**
  (350km/217.4mi – 5 days, incl. 1 day in Maastricht)

Local Drives

Use the A–Z Discovering section and the Driving Tours Map to explore The Netherlands' hidden routes in:

- **BREDA:** From Hoeven to Wilemstad; From Raamsdonksveer to Biesbosch
- **ENSCHEDE:** The Verdant Region of Twente
- **GOUDA:** The Reeuwijkse Plassen and Woerden; From Oudewater to Schoonhoven
- **HILVERSUM:** The Gooi
- **HUNEBED TRAIL:** From Emmen to Noordlaren
- **KEUKENHOF AND BULB FIELDS**
- **LEEUWARDEN:** Terp Region
- **ROTTERDAM:** To Europoort and Maasvlakte
- **SNEEK:** Friese Meren
- **UTRECHT:** Loosdrechtse Plassen

WHEN AND WHERE TO GO

When to Go

The Netherlands is a land for all seasons, and although the country is uniformly flat it is never dull, as there is a constantly changing play of light between sea and sky.

Spring – Without doubt the outstanding attractions are the bulb fields: a kaleidoscope of dazzling colours in season (*from mid-April to end of May*). The main bulb-growing areas are between Haarlem and Leiden and in the vicinity of Alkmaar. In spring the foliage of the countryside is fresh green and the trees along the canalside add a splash of colour to townscapes.
The Betuwe region is a delight when the cherry orchards are in blossom (*mid-April to end of May*) and the bright yellow of the fields of oil seed rape makes a vivid picture in the provinces of Friesland, Groningen, Overijssel and Flevoland (*mid-May to early June*).

Summer – The great stretches of sandy beach along the North Sea coast are popular with holiday-makers and locals alike. Here, as in other popular resorts and holiday areas, (Drenthe and Southern Limburg) it is always wise to book in advance as accommodation is scarce during the summer season.
The many lakes, reservoirs, canals and waterways make the country ideal for sailing and for other water sports. Throughout spring and summer flowers are everywhere: towns and villages are bright with well-tended public gardens and parks, and cheerful flower boxes and window displays enhance even the plainest façades.

Autumn – By late August and early September the dunes and heathlands are bright with the purple of heather in bloom. The forests, like those of the Veluwe, start to sport their autumnal hues.

Winter – The winter landscapes have a charm of their own, as captured by past generations of Dutch artists, and even the towns take on an uncanny stillness as they lie muffled under their first mantle of snow. In the Netherlands, frozen lakes and canals are an irresistible invitation to skate and children are not the only ones to take it up.

Weather

The Netherlands has a long coastline off the North Sea, low-lying lands near or below sea level and a network of canals and rivers, meaning its climate varies little from one area of the country to another. The coastal regions tend to have the mildest climate throughout the whole year plus the lowest rainfall, but can be extremely windy, while inland temperatures on average are higher, especially in summer. The average number of sunshine hours for the country is eight in summer, and around two in winter. The weather is changeable, so it is always best to be prepared for rain. Summer showers can be exceptionally heavy, although they may only last a short time, while in winter they may be prolonged.
Winters can be harsh with weeks of freezing conditions across the country and frequent strong gales in the coastal areas. Rivers and canals often freeze over, and local residents and visitors can be seen enjoying the traditional Netherlands winter sport of ice-skating.

Ideas for your Visit

The Netherlands has plenty to offer visitors, from city breaks and tulip-appreciation to high culture and long-distance cycling routes. The official website of the country's tourist board is a good place to begin (*www.holland.com*) because it will give you some idea of the range of possibilities. As with any trip, it pays to have some idea of what you want to see and do before you go.

BICYCLE TOURS

The Netherlands, where there are roughly the same number of bikes as people (around 16 million) and where the flat land makes for a minimum of steep climbs, is as bicycle-friendly a country as anyone could wish for. With some 17 000km/10 563mi of cycle paths the visitor is spoilt for choice, and with bicycles readily available for hire everywhere, it is not difficult to organise a day-trip or a longer excursion on two wheels. Tourist offices (see Tourist Offices) sell maps that show both bike paths and suggestions for longer routes relevant to their area.

Some lovely routes follow the rivers in the **Gelderland** region and there is a very manageable 35km/22mi signposted route starting in **Zaltbommel**. A longer route that stays close to water begins in **Tiel**, and in both these towns bicycles can be hired at the railway station. If you like the idea of staying close to the sea, consider the Wadden Sea route; it passes all the harbours that service the **Wadden Islands** and bicycles can be taken to the islands.
In the south of the country there is a signposted **Windmill Route** for cyclists that starts near Kinderdijk. Cities also have bicycle routes and the tourist offices in Amsterdam, The Hague and Rotterdam sell good maps detailing the routes.
The **Stichting Landelijk Fietsplatform** has waymarked over 6000km/3730mi of national cycle routes (**LF-routes**). These routes follow cycle paths or quieter local roads and are marked with rectangular signs with green lettering. The association publishes two main guides – one for the northern and central part of the

country and the other for central and southern Netherlands and northern Flanders – and the **Fietsideeënkaart**, which lists all the recreational cycling facilities in the Netherlands. For information contact S**tichting Landelijk Fietsplatform**, *Postbus 846, 3800 AV Amersfoort.* ☎ *(033) 465 36 56. Fax (033) 465 43 77. www.fietsplatform.nl.* Tourist offices also provide information on local cycle routes. Mountain bike enthusiasts can explore the special network of ATB-routes.

For more information on cycling in the Netherlands, 👁*see WHAT TO SEE AND DO.*

CULTURAL TOURS

A cultural tour could be planned around visits to the more important art galleries, such as the **Dutch Paintings** in the **Rijksmuseum**★★★ in **Amsterdam**, in order to view the works of, to name only some of the more famous **Dutch artists**, Van Gogh, Vermeer, Hieronymus Bosch, Frans Hals, Jan Steen and Piet Mondriaan. Such a themed tour could also take in the special exhibitions mounted by the major galleries. With half a dozen **World Heritage Sites** (👁*see World Heritage List*) and a rich miscellany of grand castles and palaces it would also be possible to plan a history-orientated tour. Alternatively, or as well as, the emphasis could be on the wonderful gardens that are to be found dotted around the country. Such a tour would be incomplete without including the baroque gardens at **Het Loo Palace**★★★ near **Apeldoorn** in Gelderland and the 5ha/12.3 acres of neo-Renaissance parkland at **Kasteel-Museum Sypesteyn** in Westbroek (👁*see UTRECHT Driving Tour*).

CITY BREAKS

The cities offer ideal short breaks, not least because of the ease of transport facilities.

Amsterdam

The centre of Amsterdam is only a short train journey away from Schiphol, the country's international airport, and in less than an hour after collecting luggage off the carousel you can have it safely unpacked in a hotel room and be on the streets of Europe's most bohemian city. Progressive, libertarian and unconventional in many respects, Amsterdam is also home to some of Europe's most famous and traditional attractions. The **Rijksmuseum**★★★ and the **Van Gogh Museum**★★★ have world-class collections of art, while smaller museums like **Rembrandthuis**★ and the **Anne Frank Huis**★★ have distinctive claims on the visitor's attention, though for very different reasons. **The Hague**★★ (👁*see DEN HAAG*) is only a short journey away by train from Amsterdam and it offers a dramatic contrast. Home to Queen Beatrix and the government, the capital is the second-largest city in the Netherlands and boasts two seaside resorts, **Scheveningen** and **Kijkduin**, only a bus ride away. In the city's major art gallery, the **Mauritshuis**★★★, hangs Vermeer's *The Girl with the Pearl Earring* and Rembrandt's *The Anatomy Lesson of Dr. Tulip*. Like Amsterdam, The Hague has a terrific range of restaurants and places to drink. (👁*see AMSTERDAM*).

Rotterdam

The attraction of Rotterdam for many visitors is its architecture. A distinct area of the city centre offers a concise introduction to the history of modern architecture. Noted buildings from the era before World War II include the **Van Nelle Factory** and the **Huis Sonneveld**, while the innovative period that came after 1945 finds expression in **Groot Handelsgebouw**, the **Kunsthal** and the **Erasmusbrug** (Erasmus Bridge). (👁*see ROTTERDAM*).

REGIONAL TOURS

The appealing landscape of windmills, dykes, flowers and green pastures that feature in old Dutch paintings can still be experienced in **noord** (north) **Holland**. The coastal region has broad, clean beaches and a relaxing atmposhere as well as the popular family seaside resort of Callantsoog (*www.callantstoog.com*). There are fishing ports like **Volendam**★, Muiden and **Medemblik** and the towns of **Hoorn** and **Enkhuizen** are redolent with the history of the Dutch East India Company (VOC) that made the country so wealthy in the 17C.

In the north of the country, the small island of **Texel**★★ offers a retreat from urban blues with its sandy beaches, nature reserves, forests and pretty villages. The island also produces a fine cheese (☙ *see NOORD-HOLLAND*).

Lower Rhine Region

The scenically attractive Lower Rhine region, where Germany and the Netherlands meet, suggests itself as a destination for a short break that is not city based. There is a dedicated website providing details of more than 30 hotels/castles in eight different cities at *www.lower-rhine.com*. The Lower Rhine landscape features forests and heathlands, secluded fens, unique river dunes and a number of nature reserves. Perfect for cyclists, the region is also suitable for hiking or horse riding as well as sailing. (☙ *see DELTA*).

Arnhem

The city of Arnhem is a good base for exploring the **east of the Netherlands** rather than a city break in its own right, notwithstanding the fact that Arnhem's city centre has its fair share of monuments, churches and squares to visit. The **Kröllller-Müller Museum**★★★, with its own Van Gogh collection, is located within the **Hoge Veluwe National Park**★★★ and is only a short drive from Arnhem. So, too, is **Burgers' Zoo**★★ and its tropical rainforest, jungle, desert and safari park sections. Arnhem was the scene of a terrible battle in World War II and the **Airborne Museum** in Oosterbeek is devoted to the event. A very different kind of museum in the region is

the open-air Afrika Museum with its authentic collection of Arfrican art. (*Berg en Dal. www.afrikamuseum.nl*).

Outdoor Activities

Opportunities in the Arnhem region come in the form of the **Veluwezoom and Hoge Veluwe national parks**. There are cycle and footpaths and for bird watchers the dunes and forests have their own rewards.

Around Leiden

The **Holland Rijnland** region, with the historical city of Leiden making a convenient base, features flowerfields, beaches and dunes and a number of quaint Dutch villages. The seaside resorts of **Noordwijk** and **Katwijk** have long sandy beaches and Noordwijk is located in the heart of the Dutch bulb-growing area. Leiden, the birthplace of Rembrandt, has a rich cultural history and a day could easily be spent taking in its sights. To stay in the region, Noordwijk, Katwijk and Leiden have a variety of accommodations, from plush hotels to self-catering bungalows. For more information about the region, its events and attractions see *www.hollandrijnland.nl* (☙ *see LEIDEN*).

Coastline

The unique **coastline** of the Netherlands is made up of the West Frisian Islands, the coast of north and south Holland and Zeeland. **Oostvoorne** has the only beach in the Netherlands where cars and motorcycles are permitted onto the sand. The **Duinen van Voorne** nature reserve here is a favourite with nature lovers.

The Dutch have a special – and not always harmonious – relationship with water and the flood barrier near **Hoek van Holland**, the only one of its kind in the world, is twice as large as the Eiffel Tower and four times as heavy. The country does not rely only on giant engineering projects to control the water; the dunes, a natural barrier between land and sea, have been turned into nature reserves in order to preserve the vital role they play in protecting the country and visitors.

KNOW BEFORE YOU GO

Useful Websites

www.holland.com
The official website of the
Netherlands Board of Tourism.
www.government.nl
The official website of the
Netherlands government.

The following websites are packed
with information about the major
cities or locations in the Netherlands:

◆ www.zuid-holland.com
◆ www.visitamsterdam.nl
◆ www. vvvdenhaag.nl
◆ www.vvvmaastricht.nl
◆ www.vvv.rotterdam.nl
◆ www.12utrecht.nl

Tourist Organisations

DUTCH NATIONAL
TOURIST OFFICES

UK & Ireland
Netherlands Board of Tourism.
*18 Buckingham Gate, London SW1
(postal address: PO Box 523, London
SW1E 6NT).* ☎*0891 871 7777 (calls
charged at premium rate) or (020)
7828 7900. Fax (020) 7828 7941.
www.holland.com/uk*

USA
Netherlands Board of Tourism.
*355 Lexington Avenue, 19th Floor,
New York, NY 10017*
☎*212-370-7360
Fax 212-370-9507
www.holland.com*

Canada
Netherlands Board of Tourism.
*25 Adelaide Street East, Suite 710,
Toronto, Ontario M5C 1Y2*
☎*416-363-1577
Fax 416-363-1470
www.holland.com*

Amsterdam
Netherlands Board of Tourism
(NBT). *Postbus 458, 2266 MG
Leidschendam*
☎*(070) 370 57 05
Fax (070) 320 1654
www.holland.com/nl*

DUTCH REGIONAL
TOURIST OFFICES

ANWB – The **ANWB** (Algemene
Nederlandsche Wielrijders Bond), the
Royal Dutch Touring Club, has offices
throughout the country. (*ANWB, Was-
senaarseweg 220, 2596 EC Den Haag.*
☎*0800 0503. www.anwb.nl (in Dutch*).

Tourist Information Centres – In the
Netherlands the **tourist information centres** are indicated by **VVV**,
three blue Vs on a white triangle. In
this guide, they are indicated by the
symbol 🄸.
These offices supply information on
a wide range of subjects, including
hotels, restaurants, campsites, rented
accommodation, youth hostels, local
events, cycling, sailing, sightseeing,
opening hours and entertainment.
They also sell tourist, cycling and
walking maps and provide currency exchange facilities as well as a
nationwide hotel reservation service.
The addresses and phone numbers
of the VVV offices in the main towns
are given in the *Discovering* section of
this guide (many are also listed in the
red-cover *Michelin Guide Benelux*) and
they are located on all town plans by
the symbol 🄸.
Most VVVs are open Monday–Friday,
9am–5pm and Saturday, 10am–noon.
In summer, the offices in major towns
are usually open for a few hours on
Sundays. Information can also be
obtained from the Netherlands Board
of Tourism website: *www.holland.com.*

International Visitors

EMBASSIES AND CONSULATES ABROAD

Australia

Consulate General of the Netherlands. *Level 23, Tower 2, Westfield Bondi Junction, 101 Grafton Street, Sydney*
☎*02 9387 6644*
Fax 02 9387 3962
www.netherlands.org.au

Ireland

Royal Netherlands Embassy, *160 Merrion Road, Dublin 4, Ireland*
☎*01 269 3444*
Fax 01 283 9690
www.netherlandsembassy.ie

New Zealand

Royal Netherlands Embassy. *PO Box 840, Cnr. Ballance & Featherston Street, Wellington*
☎*04 471 6390*
Fax 04 471 2923
www.netherlandsembassy.co.nz

UK

Royal Netherlands Embassy. *38 Hyde Park Gate, London SW7 5DP,* ☎ *(020) 7590 3200*
Fax (*020*) *7225 0947*
www.netherlands-embassy.org.uk

USA

Royal Netherlands Embassy. *4200 Linnean Avenue NW, Washington, DC 20008*
☎*202-244-5300*
Fax 202-362-3430
www.netherlands-embassy.org

EMBASSIES AND CONSULATES IN THE NETHERLANDS

Australia

Carnegielaan 4, 2517 KH Den Haag
☎ *(070) 310 8200.*
Fax (070) 310 7863.
www.netherlands.embassy.gov.au.

Canada

Sophialaan 7, 2514 JP Den Haag (*visitor address*) *or Postbus 30820,*
2500 GV Den Haag (postal address)
☎*070-311-1600*
Fax 070-311-1620
www.canada.nl

Ireland

Dr. Kuyperstraat 9, 2514 BA Den Haag
☎*(070) 363 0993*
Fax (070) 361 7604
www.irishembassy.nl

New Zealand

Carnegielaan 10, 2517 KH Den Haag
☎ *(070) 346 9324*
Fax (070) 363 2983

UK

Lange Voorhout 10, 2514 ED Den Haag
☎ *(070) 427 0427*
www.britishembassy.gov.uk

USA

Lange Voorhout 102, 2514 EJ Den Haag
☎*070-310-2209*
Fax 070-361-4688
http://netherlands.usembassy.gov

Entry Requirements

Although the Netherlands signed the Schengen Agreement ending internal border controls between member countries, which came into effect in 1995, travellers should nonetheless be equipped with proof of identity. This may take the form of a **European Identity Card** (for nationals of EU member states) or a **passport**. Holders of British, Irish and US passports require no visa to enter the Netherlands, although visas may be necessary for visitors from some Commonwealth countries and for those planning to stay for longer than three months. Visitors are advised to check visa requirements with their travel agent or with their local Dutch embassy or consulate. US citizens should obtain the booklet *Your Trip Abroad*, which provides useful information on visa requirements, customs regulations, medical care, etc. Apply to the Superintendent of Documents, Government Printing Office (*Washington, DC – 20402;* ☎ *(202) 512 1800; http://travel.state.gov*) or contact the American Consulate at *Museumplein 19, 1071 DJ Amsterdam;* ☎*020-794-0808*

Customs Regulations

Visitors from EU countries can import, tax-free, the following: 110l beer; 90l wine; 20l fortified winel 10l spirits; 800 cigarettes/400 cigars; 1kg tobacco. Visitors from non-EU countries can import, tax-free, the following: 200 cigarettes/250g tobacco/50 cigars; 1l spirits; 2l fortified or sparkling wine; 50g perfume/0.25l eau de toilette; 500g coffee; 100g tea. All other goods are exempt from tax up to 175€ per person. Anything above that will be taxed. See for more information about imports and exports.

Health

British citizens should apply for a **European Health Insurance Card** (**EHIC**) – the former E111 form is invalid – which is issued by the Department of Health. It entitles the holder to free or reduced-cost medical care for accidents or unexpected illnesses while on holiday in EU countries. This card should be presented to the relevant medical services prior to receiving treatment. For further information in the UK, contact the Department of Health: ☎ *(020) 7210 4850; www.dh.gov.uk*. Visitors are strongly advised to take out additional travel insurance to cover against any expenses not covered by the European Health Insurance Card (EHIC), as well as lost luggage, theft, cancellation, delayed departure, etc.
Non-EU travellers are advised to check with their insurance companies about taking out supplementary medical insurance with specific overseas coverage. US travellers may want to check out **Access America**: ☎*1-800 284-8300; www.accessamerica.com* or

Travel Guard International ☎*1-800 826 4919, www.travelguard.com*. Regardless of nationality, it pays to check the small print of any travel insurance policy so that you know exactly what is covered. Ensure that the necessary contact information for your policy is kept separate from your luggage.

Pets (**cats and dogs**) – A general health certificate and proof of rabies vaccination should be obtained from your local vet before departure.

Accessibility

Most public buildings, museums, galleries and theatres in the Netherlands provide facilities for disabled travellers. In this guide, the sights accessible to wheelchair users are indicated by the symbol ♿ in the Admissions Times and Charges of the *Discovering* section. Further information is available from **Nederlands Instituut voor Zorg en Welzijn** (*Catharijnesingel 47, 3511 GC Utrecht;* ☎ *(030) 230 6552; www.nizw.nl*), and the information department for disabled travellers of the **ANWB** ☎ *(070) 314 14 20*. The ANWB publishes a brochure entitled *Reiswijzer voor gehandicapten* (Travel Guide for the Disabled) which provides useful information on tourism, leisure activities and sports facilities suitable for disabled travellers. The brochure is aimed at Dutch tourists with a disability but is also useful for international visitors.
The Netherlands Railways offer a comprehensive service for the disabled traveller which includes a free escort service. The train timetables are available in braille.
For general information regarding travel for the disabled, useful information is available at *www.disabled travelersguide.com*.
In Amsterdam there is a special taxi service for disabled travellers: ☎ *(020) 696 96 40, 6910518, 6157188, 5840100, 6634811*; taxis need to be booked in advance.

GETTING THERE AND GETTING AROUND

By Plane

Various airline companies operate regular services to the international airports in the Netherlands (Amsterdam-Schiphol, Rotterdam, Eindhoven and Maastricht). These include:

KLM: ☎*0870 507 4074.*
www.klm.com; flights from London and from regional airports around the UK to Amsterdam.

British Airways: *Waterside, PO Box 365, Harmondsworth, Middlesex UB7 0GB, England*
☎*0870 850 9850*
www.britishairways.com;
flights from London airports to Amsterdam.
Reservations within the US and Canada: ☎*1-800-AIRWAYS.*

easyJet: ☎*0871 244 2366*
www.easyjet.com; flights from London Luton, Belfast, Edinburgh and Liverpool to Amsterdam.

INLAND FLIGHTS

The main airports in the Netherlands are:
- Amsterdam-Schiphol
- Rotterdam
- Eindhoven
- Maastricht

For information on internal flights, contact KLM: ☎*0870 507 4074*
www.klm.com.

By Ship

There are numerous cross-Channel services from the United Kingdom and Ireland to the Netherlands, though it may be preferable to sail to France or Belgium and then drive to the Netherlands. For details, apply to travel agencies or to:

Brittany Ferries: ☎*0870 9 076 103*
www.brittany-ferries.co.uk; sailings from the UK and Ireland to various ports in France.
Plymouth–Roscoff; Poole–Cherbourg; Portsmouth–St Malo; Portsmouth–Caen; Cork–Roscoff.

Seafrance: ☎*0871 663 2546*
www.seafrance.com
Dover–Calais

P&O Ferries: ☎*08716 645 645*
www.poferries.com
Dover–Calais, Hull–Rotterdam, Hull–Calais

DFDS Seaways: ☎*0871 522 9955*
www.dfdsseaways.co.uk
Newcastle–IJmuiden (Amsterdam)

Stena Line UK: ☎*0870 570 7070*
www.stenaline.com
Harwich–Hoek van Holland

Ferries run from the Dutch mainland to the Wadden Islands, with services from Holwerd to Ameland, Lauwersoog to Schiermonnikoog, Harlingen to Vlieland and Terschelling and Den Helder to Texel.
Further information on these services is available from the Netherlands Board of Tourism at *www.holland.com.*

By Train

Eurostar runs direct high-speed passenger trains from London to Paris and London to Brussels. The service takes only 2hrs 15min to travel from London St Pancras to Paris Nord and less than 2hrs from London St Pancras to Bruxelles Midi. ☎*0870 518 6186;*
www.eurostar.com.
From Brussels it is possible to take one of the frequent InterCity trains to

The Channel Tunnel

This tunnel under the sea is the realisation of dreams of linking Britain to mainland Europe which date back over 200 years. The Channel link consists of two single-track rail tunnels (7.6m/24ft in diameter) for passenger and freight transport, and one service tunnel (4.8m/15ft in diameter) for safety and ventilation. The tunnels are 50.5km/31mi long; 37km/23mi of which are under the Channel. Most of the tunnel is 40m/131ft beneath the seabed, in a layer of blue chalk. The trains (800m/2 624ft long) have two levels for passenger cars (capacity 118 cars per shuttle) and one level for coaches and caravans. Special services operate for heavy goods vehicles. British, French and Belgian trains, including French TGVs, also use the tunnel. Journey time through the tunnel is ideally 35min, 28min of which are in the tunnel at a maximum speed of 130kph/80mph.

Amsterdam. In the UK, **Rail Europe** will make bookings for train journeys between Brussels and the Netherlands. They can be contacted at *179 Piccadilly, London W1; ☎0844 848 4064; www.raileurope.co.uk*.

Eurotunnel runs passenger and freight services which link Folkestone to Calais in just 35min. *☎0870 535 3535; www.eurotunnel.com*.

INLAND TICKETS AND FARES

The Dutch railway system is run by the Netherlands Railways (NS). Further information and reservations are available from NS, *Postbus 2025, 3500HA, Utrecht, ☎0900 202 11 63, www.ns.nl*. Within the Netherlands, information about times, fares (day tickets, weekly tickets and season tickets), taking a bike onto the train, special offers, etc. can be obtained by phoning the public transport information office ☎*0900 9292* or by consulting the public transport information website at *www.ov9292. nl* (in Dutch).
The Netherlands has an extensive and efficient railway network. There is an InterCity network of express trains linking major cities. It is not possible to reserve seats on national train services. There are two classes (first and second). A day return is cheaper than two singles. There are numerous organised day trips and group tickets (multi, family and teenager) at reduced rates. Train tickets cannot be purchased on board.

If you arrive in a city or town by train, you can use the cheap **Train Taxi** service to travel into the centre. These are operated in 111 towns and cities, and charge a set fare regardless of the distance travelled. The taxi driver will wait (normally not for more than 10min) until he has enough passengers before setting off. Further information is available at railway stations or call ☎*0900 873 46 82*.

By Coach

Eurolines operates coach services to Amsterdam, Arnhem, Breda, Eindhoven, The Hague, Nijmegen, Rotterdam and Utrecht. For details and reservations, contact Eurolines UK, *4 Cardiff Road, Luton, Bedfordshire, England, LU1 1PP; ☎08717 818181; www.nationalexpress.com/eurolines*.

By Bus, Tram or Metro

TICKETS

A strip card (*strippenkaart*), valid for buses, trams and metros throughout the Netherlands, can be bought from post offices, railway stations and from shops displaying the strippenkaart logo. It is cheaper than buying a single ticket each time you travel by bus, tram or metro. You should either feed it into a punching machine on board the vehicle, or get the driver to stamp it, cancelling one strip per journey and one strip per zone travelled. Once stamped the strip is valid for one hour, during which you can change vehicles without having to get it restamped. City centres are one zone, and the surrounding zones are shown on maps at bus, tram and metro stops. Information on times, routes and fares is available on ☎0900 9292 or (in Dutch) at *www.9292ov.nl*.

By Car

DRIVING IN THE NETHERLANDS

When driving to the continent the ideal ports of entry for the Netherlands are Vlissingen, Rotterdam and Hoek van Holland. Depending on the point of departure it may be more convenient to land at Hamburg (seasonal service from Harwich), Zeebrugge (from Felixstowe and Kingston-upon-Hull), Ostend or Calais (both from Dover) and then drive on to the Netherlands.
To choose the most suitable route between one of the above ports and your destination, use the *Michelin Road Atlas of Europe*, or consult the Michelin route-planning service on the internet (*www.viamichelin.com*).

CAR RENTAL

Cars can be rented in most major towns and resorts. The minimum age limit is 21 although some companies maintain a minimum age of 23 and possession of a valid licence for a minimum of one year. A current driving licence is required. It is cheaper to reserve in advance rather than to pay on the spot. All the major companies (Avis, Hertz, and Europcar) are to be found in the main Dutch cities as well as local companies. The telephone numbers below are for the rental offices based at Schiphol airport in Amsterdam:
Avis ☎ *(020) 655 6050*
   www.avis.com
Europcar ☎ *(020) 316 4190*
   www.europcar.com
Hertz ☎ *(020) 502 0240*
   www.hertz.com

DOCUMENTS

Nationals of the European Union require a valid **national driving licence**. Nationals of non-EU countries should obtain an **international driving licence**, available in the US from the American Automobile Association (*www.aaa.com*) for a $10 charge. The AAA can be contacted at *AAA National Headquarters, 1000 AAA Drive, Heathrow, FL 32746-5080;* ☎*407-444-7000*. Other documents required include the vehicle's current **log book** and a **green card** for insurance. Those motorists entering the Netherlands in their own vehicles should ensure that their **insurance** policy includes overseas cover. Visitors are advised to check with their respective insurance companies prior to travel. Motorists are also advised to take out adequate accident and **breakdown cover** for their period of travel overseas. Various motoring organisations (⚓*see Breakdown service*) will be able to provide further details on options available. Bail bonds are no longer necessary, although travellers may wish to take this precaution (consult your insurance company). Members of the American Automobile Association should obtain the free brochure, *Offices to Serve You Abroad,* which gives details of affiliated organisations in the Netherlands.

ROAD REGULATIONS

Traffic in the Netherlands travels **on the right**. The minimum age for driving is 18 for cars and motorcycles and 16 for mopeds. Children under 12 are not allowed to travel in the front seat as long as there is room for them in the back. Seatbelts are compulsory in the back as well as the front of the car. Maximum **speed limits** for cars, caravans and small trailers are 50kph/30mph in built-up areas, 80kph/50mph on the open road, and 120kph/75mph on motorways (minimum speed on motorways is 70kph/45mph). Motorways (*autosnelweg*) are toll-free and all motorway junctions are numbered (see the Michelin map series). There are, however, tolls for certain bridges and tunnels (Kiltunnel and Prins Willem Alexander Brug). Priority must be given to cars coming from the right at junctions and on roundabouts, unless shown otherwise. Give way also to trams, pedestrians boarding or alighting from trams, and pedestrians crossing the road into which you are just turning. Only pass trams on the right unless there is insufficient room. Trams generally have priority. Cyclists will pass on the right and have priority over motorists when the latter want to turn off the road.

The regulation **red warning triangle** must be carried, and displayed in the event of a breakdown.

BREAKDOWN SERVICE

The main organisation is the ANWB (Algemene Nederlandsche Wielrij-ders Bond), the Royal Dutch Touring Club, which operates road patrols (Wegenwacht) on main roads. If no patrol happens to pass then phone for assistance from one of the roadside telephones to the nearest ANWB office (*alarmcentrale*) ☎*0800 08 88*. This breakdown service operates 24hrs a day. The receptionist usually speaks several foreign languages. Foreign visitors who are not in the posses-sion of a valid membership card of a club affiliated with the AIT (Alliance International du Tourisme) must pay the cost of membership. Members of the Automobile Association (AA) with a valid International Circular Letter of Credit (IRK) obtain free assistance. ANWB, *PO Box 93200, 2509 BA The Hague.* ☎*0800 0503. www.anwb.nl.*

SIGNPOSTING

In the Netherlands the names of certain European towns are often signposted in Dutch:
Belgium: Luik for Liège;
France: Parijs for Paris, Rijsel for Lille;
Germany: Aken for Aachen.

ACCIDENTS

In the event of an accident the emer-gency number for ambulance and police is ☎*112*. Emergency telephones are to be found alongside the main roads.

ROUTE PLANNING

Michelin has created a website to help motorists plan their journey. The free route planning service covers the whole of Europe – 21 countries and one million kilometres (6,21367 miles) of highways and byways – enabling browsers to select their preferred route, such as the fastest, the shortest or that recommended by Michelin. The description of the itinerary includes the distances and travel times between towns, as well as information on hotels and restaurants en route. The network is updated three times weekly, integrating road works, detours, new motorways and snow-bound mountain passes. Consult the website at **www.viamichelin.com**. Michelin map 714 covers all the Ben-elux countries at a scale of 1:400 000. Map 715 covers the Netherlands at a scale of 1:400 000 and has a compre-hensive index as well as enlarged inset maps of the conurbations of Amster-dam and Rotterdam. The Netherlands is also covered at a scale of 1:200 000 by maps 531 (northern half) and 532 (southern half) which give both road and tourist information. Map 531 has a detail map of Amsterdam and map 532 of The Hague and Rotterdam. Maps at a scale of 1:100 000 are avail-able from the ANWB and the VVV.

TOURIST ROUTES

The ANWB has organised and sign-posted about 40 itineraries ranging in distance from 80 to 150km/50 to 100mi. These routes have hexago-nal signposts and take in the most picturesque regions and interesting towns. Leaflets showing the routes and main points of interest are avail-able from the ANWB offices. Other tourist and heritage trails are organised by local authorities.

PETROL/GASOLINE

Super (*Super geload*), Super Unleaded (*Super loodvrij*), Diesel, Euro (*Eurolood-vrij*), LPG and Gas are the kinds of petrol on sale in the Netherlands: Credit cards are sometimes accepted at petrol stations, but visitors are still strongly advised to have other means of payment with them.

WHERE TO STAY AND EAT

Hotel and Restaurant recommendations are located in the Address Books throughout the *Discovering* section of this guide. For coin ranges and for a description of the symbols used in the Address Books, see the Legend on the cover flap.

Where to Stay

ADDRESS BOOKS

In this guide, Address Books have been added to the major cities and a number of towns to offer a choice of lodgings in price categories to suit all budgets. Hotels have been selected for their convenient location, character or value for money. Prices are based on a double/twin room in high season and have been marked by coin symbols in this guide that indicate price ranges. *See the legend on the cover flap for details of coin ranges*.

HOTELS

When choosing a stopover for a few hours or a few days, the current edition of the red-cover *Michelin Guide Benelux* is an indispensable complement to this. It is updated every year and offers a range of hotels and restaurants with an indication of their standard of service and comfort, their location and their prices. The prices listed are for the current year. The red symbol indicates that the hotel is particularly pleasant or peaceful. Towns underlined in red on the Michelin maps are listed in the current edition of the red-cover *Michelin Guide Benelux* with a choice of hotels and restaurants. Visitors may also like to consult the **Michelin website** (*www.viamichelin.com*).

BOOKING ACCOMMODATION

Accommodation should be booked in advance as far as possible, especially for the budget-conscious and over weekends in the spring and summer. In the case of Amsterdam, it is particularly important to book well in advance because the better hotels along the canals are often full. A wide range of accommodation can be reserved through **Bookings NL**, an organisation which offers an online booking service. Contact Bookings NL, *Weteringschans 28-4, 1017 SG Amsterdam.* (020) 712 5600. *www.bookings.com*. Once in the Netherlands, contact a VVV tourist office, which also offers an accommodation service.

RENTED ACCOMMODATION

A variety of accommodation (bungalows, log cabins, holiday cottages and apartments) from the luxurious to the rustic is available for visitors. Contact the Netherlands Board of Tourism (*see Useful Websites*) or regional VVV offices for further information. Accommodation may also be booked online through the Netherlands Board of Tourism (*www.holland.com*) and ANWB (*www.anwb.nl* – in Dutch only).

HOSTELS

These are open to young and old alike, who are members of their own national organisation or who have an international card, and offer facilities for individuals, families and groups. For general information and membership enquiries see the Hostelling International website: *www.hihostels.com*. Information and online booking is also available at *www.stayokay.com* and *www.hihostels.com*.

CAMPING

Campsites are indicated by the symbol △ on Michelin maps 715, 531 and 532. A list of campsites in the Netherlands is available from VVV tourist offices or from the Netherlands Board of Tourism. Dutch campsites are classified under the auspices of the Stichting Classificatie Kampeer-en Bungalowbedrijven. The number of stars allocated (1 to 5) refers to sanitary facilities, and the number of flags (1 to 5) concerns general and recreational facilities.

Camping in places other than official campsites is not allowed in the Netherlands. However, landowners may obtain exemptions from this law from their local councils.

Many campsites in the Netherlands have **hikers' cabins** (*trekkershut*), which can normally accommodate four people and offer rudimentary facilities. A maximum of three nights can be spent in any one cabin during the high season. Contact the ANWB or VVV for a brochure.

BED AND BREAKFAST

Most VVV offices have listings of families offering bed and breakfast style accommodation. Reservations can also be made through **Bed & Breakfast Nederland**, *Hallenstraat 12a, 5531 AB Bladel.* ☏ *(049) 733 0300. Fax (049) 733 0811. www.bedandbreakfast.nl.*

RURAL ACCOMMODATION

Visitors interested in staying on a farm should contact **Hoeve-Logies Nederland**, *Postbus 73, 2390 AB Hazerswoude.* ☏ *(017) 258 6340. Fax (017) 258 5134. www.dutch-farmholidays.com.* This organisation publishes a guide entitled *Natuurlijk… logeren op de boerderij,* which lists addresses of farms, B&Bs and apartments in the countryside.

HOLIDAY VILLAGES

The ANWB publishes a guide (also at *www.anwb.nl*, called *Bungalowwijzer,* in Dutch only) listing the addresses of holiday villages where bungalows may be rented. These are classified under the auspices of the Stichting Classificatie Kampeer- en Bungalowbedrijven. The number of stars allocated (1 to 5) refers to the level of comfort in the bungalows, and the number of flags (1 to 5) to the facilities offered in the villages. Bookings may be made through the ANWB and VVV offices.

Where to Eat

A wide variety of food is served in the Netherlands, from good local dishes to delicious international cuisine. The country's colonial past helps explain why Asia is represented particularly well, especially with with Indonesian restaurants. Chinese, Japanese, Indian and fusion restaurants are also not difficult to find. The Dutch tend to have a hearty breakfast and eat a light lunch around 12.30pm. The evening meal is usually eaten between 6pm and 7pm, although this is gradually changing and becoming a little later. Generally speaking, Dutch restaurants are not large establishments and consequently they can fill up quickly at lunchtime and early evening. It makes sense to reserve a table if a meal is to be a special occasion.

ADDRESS BOOKS

The restaurants listed in the **Address Books** for major cities and several towns in this guide have been selected for their surroundings, ambience, typical dishes or unusual character. Prices are based on the cost of an appetiser, entrée and dessert for one person, without beverage, tax or tip. As with the hotels, the selections are marked by coin symbols in this guide that indicate price ranges. *See the legend on the cover flap for details of coin ranges*.

For a wider selection of restaurants and more detailed gastronomic information, consult the red-cover *Michelin Guide Benelux*. The red Bib Gourmand found in the guide indicates a good meal at a reasonable price.

RESTAURANTS

The usual opening times for lunch are from 11am–2.30pm or 3pm and for dinner from 5.30pm–10pm or 11pm. There are some late-opening restaurants in the larger cities, but on the whole kitchens tend to close earlier than you might expect.

Neerlands Dis – The 140 restaurants of this nationwide chain are easily recognisable by their red, white and blue soup tureen emblem. They offer a selection of traditional Dutch dishes.

Tourist Menu – The restaurants displaying a blue wall plaque with a white fork serve a three-course meal (starter, main course and dessert) at a reasonable price. A booklet is available from VVV offices. It is common for many restaurants to feature a *dagschotel* (dish of the day) which will generally be good value for money.

Vegetarian – Finding a vegetarian restaurant outside the larger cities is more of a problem than one might think. Places serving traditional Dutch food are unlikely to have vegetarian choices, and often it is advisable to seek out an Asian restaurant and base your meal around the non-meat dishes on the menu. For information on vegetarian restaurants in the Netherlands see *www.happycow.net* and *www.vegetarian-restaurants.net*.

Eating with children – Children are welcome in most restaurants and child-friendly dishes are not uncommon on menus. Highchairs are often available. If dining out in the evening at a more formal restaurant, is it advisable to enquire about provision for children when making a reservation.

CAFÉS

Brown Cafés (**Bruin café**) – These traditional, dark panelled bars are famous for their atmosphere, conviviality and comfort, more typical of a cosy sitting room. They rarely open before 9am, and although some food is often available they are more a place for drinking and relaxing than eating. They are a sharp contrast to the chrome and glass designer bars popular with trendy clientele. The term 'brown café' derives from the smoky stains that accumulated on the walls, although nowadays such a colour is more likely to have come from a tin of brown paint!

Other cafés – The cafés of Amsterdam and other large towns are known for the friendly atmosphere during their cocktail hour when drinks are accompanied by small cubes of cheese and the famous small hot meatballs (*Bitterballen*).

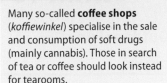

A Bit of Advice

Many so-called **coffee shops** (*koffiewinkel*) specialise in the sale and consumption of soft drugs (mainly cannabis). Those in search of tea or coffee should look instead for tearooms.

WHAT TO SEE AND DO

Outdoor Fun

CYCLING

The Netherlands is traditionally the land of the bicycle and there is no better way to discover the country at your leisure . For more information on cycling in the Netherlands (*see WHEN AND WHERE TO GO*).

Cycle lanes and paths – Cycling is very popular in the Netherlands, and accordingly the country has many special lanes and paths for cyclists (about 15 000km/9 320mi). If you follow the special cycle lanes – marked by a white bicycle on a blue sign – found in both towns and the countryside, then you won't be bothered by other traffic. Do not cycle on footpaths: cyclists are not allowed on paths designed for pedestrians, even if they are only leading their bike.

Cycling rules and special signs
- Keep to the right and overtake other bicycles or mopeds on the left. Other traffic must be overtaken on the right. Use clear hand signals to indicate a change of direction. It is in the interest of cyclists as well as motorists to be able to recognise the main signs:
- Blue circular sign with a white bicycle: bicycles (*fietsen*) and mopeds (*bromfietsen*) must use this lane;
- Rectangular sign with the mention **Fietspad** or **Rijwielpad**: an optional cycle lane for cyclists, but mopeds using their engine power are prohibited;
- Sign with **Fietsers oversteken**: give way crossing point for bicycles and mopeds.

Bicycle hire – Bicycles can be hired from most railway stations (in approximately 100 stations). Look for the blue and white square sign, which indicates there is a **NS-Rijwielshop**, where train travellers can hire a bicycle for 6€ per day. In towns there are numerous bicycle hire firms but cycle dealers and repair shops also have bicycles for hire (*fietsverhuur*).

Parking – It is advisable to lock your bike, especially in towns, and it is preferable to leave it in a guarded cycle park.

Cycling events – Information is available from Nederlandse Toer Fiets Unie (NTFU). *Postbus 326, 3900 AH Veenendaal. (031) 858 1300. www. ntfu.nl (Dutch only).* See Calendar of Events.

Cycling in Friesland

Jochen Tack/NBTC

HIKING

Hiking is popular in the Netherlands and there are numerous annual meetings. The **Four Day Walk** takes place in Apeldoorn and Nijmegen (see *Calendar of Events*), and the Tour of the Eleven Towns of Friesland leaves from Leeuwarden.

State-owned forests – Most of the forests and woods are owned by the State (*staatsbossen*) and are administered by the **Staatsbosbeheer**, a department of the Ministry of Agriculture, Nature Conservation and Fisheries. The recreational facilities provided usually include cycle paths, picnic areas and footpaths. Many trails are waymarked and differentiated by colour. Signs give the time required for each tour. Detailed information about these trails is available from: Staatsbosbeheer, *Princenhof Park 1, 3972 NG Driebergen.* ☎ *(030) 692 6111. Fax (030) 692 2978. www.staatsbosbeheer.nl (Dutch only).*

Areas of outstanding natural beauty – The **Vereniging Natuurmonumenten** association (*Postbus 9955, 1243 ZR 's-Graveland.* ☎ *(035) 655 9911. www.natuurmonumenten. nl (Dutch only)*) can provide information and booklets on walking routes, wildlife and the landscape in these areas (*Wandelen met Natuurmonumenten* by Harm Piek). The association also publishes a handbook, which is a useful reference for walkers (*Natuuren wandelgebieden in Nederland*).

Long-distance footpaths – The Netherlands offers a network (total length approximately 6 000km/3 750mi) of 33 long-distance footpaths (**langeafstandswandelpaden** or **LAW**) of 100km/60mi or longer, waymarked in white and red. The footpaths, marked in yellow and red, are **streekpaden**, which are shorter walking routes (80km/50mi to 260km/160mi) that take ramblers through a particular region or specific landscape. Information is available from **Stichting Wandelplatform-**

Waymarked cycling and walking routes

LAW, *Postbus 846, 3800 AV Amersfoort.* ☎ *(033) 465 3660. www.wandelnet.nl.*

BIRD WATCHING

The wetlands (Biesbosch National Park, the Frisian Lakes), the Wadden Islands, the many low-tide mudflats and the polderlands provide a variety of ecological habitats rich in birdlife, ideal for the amateur bird watcher. The **Oostvaardersplassen** wetland, one of the prime birding areas in Europe, is only 40km/25mi east of Amsterdam. For those interested in bird watching, the organisation to contact locally is **Vogelbescherming Nederland**, *Driebergseweg 16c, 3708 JB Zeist.* ☎ *(030) 693 7700. www. vogelbescherming.nl.*
There are tour companies that specialise in bird watching trips: see *www.birdsnetherlands.nl* for one that operates 2hr and half-day trips out of Amsterdam and provides binoculars. It takes only a half-hour train journey from Amsterdam to spot White-tailed Eagles and Eurasian spoonbills. A useful website that details the best birdwatching sites across the country is *www.natuurbeleven.nl.*

SKATING

When snow lies thickly on the ground and frost has set in, the many waterways and lakes are ideal for skating on. The website *www.skatelog.com* has a section devoted to the Netherlands, detailing where best to skate and providing general information on the activity.

LEISURE AND ANIMAL PARKS

Leisure parks and zoos attract huge interest throughout Europe, and the Netherlands has its fair share of amusement parks. See www.themeparkcity.com/EURO_neth.htm.

STEAM TRAINS

Tourist trains are operated between Apeldoorn and Dieren, Hoorn and Medemblik, as well as Goes and Oudeland. See *www.railmusea.nl* for information on all these routes.

WATER SPORTS

The Netherlands, with its rivers, canals, waterways, broads, lakes, reservoirs and the sea, provides ample opportunity for water sports. Given the country's tradition of being a sea-faring nation, the Dutch are enthusiastic sailors. There are over 300 000 boat owners (approximately one boat per 50 inhabitants) and at least 950 marinas or pleasure boat harbours throughout the country. Few places are far from a navigable waterway and one of the unexpected charms of sailing in Holland is that it is possible to sail into or through many of the town centres due to their canal networks. The most popular sailing areas are the **IJsselmeer** (high seas possible), the lakes bordering the IJsselmeer polders (calmer waters), the lakes of South Holland, the Utrecht lake district (**Loosdrechtse** and Vinkeveense) and the Frisian Lakes.

Customs formalities – On arrival and departure, visiting sailors with boats over 5.4m/18ft must report to the nearest customs harbour office which will issue the necessary sailing certificate. Boats capable of travelling at more than 20kmph/12mph should be registered at a post office and have a licence. Yachts measuring 15m/50ft in length must also carry a licence. For information on registering a boat, see *www.verkeerenwaterstaat.nl/english/pleasure%5Fcraft/background*. Insurance coverage is also compulsory. To use a sea-scooter you must be over 18 and have a Dutch licence to navigate. *http://hollandsouth.angloinfo.com/af/526/holland-south-yachts-and-sailing.html*.

Restrictions and regulations – Boaters with yachts that have high, fixed masts must look out for fixed bridges with limited headroom and remember that some bridges only open at certain hours. Many lakes have restrictions for craft with a deep draught. There are **speed limits** on many waterways and some even prohibit motorboats. At movable bridges there is often a **fee** to pay, usually well indicated, and the bridgekeeper will lower a clog (*klomp*) for you to put the fee into.

For other regulations consult the **Almanac for Water Tourism** (Wateralmanak); Part I contains general shipping rules and regulations and Part II gives information on tide timetables, opening times of bridges and locks and facilities offered by the various marinas. These almanacs have introductions in English and are available from the ANWB and some specialised bookshops. Both the ANWB and the **Netherlands Hydrographic Services** (*Hydrografische Dienst, Badhuisweg 169-171, 2597 JN Den Haag.* ☎ *(070) 316 2801. www.hydro.nl*) publish **hydrographic charts** which can be purchased from ANWB and VVV offices.

Boat hire – Motorboats and sailing boats can be hired in a number of locations in Friesland. Tjalks (flat-bottomed boats), fishing smacks and clippers are also available for hire. For lists of companies chartering boats apply to the Netherlands Tourist Board, ANWB, VVV offices or Top of Holland Yachtcharter (*Postbus 330, 9200 NL Drachten.* ☎ *(051) 258 5082. www.topofhollandyachtcharter.nl*).

Schools for sailing, windsurfing and motorboating – Almost all resorts with water sports facilities have sailing schools. Addresses are available from ANWB and VVV offices

NBTC

Veerse Meer

or from Koninklijk Nederlands Watersport Verbond.

Water skiing – This sport is subject to strict regulations and can only be practised in authorised areas. In some cases authorisation must be obtained from the local authorities.

Canoeing – The calm waterways of the Netherlands provide ideal conditions for this sport. The VVV offices can provide more information on request.

Surfing – Again the opportunities are varied, and although the Netherlands is no surfers' paradise, there are four suitable areas: see *www.globalsurfers.com* for details. Experienced surfers will enjoy the rougher waters of the IJsselmeer or the North Sea waves. The inland waters of the Utrecht Lakes and the lakes bordering the polders are also suitable for surfing.

Boat trips – For those who prefer to take it easy there are numerous boat trips to choose from. For towns with a good canal network this is a relaxing way to sightsee and is ideal for admiring all the canal houses. The following towns offer boat trips on the canals: Alkmaar, Amsterdam, Delft, Groningen, Leiden and Utrecht. Others such as Enkhuizen, Harderwijk, Kampen and Urk organise trips on the IJssel Lake while Leiden (Rhine), Maas-

tricht (Meuse to the Belgian border), Nijmegen (Waal), Rotterdam (Rhine), Venlo (Meuse) and Zierikzee (Eastern Scheldt) propose river excursions.

Fishing – Two documents are necessary: a fishing licence (*sportvisakte*) and a permit (*vergunning*). The first is on sale in post offices, VVV offices and angling shops and associations, while the second can be obtained from the local angling associations (Hengelsportverenigingen) and angling shops – addresses of these are available from the **Nederlandse Vereniging van Sportvissersfederaties** or **NVVS** (*Leijenseweg 115, Postbus 162, 3720 AD Bilthoven. ☎ (030) 605 8400. Fax (030) 603 9874. www.sportvisserijnederland. nl/sportvissers* (in Dutch only). Local information on fishing facilities is available from the VVV offices.

Useful contacts – **Koninklijk Nederlands Watersport Verbond** (KNWB; Water sports Federation), *Watersportverbond, Wattbaan 31–49, 3439 ML, Nieuwegein* (visitor address) and *Postbus 2658, 3430 GB, Nieuwegein* (*postal address*). ☎ (030) 751 3700. Fax (030) 656 4783. watersportverbond.nl (currently in Dutch only).

For information on opening times of dykes and bridges as well as sailing routes, you can call the ANWB Watersport Advieslijn on ☎ (088) 269 5020.

GOLF

The Michelin maps 531, 532 and 408 locate the country's golf courses, many of which welcome visitors. The Dutch Golf Federation's headquarters are at: *Nederlandse Golf Federatie, Rijnzathe 8, 3454 PV De Meern.* ☎ *(030) 242 6370. www.ngf.nl* (currently in Dutch only). Information on the location of golf courses in the Netherlands is available in English from the national tourist board website *www.holland.com*.

Activities for Kids Kids

There is a lot to interest children in the Netherlands, including amusement and theme parks and museums of special interest for younger visitors. Boat rides and cycling trips should also appeal and hiring bicycles for children is not usually a problem. There are also a number of zoos, eight in total, with **Apenheul** *www.apenheul.com*) near Apeldoorn (🕒*open Apr–Nov 9.30am–5.30pm; until 6pm Jul & Aug;* 🍴🛏 *16.50€ adults, 12€ 3–9yrs*) being the most enticing for kids. A useful website for checking out the possibilities in terms of kids enjoying themselves in the Netherlands is *www.travelforkids.com*. There is also a kids' corner on the national tourist board's website *www.holland.com*. In this guide, sights of particular interest to children are indicated with a Kids symbol. They include **Nederlands Openluchtmuseum**, an open-air museum in Arnhem, and **Naturalis**, a natural history museum in Leiden. Also of interest is **Spoorwegmuseum**, a railway museum in Utrecht where children can take a ride on a miniature train and, for visitors over 8 years old, a rail quest game. In Deventer there is a toy museum, and in Amsterdam the house of Anne Frank will be of interest to older children. The capital city also has **Nederlands Scheepvaartmuseum**, a ship museum where between April and October staff dress up as a captain and crew and work on the ship. They clean and scrub the deck,

sing sea chanteys and, twice a day, fire a cannon. Some of these attractions may offer discount fees for children. Places of interest for children that are not mentioned in the main text include a **Police Museum** (*Kanaal Noord 65, 7311 PM Apeldoorn;* ☎ *(055) 543 06 91)*, where young visitors can have their fingerprints taken, try on a police uniform, handle a bulletproof vest and try to solve a crime. In the town of Hengelo there is the **Techniekmuseum**, a technology museum (*Industriestraat 9, 7553 CK Hengelo;* ☎*074 243 00 54)* where children can operate some of the machinery and see a demonstration of how infra-red satellites work. In Tegelen, **Fun Forest** (*Trappistenweg 35, 5932 NB Tegelen.* ☎ *(077) 3260902; www.funforest.nl)* has 120 climbing frames along eight different circuits. They are graded according to age and start with one suitable for kids over 5; the highest is for children over 13. Safety instructions are given, the necessary equipment is supplied and children must be accompanied by a parent or adult.

The cultural attractions of The Hague will be a magnet for adults but children may find their patience tested by what is on offer. A notable exception is **Family Park Drievliet**, where there is a Ferris Wheel and an opportunity to stroke the animals at the children's farm. Another attraction is the Twistrix, a 15m/49ft-long owl train and a giant pirates' ship. (*Laan van s'-Gravenmade, 2495 AH The Haag;* ☎ *(070) 399 93 05)*.

Calendar of Events

Listed below are the most important of the many festivals held in the Netherlands; some others are mentioned in the descriptions of towns and cities in the *Discovering the Sights* section of the guide. A detailed calendar of festivals appears in leaflets produced annually by the VVV (tourist information centre) and any further information and phone numbers can be obtained from VVV offices.

JANUARY–FEBRUARY

Rotterdam — International Film Festival

IN FEBRUARY OR MARCH DURING LENT

Breda — **Carnival**
Bergen op Zoom — Carnival
Eindhoven — Carnival
Venlo — Carnival
's-Hertogenbosch — Carnival
Maastricht — Carnival
Sittard — Carnival

MARCH

Maastricht — **The European Fine Art Fair**, ☎ (073) 614 51 65

1 APRIL

Brielle — Historical Festival

LAST SATURDAY IN APRIL

Noordwijk-Haarlem — Procession of floral floats

MID APRIL TO MID SEPTEMBER

Alkmaar — Cheese Market

MAY–LATE SEPTEMBER, SUNDAYS

Tegelen — Passion Plays (2010; every five years)

LATE MAY (AROUND ASCENSION DAY)

Breda — Jazz Festival

SATURDAY BEFORE WHITSUN

Exloo — Shepherds' Feast

MAY/JUNE

Scheveningen — Sand sculpture festival

JUNE

Amsterdam — **Holland Festival** (concerts, opera, ballet, theatre). To reserve, apply to: Holland Festival, Piet Heinkade 5, 1019 BR, Amsterdam; ☎ (020) 788 2100; fax (020) 788 2102; www.holland festival.nl.
The Hague — Pasar Malam Besar (Indonesian market)
Terschelling — *Oerolfestival*
Tilburg — Festival Mundial

LATE JUNE–LATE AUGUST, THURSDAYS

Schagen — Market (West-Friese Marktdagen)

JULY

Haarlem — International Organ Festival (biennial). *Postbus 1091, 1000 BB Amsterdam. ☎ (020) 488 0479. Fax (020) 488 0478. www.organfestival.nl.*
Den Helder — National Navy Days (*Vlootdagen*)
Kerkrade — International Music Competition (quadrennial: 2009). Music competition for wind and brass bands. *Postbus 133, 6460 AC, Kerkrade; ☎ (045) 545 5000; fax (045) 535 3111; www.wmc.nl.*
Leiden — Leiden Drapers' Festival
Nijmegen — International four-day walking event (*Wandelvierdaagse*).
Rotterdam — Summer Carnival (street parade)
Tilburg — Kirmes: fair to celebrate local patron saint's day

2ND WEEKEND IN JULY

The Hague — North Sea Jazz Festival, *Postbus 3325, 2601 DH, Delft; ☎ (015) 212 1980; fax (015) 214 8393; www.northseajazz.com.*

3RD SUNDAY IN JULY

Exloo — International Festival of Ancient Handicrafts

Rotterdam Summer Carnival

JULY–AUGUST (2 WEEKS)

Frisian Lakes — Regattas: *Skûtsjesilen*

JULY AND AUGUST, WEDNESDAYS

Edam — Cheese Market

JULY AND AUGUST, SATURDAY AFTERNOONS

Kinderdijk — Windmill Days

EARLY AUGUST

Sneek — Sneekweek Regattas

3RD SATURDAY IN AUGUST

Noorwijk-Noordwijk 908 E 5 — Procession of floral floats

MID-AUGUST

Yerseke — Mussel Day

LATE AUGUST

Maastricht — *Preuvenemint* (Burgundian Food Festival)
Harlingen — Fishing Days

LATE AUGUST–EARLY SEPTEMBER

Breda — Nationale Taptoe: military tattoo
Utrecht — **Holland Festival of Ancient Music**, Postbus 19267, 3501 DG, Utrecht; ☎ (030) 232 9000; fax (030) 232 9001; www.oudemuziek.nl.

1ST SATURDAY IN SEPTEMBER

Aalsmeer — Procession of floral floats

1ST SUNDAY IN SEPTEMBER

Zundert 908 E 7 — Procession of floral floats

EARLY SEPTEMBER

Rotterdam — *Wereldhavenfestival* (festival celebrating the port)

2ND WEEKEND IN SEPTEMBER

Tiel — Fruit Parade

3RD TUESDAY IN SEPTEMBER

The Hague — State Opening of Parliament: the Queen arrives in a golden coach

4TH WEDNESDAY IN SEPTEMBER

Odoorn — Sheep market

LATE SEPTEMBER

Utrecht — Netherlands Film Festival (*Golden Calf award*)

3RD OCTOBER (FOLLOWING MONDAY IF THE 3RD IS A SUNDAY)

Leiden — Leidens Ontzet: historical procession

1ST WEDNESDAY IN OCTOBER

Leeuwarden — Show of prize Frisian bulls

3RD SATURDAY BEFORE 5TH DECEMBER

Amsterdam — St Nicholas' official arrival (*Prins Hendrikkade*)

1ST SUNDAY OF ADVENT– 1ST JANUARY

Denekamp, Ootmarsum — Blowing of midwinter horns

NATIONWIDE EVENTS

National Museum Weekend — 3rd weekend in April
Queen's Birthday Celebrations — 30th April (29th April if 30th is a Sunday)
National Mill and Cycle Day — 2nd Saturday in May
Open Monument Day — 2nd weekend in September

SPORTS COMPETITIONS

Automobile and motorcycle races – The Dutch Grand Prix takes place in Assen on the last weekend in June. Cross-country motorcycling is very popular and races on ice are held in ice skating rinks.

Cycling events – The Regional Cycle Day is held every year on the second Saturday in May. The tour of 11 Friesland towns (depart from Bolsward) is held on Whit Monday; Drenthe's 4-Day Cycling Event (Rijwielvierdaagse) is held in late July and Nijmegen's 4-Day Event in early August.

Water sports competition – Across the country different water sports activities are held throughout the summer. The most spectacular are the **skûtsjesilen**, *skûtsjes* regattas on the Frisian Lakes (late July). Among the other activities are Delta Week (Zierikzee) in late June and early July and Sneekweek in early August.

Walking – A 4-Day Walking Event takes place in Nijmegen (3rd or 4th week in July). The Frisian 11-Town Walking Event (late May) lasts five days (depart from Leeuwarden). The **6-day event** from Hoek van Holland to Den Helder is held in July.

Traditional sports – & *See also Introduction, Traditions and folklore.* Archers' processions (*boogschieten*) are held on the second Sunday in July in many towns in the Limburg province as part of the **Oud Limburgs Schuttersfeest**. Those who like ball games can watch **kaatswedstrijden** held in Frisian villages (May to September); the most important meet is held in Franeker on the fifth Wednesday in July. Annual pole vaulting championships (*fierljeppen*) are held in Friesland in late August.

Other events – The **Amstel Gold Race**, an international cycle race leaving from and returning to Maastricht, is held in April. The **Rotterdam Marathon** follows a course through the city centre in late April.

Sightseeing

INFORMATION SOURCES

The **Nederland Museumland** guide, updated every two years, lists all the museums, castles and zoos in the Netherlands. Each entry gives a brief description as well as the admission times and charges. The guide is for sale at bookshops, major museums and ANWB and VVV offices.

Details on museums and exhibitions in the Netherlands can also be obtained from the following websites:

www.holland.com: the official website of the Netherlands Board of Tourism and Conventions.

www.museum.nl: an online guide to museums with a full listing of museums.

www.travel.yahoo.com: links to all the museums that have their own websites; includes the online Museumkr@nt (museum news; mainly in Dutch).

For specific opening times of attractions and museums, consult the Admission Times and Charges in the *Discovering* section.

World Heritage List

In 1972, the United Nations Educational, Scientific and Cultural Organization (UNESCO) adopted a Convention for the preservation of cultural and natural sites. To date, more than 150 States Parties have signed this international agreement, which has listed over 500 sites "of outstanding universal value" on the World Heritage List. Each year, a committee of representatives from 21 countries, assisted by the following technical organisations: ICOMOS (International Council on Monuments and Sites); IUCN (International Union for Conservation of Nature and Natural Resources); and ICCROM (International Centre for the Study of the Preservation and Restoration of Cultural Property, the Rome Centre), evaluates the proposals for new sites to be included on the list, which grows longer as new nominations are accepted and more countries sign the Convention. To be considered, a site must be nominated by the country in which it is located.

The protected cultural heritage may be monuments (buildings, sculptures, archaeological structures, etc.) with unique historical, artistic or scientific features; groups of buildings (such as religious communities, ancient cities); or sites (human settlements, examples of exceptional landscapes, cultural landscapes) which are the combined works of man and nature of exceptional beauty. Natural sites may be a testimony to the stages of the earth's geological history or to the development of human cultures and creative genius, or represent significant ongoing ecological processes, contain superlative natural phenomena or provide a habitat for threatened species. Signatories of the Convention pledge to cooperate to preserve and protect these sites around the world as a common heritage to be shared by all of humanity.

Some of the most well-known places which the World Heritage Committee has inscribed include Australia's Great Barrier Reef (1981), the Canadian Rocky Mountain Parks (1984), The Great Wall of China (1987), the Statue of Liberty (1984), the Kremlin (1990), Mont-Saint-Michel and its Bay (France, 1979), Durham Castle and Cathedral (1986).

In the Netherlands, UNESCO World Heritage sites are:

◆ The former island of Schokland (1995)
◆ The Defence Line of Amsterdam (1996)
◆ Kinderdijk windmills (1997)
◆ Mill Network at Kinderdijk-Elshout (1997)
◆ Ir. D.F. Wouda steam pumping station (1998)
◆ Historic Area of Willemstad (1997)
◆ The Beemsterpolder, Noord-Holland (1999)
◆ The Rietveld Schröderhuis (2000)

Shopping

One of the most popular shopping items of the souvenir kind are clogs (*klompen*) and they are found everywhere, often brightly decorated and more suitable for decorating a room than wearing on the feet. Wearable wooden clogs for clomping around in are still available and garden centres and small shops sell them. Small, painted windmills and costume dolls are also a popular buy. A more serious purchase would be an item of blue-and-white Delft pottery, and the website *www.royaldelft.com* is a good place to find information on this famous Dutch product.

Pottery from Makkum and Workum is also available across the country. Top-end Dutch brands include Claudio Ferrici leather handbags: see *www.claudioferrici.com*.

Bulbs, and not just tulips, as well as horticultural items should cost less than in your home country and, as well as the famous flower market in Amsterdam, suitable shops and garden centres are not difficult to find. In springtime at The **Keukenhof** there are stalls where bulbs can be purchased and posted back to your home at reasonable prices.

Shopping hours –
🕭 *See Basic Information*

REGIONAL ARTS & CRAFTS

Silverware from Schoonhoven, **crystal** and **glass** from Leerdam and **diamonds** from Amsterdam are some of the more important products with a regional basis. When it comes to food, **cheeses** from the Netherlands have a vital regional basis and there is a rich variety, from the creamy to the crumbly, to choose from. Most good cheese shops will allow, if not invite, customers to sample their cheeses, and if you are planning to bring some home then ask for a cut from one of the big wheels of cheese on display and ask if it can be sealed airtight. Note that Gouda is not a protected name, so it can be manufactured anywhere, and most Gouda cheeses are produced on an industrial scale and are not farm products.

There are some Dutch chocolates and biscuits with venerable traditions behind them. Look for **Verkade chocolate**, first made in 1886, and Droste biscuits that were first produced in 1863.

Entertainment

THEATRE, DANCE AND MUSIC

The title of cultural capital goes to **Amsterdam** with its more than 50 museums and over 140 art galleries, not to mention 55 theatres and concert halls. The 1986 Muziektheater, part of the modern Stopera development in its attractive riverside setting, provides state-of-the-art facilities for the Nederlandse Opera and the Nationale Ballet. The vitality of the ballet company owes much to its founder, the Russian choreographer Sonia Gaskall, and also to Hans van Manen (choreographer). Its repertoire consists of traditional, classical and romantic ballets. In the summer, musicians from the two orchestras give free lunchtime concerts. Since its resplendent refurbishment, the 100-year-old **Concertgebouw** (🕭 *see AMSTERDAM*) is the perfect setting for the performances of the famous Koninklijk Concertgebouw-orkest, conducted by Riccardo Chailly. Berlage's famous Beurs building has been refurbished to serve as a cultural centre and provides a home to the Netherlands Philharmonic and Chamber Orchestras. In summer, the open-air theatre in Vondelpark is the venue for free concerts.

The Hague is home to the more contemporary culture of the **Nederlands Dans Theater** acclaimed for its adventurous performances in modern dance under the Czech-born artistic director, Jiri Kylian. The Anton Philipszaal is home to the city's **Residentie Orkest**. The refurbished **Circustheater** (1904) in Scheveningen now serves as a venue for musical extravaganzas while the redecorated Schouwburg Theatre concentrates on drama.

The North Sea Jazz Festival is a well known international event and welcomes as many as 1 000 musicians. **Rotterdam** boasts the Scapino Ballet with its narrative ballet repertoire while the **Rotterdam Philharmonic** plays at the **Doelen**.

Tickets – Tickets for major events (concerts, theatre, sports, etc.) can be obtained through most VVV offices. They can also be purchased from the **Ticket Service** on ☎ *0900 300 1250* or at **www.ticketservice.nl**. This useful website has three categories (theatre, concert and cinema) in which you can search by date, venue or title, and also has numerous links to cinema, theatre and concert venues all over the Netherlands.

CASINOS

The official gambling palaces (Holland Casinos) offer an afternoon or evening of gambling where you can try your hand at Blackjack, Punto Banco, American or French Roulette or the jackpot machines, in pleasant surroundings. There are casinos in Amsterdam, Breda, Eindhoven, Groningen, Nijmegen, Rotterdam, Scheveningen, Schiphol, Utrecht, Valkenburg and Zandvoort. Guests must be over 18 years old, carry a valid identity card and be appropriately dressed. Casinos are usually open from 1.30pm–2am. Further information is available at *www.hollandcasino.nl*.

CINEMAS

There are 1 575 cinemas across the Netherlands. Many films are shown in the original language with Dutch subtitles, but there are also plenty of Dutch films, too. Some very good films have come out of the Netherlands, particularly documentaries.

Books

HISTORY

The Dutch Revolt *by Geoffrey Parker* (2002).
A scholarly but very approachable look at relations between the Netherlands and Spain between 1572 and 1609 using original documents.
Amsterdam: A Brief Life of a City *by Geert Mak* (1999).
Using diaries and eyewitness accounts, this is an affectionate portrait of Amsterdam through the centuries, from life on the street and in the grand houses.
The Netherlands: Revolt and Independence, 1550-1650 *by Martyn Rady* (1990).
A mildly academic look at 16C-Netherlands when the area included Luxembourg, northeast France and Belgium.
A Bridge Too Far *by Cornelius Ryan* (1999).
A dramatic account of the battle for the Rhine bridges around Arnhem during World War II.
Arnhem *by Christopher Hibbert* 1998).
The Diary of a Young Girl: The Definitive Edition *by Anne Frank* (updated 2007).
The diary of a 13-year-old Jewish girl who had to go into hiding with her family to avoid being killed by the Nazis.
The Battle of the Bulge *by Charles B MacDonald* (1998).
The story of how in December 1944, 250,000 German troops took the Allied armies totally by surprise; at the time, the most serious failure of battlefield intelligence in the history of the US Army.
Patriots and Liberators *by Simon Schama* (1992).
A gripping account by a noted historian of the history of the Netherlands between 1780 and 1813.
The Embarrassment of Riches: An Interpretation of Dutch Culture in the Golden Age *by Simon Schama* (1988).
Evoking the cultural and social milieu of 17C Holland, a moral tale of tremendous material wealth coupled with anxiety and uncertainty.

TRAVEL

Through the Dutch and Belgian Canals *by P Bristow* (1988).
Of Dutch Ways *by H Colijn* (1991).
Holland *by A Hopkins* (1988).

ART AND ARCHITECTURE

Mondrian by John Milner (1994).

Vincent: the Complete Self Portraits by Bernard Denvir (1997).

From Rembrandt to Vermeer by Jane Turner (2000).

Rembrandt by Michael Kitson (1992).

Art & Home: Dutch Interiors in the Age of Rembrandt by Mariët Westermann (2003).

The Paintings of Willem Van De Veldes by MS Robinson (1990).

Dutch Painting by Christopher Brown (1993).

Vincent & Theo – Brothers in Art by Frank Grooothof (2006).

Dutch Art by Sheila D Muller (Ed) (1994).

Rembrandt's Eyes by Simon Schama (1999).

Still Life and Trade in the Dutch Golden Age by Julie Berger Hochstrasser (2007).

De Stijl 1917–1931: The Dutch Contribution to Modern Art by HLC Jaffe (1986).

Holland Frozen in Time: Winter Landscapes by Ariane Van Suchtelen (2007).

FICTION

Headlong by Michael Frayn (2000).
Erudite story featuring a philosopher turned art historian with an interest in Bruegel.

Tulip Fever by Deborah Moggach (1999).
Amsterdam in the 17C is the setting for an elegant tale of betrayal and recrimination.

Girl with a Pearl Earring by Tracy Chevalier (1999).
As the title indicates, this moving and introspective story has a Vermeer connection.

The Black Tulip by Alexandre Dumas. (2000).
Two rivals competing to grow a black tulip provides the unlikely setting for a love story.

The Assault by Harry Mulisch (1986).
A wartime setting for a tale that challenges moral assumptions.

The Two Hearts of Kwasi Boachi by Arthur Japin, Ina Rilke (2000).
Two young African princes arrive at the court of Willem I in the Netherlands in the 19C and their lives are changed forever.

Films

COMEDY

Business is Business by Paul Verhoeven (1971).
This is Paul Verhoeven's debut major film – a comedy about the lives of two prostitutes in Amsterdam.

Hush Hush Baby, written and directed by Albert ter Heerdt (2004).
A comedy about a Moroccan family that tries to find its way in contemporary Dutch society.

Schnitzel Paradise by Martin Koolhoven (2005).
A comedy about a Dutch-Moroccan worker who starts working in a restaurant kitchen and falls in love with the niece of the hotel's manager. Together, they have to overcome prejudices within both their families.

FICTION

Blood Brothers directed by Arno Dierickx (2008).
Selected for the Cannes Film Festival and based on a brutal true story, three teenagers hide a 14-year-old runaway boy in an attic before finally killing him.

Dunya & Desie directed by Dana Nechushtan (2008).
This emotive film about two best friends forced to make an important choice during a journey through Morocco was also selected for the Cannes Film Festival.

Ciske the Rat directed by Guido Peters (1984).
An award-winning film about a street child, based on a Dutch novel.

USEFUL WORDS & PHRASES

COMMON WORDS

NB: for restaurant terminology, consult the current edition of the red-cover Michelin Guide Benelux.

U	you
dag	goodbye
goedemorgen	good morning
hallo	hello
mijnheer	Mr
goedemiddag	good afternoon
mevrouw	Mrs, Ms
goedenavond	good evening
juffrouw	Miss
tot ziens	goodbye
rechts	right
alstublieft	please
links	left
dank u (wel)	thank you (very much)
ja	yes
nee	no
postkantoor	post office
postzegel	postage stamp
hoeveel/wat kost dit?	how much?
wat? waar?	what? where?
inclusief bediening	service included
en BTW	and VAT
apotheek	pharmacy
ziekenhuis	hospita
warm	hot
koud	cold

open	open
gesloten	closed
welterusten	good night
alstublieft	please
vrij	free

USEFUL PHRASES

Spreekt u engels?	Do you speak English?
Waar is/zijin?	Where is/are...?
Kunt u mij helpen?	Can you help me?
Hoe laat gaat u dicht	What time do you close?
Hoe ver is het naar?	How far is it to...?
Hoe laat gaat u open?	What time do you open?
Hoeveel kost dit?	How much does this cost?
ik versta u niet?	I do not understand
uitrit	exit
ver	far
verboden	prohibited
verboden toegang	no entry
voorrang geven	give way
werk in uitvoering	roadworks

BASIC INFORMATION

Business Hours

Banks – These are generally open Monday, 1pm–4pm or 5pm and Tuesday to Friday, 9am–4pm or 5pm. However, opening times vary a great deal from one place to another, and from one branch to another. Some banks stay open during late-night shopping.

Post offices are open Monday to Friday, 8.30am–5pm and Saturday, 8.30am–noon.

Shops – Shops are usually open Tuesday to Saturday, 9am–6pm (they tend to close earlier on Saturday, at 5pm), and are closed on Sunday and Monday mornings (sometimes all day Monday). In many towns there is late-night shopping on Thursday or Friday evening, when most shops stay open until 9pm. In Amsterdam and Rotterdam the large shops and department stores in the city centre are open on Sunday from 1pm–5pm. **Supermarkets** are open Monday to Friday, 8am–8pm, Saturday 8am–6pm and on late-night shopping nights until 9pm. They are closed on Sunday.

GWK offices are open Monday to Saturday, 8am–8pm and Sunday, 10am–4pm.

The longest opening hours, from 7am–10pm, are in the large shopping mall, Schiphol Plaza, at the airport.

Pharmacies – Pharmacies are open Monday to Friday, 9.30am–5.30pm; lists of chemists on call in the evening, at night or at the weekend are shown on the door.

Communications

To phone abroad from the Netherlands dial:

GB: 00 44
Australia: 00 61
USA/Canada: 00 1
Ireland: 00 353

followed by the area code (without the first '0') and subscriber's number. Dutch dialling codes are given in the red-cover *Michelin Guide Benelux*. The code for Amsterdam is 020, The Hague 070, Rotterdam 010, Utrecht 030 and Maastricht 043. Telephone numbers beginning with 0800 are toll-free; those beginning with 0900 are charged at premium rate calls; those beginning 0600 are mobile phone numbers.

In the Netherlands the phone boxes are green. Public telephones take both coins and phonecards. Phonecards are available from Primafoon (Dutch Telecom outlet), bookshops, newsagents, VVV offices, railway stations and post offices.

When calling the Netherlands from abroad, dial the international access code, followed by 31 for the Netherlands, then the area code (without the first '0') and the subscriber's number.

Telecentres – Amsterdam has one telecentre (KPN Telecom Telehouse, *Raadhuisstraat 48 close to the Dam.* *020 626 3871*). The centre provides facilities for making phone calls, sending telegrams, sending and receiving fax or telex messages and making photocopies. It stocks stamps and telephone cards. It is open Monday to

Sunday, 8am–2am. At Schiphol Airport there is a Communication Centre in Lounge 1 and Lounge 2. It is open daily from 6am–10pm.

SIM cards – Local SIM cards can be purchased or rented in the Arrival Hall of Schiphol Airport. For more information see *www.rentcenter.nl*.

Electricity

Electrical current – 220 volts AC. Plugs are round two-pin so, if needed, bring an adaptor in order to recharge your mobile phone or use other personal appliances. Most hotels should be able to provide one.

Emergencies

To contact **police, ambulance or fire services** 112. If you are not in an emergency situation, but you wish to contact the police 0900 88 44 (this is not a free-call number).

For **Tourist Medical Service** 5923355.

For an automobile emergency (ANWB) 0800 0888.

Remember that evidence of having made a police report is usually necessary in the event of making a claim for stolen property. Staff at your hotel should be able to direct to the nearest police station.

Mail/Post

The postage for letters and postcards is as follows:

letters and postcards within Europe = 0.72€   letters outside Europe = 0.85€ (0–20g) and 1.50€ (20–50 g)

Money

Currency – The unit of currency in the Netherlands is the Euro (€) comprising 100 cents. The euro comes in notes of 5, 10, 20, 50, 100, 200 and 500, and coins come in 1, 2, 5, 10, 20 and 50 cents and 1 and 2 euro. Note that 100, 200 and 500 euro banknotes are not that common.

Changing money and credit cards
– Traveller's cheques and foreign cash can be exchanged at post offices, banks and exchange offices (GWK) and in some coastal VVV offices. Rates of commission can vary considerably between exchange bureaux, so check before changing your money. GWK offices are found throughout the country, at major border crossing points and Amsterdam-Schiphol airport. They are usually open Monday to Sunday, early morning to late at night. Central offices include Amsterdam Central Station, Schiphol Plaza (NS-station), Antwerp-Breda border (E 19), Cologne/Oberhausen-Arnhem border (E 35), Osnabrück-Oldenzaal border (E 30).
Most GWK offices also offer a hotel booking service, tickets to major attractions, maps, tourist guides and telephone cards.
International credit cards (American Express, Diners Club, Eurocard, Visa, Access and MasterCard) are accepted in most shops, hotels and restaurants. Visitors can also obtain cash from bank machines (ATMs) using credit and debit cards. A pin number will be required to use this service.
Lost or stolen credit cards or Eurocheques should be reported to the following numbers as soon as possible:
Visa: ☎ 0800 022 3110
Mastercard/Eurocard:
☎ 0800 022 5821
American Express: ☎ (020) 504 8666
Diners Card: ☎ (020) 654 5511.
You should also report the loss or theft to the local police and to your bank.

Public Holidays

1 January
Good Friday
Easter Sunday and Monday,
30 April (Queen's Day or National Day)
Ascension Day
Whit Sunday
Whit Monday
5 May (Liberation Day)
25 and 26 December
Local festivals (&see *Calendar of events*) can also mean that various public facilities will be closed.

Reduced Rates

An annual **museum card** (*Museumjaarkaart*) gives entry to more than 400 museums all over the Netherlands. This can be bought at most affiliated museums, VVV offices and all Netherlands Boards of Tourism. The card costs Euro 15 for young people under 25 and Euro 30 for adults.

The **Euro Under 26 youth card** (CJP in the Netherlands) gives reduced rates for museums, theatres, concerts and more. Ask at VVV offices.

Smoking

Since July 2008, a smoking ban has been in force in the Dutch hospitality industry, with the exception of special "smoking rooms". On terraces, smoking is also permitted, and because the smoking rooms are not designated for smokers exclusively, this means that other activities, like drinking, eating and dancing are allowed.

Time

The time in the Netherlands is on Central European Time (Greenwich Mean Time + 1hr, EST -6hrs).

Tipping

For hotels, restaurants and shopping, the bill is usually inclusive of service charge and VAT. For taxi fares, it is customary to give a tip of around 10%.

CONVERSION TABLES

Weights and Measures

1 kilogram (kg) 6.35 kilograms 0.45 kilograms	**2.2 pounds (lb)** 14 pounds 16 ounces (oz)	**2.2 pounds** 1 stone (st) 16 ounces	*To convert kilograms to pounds, multiply by 2.2*
1 metric ton (tn)	**1.1 tons**	**1.1 tons**	
1 litre (l) 3.79 litres 4.55 litres	**2.11 pints (pt)** 1 gallon (gal) 1.20 gallon	**1.76 pints** 0.83 gallon 1 gallon	*To convert litres to gallons, multiply by 0.26 (US) or 0.22 (UK)*
1 hectare (ha) **1 sq. kilometre (km²)**	**2.47 acres** 0.38 sq. miles (sq.mi.)	**2.47 acres** 0.38 sq. miles	*To convert hectares to acres, multiply by 2.4*
1 centimetre (cm) **1 metre (m)**	**0.39 inches (in)** 3.28 feet (ft) or 39.37 inches or 1.09 yards (yd)	**0.39 inches**	*To convert metres to feet, multiply by 3.28; for kilometres to miles, multiply by 0.6*
1 kilometre (km)	**0.62 miles (mi)**	**0.62 miles**	

Clothing

Women				Men			
	35	4	2½		40	7½	7
	36	5	3½		41	8½	8
	37	6	4½		42	9½	9
Shoes	38	7	5½	Shoes	43	10½	10
	39	8	6½		44	11½	11
	40	9	7½		45	12½	12
	41	10	8½		46	13½	13
	36	6	8		46	36	36
	38	8	10		48	38	38
Dresses	40	10	12	Suits	50	40	40
& suits	42	12	14		52	42	42
	44	14	16		54	44	44
	46	16	18		56	46	48
	36	06	30		37	14½	14½
	38	08	32		38	15	15
Blouses &	40	10	34	Shirts	39	15½	15½
sweaters	42	12	36		40	15¾	15¾
	44	14	38		41	16	16
	46	16	40		42	16½	16½

Sizes often vary depending on the designer. These equivalents are given for guidance only.

Speed

KPH	10	30	50	70	80	90	100	110	120	130
MPH	6	19	31	43	50	56	62	68	75	81

Temperature

Celsius (°C)	0°	5°	10°	15°	20°	25°	30°	40°	60°	80°	100°
Fahrenheit (°F)	32°	41°	50°	59°	68°	77°	86°	104°	140°	176°	212°

To convert Celsius into Fahrenheit, multiply °C by 9, divide by 5, and add 32.
To convert Fahrenheit into Celsius, subtract 32 from °F, multiply by 5, and divide by 9.
NB: Conversion factors on this page are approximate.

Windmills in Kinderdijk
Mattes/ MICHELIN

NATURE

Geography

The area of the Netherlands, which includes huge stretches of water such as IJsselmeer and the Waddenzee, is 41 863sq km/16 163sq mi, of which 9 896sq km/3 821sq mi is reclaimed land. The longest distance from one end of the country to the other is 310km/192.6mi, from Rottum Island in the north of the province of Groningen to the south of

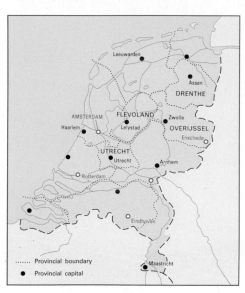

.... Provincial boundary
● Provincial capital

Limburg. Agriculture in the Netherlands is highly intensive and productive, but represents only a small percentage of the gross national product (GNP). Stock-raising is well suited to the fertile reclaimed areas. Industry, especially chemicals, metallurgy and food processing, is concentrated within the Randstad area, the Twente, Noord-Brabant and Limburg. The Netherlands relies heavily on imported raw materials and the export of its manufactured goods. Because of its privileged geographical location trade, especially goods in transit between Europe and the rest of the world, plays an important role in the Dutch economy.

HOLLAND AND THE NETHERLANDS

Over the years the name **Holland** has come to designate the whole of the Netherlands. In fact, this old province, separated since 1840 into Noord-Holland and Zuid-Holland, supplanted the other regions of the United Provinces in the 17C due to its economic prosperity and political supremacy. Napoleon I ratified the primacy of Holland by creating the short-lived kingdom of Holland in 1810. In fact, as early as the late Middle Ages the plains stretching from Friesland to Flanders were called **Lage Landen** or **Nederlanden** (Low Countries). In 1581 the United Provinces of the Netherlands (Verenigde Provinciën der Nederlanden) came into being. In 1815 this was still the name used when William I became ruler of the kingdom, which included part of Belgium. The name has remained unchanged – Netherlands – despite the secession of Belgium in 1830, and Queen Beatrix has the title of Queen of the Netherlands (Koningin der Nederlanden). The country has 12 provinces.

CLIMATE

A cloudy sky pierced by a few timid rays of sunshine or a misty horizon are typical of the climate, and were beautifully captured by the landscape artists of the 17C. The oceanic climate is humid and cool. An average of 750mm/29.5in of rain falls each year, spread over more than 200 days. The temperature is fairly cool in summer without being too harsh in winter. Winters are warmer than in the past, as proved by Avercamp's delightful 17C skating scenes; in 1795, too, the town of Den Helder fell after the French took advantage of the fact that the Dutch fleet was frozen into the ice. The westerly winds are often strong, and many of the farmhouses are protected by a screen of poplar trees.

A "Low Country"

The name Netherlands, from the Dutch 'Nederland', is very apt (*neder* = low, *land* = country). The sea is a constant threat, since more than one third of the country is below sea level. Without the protection of dunes and dykes, more than half the country would be under water during surge tides or when the rivers are in spate. The lowest point, 6.5m/21.3ft below sea level, is at Alexanderpolder, near Rotterdam.

There is a marked difference between east and west. The west of the country is a low-lying plain with an average altitude of less than 5m/16.4ft. This area is the most densely populated. In the east, on the other hand, the Veluwe Hills rise to a height of 106m/348ft at Zijpenberg to the northeast of Arnhem, and **Drielandenpunt** (321m/1 053ft), at the junction of the Dutch, Belgian and German frontiers, is the highest point. The Netherlands represents a depressed area of the earth's crust which has subsequently been filled in by alluvial deposits from the rivers and depositions from the sea.

A LAND OF WATER

The land above sea level represents only five sixths of the total area. The country is criss-crossed by a network of rivers, whose estuaries form an immense delta. In addition, the large freshwater lake, the IJsselmeer, created by the Zuiderzee Project, covers an area of

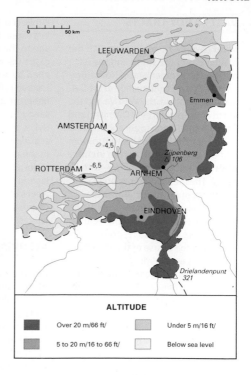

120 000ha/296 526 acres. Elsewhere, ponds, small lakes, canals, streams and ditches abound, especially in Friesland, whose flag has water lily leaves as its emblem. The percentage of land above sea level increases with the altitude from west to east. In the east the land is relatively well drained, while water tends to accumulate in the low-lying plains and polders of the west.

Topography

Apart from a few hilly regions, the Netherlands consists of an immense plain with little diversity of soil, resulting in a corresponding lack of variety in the landscape.

The polder lands are the result of man's determined intervention throughout the ages, but they also give a somewhat monotonous appearance to the countryside. However, they are one of the quintessential aspects of the country and their peacefulness, light and colour give the landscape a poetic dimension.

VAST SANDY TRACTS

Sand covers 43% of the land with the main areas in the south and the east, notably the Kempenland of Noord-Brabant, which is a continuation of the Belgian Kempenland, the **Veluwe** and the north of the provinces of Overijssel and Drenthe. In addition to agricultural land there are moorlands of heather, broom and gorse and forests (in the **vicinity of Breda** and the the Veluwe, with its pines). The great Scandinavian glaciers left tracts of **morainic material** with their telltale erratics in the undulating Utrechtse Heuvelrug and the Veluwe. The glaciers were also responsible for deflecting the course of the Rhine and Maas rivers westwards.

There are several areas of **marshland** (De Peel and Biesbosch) and lakes, for example in the south of Friesland. Unlike those in the province of Holland, these have not been reclaimed due to the infertility of their sandy soil.

DUNES

Coastal currents have caused offshore sand bars to form along the coast. The coastal **sand dunes** are of utmost importance, as they provide protection against the high tides. Marram grass is planted to stabilise the dunes, which are carefully monitored by local authorities.

Public access is restricted in certain sectors to prevent further erosion and damage to this fragile ecosystem. In some cases the chain of dunes is strengthened by a dyke. The dunes also act as reservoirs for the rainwater which then filters down to the water table. The vast sandy beaches beyond the dunes and dykes are a valuable asset for the local seaside resorts.

In the north, the Wadden Islands form an important offshore barrier. They are lashed on the north and west by the waves of the North Sea, with the calmer waters of the Waddenzee on the landward side.

ALLUVIAL DEPOSITS

Marine deposited clays cover 28% of the country, especially in the Delta area, around the great coastal estuaries and bays, and in those which have been reclaimed as polders, such as the Lauwerszee and the Middelzee, which once reached as far inland as Leeuwarden. The **fluvial clays** which cover 10% of the Netherlands are associated with the many rivers in the centre of the country and the Maas Valley, to the south of Venlo.

PEAT BOGS

In the Netherlands there are two types of peat bog. The first has formed in the lagoons on top of marine sediments. Once the peat was extracted, lakes then formed which were drained and used for agricultural purposes. In the upland region peat formed in the marshy areas; here again it was used for fuel and the land was then given over to agriculture. The provinces of Groningen and Drenthe were known for the peat colonies (*veenkoloniën*) which flourished from the 16C to the 19C.

LIMESTONE PLATEAU

The limestone landscapes of southern Limburg provide a sharp contrast to the rest of the country. Some parts of the bedrock are silt-covered (*loess*), as in the Hesbaye region of Belgium, while others appear as rocky outcrops more akin to the ancient (Hercynian) Ardennes Massif, again in Belgium.
All mining activity has now ceased in the Limburg coalfields, which are a continuation of the coal seams of Kempenland in Belgium.

The Creation of a Polder

A polder is defined as land reclaimed from the sea, a lake or marshland. The area is enclosed with dykes and then pumping begins to regulate the water level. The method has been the same since the earliest times, despite various technological developments; windmills were replaced first by steam and then by diesel engines or electrically operated pumps.

The coastal or riverside peat bogs, lying above sea level, necessitate the creation of a simple polder where all the surplus water is returned directly to the sea or the river via locks at low tide. However, when the polder lies below sea level, the water needs to be pumped into diversion canals (lodes) and thence to the sea.

A more complex type of polder is required when draining a lake. The lake is surrounded by a dyke and then a canal, which also encircles the ring dykes of neighbouring polders. The polder itself is criss-crossed with small canals linked to each other by collector canals. When the water level reaches a set height, the pump (formerly the windmill) forces the water back into the collector canals towards the peripheral canal and a network of lakes or canals serving as a temporary reservoir. The water is then discharged into the rivers and the sea, either directly or by pumping; the water level has to be constantly monitored and controlled.

When the lake to be drained was fairly deep, then a number of **windmills** (known as a gang) were required to pump the water out of the polder. The best example of this are the windmills at **Kinderdijk**.

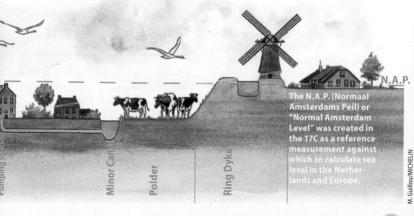

N.A.P.

The N.A.P. (Normaal Amsterdams Peil) or "Normal Amsterdam Level" was created in the 17C as a reference measurement against which to calculate sea level in the Netherlands and Europe.

Pumping Station

Minor Canal

Polder

Ring Dyke

M. Guillou/MICHELIN

The Fight Against the Sea

The history of the Netherlands tells of man's continuous struggle with the elements, against the sea, storm surges and rivers in spate. The first dunes were formed to the south of Haarlem around 5 BC, and by AD 1000 a sand bar stretched from the Scheldt to the Eems. The bar was breached at several points, creating the chain of islands now known as the Wadden Islands, and the sea inundated the peat bogs lying inland to form the **Waddenzee**.

FIRST STEPS: TERPS AND DYKES

Around 500 BC the **Frisians**, the earliest inhabitants of the coastal areas, were already engaged in their struggle with the sea. They built artificial mounds or **terps** to protect their settlements from the encroaching water. As early as AD 1200 they were building dykes and had drained a few areas of land – the very first polders – between Leeuwarden and Sneek. During the 13C there were at least 35 great floods, and large tracts of land were inundated, creating the Dollard and **Lauwerszee** in the north and the **Zuiderzee**, now IJsselmeer, in 1287.

WINDMILLS: THE FIRST POLDERS

In the 14C **windmills** were being used to drain lakes and marshes. By the 15C the rivers of Zeeland had already carved out an intricate network of peninsulas and islands, and the coastal dunes were crumbling under the assaults of the waves. The overall lack of protection was responsible for the catastrophic **St Elizabeth Flood** in 1421. Following this disaster, windmills were increasingly used in the threatened low-lying areas. Thus in Noord-Holland small **polders** appeared in Schagen in 1456 and in Alkmaar in 1564. Many of the coastal dykes of the time were the work of **Andries Vierlingh** (1507–79).

17C: A SERIES OF POLDERS

In the 17C, much of the draining of inland tracts of water was carried out by **Jan Adriaenszoon Leeghwater** (his name means low water). Leeghwater supervised the successful draining of the **Beemstermeer** to the north of Amsterdam in 1612 with the help of 40 windmills. (The Beemsterpolder has been inscribed on the UNESCO World Heritage List since 1999). The success of this initial project encouraged the Dutch to continue reclamation work, and they built the polders of **Purmer** in 1622 and **Wormer** in 1626. In 1631 the town of Alkmaar started reclaiming the **Schermermeer** in accordance with Leeghwater's instructions. This time 50 windmills were used and the work was completed in 1635. Another of Leeghwater's projects (one he never completed) was the draining of Haarlem Lake. As early as 1667, Hendrik Stevin proposed a project to drain the Zuiderzee "to evacuate the violence and poison of the North Sea." The project was only eventually completed in the 20C.

In the 18C autonomous water boards (**waterschappen**) were invested with the responsibility for building, maintaining and monitoring the country's dykes, canals and locks. These bodies still exist, but today they fall under the authority of the **Ministry of Transport and Waterways**. Steam power was introduced just before 1800, and this proved capable of pumping water over high dykes, thus replacing several rows, or gangs, of windmills. Pumping operations no longer depended on the vagaries of wind power.

THE AMBITIOUS PROJECTS OF THE 19C AND 20C

The most spectacular period of land reclamation began in 1848 with the draining of **Haarlem Lake**, which was completed four years later. Three large pumping stations were built, including that of Cruquius, which has now been converted into a museum (&see HAARLEM, Outskirts).

After the great floods of 1916 it was the turn of the Zuiderzee itself. This

THE FIGHT AGAINST THE SEA

Polders: 14-18C   Polders: 19C to the present   Dike: coastal or fluvial

great arm of the sea was closed off by the barrier dam or **Afsluitdijk** in 1932, creating the outer Waddenzee and an inland freshwater lake now known as the **IJsselmeer**. Once enclosed, work began on draining several polders around the edge (Wieringermeer, Noordoost, Zuidelijk Flevoland and Oostelijk Flevoland). The fifth polder (**Markerwaard**) was abandoned in 1986.

Other polders reclaimed in the 19C and 20C are the Prins Alexander Polder (1872) near Rotterdam and the Lauwersmeer Polder.

The most recent disaster occurred during the night of 31 January 1953, when gale force winds swept landwards at high tide; 1 865 people died and 260 000ha/642 474 acres were inundated. The success of the Zuiderzee Project encouraged engineers to find a similar way to protect the islands of Noord- and Zuid-Holland. The outcome was the **Delta Plan** (⟲ see DELTA), work

on which began in 1954. This vast project was not completed until 1998, with the building of the storm surge barrier in the Nieuwe Waterweg.

CONQUERING THE SEA

Since the 13C, about 7 050sq km/2 722sq mi have been reclaimed from the sea. Coastal dykes have been responsible for creating 4 000sq km/1 544sq mi, the IJsselmeer for another 1 650sq km/637sq mi and a further 1 400sq km/540.5sq mi has been reclaimed by other means.

However, in the early 21C, some parts of the Dutch landscape may undergo a radical change. New EU farming regulations, the surplus of floral and market garden products, and the critical level of pollution – partly caused by large-scale pig breeding – led the Dutch government to pass a bill in 1993 stipulating that one tenth of arable land should be left fallow.

Nature Conservation

In this highly industrialised and densely populated country, certain groups are very active in the protection of the environment. The Nature Conservation Society (Vereniging Natuurmonumenten) is a private organisation which acquires and preserves unspoilt coastal and rural areas. The Society currently manages more than 300 nature reserves (**natuurmonumenten**) covering a total area of 78 000ha/192 742 acres of varied habitats, including woodlands, moors, dunes and marshes. In general visitors are welcome at the reserves, and some have visitor centres, nature trails and bird hides, but there are usually restrictions. There are also 84 National Heritage Sites and 13 National Parks. State-owned forests and woodlands are managed by the Forestry Commission (Staatsbosbeheer). Recreation is encouraged and the facilities include picnic sites, nature trails and campsites.

Northern Lapwing

Eddy Van 3000/Flickr

Birds

The great variety of habitats provided by the Netherlands' seasides, hills, waters and woodlands attracts many bird species, both native and migratory (*illustrations: see WADDENEILANDEN*).

One of the most common species is the **lapwing** with its plaintive "pee-wit" cry, which is almost considered the national bird. This plump little bird is about 30cm/11.8in in length, with lustrous bronze plumage, and prefers grassy areas, especially in Friesland. Its eggs are considered a delicacy, but plans are afoot for a ban on their sale, and Queen Juliana ended the tradition whereby the first lapwing's egg to be found each year is given to the queen.

The seashores are home to **terns**, **seagulls** and other **gulls**, particularly the Black-headed Gulls, which often nest inland. Colonies of **oystercatchers**, a small black and white wader, nest along the shores while the **Grey Heron** can be seen along the canals. The **Spoonbill** is rarer but can be seen in shallow estuaries, while the **White Stork** is protected to prevent its extinction.

All sorts of **ducks** abound in the canals, ponds and marshes: the wild duck or mallard and the sheldrake with multicoloured plumage are the most common. The country's numerous **nature reserves** provide protection for a variety of species and their coastal and inland habitats. The reserves provide safe breeding and feeding grounds and facilities for scientific study. Public access is limited and usually prohibited during the breeding season (April to August).

HISTORY

Time Line

PREHISTORY

30000 BC Earliest traces of human settlement in the east of the country.
4500 Agriculturists settle in Limburg; their pottery belongs to the Spiral Meander Ware culture.
3000-2000 The megalithic Hunebed culture flourishes in the Drenthe area.
2200 A nomadic people settles to the north of the great rivers; stroke ornamented pottery ware.
2000 Bell-Beaker civilisation, notably in the Drenthe. New settlements in the alluvial areas of the delta.
1900 Bronze Age. The dead are buried in burial mounds.
800 In the east the people incinerate their dead and bury them in urnfields.
750-400 First Iron Age: Hallstatt Period.
500 First **terps** are built in Friesland and the Groningen area (👉 *see LEEUWARDEN, Terp Region*)
450 South of the Great rivers, Second Iron Age: La Tène Period.
300 Germanic and Celtic tribes arrive in the area south of the Rhine.

ROMANS – VIKINGS

57-51 South of the Rhine, **Caesar** defeats the Menapii and Eburones, Celtic tribes belonging to the Roman province of Gallia Belgica.
12 The Germanic tribe the **Batavi** settle the banks of the great rivers.

AD 69-70 Batavian uprising against the Roman garrisons.
3C Incursions by Germanic tribes: the **Franks** settle the banks of the Rhine. At this time the main tribes occupying the territory are the Franks, **Saxons** and **Frisians**.
Late 3C The area south of the Rhine belongs to the Roman province of Germania Secunda (capital: Cologne).
4C Power struggle between the Salian Franks and the Romans.
382 St Servatius transfers his bishopric from Tongeren to Maastricht and the region's gradual conversion to Christianity begins.
Early 6C The Merovingian kingdom under Clovis (465–511) extends from the north of Gaul to the Rhine.
561 The Merovingian kingdom is divided into Neustria (west of the river Scheldt) and Austrasia (east of the Scheldt; the present Netherlands).
Late 7C The Northumbrian missionary **Willibrord** evangelises Friesland.
800 **Charlemagne** is crowned Emperor of the West, a territory which covers the whole of the country and is centred on Aachen.
834 First of the **Viking** raids at Dorestad (👉 *see AMERSFOORT, The Woodlands and Heathlands of the Utrechtse Heuvelrug*).
843 **Treaty of Verdun**. The Carolingian Empire is divided into three kingdoms: Germania, Francia and, between the two, a Middle Kingdom stretching from the North Sea to the Mediterranean and including the present-day Netherlands. The Middle Kingdom (Lotharingia)

was short-lived and Lothair II received only the northern part.

879-882 Viking invasions: from their base in Utrecht they make raids into the surrounding countryside.

925 The German King Henry I, the Fowler, annexes **Lotharingia**.

959 Lotharingia is divided into Upper Lotharingia (Lorraine) and Lower Lotharingia, covering nearly all the present country.

COUNTIES AND DUCHIES

10C Bishop Balderic (919–76) extends the **See of Utrecht**.

Early 11C The **Duchy of Brabant** is founded by Lambert, Count of Leuven.

11C Creation of the county of Gelderland.

Late 11C The county of **Holland** is extended at the expense of the county of Flanders (in Zeeland) and the See of Utrecht.

Early 13C Zutphen and Veluwe become part of the county of Gelderland.

Late 13C **Floris V**, Count of Holland, conquers West Friesland.

1323 Zeeland passes from Flanders to Holland.

1350 Start of the civil war between the **Hooks** (*Hoeken* – backed by Margaret of Bavaria) and the **Cods** (*Kabbeljauwen* – backed by her son William V).

CONSOLIDATION OF BURGUNDIAN POWER

Late 14C The Duchy of Burgundy is extended northwards when **Philip the Bold** acquires Limburg and certain rights over Brabant.

1428 Philip the Good deposes **Jacoba** and makes himself ruler of Holland and Zeeland.

1473 **Charles the Bold** acquires Gelderland; the only territory not in Burgundian hands is Friesland.

THE HABSBURGS

1477 Death of Charles the Bold; his daughter and heir Mary of Burgundy marries Maximilian of Austria, one of the Habsburgs.
Mary is forced to sign the Great Privilege, a charter conferring far-reaching local powers.

1494 Philip the Fair, their son, inherits the Low Countries when Maximilian is elected Holy Roman Emperor.

1515 Charles I of Spain, son of Philip the Fair, inherits the Low Countries. In 1516 he becomes King of Spain, and then in 1519 Emperor of Germany as **Charles V**. He adds **Friesland** to the Low Countries in 1523; the See of Utrecht in 1527; Overijssel in 1528; and takes Groningen and Drenthe by force in 1536.

1543 The Duke of Gelderland cedes his dukedom to Charles V, who thus rules over nearly the whole of Europe.

1548 Charles V groups the 17 provinces of the Low Countries and the Franche-Comté into the independent Burgundian Kreis.

THE SPANISH NETHERLANDS

1555 Charles V abdicates his claim to the Low Countries in favour of his son Philip II, soon to become King of Spain.

1555-79 The **Revolt of the Netherlands**; the rise of Protestantism.

1566 The **Compromise of Breda**, also known as the Compromise of the Nobility; the Beggars protest against the Inquisition (*see BREDA*).

William the Silent depicted on a stained-glass window of St.-Janskerk, Gouda

Ph. Gajic/MICHELIN

The **Iconoclasm**, involving riots and destruction of Church property.

1567 The Duke of Alba is appointed Governor of the Low Countries.

1568 **William the Silent** raises an army; beginning of the Eighty Years' War.

1572 **Capture of Brielle** by the Sea Beggars (☙ *see BRIELLE*); Vlissingen and Enkhuizen follow.

1579 **Union of Arras** is signed by Catholic Hainaut, Artois and Douai, pledging allegiance to Philip; in reply the northern Protestant provinces form an essentially military alliance and sign the **Union of Utrecht** (☙ *see UTRECHT*).

THE UNITED PROVINCES

1581 Creation of the **Republic of the Seven United Provinces**, a federation of seven provinces, independent of Spanish rule; Philip II is deposed.

1584 William the Silent is assassinated in Delft.

1585 His second son, Maurice of Nassau, succeeds his father as Stadtholder of Holland and Zeeland. He becomes undisputed leader of the United Provinces in 1618 on the death of his elder brother.

1596 Cornelis de Houtman establishes trading relations with Java.

1598 Edict of Nantes.

1602 **Dutch East India Company** founded to trade with Asia.

1609-21 **Twelve Years' Truce** with Spain. Henry Hudson sails up the American river, later named after him, in his ship the *Half Moon*, while on a voyage for the Dutch East India Company.

1614 The name New Netherland is first used for the colony founded in the New World.

1618 **Synod of Dort**. Reprobation of the Remonstrants.

1619 Founding of **Batavia** (Jakarta) in the Dutch East Indies.

1620 The Pilgrim Fathers arrive on the **Mayflower** and establish Plymouth Colony.

1621 Founding of the **Dutch West India Company** to trade with America. Renewal of hostilities with Spain.

1624-54 Colonisation of northeast Brazil.

1625 The Dutch trading post on Manhattan Island is called Nieuw Amsterdam.

1626 Peter Minuit of the Dutch West India Company buys

Manhattan from the Indians for a pittance.

1634   Dutch West India Company establishes a trading post in Curaçao in the Antilles.

1648   Treaty of Westphalia ends the Thirty Years' War, also called the Eighty Years' War. In the **Peace of Münster** Philip IV of Spain recognises the independence of the United Provinces.

1651   The English Navigation Act augurs ill for Dutch trade.

1652   Jan van Riebeeck founds the Cape Colony.

1652-54 **First Anglo-Dutch War:** commercial and colonial rivalry lead to what is essentially a war at sea; the Dutch fleet is commanded by Admiral Tromp (*see BRIELLE*).

1653-72 Stadtholderless Period: the statesman **Johan de Witt** (*see DORDRECHT*) governs as Grand Pensionary.

1658-
1795   Colonisation of Ceylon (Sri Lanka).

1664   The English seize New Netherland and rename its capital New York after the Duke of York, later James II.

1665-67 **Second Anglo-Dutch War.** Admiral de Ruyter earns distinction as commander of the Dutch fleet. Under the **Treaty of Breda,** Dutch Guiana (Surinam) is ceded to the Dutch in exchange for control of New Netherland.

1667-68 War of Devolution led by Louis XIV; Treaty of Aachen.

1672   **William III** becomes Stadtholder of Holland and Zeeland.

1677   William marries Mary, the daughter of James II.

1672-78 War with France.

1678-79 **Peace of Nijmegen**

1685   Revocation of the Edict of Nantes.

1688   Glorious Revolution: British crown offered jointly to William and Mary following the flight of James II.

1689   William becomes King of England.

1701-13 Spanish War of Succession: alliance of several countries, including the United Provinces, against Louis XIV. **Treaty of Utrecht**.

1702   Stadtholder William III dies without an heir. The title of Prince of Orange passes to the Frisian Stadtholder, Jan Willem Friso.

1702-47 Stadtholderless Period.

1747   **William IV**, the son of Jan Willem Friso, is the first elected Stadtholder of the United Provinces.

1751-95 **William V,** William IV's son, is Stadtholder.

FRENCH DOMINATION

1795   A French army under General Pichegru overruns the country; William V flees to England; the United Provinces become the **Batavian Republic** (1795–1806).

1806   **Louis Bonaparte** becomes king of the **Kingdom of Holland** with Amsterdam as the capital.

1810-13 Louis Bonaparte abdicates; the country becomes part of the **French Empire** under Napoleon.

UNION WITH BELGIUM

Dec 1813 William VI of Orange, son of William V, becomes last Stadtholder of the Netherlands.

1815   Battle of Waterloo and the fall of Napoleon. The Congress of Vienna recognises William VI, Prince of Orange, as the King of the Netherlands (including Belgium) under the name **William I**. In addition, he becomes Grand Duke of Luxembourg. The Western seaboard of New Guinea is colonised.

1830   Brussels Revolution leads to Belgium's independence.

AN INDEPENDENT KINGDOM

1831 Parts of Limburg and Brabant are ceded to Belgium but William I only ratifies the treaty in 1839.

1839 The first **railway** line is built between Haarlem and Amsterdam.

1890-
1948 Reign of **Queen Wilhelmina**.

1932 Zuiderzee Project.

May 1940 The country is invaded by the German army. The Queen and her family leave for London.

5 May
1945 German army surrenders (see ARNHEM), and the Queen returns.

1948 Queen Wilhelmina abdicates in favour of her daughter **Juliana**. Economic Union of Benelux.

Dec 1949 Independence of the Dutch East Indies which become the Republic of **Indonesia.**

1954 Autonomy of Dutch Guiana or Surinam and the archipelago of the Dutch Antilles.

1957 The Netherlands joins the **EEC**.

1960 The **Benelux** economic union comes into effect.

Nov 1975 Dutch Guiana becomes independent as the Republic of **Surinam**.

30 April
1980 Queen Juliana abdicates in favour of her daughter **Beatrix**.

1 Jan
1986 **Aruba** is separated from the Netherlands Antilles and becomes an internally self-governing integral part of the Netherlands realm.

1986 Flevoland becomes the 12th province.

1987 Inauguration of the Oosterschelde storm-surge barrier.

1992 **Treaty of Maastricht** signed by the twelve EC members.

1998 Completion of the Delta Plan.

THE NEW MILLENNIUM

2000 The Netherlands and Belgium co-host the **Euro 2000** football championships.

2000 Parliament legalises euthanasia, setting strict guidelines for doctors.

Apr 2001 Four homosexual couples marry in Amsterdam under brand new legislation. It is the first ceremony of its kind in the Netherlands.

Jan 2002 The **euro** replaces the Dutch guilder.

Apr 2002 Following an official report that criticised its role in the Srebrenica massacre in 1995 when ill-equipped Dutch peacekeeping forces failed to stop Bosnian Serb forces from murdering thousands of Muslims, Wim Kok's government resigns.

May 2002 Anti-immigration party leader Pim Fortuyn is assassinated. Nearly a year later animal rights activist Volkert van der Graaf is sentenced to 18 years for the killing.

Mar 2004 Queen mother Juliana dies, aged 94.

Jun 2006 Prime Minister Balkenende forms a temporary minority government after his coalition collapses in a row over immigration.

Nov 2006 New coalition government formed after a general election which brings large gains for the country's Socialist Party.

Jan 2008 Controversy rages over the release of a short anti-Islam film by the Dutch right-wing politician Geert Wilders.

Ties Between the British and the Dutch

The Netherlands and Britain were two small seafaring nations with a strong Protestant tradition, in an otherwise predominantly Catholic world. They were linked politically, religiously, commercially, intellectually and artistically long before William III's reign, though it was during his time that their friendship reached its peak.

William III, **Prince of Orange**, was the nephew and son-in-law of King James II (1685–88) of England, and Stadtholder of the United Provinces. He married Mary, James' daughter, in 1677. James set about establishing Catholicism, which created nationwide unrest and dissent. The British wrote to William in June 1688 asking him to restore peace and unity to the country. William landed in October 1688, James abdicated, and Mary, the nearest Protestant claimant to the throne, was crowned jointly with William in April 1689. During their reign (1689–1702) a vogue for all things Dutch developed.

Political decisions were closely linked to commercial interests, and the Dutch, English and Scots had been exchanging naval techniques and trading together for years, in areas such as the wool and shipbuilding industries.

Once commercial links had been established between the two countries, Dutch goods and influences began appearing in Britain. These included bricks and gables, sash windows, Dutch-style gardens, marine painting and portraits, and interior decoration. Dutch influence reached its peak during William and Mary's reign with the transformation of Hampton Court and Kensington Palace, where the influence of their Dutch residence, Het Loo, is apparent. They employed Grinling Gibbons to do carvings, Daniël Marot as their architect and interior decorator, and Sir Godfrey Kneller to paint portraits; all were in some way connected with the Netherlands. Many stately homes, such as Belton, Ashdown and Easton, contained Dutch-style decorative features including carvings, tulip vases, lacquerware cabinets and upholstered cabriole-legged chairs, and reflected Mary's great love of porcelain and William's for gardens.

The Dutch tradition of religious tolerance and freedom of expression also attracted political and religious refugees from Britain. With the reign of William and Mary, a wave of tolerance spread through Britain, rendering exile to the Netherlands unnecessary.

Overseas Expansion

In the middle of the 16C, Amsterdam traders went to Antwerp to obtain goods brought back from the Indies by Portuguese ships. Since the mouth of the Scheldt was cut off by the Sea Beggars, the traders started sailing to Lisbon in 1580, the same year that Philip II of Spain invaded Portugal. In 1585 he placed an embargo on Dutch trade in Spain and Portugal. The Dutch merchants, forced to handle shipments themselves, clashed with the Spanish, Portuguese and above all the English, who were fearsome competitors in the overseas markets.

THE ROUTE TO THE EAST

While looking for a passage to India from the north of Europe, **Willem Barents** (see WADDENEILANDEN, Terschelling) discovered Novaya Zemlya in 1594 and Spitsbergen in 1596. In the same year, **Cornelis de Houtman** landed in **Java**. **Jacob van Neck** conquered the island of Mauritius in 1598. After the establishment of Batavia (now Jakarta) by **Jan Pieterszoon Coen** (see HOORN) in 1619, Java became a Dutch colony. In 1641, **Malacca** was wrested from the Portuguese, and in the following year the explorer **Abel Janszoon Tasman**, an explorer working for the East India Company, discovered the islands of **Tasmania** and **New Zealand**. Australia was first mapped by Dutch cartographers, who called it **Nieuw-Holland**. **Jan Anthoniszoon van Riebeeck** established the **Cape Colony** (South Africa) in 1652, and **Ceylon** was occupied in 1658.

THE EAST INDIA COMPANY

To coordinate the large number of trading companies sailing to the East, Johan van Oldenbarnevelt founded the **United East India Company** or **VOC** in 1602. The Company obtained a monopoly over shipping and trade to the east of the Cape of Good Hope and west of the Strait of Magellan, it soon became the biggest trading company of the 17C, with trading posts all over Asia. From these settlements, the VOC brought back costly spices (nutmeg, pepper, cinnamon, saffron, ginger and cloves) and Chinese porcelain; these were largely replaced by tea, coffee, silk and cotton from the 18C onwards. The journey from the Netherlands to Java took eight months, and to coordinate all these expeditions a central administration was set up in **Batavia**. Here, all products from Sumatra, Borneo, the Moluccas, and also India, China, Japan and Persia, were centralised for transportation to the home country, and they played a major part in creating the prosperity that was the Golden Age. The VOC was finally disbanded in 1789.

THE AMERICAS

In the 17C, Dutch trade also turned towards the New World. The first expedition was that of **Hudson** in 1609; Amsterdam merchants established a factory in **Surinam** in 1613, and **Willem Schouten** (see HOORN) discovered Cape Horn in 1616.

The **Dutch West India Company** (**WIC**), created in 1621, traded both with Africa and the Americas; the "commodities" included slaves. It set up trading posts on the coasts of both continents, and also conquered many islands in the Caribbean: Bonaire, Tobago, **Curaçao**, Sint-Maarten and the other Antilles.

In **Brazil**, **Johan Maurits van Nassau** (1604–79) was appointed governor-general (1636–44). He was a great patron of the arts and sciences, and assembled a team of academics and artists who documented the country in great detail.

The WIC concentrated mainly on southern America, but in 1624 it established **Nieuw Amsterdam** on the east coast of North America, and the Dutch colonialist **Peter Stuyvesant** became its governor shortly afterwards. Under his rule, Nieuw Amsterdam developed rapidly, but in 1664 it was taken by the English and renamed New York.

COLONIES

Many of the Dutch conquests in Asia and America were only temporary. However, they succeeded in establishing lasting settlements in **Indonesia** (until 1949) and **Surinam** (until 1975). The **Netherlands Antilles** (Curaçao, Bonaire, St Eustatius, Saba and St Martin) and **Aruba** still form part of the Kingdom of the Netherlands, having become an internally self-governing integral part of the Netherlands in 1954 and 1986 respectively.

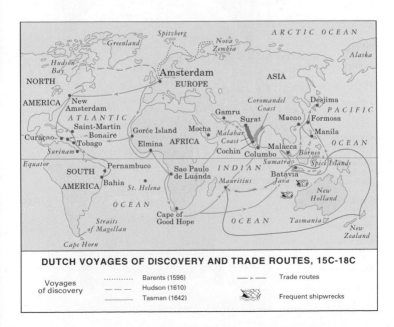

DUTCH VOYAGES OF DISCOVERY AND TRADE ROUTES, 15C-18C

Voyages of discovery	.... Barents (1596)	—▸— Trade routes
	— — — Hudson (1610)	
	——— Tasman (1642)	🚢 Frequent shipwrecks

ART AND CULTURE

Architecture

Religious Architecture

'S-HERTOGENBOSCH – Ground plan of St.-Janskathedraal (1380-1580)

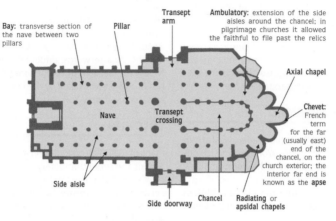

Bay: transverse section of the nave between two pillars

Pillar

Transept arm

Ambulatory: extension of the side aisles around the chancel; in pilgrimage churches it allowed the faithful to file past the relics

Axial chapel

Nave

Transept crossing

Chevet: French term for the far (usually east) end of the chancel, on the church exterior; the interior far end is known as the **apse**

Side aisle

Side doorway

Chancel

Radiating or apsidal chapels

HAARLEM – Grote Kerk or St.-Bavokerk (Chancel)

The inclusion of an ambulatory and the length of the chancel are unusual in a Gothic church in the Netherlands, suggesting French influence. The architect chose cedar wood for the stellar vaulting.

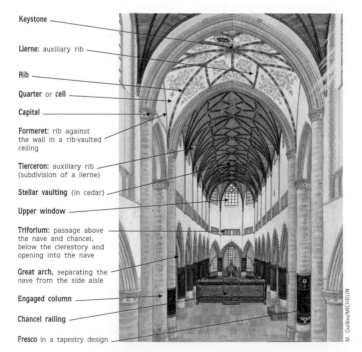

Keystone

Lierne: auxiliary rib

Rib

Quarter or **cell**

Capital

Formeret: rib against the wall in a rib-vaulted ceiling

Tierceron: auxiliary rib (subdivision of a lierne)

Stellar vaulting (in cedar)

Upper window

Triforium: passage above the nave and chancel, below the clerestory and opening into the nave

Great arch, separating the nave from the side aisle

Engaged column

Chancel railing

Fresco in a tapestry design

M. Guillou/MICHELIN

AMSTERDAM – Westerkerk (1619-31)

The Westerkerk is the last and most imposing of the three Mannerist churches built by Hendrik de Keyser commissioned by the city of Amsterdam. The two churches which predate it are the Zuiderkerk and the Noorderkerk.

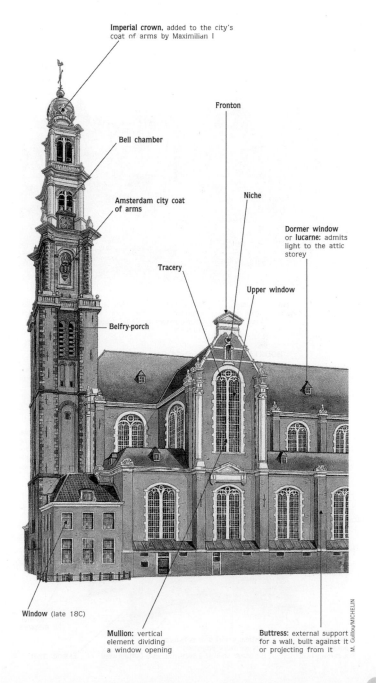

Imperial crown, added to the city's coat of arms by Maximilian I

Fronton

Bell chamber

Niche

Amsterdam city coat of arms

Dormer window or **lucarne:** admits light to the attic storey

Tracery

Upper window

Belfry-porch

Window (late 18C)

Mullion: vertical element dividing a window opening

Buttress: external support for a wall, built against it or projecting from it

M. Guillou/MICHELIN

Military Architecture

AMERSFOORT – Koppelpoort (c. 1400)

This fortified gateway is a remnant of the second enceinte around Amersfoort. It is a unique combination of a town and water gate; the latter houses a double fulling mill.

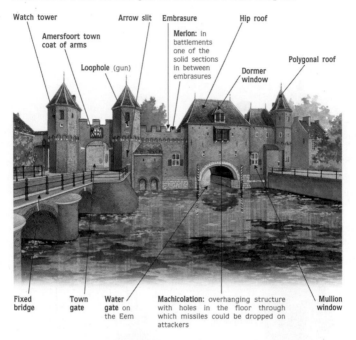

Watch tower

Amersfoort town coat of arms

Arrow slit   Embrasure

Loophole (gun)

Merlon: in battlements one of the solid sections in between embrasures

Hip roof

Dormer window

Polygonal roof

Fixed bridge

Town gate

Water gate on the Eem

Machicolation: overhanging structure with holes in the floor through which missiles could be dropped on attackers

Mullion window

BOURTANGE – Stronghold (late 16C and 17C)

The stronghold at Bourtange was designed by Adriaan Anthonisz and dates from the late 16C; the fortifications were extended and strengthened in the following century. It is one of the best examples of a fortress in the Old Dutch style.

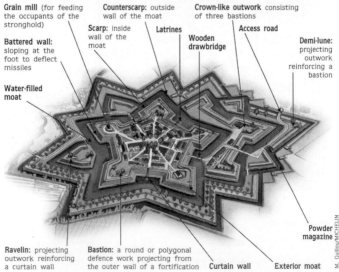

Grain mill (for feeding the occupants of the stronghold)

Battered wall: sloping at the foot to deflect missiles

Water-filled moat

Counterscarp: outside wall of the moat

Scarp: inside wall of the moat

Latrines

Crown-like outwork consisting of three bastions

Wooden drawbridge

Access road

Demi-lune: projecting outwork reinforcing a bastion

Powder magazine

Ravelin: projecting outwork reinforcing a curtain wall

Bastion: a round or polygonal defence work projecting from the outer wall of a fortification

Curtain wall   Exterior moat

M. Guillou/MICHELIN

Civil Architecture

AMSTERDAM – 18C merchant's house

The beautiful town houses along the canals of Amsterdam were built on pilotis (free-standing piles). Those commissioned by merchants in the 18C consist of a "downstairs", where the domestic staff were housed, an "upstairs", where the merchant and his family lived, and a loft in which merchandise was stored.

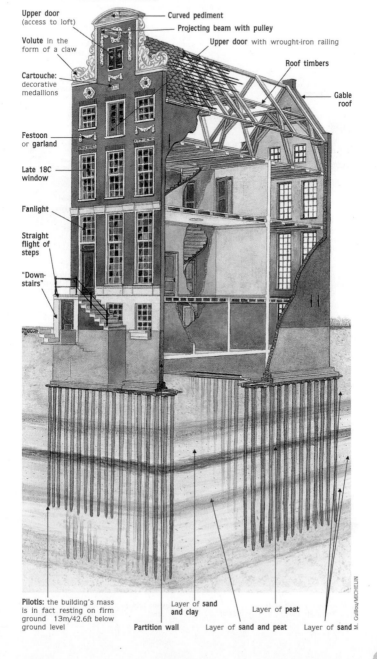

Upper door (access to loft)

Curved pediment

Projecting beam with pulley

Volute in the form of a claw

Upper door with wrought-iron railing

Roof timbers

Cartouche: decorative medallions

Gable roof

Festoon or **garland**

Late 18C window

Fanlight

Straight flight of steps

"Downstairs"

Pilotis: the building's mass is in fact resting on firm ground 13m/42.6ft below ground level

Partition wall

Layer of **sand and clay**

Layer of **peat**

Layer of **sand and peat**

Layer of **sand**

M. Guillou/MICHELIN

HILVERSUM – Town Hall (1927-31)

Hilversum town hall won international renown for architect WM Dudok. Giant cuboid forms sit on top of or next to one another, giving rise to a harmonious interplay of vertical and horizontal lines. A tall clock tower overlooks the complex.

Roof overhang, designed to accentuate the horizontal and create a play of light and shade

Tall, thin **brick;** bricks with this dimension (24 x 11.5 x 4.5cm/9.4 x 4.5 x 1.8in) came to be known as "Hilversum format"

WM Dudok's **office** with a large corner window

Tower

Gallery

Tall, narrow **windows,** surmounted by a small projecting roof; the openings are remininscent of those in a bell tower

Canopy

Row of small windows directly beneath the roof, making it seem to be floating in thin air

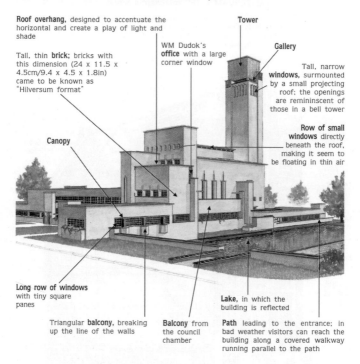

Long row of windows with tiny square panes

Triangular **balcony,** breaking up the line of the walls

Balcony from the council chamber

Lake, in which the building is reflected

Path leading to the entrance; in bad weather visitors can reach the building along a covered walkway running parallel to the path

ROTTERDAM – Erasmusbrug (1996)

This 802m/2 630ft long single pylon bridge is the work of Ben van Berkel. It was inaugurated in 1996 and consists of two approach ramps joined in the middle by a fixed metal cable bridge and a steel bascule bridge.

Cable

Pylon (139m/456ft high); this has give the bridge its nickname "The Swan"

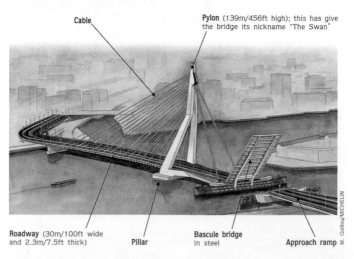

Roadway (30m/100ft wide and 2.3m/7.5ft thick)

Pillar

Bascule bridge in steel

Approach ramp

M. Guillou/MICHELIN

Traditional Structures

FARMHOUSES

The lovely farmhouses, which are scattered over the countryside, are part of the country's familiar landscape. They are largest in the polder areas.

Frisian Farmhouses

These buildings with huge roofs can be seen all over Friesland, in areas which were formerly part of Friesland, such as the north of the province of Noord-Holland, and in the province of Groningen.

Pyramid-Roofed Farmhouses
(*Stolpboerderijen*)

There are many of these in the north of the province of Noord-Holland. Their enormous pyramid-shaped roofs are reminiscent of haystacks, and the stables, barn and living quarters are all under one roof. On one side of the roof, the thatch is partially replaced by tiles forming a decorative pattern. Sometimes, in the more elaborate farmhouses, the façade has a richly decorated brick pediment. Similar buildings which are rectangular are found in southern Friesland.

"Head-Neck-Trunk" Farmhouses
(*Kop-hals-rompboerderijen*)

These can be seen in the north of Friesland and the province of Groningen. These are made up of three parts: the living quarters (the "head") are linked by a narrow section (the "neck") to a large building (the "trunk"), which includes the cowshed, barn, and in some cases a stable. Traditionally, the living quarters have a tiled roof, whereas the barn is thatched. This kind of farmhouse is often built on a mound (see LEEUWARDEN, Terp Region). At either end of the ridge of the barn roof, there is an ornamental triangular board with holes in it, which were placed there to allow owls to fly in and out of the building, nest in the hay and catch mice. The boards are often decorated with carved wooden motifs depicting two swans.

"Head-Neck" Farmhouses
(*Kop-rompboerderijen*)

These are found in the same areas as "Head-neck-trunk" farmhouses, and are similar to them except that, although the living quarters have a tiled roof, there is also some living accommodation in the thatched section. Sometimes, the back of the house gradually widens out to form the barn.

Oldambt Farmhouses

These are named after the region of **Oldambt**, in the east of Groningen province, where they were first built. They can now be seen all over the province, and have staggered side walls which merge into those of the barn. The tall, wide living quarters often have stucco mouldings around the front door, making the building look very elegant. There are small windows in the attic, and the living quarters have a tiled roof, while the barn is usually thatched. Sometimes a second or even a third barn would be attached to the first to cope with large harvests.

Hall-houses (*Hallenhuizen*)

These are the most widespread type found in the Netherlands, particularly in the provinces of Drenthe, Overijssel, Gelderland and Utrecht; they can also be seen in Zuid-Holland and in the Gooi. Inside, the ceiling rests on two rows of piles connected by crossbeams. These divide the interior into a wide central "nave" and two narrower "side aisles". All hall-houses derived from *losse hoes* or open houses. The interior consisted of one large room with no partitions and with an open fireplace; the family and cattle shared the same space, and the hay was stored on the beams beneath the roof. A separate living area for the parents was sometimes built on to the side of the house. This type of farmhouse can still be found in Twente.

Twente Farmhouses
(*Twentse boerderijen*)

In Twente and around Winterswijk (Gelderland), there are still some **half-timbered farmhouses**. The walls were formerly made from woven wicker and clay, but are now made of brick. The

Southern Limburg farmhouse

Kop-romp farmhouse

Drenthe farmhouse

Pyramid-shaped Frisian farmhouse

T-shaped farmhouse

M. Guillou/MICHELIN

Stage mill

Hollow post mill

Mill with rotating cap

Post mill

Tjasker

M. Guillou/MICHELIN

buildings have two-sided roofs with wooden gable ends.

Drenthe Farmhouses
(*Drentse boerderijen*)
These are elongated in shape, with a usually thatched four-sided roof to both the house and the barn and stable section. At the back of the building, the roof has a section taken out of it to create sufficient height for the stable doors, so that hay carts can pass through. From the 18C onwards, some farmhouses in southwest Drenthe and to the north of Overijssel had the stable doors at the back replaced by side doors in order to increase the space in the barn.

T-shaped Farmhouses (*T-huizen*)
In the Achterhoek, the IJssel area, the provinces of Utrecht and Zuid-Holland, and in Gooi, the house is set crosswise to the barn, creating a T shape. This design owes its existence to the prosperity of farmers in the fertile areas along the main rivers, who extended their houses on either side. Carts entered through the back of the building, which had a single long roof.

Local variations on the hall-type farmhouse can also be seen in Staphorst and Giethoorn. They also exist in the Krimpenerwaard and Alblasserwaard (see ROTTERDAM, Excursions), where the living quarters have a raised floor because of the risk of floods. In the provinces of Utrecht Zuid-Holland, cheese-making farms had a dairy and a cheese storage area in the basement of the house.

Transverse Farmhouses
(*Dwarshuizen*)
These farmhouses have their longest side at the front, and the rooms are side by side, with the living quarters set at right angles to the barn. They can be seen in Limburg and in the eastern part of Noord-Brabant.

Limburg
This is the only province in the Netherlands where farmhouses have a square enclosed courtyard, which is reached from the outside via a large gateway. In Southern Limburg, some of the build-ings often have black and white **half-timbered walls**.

Noord-Brabant
This province has a distinctive long-fronted style of farmhouse, lang-gevelboerderijen, with the doors and windows facing the road and a long thatched or tiled roof. Because these farmhouses often provided limited space, a Flemish barn would often be built beside them, with wooden walls and a thatched roof.

Zeeland
Here, the various buildings were kept separate. The largest was the wooden barn, which had tarred walls and white door and window frames.

WINDMILLS

There are still some 1 000 windmills in the Netherlands, and they are one of the most distinctive features of the landscape. Some overlook the old walls of towns and dykes; others stand at the entrances to villages or beside lakes. The most famous group of windmills is at Kinderdijk.

The Language of Windmills
The sails of a windmill turn anticlockwise. When stationary, their position could be used to send messages to the people of the surrounding area, as follows:
- two vertical sails (+): windmill is at rest, but ready to be operated again
- two diagonal sails (x): polder windmill, at rest for a longer period
- upper sail just to the right of vertical (x): a sign of celebration
- upper sail just to the left of vertical (x): a symbol of mourning.

Windmill Decorations
Many wooden windmills are painted green with white edging. The wind-shaft, where the sails cross, is often painted with a red and yellow or blue and white star, with a decorative board underneath stating the windmill's name and the date of its construction. When a wedding took place, the sails would be abundantly decorated with garlands and symbolic motifs.

Windmills in Kinderdijk

Main Types of Windmills

There are two main kinds of windmills: polder mills and industrial mills. **Polder mills** were used for drainage purposes, and there are none in the east of the country, where the height above sea level ensures natural drainage of water. **Industrial mills** were used for a wide variety of purposes, such as milling wheat, extracting oil, hulling rice and peppercorns, and sawing wood. Some of these are still in use.

The Oldest Type of Windmill

Originally, the only mills in the Netherlands were the watermill and the horse-powered treadmill. The first windmills appeared in the mid 13C, and may have derived from the stone-built ones used in Persia to mill corn. The body and sails rotate round a heavy fixed wooden post made out of a tree trunk, so that the mill is always facing into the wind. When the sails turn, they rotate the grindstones inside. Outside, on the side opposite the sails, a tail pole joined to the post and operated by a wheel enables the windmill to be turned round. The ladder fixed to the main body of the windmill also turns with it. Few windmills of this type remain in the country.

The First Polder Mills

The first windmill used for drainage, in about 1350, was a post-mill adapted specifically for the purpose by replacing the solid central post with a hollow one, through which the drive-shaft was placed. This was known as a **hollow post-mill**; the earliest known example dates from 1513. This had a smaller tower and a larger base to allow space for a scoop, resembling a paddle-wheel, which was used to lift the water. In most cases, however, the scoop was on the outside and the base was used as living accommodation, particularly in Zuid-Holland.

The **sleeve windmill** (*kokermolen*) was easier to turn into the wind: the wooden spindle was replaced by a sleeve, around which the sails and the top part of the windmill rotated. In Friesland, there is a smaller version of the hollow post-mill known as the **spinnekop** (spider's head) because it looks like a spider from a distance. The **weidemolentje** of Noord-Holland is even smaller. In Friesland and Overijssel, there are still a few examples of the **tjasker**, a simply constructed windmill with a tilted spindle.

Mills With Rotating Caps

Turning the whole windmill into the wind was heavy work, and the Dutch invention of the **smock mill** represented a major improvement. This had a small rotating cap and sails on a large fixed tower. The wheel used to turn the cap and sails was usually on the outside, though there was also a form in Noord-Holland where the wheel was inside the mill, making it larger.

These mills were built of wood. They often had a **thatched roof** and an octagonal shape, in which case the base was made of stone. Sometimes, the wooden frame was clad in **brick**, giving it a **truncated cone shape**.

Industrial Mills

Illustration: see ZAANSTREEK.
In the 16C, the windmill was adapted for industrial purposes. The first oil windmill began operation in Alkmaar in 1582. In 1592, Cornelis Corneliszoon of Uitgeest built the first **sawmill**, which subsequently underwent many improvements and resulted in the first **post-mill** used for sawing, which rotated on its base. Next, **hulling mills** were built to hull first barley and then, when the Dutch began trading in the Far East, rice. The first of these was built in 1639 in Koog aan de Zaan. **Paper mills** were first used in about 1600, and became more widespread in 1673 when French paper manufacturers relocated to the **Zaanstreek**.
It was here that the greatest concentration could be found until the 19C; they were specially built for making paper and sawing wood for boat-building. Most of the other different types of windmills developed in this area; they included tobacco snuffmills, hemp mills for making ropes, tanning mills for leather, spice mills mainly for mustard, and fulling mills for textiles. Most of these were very tall, with a balcony around the side and a workshop at the bottom.

Tower Mills

Industrial windmills were often built in towns, and had to be several storeys high if they were to catch the wind. Because they were so tall, the sails could not be set from the ground, and so this was done from a balcony halfway up the windmill; the miller's accommodation and the storage area were below this. Alternatively, instead of a balcony, an earth wall was built around the windmill and served the same purpose. Most tower mills were made of stone and were a truncated cone shape. In Groningen province, they had octagonal bases made of brick, and in the Zaanstreek there was a workshop in the wooden base.

Architecture and Sculpture

Over the centuries, the Netherlands has made a major contribution to Western art. Sculpture occupies a relatively modest place in the Dutch artistic heritage, perhaps due to a shortage of materials until the 20C, and so does music. But the country's architecture has been outstanding during some periods of its history, and its paintings, too, make the Netherlands a place of pilgrimage and inspiration.

ROMANESQUE ART AND ARCHITECTURE

Examples of Romanesque art and architecture can be seen throughout the country.

Rhenish-Mosan Art

This form of Romanesque developed in the Maas Valley and in particular at Maastricht, which belonged to the diocese of Liège. The style is very similar to that of the Rhine Valley, hence its name (Mosan being the adjective for Maas or Meuse).
Maastricht was an important town in the Roman era and then a place of pilgrimage where the relics of St Servatius, who died in 384, were venerated. The town has some magnificent buildings, such as the St-Servaasbasiliek and the Onze Lieve Vrouwebasiliek. In its early days, Mosan art borrowed a great deal from **Carolingian architecture**. Apart from the St-Nicolaaskapel at Nijmegen, whose shape imitated the octagonal basilica of Charlemagne in Aachen Cathedral, Carolingian churches usually have two chancels, an imposing westwork, and a court chapel. Inside, there is a flat wooden ceiling and square pillars. Construction of the **St-Servaasbasiliek** began in about 1000, starting with a westwork with two large towers decorated with Lombard arcading. The **Onze Lieve Vrouwebasiliek**, dating from the same period, also has a massive westwork, flanked by round turrets (*photograph: see MAASTRICHT*). The St-Amelbergakerk at **Susteren**, built in the second half of the 11C, is very plain.

In the 12C, Mosan architecture mellowed and became more decorative, and sculpture started appearing on the capitals, low reliefs and portals. It was during this period that both the St-Servaasbasiliek and the Onze Lieve Vrouwebasiliek were altered, and the chancel of the latter, viewed from the nave, is one of the most beautiful Romanesque achievements in the country. The original trefoiled plan of **Rolduc Abbey** in Kerkrade also shows a Rhenish influence. The Onze Lieve Vrouwe Munsterkerk at **Roermond**, although restored, retains some Rhenish-Mosan characteristics. The crypts of these Romanesque churches are often very beautiful.

Other Centres

Utrecht, which was an important bishopric in the Middle Ages, became a centre of Romanesque church architecture at an early stage. However, apart from the Pieterskerk dating from 1148, there are only a few remains of the fine Romanesque buildings erected by Bishop Bernulphus. Among the churches in the diocese of Utrecht, the Grote Kerk at **Deventer** has preserved the remains of a double transept and a westwork which links it to Mosan churches. At **Oldenzaal,** the great St-Plechelmusbasiliek is later (early 12C) and has a nave with groined vaulting supported by powerful pillars. Beginning in the mid-12C, regional versions of the Romanesque style appeared in **Friesland** and in the **province of Groningen,** where **brick decoration** was used on the outside walls of village churches (*see GRONINGEN and LEEUWARDEN, Excursions*); inside, there are often the remains of frescoes.

GOTHIC ARCHITECTURE

Gothic architecture appeared in the Netherlands during the 14C and 15C. Many churches, and some town halls, date from this period.

Churches

Noord-Brabant, a province where the majority of the inhabitants are Catholic, has most of the large churches and **cathedrals** in the country. These were

Detail of a stained-glass window, St.-Janskathedraal, 's-Hertogenbosch

built in the **Brabant Gothic style**, which resembles Flamboyant Gothic and is found in many buildings in Belgium. Their exteriors have open-work gables and crocket spires, tall windows, flying buttresses, and a tall belfry, while the interiors have a slender central nave with pointed vaulting resting on round columns with crocket capitals and a triforium.

The Grote Kerk in **Breda** (*illustration: see BREDA*) is a typical example of Brabant Gothic, as is the St-Janskathedraal in **'s-Hertogenbosch** (*illustration: see Architecture and 'S-HERTOGENBOSCH*), which was begun in the 14C and is one of the most beautiful pieces of architecture in the country, as well as being the largest. Unlike other buildings, its vaults rest not on columns but on a cluster of small columns without capitals. Brabant Gothic influenced the style of many other churches in the country. In Noord- and Zuid-Holland, the stone vault was rare and churches had flat or barrel-vaulted wooden ceilings; the only exception is the Grote Kerk in Dordrecht. Other beautiful Gothic buildings include the Hooglandse Kerk in Leiden, the Grote Kerk in Alkmaar, the Nieuwe Kerk in Amsterdam, the St-Janskerk in Gouda, and the St-Bavokerk in Haarlem (🔊 *illustration: see Architecture*). The cathedral in Utrecht unfortunately did not survive the great storm of 1672, but its elegant bell-tower, the **Domtoren**, still stands, and influenced many other bell-towers around the country, including that of Amersfoort. In the same diocese, the Gothic St-Nicolaaskerk in Kampen is also interesting.

Town Halls (Stadhuisen)

Two town halls in the Flamboyant Gothic style are particularly remarkable. That of **Gouda** is delightful, its façade a mass of pinnacles and slender spires. The town hall in **Middelburg** is sumptuous; it was built by the Belgian architect family Keldermans and shows the influence of Brussels town hall.

Sculpture

Although sculpture is not as abundant as in Belgium, there are some interesting 15C and early 16C woodcarvings. The groups by **Adriaen van Wesel** (late 15C) displayed in the Rijksmuseum in Amsterdam are carved with a remarkable sense of composition and a great strength of expression. The Brabant altarpieces are triptychs in the Flamboyant style, with a carved central panel showing very lively scenes. This is flanked by two painted panels. The altarpieces can be seen at St.-Janskathedraal in 's-Hertogenbosch and Onze Lieve Vrouwe Munsterkerk in Roermond. There are some fine examples of choir stalls, often carved with satirical themes, in churches including the Martinikerk in Bolsward and the Grote Kerk in Breda.

THE RENAISSANCE AND MANNERISM

The Renaissance reached the Netherlands at a relatively late stage, and its pure Italian form appears hardly at all. However, Mannerism (a transitional form between Renaissance and Baroque) flourished, particularly in Holland.

Architecture

This was not influenced by the Renaissance until the mid 16C. The style was brought here by Italian artists such as **Thomas Vincidor da Bologna**, who designed Breda Castle; it was then taken up by local architects. In fact, Renaissance elements were used without making major architectural changes, and the traditional Gothic plan was often retained. They were mainly apparent in details, such as shell-shaped window tympana, dormer windows with pinnacles, and octagonal turrets.

Hans Vredeman de Vries (1527–c. 1603) was a great advocate of Renaissance decoration applied to architecture, but did not do much work in his own country. His theoretical writings had an important influence on the architecture of the Low Countries. The Fleming **Lieven de Key** worked a great deal in Haarlem, where he was the municipal architect. The old meat market, or Vleeshal (1603), is his finest work. **Hendrick de Keyser** (1565-1621) was both a sculptor and architect. He built several churches, mainly in Amsterdam (including the Zuiderkerk and Westerkerk; 🔊 *illustration: see Architecture*) and large town houses (Huis Bartolotti)). De Keyser's Mannerist style, like that of Lieven de Key, also contained Baroque elements; his buildings were more monumental, with an imposing feeling of line.

Renaissance influences were particularly apparent in **Friesland**, where the penchant for geometric decoration and playful detail, which was already apparent in Romanesque churches, spread to many other buildings. The new style was used in town halls, such as those of Franeker and Bolsward, law courts (the Kanselarij in Leeuwarden), and town gateways (the Waterpoort in Sneek; 🔊 *illustration: see SNEEK*). The east and west of the country were less affected by these influences, though the weighhouse in Nijmegen is a good example of the Renaissance style.

Sculpture

Increasing numbers of **funerary monuments** were made in the Italian Renaissance style. Thomas Vincidor da Bologna made the tomb of Engelbert II of Nassau in Breda. Hendrick de Keyser continued this trend in the early 17C with the tomb of William the Silent in Delft. He also designed the bronze statue of

Het Loo Palace, Apeldoorn

NBTC/

Erasmus in Rotterdam. In **Friesland**, the Renaissance style was expressed in woodwork. Some churches, such as the Martinikerk in Bolsward and the Grote Kerk in Dokkum, have **pulpits** whose panels are carved with symbolic scenes. The remarkable 17C choir stalls of Dordrecht's Grote Kerk are also inspired by the Renaissance, and the magnificent stained glass of the St-Janskerk in Gouda is one of the finest examples of Renaissance art.

THE GOLDEN AGE

In the middle of the 17C, the playful ornamentation of Mannerism began to disappear. Architecture became dominated by symmetry and proportion, although this was much more restrained in the Netherlands than the Baroque style of other countries, and is sometimes called "**Classicism**".

One of the most famous architects of the Golden Age was **Jacob van Campen** (1595–1657), designer of **Amsterdam's town hall** (1648), which subsequently became the royal palace. This is square in shape, with severe lines softened a little by the slightly projecting façade, sculpted pediments and small tower. It is a majestic work which greatly influenced architecture throughout the country. **Pieter Post** (1608–69), who built the royal palace (Huis ten Bosch) and the Mauritshuis in The Hague based on plans by Van Campen, and the town

hall in Maastricht, continued this trend. **Jacob Roman** built Het Loo Palace in Apeldoorn in a similar style in 1685. This stately architectural style, reflecting the Golden Age, is also apparent in the town houses along Amsterdam's main canals (⊙ *illustration: see AMSTERDAM*). One of the most beautiful examples is the Trippenhuis built by **Justus Vingboons** (c. 1620–98), who worked a great deal with his brother Philips.

Many of the Protestant **churches** of this period are circular, often with a dome; one example is the Nieuwe Kerk, or Ronde Lutherse Kerk, in Amsterdam (1671). In the south of the country, some buildings were constructed using the more extravagant Baroque style; one example is the Jezuïtenkerk in Maastricht.

18C AND 19C

The French-born architect and decorative designer **Daniël Marot** (1661–1752) built a number of elegant town houses in The Hague. From now on, the French influence and the **Louis XV** and XVI styles predominated; the Rococo or Louis XV style was mainly apparent in the external sculpture, and in the grilles and imposts used to decorate the doors, though it also appeared in stucco interior decoration.

In the early 19C, architects began once again to seek their inspiration in the past; first ancient Greece and Rome (**Neoclas-**

sicism), and later the Middle Ages and Renaissance (**neo-Gothic** and **neo-Renaissance**). In **Eclecticism**, these stylistic elements were used together. One of the most important architects in this period, **PJH Cuypers** (1827-1921), introduced a form of neo-Gothic to his buildings, which included the Rijksmuseum and the central railway station in Amsterdam, and carried out radical restorations of several medieval buildings such as Kasteel De Haar. Although the architecture of earlier eras provided such a major source of inspiration for that of the 19C, it was also during this period that new materials such as cast iron and steel were first used (*see Industrial heritage*).

20C AND 21C

During the 20C and 21C, architecture has experienced something of a renaissance in the Netherlands, and there has also been a renewed interest in sculpture.

Architecture
HP Berlage (1856–1934), who built Amsterdam's Stock Exchange (1897–1903), was the precursor of Rationalism, an architectural movement which placed a great deal of emphasis on materials and function. **KPC de Bazel** (1869–1923) worked in a similar way with his building for Algemene Bank Nederland, Amsterdam.

The **Amsterdam School** (c. 1912–23) strove for a less austere architecture than that of Berlage, and **Michel de Klerk**, **Peter Kramer** and **JM van der Mey** were the great masters of urban renewal; their work made expressionistic use of brick. **WM Dudok** stood slightly apart from the Amsterdam School; he was influenced by Frank Lloyd Wright and is best known as the designer of the town hall in Hilversum ((*illustration: see Architecture*).

At the same time, the **De Stijl movement** was being founded by the painters **Piet Mondrian** and **Theo van Doesburg** and the architect **JJP Oud**. Architects such as **Gerrit Rietveld** (who also designed furniture), **J Duiker** and **B Bijvoet** also gained their inspiration from the movement, using concrete skeletonnes and superimposing and juxtaposing cube-shaped spaces to form a whole. This was known as **Nieuwe Bouwen** (New Building) or **Functionalism**, and was at its height from 1920–40. One of the highlights of this style is the Van Nelle factory in Rotterdam by the architects **Brinkman** and **Van der Vlugt**, a masterpiece in steel, glass and concrete.

Around 1950, particularly during the rebuilding of **Rotterdam**, urban planners began taking more account of local people's needs. The Lijnbaan (1952–54), designed by JH Van den Broek and **JB Bakema**, was the first pedestrian pre-

Groninger Museum

Ralph Richter/Groninger Museum

cinct in Europe. The Forum generation, as it was called, also included **Aldo van Eyck** (who built the Burgerweeshuis and Moederhuis in Amsterdam), **Herman Hertzberger** (responsible for the Vredenburg in Utrecht and the VROM building in The Hague), and **Piet Blom**, the architect of the famous cube-shaped apartments and the building known as Het Potlood, both in Rotterdam. **Wim Quist** built the Willemswerf, an office block in the same city, and various museums including the Museum Beelden aan Zee, the seaside sculpture museum in The Hague.

Rem Koolhaas (b. 1944) is one of the country's leading contemporary architects. He established a firm of international architects, the Office for Metropolitan Architecture, in Rotterdam in 1975. Koolhaas has become famous in the Netherlands for buildings such as the Nederlands Danstheater in The Hague and the Museumpark and Kunsthal in Rotterdam. He has also gained an international reputation for work such as his urban plan for the French city of Lille. The local environment and traditional building styles play an important part in the work of **Jo Coenen** (b. 1949), whose most important project has been the Nederlands Architectuurinstituut in Rotterdam. Finally, among the younger generation of architects, **Ben van Berkel** (b. 1957) designed Rotterdam's Erasmusbrug, or Erasmus Bridge, completed in 1996.

The Kop van Zuid with Luxor Theatre (right) in Rotterdam

©2006 Hannah Anthonysz/NBTC

Sculpture

Most Dutch towns and cities have used sculpture in a wide variety of materials to enliven their pedestrian precincts and parks. Many modern buildings have façades decorated with mosaics, coloured ornamentation or bronze figures.

Mari Andriessen (1897–1979) was one of the greatest Dutch sculptors of the 20C. He created the statue of a docker near the Portuguese Synagogue in Amsterdam, the monument in the Volkspark in Enschede, and the statue of Queen Wilhelmina in the Wilhelminapark in Utrecht.

Other leading contemporary sculptors are the **Fortuyn/O'Brien** duo, whose light, elegant compositions feature wooden slats wrapped in paper or silk. **Carel Visser** (b. 1928) was one of the first Dutch sculptors to work in metal, and made collage sculptures, including a wide variety of found objects. His recent work is more detailed and intricate. **Henk Visch** (b. 1950) is mainly known for his figurative sculptures, often consisting of contemplative human or animal figures with poetic titles.

The Netherlands has a leading international reputation for modern architecture and urban planning. Top Dutch and foreign architects have worked on such major projects as the Resident and Kop van Zuid developments in The Hague and Rotterdam respectively. The latter, in particular, is an absolute must for visitors interested in contemporary architecture, and more new projects are in progress there. A number of museums are also important works of architecture in their own right; they include the Groninger Museum in Groningen, the Bonnefantenmuseum in Maastricht, and Nemo in Amsterdam.

The Spanjaardsgat in Breda

Alvaro de Leiva/NBTC

Military Architecture

All over the Netherlands there are the remains of fortifications built over the centuries to defend the country against invasion.

In the Middle Ages, defensive works initially consisted of walls of earth surrounded by a ditch and a ring of stakes; later on, castles and fortresses were built. Some of the finest examples are the fortress in **Leiden**, the **Muiderslot**, and **Slot Loevestein**. As towns began to develop, so earthworks were replaced by stone walls with towers and impressive gateways. Parts of these walls can still be seen in **Amersfoort** (*illustration: see Architecture*) and **Elburg**. Typical features included machicolations and parapet walks along the tops of walls and towers, and crenels and other holes through which stones and burning pitch could be thrown.

The walls of fortified towns were not able to withstand the cannons introduced in the early 15C, and so the high walls and towers were lowered and provided with moats or earthworks which could not be breached by these weapons. The **Spanjaardsgat** in Breda is an example of this kind of construction.

The next step was to build bigger but shorter towers known as **roundels**; a fine example of these is **De Vijf Koppen** in Maastricht. However, their round shape was not very practical, since there was not enough room for armaments at the top and there was a blind spot straight in front of the roundel. As a result, Italian engineers in the early 16C developed the bastion, a five-sided projecting fortification intended to overcome the drawbacks of roundels. This new structure was soon adopted in the Netherlands.

During the Eighty Years' War, a variety of Italian-inspired changes resulted in the development of a new form of defence known as the **Old Dutch System**. The Flemish engineer **Simon Stevin** (1548–1620) developed the theoretical basis for this system. The fortifications were made of earth, so that cannon balls would simply become lodged in them, and were nearly always surrounded by a ditch in which small islands known as demilunes. The leading builder of fortifications at this time was **Adriaan Anthoniszoon** (c. 1543–1620), who worked on nearly 30 towns and forts around the country. The best-preserved examples of these are at Willemstad, Heusden, and **Bourtange** (*illustration: see Architecture*). Naarden, whose fortifications are better preserved than any other in the country, was built using the so-called **French System**, with larger bastions and a double ring of defence

In 1685, **Colonel Menno van Coehoorn** (1641–1704) designed the **New Dutch System** exemplified by Hellevoetsluis and Bergen op Zoom. This had large bastions placed close together, making the walls between them (known as curtain walls) shorter and shorter, eventually resulting in the **tenaille system** of star-shaped fortifications formed by a succession of bastions with no curtain walls (**Linie van Doesburg**).

The development of longer-range artillery meant that fortifications had to be built at increasing distances from the towns they were built to defend. Forts were built in a circle around the fortifications, as in the **Nieuwe Hollandse Waterlinie** (1840–60) around Utrecht. The main purpose of these "water lines" was to flood the land to a depth of about 40cm/15.7in to slow the enemy down; this was done using a system of sluices and quays. Forts were built in places which could not be flooded, such as the huge fort at Rijnauwen, near Bunnik. The circle of some 40 forts that form the **Amsterdam Citadel** is an average of 12km/7.4mi from the capital; one is the island fort of **Pampus** in the IJsselmeer. This famous citadel has been a **UNESCO World Heritage site** (☙see *Planning Your Trip*) since 1996. The earlier citadel of **Den Helder** was built by Napoleon in 1811.

After the First World War, defensive lines of concrete bunkers were built; the best known are the **Grebbelinie** and the bunkers on the Afsluitdijk near De Oever and Kornwerderwand (now a museum). The most prominent Second World War fortifications in the Netherlands are the long series of bunkers along the coast, which formed part of the German **Atlantic Wall**. The most recent are the Rijn-IJssellinie, built in 1951 as part of NATO defences. The project was cancelled in 1954 as a result of changes in NATO's strategic plans.

Industrial Heritage

The **Industrial Revolution** did not take place in the Netherlands until the end of the 19C. **Factories** were built, steam power began to be used, as were iron and steel. But as far back as the 17C, the Netherlands had Europe's biggest industrial area, the **Zaanstreek** (☙see *ZAANSTREEK*), where nearly a thousand windmills were used to manufacture paper, dye, and foodstuffs.

FACTORIES AND WORKERS' HOUSING

The first factories were built in Twente and Noord-Brabant, making cotton and wool. Many of these were subsequently demolished, but some have been put to new uses, such as the 19C wool factory in Tilburg, which is now the **Nederlands Textielmuseum,** and the **Jannink spinning mill** in Enschede. In the early 20C, the use of concrete, glass and steel enabled larger factories to be built, such as the **Wiebengahal** of the former Sphinx Céramique factory in Maastricht and Rotterdam's **Van Nelle factory** (1926–30). Examples of whole districts built specially to house the multitude of workers include the **Agnetapark** in Delft and Philipsdorp in Eindhoven.

MINERALS

There are still some impressive **limekilns** to be seen here and there (such as in the Zuiderzeemuseum in Enkhuizen); these were bottle-shaped structures used to burn shells to make lime. There are some fascinating remains of Zuid-Limburg's **coal industry**, including the Nulland pit in Kerkrade and the Oranje Nassau mine in Heerlen. The reconstructed **mine at Valkenbrug** gives a first-hand view of how coal was dug.

STATIONS

The oldest surviving railway station in the Netherlands is the building at **Valkenburg**, dating from 1853. **Amsterdam**'s Centraal Station was designed by PJH Cuypers (1827–1921), and the elegant Art Nouveau station at **Haarlem** is by the architect Margadant. The enormous iron roofs of such stations as 's-Hertogenbosch and The Hague were also a major technological innovation. The history of railways is chronicled in the **Nederlands Spoorwegmuseum** in Utrecht.

De Cruquius steam pumping station

PORTS

Amsterdam still has a 19C wharf with cast iron roofs, **'t Kromhout**. In Rotterdam, which was largely destroyed in 1945, there are still some old warehouses such as **De Vijf Werelddelen** (now a shopping and entertainment centre). The former headquarters of the **Holland-Amerika shipping line** (1901) on Wilhelmskade has been converted into a hotel. **De Hef**, an old lifting railway bridge, is on permanent display in the raised position.

STEAM-OPERATED PUMPING STATIONS

The first time that steam pumping stations were used was in the draining of the Haarlemmermeer (see The Fight Against the Sea). One of these was the **Cruquius**, which is now a museum. These stations were used in increasing numbers in the second half of the 19C; they included the **Vier Noorder Koggen** (now the Nederlands Stoommachinemuseum), and the Ir Lely station at Medemblik and the steam pumping station near **Halfweg**, now a museum. The **Ir. D.F. Wouda steam pumping station** just outside Lemmer is the largest in Europe; this highly impressive structure was built in 1917 and has been a UNESCO World Heritage Site since 1998.

WATER TOWERS AND LIGHTHOUSES

The oldest water tower in the country is in **Rotterdam** and dates from 1873. The oldest lighthouse, the **Brandaris** on the island of Terschelling, was built in 1594. The brick lighthouse at **Haamstede** used to be depicted on the old 250fl banknote. The **Waterleidingmuseum**, situated in Utrecht's oldest water tower, describes the history of the mains water supply in the Netherlands. The neo-Gothic water tower of **Schoonhoven** is the centre of the Zilver in Beweging initiative.

Painting

Dutch painting was initially very similar to that of Flanders, and was later influenced by Italian art. It reached its peak in the 17C, reflecting the country's increasing prosperity.

PRE-RENAISSANCE

One of the greatest of all Dutch artists was **Hieronymus Bosch**, who was active in 's-Hertogenbosch in the late 15C. His work was extraordinarily imaginative for its time (illustration: see 's-HERTOGENBOSCH). Although his vision of a world dominated by the spectre of sin was a medieval one, his realism presaged that of 17C painting, and his work has many features of modern Surrealism. Other artists had more in common with the Flemish primitives. The work of **Geertgen tot Sint Jans** is akin to miniature art. **Cornelis Engebrechtszoon** painted lively, colourful scenes full of people; a number of his works can be seen in the Stedelijk Museum De Lakenhal in Leiden. Another of the early Dutch painters was Jan Mostaert.

RENAISSANCE

Jan van Scorel, a pupil of **Jacob Corneliszoon van Oostsanen**, introduced the Renaissance to the northern Netherlands when he returned from Rome in 1524. He was the first Dutch painter to be influenced by Italian art, and painted portraits of great sensitivity, such as the

Portrait of a Young Scholar in the Museum Boymans-van Beuningen in Rotterdam, as well as rather Mannerist religious pictures. One of his pupils was **Maarten van Heemskerck**. **Lucas van Leyden**, a pupil of Cornelis Engebrechtszoon, was also influenced by the Renaissance. He painted large, carefully composed canvases such as the *Last Judgement* in the Stedelijk Museum De Lakenhal in Leiden (see LEIDEN). **Pieter Aertsen** was not at all influenced by Italian art. This great Amsterdam artist, who also lived in Antwerp for a time, painted subtle landscapes and interior scenes with still life compositions in the background. **Antoon Mor** became famous under the Spanish name of Antonio Moro, since he was the court painter to Charles V and Philip II of Spain. He later worked at the English court.

The Glorification of the Virgin by Geertgen tot Sint Jans

Museum Boijmans Van Beuningen, Rotterdam

THE GOLDEN AGE

The 17C may have been dominated by such great figures as Rembrandt, Hals, Vermeer and Ruisdael, but it had many other highly talented artists. While the Flemish continued to paint large numbers of religious scenes, Dutch art was more secular and varied, since much of it was painted for well-off middle-class homes. It also provides a remarkable record of the daily life of the period.

Group Portraits

During the Golden Age, there was a considerable demand for group portraits from bodies such as guilds, companies of the civic guard, groups of surgeons, and the governing bodies of almshouses. **Bartholomeus van der Helst** painted many traditional, formal portraits of wealthy citizens and members of the House of Orange, as well as numerous group portraits. **Frans Hals** had the nonconformist style that came with genius. Most of his large group portraits are in the Frans Hals Museum, in his home town of Haarlem. He also painted striking and lively individual portraits, such as *The Jolly Drinker*, now in the Rijksmuseum Amsterdam.

Rembrandt and his Pupils

Rembrandt also painted group portraits, such as *The Anatomy Lesson of Doctor Tulp*, now in the Mauritshuis in The Hague, but the best-known is the *Night Watch,* in the Rijksmuseum Amsterdam. This museum has an excellent collection of Rembrandt's work, notably Biblical scenes, portraits and self-portraits, with brightly lit, solemn figures against dark backgrounds. Rembrandt had a number of pupils: **Gerard Dou**, who did chiaroscuro genre paintings; **Ferdinand Bol**, one of the closest to Rembrandt in style; **Nicolaes Maes**, who used warm colours to paint calm interior scenes; **Samuel van Hoogstraten**; **Aert van Gelder**; **Carel Fabritius**, who died young, but was the most gifted of all; and **Philips Koninck**, mainly a landscape painter.

Landscape and Seascape Painters

Although Rembrandt produced many landscape drawings and etchings, he painted few landscapes. Many artists specialised in this genre; these included **Hercules Seghers**, **Salomon van Ruysdael** and **Jan van Goyen**. They painted luminous, serene compositions with wide horizons, still rivers, sunlight filtering through the clouds, and silhouetted trees, churches and windmills. The greatest landscape painter of the time, **Jacob van Ruisdael**, had a penchant for romantic scenes.

Meindert Hobbema painted tall trees with vivid green sunlit foliage, while **Cornelis van Poelenburgh** preferred Italian-style landscapes and sunsets. Sometimes landscapes were a pretext to depict human figures, as with **Albert Cuyp**; elsewhere, they included shepherds and their flocks in the case of **Nicolaes Berchem**, cows and horses in the case of **Paulus Potter**, and horses and their riders in the paintings of **Philips Wouwerman**. **Hendrick Avercamp** was slightly different: his paintings were similar to miniatures, with subtle colours bringing to life the picturesque world of ice-skaters. **Aert van der Neer** also painted winter scenes and rivers by moonlight.

Willem van de Velde the Elder, and more especially his son **Willem the Younger**, were remarkable marine painters, as were **Ludolf Bakhuizen**, **Jan van de Cappelle** and the Ghent painter **Jan Porcellis**. **Pieter Saenre-** **dam** and **Emanuel de Witte** whose work was highly appreciated during their lifetime, depict church interiors in carefully studied compositions. **Job Berckheyde** and his younger brother **Gerrit** were also painters of architecture.

Genre Pieces

Apart from some of Rembrandt's pupils, many other painters specialised in domestic interiors. **Gerard Terborch**, **Frans van Mieris the Elder** and **Gabriel Metsu** re-created domestic scenes with delicate brushwork, while Pieter de Hooch, a remarkable colourist and virtuoso of perspective, depicted the daily lives of the wealthy. **Vermeer** was neglected for a long period, but is now regarded as one of the greatest of all artists. He mainly painted interior scenes, which were realistic but extraordinarily poetic. Although simple in appearance, they make highly sophisticated use of colours, composition and light. **Adriaen**

The Milkmaid (c.1660) by Johannes Vermeer, Rijksmuseum Amsterdam

Rijksmuseum, Amsterdam/NBTC

Rijksmuseum Amsterdam

Still life with Cheeses (c.1615) by Floris Claeszoon van Dijck, Rijksmuseum Amsterdam

van Ostade was a painter of rollicking peasant scenes, and was influenced by the Flemish artist Adriaen Brouwer. Van Ostade's pupil **Jan Steen** painted similarly cheerful and humorous pictures, though with a moral message.

In Utrecht, the Italian influence which was widespread in the 16C made itself felt in the work of **Abraham Bloemaert**. One of his pupils, **Hendrick Terbrugghen**, introduced "Caravaggism" to the Netherlands along with **Gerard van Honthorst**. Their work is characterised by strong light-dark contrasts, half-length portraits of ordinary people, and people playing music. **Judith Leyster**, a pupil of Frans Hals, was also clearly influenced by Caravaggio.

Still-Life Paintings

The tradition of still-life painting had its origins in Flanders, in the work of artists such as Fyt and Snyders. It was taken up in Haarlem by **Pieter Claeszoon** and **Willem Claeszoon Heda** and **Floris Claeszoon van Dijck**. Their favourite subject was a table covered with the remains of a meal, and glasses and dishes reflecting the light. Their paintings were less crowded than those of their Flemish predecessors, with flatter colours and strictly geometrical compositions. The works of **Willem Kalff, Abraham van Beyeren** and Jan Dav-

idszoon de Heem were more colourful and Baroque.

Drawings and Prints

17C painters also produced very large numbers of drawings and prints, particularly etchings, and **Rembrandt** excelled in this form of art.

18C-20C

In the 18C, a decline set in. One notable exception was **Cornelis Troost**, an Amsterdam painter whose work was inspired by the theatre, and evokes Watteau and Hogarth. **Jacob Wit** was known for his *grisailles* (in Dutch: *witjes*), which were popular forms of household decoration among the wealthy. **Wouter Joannes van Troostwijk** immortalised the streets of Amsterdam in his paintings. In the 19C, with **The Hague School** led by **Jozef Israëls**, Dutch art enjoyed a rebirth. Nature, beaches, dunes and the lives of fishermen provided an inexhaustible source of inspiration for the artists of this school (🔍 *illustration: see Den HAAG*). **JB Jongkind** was a precursor of the Impressionists, and his paintings were full of light and atmosphere. This was also true of **George Hendrick Breitner**, who is known for his pictures of horsemen and of old Amsterdam

Counter-composition of Dissonants XVI (1925), Theo van Doesburg
Haags Gemeentemuseum, The Hague

(*illustration: see AMSTERDAM*). **Isaac Israëls**, the son of Jozef, painted beach scenes and numerous portraits.

Vincent van Gogh was the greatest figure of the late 19C. His early paintings were sombre, but under the influence of Impressionism his canvases became lighter and more colourful. From 1886 onwards he worked mainly in Paris and near Arles in Provence. Many of his masterpieces can be seen in the Kröller-Müller Museum, near Arnhem, and the **Van Gogh Museum** in Amsterdam.

Jan Toorop was born in Java. He began his career as an Impressionist, before turning to Symbolism, a movement in which he held an important place in Europe along with **Johan Thorn Prikker**. Later, Toorop briefly allied himself with the pointillists and divisionists, and also took an interest in the Art Nouveau movement, painting a large number of posters in this style.

Piet Mondrian was one of the greatest innovators of his time. He was the driving force behind the **De Stijl movement** (1917–31) and its magazine of the same name, along with **Theo van Doesburg** and **JJP Oud**. In so doing, he helped to found the constructivist movement. One of the most intriguing artists of the inter-war period was **Herman Kruyder**, whose work is highly enigmatic. **Jan Wiegers** was the leader of the Expressionist movement **De Ploeg** (1918–30), characterised by dramatic contrasts

in colour. **Hendrik Werkman** is now regarded as the most important member of De Ploeg; he introduced radical innovations in woodcuts and typography. After a brief Expressionist period, **Charley Toorop**, the daughter of Jan Toorop, subsequently adopted a realist style of painting. **Kees van Dongen** (*illustration: see ROTTERDAM*) became a famous artist in Paris.

The main exponents of **magic realism** (or **new objectivity**; 1920–30) in the Netherlands were **Raoul Hynckes, Pyke Koch** and **Carel Willink**. Their strange, near-photographic realism, tinged with surrealism, influenced many young artists. One of their contemporaries was **MC Escher** (1898–1972), the Netherlands' leading graphic artist, whose ingenious play on spaces and dimensions became world famous.

The international group of experimental artists **CoBrA** (1948-51) was named from the initial letters of Copenhagen, Brussels and Amsterdam. Its main members were the Dane Asger Jorn, the Belgian artist Dotremont and three Dutchmen, **Karel Appel, Constant** and **Corneille**. The movement advocated free, spontaneous creation, often inspired by children's drawings.

The year 1960 saw the creation of the Dutch group **Nul** (Zero) whose three principles were impersonality, detachment and objectivity. Its most important representative was **Jan Schoonhoven**, best known for his monochrome reliefs.

During the 1970s, **Jan Dibbets** and **Ger van Elk** used photography as a means of expression; Dibbets turned reality into abstraction by creating trick montages characterised by a strong sense of perspective. **Rob van Koningsbruggen** uses unconventional techniques to produce his quasi-monochrome pictures: he takes canvases painted in black, white or primary colours and rubs one or more unpainted canvases over them.

The leading artistic figures of the 1980s were **Rob Scholte** and **Marlene Dumas** who, despite their different styles, both draw inspiration from the visual imagery generated by newspapers, magazines and other media.

Decorative Arts

POTTERY AND PORCELAIN

The Museum Het Princessehof in Leeuwarden has a comprehensive collection of Dutch pottery and porcelain.

From Sandstone and Majolica to Delftware

The majolica technique was brought to Antwerp and other parts of northern Europe by Italian potters in the 16C. After the fall of Antwerp in 1585, many potters moved to the Netherlands, where majolica production subsequently flourished. Very soon, this technique replaced the traditional Rhine sandstone pottery.

In the early 17C, large quantities of **Chinese eggshell porcelain** were imported by the United East India Company. These damaged the domestic market and bankrupted many potters. Some majolica-makers switched to making tiles or domestic objects not made by the Chinese, such as mustard pots and apothecaries' jars, often imitating oriental styles of decoration. Others tried to discover the secret of eggshell porcelain, but initially they had no success. However, a few manufacturers in **Delft** and **Haarlem** did manage to make a better-quality product than traditional majolica to compete with porcelain from the Far East. This new technique, called **faience**, used a different mixture of clays to make thinner ceramics. The lead glaze

was replaced by a white tin glaze closely resembling white porcelain, and the pieces were decorated with both Chinese and Dutch motifs; Italian-inspired decoration was also popular.

When imports of Asian porcelain declined around 1650 as the result of a civil war in China, delftware enjoyed a huge success. Delft potters responded quickly to the gap in the market, and specialist faience factories began producing on a larger scale (*see DELFT*).

Frisian Majolica

In the second half of the 17C, **Makkum** (*see SNEEK, Makkum*) and **Harlingen** became the centres of Frisian majolica production, consisting mainly of tiles and tableware. This bore considerable similarities to the pottery produced in Delft, but was simpler in style and less imitative of Chinese porcelain. Also, the Frisian pieces rarely bore a manufacturer's mark; most were inscribed with the name of the client for whom they were made. Plates made in the **port of Lemmer** were particularly distinctive. The **Tichelaar factory** in Makkelum was established in the late 17C and is still in operation.

Dutch Porcelain

True porcelain was first successfully produced in the German town of Meissen in the early 18C, and other west European countries began making it shortly afterwards. Porcelain was made in the Netherlands only for a short period of about 50 years, mainly in imitation of the German variety. The typically Dutch **porcelain cabinet** was designed to display and protect these costly objects; it consisted of a tall, flat display case on a base.

The first Dutch factory was established in **Weesp**, producing Rococo forms with multicoloured decoration, but this closed ten years later. Its equipment and stock were acquired by a priest in **Loos-**

Many Dutch museums have a decorative arts section with re-creations of rooms furnished in the style of a particular period or region. Some also have **doll's houses** which are detailed reproductions of the interiors of wealthy Dutch homes during the Golden Age.

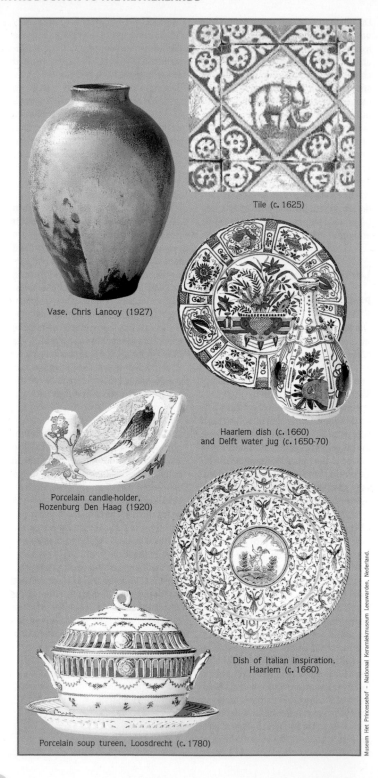

Tile (c. 1625)

Vase, Chris Lanooy (1927)

Haarlem dish (c. 1660)
and Delft water jug (c. 1650-70)

Porcelain candle-holder,
Rozenburg Den Haag (1920)

Dish of Italian inspiration,
Haarlem (c. 1660)

Porcelain soup tureen, Loosdrecht (c. 1780)

Museum Het Princessehof – Nationaal Keramiekmuseum Leeuwarden, Nederland.

drecht to provide jobs for poor people in his area, and the Loosdrecht factory produced beautifully painted tableware and ornaments between 1774 and 1784. After the priest's death, the factory moved to **Ouder-Amstel**, where it produced its own Louis XVI-style designs between 1784 and 1809. In that year it moved to **Nieuwer-Amstel** and continued making Empire-style porcelain until it closed in 1814.

Hague porcelain was made in The Hague from 1776 to 1790; porcelain imported mainly from Ansbach and Tournai was used and then painted. Dutch porcelain was of reasonably high quality, but high production costs and a limited market meant that large-scale production was not possible.

Dutch Art Nouveau

In the second half of the 19C, Petrus Regout's factory in **Maastricht** made mainly white dinner services, sometimes with printed decoration; these were strongly influenced by, and sometimes copied from, Wedgwood and other British manufacturers.

Art Nouveau did not become widespread in the Netherlands until the end of the 19C. The **Rozenburg** delftware factory in The Hague made pottery with stylised, often fanciful flower and plant motifs. The designer **TAC Colenbrander** was a great innovator who devised some highly imaginative forms and decorations. Another very successful product of the Rozenburg factory, under **JJ Kok,** was **eggshell porcelain** with very fine, naturalistic decoration. In Gouda, too, brightly coloured ceramics, known as **Gouds plateel**, were made between 1900 and 1930.

Modern Ceramics

Despite increasing Industrialisation at the beginning of the 20C, smaller-scale production of stoneware and earthenware has continued, and ceramics have become unique works of art. Leading modern Dutch ceramicists inclde Chris Lannooy, Bert Nienhuis, WC Brouwer, Johan van Loon and Jan van der Vaart.

TILES

The Nederlands Tegelmuseum in Otterlo and Museum Het Princessehof in Leeuwarden have a comprehensive collection of Dutch tiles.

Like majolica, tiles arrived in the Netherlands in the 16C via Italy and Flanders. They were initially used as **floor tiles**, but the thin tin glaze was easily damaged, and soon **wall tiles** were being made instead. These were initially painted in bright colours and decorated with geometric motifs, animals and fruit. Later, under the influence of Chinese porcelain, they were often decorated entirely in blue.

After 1750, the demand among townspeople for painted tiles tailed off almost to nothing; they preferred to decorate their walls with expensive fabrics. In the countryside, however, they remained a popular form of decoration. They depicted mainly craftsmen and women, imaginary sea creatures, children playing, soldiers and ships. Later on in the 18C, biblical and **pastoral scenes** became increasingly popular. After 1800, however, interest declined as people began using wallpaper, and also machine-produced tiles from England.

Tile Pictures

Huge tile pictures were made in the Netherlands from about 1620 until well into the 18C. These were placed either against the back of a fireplace or in other positions such as in **passageways**, on **walls** or above the **hearth**. They included beautifully painted vases of flowers; in the 18C, a wider variety of motifs was produced, including scenes from rural life, allegorical pictures, naval battles, townscapes, dogs and parrots. Tile pictures enjoyed a small-scale revival at the beginning of the 20C; they were made mainly for commercial purposes such as **shop interiors** or **advertising** on the outsides of buildings.

FURNITURE

Rijksmuseum Amsterdam has a comprehensive collection of furniture.

Middle Ages and Renaissance

The late-Gothic period produced carved oak chests, small side-tables with shelves and dressers decorated with **letterbox motifs**. From 1550 onwards, the Italian Renaissance inspired ornamentation with carved panels depicting medallions and grotesques, and heavy tables in the Flemish style (*bolpoottafels*) with turned feet widening into vase-like shapes.

Chests in the Golden Age

The most beautiful items of furniture from the late 16C and the Golden Age were linen chests. The **Dutch chest** (*Hollandse kast*) was perhaps the most common kind. It had very varied decoration: lion's heads, caryatids, friezes of foliated scrolls, grotesque masks, etc. The chest had a wide plinth, four doors and a heavy cornice decorated with a frieze of plants. Its uprights consisted of pilasters, and subsequently columns:

Zeeland chest

it was then called a columned chest (*kolommenkast*).

By the second half of the 17C magnificent chests in various kinds of wood were being made, known as **bombé chests** (*kussenkast*) because of the bulging shape of their panels, usually veneered with ebony. The chest rested on enormous ball feet. A set of five delft vases would often be placed on the cornice.

Marquetry and Inlaid Work

In the 17C and 18C, marquetry and inlays of ebony, tortoiseshell, metal and ivory became increasingly popular. Both in the Netherlands and in Flanders, they were used on inkstands and **cabinets** with numerous drawers used to store precious objects.

18C and 19C Chests

The Louis XV style, imported by the French Huguenots, was very much in vogue in the 18C, though it was freely adapted. **18C cabinets** had two doors and a base with drawers, which in the middle of the century acquired a characteristic bulge, and undulating cornices on their tops. Inlays and marquetry remained popular during this period.

At the end of the 18C, the influence of the more austere Louis XVI style became apparent; this was much more faithfully reproduced. In the 19C, the Empire style became popular following the arrival in the Netherlands of King Louis Napoleon and his wife Hortense, both of whom were very fond of Parisian fashions.

Painted Furniture

The north of the country specialised in the production of painted furniture in the 18C. This was mainly made by fish-

Dutch chest

Bombé chest

ermen in the Zuiderzee ports during the months when they did not fish, and they used methods they had seen during their travels in the Baltic or the East. This furniture was elaborately carved, and painted in bright colours in a style reminiscent of naive popular art. Many different objects were painted in this manner: chests, box beds, cradles, chairs, and even children's wooden satchels. There are fine collections of this form of furniture in the **Zuiderzeemuseum** in Enkhuizen, the **Hidde Nijland Stichting** in Hindeloopen, and the **Nederlands Openluchtmuseum** in Arnhem.

CLOCKS

After the famous scholar Christiaan Huygens invented the pendulum clock in 1656, clocks became a great deal more accurate, and **long-case** or **grandfather clocks** became increasingly popular in well-off households. These had a tall ornamented plinth containing the weights and pendulum, with the mechanism contained in a case above this and an arched pediment at the top. The dial was often painted with pictures of the night sky and moving human figures or boats; some showed the month, the day of the week, the date and the phase of the moon as well as the time. Amsterdam was a great clock-making centre in the 18C, and wall clocks in Louis XV style were also popular.

The provinces of Friesland, Groningen and Drenthe had their own distinctive form of clocks known as **stoeltjesklokken**. These had ornate openwork decoration, similar to that of the painted furniture described earlier, and the mechanism rested on a console. Zaandam clocks were more elegant.

Several museums have very fine clock collections, in particular the **Nederlands Goud-, Zilver- en Klokkenmuseum** in Schoonhoven and the **Museum van het Nederlandse uurwerk** in the Zaanse Schans to the north of Amsterdam

GOLD AND SILVERWARE

Romanesque Period
All over the bishopric of Liège in Belgium, the **gold and silversmiths of the Maasland** produced many master-

The shrine of St Servatius

Stichting Schatkamer St.-Servaas

pieces. The shrine of St Servatius in the St.-Servaaskerk in Maastricht, for example, is made of copper gilt decorated with enamel and precious stones, with depictions of Christ, St Servatius and the apostles around it. The Museum Catharijneconvent in Utrecht contains examples of **gold and silverware** that reflect the prosperity of bishops in the region during the Romanesque period; they include monstrances, pyxes, shrines, processional crosses, and books.

The Golden Age
In the 16C, and even more so in the 17C, it was a common practice among town councils, guilds and well-off ordinary people to commission finely engraved and chased silver objects to commemorate particular events. Most museums have collections of these items; they include large and small goblets, dishes, water jugs, **nautilus-shell cups** (made with a nautilus shell on a silver base), chains of office and other ceremonial items. The churches also owned much gold and silverware. Many beautiful **brandy bowls** were made during this period. They were oval in shape, with handles, and were highly decorated. The most famous silversmiths were the Van Vianen brothers.

A distinctive feature of the 17C interiors of Holland are the **brass candelabras**, also prevalent in churches.

Music

MUSICIANS

One famous Renaissance musician was **JP Sweelinck**, who was organist of the Oude Kerk in Amsterdam, and composed vocal and instrumental works. During the same period, the poet and diplomat **Constantijn Huygens** composed a number of pieces of music, as well as writing about the subject.

In the 19C, the composer and conductor **Johannes Verhulst** made an important contribution to music in the Netherlands, as did **Richard Hol**, a conductor, pianist and composer of cantatas and symphonies. One of Hol's students was **Johan Wagenaar**, an organist who composed works in his own very distinctive style. Wagenaar in turn taught the composer **Willem Pijper**, who was also known for his essays on music.

Today, the Netherlands has two of the world's leading orchestras: the Royal **Concertgebouw Orchestra** in Amsterdam, and the Residentie Orchestra in The Hague. The first conductor of the Concertgebouw Orchestra was **Willem Mengelberg**, who had a particular interest in the works of contemporary composers such as Mahler. Under his leadership, the orchestra became known for its exceptionally high standard of performance, and he was succeeded by

The organ case in Oude Kerk, Amsterdam

P. Gajic/MICHELIN

Eduard van Beinum, Bernard Haitink and Riccardo Chailly.

Organs

This instrument was first developed in Byzantium, imported into Western Europe in the 9C, and played an important part in Catholic worship from the 12C onwards. The instrument was also used in people's homes from an early stage, and therefore escaped the destruction wrought by the iconoclasm of the 16C. However, organ music was at first condemned by the Calvinist religion, and it was only in the mid 17C that it spread into Protestant churches. Numerous instruments were made during this and the following century. The sons of the famous German organ-builder **Arp Schnitger**, who had moved to Groningen, perfected the instrument in the Netherlands and built the great organ in **Zwolle**'s Grote Kerk. The impressive 18C organ of St-Bavokerk in **Haarlem**, built by **Christiaan Müller**, is one of the best-known in the world.

Most of the organ cases date from the Baroque era, and are sumptuous achievements with statues and carvings above the pipes.

Mechanical Organs

The first such instrument was a **barrel organ**, probably invented by an Italian in the 18C. A barrel covered in pins and turned by a handle raises levers which admit air to a set of organ pipes. Wheeled organs of this kind became widespread in 19C Europe. In 1892, Gavioli built the first mechanical organ to use a **perforated paper roll** instead of a barrel. Turning the handle moves a continuous sheet of perforated paper across a keyboard. The organ's repertoire was almost unlimited, since the paper rolls were interchangeable. The mechanical-organ builder **Carl Frei** established a business in Breda in 1920, but most of the instruments were imported from abroad, from Belgium (Mortier) and France (Gasparini and Limonaire Frères).

At the end of the 19C, the **dance-hall organ** became popular; this was an impressive instrument with a beautifully ornamented front. The beginning of the 20C saw the introduction of the **fairground organ**, which produced loud music intended to be heard above the hubbub of the fair. Finally, in 1945, an **electric dance-hall organ** appeared, with many built-in automatic instruments imitating the sound of a full orchestra. The **Nationaal Museum van Speelklok tot Pierement** (museum of mechanical music) in Utrecht has an interesting collection of mechanical organs (see UTRECHT).

Carillons

Countless churches and town halls in the Netherlands have carillons. These are believed to have been first used in the 15C, and are operated by barrels in a similar way to mechanical organs.

In the 17C, **François and Pierre Hemony**, famous bell-founders from Lorraine, played a very important role in the development of the carillon in the Netherlands. Of the many carillons they made, the best-known are those of the Onze Lieve Vrouwe Toren in Amersfoort, the Martini Toren in Groningen and the Domtoren in Utrecht. In 1941, a bell-founder in Heiligerlee, in Groningen province, invented an **electromagnetic system** to replace the barrel. In 1953, the Netherlands Carillon School was established in Amersfoort.

The town of Asten has an interesting **National Carillon Museum** (see EINDHOVEN: Excursions). Details of carillon concerts are given in the descriptions of individual towns.

Language and Literature

The Dutch language is spoken by about 22 million people throughout the world: in the Netherlands itself, in part of Belgium, and in the Netherlands Antilles and Surinam. Dutch is one of the western branches of the Germanic family of languages, and resembles both German and English. Frisian is not a dialect of Dutch, but a language in its own right. It was only on 29 January 1993 that Dutch was recognised by law as being the official national language, and Frisian was accorded the status of the second

governmental language. Many Dutch people speak English, French and German as well as their native Dutch.

LITERATURE: THE MIDDLE AGES

Although most literature until the Middle Ages was written in Latin, a number of mystical works were published in Dutch during the 13C, by authors including Jan van Ruusbroeck and Hadewych. Other works written in Dutch were those of the Flemish poet Jacob van Maerlant, the anonymous animal epic **Reynard the Fox**, the miracle play **Mariken van Nieumeghen**, the morality play **Elckerlyc** (*Everyman*) and the works of Thomas à Kempis.

16C-17C

The great 16C and 17C humanists wrote in Latin; they included **Erasmus, Jansenius** (1585–1638), the theologian Hugo de Groot or Grotius, and the jurist and Jewish philosopher **Spinoza** (1634–77). The country, and especially Amsterdam, became known for its liberal attitude; many foreign scholars and philosophers, such as John Locke, Descartes and Pierre Bayle, sought shelter in the Netherlands and found freedom to publish. The two great figures in Dutch literature of the period were the poet and historian **PC Hooft** (1581–1647), and the poet and dramatist **Joost van den Vondel** (1587–1679); both belonged to the **Muiderkring**, a circle of artists, writers and musicians founded by Hooft.

18C: THE AGE OF ENLIGHTENMENT

The Dutch presses continued to print the uncensored works of great foreigners, including such prophets of enlightenment as Voltaire and Diderot, but for Dutch literature this was a period of decline.

19C

Eduard Douwes Dekker, known under the pseudonym of **Multatuli**, gained an international reputation with his novel *Max Havelaar*, a satire on colonial life in

The Multatuli Museum, Amsterdam

The 1927 edition of Max Havelaar

the Dutch East Indies. **Louis Couperus** was an important novelist of the 1880 literary revival, and is best known for *Eline Vere*, dealing with contemporary life in The Hague, and *Old People* and the *Things That Pass*.

20C

Other writers of the early 20C include the historian **Johan Huizinga**, known for the lively style of his book *The Waning of the Middle Ages*, the prolific writer sometimes copied from, Wedgwood and other British manufacturers.

Art Nouveau did not become widespread in the Netherlands until the end of the 19C. The **Rozenburg** delftware factory in The Hague made pottery with stylised, often fanciful flower and plant motifs. The designer **TAC Colenbrander** was a great innovator who devised some highly imaginative forms and decorations. Another very successful product of the Rozenburg factory, under **JJ Kok**, was **eggshell porcelain** with very fine, naturalistic decoration. In Gouda, too, brightly coloured ceramics, known as **Gouds plateel**, were made between 1900 and 1930.

FRISIAN LITERATURE

The highly gifted poet **Gysbert Japicx** (1603-66) was the first to use the Frisian language in literature; a literary prize

named after him is awarded in Bolsward every two years.

Traditional Sports

Many sports from earlier times are being kept alive, and in some cases are highly popular. **Archery** is one such example; it is particularly widely practised in **Limburg**, and dates from a time when citizens felt it necessary to arm themselves against possible enemies. Members of a large number of local societies or guilds of archers congregate at an annual gathering, the Oud Limburgs Schuttersfeest (Old Limburg Archers' Festival) and give a colourful demonstration of their sport. In Friesland, **kaatsen** is a traditional ball game similar to fives, with six players divided into two teams, and the **skûtsjesilen** are spectacular annual regattas using traditional boats called *skûtsjes* (see SNEEK). Pole-vaulting (known as *fierljeppen* in Frisian) is another equally exciting traditional sport. It originates from the time when people hunting birds' eggs in the fields used to cross the many canals with the help of a long pole. In the Zeeland town of Middelburg, the sport of **ringrijderijen** has been revived. This is a tournament where riders on horseback gallop past and try to place their lances through a ring.

Skating was not only a traditional sport and pastime, but also a practical means of transport in the harsh winters of years gone by. The delightful winter scenes of the 17C Dutch master Hendrick Avercamp show how popular skating was at the time, and how sleighs were also used on the ice. Another activity that Avercamp portrayed in his paintings is **kolf**. This game was also played on ice with a club (*kolf*) and ball, and the aim was to hit a pole stuck into the ice. This game has been a subject of controversy between the Dutch and the Scots for centuries. The Dutch claim that it was the origin of the game of golf. However, the Scots claim that the early ball-and-stick version of golf was already being played on the sandy links of Scotland in 1457, when an Act of the Scottish

Parliament was passed requiring that "futeball and the golfe be utterly cryit down" in favour of church attendance and archery practice. The tradition of the

Friese Elfstedentocht, or Eleven Towns Race (⌀ *see LEEUWARDEN*), is thought to go back to the 18C.

THE COUNTRY TODAY

Economy

With the 16th largest economy in the world the Netherlands is currently enjoying a healthy, internationally oriented economic climate. In recent years the annual rate of economic growth has been above the European average and this still remains the case despite global uncertainties adversely affecting many neighbouring countries. Inflation is remarkably low, averaging around 1.5%, and unemployment remains steady at just under 3%. The economy is a free-market one and the present government is working towards making it more so all the time.

SECTORS OF THE ECONOMY

Food processing – The main focus of Industrial activity lies with food-processing and it is a very prosperous sector of the economy. Witness, for example, the familiar household name of Unilever® (a company based in the Netherlands). Next in importance comes the chemical industry, followed closely by petroleum refining (Shell® is also based in the Netherlands) and electrical machinery (the Dutch-based company Philips, is another household name around much of the world). At Slochteren, the Netherlands is also home to one of the largest natural gas fields in the world, generating profits that are measured in billions of euros.

Agriculture – Agriculture continues to play a significant role in the national economy, notwithstanding the fact that it only employs 4% of the working population. Dairy farming, including the raising of poultry and cattle, is important although more significant is the production of crops like beets and

potatoes; the country is famous for its cheese industry. Agriculture is a highly mechanised sector and feeds into the food-processing chain which, in turn, is a vital part of the country's exports. The total value of agricultural exports – over £25.4 billion ($50 billion) annually – is remarkably high for such a small country.

Probably the best-known agricultural product that is exported is based on fresh-cut plants, flowers, and bulbs, It has been estimated that two out of every three plants or flowers sent abroad comes from the Netherlands. To this surprising statistic can be added the fact that one in four of all tomatoes exported, plus one one-third of the world's exports of peppers and cucumbers are also Dutch.

Government and Administration

THE MONARCHY

The **constitution** of the Netherlands only covers the European part of the state. The country as a whole, the Kingdom of the Netherlands, has its own statutes instituting a federate political system and this includes the Caribbean islands of Aruba and the Netherlands Antilles.

Head of State – The present head of state, **Queen Beatrix**, is a member of the House of Orange-Nassau (which has ruled the country since 1815) and as monarch she retains constitutional powers. She has to co-sign every law and could in theory refuse to endorse a piece of legislation. The monarch also holds the chair of the Council of State, and as such has the role of advising the cabinet on new laws. She is also the final court for administrative law. Such power, however, is not usually practised and, like her British counterpart, the role of Queen Beatrix is largely a ceremonial one and the continuing existence of the monarchy is not a political issue in the Netherlands. The heir apparent is Willem-Alexander, her son.

POLITICAL POWER

Political power rests with a **cabinet of ministers** chosen from more than one party. No single party is able to command an overall majority when general elections take place and therefore **coalition governments** are the norm. The party with the most parliamentary seats usually gains the coveted post of Prime Minister and this has been the case for the last thirty years and more.

States-General

The parliament of the Netherlands is called the **States-General** and consists of two chambers. The one with the major legislative powers, the Second Chamber, has 150 members who are directly elected whenever a general election takes place (usually every four years, or sooner if the coalition breaks down).

The First Chamber

The First Chamber, consisting of 75 members, is elected by the representatives of the provincial assemblies which are also constituted by direct election during a general election. The First Chamber is only broadly similar in function to the British House of Lords in that it cannot directly initiate new laws but only reject them; nor does it have the power to amend legislation.

Provinces

For purposes of administration and local government, the Netherlands is divided into twelve regions, called provinces. Each province has its Governor, usually called Commissaris van de Koningin (Commissioner of the Queen). The next level of local government is formed by the division of the provinces into municipalities and there are currently 458 of these.

POLITICAL PARTIES

There are three main political parties: a conservative **Christian Democratic Appeal (CDA)** party, a social democratic grouping which is currently dominated by the **Labour Party (PvdA)** and a right-wing party called the **People's Party for Freedom and Democracy (VVD)**. For a long time, the Christian Democrats could be relied on to win enough seats to secure a place in any coalition government and at the time of a general election the unknown factor usually came down to whether a centre right or a centre left government will emerge as the next government. Recent elections have been more unpredictable and smaller parties have emerged with the ability to upset the usual arrangements between the main political groupings.

This took a dramatic and unfortunate turn in the run up to the 2002 general election when a new party, called the LPF and based around the populist right-wing politician **Pim Fortuyn**, gained considerable media attention. A week before the actual election, Fortuyn was gunned down and killed by a Dutch extremist. The political situation became quite volatile and following another general election in 2003 a new right-wing coalition government emerged to run the country. Policies to cut back on welfare spending and restrict immigration were quickly implemented. Another election followed at the end of 2006, following the collapse of the coalition, and this time the Christian Democratic Appeal party substantially improved its ratings and became the leading partner in a new cabinet.

RACE AND IMMIGRATION

Issues of race and immigration have recently done much to dent the Netherlands' famously liberal image. The political assassination of Pim Fortuyn was linked to his party's attacks on Islam in 2007, and in 2008 another political storm developed over a short film made by Geert Wilders, a very right-wing politician and leader of the relatively new PVV (Freedom) party (with nine members). Wilders has called for a ban of the Qur'an, comparing it to Hitler's *Mein Kampf*, and his film is very hostile to Islam.

Population

The Netherlands has a total population of c. 16 408 557 (2008). With a density of 395 persons per sq km/1 023 per sq mi, it is one of the most densely populated countries in the world (the United Kingdom, by comparison, has a density of 246 per sq km/637 per sq mi). A factor working against the increasing population is the low fertility rate of 1.72 children per woman.

POPULATION DISTRIBUTION

The population distribution is very uneven, and the highest densities are in the provinces of Noord- and Zuid-Holland. Together with the province of Utrecht, these form the **Randstad**, a large conurbation encompassing the country's four main cities – Amsterdam (744 740), The Hague (474 245), Rotterdam (581 615) and Utrecht (290 529) – and accounting in total for nearly eight million inhabitants.

The other main cities are Eindhoven (209 601), Tilburg (200 975), Almere (183 738), Groningen (180 824), Breda (170 451) and Nijmegen (160 732).

ETHNIC MINORITIES

The population of the Netherlands as a whole is an ethically diverse one, although over 80% of people are registered as indigenous Dutch. The two largest ethnic minorities are Indonesians and Germans (each representing just under 2.5% of the population), followed by Turks (2.2%), Surinamese (2%), Moroccan (1.9%), and Antillean and Aruban (0.8%).

Traditions and Folklore

COSTUMES

In the past, the Netherlands had a great variety of local costumes. Today, apart

NBTC

A girl in Volendam headdress

from Marken and Volendam where many people wear traditional costume during the tourist season, there are few places where it is regularly worn, and then it is mostly confined to older women.

Women's Costumes

In spite of their variety, there are common features shared by all women's costumes. They consist of a skirt, an apron and a jacket done up at the front, usually with short sleeves. Over the jacket some women wear a stiff bodice or a shawl. The costume, worn on Sundays, is always more elegant than that of other days, and on Whit Sunday in particular, women usually dress up in their finest clothes and jewellery.

Men's Costumes

Nowadays, these are worn only in a few coastal areas, such as Urk, Volendam and Zuid-Beveland. They are nearly always black, whereas in the past brighter colours were worn. The costume consists of a jacket, often double-breasted, and wide trousers or, around the Zuider Zee, knickerbockers. The shirt, which is rarely visible, is made of brightly coloured cotton with a striped or checked pattern, and has a straight collar with two gold buttonnes. These are the costume's only ornaments, except in Zuid-Beveland, where two attractive chased silver buckles are used to hold up the trousers. Men also wear a small cotton scarf knotted round the neck, and a black hat; this is often a simple cap, but in Urk it resembles a kepi, and a round hat is worn in Zeeland. Wooden clogs are usually worn as well.

Food and Drink

BREAKFAST (*ontbijt*)

Breakfast a fairly conventional meal and, at its most filling and leisurely, consists of different types of bread, spice cake, cheese, a boiled egg and a selection of cold cuts. In practice, most people rarely eat this much except perhaps at weekends as a form of brunch. A slice of toast, a drink of fresh juice or tea or coffee is a more likely repast for those setting off to work early in the morning.

LUNCH (*middegeten*)

Lunch (*middageten*) is usually taken between midday and 2pm and, although a full meal is not uncommon, a sandwich or a light dish is more likely to be eaten.

DINNER (*avondeten*)

Dinner (*avondeten*) in the evening is the main meal of the day for most Dutch families and until very recently took place around 6pm. Even today, when going out for a meal, it is not uncommon for a table to be booked for around that time. One of the few good books on Dutch cuisine is *Dutch Cooking* by Janny de Moor (Aquamarine, 2007).

A stall in Volendam selling herring

Eduard Bergman/NBTC

For dessert, pancakes are always pleasantly affordable. *Poffertjes* are sweetened pancakes, traditionally prepared using a shallow copper pan.

DUTCH CUISINE

The provinces can be better than cities like Amsterdam when it comes to experiencing traditional Dutch cuisine at its most authentic. Dishes to look out for include *stamppot*, a meat-based stew.

SEAFOOD

Any mention of typical Dutch dishes must include seafood like *haring* (raw herring), *Zeeuwse oesters and Zeeuwse mosselen* (oysters and mussels from Zeeland), *gerookte paling* (smoked eel), and *lekkerbekjes* (deep-fried breaded hake or whiting). The month of June or late in May sees the year's first catch of herring – tradition dictates their being landed in the harbour of Scheveningen near The Hague – and every restaurant is keen to ensure that it can offer the fish to its customers. *Vlaggetjesdag* (Flags' Day) celebrates the start of the new herring season, marked by the bedecking of the fishing fleets with flags. When the fresh herring are in plentiful supply after June you will see them being sold from carts on the street; the traditional way to enjoy them is to hold the fish by the tail and let it slip down your throat.

Herring does not have to be eaten raw and you can always try the pickled variety at any time of the year. *Zur haring* is a marinated version and sometimes herring is baked before being marinated.

MEAT DISHES

Meat-based dishes lay at the heart of Dutch cuisine and pork is likely to feature somewhere on the menu of most restaurants. Smoked pork sausages from Guelders – a province where the easy availability of birch and oak trees made it the first to develop smoking techniques – are a popular choice. A more acquired taste is *balkenbrij*, a pudding of sorts made from whatever is left over from a butchered pig.

Chicken and beef are also firm favourites and while usually prepared in ways that will not seem novel to the British or North Americans there are some interesting varieties. *Rookvlees*, for example, is a thinly sliced smoked beef that is typically served on a slice of buttered bread.

VEGETARIAN

The Netherlands does not have many vegetarian restaurants outside of Amsterdam but it is not difficult for non-carnivores to enjoy eating out. In the summer months salads are everywhere and can be sophisticated affairs featuring chicory, leek and bell peppers as well as the more usual ingredients. Given that English is so widely spoken, diners can always ask in a restaurant for a vegetarian dish, or a modification of something that is available, even if one is not specified on the menu.

Dutch breads are wholesome and tasty and can form the basis of a vegetarian lunch. White bread is still inordinately popular, a tradition that can be traced back to the times after World War II, when a sort of white bread was distributed to a near-starving population in the towns and western provinces. In recent years, though, brown breads and French-style varieties have become more common. Rye bread (*roggebrood*) is always available and comes in a black and coarse variety as well as a more dry version from Limburg and Brabant.

Spice cake, tasting like a sweet soda bread but made from rye flour, is also readily available and comes in various forms: with nuts, raisins or orange peel. The one you most likely to come across is *Deventer koek*, which gets its name from the town where the bread has been made since the late 16C.

CHEESES

The Netherlands is famous for its cheeses and, while there is a tendency to find your choice restricted to the Gouda or Edam kind, variety comes by way of the stage of ripening the cheese has acquired. Gouda is available as young, ripe, mature and extra-mature and the tastes are quite distinct; there is no mistaking the Parmesan-like taste of an extra-mature Gouda with that of its younger variety.

It is worth seeking out some of the goat cheeses and *boerenkaas* (farmer's cheese). When spices were first marketed in the Netherlands in the 17C, cheese-makers started to experiment with them and this accounts for the cumin-flavoured Leiden cheese and a Frisian variety (*nagelkaas*) that is made with cumin and cloves. Look out also for a hard, dry cheese made on the island of Texel.

DUTCH DRINKS

The ancient Roman writer Tacitus observed the partiality of people in the Low Countries for the taste of **beer** and he came to the conclusion that the population could be conquered by controlling the supply of it. Exaggeration aside, the Dutch do like their beer and brew many brands themselves. A good place to experience the surprising variety of Dutch beers is the De Bierkoning store in central Amsterdam at Paleisstraat 125 (☎*031 206 252 336*). Some of them are sold with a special glass from the brewery and come in a packaged form suitable for packing in your hand luggage.

Popular spirits include the juniper-flavoured **Jenever** (*corenwijn*), reputedly invented by a Dutch chemist named Sylvius de Bouve. The drink was apparently first dispensed as a medicine in the late 16C and then caught on as a favourite tipple. Other favourite drinks in the Netherlands are brandied apricots or raisins and redcurrant gin.

Dutch wine does not have an international reputation but the Slavante and Apostelhoeve vineyards, from the deep south of the country near Belgium, produce a white wine that should not disappoint.

Water is safe to drink straight from the tap anywhere in the country. Coffee-drinking is extremely popular and is usually served freshly brewed and strong. Tea is also widely consumed, and is generally taken without milk, and often with lemon.

Zandhoek, Amsterdam
P. Gajic/MICHELIN

DISCOVERING NETHERLANDS

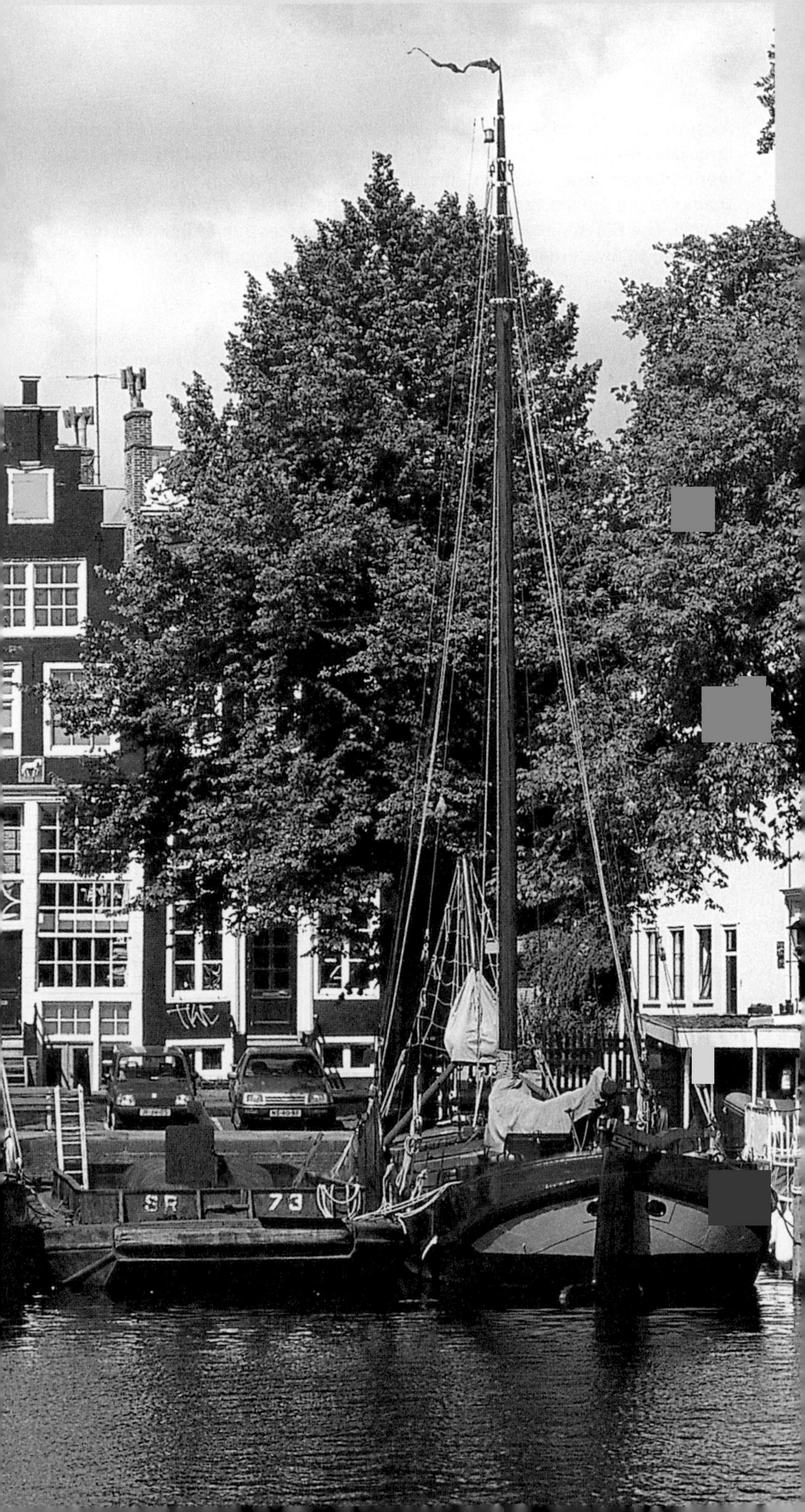

AALSMEER★

NOORD-HOLLAND

POPULATION 25 040

Aalsmeer is on the edge of the Haarlemmermeer Polder (🕭 see HAARLEM) and the large lake, the Westeinder Plassen. The town is mainly known as the home of the world's largest flower auction, where most Dutch florists buy their flowers and, thanks to the proximity of Schiphol airport, there are plenty of foreign buyers as well. The **Bloemencorso** is a famous annual procession of floral floats from Aalsmeer to Amsterdam and back (🕭 see Calendar of events).

- 🛈 **Information:** Drie Kolommenplein 1 – 1431 LA. ☎ (0297) 32 53 74. Fax (0297) 38 76 76.
- ▶ **Orient Yourself:** Aalsmeer lies just south of Amsterdam, just 7.3km/4.5mi south of Schiphol airport. Buses run every ten minutes or so from the airport. The town itself is compact and easily explored on foot.
- 🅿 **Parking:** There is plenty of parking around Aalsmeer railway station and free parking at the flower market for those visiting by car.
- 🕭 **Don't Miss:** Bloemenveiling Aalsmeer – the sheer volume of flowers and the speed with which the auction takes place are breathtaking.
- 🕐 **Organizing Your Time:** Start your visit to Aalsmeer early, and be sure to arrive at the flower auction by 7.30am to see the pre-auction action. The auction, itself, finishes by midday. Lunch is available at the auction complex, leaving time to explore Aalsmeer during the afternoon .
- 🕭 **Also See:** AMSTERDAM.

Sights

Bloemenveiling Aalsmeer★★

Legmeerdijk 313. 🕐Open Mon–Fri 7am–11am. 🕐Closed public holidays. ☞4.50€. 🕭☎0297 39 39 39. www.flora.nl.
The flower auction takes place in a huge complex of halls (766 000sq m/916 128sq yd) decorated with a stylised red tulip, the headquarters of the Aalsmeer Flower Auction, the **VBA** (Verenigde Bloemenveilingen Aalsmeer).
Visitors are advised to arrive early. The auction is open to visitors from 7.30am to 11am, but the best time to visit is before 9am. Mondays are usually the busiest

Flower auction in Verenigde Bloemenveilingen Aalsmeer

Bartruff/NBTC

The Biggest Flower Market in the World

It is fair to say that the sales figures of the VBA are impressive: a total of 19 million cut flowers and two million pot plants are sold every day. Roses are the greatest seller with 1.7 billion units, leaving tulips (569 million), chrysanthemums (421 million), gerberas (272 million) and carnations (178 million) trailing far behind. The Aalsmeer Flower Auction is the largest market in the Netherlands with an annual turnover of some six million euros. An average of 50 000 transactions are made every day.

days and Thursdays the quietest. Inside there is a **gallery** from where visitors are able to watch the auction and the activity down below on the shop floor.

Some of the halls are reserved for the arrival of cut flowers, which takes place the day before or early in the morning. The flowers are packed and loaded onto trucks elsewhere. At the centre of the halls are the **auction rooms**: four of these amphitheatres are used for selling cut flowers and can be viewed. The retail buyers sit in tiers facing dials linked to a computer. A trolley carrying a lot, or batch, of flowers is brought to the foot of one of the dials. On the dial a number

indicates the product, the producer, the quality, the size of the lot and the currency. As soon as the buyer sees the price he wants to pay come up on the dial, he presses a button to stop the countdown on the dial. The fastest – and therefore the highest – bidder gets the lot for which he has just bid. The successful bidder's number then appears on the dial as well as the number of lots bought.

Westeinder Plassen

This large lake is one of the most popular water sports centres near Amsterdam. The road that runs round it via Kudelstaart provides lovely **views**.

ALKMAAR★

NOORD-HOLLAND
POPULATION 94 216

The historic town of Alkmaar is best known for its picturesque weekly cheese market (*mid-Apr–mid-Sept*). Inside its surrounding moat, formed partly by the Noordhollandskanaal, the old town has more or less preserved its 17C plan and a number of original façades. The old fortifications have been transformed into a garden. Alkmaar is now the main market town for the agricultural regions of the Noord-Holland peninsula.

- **Information:** Waagplein 2–3 – 1811 JP. ☏072 511 42 84. Fax 072 511 75 13.
- ▶ **Orient Yourself:** A pretty town surrounded by canals, Alkmaar lies 60km/37mi notheast of Amsterdam. The town's roads radiate in a grid-like fashion.
- **Parking:** There is plenty of parking, mostly free, around Waagplein, and the roads off the pedestrianised shopping street, Langestraat.
- **Don't Miss:** Hollands Kaasmuseum, the museum that tells the story of cheesemaking, for which Alkmaar is famous the world over.
- **Organizing Your Time:** Allow two or three days to really explore Alkmaar, including an hour or so spent at the Kaasmarkt. Be sure to spend at least one evening in the town to appreciate its lively atmosphere and sample one of its fine restaurants. Include a canal tour: see the town from the water with tour boats leaving regularly from the Mient Quay, near the cheese market. It's a great way to see Alkmaar's surrounding countryside. The tours last around 45 minutes, or take a longer trip to Amsterdam or Zaanstreek.

ALKMAAR

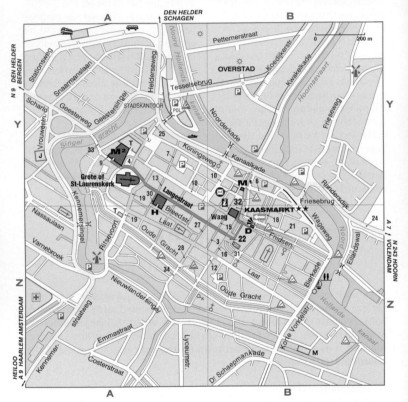

A Bit of History

Alkmaar was founded in the 10C in the middle of marshes and lakes. Its name derives either from *elk meer* or "each lake", or from *alken meer* or "auk lake", after the name of the bird which lived in the marshes.

The siege of Alkmaar – During the Eighty Years' War, which began in 1568, Alkmaar was besieged in August 1573 by 16 000 Spaniards commanded by Don Federico of Toledo, the son of the Spanish governor, the Duke of Alba.

Heavy autumn rain flooded the surrounding countryside and forced the assailants to withdraw on 8 October, after a seven-week siege. Alkmaar was therefore the first town to resist the Spanish, and for centuries it has been said that victory began in Alkmaar.

The famous cheese porters of Alkmaar

Kaasmarkt★★

🕑*Open mid-Apr–mid-Sept, Fri 10am–noon.* ☎*072 511 42 84.*
This traditional market, known since the early 17C, is held on Waagplein every Friday in summer. Early in the morning, trucks and cars bring the Edam and Gouda cheeses to the square, where they are carefully piled up. At 10am the buyers start tasting and comparing the different cheeses and haggling; they then seal their agreement with the seller by slapping hands. Next, the famous **cheese porters** (*kaasdragers*), wearing the traditional white clothes and straw hats, take over. The porters belong to an ancient guild, which is divided into four companies each identified by a different colour (green, blue, red, and yellow) and consisting of six porters and a weigher or stacker (*tasman*).

Additional Sights

Waag

The weigh-house is the former Chapel of the Holy Ghost, built at the end of the 14C and converted in 1582. On the east side, the chancel has been replaced by a Renaissance building with a finely worked gable, which since the 19C has been decorated with a painting on Auvergne lava, representing trade and industry. The tower, which was built at the end of the 16C, was modelled on that of the Oude Kerk in Amsterdam and has a carillon and working models of knights engaging in a joust every hour.

Hollands Kaasmuseum

In the Waag. Visit starts on second floor. 🕑*Open mid-Mar–Oct, daily, 10am (Fri 9am)–4pm.* 🕑*Closed public holidays.* 📷*3€.* ☎*072 511 42 84. www.kaasmuseum.nl.*
The Dutch Cheese Museum includes a collection of tools, such as decorative carved wooden cheese moulds, illustrating the history and making of cheese and butter. The display on the first floor shows how cheese is made on farms and in dairies, and explains the importance of dairy products to the Dutch economy.

Nederlands Biermuseum De Boom

Houttil 1. 🕑*Open Oct–Mar, Tue–Fri noon–5pm, Sat–Sun, 1pm–4pm.* 🕑*Closed Easter Day, Whit Sunday, 25 and 26 Dec.* ☎ *072 511 38 01. www.biermuseum.nl (in Dutch).*
A beer museum in a 17C brewery, chronicling the history of brewing. There is a tasting area in the cellar.

Huis met de Kogel

This building, the "house with the cannonball," overlooks the canal and has a corbelled wooden façade. Embedded in the gable is a Spanish cannonball from the battle of 1573.

From the neighbouring bridge there is a fine **view** of the weigh-house.

Mient

On this square and along the canal there are numerous old façades. To the south is the fish market, Vismarkt.

Langestraat

This pedestrian precinct is the town's main shopping street.

Stadhuis

Guided tour or by appointment. ☎ *072 511 42 84.*
The town hall's charming Gothic façade with its flight of steps is flanked by an elegant octagonal tower with streaks of white limestone. The adjoining building is 17C. The town hall has a collection of porcelain.

Grote Kerk or St Laurenskerk

Open Jun–mid-Sept, Tue–Sat noon–5pm. ☎ *072 514 07 07. www.grotekerk-alkmaar.nl (in Dutch).*
This is a beautiful church with three naves, a transept and an ambulatory dating from the late 15C and early 16C. It was built by members of the Keldermans family, famous architects from Mechelen in Belgium. The imposing interior has wooden vaults with beautiful 17C chandeliers.

Under the chancel vault there is a painting, the *Last Judgement,* by **Cornelis Buys** (15C–16C), known as the Master of Alkmaar. The **great organ case**★, made in 1645 by Jacob van Campen, is decorated with panels depicting the Triumph of King Saul. The **small organ**★ on the north side of the ambulatory dates from 1511; it is one of the country's oldest such instruments. Over 1 700 gravestones are embedded in the floor. The church also contains the memorial tomb of Count **Floris V**, who was assassinated in 1296. Since 1996, the building has been used for events such as organ concerts, exhibitions, trade fairs and conferences.

Stedelijk Museum

Open Tue–Fri, 10am–5pm, Sat–Sun and public holidays, 1pm–5pm. Closed 30 Apr, 25 Dec and 1 Jan. ● *4.50€.* ☎ *072 548 97 89. www.stedelijkmuseum alkmaar.nl (in Dutch).*
The municipal museum houses several interesting collections pertaining to the history of the town: 16C and 17C paintings, including a great many portraits of companies of the civic guard (schuttersstukken), and works by Maerten van Heemskerk, Pieter Saenredam, Gerard van Honthorst, Willem van de Velde the Elder and Allart van Everdingen.

Excursions

Broek op Langedijk

8km/5mi north of Alkmaar.
This is the home of Europe's oldest "drive-through" vegetable auction, the **Museum Broeker Veiling** (*open Apr–Oct, Mon–Sat 10am–5pm, Sun 11am–5pm; closed 30 Apr; ● 6.75€;* ☎ *0226 31 38 07; www.broekerveiling.nl).* From 1887 to 1973, market gardeners from the

---

Beemster, a Masterpiece of 17C Creative Planning

When the problem of high water levels and a lack of good farming land came to a head in the early 17C a group of Amsterdam merchants, enlisting the ingenious talent of hydraulic engineer **Jan Adriaenszoon Leeghwater**, decided to drain the Beemstermeer. This ambitious project was completed in 1612, providing 7 200ha/17 790 acres of fertile land. In accordance with 17C Renaissance aesthetic ideals of order, cohesion and harmony, the reclaimed land was divided into perfect squares, which in turn were divided into parcels, 185m x 930m or 203yd x 1 021yd, which was deemed ideal for farming. The geometrical landscape of roads, ditches, dykes and trees has been preserved almost intact. This explains the exceptional interest of this area. Among the fields and farmhouses with pyramidal roofs, the Amsterdam landowners had luxury country-houses built, where they came to escape the stench of the city in the summer. Some of these houses have been preserved.

"Kingdom of the Thousand Islands", as the watery surrounding area is called, transported their produce to auction by boat. Instead of wasting time loading and unloading the produce, they would simply moor at the water's edge. In 1903, the system was changed so that they were actually able to sail into the auction room!

Graft-De Rijp
17km/10.5mi to the southeast.
These two localities merged and became one municipality in 1970. **Graft** has kept its beautiful town hall built in 1613, with crow-stepped gables.

De Rijp was an important centre for herring fishing and whaling in the 16C and 17C. It has a town hall (1630) designed by **Jan Adriaenszoon Leeghwater** (1575–1650), the famous hydraulic engineer, who was born in De Rijp and claimed it was 'the finest village in Holland'. A tourist office (☎0229 67 19 79) is located on the ground floor of the town hall, in what was a weighing room, and it still has the scales used for weighing agricultural products and livestock. An original 17C fire extinguisher, made by Jan van der Heyden is also on show here. There are also a number of houses built in the regional style with wooden gables in De Rijp. The Dutch Reformed Church or Hervormde Kerk has 17C stained-glass windows.

De Beemsterpolder
22km/13.6mi to the southeast.
The Beemster Polder was declared a UNESCO World Heritage Site in 1999, as a result of its perfectly straight parcels of land and exceptional history of development. In Middembeemster the local museum, **Museum Betje Wolff** (◷open May–Sept, Tue–Fri 11am–5pm, Sat–Sun 2pm–5pm; Oct–Apr, Sun 2pm–5pm; ◚2.30€; ☎0229 68 19 68), is housed in the parsonage where the Enlightenment authoress Betje Wolff lived between 1759 and 1777.

The Dunes
Round tour of 35km/21.7mi – about 2hr. Leave Alkmaar via Scharlo.

Bergen
Also known as Bergen-Binnen (*binnen:* inner), as opposed to the neighbouring seaside town, Bergen is an agreeable holiday resort where substantial villas stand in rows along tree-lined avenues. It has a university department of extramural studies, located in the former manor house of the lords of Bergen. Bergen's popularity as a destination for Dutch holidaymakers means there are a number of hotels and restaurants in the area.

When World War II broke out, the Bergen airfield was bombed and a large number of aircraft and hangers were damaged. Following the occupation, the Germans took over the airfield and built a series of bunkers; on June 6 1944 they abandoned Bergen but the airfield was never put to use again. Remains of the German bunkers are still to be seen.

The **Bergen School** of artists was founded around 1915; its members played an important part in propagating the influence on Dutch art of artists such as Cézanne and Le Fauconnier. The **Museum Kranenburgh** (*Hoflaan 26;* ◷open Tue–Sun 1pm–5pm; ◷closed 25 Dec and 1 Jan; ◚7€; ☎072 589 89 27; www.museumkranenburgh.nl) contains work by artists including Leo Gestel, Matthieu and Piet Wiegman and Charley Toorop.

The entrance to the **Noordhollands Duinreservaat** (◷open daily dawn–dusk; ☎0251 66 22 66) is at the junction with the Egmond road. This is a nature reserve of 4 760ha/11 757 acres owned by the provincial water company, and a large number of bird species nest in the dunes.

Bergen aan Zee
This pleasant seaside resort has a coastline with long beaches and high dunes dotted with villas. From the promenade there is an extensive view over the dune landscape, with trees lining the horizon.

The **Zee Aquarium Bergen aan Zee** (Kids ◷open Apr–Sept, daily 10am–6pm; Oct–Mar, daily 11am–5pm; ◚8.50€; children 7.50€; ☎072 581 29 28; www.zeeaquarium.nl) has 43 aquariums with exotic fish and crustaceans, a large col-

Aerial view of Bergen aan Zee

lection of shells and a touch tank. The 14m/45ft-long skeleton is that of one of the sperm whales stranded on the Frisian island of Ameland in November 1997.

Egmond aan de Hoef

This village is set in the bulb field area to the south of Alkmaar. To the east, on the old Alkmaar road, beyond the church and close to the Slotkapel, the ruins of the moated **Slot van Egmond** (or Slot op den Hoef) can be seen. It was sacked in 1573. Only the red-brick foundations surrounded by water are still visible. One of its better-known owners was the famous Count of Egmond, executed in 1568 in Brussels (👤 *see DELFT*).

Egmond aan Zee ♨

This small seaside resort is in the middle of the dunes. At the foot of the Jan van Speyck lighthouse a statue of a lion symbolises the heroism of **Lieutenant Van Speijk**, who on 5 February 1831 blew up his gunboat with all on board on the Scheldt near Antwerp, rather than surrender to the Belgians.

▶ *Return to Egmond aan de Hoef.*

Egmond-Binnen

The famous **abbey** of Egmond was destroyed in 1573 and was rebuilt in 1935. Benedictine monks still live and work here.

▶ *Return to Alkmaar.*

AMERSFOORT★

UTRECHT
POPULATION 139 017
PLAN OF THE CONURBATION IN THE CURRENT RED-COVER MICHELIN GUIDE BENELUX

Amersfoort stands at the confluence of two waterways which form the navigable River Eem in the Gelderse Vallei. In the surrounding area, woodland and moorland cover the poor glacial soils, while the hills to the south, the **Utrechtse Heuvelrug**, are moraines deposited by the Scandinavian ice sheets.

Amersfoort is a delightful medieval town encircled by a double ring of canals. The whole of the town centre is a protected architectural area. In the modern northern suburb of **Kattenbroek**, there are a number of buildings designed by leading contemporary architects, including Ashok Bhalostra, Babet Gallis, Jan de Graaf, Leo Heijdenrijk, Jan Poolen, Rudy Uytenhaak and Kas Oosterhuis.

- 🛈 **Information:** Stationsplein 9 – 3818 LE. ☎0900 112 23 64. Fax 033 465 01 08.
- ▶ **Orient Yourself:** The Langestraat is Amersfoort's main shopping street and essentially cuts it in two, with much of the Old Town to the north.
- 🅿 **Parking:** Large parking areas are provided on the outskirts of town at reasonable cost, but central spaces are hard to find.
- 👁 **Don't Miss:** The Muurhuizen, a collection of houses built into the old wall of the town dating from the 1400s. They typify the character of Amersfoort.
- 🕔 **Organizing Your Time:** Allow around 4 hours to explore the Old Town, but be sure to spend a night or two to absorb the historic atmosphere of Amersfoort.
- **Kids Especially for Kids:** Children will love watching the animals at Dierenpark Amersfoort.

AMERSFOORT		Groenmarkt	BY	12	Lieve Vrouwekerhof	AZ	23
		Grote Spui	AY	14	Lieve Vrouwestr.	AZ	24
Appelmarkt	BY 2	Herenstr.	BZ	15	Nieuweweg	AY	9
Arnhemsestr.	AZ 4	Kleine Spui	AY	17	Utrechtsestr.	AZ	26
Arnhemseweg	BX 3	Krankeledenstr.	AZ	18	Varkensmarkt	AZ	27
Bloemendalse		Krommestr.	AY	20	Windsteeg	BY	30
Binnenpoort	ABY 6	Langestr.	AZBY		't Zand	AY	21

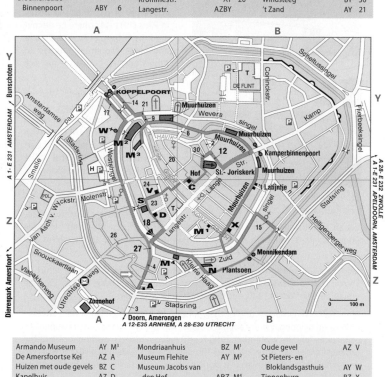

Armando Museum	AY M³	Mondriaanhuis	BZ M¹	Oude gevel	AZ V
De Amersfoortse Kei	AZ A	Museum Flehite	AY M²	St Pieters- en	
Huizen met oude gevels	BZ C	Museum Jacobs van		Bloklandsgasthuis	AY W
Kapelhuis	AZ D	den Hof	ABZ M⁴	Tinnenburg	BZ X
Mariënhof	BZ N	Onze Lieve Vrouwe Toren	AZ S		

A Bit of History

The town grew up around its 12C castle, and in 1259 it was granted civic rights. The first town wall, with its girdle of canals, dates from the 13C.
Amersfoort prospered in the 15C and 16C thanks to its thriving trade in wool and cloth and to a growing brewing industry. A second town wall was built c. 1400 and reinforced by a ring of canals, now partially replaced by the wide circular boulevard, the Stadsring. The town gate known as the Koppelpoort and other foundations at the far end of the main street, Kamp, are all that remain of the second city wall.

Old Town★

The recommended itinerary follows the line of the first town wall, where the famous **Muurhuizen**★, or wall houses, were built in the 15C. These houses are a distinctive feature of Amersfoort, and are so called because they are built into the town wall.

Krankeledenstraat

There are numerous old houses in this street; note in particular the Late Gothic **Kapelhuis** or chapel-house.

Onze-Lieve-Vrouwe-Toren★

Open Jul and Aug, Tue–Fri 10am–5pm, Sat noon–5pm. 4€. 0900 112 23 64 (VVV).

Piet Mondrian and De Stijl

Gemeentemuseum Den Haag

Gemeentemuseum Den Haag, built by H.P. Berlage

Pieter Cornelis Mondrian was born in Amersfoort in 1872. After experimenting with many different forms of painting, and a stay in Paris (1911–14) where he discovered the Cubism of Picasso, Braque and Léger, Mondrian returned to Amersfoort to look after his sick father.

During the First World War he came into contact with artists such as **Bart van der Leck**, **Theo van Doesburg** and **JJP Oud**, with whom he founded the abstract art movement called **De Stijl** ("The Style"). He passionately expounded his theories in the art periodical of the same name.

From then on his painting abandoned all subjectivity, and he used vertical and horizontal lines and the three primary colours, red, blue and yellow, together with neutral blacks, whites and greys.

Mondrian unremittingly pursued his experimentation in this genre, which is known as **Neo-Plasticism**. After a second period in Paris from 1919 to 1938, he moved to New York in 1940, and died there four years later.

Mondrian is regarded as one of the founders of geometric abstraction. His last, unfinished painting, *Victory Boogie Woogie*, was bought by the Dutch national art collections fund in September 1998 for 80 million guilders, making it one of the ten most expensive artworks ever. The painting was given to the Gemeentemuseum Den Haag, which owns the world's largest collection of works by Mondrian.

His influence can also be seen in architecture; buildings designed by Gerrit Rietveld (1888–1964), such as the 1959 **Zonnehof** (*Zonnehof 8, now a centre for modern art;* ⏰*open Tue–Sat 11am–5pm, Sat, Sun and public holidays noon–5pm;* ☎*033 463 30 34*) and the Rietveld Schröderhuis in Utrecht (ⓘ*illustration: see UTRECHT*) are directly inspired by his theories.

This beautiful 15C Gothic tower dedicated to Our Lady stands in a large peaceful square, Lieve Vrouwekerkhof. It is 98m/326ft high and has an onion-shaped dome and a carillon. The tower is all that remains of a church destroyed in 1787 by an explosion. A flower market is held every Friday morning on Lieve Vrouwekerkhof.

▶ *Take the small footbridge to cross the canal, the Lange Gracht, which divides Amersfoort in two.*

Zonnehof

⏰*Open Tue–Sat 11am–5pm, Sat–Sun and public holidays noon–5pm.* ⊚*5€.* ☎*033 463 30 34. www.dezonnehof.nl.*
This 1959 building designed by Gerrit Rietveld is home to the centre for modern art, which holds a varied collection of contemporary works and stages changing exhibits.

Hof

This spacious square is still bordered by some old houses (n° 24, for example) and is the scene of a lively market on Friday mornings and Saturdays.

St Joriskerk

🕐*Open mid-Jun–mid-Sept, Mon–Sat 2pm–4.30pm.* 🚫*Closed public holidays.* 🌐*0.50€.* ☎*033 461 04 41. www.joriskerk -amersfoort.nl.*

The Romanesque **church** of St George, dating from 1243, was destroyed by fire in 1370. It was rebuilt and then extended in 1534 into a hall church with a nave and two aisles. A finely sculpted sandstone **rood screen**, in the late 15C Gothic style, separates the nave from the chancel. The capitals and consoles in the chancel depict people and animals. Other items worthy of attention include wall paintings, a 14C baptismal font beside the pulpit and – against the Romanesque tower – a jack-o'-the-clock (Klockman) dated 1724. In the Gothic portal is a 17C surgeons' room (chirurgijnskamer).

Groenmarkt★

Several of the old houses in this pleasant square have been beautifully restored, in particular those near the adjoining square, Appelmarkt.

▶ *Follow Langestraat to Kamperbinnenpoort.*

Kamperbinnenpoort

This 13C brick gateway with its octagonal turrets stood just outside the inner town wall on the road to Kampen.
In the street to the west are some of the smaller wall houses, **Muurhuizen**, which have been well restored.

Havik

This is Amersfoort's old port, situated near the ford where the town was founded (Amersfoort means "ford on the Amer").

▶ *Continue along Muurhuizen.*

There are some interesting and quite impressive **Muurhuizen**★ between nos 217 and 243.

Armando Museum

Langegracht 36. 🕐*Open Tue–Fri 11am–5pm, Sat–Sun and public holidays, noon–5pm.* 🚫*Closed 1 Jan.*

🌐*3.50€.* ☎*033 461 40 88. www.armandomuseum.nl.*

This museum was once a church, the Elleboogkerk, and is now the showcase for the work of the Dutch artist **Armando** (1929). Exhibits include paintings, sculptures, poems and music.

Koppelpoort★

♿*Illustration: see Architecture.* 🕐*Open Jul and Aug, Tue–Fri 10am–5pm, Sat–Sun and public holidays, noon–5pm.* 🌐*2.50€. Information from the tourist office.* ♿☎*0900 112 23 64.*

This beautiful double gate, built c. 1400, includes a fortified bridge or water-gate over the Eem, a double treadmill in the centre and the gateway proper, flanked by polygonal towers. The Bag-Carriers' Guild used this as their meeting place and today it is occupied by a **puppet theatre** (🕐*performances on Sat at 2.30pm;*🌐*admission 6€;*☎*033 470 01 53; www.theatertoermalijn.nl*).

Museum Flehite

🕐*Open Tue–Fri, 11am–5pm, Sat–Sun noon–5pm.* 🚫*Closed public holidays.* 🌐*5€.* ☎*033 461 99 87. www.museum flehite.nl.*

The collections in this museum, which is housed in three wall houses, cover the history, archaeology and decorative arts of the town and the Flehite area (the eastern part of the province of Utrecht). Opposite the museum, on the Westersingel, is the chapel of the **St Pieters en Bloklands Gasthuis**, with the restored **Mannenzaal** (🕐*same opening times as Museum Flehite.* ☎*033 461 99 87*) behind it. This almshouse was built in 1530, and until 1907 the sick and poor of Amersfoort could stay here at the expense of local benefactors.

▶ *Return to the Varkensmarkt via the Westsingel, the last part of which is pedestrianised. Cross the square.*

Museum Jacobs van den Hof

🕐*Open Sat–Sun noon–5pm.* 🌐*2.30€.* ☎*033 462 57 55. www.jacobsvandenhof.com.*

This small, privately owned museum contains sculpture and drawings by Gijs Jacobs van den Hof (1889–1965).

Water-gate, Monnikendam

The fine house opposite is the School of Music and Dance (Muziek- en Dansschool).

▶ *Turn right into Kleine Haag, to reach the town walls.*

Mariënhof

This beautifully restored 16C convent now houses two restaurants. A herb garden has been created in the old convent garden.

Plantsoen

The footpath and cycle path along the top of the town ramparts lead to the Monnikendam.

Monnikendam

This graceful water-gate (1430) formed part of the outer fortifications, and overlooks the leafy gardens of patrician houses.

▶ *Take Herenstraat back to Zuidsingel and follow this to the left.*

The lovely shaded **canal**, the Zuid-singel, runs beside the gardens of the wall-houses. Cross the canal back to the wall-houses. The bridge over the **Kortegracht** is in a very picturesque **location**★, with a view of the 15C wall-house, Tinnenburg.

Mondriaanhuis

Kortegracht 11. ○*Open Tue–Fri, 10am–5pm, Sat–Sun, 1pm–5pm.* ○*Closed public holidays.* ∞*3.75€.* ☎*033 462 01 80. www.modriaanhuis.nl.*

In the house where Piet Mondrian was born and the adjoining school where his father used to be headmaster, a permanent retrospective of his work has been set up. There is a particularly interesting reconstruction of the studio in Paris where Mondrian worked from 1921 to 1936; he adapted this five-sided room to suit his own ideas of how spaces and surfaces should be divided up, using panels in primary colours where necessary.

't Latijntje

Also known as the Dieventoren or the Plompetoren, the 13C tower on the right is a relic of the first town wall. Past this tower, there is a very fine series of **Muurhuizen**★ on the right before you reach Langestraat.

Excursions

Dierenpark Amersfoort   [Kids]

3km/1.8mi to the west. Leave Amersfoort via Van Asch Van Wijckstraat. ○*Open Nov–Mar, 10am–5pm; Apr–Oct, 9am–6pm.* ∞*16€; children 13€.* ☎*033 422 71 00. www.dierenparkamersfoort.nl.*
Surrounded by woodland, Amersfoort's zoo features animals from all over the world. The Ancient City (Stad der Oudheid) with its Roman gate, arena, ziggurat (Mesopotamian stepped tower) and Egyptian temple is a place where crocodiles, tigers, lions and baboons roam.

Bunschoten★

12km/7.4mi to the north via the N 199. Leave Amersfoort via Amsterdamseweg.
Bunschoten forms one conurbation with **Spakenburg**, a small port on the edge of the freshwater lake, Eemmeer, once famous for its eel fishing.
The two villages line a street for more than 2km/1.2mi, which divides in the north to form the quays of a canal. The canal then widens into a dock where old boats, typical of the Zuiderzee, are still sometimes moored in the **old shipyard**.
The two villages are famous for the fact that some of the older women still wear the **traditional costume**★. The skirt is long, black and covered with a black apron. The distinctive feature of

the costume is the stiff, flowered panels, often of chintz, on either side of the tartan band which marks the centre of the bodice. A small white crocheted bonnet is perched on the back of the head. There is a market on the last two Wednesdays of July and the first two Wednesdays of August (known as Spakenburg Days).

The **Museum 't Vurhuus** (🕐 *open Easter–autumn half-term holiday, Mon–Sat 10am–5pm; Nov–Easter, Thu and Sat 11.30am–2.30pm; ⊛2.50€; 🕐 closed public holidays; ♿☏033 298 33 19*) gives a picture of what everyday life used to be like in Bunschoten-Spakenburg. It includes old shops, a herring smoke-house, a farmhouse and a fisherman's house.

The Woodlands and Heathlands of the Utrechtse Heuvelrug

41km/25.5mi to the south – about 3hr 30min. Leave Amersfoort to the south via Arnhemsestraat.
The road crosses the heathland known as the **Leusder Heide** and the woodlands of the Utrechtse Heuvelrug, the southern part of which has been designated a National Park.

▶ *Turn right at the Utrecht-Woudenberg junction of the N 227.*

Piramide van Austerlitz (Austerlitz Pyramid)
In 1804, Napoleon ordered his unemployed troops to build a sand pyramid here. It was restored in 1894, and a flight of steps and a small memorial were added.

Kasteel Huis Doorn
South of Doorn along the N 227. ☚☛By guided tour only (1hr). 🕐Open mid-Mar end Oct, Tue–Sat 10am–5pm, Sun 1pm–5pm; Nov–mid-Mar, Tue–Sun 1pm–5pm. 🕐Closed 25 Dec and 1 Jan. ⊛5.50€. ☏0481 421 456. www.huisdoorn.nl.
Surrounded by moats, set in the middle of a lovely park, this castle was the home of the ex-Kaiser of Germany **Wilhelm II** from 1920 to his death in 1941. The original castle was built in the 14C by the

Bishop of Utrecht to defend his territory and was altered in 1780. The tower on the southwest side is part of the medieval castle. Now a **museum**, the castle contains souvenirs of Wilhelm II, who brought his **collections**★ (paintings, tapestries) from the imperial palaces, displayed in a setting that has remained unchanged since the Kaiser's death.

Wijk bij Duurstede
Marktplein, the market square, is overlooked by the church, **Grote Kerk**, with its incomplete square tower, and the town hall (1662). **Museum Dorestad** (*Muntstraat 42; 🕐open Tue–Sun 1.30pm–5pm; 🕐closed 25 Dec and 1 Jan; ⊛2.50€; ☏0343 57 14 48; www.museumdorestad.nl*) traces the history of the town and the excavations on the site of Dorestad.

Amerongen
A peaceful place between the Rhine and the Utrechtse Heuvelrug, where tobacco was formerly cultivated; typical wooden tobacco-drying sheds can still be seen here. The Gothic **church** has a tall 16C tower with limestone courses. On the square, with its lovely restored rustic houses, an oak tree was planted in 1898 in honour of Queen Wilhelmina. The **Amerongs Historisch Museum** (🕐 *open Apr–Oct, Tue–Thu 1pm–5pm; ⊛1.50€; ☏0343 45 65 00*) is housed in an old drying shed and gives an insight into the history of tobacco-growing in the area.

Not far away, in Drotestraat, stands the famous castle, **Kasteel-Amerongen** (☚☛group tours; ⊛7.50€; ☏0343 45 42 12; www.kasteel-amerongen.nl). After the first castle was destroyed by the French army in 1673, its owner Godard van Reede had a new castle with double moats built on the same site.

Near **Leersum,** the **De Leersumse Plassen** lakes (🕐 *open mid-Jul–mid-Mar, dawn–dusk; ☏030 602 86 61*) are favourite breeding grounds with birds. The landscape is made up of heathland and fens, which used to cover a large part of the Utrechtse Heuvelrug.

AMSTERDAM★★★

NOORD-HOLLAND
POPULATION 743 027
LOCAL MAP SEE IJSSELMEER
PLAN OF THE CONURBATION IN THE CURRENT RED-COVER MICHELIN GUIDE BENELUX

Amsterdam, the biggest city in the Netherlands, lies on the banks of two rivers, the IJ and the Amstel. One of the best ways of getting to know this unique metropolis is by strolling along the picturesque canals with their narrow brick houses, some of them gradually sinking because they are built on piles to cope with the marshy subsoil. The numerous houseboats moored on the canals reflect the difficulty of building new housing in the old city centre. The lack of tall buildings and wide roads gives Amsterdam a small-town atmosphere. Another of its most striking features is the dominance of the bicycle as a means of transport; hiring a bike is the ideal way of exploring the city's byways.

Apart from its international importance as a port, Amsterdam is a city of great cultural wealth, including major exhibitions in the Rijksmuseum and the Stedelijk Museum, numerous art galleries in and around Nieuwe Spiegelstraat, concerts by the world-famous Concertgebouw Orchestra, the Hollandfestival of theatre, music and other genres, the Prinsengrachtfestival outside the Pulitzerhotel in summer, and the Uitmarkt, heralding the beginning of the new theatre season.

The city has some of the best nightlife in the world: cosy "brown cafés", trendy alternative bars, discos, night-clubs, and of course the infamous red-light district, the Walletjes. Amsterdam is a very outward-looking and tolerant city. As elsewhere in the Netherlands, many coffee shops sell soft drugs legally.

- **Information**: Stationsplein 10 and 15. ☎020 551 25 25. www.amsterdamtourist.nl.
- **Orient Yourself:** The best place to get your bearings in Amsterdam is Centraal Station. Directly ahead of you is the Damrak, one of the main shopping and commercial streets in the city, and the ideal place to explore the roads that radiate from it, while either side is part of the grid-like canal network for which Amsterdam is famous.
- **Parking:** There is parking for both cars and bicycles around Centraal Station, along with car parks and off-street parking throughout the city, but it is expensive. Free parking can be found at park and ride centres on the outskirts.
- **Don't Miss:** Taking a boat ride through the canals – the view of the tall, medieval buildings and the sheer size of the port are best viewed from the water.
- **Organizing Your Time:** Amsterdam is a surprisingly compact city, but there is a lot to see. It is possible to see most of the main tourist sights in a long weekend, but to really appreciate it, stay longer or visit several times. Find some time to visit Ouderkerk aan de Amstel, a traditional Dutch village a short distance away, ideally reached by canal boat.

A Bit of History

The first documented mention of the city dates from 1275, when Count Floris V of Holland granted toll privileges to this herring-fishing village, situated on two dykes joined by a dam at the mouth of the Amstel River. Amsterdam developed in stages round the original village centre, the present-day Dam square. It was awarded its city charter in about 1300, and was annexed by William III to the county of Holland in 1317.

In 1345, following a miracle in which a Eucharistic host was left undamaged in a fire, Amsterdam became an important place of pilgrimage. In 1428 the town, together with the county of Holland, passed into the hands of the Duke of Burgundy, Philip the Good. The use of the imperial crown in the city's coat of arms was sanctioned in 1489 by Emperor Maximilian for the support given by the city to the Habsburg monarchs.

The beginning of prosperity – A period of great affluence began in the late 16C. After Antwerp had been pillaged by the Spanish in 1576, the town's rich merchants took refuge in Amsterdam, bringing their diamond industry with them. Once Amsterdam had been freed from Spanish rule by the Union of Utrecht in 1579, the town became very prosperous, not least because of the large-scale influx of immigrants. Later, at the end of the 16C, the Marranos arrived from Spain and Portugal; these were Jews who had been forcibly converted to Catholicism but continued to practise their own religion in secret. The authorities granted them extensive privileges in order to encourage their trading activities.

The Golden Age – The 17C marked the height of Amsterdam's powers. Following in the wake of the Portuguese, the Dutch began a period of overseas expansion, and only a few years later their sailing ships were trading all over the Far East. In 1602 they founded the East India Company (Verenigde Oost-indische Compagnie, or VOC), followed in 1621 by the West India Company. A Dutch settlement was established at Nieuw Amsterdam; this was later renamed New York by the British. The Wisselbank, created in 1609, was one of Europe's first banks, and the Stock Exchange was built in 1608 by Hendrick de Keyser.

In 1610 it was decided to build the three main canals, the Herengracht, Keizersgracht and Prinsengracht, and these were soon lined with the mansions of wealthy merchants. The town was surrounded with a high wall on which a number of windmills were built.

Rembrandt, who was born in Leiden, came to live in Amsterdam in 1630, and was buried in the Westerkerk in 1669.

In 1648, when the Treaty of Münster ended the Eighty Years' War with Spain, the independence of the United Provinces was officially recognised.

The growth of navigation led to an increased demand for maps and globes, and their manufacture became one of Amsterdam's specialities. The city acquired a leading reputation in this area, partly as a result of the work of famous geographers such as Hondius, who published a new edition of Mercator's famous atlas in 1605.

Canal houses in Amsterdam

NBTC

Ice skating in Amsterdam

The Revocation of the Edict of Nantes in France in 1685 resulted in the arrival of a large number of Huguenots, who contributed to the city's prosperity.

French occupation – Such was Amsterdam's accumulated wealth that for a long time it withstood the effects of the economic decline of the 18C. Although the city had contrived to repel an attack by Louis XIV's troops in 1672 by opening the locks which protected it, it could do nothing in 1795 against Pichegru's army. In 1806, Napoleon made his brother Louis Bonaparte King of Holland. Louis settled in Amsterdam, which became the capital of the kingdom. The country became a part of France in 1810, and was decreed by Napoleon to be the third city of the French Empire and seat of the local government of the Zuiderzee département. However, Amsterdam was seriously hit by Napoleon's blockade of Britain, the Continental System, which ruined its trade. In November 1813, the population revolted and recognised the Prince of Orange, William I, as their sovereign on 2 December 1813.

Economic reawakening – It was only in the second half of the 19C that the city emerged from a long period of economic lethargy. The city walls were demolished and the opening of the Noordzeekanaal in 1876 provided a major boost to overseas trade. In 1889 the Centraal Station was built. The diamond industry also began to flourish again.

The early 20C – In 1903 the new Stock Exchange by **Berlage** was completed, marking the beginning of a new era of architecture. Shortly before World War I, the city began expanding and new suburbs were built. The **Amsterdam School** of architecture developed a new style of building, mainly after World War I. The central figure of this movement was **Michel de Klerk**. He, along with **Peter Kramer** and **JM van der Mey**, designed a great deal of local authority housing, particularly to the south of **Sarphatipark** and to the west of **Spaarndammerstraat**. They tried to break the monotony of façades by using asymmetry and differences in level, and to reduce the severity of straight lines by introducing sections of curving walls. The last war hit the city badly. Under the five-year German occupation, nearly 80 000 Jews were deported to concentration camps; only 5 000 survived.

Amsterdam after 1945 – Since the war, Amsterdam has staged a magnificent recovery from its ordeal. It is now a major industrial city, part of the huge **Randstad conurbation**. Its industries include medical technology, metals, printing, food, and of course tourism. The **RAI,** built on Europaplein in the 1960s, hosts many international con-

Address Book

For coin ranges, see the Legend on the cover flap.

WHERE TO STAY

The following hotels have been selected for their facilities, location, character or value for money. The **red-cover Michelin Guide Benelux** gives a more detailed list of hotels in each area.

YOUTH HOSTELS

Non-members can stay in youth hostels on payment of a supplement, and there is no age limit. Information from *www.stayokay.com.*

Stayokay Amsterdam Stadsdoelen – *Kloveniersburgwal 97, 1011 KB. ☎020 624 68 32. 170 beds.* Right by the red-light district.

Stayokay Amsterdam Vondelpark – *Zandpad 5, 1054 GA. ☎020 589 89 96. 536 beds.* The busiest and best-located youth hostel.

Stayokay Amsterdam Zeeburg – *Timorplein 21, 1094 CC. ☎020 551 31 55. 528 beds.* Located in the east of Amsterdam.

HOTELS

Aalders – *Jan Luijkenstraat 13-15, 1071 CJ. ☎020 673 40 27. www. hotelaalders.nl. 53 rooms.* Simple but comfortable hotel close to the Stedelijk Museum, the Van Gogh Museum and the Rijksmuseum.

Amstel Botel – *Oosterdokskade 2-4, 1011 AE. ☎020 626 42 47. www. amstelbotel.com. 175 rooms.* This cruise ship lies right by the station (Centraal Station) and is well-appointed.

Arena – *'s-Gravesandestraat 51, 1092 AA. ☎020 694 74 44. www. hotelarena.nl. 127 rooms.* This hotel near Oosterpark is housed in a former orphanage dating from 1890. The rooms are spacious, the fixtures and fittings are simple and modern. A café-restaurant with a terrace overlooking the garden and a night-club also form part of the same complex. The hotel has its own private car park.

La Casaló – *Amsteldijk 862,1079 LN, ☎020 642 36 80. 4 rooms.* Each of the rooms in this floating hotel is in a different style: Dutch, Asian, African

and Caribbean. You can have breakfast outside in fine weather.

Piet Hein – *Vossiusstraat 53, 1071 AK. ☎020 662 72 05. www. hotelpiethein.nl. 37 rooms.* Comfortable hotel right by Vondelpark and the main museums.

Nicolaas Witsen – *Nicolaas Witsenstraat 4, 1017 ZH. ☎020 623 61 43. www.hotelnicolaaswitsen.nl. 31 rooms.* Comfortable hotel in a quiet street at walking distance from the main museums and the busy area around Rembrandtplein and Leidseplein.

Toro – *Koningslaan 64, 1075 AG. ☎020 673 72 23. www.hoteltoro. nl. 22 rooms.* This early 20C villa on the edge of Vondelpark has a pleasant atmosphere and an attractive lake view from the terrace.

Ambassade – *Herengracht 341, 1016 AZ. ☎020 555 02 22. Fax 020 555 02 77. www.ambassade-hotel.nl (also in English). 59 rooms.* This stylish hotel is superbly located in a group of 17C houses on the Herengracht, close to the tourist centre.

American – *Leidsekader 97, 1017 PN. ☎020 624 53 22. www. amsterdamamerican.com. 174 rooms.* Well known hotel on Leidseplein. Its magnificent Art Deco-style brasserie is frequented mainly by politicians and leading figures in the arts.

Amstel – *Prof. Tulpplein 1, 1018 GX. ☎020 622 60 60. www.amstel hotel.nl. 79 rooms.* This luxury hotel on the banks of the Amstel has one of the Netherlands' most famous restaurants, La Rive. It also boasts a fitness club complete with pool, jacuzzi, sauna, gymnasium and steam room.

Canal House – *Keizersgracht 148, 1015 CX. ☎020 622 51 82. www. canalhouse.nl. 26 rooms.* This very elegant 17C hotel is full of antiques; each room is furnished differently. Breakfast is served in the dining room overlooking the garden.

Hotel de l'Europe – *Nieuwe Doelenstraat 2, 1012 CP. ☎020 531 17 77. www.leurope.nl (also in English). 100 rooms.* This famous hotel of Victorian grandeur is close to the historic centre

NBTC

Hotel Amstel

of Amsterdam. The Excelsior restaurant, known for its outstanding wine cellar, has a unique view of the Amstel. The hotel also has a heated indoor pool, a solarium and a fitness club.

Pulitzer – *Prinsengracht 315-331, 1016 GZ.* ☎*020 523 52 35. Fax 020 627 67 53. www.pulitzer.nl (also in English). 230 rooms.* This magnificent hotel on Prinsengracht was created from twenty-five 17C and 18C houses. It has an inner courtyard, a restaurant, a piano bar and a café.

The Grand – *Oudezijds Voorburgwal 197, 1012 EX.* ☎*020 555 31 11. www.thegrand.nl. 169 rooms.* This luxury hotel is housed in the former Prinsenhof. The rooms overlook either the canal or the inner courtyard.

WHERE TO EAT

The capital offers a huge variety of eating experiences. The following restaurants have been selected for their food, decor and/or distinctive setting. The **red-cover Michelin Guide Benelux** contains a larger selection of restaurants, with a gastronomical emphasis.

Cobra – *Museumplein.* ☎*020 470 01 14. www.cobracafe.nl.* Everything about this café-restaurant is inspired by the Cobra art movement: the artwork on the walls, the chairs, even the floor and the wine labels. The tableware was designed by Corneille, founder member of the movement.

Also a sushi bar, shop and a large terrace in the summer months.

Haesje Claes – *Spuistraat 275.* ☎*020 624 99 98. www.haesjeclaes.nl.* Simple Dutch food, generous portions, and excellent value for money.

In de Waag – *Nieuwmarkt 4.* ☎*020 422 77 72. www.indewaag.nl.* This pleasant café-restaurant is in the city's historic weigh-house (waag). The menu emphasises fish from the IJsselmeer, and there is also a wine bar, a reading table and a large terrace in summer. **Kantijl & De Tijger** – *Spuistraat 291-293.* ☎*020 620 09 94. www.kantjil.nl/restaurant.htm.* Indonesian.

Sea Palace – *Oosterdokskade 8.* ☎*020 626 47 77. www.sealpalce.nl.* Floating Chinese restaurant with a great view of Amsterdam.

Tom Yam – *Staalstraat 22.* ☎*020 623 48 29.* Stylish restaurant with a Zen garden and an exotic mixed cuisine.

Bordewijk – *Noordermarkt 7.* ☎*020 624 38 99. Open evenings only.* Trendy restaurant in the Jordaan serving contemporary cuisine.

Café Roux – *Oudezijds Voorburgwal 197.* ☎*020 555 35 60.* This restaurant, on the ground floor of The Grand hotel, serves good food in a beautiful Art Deco setting. By the entrance is a mural by Karel Appel.

De Gouden Reael – *Zandhoek 14.* ☎*020 623 38 83.* Superbly located restaurant on the old harbour; a weekly changing menu of French local dishes.

De Rode Leeuw (Hotel Amsterdam) – *Damrak 93.* ☎*020 555 06 66. www.hotelamsterdam. nl (in English).* Brasserie on the busy Damstraat, serving Dutch specialities such as kapucijners, kidney beans served with bacon and onion.

De Vijff Vliegen – *Spuistraat 294–302.* ☎*020 624 83 69.* Dutch cooking in an atmospheric, typically Amsterdam setting; a jumble of little rooms, beautifully decorated in 17C style.

Le Garage – *Ruysdaelstraat 54–56.* ☎*020 679 71 76. www.restaurantlegarage.nl.* Modern brasserie with an artsy atmosphere and international clientele. The owner has a cooking programme on Dutch television.

Indrapura – *Rembrandtplein 40.* ☎*020 623 73 29. www.indrapura.nl.* Indonesian restaurant.

OUT AND ABOUT IN AMSTERDAM

Amsterdam is believed to have around a thousand cafés, renowned for their friendly and cosy atmosphere. Some serve snacks and simple meals.

The area around **Leidseplein** and Rembrandtplein is particularly busy in the evenings. The Stadsschouwburg, or municipal theatre, is located on the former; the area also has a wealth of small theatres, cafés, cinemas and discos, as well as the Holland Casino. **Rembrandtplein** is mainly known for its restaurants and clubs.

CAFÉS

Brown Cafés

Brown cafés are a typically Dutch phenomenon, so named because of their nicotine-stained ceilings and wooden interiors. They are often not very large, and so tend to get crowded quickly. The most authentic brown cafés are in the city centre and the Jordaan.

Café Hoppe – *Spui 18–20.* ☎*020 420 44 20.* A meeting place for writers, journalists and other denizens of the literary world; in summer, customers also spill out onto the pavement.

De Admiraal – *Herengracht 319.* ☎*020 625 43 34.* This café makes its own gin in one of Amsterdam's oldest distilleries.

't Papeneiland – *Prinsengracht 2.* ☎*020 24 19 89.* This is one of the city's most romantic brown cafés, with Delft tile decoration, an old-fashioned stove and a delightful waterside location.

't Smalle – *Egelantiersgracht 12.* ☎*020 344 45 60.* A tiny café with a terrace overlooking the canal.

Proeflokalen

Proeflokalen are a relic of the 17C, when merchants came to sample drinks being sold by importers; *proeflokaal* simply means "tasting place." Today, you can taste gin and other spirits here before making a purchase.

De Drie Fleschjes – *Gravenstraat 18.* ☎*020 624 84 43.* This *proeflokaal* is always pleasantly busy, with a throng of people at the bar, and walls lined with carafes of exotically named drinks like crème de roses, parfait amour and ratafia.

A proeflokaal: "De Drie Fleschjes"

P. Gajic/MICHELIN

Wynand Fockink – *Pijlsteeg 31 (near Dam).* ☎*020 639 26 95.* Wynand Fockink offers a wide selection of gin and other local spirits, with the chance to try before you buy. There is also an attractive courtyard.

Café Américain – *Leidsekade 97 and Leidseplein 26.* ☎*020 556 30 09.* An Amsterdam institution; despite its rather high prices, this wonderful brasserie is a must for lovers of Art Deco.

Café Dantzig – *Zwanenburgwal 15.* *☎020 620 90 39*. Large café with a terrace on the Amstel and a separate reading area. A good place to put your feet up after a visit to the Waterlooplein flea market.

Café Luxembourg – *Spui 24.* *☎020 620 62 64. www.cafeluxembourg. nl*. Actually somewhere part-way between a brown café and a French-style café; at its best in the late morning, though it also serves a great breakfast.

De Jaren – *Nieuwe Doelenstraat 20-22.* *☎020 625 57 71*. This huge modern café is particularly popular with young locals; its delightful two-level terrace on the Amstel gets packed in fine weather.

De Kroon – *Rembrandtplein 17. ☎020 625 20 11*. This is an Amsterdam land-mark, with a very varied clientele. The room on the first floor is a sight in itself, and the terrace has an enjoyable view of the square.

BARS

Café de Sluijswacht – *Jodenbreestraat 1. ☎020 625 76 11. www.sluyswacht. nl*. This cheerful little waterside café lies opposite the Rembrandthuis, and the terrace offers a view of the Oude Schans. Don't worry if you've had a glass or two and things look a little strange; it's the building that's leaning at an angle, not you.

De Prins – *Prinsengracht 124.* *☎020 624 93 82. www.deprins.nl*. Pleas-ant café with terrace, right by the Anne Frank Huis.

Walem – *Keizersgracht 449.* *☎020 625 35 44*. Attractive designer interior with a garden at the back.

Morlang – *Keizersgracht 451.* *☎020 625 26 81*. Next door to Café Walem. An often busy place, with a youngish clientele and a scenic water-side terrace.

VOC – *Prins Hendrikkade 94-95.* *☎020 428 82 91*. This café has two rooms, one furnished with antiques and the other used as a reading room. It also has two terraces, one beside the water.

COFFEE SHOPS

Although you can actually go into a coffee shop just for a drink, their main purpose is to sell legal soft drugs such as hashish and marijuana.

NIGHTLIFE

Day by Day is published monthly, and gives full listings of music, dance, theatre and other events. It is available in VVV tourist offices.

You can book tickets direct or through **VVV Theatre Ticket Service** (*Centraal Station, Leidseplein* or *Stadionplein*) or **Amsterdams Uit Buro: AUB Ticket-shop** in the theatre (*Stadsschouwburg*) on Leidseplein (*daily 10am–6pm. www. uitburo.nl* or through the **Uitlijn** ticket line, *☎0900 01 91* (*daily 9am–9pm*).

Clubs – **Escape** (*Rembrandtplein 11; ☎020 622 11 11; www.escape.nl*) is Amsterdam's biggest club; iT, Amstel-straat 24, is an extravagant venue with go-go girls, drag queens, and special gay evenings.

Casino – **Holland Casino** *Max Euweplein 64. ☎020 620 10 06. www.hollandcasino.nl*.

Jazz, rock, pop concerts – **Amster-dam ArenA** (*Huntum 2; ☎020 311 13 33; www.amsterdamarena.nl*) – performances by big international names; **Bimhuis** (*Oude Schans 73; ☎020 623 13 61; www.bimhuis.nl*) – a must for jazz lovers; **De Melkweg**, (*Lijnbaansgracht 234; ☎020 531 81 81; www.melkweg.nl*) – concerts and dance nights in an old dairy; **Paradiso** (*Weteringschans 6; ☎020 626 45 21; www.paradiso.nl*) – dancing and rock concerts in a former church.

Classical music and opera – **Konin-klijk Theater Carré** (*Amstel 115-125; ☎020 625 52 25; www.theatercarre.nl*) – circus, variety, musicals; **Muz-iektheater** (**Stopera**) (*Amstel 3; ☎020 625 54 55; www.muziektheater. nl*) – performances by the Nederlandse Opera, the Nationale Ballet and the Nederlands Dans Theater; **Stadsschou-wburg** (*Leidseplein 26; ☎020 624 23 11; www.stadsschouwburgamsterdam. nl*); **Beurs van Berlage** (*Damrak 213; 020 530 41 41; www.beursvanberlage. nl*) – concerts by the Netherlands Philharmonic Orchestra and others; **Concertgebouw** (*Concertgebouwplein 2-6; ☎020 671 83 54; www.concert gebouw.nl* (*also in English*) – home of the world-famous Royal Concertgebouw Orchestra; **Felix Meritis** (*Keizersgracht 324; ☎020 623 13 11; www.felixmeritis.nl*) – classical concerts in a magnificent 18C auditorium.

SHOPPING

Most shops are closed on Monday mornings. Many, particularly in the city centre, are open until 9pm on Thursdays.

DEPARTMENT STORES AND SHOPPING CENTRES

De Bijenkorf, *Damrak 1. ☎0900 09 19. www.bijenkorf.nl*; **Magna Plaza Center**, *Nieuwezijds Voorburg-wal 182; www.magnaplaza.nl* – an upmarket indoor shopping centre with around 40 shops; **Metz & Co**, *corner of Keizersgracht and Leidsestraat; ☎020 624 38 28* – design, gifts, etc.; **Vroom and Dreesmann**, *Kalverstraat 201; ☎0900 235 83 63; www.vroom endreesmann.nl.*

FASHION

There are plenty of exclusive and trendy fashion stores, luxury shoe shops and jewellers in the **Museum District**, and particularly in P.C. **Hooftstraat** and **Van Baerlesstraat.** The pedestrianised **Kalverstraat** and Nieuwendijk have many more down-to-earth clothes shops.

DIAMOND FACTORIES

Ten of these are open to the public. Information from the VVV, *☎0900 400 40 40.*

Antiques – Most of the antique shops are located around the main canal area (Singel, Herengracht, Keizersgracht and Prinsengracht), and more especially in **Spiegelstraat, Nieuwe Spiegelstraat** and **Kerkstraat.**

MARKETS

Even if you don't buy anything, the markets are a great place for people watching.

Albert Cuypmarkt – *Albert Cuypstraat; Mon–Sat 9.30am–5pm;* general goods.

Flower market – *Singel, between Muntplein and Koningsplein; Mon–Sat 9.30am–5pm.*

Book market – *Oudemanhuispoort, Monand Sat 10am to 4pm; Spui, Fri 10am–6pm.*

The flower market

C. Bastin, J. Evrard/ MICHELIN

Flea market – *Waterlooplein; Mon–Sat 9am–5pm.*

Antiques market – *Nieuwmarkt; May–Sept, Sun–Fri 9am–5pm.*

Indoor flea market – *Looiersgracht 38, Sat and Sun 11am–5pm.*

PRACTICAL INFORMATION

General information – The VVV tourist office has branches in and opposite the **Centraal Station**, on the corner of **Leidseplein** and **Leidsestraat**, and at **Schiphol**. These are all open daily, *☎0900 400 40 40; www.visitamsterdam. nl.* At any of the offices you can purchase the **I am Amsterdam Card** (*www. iamamsterdamcard.com*), *which covers entrance to museums, a canal cruise and all public transport in the city: 33€ for 24hrs, 43€ for 48hrs or 53€ for 72 hrs.*

Parking – Parking is very difficult and expensive in Amsterdam, and is free only after noon. If you break the rules, you risk getting ticketed or even clamped; in the latter case, call the **clamping assistance** line on *☎020 553 07 00.* You can avoid all these problems by buying a daily parking permit from your hotel or using one of the (equally expensive) **multi-storey car parks.** There is free parking at the **park and ride centres** on the outskirts of the city, though their isolated location means that parking here at night is not recommended.

PUBLIC TRANSPORT

Information and tickets, including one-day travelcards and strippenkaarten (strips of tickets), are available from the VVV tourist office; *for more information, see www.gvb.nl.*

GUIDED TOURS

The **VVV** organises a great variety of guided tours.

BIKE HIRE

Renting a **bicycle** (*Hire firms only: Bike City – Bloemgracht 68-70; ☎020 626 37 21; www.bikecity.nl; Holland Rent-a-Bike – Damrak 247; ☎020 622 32 07; MacBike, Mr Visserplein 2 – ☎020 620 09 85; www.macbike. nl. Yellow Bike – Nieuwezijds Kolk 29; ☎020 620 69 40; www.yellow bike.nl*) is definitely the best way to get around and avoiding parking problems.

Canal bikes (*information from Canal-bike, Weteringschans 24; ☎020 623 98 86; www.canal.nl*) are available for hire.

BOAT TRIPS

Boat trips on the canals leave from various points in the city. *For further information, see below.*

The **Museum Boat** (*Leaves from Centraal Station. Seven stops near the main museums. Daily, 10am–6pm. Day ticket adult 15€ (after 1pm 12.50€). Information from Rederij Lovers ☎020 530 10 90. www.lovers.nl*).

---

gresses and trade fairs, and the **World Trade Centre** near the Station Zuid was inaugurated in 1985.

The canal from Amsterdam to the Rhine (Amsterdam-Rijnkanaal), completed in 1952, has contributed to the development of the port. The completion of a road tunnel under the IJ in 1968 improved communication between the city centre and the area to the north of the port; the first Metro line was opened in 1976. The town has seen the development of such modern suburbs as **Buitenveldert** to the south and **Bijlmermeer** to the southeast. However, the housing problem remains acute, and the city is continuing to expand (**Java-eiland**, **KNMS-eiland**). Another typical feature of the city are the 2 400 picturesque houseboats lining 36km/22mi of quays. Amsterdam has two universities and numerous higher educational institutions.

Old Amsterdam★★★

Nieuwe Zijde★★

Centraal Station

The huge central station on three artificial islands in the River IJ aroused great controversy when it was built between 1881 and 1889, mainly because it blocked off the view of the port. Designed by the architects **PJH Cuypers** and **AL van Gendt**, it is now one of the city's best-known buildings.

▶ *The busy Damrak leads to the Dam.*

Dam★

The Dam, Amsterdam's main square, is at the junction of the two large central thoroughfares, **Damrak** and Rokin, on the site of the dam across the Amstel. Overlooking this very busy square are the Royal Palace and the Nieuwe Kerk. The Nationaal Monument (1956, Raedeker) symbolises humanity's suffering in times of war and has become a popular meeting-place.

Koninklijk Paleis★ (Royal Palace)

○━*Closed for renovation until 2009. For information, see www.koninklijkhuis.nl.*
The town hall became the Royal Palace in 1808 during the reign of Louis Bonaparte. This imposing classical building was built on 13 659 wooden piles. The east and west façades are topped by tympana carved by Artus I Quellin, of Antwerp, who also decorated the interior. On the ground floor is the **Vierschaar**, the courtroom where death sentences used to be passed. The public could watch the proceedings through grilles.

In the **Burgerzaal**★ (citizens' room) on the first floor, the floor decoration depicts the eastern and western hemispheres. There is also a famous sculpture by Artus I Quellin of Atlas holding the celestial globe on his shoulders. It was in the Council Room (**Schepenzaal**) that Queen Juliana abdicated in 1980.

Nieuwe Kerk★★

🕐*Open daily, 10am–6pm (Thu 10pm).* 🕐 *Closed 25 Dec, 1 Jan.* 👁*10€.* ☎*020 638 69 09. www.nieuwekerk.nl.*

The Protestant New Church is the national church of the Netherlands. It is here that the country's sovereigns are crowned. This lovely Late Gothic building was pillaged and gutted by fire several times. After the fire in 1645 its tower, designed by Jacob van Campen, remained unfinished. Today the building is used as a cultural centre, where all kinds of activities are organised, including major **exhibitions**.

The church has a massive mahogany **pulpit★★** carved by Vinckenbrink in 1649, and a copper **chancel screen★** which is a masterpiece of Johannes Lutma, the Amsterdam gold and silversmith. The main **organ case★★** (c. 1650) was designed by Van Campen. The church contains the tombs of several Dutch admirals, including that of **Michiel de Ruyter★**, the commander of the fleet in the Second and Third Anglo-Dutch Wars, by the Belgian sculptor Rombout Verhulst. The poet Vondel and the famous bell-founders François and Pierre Hemony were also buried here.

Madame Tussaud Scenerama

Dam 20. 🕐*Open daily 10am–5.30pm; July and Aug 10am–9pm.* 🕐*Closed 1 Jan, 30 Apr and 31 Dec.* 👁*19.95€.* ☎*020 522 10 10. www.madametussauds.nl.*

Here modern technology, including audio-animatronics, is used to create a fascinating museum illustrating mainly life during the Golden Age, as depicted in the paintings of Rembrandt, Vermeer and Jan Steen. There is also a fine **revolving model** of 17C Amsterdam. The exhibition ends with many well-known figures from the Netherlands and abroad.

Kalverstraat

This bustling pedestrian precinct is the most important shopping street in Amsterdam.

Amsterdams Historisch Museum★★

Access via Kalverstraat 62, Sint-Luciën-steeg 27 or Gedempte Begijnensloot (*Gallery of the Civic Guards*). 🕐*Open Mon–Fri 10am–5pm, Sat–Sun and public holidays, 11am–5pm.* 🕐*Closed 1 Jan, 30 Apr and 25 Dec.* 👁*7€.* ☎*020 523 18 22. www.ahm.nl.*

This museum is housed in a 15C former orphanage. On the left of the entrance in Kalverstraat is the boys' playground; the cubbyholes where they used to keep their belongings are in the east wing. Opposite, a building in the classical style hosts temporary exhibitions. In **St Luciënsteeg** a small gateway is surmounted by the city's coat of arms. On one wall there is a large collection of picturesque **façade-stones**, and there is also a free **gallery of schutterstukken★**, group portraits of companies of the civic guard.

The entrance to the museum is through the second courtyard, formerly reserved for the girl orphans.

▷ *Follow the rooms in numerical order; these are spread over several floors and retrace the history of Amsterdam chronologically and thematically.*

An illuminated map shows the city's remarkable expansion. The city was built on sand, erected a town hall and fairly rapidly began to trade with the rest of the world. In 1345 a miracle made it a centre of pilgrimage, and then Amsterdam was subjected to Spanish rule. During this period it began to extend its influence around the world. The ships and merchandise from the Dutch East India Company and other companies flooded the city. At its peak, it built a new town hall, the present Royal Palace. The city began attracting many artists, who were commissioned by the rich merchants to paint portraits and landscapes. Large numbers of buildings were constructed, including several churches. Although the town had become wealthy, it did not forget those living in poverty: charitable institutions abounded, and their regents, or governors, liked having their portraits painted. In the 18C, despite strong competition from foreign countries, Amsterdam still occupied a prominent position in the world of the arts. In 1795

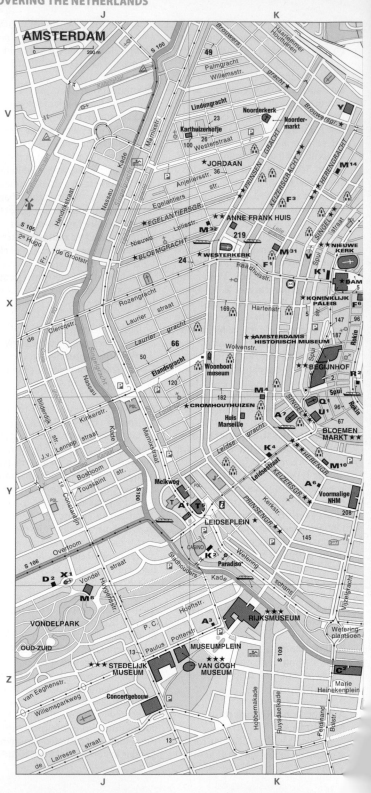

AMSTERDAM

0 — 200 m

JORDAAN

Lindengracht
Noorderkerk
Noorder-markt
Karthuizerhofje
Westerstraat
Anjeliersstr.
Egelantiersstr.
Egelantiers
★★ ANNE FRANK HUIS
Nieuwe
Leliestr.
BLOEMGRACHT
★ WESTERKERK
★★ NIEUWE KERK
Raadhuisstr.
★ DAM
★ KONINKLIJK PALEIS
Hartenstr.
★ AMSTERDAMS HISTORISCH MUSEUM
Rozengracht
Laurier straat
Wolvenstr.
★ BEGIJNHOF
Laurier gracht
Elandsgracht
Woonboot museum
★ CROMHOUTHUIZEN
Huis Marseille
BLOEMEN MARKT ★★
★ HERENGR
Melkweg
LEIDSEPLEIN
Kerkstr.
Voormalige NHM
CASINO
Paradiso
Wetering
Vondel straat
VONDELPARK
OUD-ZUID
Hooftstr.
RIJKSMUSEUM ★★★
P. C.
Paulus Potterstr.
MUSEUMPLEIN
STEDELIJK MUSEUM ★★★
★★★ VAN GOGH MUSEUM
Concertgebouw
Marie Heinekenplein
van Eeghenstr.
Willemsparkweg
de Lairesse straat

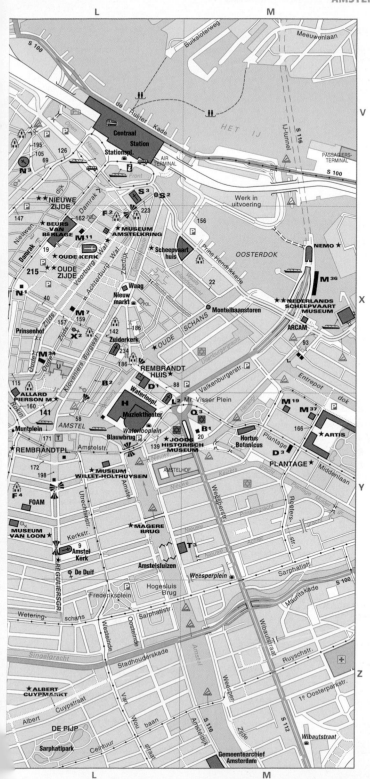

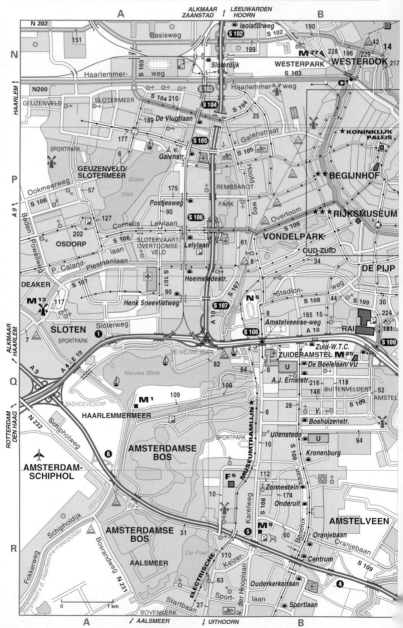

Map of Amsterdam showing Oostelijke Eilanden, Oost Watergraafsmeer, Duivendrecht, Ouder-Amstel, Ouderkerk a/d Amstel. Directional references: HOORN LEEUWARDEN, HOORN PURMEREND, ALKMAAR LEEUWARDEN, HOORN, APELDOORN HILVERSUM, UTRECHT ARNHEM.

the French arrived; the towns lost their independence but the country was unified. At the end of the 19C, Amsterdam experienced something of a population explosion. New developments sprang up, including the Rijksmuseum. After the horrors of World War II, Amsterdam went back to being the dynamic city it had once been and it has remained so ever since. As you leave, visit the **17C Regents' Room** left of the entrance; this is where the directors of the orphanage met.

Begijnhof★★

The Beguine convent is a haven of peace in the heart of the city. Founded in the 14C, it is one of the few such institutions remaining in the Netherlands (*see BREDA*). Beguines are women belonging to a lay sisterhood; although they take no vows, they devote themselves to religious life and wear a habit. The tall 17C and 18C houses with small front gardens are arranged around an area of grass where the former church of the Beguines stands. This has belonged to the English Presbyterian community since 1607. Nos 11, 19, 23 and 24 have beautiful sculpted façade-stones, while the tall and elegant house at n° 26 was that of the mother superior of the Beguinage. At n° 29 there is a hidden Catholic chapel, built by the Beguines in 1665. Not far away is the city's oldest house, no 34, dating from the 15C and with a wooden **façade**★; note the large number of façade stones incorporated into the wall of the courtyard on the left.

Begijnhof

Oude Zijde★★

Sint-Nicolaaskerk

This domed neo-Baroque-style Catholic church is situated very close to the Centraal Station. The church was built in 1887 and designed by AC Bleys.

Schreierstoren

This tower, known as the "weeping tower", formed part of the city wall. Legend has it that sailors' wives came to say goodbye to their husbands; hence the name.

There is a bronze plaque commemorating the Englishman, **Henry Hudson**, who discovered the American river which bears his name while working for the Dutch East India Company in 1609.

Huis Leeuwenburg

14 Oudezijds Voorburgwal.
This picturesque 17C house has a stepped gable of rust-coloured brick. A carved façade-stone depicts a fortified castle sheltering a lion. From the bridge over the lock where the two canals meet, there is an attractive **view**★: on one side, the Oudezijds Kolk, and the dome of the Catholic Sint-Nicolaaskerk, and on the other side the Oudezijds Voorburgwal, with its lovely series of old façades, and the Oude Kerk in the distance.

The hall, Museum Amstelkring Ons' Lieve Heer op Solder

Museum Amstelkring Ons' Lieve Heer op Solder★ (Our Lord in the Attic Chapel)

○*Open Mon–Sat 10am–5pm, Sun and public holidays, 1pm–5pm.* ○*Closed 1 Jan and 30 Apr.* ⊙*7€.* ☎*020 624 66 04. www.museumamstelkring.nl.*

After the Union of Utrecht in 1579, when the Catholics were driven out of their churches by the Reformation, they were forced to celebrate mass in private houses. Although this was officially prohibited, in practice the authorities turned a blind eye (a 17C example of Amsterdam's spirit of tolerance and liberalism). This secret chapel fitted out in the attics of two houses was used for Catholic worship from 1663 until the construction of the new St Nicolaaskerk in 1887. Services and concerts are sometimes held here.

The staircase leading to the 2nd floor passes in front of the hall, which is in pure 17C Amsterdam style, and the curate's room with a box bed. The **church**, whose two superimposed galleries occupy the 3rd and 4th floors of the houses, has interesting 18C furnishings.

Oude Kerk★

○*Open Mon–Sat 11am–5pm, Sun 1pm–5pm.* ○*Closed 30 Apr, 25 Dec, 1 Jan and festivities (check website for details);* ⊙*5€ (extra 5€ to visit the tower; weekends only).* ☎ *020 625 82 84. www.oudekerk.nl.*

The present Old Church, dedicated to St Nicholas, was built in 1306. It is the oldest in the city. In the 16C the bell-tower was topped by an elegant spire whose carillon was in part cast by François Hemony; there is an excellent **view**★★ from here.

The Lady Chapel has three fine **stained-glass windows**★ (1555). The **organ loft**★ above the entrance to the nave was made in 1724 by Jan Westerman. In 1642 Rembrandt's wife Saskia was buried here, and the church is the final resting-place of many famous people, including the painter Pieter Aertsen, the writer Roemer Visscher, the architects Justus and Philips Vingboons and the composer JP Sweelinck.

The church hosts various cultural events, such as organ recitals, exhibitions and theatre performances. During these times, admission fees may increase.

The Walletjes★★

The area between Warmoesstraat, Damstraat, Oude Doelenstraat, Kloveniersburgwal, Nieuwmarkt and Geldersekade.

This is Amsterdam's **red-light district**. The locals sometimes use the word 'Walletjes' to describe this district frequented by seafarers from the 14C onwards. The word means "small walls" and refers to the fact that the shop windows displaying the ladies' charms are sometimes half-concealed in old, very narrow streets (particularly to the south of Oude Kerk). The days of the seafarers and distilleries have gone, however, and today the industry, although equally colourful, has become much less lighthearted, with a mass of sex shops and stores selling pornographic videos. The area is not dangerous – indeed avoiding it would mean missing out on a large section of the historic centre – but visitors should nevertheless be on their guard as the area is well known for pickpockets and bag-snatchers.

Nieuwmarkt

Amsterdam's oldest market square lies between the Chinese district (*Zeedijk and the surrounding area*) and the red-light district.

Waag or St Anthoniespoort

This imposing fortified gateway (1488), flanked by towers and turrets, was converted into a weigh-house (waag) in 1617 and restored in 1996. The top floor served as an anatomy theatre, where surgeons and their students could attend public dissections, often on the corpses of criminals who had been condemned to death. Rembrandt's famous painting, *The Anatomy Lesson of Dr Jan Deyman* (now in the Amsterdams Historisch Museum), documents the lecture given by Dr Deyman in 1656. The building also has a café-restaurant.

Trippenhuis

Kloveniersburgwal n° 29.

This elegant classical edifice was built in 1662 by Justus Vingboons for the Trip brothers, who were cannon manufacturers; the chimneys are in the shape of mortars. The small picturesque house next door at **n° 26** is thought to have been built for the Trip brothers' coachman, using the stone left over from the main house.

Universiteitsmuseum de Agnietenkapel

Oudezijds Voorburgwal 231.

Near the Oudemanshuispoort, the **Agnietenpoort** leads to this chapel, once the home of the Athenaeum Illustre of 1632, a predecessor of the university. The buildings are currently being used by the university, and temporary exhibitions are held here.

Grimburgwal

This canal was built in the early 14C and marked the southern boundary of the city. The beautiful **Huis op de Drie Grachten**★ (House on the Three Canals), dating from 1609, stands at the confluence of the Oudezijds Voorburgwal, the Oudezijds Achterburgwal, and the Grimburgwal.

Allard Pierson Museum★

Open Tue–Fri 10am–5pm, Sat–Sun and public holidays, 1pm–5pm. Closed 1 Jan, Easter Day, 30 Apr, Whitsun, 25 Dec. 5€. 020 525 25 56. www.uba.uva. nl/apm.

This archaeological museum, part of Amsterdam University, has a remarkable collection of antiquities. The first floor contains items from Egypt (such as **funerary masks**★, sculptures and Coptic textiles), the Middle East (Iranian pottery and jewellery), Syria, Anatolia, Palestine and Mesopotamia (including cylinder-seals and cuneiform writings). The second floor is devoted to Greece, Etruria and the Roman empire. The collection includes the **Amsterdam Kouros**★ (c. 590 BC), ceramics (including **red-figure jars**★), a Roman sarcophagus (c. AD 300) and various items of Etruscan earthenware and sculpture.

Between the Flower Market★★ and Rembrandtplein★

Muntplein

This busy square is dominated by the Mint Tower, **Munttoren**. The tower, the remains of a 17C gateway, has a Baroque spire which was added by Hendrick de Keyser and which has a **carillon**. In 1672, during the war against France, money was minted here.

Bloemenmarkt★★
(Flower Market)

This colourful market, located at the southern end of the Singel and in existence since 1862, offers passers-by a wide selection of cut flowers and bulbs as well as clogs and other souvenirs.

Tuschinskitheater

Reguliersbreestraat 26–8.
This beautiful cinema in genuine Art Deco style was built in 1921 by HL de Jong. Note particularly the expressive **front façade**, the very beautiful carpet in the foyer, and the overwhelming **interior**★ of the Tuschinski 1 auditorium. Opposite, the building that was once the Cineac cinema (1934, J Duiker) is now a restaurant. The exterior is a good example of the differences between Art Deco and Functionalism.

Tuschinskitheater – Art Deco detail

P. Gajic/MICHELIN

Rembrandtsplein★

This square is a popular destination for local people out for an evening stroll. Many large cafés surround the square, with its statue of **Rembrandt** by Royer (1852).

Thorbeckeplein

With its many night-clubs, this square is very busy in the evenings.

In and Around Waterlooplein

Waterlooplein

On this large square, which has a lively **daily market** (second-hand clothes and furniture, ethnic jewellery, textiles, etc.), stands the **Mozes- en Aäron Kerk**. This Catholic church (1837–41) is used for exhibitions and concerts. The southern part of the square is occupied by the highly controversial **Stopera** (1987) (from *stadhuis* and *opera*). This modern complex includes the **Muziektheater** and the **Stadhuis**, or city hall, both designed by the Austrian architect Wilhelm Holzbauer and the Dutchman Cees Dam. The 1 689-seat theatre is home to the Nederlandse Opera and the Nationale Ballet. In the passage between the stadhuis and the opera house is a replica of the Normaal Amsterdams Peil (standard watermark).

The black marble **monument** standing in front of the city hall at the corner of the Amstel and the Zwanenburgwal commemorates the resistance by Jewish citizens who lost their lives during World War II.

Museum Het Rembrandthuis★

Jodenbreestraat 4–6. ◐ Open daily 10am–5pm (Fri 10am–9pm). ◑ Closed 1 Jan. ◉ 8€. ☎ 020 520 04 00. www. rembrandthuis.nl.
Rembrandt's house is situated at the heart of the old Jewish quarter. **Rembrandt** bought it in 1639 for 13 000 guilders and lived and worked here, producing large numbers of works in his studio on the first floor, until his creditors sold the house and contents by auction in 1658. The interior has been faithfully reconstructed using the inventories made up at the time of the

sale. The various rooms evoke the way in which Rembrandt lived and show where he received his clients and sold his paintings, where he found his inspiration (in the Kunst Caemer), and where he introduced his pupils to painting and etching.

One wing has a rotating exhibition of about 290 etchings. The rooms open to the public will convince even the most hardened detractor of etchings that Rembrandt was an exceptionally talented engraver, whose work was depicted with unadulterated realism.

Temporary exhibitions exploring various aspects of his work and examining the work of his contemporaries (Dirck Sandvoort, Ferdinand Bol and Pieter Lastman) are also held.

Oude Schans★

The **Montelbaanstoren** stands on this attractive canal. This tower, along with the St Anthoniespoort, was part of the city walls in the 16C.

Zuiderkerk

🕐Open Mon–Fri 9am–4pm, Sat noon–4pm. 🕐Closed public holidays. No charge. ♿ ☎ 020 552 79 87. www.zuiderkerk. amsterdam.nl

The first church built in Amsterdam after the Reformation was designed by Hendrick de Keyser and constructed between 1603 and 1611; it is flanked by a **tower**★ (1614). At present, the church is used as an information centre for the department of housing and town and country planning.

Further along, at 69 St Antoniesbreestraat, is the beautiful **Huis de Pinto**, which was built c. 1680 and once belonged to a rich Jewish merchant.

Joods Historisch Museum★

🕐Open daily, 11am–5pm (also 25 and 26 Dec), 1 Jan noon–5pm. 🕐Closed Yom Kippur. ☜ 7.50€. ♿ ☎ 020 531 03 10. www.jhm.nl.

The Museum of Jewish History is housed in a complex of four synagogues on Jonas Daniël Meijerplein. The first one on the site was the Grote Synagoge, built in 1671, but as the congregation expanded new ones were built on neighbouring plots: the upstairs, or Obbene Sjoel,

in 1685, the third, or Dritt Sjoel, in 1700 and the new or Nieuwe Synagoge in 1752. The latter is recognisable by the Ionic columns at the entrance and by the domed roof.

The **Nieuwe Synagoge** examines five aspects of the "Jewish identity": religion; Israel and Zionism; war, persecution and survival; history; and mixing of cultures.

The **Grote Synagoge**★ or Grand Synagogue still has the marble Ark of the Covenant given to the community in 1671. Various themes, such as the Jewish Year and its feast days and the Bar mitzvah, are explained through displays of items used in worship and ceremonials (silver plate, lamps, clothes, decorations for the Torah). The galleries are devoted to the socio-economic history of the Jewish people in the Netherlands. The renovation work brought to light a **mikveh**★, a bath used for ritual purification.

Portugees-Israëlitische Synagoge★

🕐Open Apr–Oct, Sun–Fri 10am–4pm; Nov–Mar, Sun–Thu 10am–4pm, Fri 10am–3pm. 🕐Closed Jewish festivals. ☜6.50€. ☎020 624 52 22. www.esnoga. com.

This massive brick building, lit by tall windows, was built in 1675 by Elias Bouman as a place of worship for three Portuguese congregations which had just united.

The interior remains as shown in Emmanuel de Witte's painting in the Rijksmuseum, with wide wooden barrel vaults supported by very high columns, galleries for the women, the Ark of the Covenant, and large **copper chandeliers**. There is no curtain (Parochet) in this synagogue, as this feature was unknown in the Jewish tradition of Spain and Portugal.

Sand is regularly sprinkled on the floor to absorb the humidity and muffle the noise of footsteps, and just as in the 17C, the synagogue has no electricity or heating. One of the most important Jewish libraries in the world is attached to this place of worship.

De dokwerker, the statue of a docker by **Mari Andriessen** in the square in front of the synagogue, commemorates the strike launched by the dockers on 25 February 1941 in protest against the deportation of Amsterdam's Jewish population.

Blauwbrug

The "blue bridge" dates from 1883 and is a copy of the Alexandre III Bridge in Paris; it has a view of the Magere Brug to the south.

Magere Brug★

The "thin bridge" is a picturesque wooden drawbridge across the **Amstel**, dating from the end of the 17C and still manually operated. It is attractively lit at night during the summer months. The wooden 18C **Amstelsluizen** or Amstel sluices refresh the water in the city's canals twice a week in winter and four times a week in summer. The large building to the east of the Magere Brug is the **Koninklijk Theater Carré**, which dates from 1887.

The Canals★★★

In 1586, the town council decided to launch the building of the **Grachtengordel** (*gracht* means "canal" and *gordel* "belt"), a vast ring of four concentric canals to the west and south of the historic town centre. The plan included, first the widening of the existing **Singel** and then the digging of the **Herengracht** (1586–1609), the **Keizersgracht** (1612) and the **Prinsengracht** (1612) respectively. These canals, 25m/8ft wide, then stretched from the Brouwersgracht to the current Leidsegracht, which was dug in 1664. As the population continued to grow, work on extending the ring of four canals eastwards began in 1662. It was completed in 1665.

The canal-side houses

Most of the houses which line the canals in the centre of the city were built in the 17C and 18C by wealthy merchants. Although somewhat similar in appearance, with their narrow façades and

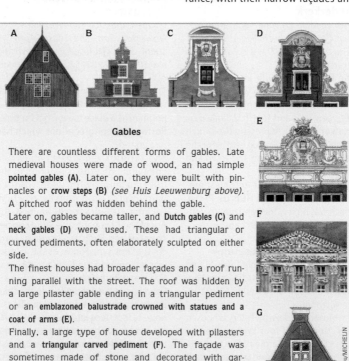

Gables

There are countless different forms of gables. Late medieval houses were made of wood, an had simple **pointed gables (A)**. Later on, they were built with pinnacles or **crow steps (B)** *(see Huis Leeuwenburg above)*. A pitched roof was hidden behind the gable.

Later on, gables became taller, and **Dutch gables (C)** and **neck gables (D)** were used. These had triangular or curved pediments, often elaborately sculpted on either side.

The finest houses had broader façades and a roof running parallel with the street. The roof was hidden by a large pilaster gable ending in a triangular pediment or an **emblazoned balustrade crowned with statues and a coat of arms (E)**.

Finally, a large type of house developed with pilasters and a **triangular carved pediment (F)**. The façade was sometimes made of stone and decorated with garlands. The many warehouses mostly have a simple, undecorated **spout gable (G)**.

M. Guillou/MICHELIN

front steps, they differ in colour and in the way their gables are decorated. Beams with pulleys project over the pediments: the narrow staircases make it impossible to bring in furniture.

Boat tours★

Information from the various operators: **Rederij Lovers**, *Prins Hendrikkade 25.* ☎ *020 530 10 90. www.lovers.nl;* **Rederij Kooij**, *opposite Rokin 25.* ☎ *020 623 38 10. www.rederijkooij.nl;* **Meyers Rondvaarten**, *Damrak Steiger 4–5.* ☎ *020 623 42 08. www.meyersrond-vaarten.nl;* **Amsterdam Canal Cruises**, *Nicolaas Witsenkade 1a;* ☎ *020 626 56 36. www.canal-cruises.nl.*

A boat tour offers an excellent view of the most important canals as well as part of the port. The route varies according to which locks are open.

Singel★★

Nieuwe Kerk or Ronde Lutherse Kerk

The high-domed New Church or Round Lutheran Church from 1671 has been converted into a **concert hall** and **conference centre**.

N° 7

This house, the width of a door, is often said to be the narrowest in the city. It is in fact the rear access to a house in Jeroenensteeg.

Bloemenmarkt★

The flower market is at the end of the Singel.

Herengracht★★★

This is the most important of the four canals and is where wealthy merchants came to live. The houses vie with one another in their rich decoration, and particularly that of their gables.

N° 168: Theatermuseum

⊙*Open Mon–Fri 11am–5pm, Sat–Sun 1pm–5pm.* ◉ *4.50€.* ☎ *020 551 33 00. www.tin.nl.*

The theatre museum forms part of the Netherlands Theatre Institute and is located in four houses along the Herengracht (*n°s 168–174*). Number 168 has

Staircase in the Theatermuseum

P. Gajic/MICHELIN

a fine stone **neck gable**★ designed by **Philips Vingboon**. Dating from 1638, it is the oldest gable of its kind in Amsterdam.

The **interior**★★, in Louis XIV style, is richly decorated with stucco, murals and ceiling paintings, many of them by **Jacob de Wit**. There is also an ornamental spiral **staircase**★ leading from the basement to the attic.

The museum's permanent display includes costumes, posters, props and an audio-visual archive. Temporary exhibitions are also held here.

The **Huis Bartolotti**★ next door at n° 170 was built by Hendrick de Keyser around 1617. The combination of brick and freestone on the frontage is typical of what is referred to as the Dutch Renaissance style.

N°s 364, 366 and 370: Cromhouthuizen★

Philip Vingboons built this fine row of four houses with neck gables in 1662. The gracious buildings, Baroque as regards their decoration, were commissioned by Catholic merchant Jacob Cromhout (*see the façade-stone at n° 366*). Housed in a 17C canal-house at n° 366 is the **Bible Museum** (⊙*open Mon–Sat 10am–5pm, Sun and public holidays 1pm–5pm;* ⊙*closed 1 Jan and 30 Apr;* ◉*7.50€;* ☎ *020 624 24 36; www.bijbels museum.nl*).

Nᵒs 386 to 394★

A lovely series of façades. At nᵒ 394, below a graceful gable, a **façade-stone** depicts the four sons of Aymon, mounted on their horse Bayard.

Gouden Bocht

The large, elegant houses on the second bend in the Herengracht are known collectively as the "Golden Bend". In the 17C, this was the area favoured by wealthy Amsterdam citizens who could afford double-fronted houses; these are now mostly occupied by banks and consulates.

Nᵒ 475★

This house (1731) with a stone façade was built by **Daniël Marot** and decorated by Jan van Logteren.

Nᵒ 497: Kattenkabinet

Open Tue–Fri, 10am–2pm, Sat–Sun, 11am–5pm. Closed 1 Jan, 25 and 26 Dec. 5€. 020 626 53 78. www. kattenkabinet.nl.

The Cat Gallery, located in a beautiful 17C house, holds temporary exhibitions consisting mainly of works of art depicting cats.

Nᵒ 476★

This elegant mansion was built around 1740. It has a very fine façade with six Corinthian pillars and decorative festoons. The open-work attic above the main part of the building has a balustrade decorated with the owner's blazon and an eagle above.

The **ABN-AMRO Bank** building (1923) on the corner of Vijzelstraat is by the architect **De Bazel**, a contemporary of Berlage.

Nᵒ 605: Museum Willet-Holthuysen★

Open Mon–Fri 10am–5pm, Sat–Sun and holidays, 11am–5pm. Closed 1 Jan, 30 Apr, 25 Dec. 5€. 020 523 18 22. www.willetholthuysen.nl.

This mansion, built between 1685 and 1690, has a series of elegantly furnished rooms evoking the lifestyle of rich merchants of the time. The kitchens, the men's smoking room, the bedroom and

the collector's room contain paintings, pottery, glassware and gold and silver. The **garden**★ has been restored to the original design of **Daniël Marot**.

Keizersgracht★★

Nᵒ 123: Huis met de Hoofden★

This attractive restored brick house dates from 1622. Its façade is similar to that of the Huis Bartolotti, and is decorated with six sculpted heads of Roman gods; hence its name, "house of the heads".

Nᵒ 672: Museum Van Loon★

Open Wed–Mon. 6€. 020 624 52 55. www.musvloon.box.nl.

This stately mansion was built in 1671 by Adriaan Dortsman, and has been altered on various occasions since; it once belonged to the painter **Ferdinand Bol** (1616–80). It has a stairwell decorated in stucco with magnificent **banisters**★ from the second half of the 18C, and numerous portraits. There is also a small Classical-style coach house in the lovely French-style **garden**★.

Prinsengracht★★

Westerkerk★

Illustration: see Architecture. Open Apr–Sept, Mon–Fri 11am–3pm. 020 624 77 66. www.westerkerk.nl.

This Renaissance church was built between 1620 and 1631 by **Pieter de Keyser**, based on the plans of his father Hendrick. It is the largest Protestant church in the city.

The remarkable carillon (*played Tue midday–1pm*) in the 85m/280ft **bell-tower**★★ dates from 1638 and is the work of **François Hemony**. The fine **view**★ from the top of the tower takes in the central canals and the Jordaan district.

The church **interior** is very plain; the nave has wooden barrel vaulting and the twelve chandeliers are copies of the original ones. The magnificent painted organ panels are the work of **Gerard de Lairesse**.

Rembrandt was buried here in 1669, one year after his son Titus, though the exact location of his tomb is not known.

Façade Stones

After the huge fire of 1452, all new houses were required to be built of stone with tiled roofs. In the absence of house numbers, a small sculpted façade stone was used, showing the emblem of the owner or the symbol of their trade. This practice ended when house numbering was introduced by the French. Such façade stones are still sometimes used today; this example in mirror writing dates from 1972.

P. Gajic/MICHELIN

On the pavement behind the church **Westermarkt** stands the **Homomonument**, commemorating gay men and women who died in the Nazi concentration camps.

Anne Frank Huis★★

Open mid-Mar–mid-Sept, daily 9am–9pm (Sat and all of Jul–Aug 10pm); mid-Sept–mid-Mar, daily 9am–7pm. Closed Yom Kippur. 7.50€. 020 556 71 00. www.annefrank.nl.

This narrow building erected in 1635 extends back a considerable way, and has an extension behind it which was enlarged in 1740. It was here that **Anne Frank's** father, a German Jew who emigrated in 1933, hid seven members of his family and friends in July 1942. They were betrayed, arrested and sent to Auschwitz in August 1944; only the father returned. The moving diary kept by his 13-year-old daughter was found in the house, and displays a rare sensitivity.

A revolving bookcase reveals a secret passage which leads to the bare rooms where the family hid. In the attic and in an adjoining house are exhibitions on Anne's life, and on war, Nazism and anti-Semitism, as well as temporary displays related to these issues.

Reguliersgracht★

This delightful canal built in 1664 provides one of the most attractive **views**★★ of any of Amsterdam's waterways. From the bridge spanning the canal beside Kerkstraat, the view encompasses the seven bridges across the Reguliersgracht.

Leidseplein★

This is possibly the liveliest square in Amsterdam. There are many theatres in the area, including the well known municipal theatre, the **Stadsschouwburg,** as well as restaurants and nightclubs. The **American Hotel,** dating from 1902, combines elements of Art Nouveau and the Amsterdam School, as well as a beautiful art deco café.

Max Euweplein is the home of the **Holland Casino**.

Further on, at n° 6 Weteringschans, is the **Paradiso**, a disused church which is now a popular venue for musical events. Behind the Stadsschouwburg (municipal theatre) a former dairy now houses the **Melkweg** cultural centre (*Lijnbaansgracht 234a*).

The long and pleasant pedestrian street Leidsestraat links Leidseplein to the city centre.

The Museum District
Allow 1 day minimum

Rijksmuseum★★★

Open daily 9am–6pm (Fri 8.30pm). Closed 1 Jan. 10€. 020 674 70 47. www.rijksmuseum.nl.

The famous national museum was founded by Louis Napoleon, the brother of Napoleon Bonaparte, in 1808. The present building was constructed between 1876 and 1885 by PJH Cuypers in a style combining neo-Gothic and neo-Renaissance features. It includes an exceptional collection of 15C–17C paintings, including magnificent works by Rembrandt and Vermeer, and also has important departments of sculpture and decorative arts, Dutch history, prints, Asiatic art, costumes and textiles.

A major restoration of the main building is underway and during this time the Rijksmuseum is only displaying the best of its permanent collection, entitled 'Rijksmuseum, The Masterpieces', in the new Philips Wing. Many, but not all, of the paintings mentioned below are on show.

Dutch paintings★★★ (15C–17C)

The collection of **pre-Renaissance** paintings includes works by **Geertgen tot Sint-Jans**, such as his *Adoration of the Magi;* Jan Mostaert, whose painting of the same subject is set amid an Italian Renaissance scene; the Master of Alkmaar, famous for his *Seven Works of Charity*; and Jacob Corneliszoon van Oostsanen, whose ornamental style is apparent in his triptych of the *Adoration of the Magi.*

In the **Renaissance** section, **Lucas van Leyden**'s *Adoration of the Golden Calf* shows great mastery of composition; **Jan van Scorel** depicts a *Mary Magdalene* of very Italian elegance. The art of Pieter Aertsen is more realistic, while Antonio Moro's portraits show considerable restraint. Both Cornelis Corneliszoon van Haarlem and Abraham Bloemaert are representatives of **Mannerism**. There is also a still-life with flowers by Jan ("Velvet") Brueghel as well as some lovely landscapes by the Antwerp painter, Joos de Momper.

In the **Golden Age**, painting styles varied a great deal. Hendrick Avercamp specialised in winter scenes, such as *Winter Landscape*. **Frans Hals** produced outstanding portraits such as that of *Isaac Massa and his Wife,* while the vivid and rapid brushwork of *The Jolly Drinker* is reminiscent of Impressionism.

Paulus Potter chose to depict animals, while **Jan Steen** specialised in cheerful domestic scenes (*The Feast of St Nicholas, Woman at her Toilet*).

Other leading landscape artists included **Jacob van Ruysdael** (*The Windmill at Wijk bij Duurstede,* and *View of Haarlem,* and **Meindert Hobbema** (*Watermill*). Adriaen van Ostade was more interested in villagers and their daily lives (*Peasants in an Interior: The Skaters*).

The four works by **Vermeer** are all masterpieces: *The Little Street* (c. 1658),

The Mill at Wijk bij Duurstede (c. 1670) by Jacob van Ruisdael

©Rijksmuseum, Amsterdam

"The Night watch (1642) by Rembrandt van Rijn, Rijksmuseum, Amsterdam

©Rijksmuseum, Amsterdam

painted from the windows of his house; *The Milkmaid* (c. 1660), pouring milk with a measured gesture; *Woman in Blue Reading a Letter* (c. 1662), in luminous blue tones; and finally *The Love Letter* (c. 1666).

Portraits by Terborch include a *Self-portrait with Pipe* by Gerrit Dou, and a sentimental scene by Metsu, *The Sick Child*. **Pieter de Hooch** is famous for his geometric interiors (*The Pantry*). Also on show is *Girl at a Window: The Daydreamer* by Nicolaes Maes.

The best-known work by **Rembrandt** on show is *The Militia Company of Captain Frans Banning Cocq and Lieutenant Willem van Ruytenburch,* known as **The Night Watch**. Commissioned by a company of the civic guard, this enormous group portrait was completed in 1642 and displayed in the company's headquarters in Kloveniersburgwal, before being transferred to Amsterdam's town hall in 1715. At that time, it was made smaller by cutting large strips off the edges. During World War II, it was hidden in caves near Maastricht (*see MAASTRICHT, Outskirts*). It owes its name to the darkened varnish, which was cleaned in 1947, but the painting in fact depicts the company in broad daylight.

The guards are shown in great agitation, as though taken by surprise; the captain is giving the signal to depart, and some of the guards have their faces half hidden, resulting in a very original group portrait. There are a number of details which add to the feeling of spontaneity: the little girl with a bird attached to her belt walking through the group, the barking dog, the dwarf running, and the man with a helmet covered with leaves. Spots of bright colour offset the rather grey tones of the guards' uniforms: the bright yellow of the girl's and the lieutenant's costumes, the red outfit of the guard reloading his gun, and the captain's red scarf.

The pictures from the **Italian School** include numerous Primitives, such as a remarkable *Madonna of the Lily* by Fra Angelico and a *Mary Magdalene* by Crivelli. There are some interesting portraits by the Florentine painter Piero di Cosimo and views of Venice by Guardi. Works from Spain include a lovely *Virgin and Child* by Murillo.

The Flemish paintings include two works by **Rubens**.

There are major paintings by Dutch masters from the second half of the 17C; the late works by Rembrandt are particularly noteworthy. *The Portrait of Titus in a Monk's Habit* dates from about 1600. The *Self-Portrait as the Apostle Paul* (1661) shows Rembrandt as a disillusioned old man, while the portrait of a couple known as *The Jewish Bride* (1668–69) is full of light and tenderness. *The Syndics,* a masterpiece dating from 1662, shows the inspectors of the Drapers' Guild grouped behind a table with a warm red tablecloth. Although their expressions are serious, this portrait is full of life.

There is a work by Nicolaes Maes, a contemporary of Rembrandt: *Old Woman at Prayer.* Another of his pupils who was greatly influenced by the master was Aert de Gelder (*Portrait of Ernst van Beveren*). Albert Cuyp was a very versatile landscape painter whose compositions featured shepherds, cattle and small human figures.

Sculpture and Decorative Arts★★★

The museum has a rich collection of furniture and works of art from the 15C to the 20C.

Particularly worthy of note among the collection of sculpture from the Low Countries are the series of **bronze statuettes** (Brabant, 1476) used to decorate the tomb of Isabella de Bourbon, representing the mourning family of the deceased, and **Adriaen van Wesel**'s *Death of the Virgin* from the same period, as well as a rood screen made in about 1500. The **Annuncia-**

Girl in Kimono (1894) by George Breitner

Rijksmuseum, Amsterdam

tion of the Virgin Mary by the German sculptor **Tilman Riemenschneider** is typically late Gothic, while the 16C Brussels wall tapestry *The Triumph of Fame over Death* shows the influence of the Italian Renaissance. Other notable 17C works include the tapestry *Noah's Ark,* produced in Brussels and a terracota bust by **Hendrick de Keyser**. The **treasury** contains fine goblets, bowls, dishes and jewellery. Note the map of the Iberian Peninsula and the **chess set**. Other items of interest are a Renaissance oak cabinet, engraved glassware, a Colonial ebony bed, delftware, a bombé chest and a lacquer cabinet.

Of particular interest are the finely detailed **dolls' houses**, the 18C canopy beds; the 1730 **apothecary's chest** thought to originate from Delft; the **Meissen porcelain**; the fine inlaid bureau and the enamelled snuffboxes

There are examples of engraved glass, 18C furniture, Art Nouveau jewellery, a 1909 Art Nouveau drawing room and porcelain from Weesp and Loosdrecht.

Dutch history★★

Art is used in an interesting and pleasant way to retrace the history of the Netherlands from the Eighty Years' War through to World War II. The **VOC-Galerij** tells the story of the East India Company through the eyes of the men who sailed its ships. The Netherlands were a formidable power at sea and this was mainly due to admirals such as Maarten Tromp and Michiel de Ruyter. Works include a Japanese roller painting depicting cannibals and Dutch naval officers, bear witness to the Dutch presence in the East. The painting by the French artist Pierre-Paul Prud'hon, *Rutger Jan Schimmelpenninck, his Wife and Children* was painted in 1802. Schimmelpenninck was the Ambassador of the Batavian Republic in Paris. The huge painting, *The Battle of Waterloo, 18 June 1815* by JW Pieneman recalls the victory over Napoleon. The chair used by William III at his inauguration in the Nieuwe Kerk in 1849 is also on display.

Vincent van Gogh

Born in Zundert, near Breda, Van Gogh began sketching as a child, but only became conscious of his vocation at the age of 27. He then threw himself into drawing, before taking up oil painting the following year in The Hague.

At first, Van Gogh was inspired by the dark landscapes and thatched cottages of the Drenthe region. Later on, he and his parents moved to a presbytery in the village of Nuenen (*see EINDHOVEN, Excursions*). Here, he produced a series of portraits of peasants, with strikingly intense expressions, which served as studies for *The Potato Eaters* (1885).

Van Gogh Museum/NBTC

Van Gogh, Self-portrait with a straw hat (1887)

After a stay in Antwerp, the artist moved to Paris in February 1886. During 1887 and 1888, under the influence of the Impressionists, he began using brighter colours in his paintings. Examples include *View of Paris from Theo's Room, Cornfield with a Lark, Road beside the Seine at Asnières*, and numerous self-portraits, including *Self-Portrait at the Easel*. Van Gogh also painted landscape paintings influenced by Japanese art.

During the period from 1888 to 1889, he strove to reproduce the bright, contrasting colours he saw in Arles, with paintings of Provençal orchards, *The Zouave, Pont Langlois with Road beside the Canal* and *Sunflowers*.

The first signs of mental illness began to be reflected in his paintings of windswept cornfields and twisted olive trees and cypresses, all in more muted colours. This illness resulted first in a stay in Arles hospital and then in his admission to the mental hospital at St Rémy-de-Provence from 1889 to 1890, where he painted his room in Arles as he remembered it. In 1890, after a quiet period in Auvers-sur-Oise, near Paris, Van Gogh painted the moving *Cornfield with Crows*. On 27 July of the same year, he shot himself in a fit of depression, and two days later the artist's stormy life came to a premature end.

Prints room★★
(Rijksprentenkabinet)

The museum possesses over a million drawings and engravings from the 15C to the present day, including the largest collection of etchings by **Rembrandt**, a rare collection of engravings by **Hercules Seghers** and a large number of oriental woodcuts.

Dutch painting★ (18C–19C)

18C paintings were hung at the time in rows, one above the other, and this is illustrated in the work of Adriaan de Lelie: *The Gallery of Brentano in his house on Herengracht*. Most of these paintings are rather formal portraits of elegant women, and men in wigs. The works by Cornelis Troost deserve special attention. The pastels collection includes works by the Swiss artist Jean Etienne Liotard and portrait miniatures. The rooms dedicated to the 19C cover the Napoleonic era (PG van Os), Dutch Romanticism (Barend C Koekkoek; WJJ Nuyen's *Shipwreck on a Rocky Coast*) and the Hague School (Weissenbruch; J Maris's Feeding the Chickens; Josef Israëls; and A Mauve (*illustration: see Den HAAG*). George Breitner, Isaac

Israëls and Jacobus van Looy (*Summer Luxury*) are important representatives of Amsterdam Impressionism.

Costume and textiles

A changing selection of items from the collection are usually displayed, including 18C and 19C Dutch costumes, oriental carpets, lace and linen damask.

Asiatic art★

This particularly interesting department displays a changing selection of more than 500 objects from the Indian subcontinent, Cambodia, Indonesia, Japan and China. The 12C bronze, *Shiva*, Lord of the Dance, represents India. One of the most striking small sculptures is the 7C or 8C *Buddha Shakyamuni* found in Indonesia. The Chinese sculptures include an elegant, relaxed-looking seated Buddha, and some magnificent porcelain. Highlights of the Japanese collection include ceramics for the tea ceremony, lacquer items and delicately painted screens.

Van Gogh Museum★★★

Open daily, 10am–6pm, Fri 10am–10pm. *Closed 1 Jan.* 12.50€. 020 570 52 00. www.vangogh museum.nl.

This museum (1973) is home to the world's largest Van Gogh collection. It was designed by the architect **Gerrit Rietveld**. It has over 200 **paintings** and around 600 **drawings** by Vincent van Gogh (1853–90), as well as the **letters** he wrote to his brother Theo and **works by contemporaries** such as Toulouse-Lautrec, Gauguin, Chaval and Redon. The painting collection traces the artist's development from the sombre canvases of his early career to the violent tonalities of his last years. In the oval pavilion behind the museum, temporary exhibitions of late 19C art are held, which seek to give a greater insight into the world of art in Van Gogh's time. On **Friday nights**, the museum becomes a popular meeting spot, with a bar, DJ, video projections and comfy chairs.

Stedelijk Museum★★★

The Stedelijk Museum is usually housed in Paulis Potterstraat (closed for renovation). Until Oct 2008 its temporary location is the Post CS-building, near the Centraal station. From Oct 2008–Dec 2009 the temporary locations are the Nieuwe Kerk, Van Gogh Museum and Rijksmuseum. See website for opening details. 9€. 020 573 29 11. www.stedelijk.nl.

Built in 1895 and enlarged in 1954, this modern art museum has a very varied collection covering the period from 1850 to the present day. This includes paintings, sculpture, drawings and prints, applied art and industrial design, posters and photographs. There are also paintings by artists such as Cézanne, Kandinsky, Malevitch, Chagall, Mondrian, Picasso, De Kooning and Lichtenstein. Recent trends in European and American art are also well represented, and the museum also holds major exhibitions and other events.

In and Around the Vondelpark

Vondelpark

This park (48ha/120 acres), named after the famous 17C Dutch poet and dramatist Joost van den Vondel, is located between Singelgracht and Amstelveenseweg. It was laid out between 1864 and 1874.
It is popular with walkers, cyclists and horse-riders, and has a fine collection of over 120 kinds of tree, including chestnuts, oaks, poplars, swamp cypresses and catalpas, as well as vast lawns, a rose garden and sparkling lakes and fountains. In summer, free concerts are given in the open-air theatre (**openluchttheater**), and the **Filmmuseum** (*open Mon–Fri 9am–10.15pm, Sat–Sun one hour prior to first performance until 10.15pm;* 7.80€ *per performance;* 020 589 14 00; www.filmmuseum.nl) is also located in the park.

Concertgebouw

The famous concert hall (1888) is the home of the Royal Concertgebouw Orchestra; the title "Royal" was bestowed by Queen Beatrix to mark the orchestra's centenary.

Hollandse Manege

A.L. van Gendt, the architect of this riding school dating from 1882, was clearly influenced by the Spanish Riding School in Vienna. The Neoclassical building is decorated with stucco and cast iron and is still in use.

The Jordaan★

This area dates from the 17C, and has been thoroughly restored over recent years. Its many warehouses have been converted into apartments, and the area is full of attractive shops and cafés. The Jordaan's picturesque nature has made it popular with students, artists, and the well-off middle classes. It was originally inhabited by French immigrants, and its name is believed to derive from the French word jardin, a term thought appropriate given the many flower and vegetable gardens dotted across the area.

Noorderkerk

Built in 1623 by Hendrick de Keyser, this church is in the shape of a Greek cross. A **farmers' market**, selling organic fruit and vegetables, is held in Noorderplein on Saturday and on Mondays there is a **general market**.

Brouwersgracht★

The Brewers' Canal is lined with attractively restored warehouses. Nºs 172 to 212 are particularly interesting. Nº 118, the De Kroon warehouse, has a carved stone on its façade depicting a crown, which is what its name means. There is a row of houses with crow-stepped gables dating from 1641 near the bridge where Brouwersgracht and **Prinsengracht** meet. The popular Papeneiland, a small brown café, is located here.

Karthuizerhofje

Entrance via Karthuizerstraat nº 173 or after no 85.
These delightful almshouses, the biggest in Amsterdam, were built in 1650 by the municipal architect, Daniël Stalpart.

Claes Claeszoon Hofje

A 17C almshouse (*entrance at Eerste Egelantiersdwarsstraat nº 3*) with a picturesque inner courtyard.

Egelantiersgracht★

This canal, with its beautiful 17C and 18C houses, has retained the typical charm of yesteryear.

Bloemgracht★

This canal, sometimes ironically called the Herengracht of the Jordaan, used to be occupied by dyers and paint makers. There are three magnificent houses with stepped gables, nºs 87 to 91, and many others have **façade stones**, including nos 19 (a pelican), 23 (a unicorn), 34 (a trout) and 77 (a sower).

The Plantage★

This eastern residential area was developed in the 19C, and takes its name from the area's many parks.

Hortus Botanicus

Open Mon–Fri 9am–5pm, Sat–Sun and public holidays 10am–5pm (Dec–Jan 4pm, Jul–Aug 7pm). Closed 1 Jan and 25 Dec. 7€. 020 625 90 21. www.hortus-botanicus.nl.
The botanical garden was created in 1682 for the cultivation of medicinal plants. In addition to the outdoor part of the garden, there is also a greenhouse representing three different climatic zones, and a palm house.

Nationaal Vakbondmuseum

Open Tue–Fri 11am–5pm, Sun 1pm–5pm. Closed public holidays. 2.50€. 020 624 11 66. www.deburcht-vakbondsmuseum.nl (in Dutch).
The national trade union museum is located in the headquarters of the Dutch diamond workers' union, founded in 1894 by Henri Polak. The imposing building was designed in 1900 by **Hendrik Petrus Berlage**, and soon gained the nickname of Burcht van Berlage (Berlage's Castle). The magnificent **staircase**★, council chamber and boardroom are particularly worth

Storkes in Artis

Eduard Bergman/NBTC

seeing, and the museum itself is devoted to the history of the trade union movement.

Artis★★ [Kids]

🕙*Open summer, daily 9am–6pm; winter, daily 9am–5pm.* 👁*17.70€; children 14.50€.* ♿☎*020 523 34 00. www.artis.nl.*
Founded in 1838, this is one of Europe's oldest zoos. It has some 6 000 animals including small mammals, big cats, insects, sea-lions, gorillas and polar bears. A few sections are of particular interest: the new **African Savannah**, the reptile pavilion, the ape enclosure, the noisy aviary and the 'Jungle by Night'. The newly restored **aquarium**★ brings to light the colourful world of the coral reefs as well as showing what lives in Amsterdam's canals. In the **Zoological Museum** in the same building, temporary exhibitions are held. The lecture theatre contains the **Heimans Diorama,** where the dune ecosystem is explained in a 15-minute presentation. Artis also has a **Geological Museum,** with exhibitions on the Earth's history and collections of minerals, precious stones and crystals, a **planetarium** with shows specially adapted to children, hothouses, and an animal sanctuary.

Verzetsmuseum★

🕙*Open Tue–Fri 10am–5pm, Sat–Sun and public holidays noon–5pm.* 🕙*Closed 1 Jan, 30 Apr, 25 Dec.* 👁*6.50€.* ♿☎*020 620 25 35. www.verzetsmuseum.org.*

This interactive museum uses film and sound recordings, photographs and a wide range of authentic objects to lead visitors on a journey through the occupied Netherlands of World War II. The terror and horror as well as the daily lives of the people during that wartime period are vividly brought to light. As visitors walk through the reconstructed streets and houses they are given answers to questions such as what happened on the ground during an air raid; how did the propaganda machine of Nazi Germany operate; how did the resistance movement manage to get secret messages through; and how were false documents made? The letters of farewell thrown from the deportation trains and the yellow Stars of David recall the deportation of more than 100 000 Jews. And the resourcefulness and creativity of people during times of war are illustrated through items such as radios, chess sets and small Christmas trees, all made by prisoners of war during their confinement.

Hollandsche Schouwburg

🕙*Open daily 11am–4pm.* 🕙*Closed Yom Kippur.* 👁*No charge.* ♿☎*020 531 03 40. www.jhm.nl. www.hollandscheschouwburg.nl.*
This former theatre was used during the war as a transit camp for Jews, and has a memorial to those who died.

Muiderpoort

This gate (1771) is the one through which Napoleon entered the city.

Tropenmuseum★

🕙*Open daily 10am–5pm, 5, 24 and 31 December 10am–3pm.* 🕙*Closed 1 Jan, 30 Apr, 5 May and 25 Dec.* 👁*7.50€.* ♿☎*020 568 82 00. www.kit.nl/tropenmuseum.*
The Museum of the Tropics is part of the Royal Tropical Institute, and is an excellent source of information about the cultures of Africa, Asia, the Middle East, Oceania and Latin America. The displays include works of art, a wide variety of everyday objects, reconstructions of homes and shops, and photographs, slide shows and music, all working together to give visitors an insight into life in

tropical and subtropical countries. The Kindermuseum (**children's museum**) holds two-year exhibitions for young people aged six to twelve.

The Port Area

Oosterdok

Nederlands Scheepvaartmuseum★★

⚓*Closed for renovation until 2009.* ☎*020 523 22 22. www.scheepvaartmuseum.nl.* The museum's **Amsterdam**★★, a replica of an 18C merchant ship belonging to the Dutch East India Company, remains open but has been towed to Nemo.

Nemo★   Kids
🕐*Open Tue–Sun (Jul–Aug daily) and school holidays, 10am–5pm.* 🕐*Closed 25 Dec, 1 Jan and 30 Apr.* ⌨*11.50€; children 11.50€.* ♿☎*0900 919 11 00. www. e-nemo.nl.*
Bright green and shaped like the bow of a ship, this science and technology centre was designed by the Italian architect **Renzo Piano**. It provides hands-on displays on subjects as varied as medicine and money, and is particularly suitable for children. There is a beautiful **view**★★ of the city from the roof.

Prins Hendrikkade
On the corner of this quay and the Binnenkant is the impressive **Scheepvaarthuis**★, or Shipping House. This was built in 1916 by the principal architects of the Amsterdam School, Van der Mey, Michel de Klerk and PL Kramer. From the bridge to the east, there is a fine **view** of the Montelbaanstoren (1512).

Entrepotdok
On this canal stand 84 warehouses dating from between 1708 and 1829 and rebuilt in the 1980s for use as offices, low-cost housing, and cafés. The development is a fine example of sensitive urban renewal.

Westerdok

Realeneiland
This is one of the "islands" in the western part of the port, lined with warehouses. On **Zandhoek**, overlooking the Westerdok, is a row of restored 17C houses with attractive facing-stones.

Spaarndammerbuurt
Corner of Zaanstraat and Oostzaanstraat.
This beautiful, low-cost housing area was designed in the 1920s by **Michel de Klerk**. It is one of the finest creations of the Amsterdam School of architecture. The **Het Schip**★ apartment block in Hembrugstraat has an expressionist-style tower.

©Jurjen Drenth/NBTC

Scheepvaartmuseum

Heineken Brewery, built in 1864

The Pijp

This area is actually an island linked to the rest of the city by 16 bridges. It was a working-class area in the 19C, and its long, narrow streets (in fact filled-in canals) have given it its nickname of the "pipe", while its cosmopolitan population has also led it to be called the Latin Quarter of Amsterdam. The Pijp is a lively area full of cafés, restaurants and shops.

Heineken Experience
Open Tue–Sun, 10am–6pm. Last ticket sales 5pm. Closed 25 Dec and 1 Jan. 10€. 020 523 96 66. www.heineken experience.com
The brewery was built in 1864, and has been open to the public since 1988. There is a tour describing the history of the company and the methods used to brew beer; a free sample is available at the end.

Albert Cuypmarkt★
This colourful market in the 3km/1.8mi long Albert Cuypstraat has been in existence since 1904, and sells just about anything, from fruit to clothing, from all over the world.

De Dageraad★
Area around Pieter Lodewijk Takstraat.
This complex of 350 workers' apartments was built between 1919 and 1922 by **Michel de Klerk** and Piet L Kramer for the De Dageraad housing association. Its unusual forms, undulating orange-tiled roofs and rounded beige brick façades make it one of the finest products of the **Amsterdam School**.

Excursions

Ouderkerk aan de Amstel
This picturesque village is a popular Sunday outing for people from Amsterdam. To the north is a **stage mill**.

Amstelveen
A modern commuter district which has been the home of the **Cobra Museum voor Moderne Kunst**★ (*Sandbergplein 1; open Tue–Sun 11am–5pm; closed 1 Jan, 30 Apr and 25 Dec; 9.50€; children 5€; 020 547 50 50; www.cobra-museum.nl*) since 1995. This surprisingly light building designed by **Wim Quist** houses a fine collection of modern art, including works by the **CoBrA movement**. This international movement (its name derives from **C**openhagen, **B**russels, **A**msterdam) was established in Paris in 1948 by a Dane, **Asger Jorn**; two Belgians, **Christian Dotremont** and **Joseph Noiret**; and the Dutch artists **Appel, Constant** and **Corneille**. They sought to break away from the dullness of neo-traditional post-war art by taking their inspiration from folk and primitive art and, most importantly, from drawings by children and mentally

ill people. This resulted in spontaneous, experimental, colourful and often cheerful works. The museum does not have a permanent exhibition; the pieces are shown in rotation. Related movements, such as the Dutch groups **Vrij Beelden** and **Creatie**, are also represented. Together, they give an excellent overview of abstract and semi-abstract art in the Netherlands between 1945 and 1955. The museum also holds exhibitions of contemporary art.

Amsterdamse Bos

This is Amsterdam's main woodland area: an immense park with lakes offering boating, and fishing with a permit.

Schiphol

Amsterdam's international airport, a leading European transit point, lies 4.5m/14ft below sea level in what used to be a bay of the Haarlemmermeer. Not far from the runways is the **Aviodome** (*open Tue–Sun 10am–5pm; closed 25 Dec and 1 Jan; 14.90€; 0900 284 63 76; www.aviodome. nl*), a distinctive building with an aluminium domed roof, housing a collection of items from the National Aviation Museum. The history of air travel is traced using models, and special attention is given to Dutch aircraft constructor **AHG Fokker** and his work. There is a cinema in the basement.

Sloten

This village (11C), still has a boundary post dating from 1794 laying down the outer limit beyond which the city of Amsterdam must not expand. The **Molen van Sloten** (*open daily 10am–4pm; closed 1 Jan, 30 Apr, 25, 26 Dec; 020 669 04 12; www.molen vansloten.nl*) is a polder mill from 1847 erected here in 1989; a tour explains how it works. There is also a Coopery Museum here.

Round Tour North of Amsterdam

▶ *65km/40mi – About 4hr. Leave Amsterdam by Mauritskade. After the second bridge (Schellingwouder Brug), turn off towards Schelling-*

woude, then pass under the road towards Durgerdam.

Just before **Durgerdam** there is an excellent **view**★ of the village. There is an attractive square church with a pyramid-shaped roof and a clock tower.

Marken★ – *See MARKEN.*

Monnickendam

This small port was formerly renowned for its eels. The town is overlooked by the 16C brick tower, the **Speeltoren** (*open Tue–Sat 11am–4.30pm, Sun 1pm–4.30pm; 1.50€; 0299 65 22 03; www.despeeltoren.nl*). Opposite, the town hall or **stadhuis** is an 18C patrician house with a decorated pediment; note the snake-shaped balustrades.
Nearby, in Middendam, stands the **Waag** (weigh house): a small building dating from about 1600 with pilasters and an elaborately carved gable. To the south, the Gothic **Grote Kerk**, or **St Nicolaaskerk**, is a triangular hall church with a fine 16C carved wooden choir screen.

Volendam★ – *See VOLENDAM.*

Edam – *See EDAM.*

Broek in Waterland

This village has brightly painted 17C and 18C houses, some of which are U-shaped, and some have two doors; the front door used only for weddings and funerals. On the edge of the lake, the Havenrak, is the small white pagoda-shaped pavilion where Napoleon was received when he visited the village in 1811, the **Napoleonhuisje**.
The **church** by the canal was burned down by the Spaniards in 1573, and rebuilt between 1585 and 1639. In the north aisle, an interesting stained-glass window (c. 1640) recalling these events.

▶ *Return to Amsterdam via the S 116.*

APELDOORN

GELDERLAND
POPULATION 155 328
TOWN PLAN IN THE CURRENT RED-COVER MICHELIN GUIDE BENELUX

The town of Apeldoorn, with its broad, shady lanes and many parks, lies in the heart of the Veluwe. A market is held in the square outside the new town hall on Mondays, Wednesdays and Saturdays.

A tourist steam train, the **Veluwsche Stoomtrein** (*Departs Jun, Thu; mid-Jul– late Aug and during autumn half-term, Mon–Fri. ☞16€ (single). ☎055 506 19 89. www.stoomtrein.org*), **runs southwest from Apeldoorn to Dieren** (*23km/14mi*).

- 🛈 **Information:** Stationsstraat 72 – 7311 MH. ☎0900 168 16 36.
- ▶ **Orient Yourself:** Apeldoorn is about 97km/60mi east of Amsterdam.
- 🅿 **Parking:** Finding space is only a problem on market days.
- 🕓 **Organizing Your Time:** An hour will suffice to see the town itself, but allow longer to see the Nationaal Museum Paleis Het LOO and Deventer, too.
- 🄺🄸🄳🅂 **Especially for Kids:** The apes or Dajak Farm at Apenheul.

Sights

CODA Museum, Vosselmanstraat 299, Apeldoorn

🕓*Open Tue–Fri 10am–5.30pm (until 8.30pm Thu), Sun and public holidays 1pm–5pm.* 🕓*Closed Easter Sunday, Whitsun, 25 Dec and 1 Jan.* ☞5€. ☎055 526 84 00. www.coda-apeldoorn.nl (*in Dutch*).

The local museum is located in the old town hall; it documents the history of the town and the surrounding area.

Apenheul★★/Berg en Bos 🄺🄸🄳🅂

4km/2.5mi to the west. Leave Apeldoorn via Kennedylaan and JC Wilslaan. 🕓*Open mid-Mar–Oct, daily 9.30am–5pm; Jul, Aug and weekends in May, Jun & Sept until 6pm. Berg en Bos nature reserve closes 1hr after Apenheul.* ☞16.50€; children 12€. ☎055 357 57 57. www.apenheul.nl (*in Dutch*).

Apenheul means "apes' refuge", and most of the apes here, representing 30 different species, are able to roam freely in the woodlands. They include rare woolly monkeys, over 120 squirrel monkeys, Barbary apes and half-apes from Madagascar, which spend their time swinging through the trees or crowding round visitors. The larger animals, such as the **gorillas**, the orangutans and the bonobos live on separate islands. Feeding time is a particularly good time to see them. There is also a separate tropical animals section for children, *Dajak Farm*. The **Berg en Bos** (hill and forest) nature reserve is ideal for walks.

Excursion

Kasteel Cannenburch

In Vaassen; 9km/5.6mi north of Apeldoorn via the road to Zwolle towards Epe.
🕓*Visit by guided tour only (1hr): mid-Apr–Oct, Tue–Fri 10am–5pm, Sat–Sun 1pm–5pm; also Easter Monday, Whit Monday & 26 Dec, 10am–5pm.* 🕓*Closed Nov–mid-Apr and 30 Apr.* ☞4€. ☎057 857 12 92. www.mooigelderland.nl.

This moated castle was built in 1543 in Renaissance style by **Maarten van Rossum**, the bloodthirsty commander of Karel van Gerle's army. After his death the castle was occupied by the Van Isendoorn family, who extended and refurbished it during the 17C and 18C. The interior, now fully restored to its 18C appearance, is an excellent example of a stately home that has been inhabited by the same family for centuries.

ARNHEM

GELDERLAND P
POPULATION 142 636
PLAN OF THE CONURBATION IN THE CURRENT MICHELIN RED GUIDE BENELUX

Arnhem is the capital of the province of Gelderland, which used to be called **Gelre** when it was a duchy. Situated on the Neder Rijn or Lower Rhine, by the confluence with the IJssel, Arnhem is an important road junction and a major industrial and retailing centre. It is, however, first and foremost an administrative centre. Also referred to as the **Tuinstad** or **Garden City** because of its many green spaces and its favourable position at the southern foothills of the Veluwe, Arnhem is a pleasant place to explore on foot, in particular the pedestrianised area in the city centre and the parks. Arnhem is also known for its **Arnhemse meisjes**, biscuits made of sweet puff pastry.

- **Information:** Velperbuitensingel 25 (Musis Sacrum), 6828 CV. ☎0900 11 22 344. www.vvv.arnhem.nl.
- **Orient Yourself:** Arnham's Centraal Station lies to the north west of the town, and is a good place from which to get your bearings. Head to the Grote Kerk area, the heart of Arnham, via Willensplein, a long street of shops and eateries.
- **Parking:** Arnham provides ample parking for motoring visitors in parks or beside the river, mostly free of charge.
- **Don't Miss:** Duivelshuis, one of Arnham's oldest houses and one of the very few to survive the wartime bombings.
- **Organizing Your Time:** Allow a day or two to tour the town's array of interesting museums and cemeteries. Take an hour or so to enjoy National Park Veluwezoom, a large area of forest and parkland that contains a castle, museums and a number of villages.

A Bit of History

A coveted duchy – Arnhem was a prosperous town trading in goods along the Rhine and the IJssel, and belonged to the Hanseatic League. Gelre became a duchy in 1339. Arnhem was taken by Charles the Bold in 1473, and then by Emperor Maximilian (Charles the Bold's son-in-law) in 1505. Invaded by Emperor Charles V, the duchy was defended by **Charles of Egmont**, who was killed in battle in 1538. His successor ceded his rights to the duchy to Charles V in the Treaty of Venlo (1543). In 1585, under the reign of Philip II (Charles V's son), the town was taken from the Spanish. It passed to the French during the 1672–74 war, and then to the Austrians between 1795 and 1813.

Prior to World War II, Arnhem was one of the favourite retirement places for colonials returning from Indonesia; their substantial residences are dispersed throughout the woods.

The Battle of Arnhem (17–27 September 1944) – The name Arnhem is associated with one of the most tragic episodes in the liberation of the Netherlands. The aim of **Operation Market Garden** was to gain access to the Ruhr via a corridor north from the Belgian border across the three great rivers. On 17 September 1944 more than 10 000 English soldiers were parachuted into **Oosterbeek**, west of Arnhem. They were to march on Arnhem to take the bridge over the Neder Rijn, and hold it until the 20 000 Americans and the 3 000 Poles parachuted to the south were able to cross the Maas at Grave and the Waal at Nijmegen. General Montgomery, who directed Operation Market Garden, counted on surprise to disorganise the enemy. Unfortunately, the plan was not successful. On 18 September, thick fog enveloped Arnhem, making help impossible. Only a few battalions of parachutists from Oosterbeek had reached the town. After nine

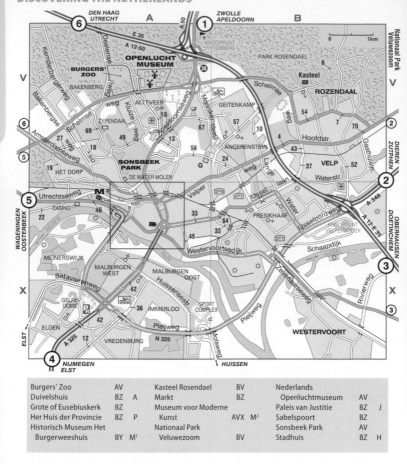

Burgers' Zoo	AV		Kasteel Rosendael	BV		Nederlands	
Duivelshuis	BZ	A	Markt	BZ		Openluchtmuseum	AV
Grote of Eusebiuskerk	BZ		Museum voor Moderne			Paleis van Justitie	BZ	J
Her Huis der Provincie	BZ	P	Kunst	AVX	M²	Sabelspoort	BZ
Historisch Museum Het			Nationaal Park			Sonsbeek Park	AV
Burgerweeshuis	BY	M¹	Veluwezoom	BV		Stadhuis	BZ	H

days of desperately hard fighting, the **Red Devils**, who had not managed to capture the bridge, left 2 000 dead and more than 5 000 wounded or missing in the ruins of the town. On the other hand, 500 soldiers were given shelter by the townspeople and 2 300 were evacuated towards the south during the night of 25–26 September. In the meantime, the progress of armoured divisions effecting a junction had been held up by several German attacks. The crossing of the Maas at **Grave** (19 September) and the Waal at **Nijmegen** (20 September) made it possible for the Allies to come within sight of Arnhem, but it was too late. The bridge over the Neder Rijn was, according to Browning, "a bridge too far". For more details read *A Bridge Too Far* by Cornelius Ryan. Arnhem was liberated by the Allies on 8 April 1945, shortly before the German capitulation.

Boat tours
Depart mid-Apr–late Oct. Information from tourist office. ☎0900 11 22 344. On the Gelderland rivers.

Sights in the City Centre

Markt
This long square is bordered by the Law Courts, the **Paleis van Justitie** and, at the end, by the Gelderland seat of government, the **Huis der Provincie**. This was destroyed during the war and a simple new building with an inner courtyard was constructed by JJM Vegter in 1954. Adjoining it is the **Sabelspoort**, a 14C fortified gateway (altered in 1645), which is all that remains of the town's ramparts.

ARNHEM

Airbonepl.	BZ		Ir. J. P. van Muylwijkstr.	BY	25	Ringallee	BV	54
Amsterdamseweg	AV	AY	Jacob Marislaan	AV	27	Rivierweg	BX
Apeldoornsestr.	BY	3	Jansbinnensingel	BY	28	Roermondspl.	AY
Apeldoornseweg	AV		Jansbuitensingel	BY		Roggestr.	BY	55
Arnhemsestraatweg	BV	4	Janspl.	ABY	30	Rosendaalseweg	BV	57
Bakenbergseweg	AV		Jansstr.	ABY	31	Schaapdijk	BX
Bakkerstr.	BYZ		Johan de Wittlaan	AX	33	Schelmseweg	ABV
Batavierenweg	AX		John Frostbrug	BZ		Sonsbeeksingel	BY
Beekhuizenseweg	BV	6	Kemperbergerweg	AV		Sonsbeekweg	BY
Beekstr.	BYZ		Ketelstr.	BY	34	Steenstr.	BY
Bergstr.	AY		Kleine Oord	ABZ		Sweerts de Landastr.	AY
Beukenweg	BV	7	Kluizeweg	AV		Thomas a Kempislaan	AV	58
Bloemstr.	BY		Koningspl.	BY		Trans	ABZ
Boulevard Heuvelink	BZ	8	Koningstr.	BYZ		Turfstr.	BZ
Bouriciusstr.	AY	9	Koppelstr.	AX	36	Utrechtsestr.	AY
Broerenstr.	BZ		Lange Water	BVX		Utrechtseweg	AX
Bronbeeklaan	BV	10	Lerensteinselaan	BV	37	van Heemstralaan	AV	18
Burg. Matsersingel	AX	12	Looierstr.	BY	39	van Oldenbarneveldtstr.	AX	45
Cattepoelsweg	AV	13	Molsweg	BX		Velperbinnensingel	BY	60
Deelenseweg	AV		Monnikensteeg	ABV		Velperbuitensingel	BY	61
Eusebiusbinnensingel	BZ	16	Nelson Mandelabrug	AZ		Velperpl.	BY
Eusebiusbuitensingel	BYZ		Nieuwe Plein	AY		Velperweg	AXBV
Gasthuisln	BV		Nijmeegseweg	AX	42	Vijzelstr.	ABY	63
Heijenoordseweg	AV	19	Nordlaan	BV	43	Voetiuslaan	ABX	64
Hommelstr.	BY		Onderlangs	AX	46	Walburgstr.	BZ	66
Hoofdstr.	BV		Oranjewachtstr.	BZ	48	Waterstr.	BV
Huissensestr.	AX		Oude Kraan	AY		Weerdjesstr.	AZ
Hulkesteinseweg	AX	22	P. Krugerstr.	ABY		Weg achter het Bos	AV	67
Huygenslaan	BV	24	Parkweg	AV	49	Westervoortsedijk	ABX BZ
IJssellaan	BX		Pleijweg	ABX		Willemspl.	AY
IJsseloordweg	BX		President Kennedylaan	BV	52	Zevenaarseweg	BX
			Rijnkade	AZ		Zijpendaalseweg	AY AV	69
			Rijnstr.	AY		Zutphensestraatweg	BV	70

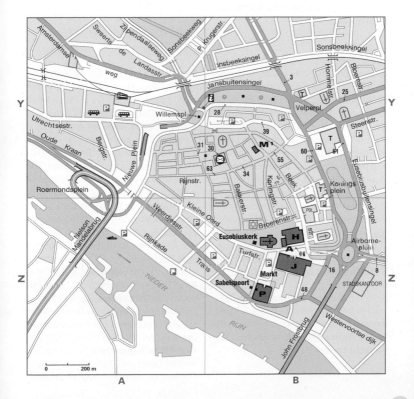

Grote Kerk or Eusebiuskerk

🕐 *Open Tue–Sat 10am–5pm (11am–4pm winter), Sun and public holidays noon–5pm (4pm winter).* ☎026 443 50 68. www.eusebius.nl (*in Dutch*).

This 15C church by the square (Markt) was destroyed during the Battle of Arnhem. Both the church and its tower (93m/305ft) were rebuilt in the neo-Gothic style; the upper part is in a more modern style.

The tower has a new 53-bell carillon, the largest in western Europe, and a small carillon of seven bells. A panoramic glass lift takes visitors up between the bells to a height of 73m/240ft, where there is a magnificent **view**★ of the town and the surrounding area.

The richly decorated **mausoleum** of Charles of Egmont, the last Duke of Geldern, dates from 1538. Look out for the "man in the box" against the pillar beside the tomb. Also of interest is the tomb of Jodocus Sasbout (1546) to the right of the large Salvator Clock. The inscription "Homo Bulla" (man is a soap bubble), the young woman and the decaying body all symbolise the transience of life.

Duivelshuis

The Renaissance Devils' House was built in 1545 and later greatly restored in 1829; it suffered no damage during either World War. It takes its name from the strange statue and grotesque heads which decorate its walls.

The building was the last dwelling place of the bloodthirsty general **Maarten van Rossum**, chief of the armies of the Duke of Gelderland, Charles of Egmont, and adversary of Emperor Charles V. According to legend, Van Rossum had these demons carved to offend the magistrates of Arnhem, who refused to allow him to pave his front steps with gold. Formerly the town hall, the house is still occupied by various municipal departments.

Behind is the new **stadhuis** (town hall) built in 1964 and designed by J. J. Konijnenburg. In the distance is the restored 14C **St Walburgiskerk**, which has two different towers.

Historisch Museum Het Burgerweeshuis★

🕐 *Open Tue–Fri 10am–5pm, Sat–Sun and public holidays 11am–5pm.* 🕐*Closed 30 Apr, 25 Dec and 1 Jan.* 🔖3.75€. ☎026 337 53 00. www.hmarnhem.nl.

This beautifully restored 18C mansion was used as a public orphanage (*burgerweeshuis*) from 1844 to 1920. Today, it houses a rich collection of decorative arts: 15C Arnhem **guild silverware**★, oriental porcelain, glass, rare local pottery and 17C paintings. The **Rococo-style regentenkamer** (boardroom) has oil-painted wall-hangings showing three episodes from the life of Alexander the Great. The picture of Pallas Athene and Mercury (the god of trade) on the stucco ceiling reminds us that the mansion was built for a successful soap dealer. The first floor, where temporary exhibitions are also held, houses a collection relating to local topography and a collection of 19C paintings, silverware and tobacco boxes. The top floor chronicles the story of Arnhem using archaeological finds, paintings, photographs and videos.

Sights Outside the City Centre

Museum voor Moderne Kunst★

🕐 *Open Tue–Fri 10am–5pm, Sat–Sun and public holidays 11am–5pm.* 🕐*Closed 30 Apr, 25 Dec and 1 Jan.* 🔖7€. ☎026 351 24 31. www.mmkarnhem.nl.

A former 19C men's club, standing on a hill overlooking the Rhine, houses Arnhem's museum of modern art. The museum has interesting collections of modern and contemporary art, with the emphasis on Dutch artists, and has a policy of ensuring that at least half its acquisitions are by female artists. The museum holds around 20 exhibitions a year. The permanent collection includes work by **magic realists** (Carel Willink, Raoul Hynckes, Pyke Koch) and **contemporary artists** such as Dick Ket, Wim Schuhmacher and Charley Toorop. There are also a number of fine paintings by the artist Jan Mankes (1889–1920) and by the **New Figuratives** (Roger Raveel, Reinier Lucassen, Alphons Freymuth). The new garden room houses the post-war applied art and design section. This includes ceramics, glass and other design, as well as the country's largest collection of Dutch post-1960 **jewellery**. The garden, which also has a beautiful view of the Rhine, has a collection of old and contemporary sculpture.

Sonsbeek Park★

This park of 75ha/185 acres, together with the adjoining Zypendaal and Gulden Bloem Parks, is one of the most beautiful landscaped parks in the Netherlands. It was declared a national monument in 1963. It is an undulating area with woodlands, large meadows, a string of streams, lakes, a castle and a 16C watermill, De Witte Molen. The barn beside this houses a visitors' centre. Elegant early 20C houses are located around the park.

Nederlands Openluchtmuseum★★

⊙*Open late Mar–Oct, daily 10am–5pm; early Dec–mid-Jan, noon–8pm, mid-Jan–late Mar, park only.* ◈*13.60€.* ♿☎ *026 357 61 00. www.openlucht museum.nl.*

This open-air folklore museum is set in 44ha/109 acres of splendid wooded parkland. Around 80 authentic farmhouses, cottages, barns, windmills, workshops, a schoolhouse, a church and a steam-operated dairy factory

(*see Introduction, Industrial heritage*) have been assembled here to illustrate rural architecture and life in the past. The buildings, from all over the Netherlands, are decorated and furnished authentically. Demonstrations of a variety of handicrafts add interest to the visit. The buildings from some of the provinces are grouped together, as in the case of the handsome half-timbered farmsteads from Limburg (nos 100–104) or the farmhouses from Gelderland (nos 1–19). However, the most picturesque corner is probably the one representing **Zaanstreek** with its very characteristic houses. The green-painted buildings with variously shaped gables are attractively decorated with white trims. The calm waters of the nearby pond are reminiscent of the Zaan and are spanned by a wooden lever-bridge and bordered by two windmills.

Visitors first arrive at the **entreepaviljoen**, a recently renovated pavilion affording a splendid view of the park and several windmills – the taller ones are grain mills while the smaller ones are typical examples of polder mills. Like the **Collectie Centrum**, it contains a number of exhibition rooms where temporary exhibitions of pottery, ornamental folk art, traditional costumes, farming tools and other items are held on a rotational basis. On the lower floor is the entrance to the spectacular **Holland-**

Nederlands Openluchtmuseum illustrates life in the past

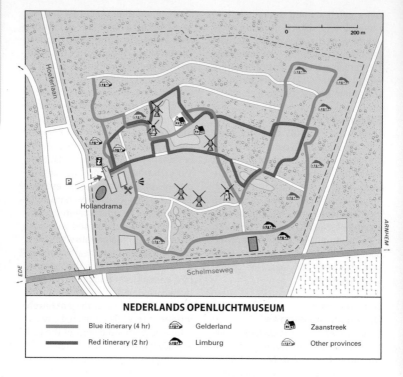

NEDERLANDS OPENLUCHTMUSEUM

	Blue itinerary (4 hr)		Gelderland		Zaanstreek
	Red itinerary (2 hr)		Limburg		Other provinces

Rama, a simulator-type capsule in which visitors are taken on a virtual sightseeing tour. Film, sound, light, smell and even temperature-changes bring to life a variety of landscapes, towns and cities, and interiors.

Burgers' Zoo★★ Kids

◷ Open Apr–Oct, daily 9am–7pm; Nov–Mar, daily 9am–5pm. ⊜16.50€; children 14.50€. ☎026 442 45 34. www.burgers zoo.nl.

In this exceptional zoo ("burgers'" means "people's"), artificial ecosystems have been created so that visitors can see animals in their natural habitat.

Burgers' Desert (7 500sq m/9 036sq yd) recreates the North American desert, complete with rocks, sand dunes and cactuses. This is home to turkey vultures, lynxes, collared peccaries, and colourful hummingbirds. A cave area containing nocturnal animals and an "abandoned mineshaft" lead from the desert to the tropics.

Burgers' Bush, an enormous greenhouse, re-creates the ecosystem of a tropical forest, with trees and plants from Asia, Africa and South America. These include rice, sugar cane, pineapple, vanilla, banana and coffee plants as well as mahogany and rubber trees. Amid this colourful vegetation, complete with a waterfall and suspension bridges, live the more timid animals such as butterflies, exotic birds, manatees and caimans.

The next stage in this journey of discovery is the tropical beach and lagoon of **Burgers' Ocean**. A coral cave provides a first-hand view of an extraordinary undersea world: corals, sponges, sea anemones, starfish and a wealth of other creatures. Hundreds of colourful fish accompany the visitor on to an impressive 20m x 6m (66ft x 20ft) panorama showing life in the dark depths of the ocean, where sharks, rays, and jellyfish lurk.

Finally, **Burgers' Safari** is a place where giraffes, zebras, ostriches, rhinoceroses and antelopes roam freely. The wild animal enclosure is home to lions and cheetahs. There is also a group of chimpanzees (which is being closely studied), large numbers of birds of prey, a nocturnal animal house and **Burgers' Mangrove**. All of this is great fun for children.

Nationaal Park Veluwezoom★

▶ *Round tour of 20km/12.4mi. Leave Arnhem by Beekhuizenseweg.*

The Veluwezoom National Park is a vast area (4 600ha/11 362 acres) of pine and silver birch forest and undulating heathland situated to the north of Arnhem on the edge (zoom) of the Veluwe. The park has many footpaths and cycle routes, and there are several car parks.

Rozendaal
A small 18C castle, **Kasteel Rosendael** (guided tours only, Tue–Sat 11.30am, 1pm, 2.30pm and 4pm, Sun also 1.45pm and 3.15pm; closed 30 Apr; 5.50€;

026 364 46 45.) flanked by a 14C tower, stands on the edge of a lake in the heart of its own **park**. Several furnished rooms are open to the public. The gallery of shells is also worth a visit.

The road climbs and descends as it crosses the forest, goes through the hamlet of **Beekhuizen** and then climbs to an altitude of approximately 100m/328ft to the **Posbank** where several viewing points offer good **panoramas**★ of the rolling heathland stretching away to the horizon. There are many footpaths and the area makes good walking country.

▶ *The road then descends to Rheden.*

The **Visitor Centre** (open Tue–Sun 10am–5pm; closed 25 and 31 Dec; 026 497 91 00) occupies an old farmhouse on Heuvenseweg. Ramblers will be able to find detailed maps here. The exhibition introduces visitors to the beauty of this area through the eyes of a badger, a black woodpecker and a red deer.

▶ *On the N348, turn left towards Dieren.*

C. Bastin, J. Evrard/ MICHELIN

Kasteel Rosendael

De Steeg

To the east of the village, the 17C **Kasteel Middachten**★ (◔ *castle open Jan–Jul, Mon–Sat 1pm–4pm; mid-Dec–Christmas, 11am–7pm;* ✆8€; *garden open mid-May–mid-Sept, Sun–Tue 10.30am–4.30pm;* ✆5€; ✆026 495 49 98; www.middachten.nl (in Dutch only)*) is surrounded by a double moat. There is a fine view of the castle from the large garden. Inside, the original furnishings have been preserved, including portraits, miniatures, and a library.

▶ *Returning to Arnhem by the N348, there is another moated castle, Kasteel Biljoen, on the left just before Velp.*

The Southern Veluwezoom

▶ *25km/15.5mi to the west – 2hr 30min. Leave by ⑤ on the town plan.*

Oosterbeek

To the north of this small town, on the road to Warnsborn just after the railway, is the **Airborne Kerkhof** war cemetery. This is the last resting place of the Allied troops who fell during the Battle of Arnhem; there are more than 1 700 gravestones (1 667 British and 79 Polish).

The Huize Hartenstein (*Utrechtseweg 232*) was the headquarters of General Urquhart, the commander of the 1st British Airborne Division, in September 1944. It houses the **Airborne Museum** (◔ *open Apr–Oct, Mon–Sat 10am–5pm, Sun noon–5pm; Nov–Mar, Mon–Fri 11am–5pm, Sat–Sun, noon–5pm;* ◔ *closed 25 Dec and 1 Jan;* ✆5.50€; ✆026 333 77 10; www.airbornemuseum.com), which covers Operation Market Garden and the Battle of Arnhem. General Urquhart's headquarters have been reconstructed in the cellar.

To the south, on the banks of the Rhine, the terraces of the **Westerbouwing** (restaurant) offer a fine view over the river and the Betuwe with its orchards.

▶ *Drive towards the north bank of the Rhine.*

Doorwerth

This village was badly damaged in 1944 during the Battle of Arnhem.

Kasteel Doorwerth, in its riverside setting, dates originally from 1260 but was enlarged c. 1600. This massive square castle and its outbuildings are still encircled by moats. In the north and east wings, several furnished rooms and exhibition rooms are open to visitors. The south wing houses the **Museum voor Natuur- en Wildbeheer** (◔ *open Apr–Oct, Tue–Fri 10am–5pm, Sat 1pm–5pm, Sun 11am–5pm; Nov–Mar, Wed–Sat 1pm–5pm, Sun 11am–5pm;* ◔ *closed 30 Apr, 25, 31 Dec and 1 Jan;* ✆5€; ✆026 333 25 32), or museum of nature and game conservation, with exhibitions on the various aspects of hunting and game. The fine collections of weapons, stuffed animals, pictures and photographs are attractively displayed.

▶ *Continue towards Renkum and pass under the motorway to take the road to Wageningen.*

Wageningen

On the **Grebbeberg**, 5km/3mi west of Wageningen, there is a **Dutch military cemetery** commemorating the battle that took place here in 1940. A path opposite leads to the **Koningstafel** or "king's table", which has a view over the Rhine and the Betuwe. It was one of King Frederick V of Bohemia's favourite walks; he took refuge in the Netherlands after having been defeated by the Austrians in 1620.

Rhenen   Kids

Rhenen is known for its large zoo, the **Ouwehands Dierenpark** (◔ *open Apr–Sept, daily 9am–6pm; Oct–Mar, daily 9am–5pm.* ✆18€; *children 15€;* ♿✆0317 65 02 00. www.ouwehand.nl), with over 1 600 animals. A large aviary of exotic birds, a primate house, a dolphinarium and an aquarium add to the interest of the visit. Brown bears and wolves roam free in the bear forest and can be observed from a walkway.

ASSEN
DRENTHE Ⓟ
POPULATION 64 320
TOWN PLAN IN THE CURRENT RED-COVER MICHELIN
GUIDE BENELUX

Assen owes its existence to a nunnery, founded in the 13C, of which one can see the chapel (the old town hall) on the main square or Brink. Today, this modern and spacious town is laid out beside **Asserbos**, a pleasant woodland area to the south. The area is known for its many megalithic monuments (ⓒsee HUNEBEDDEN).

- **Information:** Marktstraat 8–10 – 9401 JH. ☎0592 31 43 24. www.assen.nl.
- ▶ **Orient Yourself:** In the northeast of the country, capital of Drenthe province.
- Ⓟ **Parking:** Parking should not be a problem.
- Ⓓ **Don't Miss:** The archaeological finds exhibited in the Drents Museum
- Ⓞ **Organizing Your Time:** Half a day could pass easily with the excursion.

A Bit of History

Until 1602 members of the States or Provincial Assembly of Drenthe met out of doors, in the Germanic style, at the **Balloërkuil** where they dispensed justice. Due to its central location Assen was chosen as capital of the Drenthe in 1809 during the reign of Louis Bonaparte.

Sight

Drents Museum★★
Brink 1. ⓄOpen Tue–Sun 11am–5pm. ⓄClosed 25 Dec and 1 Jan. ⊜5€. ☎0592 31 27 41. www.drentsmuseum.nl.
The museum has a very wide-ranging collection and there is a particularly interesting historical and **archaeological section**★ with an outstanding display on prehistoric times. This includes a large number of artefacts from the local burial mounds known as hunebedden (ⓒsee HUNEBEDDEN), fields of funerary urns, and objects preserved by peat bogs, such as a canoe from 6 300 BC (discovered in Pesse, south of Assen) and 3C and 5C bodies including that of a strangled girl from Yde.
The extensive collection of **decorative arts** (furniture, everyday objects and ceramics), as well as the local **silver**, **period rooms** and **textile collection**, provide a detailed picture of local

life, while the paintings by the **Hague masters** and the selection of prints and drawings from the historical topographic atlas show the Drenthe landscape at its best.
Finally, the museum has an important collection of **art from around 1900**, in which Art Nouveau and Art Deco are particularly well represented. In addition, it holds regular temporary exhibitions.

Outskirts

Rolde
6km/3.7mi to the east – local map ⓒsee HUNEBEDDEN. In a wood to the west of Rolde is a former place of assembly, **Balloërkuil**, an open clearing several metres below ground level. Beyond the church, turn left onto a paved path signposted "hunebedden." In a wood there are two of these **burial mounds** (D 17/18); one of them is covered with seven slabs.

Hooghalen
9km/5.6mi to the south.
In Hooghalen, turn left onto the Amen road. The **Herinneringscentrum Kamp Westerbork** (Ⓞopen Mon–Fri 10am–5pm, Sat–Sun 1pm–5pm; Jul–Aug 11am–5pm; ⊜4.50€; ☎0593 59 26 00; www.kampwesterbork.nl) commemorates the

Drenthe

For a long time this province was ill-favoured. The Scandinavian glaciers, which spread over the north of the Netherlands, left a sandy and not very fertile soil. In places it is covered with **heathland** with a few clumps of oak or pine. In the wetter areas, **peat** developed on the poor morainic soils left by the glaciers. Drenthe was at one time the largest peat-producing region and local peat working has left a dense network of canals, built to transport the peat. Today much of the area has been brought into cultivation, by clearing and the judicious use of fertilisers, and the region now has a very different aspect. Sheep moors have given way to pastures or plantations of conifers. Well fertilised peat bogs, with sand and the upper layer of peat, can make good arable land for growing potatoes, cereals and market garden produce; many ex-colonials have taken over farms in the area. The farmhouses in Drenthe are very picturesque with their vast thatched roofs, and are for the most part hall farmhouses (see Introduction, Farmhouses).

war and the persecution of Jews in the Netherlands using photographs, films, drawings, objects and monuments. Anne Frank was deported from Westerbork to Auschwitz.

Excursion

Norg, Leek and Midwolde

▶ *27km/16.7mi via the N 373; turn right after 3km/1.8mi.*

Norg
This charming Drenthe village with thatched cottages is built around the Brink, a large shady square. It has a small Gothic church with a saddleback roof.

Nationaal Rijtuigmuseum, Kasteel Nienoord

Leek   Kids
To the north of town the moated manor of **Kasteel Nienoord** stands in extensive parkland. It was rebuilt in 1887 and it now houses the National Carriage Museum, or **Nationaal Rijtuigmuseum** (open May–Oct, Tue–Sat, 10am–5pm, Sun 1pm–5pm; closed public holidays; 4.50€; 0594 51 22 60. www.rijtuig museum.nl). This includes many unique carriages (some drawn by goats), royal children's carriages and 17C to 20C sledges. Paintings and travel requisites (saddles, whips, harnesses, livery coats) also form part of the collection. There is a further collection of stagecoaches in a modern building.

Midwolde
The small brick **church** with a saddleback bell-tower contains a fine **marble tomb**★ made by Rombout Verhulst in 1669 for Anna van Ewsum. The young woman is shown leaning gracefully over the mortal remains of her husband. The cherubs in white marble represent the couple's children. In place of the seventh cherub there is now a statue of Anna van Ewsum's second husband; this statue by Bartholomeus Eggers was added in 1714.

BERGEN OP ZOOM

NOORD-BRABANT
POPULATION 65 454
LOCAL MAP SEE DELTA
TOWN PLAN IN THE CURRENT RED-COVER MICHELIN GUIDE BENELUX

In the Middle Ages Bergen op Zoom was already the venue for two important annual fairs, and in 1287 it became the chief town of an independent fiefdom. The old port, today partially filled in, was once linked to the Oosterschelde. Situated in a forested area of heathland and dunes of drifting sand, Bergen op Zoom has become renowned for its asparagus. Its carnival is also well known (🕭 *see Calendar of events*).

- **Information:** Grote Markt 1 4611 NR, Bergen op Zoom. ☎0164 277 4 82.
- ▶ **Orient Yourself:** Bergen op Zoom is in the southwest of the country, close to the sea.
- 🕐 **Organizing Your Time:** An hour or two is sufficient to walk around the town and visit the museum.
- **Kids Especially for Kids:** The fairground collection in the museum.
- 🕭 **Also See:** MIDDELBURG.

A Bit of History

The town was long regarded as invincible after withstanding two sieges by the Spanish: in 1588 by the Duke of Parma, Alessandro Farnese, then again in 1622 when it was besieged by Spinola's troops. However, Bergen was unable to withstand the French army in 1747, during the Austrian War of Succession. The ramparts were demolished in 1868 and the boulevards mark their former location.

Markiezenhof

Sights

Grote Markt

The **Stadhuis** (*town hall;* ◷*open May–Sept, Tue–Sat 1pm–4.30pm;* ◷*closed public holidays and Oct–Mar;* ⊚*1€;* ☎*0164 25 18 59*) stands on Grote Markt and comprises three buildings; the one in the middle and the one on the right have attractive limestone fronts and date from 1611. They have a perron bearing the **town's coat of arms**; two savages support the coat of arms crowned by a coronet, and the arms themselves show three St Andrew's crosses and three hills (Bergen means "hills").

Near Grote Markt, there is a massive **bell-tower** (14C), which locals call De Peperbus (the Pepperpot).

Markiezenhof★

Steenbergsestraat 8. ◷ *Open year-round Tue–Sun 11am–5pm.* ◷*Closed Easter Sunday, 25 Dec and 1 Jan.* ⊚*5€; children (6–12yrs) 2.50€.* ☎*0164 277 077. www.markiezenhof.nl.*

Antonie and Rombout Keldermans, from the famous family of architects in Mechelen, built this 15C and 16C palace for the marquises of Bergen op Zoom. it is one of the finest Late Gothic town palaces in western Europe. The main façade is of brickwork, patterned with string courses. The palace is now a cultural centre and includes a **museum**, an art gallery, a library and a restaurant. There is also a small, picturesque arcaded courtyard. The **Hofzaal** or great hall is remarkable for the carved stone chimneypiece (depicting St Christopher) of 1522, and for its paintings, furniture and silverware, giving an idea of the elegant environment in which the marquises lived. In the garden wing, which was rebuilt in 1706 in the Classical style, there are lovely period rooms. The second floor is devoted to the history of Bergen op Zoom, and includes a **fairground** collection, which children will find particularly appealing.

BOLSWARD★

FRYSLÂN
POPULATION 9 607
LOCAL MAP SEE SNEEK

Bolsward, or Boalsert in Frisian, is one of the eleven towns of Friesland. The date of its foundation is inscribed on a façade stone of the town hall: 713. Its name is believed to mean "the land of Bodel, surrounded by water;" the ending "ward" or "werd" refers to a small mound.

- ▤ **Information:** Marktplein 1 – 8701 KG. ☎0515 57 27 27. www.bolsward.nl.
- ▸ **Orient Yourself:** The town is 12.2km/7.5mi west of Sneek.
- ▣ **Parking:** It is always possible to find a parking space.
- ⊛ **Don't Miss:** The grand interior of the town hall.
- ◷ **Organizing Your Time:** An hour at least; perhaps a picnic near the marina.
- ◔ **Also See:** Leeuwarden, Terpenland.

A Bit of History

In the past Bolsward was linked to the Zuiderzee and it grew rapidly to become a prosperous and powerful town. In the 11C it was granted the privilege of minting coins and became a Hanseatic town.

Today it is a peaceful place in the middle of an area of rich pastureland. Every three years, the town awards a prize for Frisian literature named after **Gysbert Japicx** (1603–66) who was the first literary writer to use Frisian; written Frisian had been obsolete for many years.

Sights

Stadhuis★

⏱ *Open Apr–Jun and Sept–Oct, Mon–Fri 9am–noon, 2pm–4pm; Jul and Aug, Mon–Sat 10am–5pm.* 🎫*1€.* ☎ *0515 57 87 87.*

The town hall is an elegant Renaissance construction dating back to the years 1614–17. The centre of the street front has a gable surmounting a fine 18C perron decorated with two lions bearing the town's coat of arms. At the top there is a tall octagonal clock tower with a **carillon**. In the **council room** there is a splendid carved door by the cabinetmaker Japick Gysberts, who also undertook the decoration of the lovely wooden chimney piece framed by stone telamones. One of the rooms on the first floor, with great timber beams supporting the weight of the tower, houses a collection of antiquities, including Frisian silverwork, traditional costumes, and artefacts from archaeological excavations.

Martinikerk

⏱ *Open Mon–Fri 10am–noon, 1.30pm–5pm; Jul and Aug also open Sat 2pm–4pm.* ☎*0515 57 22 74.*

This large Gothic church was built in the middle of the 15C and, like most Frisian churches, has a saddleback roof. Inside, great round piers support the vaulting of the three naves. The **choir stalls**★ (late 15C) have interesting wood-carvings combining realism with a degree of naïvety. The scenes which are shown on the lateral partitions are particularly noteworthy. Equally interesting are the figures on the high backs, the picturesque illustrations of parables shown on the misericords, the figures on the cheekpieces, and the grotesque figures of the lecterns. The **pulpit**★ (17C), with a tiered canopy, is decorated with elegant motifs in the Frisian style. The central panel depicts a Bible and the signs of the Zodiac; the other panels depict the seasons. The church's remarkable acoustics make it a popular venue for recording music. Note the church floor embedded with tombstones.

Bolsward marina

Excursion

Witmarsum

10km/6.2mi to the northwest.

Near the main road there is a statue of **Menno Simonszoon** (1496–1561). He was born in Witmarsum and became vicar of Pingjum, then the parish priest of his native town and, finally, in 1536, turned his back on Catholicism to become an Anabaptist. He founded the *doopsgezinden* brotherhood or **Mennonites**. In 1539 he summarised his doctrine, which was more pacific than that of John of Leiden: belief in the Bible, rejection of the baptism of children, an emphasis on personal piety, and a refusal to obey all the established Church's dogma. The Mennonite religion spread to Germany, Switzerland and North America, where it still has its adherents.

The Mennonites of Witmarsum meet in a small church, the **Menno-Simonskerkje** (⏱*open daily 10am–4pm by appointment;* ☎*0517 53 19 59*), which was rebuilt in 1961. The prayer area has a portrait of Menno Simonszoon, and the sacristy has various objects commemorating him.

BOURTANGE

GRONINGEN
POPULATION 530

Bourtange, close to the German border, is one of the best-preserved fortified villages in the Netherlands. Lying on the extensive marshes to the east of Groningen, it was built during the Eighty Years' War by **Adriaan Anthoniszoon** for Prince William of Orange, who hoped that it would enable him to free Groningen from Spanish occupation. Bourtange was not completed until 1593 through lack of money. When Groningen surrendered a year later, Bourtange became part of the frontier fortifications. Because of its strategic position, it was considerably expanded and reinforced.

- **Information:** W. Lodewijkstraat 13 – 9545 PA. ☎0599 35 46 00. www.boutange.nl (in Dutch and German).
- **Orient Yourself:** Bourtange is a compact village arranged within the boundaries of a fort and two moats. Visit the tourist office (signposted) first and you can orient yourself within minutes.
- **Don't Miss:** The chance to walk along the wall and observe the surrounding countryside from it high vantage point.
- **Organizing Your Time:** Bourtange is ideal for a leisurely day's outing or an afternoon visit.

A Bit of History

Until 1851, Bourtange was a military fort permanently occupied by some 300 soldiers and their families. Later it was turned over to civil use and the fort fell into disrepair.

Bourtange was made a listed monument in 1967, and extensive rebuilding has restored it to its appearance in 1742, when it was at its largest.

Sights

The fortifications may be visited at any time. The museums, exhibitions and slide show are open from Apr–Oct, Mon–Fri 10am–5pm, Sat–Sun 11am–5pm; Nov–Mar, Sat–Sun 12.30pm–4.30pm. Information from Westerwolde Tourist Office (Bourtange fortress dept) ☎0599 35 46 00.

Bourtange fortress★ is a classic example of a fortress built in the style of the **Old Dutch System** (⊙*illustration: see Architecture*). The core consists of a bastioned pentagon surrounded by two moats. The fort has been carefully restored to give visitors an idea of how it looked in the 18C, complete with drawbridges and cannons.

The only access to the fort is via two narrow paths following a complicated route of bridges and outworks to the Marktplein, or market square. From here 10 streets radiate outwards to the bastions and the main ramparts. This layout made it possible for troops to move around quickly and to be seen by their commanders.

The **Museum De Baracquen**, a reconstructed barracks, contains items found in the fortress.

The **protestant church**, the former synagogue, an officer's apartment and the horse mills can also be visited, and the former powder magazine has an informative slide show about the fortress. Inside the fortress there is a windmill, replacing an earlier one that was privately purchased and taken away in 1832. The new windmill is supposed to be an exact copy of the original structure.

A gruesome reminder of the past, a gallows, stands in a field outside the fortress; thought to have been placed there as a warning to any enemy. to discourage the enemy.

To reach the gallows, follow the sign the Munster Gate .

BREDA★

NOORD-BRABANT
POPULATION 170 491
PLAN OF CONURBATION IN THE CURRENT RED-COVER MICHELIN GUIDE BENELUX

At the confluence of the Mark and the Aa, Breda was formerly one of the country's main fortified towns and the centre of an important barony. Today it is a dynamic city and a great commercial and industrial centre. Benefiting from its position on one of the main access routes into the country, it is a welcoming stopping place with large pedestrian precincts. With numerous parks, Breda also has very attractive suburbs and large areas of woodland, such as the **Liesbos** to the west and the **Mastbos** to the south. To the east, **Surae** is a recreational park with a bathing area.

In February Breda holds its well-known **carnival** (*see Calendar of events*). In May there is the International Jazz Festival and at the end of August the Taptoe, a military music festival (*see Calendar of events*). The month of October brings the Breda Flower Show, held in the Grote Kerk.

- **Information:** Willemstraat 17 – 4811 AJ. www.vvvbreda.nl.
- ▶ **Orient Yourself:** Start at the station, which lies conveniently close to the tourist information centre, and head through Valkenberg park to the main shopping and restaurant centre of Breda.
- **P Parking:** Car parks are plentiful around the town, especially close to the station and the shopping areas (fees apply).
- **Don't Miss:** The newly-restored Grote Kerk, a magnificent Gothic style church in Grote Markt.
- **Organizing Your Time:** Breda is a shoppers' and diners' paradise, and is ideal for a leisurely break of two or three days, but be sure to allow around 45 minutes to see the Grote Kerk. While here, visit Kasteel Bouvigne, a pretty 17C castle just 4km/2.5mi or so from Breda.

A Bit of History

The residence of the House of Nassau – Breda obtained its city rights in c. 1252. It became part of the Breda barony, but in 1404 this passed to the Nassau family, who adopted Breda as their family seat. The 13C fortifications were rebuilt (c. 1535) by Count Henry III of Nassau, and the ring of canals mark the former alignment of the walls, which were destroyed shortly after 1870.

The Compromise of Breda – Although the treaty was actually concluded in September 1556 at Spa (now Belgium), the Compromise of Breda (or of the Nobility) was signed in Breda Castle in 1566. Its aim was to abolish the Inquisition. Following this meeting a delegation of about 300 nobles set out for Brussels to petition the Governor, Margaret of Parma, to convene the States General and change the edicts against heretics (i.e. the Protestants). She burst into tears; her counsellor, the Count of Berlaymont, responded in jest with the phrase: "What, Madam, afraid of these *gueux* (beggars)?" This taunt did not displease the Calvinists, who from then on took the name **beggars** for their movement and the beggar's bowl as the symbol of their fight against Spanish rule. The Calvinists' actions then knew no bounds: in August the **Iconoclasm** was unleashed, and churches were pillaged and statues destroyed. In 1567 Philip II of Spain sent the tyrannical Duke of Alba as governor-general to punish the rebels, root out heresy and re-establish royal authority in the Spanish Netherlands.

An ardently disputed stronghold – In 1581 Breda was pillaged by the Spanish,

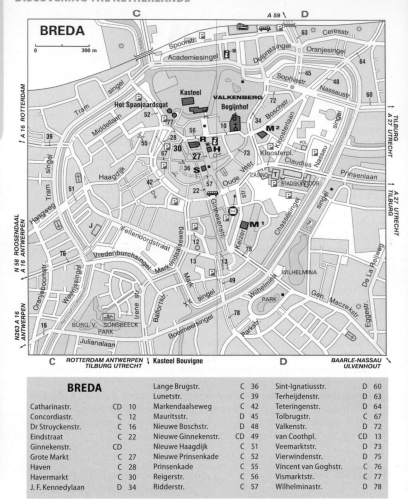

who occupied the castle, the family seat of William the Silent.

In 1590, Maurice of Nassau took the town by surprise, 70 of his men having been able to enter by hiding under a load of peat in a barge belonging to Adriaan van Bergen.

In 1625, after a long siege, Breda surrendered to the Spanish commanded by the Marquis of Spinola. This episode was immortalised by Velázquez in *The Surrender of Breda-Las Lanzas* (1634–35). The town was recaptured in 1637 by the Prince-Stadtholder Frederick Henry.

The **Treaty of Breda** of 1667 ended the Second Anglo-Dutch War (1665–67) and confirmed English possession of Nieuw Amsterdam, which became New York. The negotiations and the signing of the treaty took place in the castle.

During the French Revolutionary Wars, the town was once again under siege in 1794, this time by Pichegru, but only surrendered when the whole country was occupied. It became part of the Deux-Nethes *département* (with Antwerp as its county town) until 1813: that year, at the approach of the Russian vanguard, the French garrison sallied out but the population of Breda prevented their return.

On 11 and 12 May 1940 Breda marked the most northerly point of the Allied advance into the Netherlands; Breda was liberated by the Allies in October 1944.

Grote Kerk or Onze-Lieve-Vrouwekerk★

Grote Kerk, Breda

Open mid-Apr–Oct, daily 10am–5pm; Nov–mid-Apr, Mon–Fri 10am–5pm. ☎076 521 82 67.

The church is an imposing 15C–16C edifice in the Brabant Gothic style. With three naves, it was enlarged in the 16C by the addition of a number of chapels and an ambulatory. Its tall **bell-tower**★ of 97m/318ft with a square base and octagonal top is surmounted by an onion-shaped dome. The **carillon** has 49 bells.

The interior, with its typical Brabant Gothic-style columns – their capitals decorated with crockets – and with a triforium, contains numerous tombs. The most striking one is the **tomb**★ of Engelbracht II of Nassau (1451–1504) and his wife in the Chapel of Our Lady, to the north of the ambulatory. This Renaissance alabaster monument was probably designed by Thomas Vincidor of Bologna. The recumbent statues lie under a slab held up by four figures; they depict Julius Caesar (representing military courage), Regulus (magnanimity), Hannibal (perseverance) and Philip of Macedonia (prudence). Engelbracht's armour lies on top of the slab. The vault under the tomb contains the mortal remains of **René de Chalon**, Henry III of Nassau and Anna van Buren, William of Orange's first wife.

The 15C wooden chancel stalls are carved with satirical motifs illustrating vices, proverbs, etc. Other unusual reliefs were added after 1945. In the north transept there is a triptych by Jan van Scorel and at the end of the south aisle there is a bronze baptismal font (1540) made in Mechelen, Belgium, of Gothic construction with Renaissance motifs. The organ case is decorated with a 17C painting depicting David and Goliath and the Ark of the Covenant. The organ, a fine instrument with its oldest parts

dating from the 16C, can be heard when **concerts** are held.

Additional Sights

▶ *Leave from the point where Nieuwe Prinsenkade becomes Prinsenkade.*

From here there is a lovely view of the Grote Kerk's bell-tower.

Het Spanjaardsgat

These remains of the fortifications, known as the Spanish Gap, consist of two large towers with small onion-shaped domes flanking a watergate, which was used to drain the moat.

Hidden behind the thick walls is the **castle** (⌕ *guided tours only (2hr); information from Breda Tourist Office* ☎076 522 24 44), an immense building with numerous windows, surrounded by a moat; the north façade (visible from the Academiesingel) is flanked by octagonal turrets. Since 1828 it has been occupied by the Royal Military Academy. This old fortified castle was redesigned from 1536 onwards by **Thomasso Vincidor da Bologna**, and was William the Silent's favourite retreat until his departure for the revolt which was declared in 1567. It was here that the Compromise of Breda was signed by the nobles.

Havermarkt

This charming little square in front of Grote Kerk was at one time the hay market. There are several busy cafés around the square.

Valkenberg★

This pleasant park with its magnificent trees was once part of the castle grounds. Nearby the Beguine convent, or **Begijnhof** (1535), comprises simple houses arranged round a courtyard with a herb garden and a chapel.

The Beguines are a Catholic community, but unlike nuns they make no vows.

At the entrance is the covent's former chapel, which has become a Walloon Church, **Waalse Kerk**. The Frisian, **Peter Stuyvesant** (1592–1672) was married here; he was the last Dutch governor of Nieuw Amsterdam (New York) from 1647–64.

Grote Markt

From the middle of this large square there is a fine view of the Grote Kerk. On Tuesday and Friday evenings a general market is held here and a flea market on Wednesdays.

The **Stadhuis** (town hall; ◷open Tue–Fri 9am–4.30pm; ☎076 529 40 55), dating from the 17C, was rebuilt in 1767. It contains a copy of Velázquez's painting, **The Surrender of Breda**, the original of which is in the Prado Museum in Madrid.

To the south of the square, at n° 19, is **Het Wit Lam** (The White Lamb), the former meat hall and premises of the crossbowmen's guild. The pediment of the façade bears the date 1772 and a depiction of St George slaying the dragon.

De Beyerd Museum

Boschstraat 22. ◷*Open Tue–Fri 10am–5pm, Sat–Sun 11am–6pm.* ☎*076 529 99 09. www.museumdebeyerd.nl.*

This former almshouse has been transformed into a graphic design museum, a centre for the visual arts (Centrum voor beeldende kunst). The centre also organises temporary exhibitions on architecture, ceramics, photography and graphic design.

Breda's Museum

◷*Open Tue–Sun10am–5pm.* ◷*Closed 25 Dec and 1 Jan.* ✆*3.50€.* ☎*076 529 93 00. www.breda-museum.org* (*in Dutch*).

The rich history and archaeology of the barony of Breda is chronicled in this former police barracks. The story of Breda as a bishopric is also traced in an important collection of religious art, including statues of saints, paintings, church silver and richly decorated textiles. There is a display of local arts and crafts, and temporary exhibitions are held.

Excursions

Kasteel Bouvigne

3.8km/2.3mi. Leave to the south along Ginnekenweg for 3.5km/2.2mi, then turn right onto Duivelsbruglaan. ⊶*The castle itself is not open to the public.* ◷*Gardens open Mon–Fri 9am–4pm.* ◷*Closed public holidays.* ✆*1€.* ♿☎*076 564 10 00.*

This castle stands on the edge of the **Mastbos**, a lovely wood criss-crossed with cycle paths and rides. The moated castle was built in 1612, and it is flanked by a high octagonal turret with an onion-shaped dome. The gardens are open to visitors (♿ *see above*).

Baarle-Nassau

28.7km/17.8mi to the southeast on the N639.

This village is both Dutch and Belgian; the Belgian part, Baarle-Hertog, consists of some thirty enclaves on Dutch soil. In the 12C the village of Baerle was divided in two; the southern part was ceded to the Duke of Brabant (Baarle-Duc or Baarle-Hertog), and the northern part was united to the Breda barony and called Baarle-Nassau. At present each community has its own town hall, church, police station, school and post office. The border is so complicated that houses of different nationalities stand side by side: a small flag alongside the house number indicates the nationality of each household.

Hoeven
Kids

18.6km/11.5mi west by the N 58.
In the observatory, **Quasar**, **Het heelal dichtbij** (🕐*open Jul–Aug, Fri 7.30pm–10pm, Sun 2pm–5pm, Sept–Jun Fri 7.30pm–10pm, Sun 2pm–5pm;* 🕐*closed 25 Dec and 1 Jan.* ☞*6.80€; children 5.70€.* ♿☎*0165 50 24 39. www.quasar heelal.nl*), visitors are invited – as the name suggests – to take a close look at the universe and all its secrets. The building also houses a **planetarium** and various telescopes.

Oudenbosch

23.5km/14.6mi west by A 58.
This village, also known as Klein (Little) Rome, is overlooked by the enormous **Basiliek van de HH Agatha en Barbara**. It was built by PJH Cuypers in 1867–80, as a smaller version of St Peter's in Rome. The dome, however, is 68m/224ft high. The façade (1892) is a copy of the west front of the Basilica of St John Lateran in Rome. The interior was decorated by an Antwerp sculptor.

Nederlands Zouavenmuseum

🕐*Open May–Sept, Tue, Thu and the first and third Sun of the month, 2pm–5pm; Oct–Apr, Tue and the first Sun of the month, 2pm–5pm.* 🕐*Closed public holidays, Carnival and between Christmas and New Year.* ☞*2.50€.* ☎*0165 31 34 48. www.zouavenmuseum.nl.*
The Museum of Pontifical Zouaves, tells the story of the 3 200 Dutch people who, in the 19C, volunteered to defend the Papal States in Italy.

Willemstad

43km/26.7mi to the northwest by the A 16 and A 59, on the edge of Lake Brabant.
This fortified town in the shape of a seven-pointed star dates from 1583. It is one of the finest example of a fortress in the Old Dutch style and owes its name to its founder, William of Orange. Willemstad was designed by **Adriaan Anthoniszoon**. Today it has a marina which is very popular with holidaymakers. The **Prinsenhof** or Mauritshuis (*now the home of the tourist information office*) was built for Prince Maurice of Orange. It stands in its own park within the old town walls, which have remained intact.

There is a small historical collection. The octagonal **church**, **Koepelkerk**, was completed in 1607 and claims to be the first Protestant church in the Netherlands. The 17C **former town hall** stands close to the harbour, and a little further along is the **d'Orangemolen**, a tall white-walled mill dating from 1734.

Driving Tour

From Raamsdonksveer to Biesbosch★

Raamsdonksveer

25km/15.5mi southwest of Breda by the A 59.
The **Nationaal Automobielmuseum**★ (🕐*open Easter–Oct, Tue–Sat 10am–5pm, Sun and public holidays, 11am–5pm;* ☞*10€;* ☎*0162 58 54 00; www.louwman collection.nl*) is near the Geertruidenberg exit of the A 27 motorway. With over 200 vehicles on display, it traces the history of the car from its origins to the present day. A number of carriages, sledges and motorcycles add to the interest of the main collection. The hall to the left of the entrance contains cars by the Dutch manufacturer, Spyker. The Ahrens-Fox fire engine is American-built, and Elvis Presley owned the bright red Cadillac (1976). The area to the right of the entrance includes such pioneers of the road as the Peugeot Double Phaeton (1894), the Benz Victoria (1899) and the Panhard & Levassor (1895). There is also a 1907 steam-operated street-sweeping machine which belonged to the city of Amsterdam. Among the serried ranks of models and racing cars in the other halls, look for the magnificent **Auburns Duesenbergs and Cords**★★★ of the 1920s and 1930s.

▶ *2km/1.2mi. Head north out of Raamsdonksveer and along Keizersdijk, left onto the N 623 across the water, then bear left for a short distance.*

Geertruidenberg

This small fortified town on the Amer is organised round a triangular **square** overlooked by the massive tower of

St Geertruidskerk. The **stadhuis** has a lovely 18C façade overlooking the square.

> *6km/3.7mi. Go east on the N 623, across the water, then take the first exit north onto Sluizeweg for 1.8km/1mi.*

Drimmelen

Drimmelen stands on the banks of the Amer and has become an excellent water sports centre attracting increasing numbers of tourists; it is also popular with anglers. The **marina** can accommodate up to 1 400 boats. The **Biesbosch Informatiecentrum** provides information on the **Biesbosch** national park.

De Biesbosch★   Kids

Biesbosch (or Biesbos) was made a National Park in 1994 and consists of three parts, stretching across the area of Noord-Brabant and Zuid-Holland. The **boat tours**★ (*By reservation only. Information: Biesbosch Informatiecentrum Drimmelen. ◐open Tue–Sun 10am–5pm; ☎0162 68 22 33; www.biesbosch.org*) give a good overall view of the region.

Although very busy with pleasure boats, the Biesbosch is rich in birds. Reeds, rushes and grassland are the main vegetation on the many small islets. Recreational facilities in the Biesbosch include rowing, sailing and canoeing.

Biesbosch Museum   Kids

Hilweg 2, 12km/7.4mi west of Werkendam. ◐Open Tue–Sat 10am–5pm, Sun and public holidays, noon–5pm. ◐Closed 25, 31 Dec and 1 Jan. ⌫3.25€; children 2.35€. ☎0183 50 40 09. www.biesboschmuseum.nl.

In this museum, visitors can find out about the origins of the area and its wealth of flora and fauna.

BRIELLE

ZUID-HOLLAND

POPULATION 17 000

Brielle, generally known as Den Briel (pronounced bril), stands on the island of Voorne. This fortified historic town was once a busy port at the mouth of the Maas.

- **Information:** Markt 1 – 3231 AH. ☎0181 47 54 75. www.vvvbrielle.nl.
- **Orient Yourself:** Brielle's main roads radiate from the ferry terminal where foot passengers and cyclists arrive on the island, so orientation is quick and straightforward.
- **Parking:** There are a number of areas reserved for parking.
- **Don't Miss:** St Catharijnekerk, the Gothic-style church that dominates the skyline of the town.
- **Organizing Your Time:** Spend two or three hours to admire Brielle's beautiful period houses, its fortifications and its quaint quaysides.
- **Also See:** ROTTERDAM.

A Bit of History

On 1 April 1572 the Sea Beggars (*Gueux de Mer or Watergeuzen*), with the support of William the Silent, left England and landed at Brielle. This was the signal for the uprising of Holland and Zeeland against the Spanish occupation. In July 1572, 19 priests were executed in Brielle of which 16 had just been made prisoners by the Sea Beggars at Gorinchem. Known as the "martyrs of Gorkum", they have been canonised. Each year, on 1 April, Brielle commemorates the taking of the town by the Sea Beggars with a costumed parade and a series of plays. Brielle was the birthplace of Admiral **Maarten Tromp** (1598–1653), famous for his victory against the Spanish at the Battle of the Downs in 1639.

Today, it is a tourist centre benefiting from the proximity of **Brielse Meer** to which it is linked by a ferry for pedestrians and cyclists.

Sights

Reminders of the past include fortifications, laid out as an esplanade, and peaceful quays bordered with old houses, like **Maarland** to the north of the town. At the far eastern end of Maarland, beyond a bridge, there is a fine **view** over the docks and the tower of the Gothic church, St Catharijnekerk.

Historisch Museum Den Briel

◔*Open Apr–Oct, Tue–Fri 10am–5pm, Sat 10am–4pm, Sun noon–4pm; Nov–Mar, Tue–Sat 10am–4pm.* ◉*2€.*

☎*0181 47 54 75. www.historischmuseum denbriel.nl.*

Behind the 18C stadhuis, on the **picturesque Wellerondom** square, this small museum, installed in a former prison and weigh-house, is devoted to the turbulent history of the town and the island of Voorne.

Grote Kerk or St Catharijnekerk

◔*Open May–Sept, daily 10.30am–4.30pm; rest of the year by appointment.* ◉*1€.* ☎ *0181 47 54 75 (VVV). www. catharijnekerk.nl.*

Although this church was started in the Brabant Gothic style in the 15C, it remains unfinished. It has a massive stone tower 57m/187ft high. The carillon, cast in 1660 by one of the Hemonys, has been enlarged and now has 48 bells.

DELFT★★

ZUID-HOLLAND

POPULATION 95 300

PLAN OF THE CONURBATION IN THE CURRENT RED-COVER MICHELIN GUIDE BENELUX

The town of Delft is known the world over for its blue and white ceramics, delftware. With its tree-lined canals, famous monuments and museums, Delft is also one of the Netherlands' most charming towns. It was the home town of the jurist **Grotius**, as well as the artist **Vermeer** and the naturalist **Antonie van Leeuwenhoek** (1632–1723) who, thanks to the microscopes which he perfected, made a multitude of discoveries in both botany and zoology.

- ▯ **Information:** Hippolytusbuurt 4, 2611 HN. ☎015 215 40 51. www.delfttoerisme.nl.
- ▶ **Orient Yourself:** Delft is 13.8km/8.6mi southeast of Den Haag and 38.8km/24mi southeast of Aalsmeer. Once in Delft, head for the Markt because from here whichever road you take you will come across one of Delft's many treasures, including the Oude Kerk and Nieuwe Kerk. The station is a 15-min or so walk away along a busy road.
- ▯ **Parking:** Delft is geared up for visitors and provides many car parks, although off-street parking can also be found. Parking permits cost 1.60€ per hour.
- ☺ **Don't Miss:** Oude Kerk; this mighty church contains the tomb of Delft's most famous son, the painter Vermeer. Nearby, the Nieuwe Kerk houses the Dutch Royal family crypt.
- ◔ **Organizing Your Time:** Delft can be explored in just a few hours, but an overnight stay will mean you can sample one of its fine evening restaurants.

A Bit of History

A prosperous city – Delft, which means moat, was probably founded in 1074. Count William II of Holland granted

the city its charter in 1246, and Delft reached the peak of its prosperity in the 13C and 14C based on the cloth trade and its brewing industry. At the end of the 14C the town's authorities decided to build a canal linking the city to the Maas to facilitate the transportation of its products. Slowly the small town of Delfshaven grew up around the newly established port, which became part of Rotterdam in 1886. In 1428 Jacoba or Jacqueline of Hainaut (*see GOES*) signed the **Treaty of Delft** by which she gave her territories of Holland, Zeeland and Hainaut to Philip the Good, while keeping the title of countess. The ramparts were built in the 15C. Delft was extensively damaged by the large fire of 1536 and it has few edifices dating from before the 16C. In 1654, the explosion of a powder magazine completed the destruction.

Today Delft is an intellectual centre, due to its schools of Natural Sciences, its hydraulic laboratories and its Technical University. A nuclear reactor was built in 1963 for research and development purposes. The modern university buildings are in the southwest of the town.

The father of international law – Hugo de Groot or **Grotius** (1583–1645), one of the greatest intellectuals of his time, was born in Delft. He was a theologian, philosopher, politician, diplomat and poet, but is best known for his legal writings and notably his *De Iure Belli ac Pacis* (*On the Law of War and Peace* – 1625) which became the accepted authority on matters of civil rights and earned its author the sobriquet "father of international law." Following the Synod of Dort, Grotius, who was a Remonstrant and follower of Oldenbarnevelt, was imprisoned in Slot Loevestein. He managed to escape and went to live in Paris, where in 1634 he became the Swedish Ambassador to France.

Johannes Vermeer (1632–75) – Delft and its townspeople were the whole universe of Vermeer, one of the Netherlands' greatest Old Masters, who was born and died in Delft.

Early on he applied himself to painting scenes of daily life, and he is one of those who, without giving up the realism current at the time, revolutionised pictorial art. Vermeer avoided the anecdotal and his subject matter tended to be banal and everyday, however he displayed an extraordinary sense for composition, geometry, for the use of unctuous matter, vivid tones (lemon yellow, sky blue) remarkably blended, and above all, for the marvellous light effects for which Vermeer is the great virtuoso. This play of light is particularly fine in the famous *View of Delft* or in the portraits of women suffused with light and grace like the *Girl with a Pearl Earring* (*Illustration: see Den HAAG*) and *The Lacemaker*. The Mauritshuis in The Hague and the Rijksmuseum in Amsterdam have the greatest number of works by Vermeer, who was not in fact a prolific artist.

His contemporary, **Pieter de Hoogh** or **Hooch** (1629–84) was born in Rotterdam and spent a long time in Delft before going to Amsterdam. He depicted the life of the well-to-do bourgeois seen in interiors with open doors and windows, creating clever perspectives and light effects on the floor.

Delftware

Illustration: see Introduction, Decorative Arts.

In the second half of the 17C Delft acquired a reputation for making ceramics, a craft which soon spread over all of Europe. Heir to the Italian majolica techniques, delftware is tin-glazed earthenware and characterised by its remarkable lightness and its particularly shiny aspect, due to the application of a translucent coating.

At first Delft was known for its monochrome painting of blues on a white background; this is still one of the characteristics of delftware today (**Delfts blauw**).

At the end of the 17C the production became more varied, polychrome appeared, and there was not a design or shape, coming from China or Japan, which the Delft artists did not try out in order to satisfy the tastes of European clients fascinated by the Orient.

In the 18C the influence of Sèvres and Meissen porcelain expressed itself in objects with mannered outlines and decoration, while some of the pieces remained faithful to traditional Dutch scenes where one sees small boats

William the Silent

William was born in 1533, in Dillenburg Castle in Germany, to Count William of Nassau and Juliana of Stolberg. On the death of his cousin **René de Chalon** (1544) William the Silent (*illustration: see Introduction, History*) inherited his possessions in France and in the Low Countries, and took his title of **Prince of Orange** as well as his motto *Je maintiendrai* (I shall maintain). In 1559, Philip II of Spain made him **Stadtholder** of the provinces of Holland, Zeeland and Utrecht.

Philip II took measures to repress the Calvinists and in so doing encouraged the growth of an opposition movement, which was led by William of Orange and the **Counts of Egmont and Hornes** In 1566 the Iconoclasm (*see BREDA*) began. William, convinced he was under threat, fled to Dillenburg (1567). The Counts of Egmont and Hornes were less lucky, they were executed in Brussels in 1568. In 1570 William, who had been brought up as a Catholic, became a Calvinist and he then began to give open support to the Beggars campaigns, both on land and sea. The capture of Brielle by the Sea Beggars on 1 April 1572 was only the beginning of a long and bitter conflict. The States of Holland met in Dordrecht in July and approved the revolt and acknowledged William of Orange as Stadtholder (*see DORDRECHT*).

From 1572 onwards the prince often resided in Delft. In 1579 by the Union of Utrecht the provinces of Holland, Zeeland, Utrecht, Gelderland and Zutphen decided to join the fight; the other provinces followed suit fairly soon afterwards.

In 1581 Philip II offered a reward for the assassination of the prince; William of Orange retaliated with the well-known *Apologie*. He sought support from François of Anjou, brother of King Henri II of France, but the latter died (1584) before he could help. On 10 July 1584 William the Silent was assassinated in the Prinsenhof in Delft.

sailing on the canals spanned by hump-back bridges.
At the beginning of the 18C delftware reached its peak. But a decline set in rapidly, caused mainly by English competition and porcelain, made first in Germany and later throughout Europe. However, production continues today in several local factories.

Walking Tour
Map, see DELFT

Historic Centre★★
Allow half a day

Markt
This long, narrow square stretches from the Nieuwe Kerk to the Stadhuis. In the middle stands a statue of Grotius.

Nieuwe Kerk★
Open Easter–Oct, Mon–Sat 9am–6pm; Nov–Mar, Mon–Sat 11am–4pm. 3.20€. 015 257 02 98. www.nieuwe erk-delft.nl.

This Gothic church (1381) has a brick tower crowned with a stone spire whose top has weathered to black. The carillon has bells cast by one of the Hemonys. The church contains the crypt of the

Making Delftware

Address Book

For coin ranges, see the Legend on the cover flap.

WHERE TO STAY

This beautiful old town has many hotels in historic buildings; the following is a selection.

De Plataan – *Doelenplein 10, 2611 BP. ☎015 212 60 46. www.hotelde plataan.nl. 25 rooms.* This hotel has a great deal of character. The rooms – and in particular the bridal suites – are furnished with refreshing originality: beds in the shape of a sycamore leaf (the hotel is called the Sycamore), and entire rooms decorated in Turkish style. The hotel also has apartments for guests who wish to stay for longer periods. Breakfast is served in the welcoming Living Room Café Quercus.

Herberg de Emauspoort – *Vrouwenregt 9, 2611 KK. ☎015 219 02 19. www.emauspoort.nl. 23 rooms.* The rooms in this family hotel are pleasantly furnished. For those who are looking for something slightly out of the ordinary, however, two old-fashioned gypsy caravans have been set up in the inner courtyard, fully equipped with shower, toilet and television. And a breakfast of fresh home-baked rolls ensures that guests start the day on the right footing.

Leeuwenbrug – *Koornmarkt 16, 2611 EE Delft. ☎015 214 77 41. www.leeuwenbrug.nl. 36 rooms.*This hospitable and typically Dutch hotel is located in two mansions in the heart of the town, and has comfortable rooms of various sizes.

Johannes Vermeer – *Molslaan 18–22, 2611 RM. ☎015 212 64 66. http://bb.go.nl/hotel/Vermeer. 25 rooms.* Set in a quiet location, the Johannes Vermeer lives up to its name, with large reproductions of the Old Master's work decorating the walls of the brasserie. The rooms are comfortable and look out over the old town centre at the back. The restaurant is fitted out in the typical style of Holland, with a wonderful array of copper kettles suspended from the ceiling.

Bridges House – *Oude Delft 74, 2611 CD. ☎015 212 40 36. www.bridges-house.nl. 7 rooms.* This fine canalside building is where Jan Steen lived between 1654 and 1656. Today it is a small but elegant luxury hotel. The hotel and the spacious rooms are tastefully decorated in the English style.

BW Museumhotel Delft – *Phoenixtraat 50A, 2611 AM. ☎015 215 30 70. www.museumhotel.nl. 63 rooms and 3 suites.* The Residence, the splendid annexe of the Delft Museumhotel, is housed in a row of smart 17C canalside houses with an attractive courtyard. It is full of antique and modern objets d'art, and the modern rooms, lounge and garden contain displays of contemporary ceramics. Almost a museum, it is also a top-class hotel.

WHERE TO EAT

De Klikspaan – *Koornmarkt 85. ☎015 214 15 62. www.klikspaandelft. nl.* Excellent food served in an old canalside warehouse. The restaurant is called 'the telltale' after the resident parrot, but don't worry; the bird is the very model of discretion.

Le Vieux Jean – *Heilige Geestkerkhof 3. ☎015 213 04 33. www.levieuxjean.nl.* Typically Dutch décor, but typically French cuisine.

De Zwethheul – *Rotterdamseweg 480 (5km/3mi southeast of Delft). ☎010 470 41 66. www.zwetheul.nl.* Although this restaurant is outside the centre, it is worth a detour. Apart from its superb view of passing boats, and its pleasant terrace, the food is excellent. Treat yourself!

Van der Dussen – *Bagijnhof 118. ☎015 214 72 12.* This trendy restaurant is housed in the superb 13C Bagijnhofje, or almshouses, and offers tasty exotic cuisine in a historic setting.

L'Orage – *Oude Delft 111b. ☎015 212 36 29. www.restaurantlorage. nl (in Dutch).* Arts restaurant with good food and a beautiful town-centre location. Good value for money.

NBTC

Delftware on display

PRACTICAL INFORMATION

General information – VVV Delft, *Toeristen Informatie Punt Delft,Hippolytusbuurt 4, 2611 HN Delft.* ☎*0900 515 15 55. www.zuid-holland. com* has information on sights, excursions, cultural events, restaurants, maps, etc. It also publishes a brochure listing the town's hotels, pensions and campsites.

PUBLIC TRANSPORT

All parking in the town centre is either metered or pay and display. **Daily parking permits** are available for *1.60€* per hour at the VVV. The main sights in the historic town centre are within walking distance of one another. A **Delft City Card** covers public transport and entrance to the museums: *12.99€ for 24 hours.*

TOURS AND WALKS

Guided walking tours leave daily from Apr–Sept at 11.30am, Tue, Wed, Fri and Sat at 2pm. Cost is 10€ per person. The starting point and registration point is the Tourist Information Point at Hippolytusbuurt 4 in Delft. You can register up to 30min before departure. There is also a **tour by horse-drawn tram**. The tram departs every half hour outside the town hall at the Markt during schoolholidays Fri–Wed. Outside schoolholidays the tram departs only during the weekend. Reservations are required: ☎*015 256 18 28. www. delftsepaardentram.nl.*

BOAT TRIPS

Touring the historic town centre, these leave from outside Koornmarkt 113. Trip lasts 45min. ☎*015 212 63 85, Apr–Oct, daily. www.rondvaartdelft.nl (in Dutch).*

Markets – A **general market** takes place on Markt on Thursdays, while the **Brabant Peat Market** takes place on Saturdays. Plant and flower sellers set out their wares on Hippolytusbuurt on Thursdays, and a **flea market** is held along the canals every Saturday from mid-April–end of September. **Delft Specialities** – The town still has a few factories making delftware by traditional methods. The following are open to the public:

De Koninklijke Porceleyne Fles Anno 1653 Royal Delft, *Rotterdamseweg 196.* ☎*015 251 20 30. www.royaldelft.com.*

De Delftse Pauw, *Delftweg 133.* ☎*015 212 49 20. www.delftsepauw.com.*

Aardewerkatelier de Candelaer *Kerkstraat 14.* ☎*015 213 18 48. www.candelaer.nl*

princes of the House of Orange. Only a few members of this family were not buried here: Stadtholder and King of England, William III, lies in Westminster Abbey, John William Friso in Leeu-

warden, Philip-William, eldest son of William the Silent, in Diest (Belgium). The interior is plain, with three naves and squat columns supporting wooden arches. The well-lit nave contrasts with

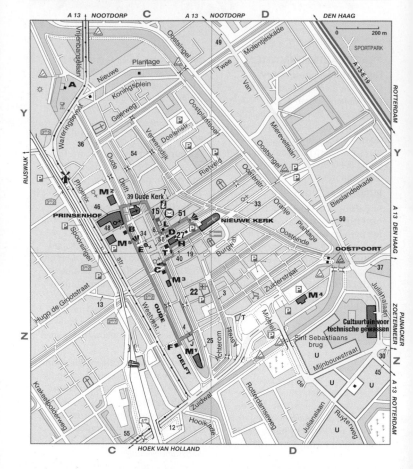

the more sombre light reflected by the rich stained-glass windows (1927–36, WA van Konijnenburg) of the transept and the wide ambulatory. The glazing depicts figurative motifs in warm colours. The exception is the stained-glass window portraying Grotius, in the north transept, by the master **Joep Nicolas** (1897–1972) with its muted grey and blue tones.

The **mausoleum of William the Silent**★ stands in the chancel, above the royal crypt. This imposing Renaissance edifice in marble and black stone was made by Hendrick de Keyser from 1614–21. In the middle of a peristyle quartered by great allegorical figures, the prince lies in full-dress uniform, under the eyes of a bronze Fame. At his feet lies his ever-faithful dog. At the head of the recumbent marble statue, a bronze statue depicts William the Silent in armour.

In the centre of the chancel, the entrance to the House of Orange's crypt is indicated by a large emblazoned slab. In the ambulatory, paved with tombstones, is the mausoleum of King William I by William Geefs (1847) and further on a simple monument to Grotius (1781), and another by the Italian sculptor Canova to Prince Willem George Frederik, can be seen.

From the penultimate platform of the **tower** there is a **panorama**★ over the new town which lies beyond the ring canal. Both the Technical University and the nuclear reactor are quite easy to pick out, and away on the horizon are Rotterdam and The Hague.

Stadhuis

Markt 87. &☎*015 260 29 60.*
The old town hall burnt down in 1618, and it was rebuilt two years later by Hendrick de Keyser. Since the 1960s restoration it has recovered its 17C aspect with its mullioned windows set in lead and its low shutters. The shell-decorated façade fronting the square is dwarfed from behind by the old 15C keep, all that remains of the original stadhuis. There is a fine view of the Nieuwe Kerk and its tower at the far end of the square.

Waag

The weigh-house (1770) has been transformed into a café. Nearby is the meat hall, **Vleeshal**, the façade of which is appropriately adorned with two ox heads (1650).

Koornmarkt

Cross the canal.
This is the landing stage for the boat trips mentioned above. At n° 81 there is a lovely Renaissance-style house with medallions, called De Handboog (the

bow). At n° 67 the 18C patrician house, where the painter **Paul Tetar van Elven** lived (1823–96), is now a **museum** (⊙*open late Apr–late Oct, Tue–Sun 1pm–5pm;* ☞*3€;* ☎*015 212 42 06*) containing furniture, paintings by Van Elven and his contemporaries, and ceramics.

Legermuseum★

Enter through Korte Geer, the continuation of Koornmarkt. ⊙*Open Tue–Fri 10am–5pm, Sat–Mon and public holidays noon–5pm.* ⊙*Closed 25 Dec and 1 Jan.* ☞*7.50€.* ☎*015 215 05 00. www. legermuseum.nl.*

The two former arsenals housing the Army Museum date from 1602 and 1692; they used to belong to the States of Holland and Western Friesland. The third building was used as a warehouse by the Dutch East India Company.

The historical exhibition in the "gebouw 1692" (1692 building) retraces the evolution of the Dutch army through the ages. Impressive collections illustrate the different stages of development of national military history: weapons, armour, uniforms, headgear, banners, trappings, means of transport, paintings and scale models. These cover the Roman and medieval periods, the Eighty Years' War, in which the army reformer Maurice of Orange and his half-brother Frederick Henry distinguished themselves, the French domination (1795–1813) and its upheavals, the Belgian Revolution (1830), and the two World Wars. The post-war events relative to Indonesia and the Cold War are also represented.

The 1602 building focuses more specifically on V weapons, and holds temporary exhibitions.

Oude Delft★

The sombre water of the canal shaded by lime trees, the humpbacked bridges and the elegant façades make an attractive picture. At n° 39 the lovely house of the Dutch East India Company, **Oostindisch Huis**, has been restored. The façade carries the company's coat of arms and its initials: VOC. The weathervane is shaped like a ship.

▶ *Turn back and follow the quay.*

One soon sees the slightly leaning spire of the **Oude Kerk**. Built of a sombre-coloured brick, it is flanked by four pinnacles, and is crooked, earning it the nickname of Scheve Jan, Crooked Jan. On the opposite quay there is the charming Gothic chapel, Kapel van het H Geeststuzusterhuis.

From Nieuwstraat Bridge there is a fine **view**★ over the canal. At n° 167 the Delft Water Board, **Hoogheemraadschap van Delfland**, an old patrician house (c. 1520), displays a sumptuous Renaissance stone façade decorated with sculptured tympana. The portal is topped with polychrome armorial bearings.

Number 169, **Het Wapen van Savoyen**, has a fine façade emblazoned with the arms of the House of Savoy and contains the local archives.

Prinsenhof★

No 183. Enter from St Agathaplein, reached through a gateway on Oude Delft. ◷*Open Tue–Sat 10am–5pm, Sun and public holidays 1pm–5pm.* ◷*Closed 25 Dec and 1 Jan.* ⊕*6€.* ☎*015 260 23 58. www.prinsenhof-delft.nl* (*in Dutch*).

The relief above one of the former gates on Oude Delft is a reminder that in the 17C the Prinsenhof was converted into a cloth market. It originally included a convent (**St Agatha**) before becoming, in 1572, the residence of **William the Silent**, who was assassinated here on 10 July 1584 by Balthazar Gerard. The Moordhal, or Assassination Hall, still has two bullet holes at the bottom of the stairs to the first floor. The palace (Prinsenhof: the Prince's Court) now houses a **museum** with important historical collections relating to the Eighty Years' War and the House of Orange-Nassau.

🙂 A Bit of Advice 🙂

CITY CARD THE HAGUE – DELFT

Get one- or two-days' bus and tram travel between the Hague and Delft with this City Card. Presenting this card gives you discounts on entry to the top 30 tourist attraction sights in the Hague and Delft.
www.citycardthehaguedelft.com/en.

The Historical Room on the first floor has angel figures on the ceiling and numerous portraits on the walls. The museum also has many still-lifes and schutterstukken (portraits of companies of the civic guard) and some fine tapestries. The buildings, in Late Gothic style, date from the 15C and 16C and are grouped around two courtyards. After the Reformation, the chapel of the old monastery was given to the Wallonian Reformed Church and services were held in French for Protestants who had fled from the southern Netherlands.

Volkenkundig Museum Nusantara

◷*Open Tue–Sat 10am–5pm, Sun and public holidays 1pm–5pm.* ◷*Closed 25 Dec and 1 Jan.* ⊕*6€.* ♿☎*015 260 23 58. www.nusantara-delft.nl* (*in Dutch*).

Nusantara means "island kingdom between two hemispheres", and the museum's collection is devoted to the history and cultures of Indonesia. It includes such items as statues, masks, weapons, textiles, brassware, shadow puppets, jewellery and Javanese gamelan instruments.

Museum Lambert van Meerten★

◷*Open Tue–Sat 10am–5pm, Sun and public holidays 1pm–5pm.* ◷*Closed 25 Dec and 1 Jan.* ⊕*6€.* ☎*015 260 23 58. www.lambertvanmeerten-delft.nl* (*in Dutch*).

This beautiful 19C canalside mansion has a magnificent collection of **Dutch and foreign tiles**★ from the 16C to 19C. The attractive little passageway from the hall to the vestibule is decorated with Gothic and Renaissance-style motifs, while the monumental staircase depicts a naval battle between French, English and Dutch ships. Other tiles and tile pictures depict flowers, animals, and traditional crafts. The museum also has collections of delftware, furniture and other items from the estate of the industrialist Lambert Van Meerten (1842–1904).

Oostpoort

Oude Kerk

🕐*Open Easter–Oct, Mon–Sat 9am–6pm; Nov–Mar, Mon–Sat 11am–4pm.* 🎟*3.20€.* ☎*015 212 30 15. www.oudekerk-delft.nl.* This 13C church is reflected in the waters of the Oude Delft canal. Since the 16C it has had three chancels and the beginning of a transept. The tower, which leans, embedded in the main nave, is built on the foundations of a watch tower. It has the second-biggest bell in the Netherlands (9t). Numerous memorial slabs are set in the pavement. The finely carved Renaissance pulpit resembles the one in the Grote Kerk in The Hague. The stained-glass windows (1972) were made by **Joep Nicolas**. Several famous people are buried in this church. In the main chancel Admiral Piet Hein is shown lying in full armour: it is the work of Pieter de Keyser, the son of Hendrick. In the chapel near the north chancel is the Baroque mausoleum of Admiral Tromp by Rombout Verhulst.

Hippolytusbuurt

This tree-lined canal is one of the oldest in Delft. On the corner of Hippolytusbuurt and Camaretten is the fish market (still in operation), next to which stands the former meat market. Opposite this is a 16C house (Kaaskop)w with crow-stepped gables.

Voldersgracht

This is a picturesque canal, lined on the south side by a few corbelled houses. From the second bridge, there is a fine **view** of the Nieuwe Kerk's tower.

Additional Sights

Oostpoort★

Formerly called St Catherine's Gate, it is the only gate remaining from the town walls. Flanked by two slender turrets (15C and 16C), there is a fine view from the picturesque white lever bridge. A canal passes under the annexe.

Cultuurtuin voor technische gewassen

🕐 *Open Mon–Fri 8.30am–5pm, Sat 10am–3pm.* 🕐*Closed public holidays.* ☎*015 278 23 56.* This botanical garden has been used to grow a wide variety of plants for Delft Technical University since 1917. Its purpose is purely scientific and educational. It has glasshouses with tropical and sub-tropical plants, and there are also two short walking routes for visitors to the tree and herb garden.

DELTA★

ZUID-HOLLAND – ZEELAND

In the coastal provinces of Zuid-Holland and Zeeland the estuaries of the Rhine, Maas and Scheldt form a complicated network of islands, headlands and channels known as the Delta.

▶ **Orient Yourself:** If travelling from Rotterdam take the A29 to the Delta, which leads to a series of roads linking the islands. You can then explore the waterways and islands with ease.

P **Parking:** Plenty of free off-street parking and viewing points.

Don't Miss: The Oosterschelde storm surge barrier; it's a powerful structure. Also take a trip to Renesse, which has a sandy beach and a pretty coastal walk.

🕐 **Organizing Your Time:** Allow a day to explore the islands.

Kids **Especially for Kids:** Older children will be impressed by the technology.

A Bit of History and Geography

At the mouth of three great rivers – The **Rhine** divides into two branches as it crosses the Netherlands, the Neder Rijn and the Waal. The **Neder Rijn** (Lower Rhine) becomes the Lek, then the Nieuwe Maas before entering the Nieuwe Waterweg. The **Waal**, the main arm of the Rhine, flows into the Lek and the Maas. The **Maas**, which has several other names (Bergse Maas, Amer), flows into the Hollands Diep. The Oosterschelde is a former estuary of the **Schelde** (Scheldt), which presently flows into the Westerschelde.

The rivers thread their way between the islands. some of which have become peninsulas.

A region under constant threat – The islands built up slowly towards the end of the Middle Ages as the rivers deposited sediments. They are generally very low lying, many below Amsterdam Reference Level and most under 5m/16ft. The coastline is protected by high dunes, while the banks of the rivers are strengthened by dykes. Several times throughout history these have proved vulnerable when the great surge tides swept inland.

Aerial view of the Delta works

On the feast day of **St Elisabeth** (19 November) 1421, the flood waters inundated the entire Delta and swept as far inland as Dordrecht and the Biesbosch area. Six villages were inundated and 10 000 lost their lives.

There was another great disaster on the night of 31 January 1953 when, under the combined effects of low atmospheric pressure and high tides, the water breached the dykes in several places. Once again the islands were inundated; 1 835 died and a further 500 000 were left homeless.

The effects were felt as far inland as the Hollandse IJssel.

The Delta Plan – Three years after the tidal wave of 1953, two options were under discussion to prevent the recurrence of similar tragedies: heighten the existing dykes or dam the major estuaries and inlets of the Delta. In 1958 the Delta Plan was incorporated in an Act of Parliament.

Four main dams, two with locks, closed off the inlets of the North Sea and several secondary dams closed off the estuaries further inland. The **secondary dams** afforded initial protection from high tides during the construction of the main dams. Once the main dams were finished the importance of the secondary ones diminished, although they proved a considerable asset to the road network.

The completion in May 1997 of the storm barrier in the Nieuwe Waterweg, which flows through Rotterdam, meant that the Delta Plan had been implemented in full after nearly forty years. The Westerschelde, which gives access to the port of Antwerp, is now the only inlet that remains open.

The dams have many advantages: they shorten the coastline by approximately 700km/435mi, and they form freshwater lakes inland (e.g. Haringvlietdam and, further to the east, two auxiliary dams, Philipsdam and Oesterdam). They reduce the seepage of salt water into the water table, limit the risk of floods, form ideal stretches of water for recreational purposes, improve the road network and encourage the development of the region.

BOAT TRIPS

Various boat trips are available in the northern part of the Delta, leaving from Rotterdam (see ROTTERDAM) and Willemstad, or further along the Oosterschelde from Zierikzee (see ZIERIKZEE) or WaterLand Neeltje Jans.

The Delta Plan also included the raising and strengthening of existing dykes along navigable waterways and the development of the Biesbosch area.

The Scheldt-Rhine Canal, to the east of the Delta, was completed in 1975 and links Antwerp to the Volkerak, a distance of 37km/23mi.

Dams and bridges – Already by 1950 the Brielse Maas, downstream from Rotterdam, had been transformed into a lake called the Brielse Meer (see BRIELLE). Since it was necessary to leave the New Waterway open for navigation a storm surge barrier, **Stormvloedkering Hollandse IJssel** was built between 1954 and 1958 on the Hollandse IJssel near Krimpen aan de IJssel in the eastern suburbs of Rotterdam. The reserve lock (120 x 24m/394 x 79ft) alongside is for larger vessels and ships in general when the gates of the storm surge barrier are closed. Following the completion of the storm barrier in Nieuwe Waterweg in 1997, the Rotterdamse Waterweg can now also be fully closed (see ROTTERDAM, Excursions). The Haringvliet estuary was closed off by the **Haringvlietdam** while further inland the secondary **Volkerakdam** linked Overflakkee to the province of Noord-Brabant. Built between 1957 and 1969, the dam has three large sluice caissons and is itself linked to **Haringvlietbrug** which spans the waterway to the north towards Beijerland.

To the west, the Brouwershavense Gat Channel is closed by the **Brouwersdam** with inland the **Grevelingendam** on the waterway of the same name. The latter links Duiveland and Overflakkee, and when it was built in 1958–65, 170 000 tonnes of rubble were tipped as infill from the gondolas of a cableway. The **Philipsdam** is a prolongation to the southeast.

The year 1986 saw the completion of the Oosterschelde Storm Surge Barrier, **Stormvloedkering in de Oosterschelde** In the event of a bad storm or when the water level reaches a critical point, it is now possible to close off this estuary, the widest (9km/5.6mi) and the deepest (40m/131ft) in the Delta. Two dams east of the estuary, **Oesterdam** (1986) and Philipsdam protect the Scheldt-Rhine Canal from tidal flow. The Oosterschelde is also spanned by the **Zeelandbrug**

The saltwater channel, Veerse Meer, to the south of Noord-Beveland is closed off by **Veerse Gatdam** which is backed up by a secondary dam, **Zandkreek-dam**, on the saltwater Zandkreek channel between Noord- and Zuid-Beveland. Built between 1956 and 1960, the 800m/2 625ft long dam has a lock (140 x 20m/459 x 65ft) spanned by a swing bridge for traffic.

Two companies provide regular boat services across the estuary. There is a project under discussion to build a tunnel.

The Storm Surge Barrier★★★

Construction of the storm surge barrier began in 1976, and was completed ten

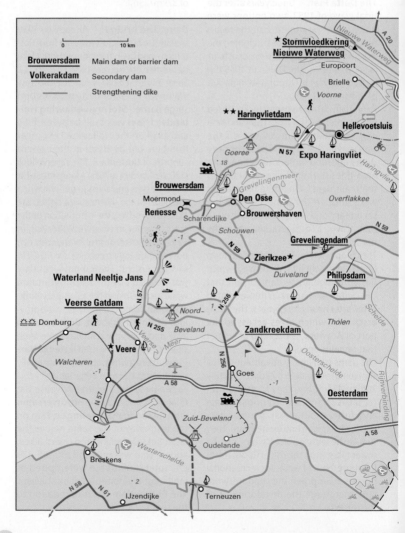

years later. The road running along the dam was opened in 1987. This gigantic and unique structure is 3km/1.8mi long. It is built across three tidal channels of the Oosterschelde and two artificial islands which were originally used as construction bases.

The original project involved the river being completely closed off, but this was changed to keep the link with the sea open. The barrier consists of 65 prefabricated concrete piers and 62 sliding steel gates. Each pillar is 30 to 38m/99 to 125ft high, and weighs up to 18 000 tonnes. The gates are normally raised, but can be closed in less than an hour in the event of high water or a storm. This construction preserves 75% of the tidal flow in the Oosterschelde and thus the unique estuary habitat with its fish and its oyster and mussel beds.

Ir. Topshuis on the former artificial island of Neeltje Jans (also home to the theme park **WaterLand Neeltje Jans** (◷*open Apr–Oct, daily 10am–5.30pm; Nov–Mar, Wed–Sun 10am–5pm;* ◷*closed 25, 31 Dec and 1 Jan.* ≈*summer 18€; winter 13.50€ (free admission up to 3 years old);* ♿☎*0111 65 56 55; www.neeltjejans.nl*) houses the central control room as well as the **Delta-Expo** exhibition, which gives an idea of the importance of the Delta Project to the area as a whole and the history of land reclamation and hydraulic engineering in the Netherlands. A working model reproduces the 1953 floods and explains the safety measures implemented since then. The film *Delta Finale* recounts the successive stages of the development of the dam: the making of the different prefabricated elements; the preparation of foundations in the sandy channel bed; the floating and sinking into position of the concrete piers; and finally, the fitting of the computer-controlled sluice gates. The **tour** of one of the pillars of the dam is also worthwhile, particularly at high tide; access to the upper girder is through the control room. Note the powerful current: in the Oosterschelde each tide displaces 800 million cu m/ 28 251 733 37cu ft of water. The futuristic **Waterpaviljoen** uses light, sound and image effects to show the cycle of water movements. In summer, there are nature walks on the island, and it is also possible to climb one of the pillars or go on a tour of the Oosterschelde; for children there is the **Waterspeelplaats** (water playground).

Hellevoetsluis to Veere

99km/62mi – allow a day

Hellevoetsluis
This small village on an inlet of the sea, Haringvliet, has a marina.

Haringvlietdam★★

This major civil engineering project was undertaken from 1955 to 1971.

Initially an artificial construction site was built in the middle of the estuary and surrounded by an encircling dyke. A cableway was used in the final stages, a method that had already been used on the Grevelingendam. Concrete blocks were tipped from the gondolas into the final channel to be dammed. All of 5km/3mi long, the Haringvlietdam has 17 drainage sluices of 56.5m/185ft, the largest in the world. Their gates take 20min to open using a hydraulic press system with 68 presses set within the 16 pillars and the abutment piers. Normally these sluice gates are closed and the water is forced back to the Nieuwe Waterweg. The drainage locks help to achieve a balance between fresh and saltwater.

A shipping lock has been made near the small port to the south. At **Expo Haringvliet** (◐open Apr–Sept, daily 10.30am–5pm; Oct–Mar, daily 11.30am–5pm; ☎0187 49 99 13; www.expoharingvliet.nl (in Dutch)) visitors are shown how the locks are constructed and how they work. They also get a chance to look around one of the engine rooms.

Brouwersdam

The dam was built from 1963 to 1972 between the islands of Goeree and Schouwen; there is no lock. To complete the north channel, sluice caissons were made, the same system which had been used for the first time when building the Veerse Gatdam. The south channel, Brouwershavense Gat, was filled in using the cableway system whereby 15-tonne loads of concrete blocks were dropped each time by the gondola.

Renesse

This small village on the north coast of the island of Schouwen has a lovely sandy beach. Just to the east is a fine 16C–17C manor, **Slot Moermond**, which is now a hotel and restaurant.

Den Osse

This recent marina is well hidden by the dykes.

Brouwershaven

This was originally a prosperous port trading in beer from Delft (*brouwer:* brewer); however life today revolves around its small pleasure boat harbour.

This was the home town of the statesman, **Jacob Cats** (1577–1660), nicknamed Father Cats, who was Grand Pensionary of Holland and West Friesland from 1635 to 1651. He was also known for his poetry.

Brouwershaven has a lovely Gothic church, the **Grote Kerk**, **or St Nicolaaskerk** (◐open Whitsun–Aug, Mon–Sat 1.30pm–4.30pm; ☎ 0111 69 19 25 58). The pulpit and font screen are in the Rococo style. The **stadhuis** (town hall) of 1599 has a highly decorated Renaissance façade.

Zierikzee★ – ◐See ZIERIKZEE.

Storm Surge Barrier★★★ –
◐ See DELTA, The Storm Surge Barrier.

Zeelandbrug★

In 1955 this bridge was built to link Zierikzee to the former island of Noord-Beveland. The crossing was paralleled with the opening of the road along the Oosterschelde Barrier. This impressive feat of engineering bridges the 5 022m/16 476ft waterway in 50 arches at a height of 17m/55.7ft above water level. The swing bridge on the Schouwen-Duiveland side gives passage to boats with tall masts.

Veerse Gatdam

This dam was built (1958–61) west of Veere on the island of Walcheren to the former island of Noord-Beveland. It is 2 700m/8 858ft long and, despite a protective sandbank, is very exposed to storms, due to its northwesterly orientation. It was the first dam to use sluice caissons; these were placed on the bed of the channel and the sluice gates were then closed at slack water, which prevented the formation of a destructive current. Another small saltwater and tideless lake, the Veerse Meer, lies between this dam and the Zandkreekdam to the east.

Veere★ – ◐See VEERE.

DEVENTER★

OVERIJSSEL

POPULATION 88 000

PLAN OF THE CONURBATION IN THE RED-COVER MICHELIN GUIDE BENELUX

Deventer stands on the east bank of the IJssel in the south of the province of Overijssel. This former Hanseatic town has a historic centre full of character which is witness to a rich past. Today it is a lively university town and commercial centre, and the home of the famous gingerbread, **Deventer Koek.**

- **Information:** De Waag – Brink 56. ☎0570 69 37 81. www.vvvdeventer.nl.
- **Orient Yourself:** The station lies to the north of the town. Directly in front is Keizerstraat, a long road that leads to the Brink, a square at the heart of Deventer.
- **Parking:** Car parks are dotted at numerous locations around the town and are well signposted (fees apply), or free beside the river.
- **Don't Miss:** The Waag, a beautiful, restored 16C weigh house that stands in the centre of the Brink.
- **Organizing Your Time:** Allow around two hours to explore Deventer town centre, although for a leisurely break spend some time at one of its fine hotels. Allow a few hours to visit Holten, a town 26km or so from Deventer and site of the Holterberg, a high wooded area on the edge of the Scandinavian glaciers.
- **Especially for Kids:** A visit to Bussink's Koekwinkel for the gingerbread.

A Bit of History

As early as the 9C Deventer was a prosperous port. At the end of the 9C, the town became the residence of the Utrecht bishops, who fled from their city threatened by the Vikings. The remains of an 11C episcopal palace have been found in Nieuwe Markt. The town soon played an important religious role. The theologian **Gerhard Groote** (1340–84), born in Deventer, was the innovator of a spiritual movement, the **Devotio Moderna** (modern devotion). One of his pupils, following the wishes of his master, founded in Deventer c. 1384 the first monastery for the **Order of the Brethren of the Common Life** a community devoted to the education and care of the poor, which had a great intellectual influence in Europe. Those who passed through this school included Thomas à Kempis (*see ZWOLLE*), Pope Adrian VI (*see UTRECHT*), Erasmus in 1475–76 and Descartes in 1632–33.

In the 16C the artist Hendrick Terbrugghen was born in Deventer. At the end of the 17C, the painter Gerard Terborch, born in Zwolle, came to work here, dying in 1681.

In the 16C and 17C printing was an important enterprise in the town; many incunabula had already been produced here in the 15C.

Today, on the first Sunday in August, Deventer hosts the great book market, **Grootste Boekenmarkt van Europa** Deventer is also an Old Catholic Episcopal See (*see UTRECHT*).

River IJssel and the town of Deventer

Town Centre

Brink

This is the name given to the main square of the town and is typical of all localities of Saxon origin. A market is held here on Friday mornings and Saturdays, and the many outdoor cafés provide a pleasant place to linger in the summertime. At nºs 11 and 12 there is an early 17C façade decorated with shells. The richly decorated **Penninckhuis** (nº 89) dates from 1600. Number 84 is the original **Bussink's Koekwinkel** where Deventer's delicious gingerbread is still sold.

Waag★

This is a large, slightly leaning weigh-house built in 1528 in the Late Gothic style and complemented in 1643 by the addition of a tall perron resting on arcades. On the right side wall hangs a huge cauldron in which, it is said, counterfeiters used to be boiled.

The building contains the **Historisch Museum Deventer** (*Brink 56, 7411 BV Deventer;* ◷*open Tue–Sat 10am–5pm, Sun and public holidays 1pm–5pm;* ◷*closed Good Friday, Easter Sunday, Whitsun, 25 Dec and 1 Jan;* ◎ *4€;* ♿☎*0570 69 37 80*), displaying several collections related to the town's history. Note the *Four Evangelists* by Hendrik ter Brugghen, the remnants of a 17C majolica oven and the bicycles, believed to be the oldest in the Netherlands.

De Drie Haringen★

This merchant's house (1575), known as the House of the Three Herrings, has a fine Renaissance façade decorated with a façade stone depicting three herrings.

Speelgoed- en Blikmuseum [Kids]

◷*Open Tue–Sat 10am–5pm, Sun and public holidays 1pm–5pm.* ◷*Closed Good Friday, Easter Day, Whitsun, 25 Dec and 1 Jan.* ◎ *4€; children 1€.* ☎*0570 69 37 86.*

The biggest public collection of toys in the country has been set up in two medieval houses. Most of the exhibits were made after 1860: construction sets, train sets, dolls, games and mechanical toys. One section presents a range of packaging tins, manufactured in the Netherlands between 1800 and 1980.

▶ *Retrace your steps and turn right into Bergstraat.*

Bergstraat★

This street, situated in the **Medieval Bergkwartier**★★ (Berg meaning hill) comprises several beautifully restored old houses in the Gelder-Overijssel style, which is a mixture of Gothic and Renaissance. It affords a lovely view of the two towers of the Bergkerk.

St Nicolaas or Bergkerk

◷*Open Tue–Sun 11am–5pm.* ◷*Closed 25 Dec and 1 Jan.* ◎*No charge.* ☎*0570 61 85 18.*

Building started c. 1200 and the two great west front towers date from that period. In the 15C the rest of the building was remodelled in the Gothic style. In 1991 the church was turned into an exhibition area, forming an elegant setting for the **13C paintings**★ that are on display.

▶ *Return to Brink via Kerksteeg – at the end of Kerksteeg, turn around and stop a moment to take in the view – and Menstraat. Polstraat then leads to Grote Kerkhof.*

Grote Kerkhof

The Grote Kerk and Stadhuis are both on this square.

Stadhuis

◷*Open Mon–Fri 9am–5pm.* ◷*Closed public holidays.* ☎*0570 64 99 59.*

The town hall complex (greatly restored) is in three parts: the Raadhuis, the Wanthuis (also partly on Polstraat), and the Landshuis, which has a brick façade (1632) topped by a pinnacled gable. The joint façade of the Raadhuis and the Wanthuis dates from 1693; its architect, Jacob Roman, also designed Het Loo Palace in Apeldoorn.

In the hall several 17C and 18C group portraits of guilds are exhibited. A room on the first floor of the Raadhuis has a lovely canvas by Terborch: entitled **The Aldermen's Council**, it was painted in 1657.

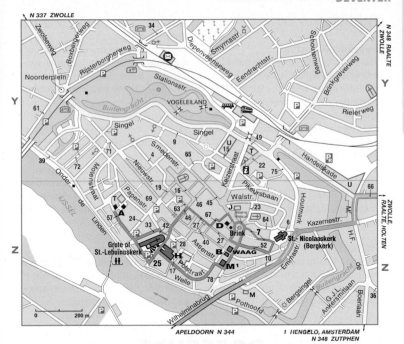

Grote Kerk or St Lebuïnuskerk

🕐*Open during summer season Mon–Sat 11am–5pm; winter Mon–Sat 11am–4pm.* ☎*0570 61 37 44.*

It bears the name of Lebuin, the Saxon apostle, who built a church here in the 8C. The Romanesque church was converted after 1235 and then again in the 15C in the Gothic style. It is a vast building flanked to the west by a tower topped with a lantern designed by Hendrick de Keyser.

Its carillon, which was cast by one of the Hemonys, can be heard during concerts. From the top of the **tower** (219 steps; 🕐*open Jul–Aug, Mon–Sat*

1pm–5pm; 🕐*closed public holidays;* ☎*0570 61 37 44)* there is a lovely view of the town.

In the hall-type interior the remains of a double transept can still be seen. The stellar vaulting has paintings round the keystones (16C). Other paintings can be seen, notably under the porch near the tower; the Bearing of the Cross dates from the 16C. The 19C great **organ** has 3 000 pipes.

The Romanesque crypt (1040), under the chancel, is remarkable with its six short pillars, cabled or decorated with geometric motifs.

Additional Sight

Buyskensklooster

This early 15C building has recovered its brickwork walls. It is the former convent of St Agnes where the Sisters of the Common Life lived, following the rules set down by Gerhard Groote. It contains the town archives, **Gemeentelijke Archiefdienst** (n° 3) and a library, the **Atheneumbibliotheek**.

Excursion

26km/16mi to the east via Snipperlingsdijk

Holten

This town, situated in the Salland region, attracts many tourists, drawn by the wooded and sandy heights of the **Holterberg** (alt 60m/200ft), which marks the southern limit of the Scandinavian glaciers.

On the Holterberg, there is the **Natuur-diorama Holterberg**★ (*open Apr–Nov daily 10am–5pm, Sun 11am–5pm; Nov–Mar Sun, Wed and school holidays 1pm–5pm; closed 25 Dec, 31 Dec and 1 Jan; 9.75€; 0548 36 19 79; www.museumholterberg.nl (in Dutch)*.) About 10 large **dioramas**★ bring to life ecosystems and their fauna, many of which are still to be found locally .

In a nearby clearing is the **Canadian military cemetery** with 1 496 graves of Canadians killed in the Second World War.

Markelo

At the beginning of the 20C an important field of funeral urns was found north of Markelo. Markelo has an **open-air theatre** De Kösterskoele.

DOESBURG

GELDERLAND

POPULATION 11 602

Doesburg, an old stronghold of the Zutphen earldom, was a prosperous commercial town in the Middle Ages and a member of the Hanseatic League in 1447. This lovely town in the Achterhoek (*see ZUTPHEN, Excursion*) has kept several of its Gothic and Renaissance façades.

- **Information:** Kerkstraat 6 – 6981 CM. 0313 47 90 88. www.vvvdoesburg.nl (in Dutch)
- ▸ **Orient Yourself:** In the east of the Netherlands, in the province of Gelderland at the confluence of the IJssel and the Oude IJssel.
- **Parking:** Finding a parking space in town is not usually a problem.
- **Don't Miss:** The excursion to the castle at Heerenberg is worthwhile.
- **Organizing Your Time:** Allow up to two hours of your time for the excursion.
- **Especially for Kids:** Huis Bergh, though not its collections, will appeal to children.

Sights

Grote Kerk or Martinikerk

Open Apr–Sept, Mon–Sat 2pm–5pm. 0313 47 90 88. www.martinikerkdoesburg.nl (in Dutch).

This Gothic church dedicated to St Martin (15C) is lit by tall Flamboyant windows. Its high **tower** was destroyed in 1945, but has been rebuilt and has a carillon. Organ concerts are given in summer.

Waag

Now a restaurant – and an inn for as far back as the 15C – this attractive weigh-house (1478) has tall picture windows with painted shutters, topped by tym-

pana and a gable decorated with pinnacles. Inside, in a typical setting, the weigh-house scales can be seen.
There are other interesting houses in the same street, notably the **Baerkenhuizen** (nos 29–31), two Renaissance buildings of 1649.

Stadhuis

Opposite the Waag, the town hall dates from the 15C. Of particular interest are its front and rear façades.
The **Streekmuseum De Roode Tooren** is at nos 9–13 in the same street. Reconstructions include a room where a cigar-maker chopped tobacco and an old grocer's shop. Note the scale model of a pontoon bridge: near Doesburg the banks of the IJssel were linked by this type of bridge until 1952. ○*Open Tue–Fri 10am–noon, 1.30pm–4.30pm, Sat 1.30pm–4.30pm; Jul and Aug also open Sun 1.30pm–4.30pm.* ○*Closed 1 Jan, Easter Sunday, Whitsun and 25 Dec.* ✆*No charge;* ☎*0313 47 42 65.*

Doesburgsch Mosterden Azijnmuseum

Boekholtstraat 22. ○ *Open Tue–Fri 10am–5pm, Sat 11am–4pm.* ○*Closed 30 Apr, Easter Day, 25 Dec and 1 Jan.* ✆*1.50€; children 0.75€.* ☎*0313 47 22 30.*
In this factory, founded in 1457, mustard is prepared according to traditional methods using small wooden barrels.

Excursion

22km/14mi to the southeast

Doetinchem

This town, situated in the heart of the Achterhoek (✆*see ZUTPHEN*), formerly belonged to the Zutphen earldom. It was badly damaged by a bombardment in 1945. Today, it is a modern industrial and commercial town.

's-Heerenberg

This village close to the German border is dominated by the imposing castle, **Huis Bergh**★★ (○*opening times vary and are subject to alteration; best to confirm in advance;* ○*closed Carnival, 25, 31*

☺ **A Bit of Advice** ☺

If you want to take some time out for a cup of tea, Croissanterie La Fleur (*Kerkstraat 16*) is a cosy coffee shop/restaurant with a garden terrace. Access is through an old sweet shop .

Dec and 1 Jan; ✆*7.50€;* ☎*0314 66 12 81; www.huisbergh.nl*). Built in the 13C by the Van den Bergh family, this moated castle has undergone much alteration work, mainly in the 17C, and has burnt down twice. The first fire was in 1735 and led to the Van den Bergh family moving out. Between 1798 and 1840 the castle served as a seminary and in 1912 it was purchased by a private owner who began renovation work, but misfortune struck again in 1939 when another fire caused extensive damage. In 1946 its last owner, a keen collector, bequeathed the castle and its contents to a trust. The interior comprises a valuable **collection of antique furniture**★★ Old Dutch and Flemish paintings, illustrated manuscripts (the earliest dates to the late 13C) and carvings of wood and ivory. Particularly notable are the Early Gothic Italian paintings, including a work by Duccio, making up the Netherlands' largest collection in private hands of early Italian paintings. The coin collection and the weapons room can also be viewed. Look out also for the lovely stained glass, *One of the three kings* by Ecole de Chartres, that dates back to the beginning of the 13C.
The roof of the tower affords a fine view of the outwork and the steward's house (now a teashop), the 15C **Mint**, where coins were struck until 1580, and the Medieval parish church.
The castle grounds, 'De Plantage', were first laid out in the 18C and the oldest oak trees to be seen date from 1785. The grounds make a pleasant walk and the website gives information on longer walks and cycles in the vicinity (www. huisbergh.nl).

DOKKUM

FRYSLÂN
POPULATION 13 145
LOCAL MAP SEE LEEUWARDEN

The small town of Dokkum was once a flourishing port. Today it hides behind the remains of its tree-covered ramparts, from which only a few bell-towers and tall mills emerge. As the town is built on a mound, it has several steeply sloping streets.

- **Information:** Op de Fetze 13 – 9101 LE. ☎0519 29 38 00. www.vvvdokkum.nl (mostly in Dutch).
- ▶ **Orient Yourself:** Dokkum is in the north of Friesland, near the coast.
- **Parking:** Parking is rarely a problem.
- **Don't Miss:** The view from the bridge offers a classic Netherlands scene.
- **Organizing Your Time:** A lunchtime visit suggests itself.
- **Also See:** LEEUWARDEN.

A Bit of History

St Boniface and his 52 companions were murdered here in 754. This English-born missionary came to Friesland in 716 to convert the people to Christianity; he then attached himself to St Willibrord in Utrecht. He was killed during his second mission to Friesland, and is buried in Fulda, Germany, where he had founded a monastery.

Sights

Zijl
From this wide bridge, there is a fine **view** over Klein Diep (meaning small canal) bordered by a mill, and the Groot Diep (large canal). The simple 17C **stadhuis** (town hall) has a white clock tower and a 19C Neoclassical façade. On the other side of the canal are three lovely early 17C houses with crow-stepped gables which have been well restored.

Museum Het Admiraliteitshuis
Diepswal 27. ◔*Open Tue–Sat 1pm–5pm.* ◔*Closed public holidays.* ☜*3.50€.* ☎*0519 29 31 34. www.museumdokkum. nl (mostly in Dutch).*
This regional museum is installed in the former Admiralty House (1618) and a neighbouring 18C house; note the Admiralty House's small Renaissance-style portal. The collections are varied: Dokkum silverwork, a Frisian sledge of carved wood, paintings, antique chests, items excavated from ancient burial mounds, local costumes, 19C toys, and Frisian folk art.

Grote Kerk or St Martinuskerk
◔*Open Jun–mid-Sept, 2pm–5pm. Contact the verger for other times:* ☎*0519 29 23 94/0622 81 28 75.*
A mound and a church were erected here to commemorate the murder of St Boniface. The present building in the Gothic style has a chancel dating from the 15C. Inside the elevation over the side aisles includes a very tall gallery. A great number of tombstones are embedded in the floor; note the Frisian pulpit with elegant carved panels portraying a lion, a pelican and a falcon.

Bonifatiuskapel
Leave Dokkum to the south in the direction of Leeuwarden and once beyond the lever bridge take the second road on the left. ◔*Open Jun–Sept, daily 2pm–5pm.* ☎*0519 29 23 94.*
In the middle of the square stands the statue (1962) of St Boniface, shielding his head with his Bible from his Frisian attackers. The chapel dedicated to St Boniface (1934) in the small park is the centre for a popular annual pilgrimage (◔*see Calendar of events*).

DORDRECHT ★
ZUID-HOLLAND
POPULATION 119 000
PLAN OF THE CONURBATION IN THE RED-COVER MICHELIN GUIDE BENELUX

In the south of the province of Zuid-Holland, Dordrecht, which the Dutch familiarly call Dordt, is an important river centre between the Beneden Merwede, a branch of the Rhine, the Noord, the Dordtse Kil and the Oude Maas. It is also a great pleasure boat harbour with many yachts anchored at quaysides, both within the town and outside. The old town has kept its colourful quays, its canals and its old façades, while the southern quarters are noted for their bolder constructions.

- **Information:** Spuiboulevard 99. ☎ 078 632 24 40. www.vvvdordrecht.nl.
- ▶ **Orient Yourself:** One of the best places to begin a tour of Dordrecht is at the Grote Kerk, which overlooks a marina beside the Oude Maas. From here, head towards the town hall (signposted) and you are in the heart, and the most interesting part, of the town.
- 🅿 **Parking:** There are many car parks on the outskirts of Dordrecht, or you can park at the station, but be prepared for a 20-minute walk into town.
- **Don't Miss:** The Museum Mr Simon van Gijn (Museum van Gijn) is well worth seeing; it houses a fascinating collection of artefacts from the 18th and 19th centuries.
- 🕐 **Organizing Your Time:** The old town is worth spending at least a half day exploring, and the town easily offers enough things to do for a couple of days' stay. While here, make sure you visit Hollandse Biesbosch, an outstanding natural park just 5km/3mi or so from Dordrecht.

Bit of History

In 1220 Dordrecht acquired city rights from the Count of Holland, William I. Because of this, it is considered the oldest town in the earldom.

The 14C was a period of great prosperity for Dordrecht due to the privilege of applying stop-over tolls, which from 1299 were levied on goods coming from the Rhine. The 15C, on the contrary, was a time of disaster: there was the unsuccessful siege in 1418 by Count John of Brabant as part of the struggle between the Hooks and Cods; the St Elisabeth's Day Flood of 1421 which isolated the town making it an island; the great fire of 1457 and then its capture in 1480 by John of Egmont. In the 16C the town recovered its splendour.

The cradle of independence – It was in the Dordrecht Court of Justice (Het Hof) that the first free assembly of the Holland and Zeeland States was held in July 1572. In Dordrecht the delegates of the twelve confederate states of Holland and the nobility decided to deliver the country from the Duke of Alba's armies, and they proclaimed William the Silent as stadtholder (*stadthouder* in Dutch). In this way they laid the foundation for the future United Provinces (see Introduction, Time Line).

Synod of Dort – Dordrecht was also the meeting place in 1618–19 of the great synod of Protestant theologians who came to settle the controversy that had arisen between the moderate **Remonstrants** or Arminians, supporters of Arminius, and the **Gomarists** supporters of **Gomarus**. The latter group won, with the help of Maurice of Orange, and carried out bloody persecutions on their opponents, such as Oldenbarnevelt (see AMERSFOORT) and Grotius (see DELFT). At this synod the union of all Protestant churches in the country took place, except for the Remonstrants, and a joint doctrine (canons of Dort) was established.

The De Witt Brothers

Dordrecht was the birthplace of the De Witt brothers, distinguished 17C statesmen. **Johan de Witt** (1625–72) became the Grand Pensionary of Holland in 1653. Although he was an excellent administrator, he had less success in foreign affairs. He was unable to avoid the defeat of the Dutch fleet by England in 1654, which marked the end of the First Anglo-Dutch War. In addition he was hostile to the predominance of the House of Orange, and as a result he was quite unpopular for being out of step with popular opinion. After having won the Second Anglo-Dutch War (1665–67) and withstood the War of Devolution led by Louis XIV (1667–68), Johan de Witt managed to get approval for the **Perpetual Edict** of 1667, which abolished the Stadtholdership and thus the Orangist power in the province of Holland.

However, in the same year (1672) that Louis XIV and Charles II united against the United Provinces in the Third Dutch War, the people, feeling threatened, repealed the Perpetual Edict; William of Orange was elected Stadtholder as William III and army commander. Finally, **Cornelis** the brother of Johan de Witt and burgomaster of Dordrecht in 1666, was wrongly accused of conspiring against William III and was imprisoned in the Prison Gate in The Hague. While visiting him, Johan de Witt was the victim of an uprising and was murdered with his brother near the prison (*see Den HAAG*).

Birthplace of 17C painters – A number of 17C painters were born in Dordrecht. Some of them were Rembrandt's students. **Ferdinand Bol** (1616–80) went to live in Amsterdam where he worked in Rembrandt's studio. His works, notably the numerous portraits tinged with seriousness, are very like those of his master, for their chiaroscuro, the abundance of impasto and the harmony between warm colours.

Nicolaes Maes (1634–93) was also influenced by Rembrandt, whose pupil he was from 1648–52 in Amsterdam. More realist than Rembrandt, he chose ordinary people, modest subjects and scenes in which he was able to evoke a degree of endearment. Towards the end of his life he changed to painting fashionable portraits.

Samuel van Hoogstraten (1627–1678) studied with Rembrandt, then after having travelled a great deal in Europe, returned to his birthplace. He painted mainly portraits and interior scenes.

Godfried Schalcken (1643–1706) was one of van Hoogstraten's pupils.

Aert van Gelder (1645–1727) was first a pupil of van Hoogstraten, then of the ageing Rembrandt in Amsterdam. His biblical scenes owe a lot to the technique of the great master, notably the sumptuous clothes and the slightly theatrical composition.

Albert Cuyp (1620–91) was influenced by Jan van Goyen and painted landscapes with luminous backgrounds, immense skies and in the foreground horsemen or peaceful herds of cattle.

Old Town★

Allow half a day

Grote Kerk or Onze-Lieve-Vrouwekerk★

Open Apr–Oct, Tue–Sat 10.30am–4.30pm, Sun and public holidays, noon–4pm; rest of the year, hours vary. No charge. 078 614 46 60. www.grotekerk-dordrecht.nl.

Grote Kerk, Dordrecht

Legend has it that the church was started by a young girl, St Sura, who, wishing to build a chapel to the Virgin and possessing only three daalders, saw each time she prayed that three new coins were miraculously added to her treasure. The present church, which is Protestant, was built between 1460–1502 in Brabant Gothic style. The massive tower has remained unfinished because of subsidence on the north side. It ends in a terrace with four clock faces. The carillon (1949) consists of 53 bells.

Interior

It is very large (108m/354ft long) and imposing with its 56 pillars topped with typical Brabant crocket capitals. The oak **choir stalls**★ were finely carved by the Fleming Jan Terwen between 1538 and 1542 in the Renaissance style, and are among the most beautiful in the country. The low reliefs above the backs of the last row on the north side depict secular triumphs, notably those of Emperor Charles V; those on the south side portray religious triumphs. Also worthy of note are the cheekpieces and misericords. The Baroque chancel screen (1744) is elegant. In a chapel of the ambulatory on the east side, three stained-glass windows depict episodes in the town's history: the flood of 1421, the fire of 1457 and the capture of the town in 1480. The pulpit (1756) with a marble base is in the Rococo style, and the **organ** was built in 1671.

Tower

279 steps. Open Apr–Oct, Tue–Sat 10.30am–4.30pm, Sun and public holidays noon–4pm; July and Aug also open Mon noon–4pm; Nov–Mar, Sat–Sun 1pm–4pm. 078 614 46 60.
On the way up, take the chance to get a closer look at the 1626 clock. From the top terrace, there is a superb **view**★★ over the old town where the houses huddle together alongside the canals and docks. Note the length of the roofs; land bordering the canals was so expensive that houses were built backwards from the canal with façades as narrow as possible. Further in the distance are the rivers that surround the town.

To the right of the tower, the Leuvebrug over the Voorstraathaven has four **low reliefs** sculpted in stone in 1937 by **Hildo Krop** (1884–1970); they depict a prisoner, a baker, a dairywoman and an apothecary-surgeon in Naïve style.

Blauwpoort or Catharijnepoort

Near this very plain gateway, dating from 1652, there are warehouses and a beautiful patrician house with a perron, the 18C **Beverschaep**: its door is topped by a naiad and a triton embracing one another; on the pediment a sheep (schaap) and a beaver (bever) support the coat of arms.

Nieuwehaven

Pleasure boats find shelter in this dock with tree-lined quaysides.

Museum Mr Simon van Gijn★

Open Tue–Sun 11am–5pm. Closed 24 Dec and 1 Jan. 6€. 078 639 82 00. www.simonvangijn.nl.
This lovely residence (1729) and its contents were bequeathed to the town by the banker **Simon van Gijn** (1836–1922), a great art collector. It contains rooms with rich furnishings, paintings, silver, glass and porcelain. The 2nd floor has temporary exhibitions and a selection of prints and drawings from the Gijn Atlas. On the top floor is a collection of 19C toys, including dolls, dolls' shops and houses, and children's dinner services. From the quay on the north side, there is a fine **view** of Nieuwehaven and part of the Grote Kerk. There is also a lovely view in the other direction over Kuipershaven, which is lined with warehouses.

Kuipershaven

Numerous barges are crammed in to the coopers' quay, which specialised in the wine trade. At nos 41–42, a barrel is shown on the grill above the door. In the transom window of no 48 a basket is depicted.

Groothoofdspoort

This was the main gate (1618) to the town. It is topped by a dome.
From the quay, situated on the north side, there is a fine **view**★ over the wide

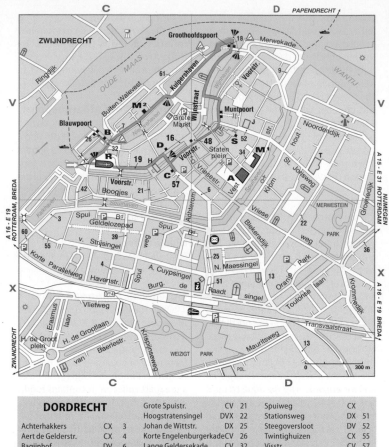

DORDRECHT			Grote Spuistr.	CV	21	Spuiweg	CX	
			Hoogstratensingel	DVX	22	Stationsweg	DX	51
Achterhakkers	CX	3	Johan de Wittstr.	DX	25	Steegoversloot	DV	52
Aert de Gelderstr.	CX	4	Korte Engelenburgerkade	CV	26	Twintighuizen	CX	55
Bagijnhof	DV	6	Lange Geldersekade	CV	32	Visstr.	CV	57
Blauwpoortspl.	CV	7	Museumstr.	DV	34	Voorstr.	CDV	
Bleijenhoek	DV	9	Oranjelaan	DX	36	Vriesestr.	DV	
Dubbeldamseweg	DX	13	Papeterspad	CX	39	Wilgenbos	CX	60
Groenmarkt	CV	16	Prinsenstr.	CV	42	Wolwevershaven	CV	61
Groothoofd	DV	18	Riedijk	DV	46			
Grote Kerksbuurt	CV	19	Schefferspl.	CDV	48			

Arend Maartenshof	DV	A	Dordrechts Museum	DV	M¹	Museum Mr. Simon		
Beverschaep	CV	B	Grote of Onze-Lieve-			van Gijn	CV	M²
De Crimpert Salm	CV	C	Vrouwekerk	CV	R			
De Sleutel	CV	D	Het Hof	DV	S			

confluence of the Merwede, the Noord and the Oude Maas Rivers.

On the other side of the gate near the lever bridge, the **Wijnhaven** (wine port), a harbour for pleasure boats, and the small bell-tower make a colourful picture.

Wijnstraat

This unevenly paved street lined with picturesque houses, all lop-sided, is another association with the wine (*wijn*)

trade. Some houses are Renaissance, still with crow-stepped gables (nᵒs 73–75; with the emblem of a cock: nᵒ 85), while others are in the Louis XIV style (nᵒ 87).

▸ *Cross the canal.*

The city's oldest residences line this canal in the central area.

Voorstraat

In this busy shopping street are some interesting façades: note the lovely Rococo décor at n° 178 and the **Muntpoort** at n° 188, dating from 1555.

At the beginning of the pedestrian precinct, on the left near the Augustijnenkerk, at n° 214 a porch gives on to **Het Hof** the former Court of Justice where the States General met in 1572.

Scheffersplein

This is the market place; in it is a statue of the painter Ary Scheffer.

Visstraat

This street, whose name means Fish Street, leads to Dordrecht's very modern commercial quarter. At n° 7 there is a lovely small Renaissance house, **De Crimpert Salm** (1608), with an elaborate façade with a stone depicting a salmon (zalm) and a gable topped with a lion.

▶ *Cross the bridge towards Groenmarkt.*

Views over the canal, which is narrow here, and the old town hall, a white Neoclassical building. On the bridge there is a monument (1922) to the De Witt brothers.

Groenmarkt

Former vegetable market. On the right, at n° 39, the **De Sleutel** house has a façade decorated with a key (sleutel) and tympana with recessed orders. Dating from 1550, it is reputedly the oldest in the town. At n° 53, there is a fine façade with ogee-shaped tympana.

Grote Kerksbuurt

The house at n° 56 has a charming façade.

Additional Sights

Dordrechts Museum

Open Tue–Sun 11am–5pm. Closed 25 Dec and 1 Jan. 6€. 078 648 21 48. www.museum.dordt.nl.

This museum contains works by 17C artists who were born in the town, namely Albert Cuyp, Nicolaes Maes and Samuel van Hoogstraten. Dutch Romanticism is present, as well as pictures illustrating The Hague School and the Amsterdam School. In the section on 18C and 19C art, special attention should be given to the biblical scenes and portraits of **Ary Scheffer**: *Self-portrait at the Age of 43* (1883) and especially *Frédéric Chopin*, a remarkable picture of the great composer (1847). Various 20C artistic movements, such as magic realism and CoBrA , are also represented in the museum's collections.

Arend Maartenshof

This old almshouse (1625) has kept its original character with small low houses surrounding a courtyard.

Boat trips

For information and reservations, contact the tourist office.
www.vvvdordrecht.nl.
Dordrecht is the departure point for boat trips through the Biesbosch.

Excursion

Hollandse Biesbosch

8km/5mi east of Dordrecht. Via the N 3, take the Hollandse Biesbosch turn-off.
This is the northern section of De Biesbosch National Park (*see BREDA, Excursions*). In the **visitor centre** (*Baanhoekweg 53, 3313 LP Dordrecht; open Sept–Apr, Tue–Sun 9am–5pm; May and Jun Mon 1pm–5pm, Tue–Sun 9am–5pm; Jul and Aug, daily 9am–5pm; closed 25 Dec and 1 Jan; No charge; 078 630 53 53; http://cms.dordrecht. nl/biesbosch or www.biesbosch.rog*), an exhibition and slide show give an account of the origins of the area and its inhabitants. Outside the visitor centre there is a special place from which visitors can watch beavers at work and at play. Biesbosch also has plenty to offer walking and boating enthusiasts.

EDAM

NOORD-HOLLAND
POPULATION (WITH VOLENDAM) 28 000

An important cheese centre, Edam is a small, quiet and charming town, criss-crossed by canals still lined with a few fine 17C houses. It is overlooked by the **Speeltoren** a tall tower with a carillon, all that remains of a church demolished in the 19C. The town was formerly a busy port on the Zuiderzee, known for its shipyards.

- **Information:** Damplein 1 – 1135 BK. ☎0299 31 51 25. www.vvv-edam.nl.
- ▶ **Orient Yourself:** Head for the tourist information centre, which lies in the heart of the town; all the roads and canals radiate from here in a grid-like fashion.
- **Parking:** Parking in Edam is mostly off-street and free.
- **Don't Miss:** The Grote Kerk, which houses some valuable stained glass windows, and the Edams Museum, complete with a floating cellar.
- **Organizing Your Time:** Edam can be explored in around two hours comfortably.
- **Also See:** Volendam, where traditional costumes are still worn although these days mostly for the many tourists who visit the pretty harbourside village. It is around 5km/3mi from Edam.

Sights

Damplein

The main square on either side of the Damsluis, laid out in 1624, is overlooked by the 18C **stadhuis** (town hall) with its clock tower.

A lovely 16C house, built around 1530 and the oldest brick building in the town, with a shop at the front, contains the small local museum, the **Edams Museum** (open Apr–Oct, Tue–Sat 10am–4.30pm, Sun and public holidays 1pm–4.30pm; 3€; ☎029 937 26 44; www.edamsmuseum.nl (in Dutch)) It has a quite exceptional feature: a cellar that floats on groundwater.

Edam Cheese

Originally made in Edam, the famous cheese is now made in several other regions. It is prepared with slightly skimmed milk and is similar in texture to Gouda, but differs in its easily identifiable shape: a ball with a yellow crust, covered with a thin red coating if it is for export. Dutch Edam has been exported since the 16C.

Kaasmarkt

This square is the site of the former cheese market. Cheese was sold her from about 1778 until 1922 and the tradition has been restored as a tourist attraction during July and August on Wednesdays. The **Kaaswaag** (open Apr–Oct, daily 10am–5pm; ☎0299 31 51 25), where cheese was weighed, is decorated with painted panels and now houses an **exhibition** on cheese-making.

Grote Kerk or St Nicolaaskerk

Open Apr–Oct, daily 2pm–4.30pm. ☎0299 31 51 25.

The 15C church has lovely early 17C stained-glass windows and a fine organ. Two major fires in the town, in 1602 and 1699, were first thought to have been caused by lightning striking the church tower. As a result, when the church was being repaired in the early 18C, the height of the tower was reduced and anchors in the shape of numerals were added to the walls.

EINDHOVEN

NOORD-BRABANT
POPULATION 206 500
TOWN PLAN IN THE CURRENT EDITION OF THE MICHELIN GUIDE BENELUX

This industrial centre continues to grow. In 1900 Eindhoven had barely 5 000 inhabitants; now it is the fifth largest city in the Netherlands. Textile and cigar factories began appearing here in the early 19C, but by the end of the century they had been supplanted by Philips and, in 1928, by Van Doorne's Aanhangwagen Fabrieken, better known as DAF. Because of its industrial importance, Eindhoven was bombed several times during the Second World War, and hardly any historic buildings survived.

- **Information:** Stationsplein 17 – 5611 AC. ☎0900 11 22 363. www.vvveindhoven.nl.
- ▶ **Orient Yourself:** Eindhoven is fashioned in a modern grid-like network of roads that often lead to industrial areas. As a visitor, head for the town hall where most of the attractions are located in the immediate area.
- **Parking:** Eindhoven has many car parking areas (fees apply), complemented by off-street parking which is often free.
- **Don't Miss:** The Stedelijk Van Abbemuseum; its collection of paintings from some of the world's greatest artists is quite outstanding.
- **Organizing Your Time:** Allow three hours to see the main attractions of Eindhoven. Allow a further hour to visit Nuenen, where the life of Vincent van Gogh is celebrated remarkably well. It is around 8km from Eindhoven.
- **Especially for Kids:** The vehicles in the DAF museum, the environment education centre and the openair museum should all appeal to children.

A Bit of History

The "city of light" – Eindhoven owes its spectacular expansion mainly to Philips, which expanded from a simple light bulb factory into an international electronics giant.

On the eastern edge of the city, on Noord-Brabantlaan, stands the **Evoluon**, a huge building (1966) supported by 12 V-shaped concrete pillars and resembling a large flying saucer. It was designed for Philips' 75th anniversary by the two architects, Kalff and De Bever, and is currently used as a conference centre.

A modern city – Eindhoven is a pleasant city, with particularly attractive pedestrian precincts. As the visitor drives into the city from a northerly direction, the sculptural installation entitled **Flying Pins** by Claes Oldenburg and Coosje van Bruggen, situated at the top of the Kennedylaan and Fellenoord, is a real eyecatcher. It consists of 10 tenpins (7m/23ft high) that fly around. The

city is well provided with recreational activities, with parks like the **De IJzeren Man** the environment education centre **Milieu Educatiecentrum Eindhoven** (*Genneperweg 145;* ◷*open Tue–Fri 9am–5pm, Sat–Mon and public holidays 1pm–5pm;* ◷*closed Easter Sunday, Whitsun, 25, 26 Dec and 1 Jan;* ⊝*no charge;* ☎*040 259 47 00; www.mecehv. nl*) is also worth a visit

The Eindhoven carnival is always a lively and popular event (⒝ *see Calendar of events*). The city also has one of Europe's leading technical universities.

Van Abbemuseum★

Bilderdijklaan 10. ◷*Open Tue–Sun 11am–5pm.* ◷*Closed 25 Dec and 1 Jan.* ⊜*8.50€.* ♿ ☎ *040 238 10 00. www.vanabbe museum.nl.*
The museum has a rich collection of paintings and sculpture from 1900 to the present, concentrating especially on contemporary art since 1945.

NBTC

Van Abbemuseum

The collection consists of an overview of modern art: the Cubism of Picasso, Braque and Juan Gris; Orphism or poetic interpretation of the real with Delaunay, Chagall and Fernand Léger; the De Stijl movement with Mondrian and Van Doesburg; Constructivism with a great number of works by El Lissitzky; the Expressionism of Kokoschka, Kandinsky and Permeke; and Surrealism with Miró, Ernst, Pieter Ouborg, and Francis Bacon.

Postwar artists include French abstract painters such as François Bazaine and

Philips and Eindhoven: a Company Town

In 1891, Gerard Philips set up a light bulb assembly plant on Emmasingel. After five difficult years his brother Anton (whose statue now stands at the railway station) came to his aid, and from then onwards the business took off in a big way. The factory began making radio valves, X-ray tubes and medical equipment, and exporting them across Europe. In 1914 Gerard set up the natural sciences laboratory Natlab, which has since been responsible for many important forms of new technology. Later, in collaboration with DAF, Philips established the Technical College (1955), now Eindhoven Technical University.

By 1929, Philips had 20 000 employees and provided jobs for 70% of the local workforce. It opened new factories and offices on Emmasingel and Mathildelaan with names like De Witte Dame (The White Lady), De Bruine Heer (The Brown Man) and De Lichttoren (The Lighthouse). The city council could not keep up with this dramatic expansion, and Philips began building its own facilities for employees and their families: a theatre, library, schools, and most importantly housing, such as the Philipsdorp garden village on Frederiklaan (*see Introduction, Industrial heritage*). The company also set up its own sports club, Philips Sportvereniging, whose football team is one of the country's best-known.

However, the close ties between Philips and Eindhoven ended in 1998, when the company moved its headquarters to Amsterdam. Now new uses are being sought for its many buildings. De Witte Dame and De Bruine Heer will house offices, apartments, small businesses, the Design Academy, the European Design Centre and the public library. The small light bulb factory opposite, where it all began, is now open to the public.

Serge Poliakoff (1906–1969) of the École de Paris.

The CoBrA movement is represented by Christiaan Karel Appel, Asger Jorn and Pierre Corneille. There are also works by Jean Dubuffet and Antoni Tàpies, Victor Vasarely, Lucio Fontana, Klein, the Zero group (Heinz Mack, Chloe Piene and Günther Uecker), and the Americans of Pop Art including Morris Louis, Robert Indiana and Frank Stella.

Conceptual Art and contemporary German painting (Anselm Kiefer, Georg Baselitz, A R Penck) are also represented.

Additional Sights

The centre
The area between Vestdijk and Keizersgracht houses the modern **Muziekcentrum Frits Philips** and the **De Heuvel Galerie** shopping centre.

Museum Kempenland
St Antoniusstraat 5–7. ⏱*Open Tue–Sun, 1pm–5pm.* ⏱*Closed Easter Day, 25 Dec and 1 Jan.* 🎫*2.50€; children 1.25€.* ☎*040 252 90 93. www.museumkempen land.nl (in Dutch).*
This museum, housed in the old Steentjeskerk, evokes the history and customs of the town and its hinterland, Kempenland. The collections concern archaeology, beliefs, textiles and handicrafts.

DAF Museum
Tongelresestraat 27. ⏱*Open Tue–Sun 10am–5pm.* ⏱*Closed Easter, Whitsun, 24, 25, 31 Dec and 1 Jan.* 🎫*5€.* ☎*040 244 43 64. www.dafmuseum.nl.*
A collection of some 50 lorries, buses and semi-trailers, and some 40 cars, chronicles DAF production from 1928 to the present day. A permanent exhibition is devoted to Charles Burki who worked as a freelance designer for DAF for 30 years.

Historisch Openluchtmuseum Eindhoven
Boutenslaan 161b. ⏱*Open Apr–Oct, daily 10am–5pm. Nov–Mar, Sun 1pm–5pm.* ⏱*Closed 25, 26, 31 Dec and 1 Jan.* 🎫*7€; children 3.50€.* ☎*040 252 22 81.*

www.historisch-openluchtmuseum-eindhoven.nl (in Dutch).
This settlement from the Iron Age (750–50 BC) has been reconstructed on the basis of excavations in Noord-Brabant and Kempen, using simple tools and natural materials. Actors re-enact the daily activities of the Iron Age: there is a forge with a blacksmith at work, a weaving-shed where wool is being dyed, ovens where pots are being fired and bread baked, people working in the fields, and a cattle pen where pigs are being reared. The museum particularly comes to life at weekends and when special events are held.

Excursions

Nuenen
8km/5mi northeast of Eindhoven.
This town preserves the memory of **Vincent van Gogh** (🎫*see AMSTERDAM, Museum district*) who came to live in the presbytery where his parents lived. He lived here from December 1883 to November 1885, and it was then that he made a large number of studies of peasants' heads which he would later use in his great canvas *The Potato Eaters*. Two monuments and the **Van Gogh Documentatiecentrum** (⏱*open Tue–Sun 11am–4pm;* ⏱*closed public holidays;* 🎫*3€;*☎*040 283 96 15*), containing some hundred photographs of paintings and drawings from the years Van Gogh spent in Nuenen, preserve the memory of his time here.

Kasteel Heeze
12km/7.4mi southeast of Eindhoven. 🚶*By guided tour only. Tours Mar–Oct, Sun 2pm and 3pm, Wed 2pm. Jul–Aug also Wed 3pm.* ☎*040 226 44 35. www.kasteelheeze.nl (in Dutch).*
This 17C castle, designed by Pieter Post, has been the home of the Van Tuyll family for more than 200 years. Behind the castle lies the original 15C castle Eymerick. Inside, the drawing rooms with their fine tapestries, a bedroom and a bathroom can be viewed.

Helmond

38km/24mi. Leave to the northeast by the A 270. This is an active textile manufacturing centre.

Kasteel Helmond★ is an imposing medieval **castle** consisting of a quadrilateral building with an inner courtyard, an encircling moat and a park. The castle houses the **Gemeentemuseum** (Municipal museum; ◷*open Tue–Fri 10am–5pm, Sat–Sun and public holidays, 1pm–5pm;* ◷*closed Carnival, 25 Dec and 1 Jan;* ✏4€; ☏0492 58 77 16; www. gemeentemuseumhelmond.nl).

Asten

To the northwest of this village lies the **Beiaard- en Natuurmuseum Asten** (◷*open Tue–Fri 9.30am–5pm, Sat–Mon 1pm–5pm;* ◷*closed Carnival, 25 Dec and 1 Jan;* ✏4.70€; ☏0493 69 18 65; www.carillon-museum.nl), a museum of carillons and natural history.

The **carillon section**★ has information on bell-making, a collection of bells from all over the world, and clocks, carillons and chiming mechanisms, some of which can be played.

The natural history section displays dioramas with stuffed animals, butterflies and insects from De Groote Peel.
There is also a peat-bog garden and a bat cellar.

Nationaal Park De Groote Peel★

Access to the south by Moostdijk, near Meijelse Dijk. ◷*Open daily, dawn–dusk.* ☏ *0495 64 14 97. www.nationaal-park degrootepeel.nl.*
To the southeast of Asten stretches a large marshy area (1 400ha/3 460 acres) called **De Peel** (*peel* meaning marsh). This **peatland nature reserve** has been a **protected national park** since 1985. It has one of the most varied bird populations in western Europe
The visitor centre, **Bezoekerscentrum Mijl op Zeven** (◷*open Tue–Sun 10am–5pm; Jul–Aug, daily 10am–5pm;* ◷*closed 25 Dec and 1 Jan;* ☏0495 64 14 97), has documentation on the nature reserve itself and the local flora and fauna.

EMMEN

DRENTHE
POPULATION 108 500
LOCAL MAP SEE HUNEBEDDEN

The prosperous market centre of Emmen is a pleasant town bordered to the north and the east by fine forests. The southern end of the Hondsrug has numerous hunebedden, prehistoric funerary monuments.

- 🛈 **Information:** Hoofdstraat 22, 7811 EP. ☏0591 61 30 00. www.vvvemmen.nl (in Dutch and German).
- ▶ **Orient Yourself:** Emmen's heart, and most of its attractions for the visitor, are located in the immediate area of the tourist information office in Hoofdstraat. It is an ideal area from which to begin a tour of the town.
- 🅿 **Parking:** Emmen is a modern town that provides car parks (various fees apply) for its visitors.
- ☺ **Don't Miss:** Noorder Dierenpark, this remarkable zoo is well worth visiting when in Emmen. It is home to rare butterflies, apes, crocodiles and a whole host of species from the African continent; a cafeteria provides a welcome break. Orvelte, a charming village (no cars allowed) where traditional crafts and agricultural procedures are still performed as part of day-to-day life is also worth a visit.
- ◷ **Organizing Your Time:** Two hours or so could be spent exploring Emmen, but be sure to allow at least a half day in the zoo.
- Kids **Especially for Kids:** The children's farm and interactive displays at the Noorder Dierenpark zoo.

Sights

Hunebed of Emmer Dennen★ (D 45)
Access by Boslaan, direction Emmer Compascuum. It is situated near a large crossroads and is well signposted.
This remarkable hunebed, an alleyway covered with six enormous slabs encircled by uprights, was erected on a mound in the middle of the forest.

Hunebedden along the Odoorn road
Coming from the centre of Emmen towards Odoorn, after the last farm, bear left on a path signposted "hunebed." Between the trees there is a **long grave**★ (D 43). A few hundred yards further to the north, on the left-hand side of the road, there is a small hunebed (D 41) covered with capstones.
On leaving Emmen, on the right, a lane marked *hunebedden* goes through the forest to a large clearing of heather. Three hunebedden (D 38/40) stand in this lovely setting.

Noorder Dierenpark★   Kids
Open daily from 10am. 18.50€. 0591 85 08 50. www.zoo-emmen.nl (in Dutch and German only).
This zoo is particularly interesting for its great variety of species. The starting point is **Biochron**, where the beginning of life on Earth is explained. Visitors then walk from one continent to another. The seal pool and the **African House** with crocodiles and naked mole-rats are other attractions. A 1.5ha/4 acre area of **African Savannah** is home to giraffes, zebras, antelopes, rhinoceroses, cranes, and impalas, and beneath the children's farm there is also a new "sewer" full of rats.

Excursions

Noorsleen★, Schoonoord and Orvelte★ – 40km/ 25mi to the west – local map See HUNEBEDDEN.

Noordsleen
This charming village of the Drenthe, with a restored mill, has two hunebedden. *Access by the small road to Zweeloo and a lane on the right signposted "hunebedden" (D 51).* On the left is a small covered alleyway, still topped by three capstones (four have disappeared). Further on the right, the **hunebed**★ (D 50) shaded by a large oak which grows in its centre is better preserved.

Schoonoord
3.5km/2mi to the south of the locality, in the woods near a riding centre, a hunebed (D 49) has been partially reconstructed. Above, the heather-covered ground forms a mound and hides the large slabs which form the hunebed's roof.

Orvelte★
This car-free **museum-village** (*open Apr, Jul, Aug, daily 10am–5pm; May, Jun, Sept, Oct, Tue–Sun 10am–5pm; 0593 32 23 35; www.orvelte.net (in Dutch))* in the heart of the Drenthe comprises a collection of typical farmhouses and barns with thatched roofs. Many of the villagers still go about the traditional agricultural activities and keep alive traditional crafts and trades, including miller, blacksmith, clog-maker and potter.

Coevorden
21km/13mi to the southwest.
An old fortified town designed by **Menno van Coehoorn** Coevorden has kept several interesting monuments. The **castle** is a fine building and part of it is occupied by the town hall; in the basement there is a restaurant. Near Markt (*Friesestraat nº 9*), there is a picturesque late-Renaissance **house** with voluted gables and ornamentation: bright red shells, heads of women, cherubs, Moors, and inscriptions. On Marktplein, facing the docks are the three 17C roofs of the Arsenal (restored), which contains the local museum, **Gemeentemuseum Drenthe's Veste** (*open Tue–Fri 10am–5pm, Sat 10am–3pm; closed public holidays; 3.50€; 0524 51 62 25; www.museumcoevorden.nl (in Dutch)).*

ENKHUIZEN★

NOORD-HOLLAND
POPULATION 17 500

Enkhuizen was the main Frisian settlement and seat of their chiefs until 1289 when West Friesland passed to the counts of Holland. The town had one of the largest herring fishing fleets which brought great prosperity; three herrings figure on the town's coat of arms. Enkhuizen is linked to Lelystad, the main town of Flevoland, by the dyke road (*31km/19mi*). This was originally to have enclosed the fifth and last polder around the edge of the IJsselmeer (*local map see IJS-SELMEER*), but the Markerwaard project was abandoned in 1986.

- **Information:** Tussen Twee Havens 1 – 1601 EM. ☎0228 31 31 64. www.vvvenkhuizen.nl.
- **Orient Yourself:** From the station (which is on the main line to and from Amsterdam) head north to the town centre and follow the signs to the Westerkerk. It is central to all the main attractions Enkhuizen offers its visitors.
- **Parking:** Town centre car parks (fees vary) are plentiful and there's free parking the further you go out of central Enkhuizen.
- **Don't Miss:** The Westerkerk; it is a beautiful 16C Gothic style church with a free-standing tower made of wood. It is worth venturing inside to admire its eleborate interior.
- **Especially for Kids:** The open-air museum is the main draw.
- **Organizing Your Time:** Allow around 5 hours to really absorb the character of the old town, but stay overnight if you want to sample one of Enkhuizen's fine restaurants.

Boat trips

Leave from Spoorhaven for Stavoren three times a day. Information from ☎0228 32 66 67. To Urk (1hr 30min): late Jun–early Sept, Mon–Sat, three times a day. Information from ☎0228 31 31 64. www. veerboot.info.
Boats leave from Spoorhaven for Stavoren, Urk and Medemblik (in combination with the steam tram).

A Bit of History

Enkhuizen was fortified in the mid 16C, and it was one of the first towns to revolt against the Spanish in 1572. In the 17C the town had approximately 50 000 inhabitants, but as the port began to silt up in the 18C, Enkhuizen's maritime activities started to dwindle. Once they had ceased entirely with the building of the Barrier Dam in 1932, the town looked to its rich agricultural hinterland for a living and today it is an important market town and centre for bulb-growing.

The marina is also an important asset of the town.

Old Town★

Enkhuizen has numerous 17C façades in Renaissance style, their fine decoration bearing witness to its former prosperity.

Westerstraat
This is the town's main street. There are lovely façades, notably that of no 158 to the north, dating from 1617 with the town emblem on a gable: a young girl bearing a coat of arms depicting three herrings.

Westerkerk or St Gomaruskerk
Westerstraat 138. ◷Open end Jun–mid-Aug, Wed–Sat 1pm–5pm; www.westerk erkenkhuizen.nl.
This hall church was completed in 1519. Its free-standing wooden tower built in the 16C on a stone base was rebuilt in the 19C in the Neoclassical style. Inside, the

Enkhuizen city gate

three naves are covered with a wooden vault. There is also a fine wooden **rood screen**★ with six richly carved panels (16C), a pulpit (16C), which is a replica of the one found in the Grote Kerk in The Hague, and a 1547 organ case.

Opposite the church is the former Mint of West Friesland, **West-Friese Munt**, with a lovely, finely decorated façade dating from 1617. Further on at n° 109, the façade of the Orphanage, or **Weeshuis**, has been rebuilt in the style of the original façade (1616).

▶ *Turn right to take Melkmarkt and Venedie.*

Dijk

At n° 32, a house (1625) displays the motto: "Contentement passe rychesse" (happiness is worth more than riches).

Drommedaris★

This imposing and well-known building (now a café and restaurant) which was part of the town walls was, like the one in Hoorn, intended for keeping watch over the entrance to the port. It consists of a circular tower and an adjoining gatehouse. Note the decoration above the doorway. It has a carillon cast by Hemony, which is one of the best in the country. From the top there is a **panorama**★ of Enkhuizen,

its port, the IJsselmeer lake and in the distance Friesland.

From the quay to the south of the tower, there is a fine **view**★ to the east over the docks (Zuiderspui) and the backs of houses with picturesque wooden oriels overlooking flowered gardens.

Zuiderspui

This short street has some interesting façades: n° 1 has five coats of arms, from left to right can be seen those of Hoorn (a horn), the House of Orange, West Friesland, Enkhuizen and Medemblik. This is the home of the **Flessenscheepjesmuseum** (◷open Jan–Oct, daily noon–5pm, weekends only early Jan–mid-Feb; ◷closed 25 Dec, 26 Dec and 1 Jan; ⊚3€; ☏0228 31 85 83), which contains over 500 large and small bottles with ships inside. A video film shows how the ships were put inside the bottles.

Breedstraat

Several houses have interesting façade stones, notably n° 81, called Den Kuiser Maegt (the young girl from Enkhuizen), depicting the town's coat of arms; no 60, an old boat, and no 59, a young girl also holding the town's coat of arms.

Stadhuis

The town hall is an imposing building dating from 1686. The interior is deco-

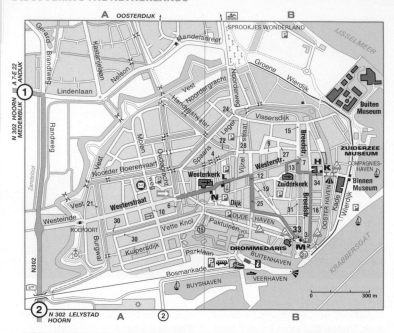

rated with painted ceilings, tapestries and murals.

On the corner of Zwaanstraat stands the **old prison** a small building, which today functions as exhibition space and whose picturesque façade dates from 1612.

Zuiderzeemuseum★★   Kids

⊙Open Apr–Oct, 10am–5pm. ⊙Closed 25 Dec and 1 Jan. ☞12.50€; children 7.50€. Combined ticket 11.50€; children 9€. ♿☎0228 35 11 11. www.zuider zeemuseum.nl.

The Zuiderzee Museum is made up of two sections: an indoor and an outdoor museum.

Binnenmuseum★★

The indoor museum consists of twelve linked buildings around three court-yards. Some are 17C houses and ware-houses formerly belonging to the Dutch East India Company. The covered reception hall is reached via the first court-yard, which preserves much of the atmosphere of the Golden Age, and the second, where the ship collection is visible through a glass wall.

The museum has a variety of permanent and temporary **exhibitions**. One, entitled **Walvisvaart**, uses maps, paintings (including the life-size Catching a whale off the coast of Spitsbergen, Storck, 1690), tools and various objects to evoke the whaling industry, highly active in the region from the 17C to the 19C. The ship collection in the **Schepenhal** has a number of old vessels, including woo-den sailing boats which used to cruise along the Zuiderzee, a flat-bottomed

Zuiderzeemuseum, Enkhuizen

Zuiderzeemuseum

fishing boat and a vessel from Urk which was pulled along the ice.

The beautifully restored **pepper store** looks and smells just as it did when it was owned by the East India Company in the 18C. Other exhibitions deal with fishing in the **North Sea and Zuiderzee** the region's constant **battle against the water** (including a computer animation on the subject of the Afsluitdijk), and **water transport**. Together, they give a varied picture of seven centuries of Zuiderzee history.

Buitenmuseum★★   Kids

Wierdijk 12–22. ⏲Open daily. 10am–5pm. 🎟12.50€; 7.50€. www.zuiderzee museum.nl (in Dutch only).

This museum is a reminder of daily life in the old Zuiderzee fishing ports between 1880 and 1932, completion date of the Barrier Dam (Afsluitdijk). More than 130 shops, houses and workshops from around 30 localities have been reconstructed to make up this charming **village-museum**. Everything in the museum conspires to evoke life in bygone days: the furniture, the tools, the layout of the gardens, the church from old Wierengen Island and the reconstruction of Marken port in 1830. Visitors may buy old-fashioned sweets, go for a ride on an old boat, or see the sailmaker, ropemaker and fish curer at work. Shops and manufacturing are also well represented: there is a spice shop, a butcher's, a pharmacy, a steam laundry, an agricultural credit bank and even three lime kilns.

Children can dress up in a traditional costume during their visit, and there is a **children's island** where they can investigate how children lived in Marken around 1930.

There is also a **nature reserve** attached to the museum, containing plants, birds and a duck enclosure .

▶ *Return to Westerstraat.*

Here, too, there are also lovely gables, shop signs and façade stones (a cooking pot, a bull's head, and more.).

The Gaper, a Typically Dutch Phenomenon

In the Art Nouveau pharmacy, De Grote Gaper, there is a colourful collection of heads with their tongues sticking out. These humorous images, known as gapers, were used as shop signs by Dutch pharmacists. They were a reminder that people had to open their mouths wide when taking the medicines they sold, and of course patients also had to show their tongues to the doctor.

ENSCHEDE

OVERIJSSEL
POPULATION 154 888

Enschede, situated in the green countryside of the Twente region, is the largest town in Overijssel province. An important industrial centre, it specialises mainly in textiles.

- **Information:** Oude Markt 31 – 7511 GB. ☎053 432 32 00. www.vvvenschede.nl (in Dutch and German).
- ▶ **Orient Yourself:** Enschede is a city in the east of the country, in the province of Overijssel.
- **Parking:** Use the parking areas indicated around town.
- **Don't Miss:** Learning about Enschede's history at Museum TwenteWelle.
- **Organizing Your Time:** There is a lot to see, so an overnight stay is a possibility. See www.hotels.nl/en/enschede for more information
- **Especially for Kids:** The open-air museum at Ootmarsum.

A Bit of History

Enschede's rapid expansion was due to the development of industry only started at the beginning of the 19C. Severely damaged by fire in 1862 and bombarded in 1944, it is, today, a modern city. On 13 May 2000 the town was hit by another disaster, when there was an explosion at a fireworks factory, killing 21 people and destroying nearly 400 homes The vast campus of Twente University, founded in 1964, lies to the northwest of the town.

Six-year-old-girl (1594) by Jan Claesz

Collection Rijksmuseum Twenthe, Enschede/Photo by R. Klein Gotink

Rijksmuseum Twenthe★

Open Tue–Sun 11am–5pm. Closed 25 Dec and 1 Jan. ◉4€; children free. ☎053 435 86 75. www.rijksmuseumtwenthe.nl.
The museum boasts a large collection of art and decorative arts.

Old Masters and Applied arts★

Right-hand wing. The pre-20C and decorative arts section in the right-hand wing is an atmospheric display in differently-coloured rooms. It includes superb medieval **manuscripts** and **late-Medieval painting** and there are also **16C and 17C landscapes** by Brueghel the Younger, van Goyen, Ruysdael and Avercamp. There are works by Jan Steen, Teniers and Terborch, and etchings by Rembrandt. The **18C** is well represented and there is also a collection of glass, silver and furniture from this period. This section ends with **Impressionism** (Jongkind, Monet, Sisley) and an early work by Mondrian.

▶ *Return to the entrance via the passageway alongside the courtyard. From here, the collection of modern and contemporary art can be viewed in chronological order in the left-hand wing.*

Twente and the Textile Industry

The ready availability of water made it possible to wash the fibres and work the looms. Twente formerly specialised in the processing of linen, which was cultivated, retted, spun and woven on the spot. **Almelo** was the centre of this activity. Twente linen was exported to Norway and to Russia where the Vriezenveen (*7km/4.3mi to the north of Almelo*) merchants had founded a colony near St Petersburg. In the 18C, linen was replaced by cotton which was less costly; at the same time they produced in large quantities a twill of linen and cotton called bombasine (*bombazijn*). In the early 19C weaving and spinning production were industrialised with the development of looms driven by steam power.

The metallurgical industry also developed greatly at this time: in 1960, together with the textile industry, it represented 86% of the town's industrial activity. Since then the development of artificial fibres, foreign competition and economic recession have caused the decline of the textile industry. Iron and steel manufacture and processing, the building industry, the tertiary sector and technology are currently the region's developing industries.

Modern and contemporary art

Left-hand wing. Here, the emphasis is on the development of Dutch art, including **expressionists**, the Cobra group and the **Hague experimental** and informal artists such as Ouborg and Wagemaker. **Systematic serial and fundamental art** from the 1960s and 70s is also represented, as well as some contemporary painters from the Netherlands.

Additional Sights

Museum TwentseWelle

🕐*Open Tue–Sun 10am–5pm* 🕐*Closed 1 Jan, Easter Day, 30 Apr, 5 May, 25 and 31 Dec.* ✆6€. ☎*053 480 76 80. www.twentsewelle.nl.*
This new museum merges the former Museum Jannink and Natuurmuseum The museum's collections illustrate the history of the Twente since 1600, with the emphasis on the textile industry over the past 150 years. The natural history section displays rocks, fossils, etc. and **dioramas** show the main species of mammals and birds found In the Netherlands.

Volkspark

In the southeastern part of this park, one of the many green areas of Enschede, there is a monument erected to the memory of victims of World War II: a group of bronze statue by the sculptor **Mari Andriessen**.

Stadhuis

The town hall was built in 1933 by G Friedhoff, who was influenced by Stockholm's town hall. This rather austere brick building is flanked by a tall, square bell-tower with slightly bulging walls.

Hervormde Kerk

This sandstone Reformed Church stands on Markt, the town's main square. It was begun c. 1200 and enlarged in the 15C but has kept its great Romanesque **tower** (13C), with its paired openings.

Driving Tour

The Verdant Region of Twente

▶ *Round trip 80km/50mi. Leave by ① on the town plan and allow about 5hrs.*

The route crosses the northern part of **Twente**. Known for its industrial activities, Twente is also a verdant region where the land, cut by waterways, is divided into pastures and magnificent forests.

Oldenzaal

This small industrial town, near the German frontier, is an old, once fortified settlement, which has kept its concentric streets around a lovely Romanesque basilica, the **St Plechelmusbasiliek**

(🕐 *open Jun–Aug, Tue and Thu 2pm–3pm, Wed 2pm–4pm; Sept, Wed 2pm–4pm.* ☎*0541 51 40 23 (VVV)*), dedicated to the Irish saint, St Plecheln.

Not far away is **Museum Het Palthehuis** (*Marktstraat 13;* 🕐 *open Tue–Fri 10am–5pm, Sat–Sun 2pm–5pm;* 🕐 *closed 1 Jan, Easter, Ascension Day, Whitsun and 25 Dec;* ☜*3€;* ☎ *0541 51 34 82; www. palthehuis.nl*). This 17C Baroque house displays traditional objects in period rooms.

Denekamp

This small town, situated in one of the loveliest parts of Twente, has kept its strange tradition of *midwinterhorens*, which translated means horns of midwinter. They are horns of carved wood which are blown at the approach of Christmas (ⓘ*see Calendar of events*) in Twente villages. Near the town stands a castle, **Kasteel Singraven** (👁️•*guided tours only, Apr–Nov, Tue and Wed at 11am, 2pm and 3pm;* 🕐 *closed public holidays;* ☜*6€;* ☎*0541 35 19 06; www. singraven.nl (in Dutch and German)*).

Ootmarsum★

This charming village with concentric streets is built on a mound, round a Gothic church. Some of the houses have elaborately decorated Renaissance façades and wooden gables. On Kerkplein stands the **Church of St Simon and St Judas**. Worthy of note are the wooden statue of the Virgin (c. 1500) at the end of the north side aisle and the modern stained-glass windows. Ootmarsum also has two small museums: the **Onderwijsmuseum Educatorium** (🕐*open Feb–Dec, Tue–Fri 10am–5pm, Sat–Mon 2pm–5pm;* 🕐 *closed Easter and 25 Dec;* ☜*3€;* ☎*0541 29 31 29; www.educatorium.nl*) which deals with the history of education, and the open-air **Openluchtmuseum Los Hoes** (🕐 *open Feb–Nov, 10am–5pm; Dec–Jan, Sat–Sun 10am–5pm;* 🕐 *closed 1 Jan and 25 Dec;* ☜*4.50€;*

☎*0541 29 30 99; www.openluchtmuseum ootmarsum.nl*).

This includes a number of barns and a carriage works around an old farmhouse of the "los hoes" type (ⓘ*see Introduction, Traditional Structures*). This gives a fine picture of how local farmers lived and worked around 1900.

▷ *Take the road to Almelo.*

Kuiperberg

From the belvedere on top of the Kuiperberg (alt 65m/213ft) there is a **view** over Ootmarsum and the wooded countryside.

▷ *Continue to Delden via Almelo and Borne.*

Delden

Kasteel Twickel stands to the north of the town, surrounded by moats and lovely **gardens** (🕐*open May–Oct, Tue–Sat 11am–5pm; last entry 4pm;* ☜*5€;* ☎*074 376 10 20; www.twickel.nl*).

The **Grote Kerk or St Blasiuskerk**, a Gothic-style sandstone hall-church, has a heavy square tower.

The old town hall (*Langestraat 30*) houses both the VVV and a small salt museum, the **Zoutmuseum** (🕐*open May–Sept, Mon–Fri 11am–5pm, Sat–Sun 2pm–5pm; Oct–Apr, Tue–Fri 2pm–5pm, Sun 2pm–5pm;* 🕐*closed 31 Dec, 1 Jan, 30 Apr, Whitsun;* ☜*3.50€;* ♿☎*074 376 45 46; www. zoutmuseum.nl (in Dutch)*). Located not far

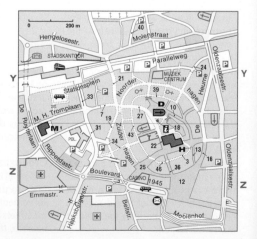

ENSCHEDE

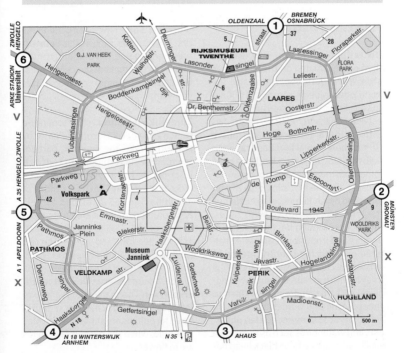

from the country's main rock salt deposits, it explains the origin, extraction and use of salt, as well as its importance to humans, animals and plants.

▶ *Return to Enschede by ⑥ on the town plan.*

FLEVOLAND ★

FLEVOLAND
POPULATION 370 700
LOCAL MAP SEE IJSSELMEER

Flevoland is in fact two polders (Oostelijk Flevoland and Zuidelijk Flevoland) which represent the most recent achievements in the Zuiderzee reclamation project (*see IJSSELMEER*).

- ⓘ **Information:** www.golelystad.nl/uk.html and www.flevoportal.nl.
- ▶ **Orient Yourself:** Flevoland covers a large area around and north of Amsterdam. It lies on either side of the IJsselmeer river and affords a network of roads to enable visitors to explore its remarkably flat landscape.
- Ⓟ **Parking:** There are many opportunities to park, usually free, at viewing areas or off-street.
- ☺ **Don't Miss:** The chance to tread the decks of the *Batavia*, a replica of a 17C merchant ship.
- ◔ **Organizing Your Time:** Allow most of a day to travel around and really explore Flevoland, including a wander around Flevoland's many windmills, open to the public.
- **Kids** **Especially for Kids:** Walibi World's Bugs Bunny World where children are welcomed by Looney Tunes cartoon characters and can enjoy amusement rides.

A Bit of History

Oostelijk Flevoland – This was the third polder created on the IJsselmeer, after Wieringermeer Polder and the Noordoost polder. An area of 54 000ha/133 437 acres, it was dyked and drained between 1950 and 1957. The largest part of this polder is destined for agriculture (75% of the area; mainly oilseed rape and bulbs) while 11% of the land has been turned into meadows and woods, 8% for housing and the rest alloted to canals, roads and dykes. Before being exploited, the land was first sown with reeds. Farmhouses hidden behind screens of poplars and enormous barns are scattered over this flat countryside, criss-crossed by clusters of young trees. Tall trees indicate an already old dwelling-place. In the fields drained by ditches, sheep, cattle and ponies graze. There are numerous lapwings, golden pheasants and water birds such as the coot, a small dark wader whose black head has a white spot.

Since 1960 towns and villages have sprung up: Lelystad, Dronten, Swifterbant, Biddinghuizen; piles placed on a sand bed ensure the stability of the construction. Wide straight roads cut across the polder. Some have been built on the ring dykes. Lakes such as the **Veluwemeer**, separating the polder from the Zuiderzee's former coast, act as regulators and have become recreational lakes with bathing areas.

Zuidelijk Flevoland – It is separated from the Oostelijk Flevoland Polder by a security dyke, the Knardijk, parts of the road being forbidden to traffic. It is surrounded by a dyke built between 1959 and 1967. In 1968 this polder of 43 000ha/106 255 acres had largely been drained. Half the area is devoted to agriculture, 25% to dwelling areas, 18% for meadows and woods. The rest is taken up by canals, dykes and roads. To the north, near Oostvaarders dyke, there is a nature reserve, **De Oostvaardersplassen** This marshland is a refuge for birds including some very rare species. The polders are at their best in May and June, when the oilseed rape fields are in flower.

Lelystad

Lelystad, capital of Flevoland, bears the name of the engineer Cornelis Lely (◔ *see IJSSELMEER*) and consists mainly of individual houses and bungalows interspersed amid the greenery. The **Agora** community cultural centre, comprising a cinema and library, marks the centre of town.

Lelystad is linked to Enkhuizen by a dyke, Markerwaarddijk (*31km/19mi*) with a road running along the top. The Oostvaardersdiep, a canal 300m/985ft wide, forms a waterway stretching between Amsterdam and the northern part of the country. The Houtribsluizen, two large locks spanning the Oostvaardersdiep, separate the Markermeer from the IJsselmeer.

Nieuwland Erfgoedcentrum `Kids`

⏰*Open Tue–Fri 10am–5pm, Sat–Sun 11.30am–5pm; also Mon Jul–Aug.* 🚫*Closed 25 Dec, 1 Jan.* ✎*7.50€; children 3.50€.* ☎*0320 26 07 99. www.nieuwland erfgoedcentrum.nl.*

This museum stands near the locks, and houses a permanent exhibition on the reclamation work carried out on the Zuiderzee. The history of the region's relationship with water is chronicled using historic film and sound recordings, models, interactive computer programs, etc., and deals with subjects as varied as fishing, trade, geology and early cultures. The construction of dykes, the creation of polders and their first inhabitants are all covered. The large "Playing with Water" model is specially designed for children.

Batavia-dock – Nationaal Scheepshistorisch Centrum★

⏰*Open daily 10am–5pm (8pm July and Aug).* 🚫*Closed 1 Jan and 25 Dec.* ✎*9.75€.* ☎*0320 26 14 09. www.bataviawerf.nl.*

Set up next to the information centre is the **Batavia**★, a replica of a merchant ship belonging to the Dutch East India Company. The original vessel was built in Amsterdam in 1628. During her maiden voyage, she ran aground on some reefs off the west coast of Australia; some of the 341 crew managed to survive the shipwreck. The wreck itself has since been salvaged, and is now on display in the West Australian Maritime Museum in Fremantle. The reconstruction of the ship was the work of a group of young people undergoing specialised training,

and began in 1985. Since the launch of the replica the dock has expanded into a shipbuilding centre using traditional techniques. Apart from the Batavia, two other vessels are on display: the Flevoaak, a modern version of a traditional barge, and a replica of De Zeven Provinciën, begun in 1995. This was the famous flagship of Admiral Michiel de Ruyter, built in 1665 and one of the largest of its time. The guided tour begins with a film in the visitor centre, and then takes visitors to see the boat and the workshops where the pulleys, sails and carved wooden sculptures are made; these recreate the atmosphere of Holland's Golden Age. The tour ends with a visit to the Batavia itself, showing how a 17C merchant vessel was a combination of a warehouse, a fortress and a community of individuals.

The **Nederlands Instituut voor Scheeps- en Onderwaterarcheologie** (Dutch Institute for Maritime Archaeology) and the **Nederlands Sportmuseum** are located beside the dock. In the **Expertisecentrum**, which looks like a ship's hull turned upside down, sections of shipwrecks – some excavated, others simply found – are examined and preserved. In time, a number of 'pavilions' will be erected between this centre and Batavia dock which will deal with a variety of maritime topics. The first of these is the **Beurtvaarderspaviljoen**, which gives an insight into the life and work of bargemen assigned to regular service and has a 17C wreck on display.

The Batavia (detail)

Aviodrome `Kids`

To the north of Lelystad on the Airship Plaza site. ◷*Open Tue–Sun 10am–5pm.* ◷*Closed 1 Jan and 25 Dec.* ⌐*14.90€; children (4–12yrs) 12.90€.* ☎*0900 284 63 76. www.aviodrome.nl.*

This museum chronicles the history of hot-air ballooning and aviation from 1783 to the present day. Exhibits include a gondola from an airship, hot-air balloon baskets and items from the Graf Zeppelin. A 'time machine' takes visitors back to 1896, recording key events in Dutch aviation history. Visitors can board the 'Pelikaan', a simulated pre-war KLM Fokker airliner and in the 'top-down' theatre visitors take on the role of passengers in a hot air balloon.

In the Fokker S11 'Instructor' you get the chance to take part in air acrobatics; a pilot loops and rolls the plane, so you need a strong stomach!

A movie theatre offers wide-screen aviation films and outside in a hangar stands a Douglas DC-2 'Uiver', the last flying DC-2 in the world. There is also a reconstruction of the Amsterdam Airport terminal building from the 1920s.

Flights in historic aircraft (the Fokker Friendship and a Catalina PH-PBY) as well as a hot-air balloon can be arranged if booked in advance.

Natuurpark Lelystad

To the east of Lelystad.

One of the exhibits in this park is a **shipwreck** dating from 1878. It has been left where it was found during drainage of the polder in 1967 and part of its cargo of bricks can be seen nearby. Elsewhere in the park, a prehistoric settlement has been reconstructed.

Additional Sights

Almere

This municipality (made up of Almere Haven, Almere Stad and Almere Buiten, Almere Hout, Almere Poort and Almere Overgooi), to the south of Flevoland and bordering the Gooimeer, was founded in 1975 and has 182 500 inhabitants; estimated to increase to 240 000 inhabitants by 2020. Almere Hout, Almere Poort and Almere Overgooi are very

recent developments. Almere, referred to as the Netherlands' 'most American city', is particularly known for its architecture, which gives every district and neighbourhood its own individuality. A number of well-known architects, including Cees Dam and Rem Koolhaas have contributed to the project. In **Museum De Paviljoens** (`Kids` *Odeonstraat 5;* ◷*open Wed, Sat noon–5pm, Thu and Fri noon–9pm, Sun 10am–5pm;* ◷*closed 1 Jan and 25 Dec;* ⌐*3€;* ☎*0365 45 04 00; www.depaviljoens.nl*) three wagon-like pavilions on stilts house temporary exhibitions of contemporary art. ☞Every Sunday, at 10am, 11am and noon, there are free guided tours of an educational kind; more suited to parents with their children than adults alone.

Walibi World `Kids`

◷*Open May–Jun, daily 10am–6pm; Jul and Aug, daily 10am–10pm; Sept and Oct, Fri–Sun 10am–6pm.* ⌐*27€; children 24.50€.* ☎*0321 32 99 99. www. walibiworld.nl (in Dutch).*

This amusement park is located on the Veluwemeer in the district of **Biddinghuizen**. The many attractions offer plenty of choice for thrill-seekers, including a variety of **roller coasters**, a white-water ride, the rotating G-Force ride and the blood-curdling Space Shot. In **Bugs Bunny World** children are welcomed by Looney Tunes cartoon characters. There are also a variety of shows, including stunt shows, and other family attractions. Six Flags Holland also has a holiday village with chalets.

Dronten

This town, standing right in the heart of the polder, was planned round a church with an openwork tower and a community centre, **De Meerpaal**. This immense glass hall, built in 1967 by Frank van Klingeren, is effectively an extension of Marktplein.

The planning of Dronten took place in the early 1950s and building work got underway in 1960. In 1995 the 18th World Scout Jamboree was held just outside the town, and nearly 30 000 scouts and staff from 166 countries gathered for the occasion.

FRANEKER★

FRYSLÂN
POPULATION 13 000

This charming small Frisian town (Frjentsjer) is the capital of te Franckeradeel municipality. Founded in 800AD, it had a famous university, founded in 1585, where Descartes became a student in 1629. It was closed in 1811 during the reign of Louis Bonaparte.

- **Information:** Dijkstraat 26 8801 LV. ☎0900 540 00 01. www.friesekust.nl (in Dutch).
- ▶ **Orient Yourself:** Franeker is 20km/12.4mi west of Leeuwarden. The town is not large and most of its visitor attractions lie around the Dijkstraat area, home to the tourist information office and the town's interesting selection of shops.
- **Parking:** Parking spaces can usually be found off-street around the town, plus there are a few inexpensive designated car parks.
- **Don't Miss:** Eise Eisinga Planetarium, which is by far Franeker's foremost attraction.
- **Organizing Your Time:** Two or three hours will give you time to see most of Franeker.
- **Especially for Kids:** Older children may appreciate the planetarium.

Sights

Stadhuis★

ⒸOpen Mon–Fri 2pm–5pm. ⒸClosed public holidays. ☎0517 38 04 80.
The town hall is a splendid building in the Dutch Mannerist style, dating from 1591, with a double gable; it is topped by an elegant octagonal tower. The Council Chamber or Raadzaal and the Registrar's Office, Trouwzaal, are hung with 18C painted leather, in rich colours.

Eise Eisinga Planetarium★

ⒸOpen Tue–Sat 10am–5pm, Sun 1pm–5pm; Apr–Oct, also open Mon 1pm–5pm. ⒸClosed 1 Jan and 25 Dec. ◉4.50€; children (under 14) 3.75€. ☎0517 39 30 70. www.planetarium-friesland.nl.
At a time when a number of his contemporaries feared the end of the world due to the exceptional position of the stars, the Frisian **Eise Eisinga** decided to prove that the situation was not dangerous. This wool-comber, who

Eise Eisinga Planetarium

NBTC

had been interested in astronomy since childhood, built in 1774–81 an ingenious system whereby the movement of the stars was depicted on his living room ceiling. Eisinga represented with surprising precision the celestial vault as known by 18C astronomers. This planetarium, whose movement can be seen in the attic, is the oldest European one in working order.

The charming House of the Corn Porters, **Korendragershuisje**, can be seen at the end of Eisingstraat.

Museum Martena

Voorstraat 35, 8801 LA, Franeker. ⏰*Open Tue–Sat 10am–5pm; Apr–Sept also open Sun 1pm–5pm.* ⏰*Closed 31 July, 25 and 26 Dec.* 5€. ☎0517 39 21 92.

The exhibits in this museum, installed in the Waag (weigh-house) and the large adjoining 17C and 18C houses, include a tribute to **Anna Maria van Schurman** (1606–1678). A celebrated entomologist and draughtsman, who belonged to the Labadist community founded by the French émigré **Jean de Labadie** (1610–1674), she advocated bringing Protestantism back to Primitive Christianity. The history of the former university is illustrated by portraits of professors and a "xylotheque" – an out-

standing collection of wood samples presented in the form of books, presented to Franeker University by Louis Bonaparte in about 1810. The museum also displays several splendid collections of Frisian silver, porcelain and glass. Note the miniature charity fête by J Kooistra. It also holds temporary exhibitions on modern art.

In the same street, at n° 35, the **Martenahuis** was built in 1498.

Martinikerk

This Gothic church has 15C paintings, and figures of saints on the pillars. The floor is strewn with finely sculptured tombstones in the Frisian style.

Weeshuis

The former orphanage's door is topped with 17C inscriptions.

Nearby, the **Cammingha-stins** is a lovely 15C and 16C residence, now housing the **Kaatsmuseum** (⏰*open mid-May–Sept, Tue–Sat, 1pm–5pm;* ⏰ *closed public holidays.* 2€; ☎0517 39 39 10), which uses photographs, prizes, emblems and a variety of documents to give visitors an insight into the popular Frisian ball game – similar to the British racquet game, fives – called Kaatsen.

GIETHOORN★★

OVERIJSSEL

The picturesque village of Giethoorn stands in the middle of the vast bogland area known as De Wieden.

- **Information:** Eendrachtsplein 1, 8355DL. ☎0900 567 46 37. www.vvvgiethoorn.nl.
- ▶ **Orient Yourself:** Giethoorn is a small village with a network of roads that hop back and forth across canals. Beulakerweg is a good place to get your bearings, but it is unlikely you will get lost here.
- 🅿 **Parking:** There is no parking in Giethoorn: the village can only be explored on foot.
- 👁 **Don't Miss:** Museumboerderij 't Olde Maat Uus, a museum that tells the story of how Giethoorn was created by man against nature.
- 🕐 **Organizing Your Time:** It is well worth venturing to Giethoorn for a relaxing afternoon's stroll in this outstandingly pretty village. Make time to visit Wanneperveen, a village 26km/16mi or so from Giethoorn, which has many thatched cottages and a notable town hall.
- **Kids Especially for Kids:** A punt on the river.

NBTC

Punting at Giethoorn

A Bit of History

Peat used to be dug here on a massive scale, creating the many lakes in this region. To transport the turf, long canals and ditches were cut, along which thatched farmhouses and peat-cutters' houses were subsequently built. Giethoorn owes its name to the great number of goats' horns (*geitehoorns*) discovered by the original settlers when they started to dig for peat.

Visit

A lakeside village – The pretty thatched cottages of Giethoorn face onto the canals spanned by hump-backed bridges or simple footbridges. The bicycle is the most popular form of transport here, although many locals use flat-bottomed punts (punters). Even bridal processions can be seen punting along the canals.
The restored working farm museum, **Museumboerderij 't Olde Maat Uus** (Kids ⊙*open May–Oct, daily 11am–5pm (Sun from noon); Nov–Apr, Sun and during school holidays noon–5pm; ☜3€; children 1€; ☎0521 36 22 44; www.old-emaatuus.nl (in Dutch)), tells the story of life in Giethoorn during the 19C.

Kameeldak roofs – The *hallenhuizen* or hall-houses (*⊚ see Introduction, Farmhouses*) are remarkable for their thatched hump-backed roofs. When more and more land was reclaimed the grain yields increased and the farmers had to extend their storage space. Since land was at a premium they extended upwards and as a consequence the farm buildings became taller than the farmhouse. Roofs with this change in level were called camel-backed (*kameeldak*). Another characteristic of these farms is that they have no carriage entrance as everything was transported by water. Hay was stored in the barn above the boat house.

The Legend of Kaatje

Kaatje (Little Kate) was an innkeeper who made her fortune back in the 18C. Her bronze statue stands by the lock in Blokzijl, and it is said that stroking her head with your left hand will bring you luck. If it is wealth you are after, then you must stroke her head with your right hand. But beware: anyone who tries to be too clever and uses both hands can expect punishment from Vrouwe van Blokzijl.

Kaatje bij de Sluis

If you are hoping for some culinary luck, then try the gourmet restaurant Kaatje bij de Sluis.

The lakes – The meres, which stretch to the east and south of the village, are vast stretches of water scattered with small reed-covered islands. The entire area is a unique ecological habitat rich in birdlife, and is a haven for recreation.

Excursions 28km/17.4mi

Wanneperveen

8.7km/5.4mi southeast of Giethoorn.
In this small town thatched cottages run for several miles alongside the road. Not

😊 A Bit of Advice 😊

No cars are allowed into the village and it must be explored on foot or by boat. Punts, motor boats, canoes and sailing boats can be hired at various points in the village and boat excursions are available. The village stretches along both sides of the Dorpsgracht, which is almost 7km/4.3mi long. The busiest part during the tourist season lies between the Centrum-Dorp turn-off and the Zuid turn-off. If you want to avoid the crowds of day-trippers – particularly in the summer months – then seek out the nearby village of Dwarsgracht and hamlet of Jonen on the other side of the canal.

far from the village's west entrance lies the **cemetery**; its free-standing bell-tower, scantily built with a few beams, is characteristic of Southern Friesland. In the main street, at n° 83, note a lovely house with a crow-stepped gable; this is the **old town hall** (1612).

Vollenhove

13km/8mi west of Wanneperveen.
The bastions of the old town ramparts are visible near the church, where pleasure boats are now moored. On **Kerkplein** stand a few fine buildings: **St Nicolaaskerk**, a Late Gothic church; the **Klokketoren** which was used as a prison; adjoining the bell-tower is the **old raadhuis** (town hall), dating from 1621 and now converted into a restaurant; finally the lovely façade of the **Latin School** – dating from 1627 and now used as a bank – has crow-stepped gables and an entrance with two carved stelae in front. The new town hall is housed in the 18C **Oldruitenborgh** manor house, opposite a church, Kleine Kerk, which stands in the midst of a fine garden, the **Historische tuin Marxveld**. In the adjoining Bisschopstraat is Vollenhove's antiquities collection, **Oudheidkamer**

Blokzijl★

6.5km/3.7mi north of Vollenhove.
This was also one of the prosperous old ports on the Zuiderzee and the Dutch East India Company used it as a haven for its East Indiamen. Today it has pleasure boats which cruise past the lovely 17C houses on the water-front.
The **Gildenhuys** (🕐 *open May–mid-Sept and during the autumn half-term holiday, Mon–Sat 1.30pm–4.30pm; Jul and Aug, Mon–Thu 7pm–9pm. ⌨2€. ☎0527 29 13 81*), in the picturesque Kerkstraat, displays the handicrafts that used to be practised in the town. A little further on the 17C **Grote Kerk** (*Information from VVV; ☎0527 29 14 14*) was one of the country's first Protestant houses of prayer. The **interior**★ with its wooden ceiling and pulpit – equipped with its very own hourglass to remind the preacher that the patience of the congregation did have limits – is also well worth a visit.

GOES

ZEELAND

POPULATION 36 600

LOCAL MAP SEE DELTA

The former port of Goes owed its prosperity to salt mining and the madder industry (the production of a red dye). Through the location of its canals it has preserved the layout of its 15C ramparts. Today Goes is the main centre of Zuid Beveland. The town is surrounded by meadows and orchards and it is linked to the Oosterschelde by a canal. A historic **steam train** (*departs Apr–Jun, Sun at 11am and 2pm; Jul and Aug, Sun–Fri at 11am, 2pm and 4pm; Sept and Oct, Sun at 2pm. 0113 27 07 05; www.destoomtrein.nl (in Dutch)*) **runs between Goes and Oudelande (south of Goes).**

- **Information:** Stationsplein 3 – 4461 HP. 0900 168 16 66. www.vvvzeeland.nl.
- **Orient Yourself:** Goes is 45.5km/28mi west of Bergen op Zoom, via the A 58.
- **Parking:** Parking here is not usually a problem.
- **Organizing Your Time:** An hour will be sufficient.
- **Also See:** MIDDELBURG.

Market day – The weekly market on Goes's Grote Markt (*Tuesdays; see Introduction, Traditions and folklore*) gives the occasional opportunity of seeing the Zeeland costumes of Zuid-Beveland.

Sights

Grote Kerk★

Open Mon–Sat 9am–noon, 1pm–6pm. 0113 21 67 68.
Part of the church dates from the 15C and was altered in early 17C after a fire. The **north portal** is finely decorated in the Flamboyant style; inside, note the 17C **organ**.

Historisch Museum De Bevelanden

Singelstraat 13, 4461 HZ Goes. Open Tue–Fri 1pm–5pm, Sat noon–4pm. Closed public holidays. 4€, 0113 22 88 83. www.hmdb.nl (in Dutch).
Housed in a former orphanage, this museum has a varied collection including traditional Beveland costumes and 17C paintings depicting archers. On the right of the museum is the former almshouse, **Oude Mannen- en Vrou-** wenhuis (1665). The depictions above the portals bear witness to the building's former use.

Turf- en Kleine Kade

To the north of Grote Markt.
These quays are lined with some fine houses.

Excursions *15km/9.3mi east – local map see DELTA*

Kapelle

The **Dutch Reformed Church** with its imposing 14C brick bell-tower and corner pinnacles is visible from afar, across the low-lying polderland.
In the nave, note the decorated balusters and heads of satyrs from the 15C.

Yerseke (or Ierseke)

This small port specialises in the culture and trade of oysters, mussels and lobsters and boasts the only mussel auction in the world. On the third Saturday in August the annual mussel festival, **Mosseldag Yerseke**, takes place, where everyone can sample the mussels free of charge.

GORINCHEM

ZUID-HOLLAND
POPULATION 34 282

On the borders of three provinces (Zuid-Holland, Noord Brabant and Gelderland), Gorinchem, often called **Gorkum**, is an important waterway junction. It lies at the confluence of two large rivers, the Waal (branch of the Rhine) and the Maas, as well as the Merwedekanaal, and a small river, the Linge. It has a large marina to the west.

- **Information:** Grote Markt 17 – 4201 EB. ☎0183 63 15 25. www.vvvgorinchem.nl. (in Dutch).
- **Orient Yourself:** Situated close to the junction of the A27 and the A15.
- **Parking:** There is ample parking space in the town.
- **Don't Miss:** The temporary exhibitions at the Gorcums Museum are usually worth checking out.
- **Organizing Your Time:** Less than an hour in town but allow for the excursion.

A Bit of History

Hooks and Cods – Gorkum dates from the 13C and because of its strategic position it has suffered numerous sieges.

In 1417 it was the site of a ferocious fight between the Hooks (Hoeken), supporters of **Jacoba** (&see GOES) who had inherited the town, and **Willem van Arkel** on the side of the Cods (Kabeljauwen). Van Arkel wished to reconquer the town, which had belonged to his father. He lost his life during a skirmish in the city.

Gorkum was one of the first strongholds wrested from the Spanish by the Beggars in 1572. Among the prisoners taken by the Beggars there were 16 priests who were executed at Brielle the same year; they are known as the martyrs of Gorkum.

Gorinchem was the birthplace of the 16C painter **Abraham Bloemaert**, who spent most of his life in Utrecht.

Historic Centre

The historic core is girdled by the star-shaped outline of the bastions and ramparts which have been transformed into an esplanade. It is crossed by the River Linge, which forms a picturesque harbour, the **Lingehaven**.

Grote Markt

The old Neoclassical **town hall** (1860) houses the VVV tourist information office and the **Gorcums Museum** (&open Tue–Sat 10am–5pm, Sun 11am–5pm (1pm Oct–Mar); &closed 1 Jan and 25 Dec; &☎0183 63 28 21; ⊚2.50€; www.gorcumsmuseum.nl), which has a collection of paintings, sculptures, models, toys and silver chronicling the town's history. The town's collection (Stadscollectie) consists mainly of works by modern and contemporary local artists, including Ad Dekkers, which are displayed in temporary exhibitions.

At nº 23 Grote Markt is the **Hugo de Grootpoortje**, a small Baroque structure which is all that remains of the house where the famous jurist and scholar, Hugo Grotius, fled after escaping from prison in Slot Loevestein (&see Excursions).

Groenmarkt

The 15C **Grote Kerk or St Maartenskerk** is located in this square. The church's tall early 16C Gothic tower, **St Janstoren** (Information from VVV; ☎0183 63 15 25),is particularly worth seeing. The builders realised during its construction that the tower was leaning to one side, but all they could do was adjust the top part of the tower accordingly.

GORINCHEM		Hoge Torenstr.	15	Pompstr.	28
		Hoogstr.	16	Robberstr.	30
Appeldijk	3	Kalkhaven	14	Tolsteeg	31
Blauwe Torenstr.	4	Kelenstr.	18	Torenstr.	33
Boerenstr.	6	Kruisstr.	19	Vijfde Uitgang	34
Bornsteeg	7	Langendijk	21	Visbrug	36
Burgstr.	9	Lombardstr.	22	Vismarkt	35
Dalembolwerk	10	Molenstr.	24	Walstr.	37
Gasthuisstr.	12	Nieuwe Waalsteeg	25	Westwagenstr.	39
Groenmarkt	13	Peterburg	27	Zusterhuis	40

Burgerkinderenweeshuis	A	Hugo de Grootpoortje	S
Gorcums Museum	M	Huis 't Coemt al van God'	V

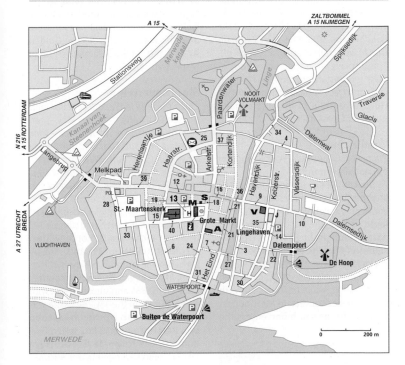

Burgerkinderenweeshuis

On the 18C façade of the old orphanage, also called **Huize Matthijs-Marijke**, a carved stone depicts Christ and children, between the founders of the orphanage.

Huis " 't Coemt al van God"

A narrow-fronted house with a crow-stepped gable, decorated with Renaissance-style medallions (1563).

Dalempoort

This lovely, small rampart gateway, square with a high roof topped by a pinnacle, dates from 1597. It is the only one of the town's four gateways to remain. From here, the tall wall mill called **De Hoop** (meaning Hope 1764), is visible.

Buiten de Waterpoort

This tree-lined esplanade stretches from the south of the old water-gate (Waterpoort), which was closed in 1894 to enlarge the road. Boat trips leave from this landing stage. There is a fine **view** over Dalempoort, the mill and the river. To the southeast, on the opposite bank, the tall bell-tower of the church of Woudrichem and the pink brick Slot Loevestein rise above the greenery.

Excursions

Leerdam

17km/10.5mi to the northeast.
Leave via Spijksedijk.

This town, situated on the Linge, has been the main glass-making centre in the Netherlands since the first glassworks was established here in 1795. To the southwest, in a villa on the Oosterwijk road (Lingedijk 28), is the **Nationaal Glasmuseum** (◷*open Tue–Sat 11am–5pm, Sun noon–5pm;* ◷*closed public holidays.* ⊜*4.50€;* ☎*0345 61 27 14; (in Dutch) www.nationaalglasmuseum.nl).* This displays interesting collections of glass and crystal from Leerdam (19C and 20C) and from various other countries (18C, 19C, and 20C). Leerdam also has a number of glass galleries.

Woudrichem

21km/13mi to the south. Leave Gorinchem by Westwagenstraat.

At the confluence of the Rhine (Waal) and the Maas, this small fortified town, commonly called **Workum**, is still enclosed in its encircling bastioned ramparts. Through the Peace of Woudrichem in 1419, John of Bavaria obtained important rights over the territories of his niece, Jacoba (ↆ*see GOES*). Workum has a small pleasure boat harbour with a ferry to Slot Loevestein for foot passengers. To the south one enters the

town by **Koepoort**. On the right is the squat **tower** of the Late Gothic church, the walls of which are decorated with medallions. Near the 15C prison gate, **Gevangenpoort**, in Hoogstraat, the **Oude Raedthuys** (nº 47) has a graceful Renaissance-style façade with a crow-stepped gable. In the same street, at nº 37, note a façade stone depicting an axe chopping wood, and opposite, twin houses of 1593 and 1606, whose façade stones are sculpted to depict a golden angel and a salamander. Note also the inscriptions, "In the Golden Angel" and "In the Salamander", their respective names.

Slot Loevestein★

Catch the ferry in Woudrichem (for foot-passengers only). ◷*Open May–Sept, Tue–Fri 10am–5pm, Sat–Mon 1pm–5pm; Oct and Apr, Sat, Sun, Wed 1pm–5pm; Nov–Mar, Sat, Sun, Wed 1pm–4pm.* ◷*Closed 1 Jan, 25, 26 and 31 Dec.* ⊜*6.80€.* ☎*0183 44 71 71. www.slot loevestein.nl.*

This solid fortress in pink brick is flanked with four square towers and surrounded by moats and ramparts. Slot Loevestein was built between 1357 and 1368 by Dirk Loef van Horne. The Count of Holland, Albrecht van Beieren (of Bavaria), seized it in 1385 and surrounded it with an enclosure. In the 15C the castle was transformed into a prison by **Jacoba van Beieren** who had just seized Gorkum. In 1619 **Hugo de Groot** (ↆ*see DELFT*), who had been taken prisoner the previous year, was imprisoned in Loevestein. There he devoted himself to the preparation of legal and theological works. His escape remains legendary. He managed to escape in March 1621 by hiding in a chest which had been used to bring him books. Inside the castle, it is possible to visit large rooms with lovely chimneypieces. In one of these rooms is the chest used by Hugo de Groot for his escape.

Kouprianoff/ MICHELIN

Slot Loevestein

GOUDA ★

ZUID-HOLLAND
POPULATION 71 873

Gouda (pronounced howdah) owes its fame to the stained glass in the church, its cheese, its syrup waffles, its pipes and its pottery. Situated at the confluence of the Hollandse IJssel and the Gouwe, this peaceful town is criss-crossed by several canals.

- **Information:** Markt 27 – 2801 JJ. ☎0182 58 32 10. www.vvvgouda.nl.
- ▶ **Orient Yourself:** The moment you arrive in Gouda head straight for the Markt, because from this rather striking marketplace, one of the largest in the Netherlands, all of Gouda's attractions can be found in a radius of less than a mile (1km).
- **Parking:** Gouda welcomes visitors and provides inexpensive car parking facilities on the outskirts of town, within easy walking distance.
- **Don't Miss:** Kaasexposeum, a museum that tells the story of cheese and how important the industry has always been to Gouda.
- **Organizing Your Time:** Gouda is the ideal place to spend a day, although some fine hotels tempt an overnight stay. Allow three hours to explore the old town centre and another three hours to visit Reeuwijkse Plassen, an area of outstanding beauty and a magnet for water-sport enthusiasts.

A Bit of History

In the Middle Ages, Gouda, then called Ter Gouwe, developed under the protection of its castle, which was destroyed in 1577. In the 15C, brewing and trading brought great prosperity to Gouda, while the 16C marked a decline. The town picked up again in the 17C due to the cheese trade and the manufacture of pipes introduced by English mercenaries. Today there is also the production of candles – Gouda having the biggest factory in the country – and pottery. Gouda is the home town of **Cornelis de Houtman** (c. 1565–99), who was in charge of an expedition to the East (1595–7) and founded the first Dutch trading post in East India (Indonesia) on the island of Java.

Boat trips
Depart Jul and Aug. Information from VVV ☎0182 51 36 66.
Tours are organised to the Reeuwijk Lakes.

The Old Town Centre ★

Markt
In the centre of the main square stands the stadhuis with its picturesque tall silhouette. Number 27, the Arti Legi, houses the tourist information centre.

Stadhuis ★
Open Mon–Fri 10am–noon, 2pm–4pm. ☎0182 58 87 58.

Stadhuis in Gouda

NBTC

The lovely mid-15C Gothic town hall was restored in the 19C and 20C.

It has a very decorative sandstone façade on the south side with a gable, flanked by turrets and adorned with a small balcony. The staircase in front is in the Renaissance style (1603). On the east side is a **carillon**, whose small figures come to life every half hour; it depicts the scene of Count Floris V of Holland granting the city charter to Gouda in 1272. The interior of the Registrar's Office (Trouwzaal) is worth visiting; it is decorated with tapestries woven in Gouda in the 17C.

Waag

The Classical-style weigh-house, designed by **Pieter Post** was commissioned in 1667 and completed two years later. At first, only the ground floor was used for weighing and the upper storey was used by the city militia. The building's façade is decorated with a low relief depicting the weighing of cheese which, from 1850, was the only product weighed here. It now houses the **Kaaswaag** (*open Apr–Oct, Tue–Wed, Fri–Sun 1pm–5pm, Thu 10am–5pm; 3.50€; 0182 52 99 96*), a museum tracing the development of the cheese and dairy industry in the Netherlands as a whole, and Gouda in particular. The first floor is devoted to various Gouda crafts, from candle-making to pottery, and displays a scale model of the Markt as it looked in 1900. The second floor has an exhibition on cheesemaking. Craft demonstrations take place regularly in the museum, and every Thursday, from June to August, cheesemaking is in progress between 10am and 12.30pm. The museum shop, which can be entered (admission-free) from the street, sells traditional Gouda Farm Cheese.

Behind the Waag the lovely **Agniet-enkapel** has been restored.

St Janskerk★

Open Mar–Oct, Mon–Sat 9am–5pm; Nov–Feb, Mon–Sat 10am–4pm. Closed 1 Jan, 25 and 26 Dec. 2€. 0182 51 26 84. www.vrtour.nl/stjans kerkgouda.

Gouda Cheese

Gouda is one of the most famous cheeses in the Netherlands (the other is Edam). Marketed in Gouda, it is either factory-made or from farms (its name then becomes *boerenkaas,* meaning farm cheese).

Gouda is made with fresh or pasteurised (when it is factory-made) cow's milk. It is either young, medium or old. The indication *volvet 48+* means that its fat content is at least 48%.

Other specialities of the town are *siroopwafels* (syrup waffles).

NBTC

GOUDA

Achter de Vismarkt	Z 3
Achter de Waag	Y 5
Agnietenstr.	Y 4
Burg. Martensstr.	Z 7
Dubbele Buurt	Z 9
Groeneweg	Z 10
Hoogstr.	YZ 12
Houtmangracht	Y 13
Jeruzalemstr.	Z 15
Karnemelksloot	Y 16
Kerkhoflaan	Z 17
Kleiweg	Y
Koepoort	Z 18
Korte Groenendaal	Z 19
Korte Tiendeweg	Z 21
Lange Groenendaal	Z 22
Lange Noodgodstr.	Z 24
Lange Tiendeweg	YZ 25
Nieuwe Markt	Y 27
Nieuwe Veerstal	Z 28
Peperstr.	Z 31
Schielands Hoge Zeedijk	Z 32
Spoorstr.	Y 33
Tuinstr.	Z 34
Vlamingstr.	Z 36
Vredebest	Y 37
Walestr.	Z 39
Wijdstr.	Z 40
Wilhelminastr.	Y 42
Zeugstr.	YZ 45

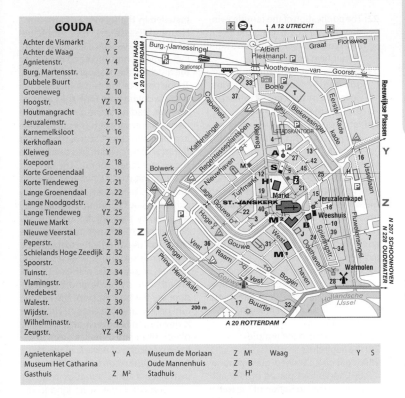

Agnietenkapel	Y A	Museum de Moriaan	Z M¹	Waag	Y	S
Museum Het Catharina		Oude Mannenhuis	Z B			
Gasthuis	Z M²	Stadhuis	Z H¹			

Founded in the 13C, the church of St John was destroyed by fire three times. Each time it was rebuilt and extended, and it is now the longest church in the Netherlands, measuring some 123m/134.5yd. Fronted by a small tower – the remains of the original church – it is surrounded by numerous pointed gables enhanced by large stained-glass windows. The interior of this Late Gothic cruciform basilica with wooden barrel vaulting is very light, and sober in the extreme.

Stained glass★★★ (Goudse Glazen)

The church is renowned for its magnificent collection of 70 stained-glass windows. Forty were spared by the Iconoclasts, the others were made after the Reformation. The largest, of which there are 27, were donated by the king, princes, prelates or rich bourgeois. The 13 most remarkable stained-glass windows, in both the eastern and the central parts of the church, are attributed to the **Crabeth brothers** (Dirck and Wouter) who made them between 1555 and 1571 when the church was Catholic. They illustrate biblical subjects. The works of the Crabeth brothers are numbered:

5: The Queen of Sheba pays a visit to Solomon

6: Judith beheading Holofernes

7: Dedication of Solomon's temple and the Last Supper (a present from Philip II, king of Spain, and Mary Tudor, queen of England)

8: Heliodorus, temple thief, chastened by the angels

12: Nativity

14: Sermon of St John the Baptist (Gouda's patron saint; his colours, white representing purity and love, and red symbolising suffering, appear in the town's coat of arms)

15: Baptism of Jesus (the oldest window, 1555)

16: First sermon of Jesus

18: Jesus's message to St John in prison

22: The purification of the temple (window donated by William the Silent and symbolising the Church's fight for purification)

23: Elijah's sacrifice and the Ablutions, donated by Margaret of Parma, governor of the Low Countries at the time of the revolt

30: Jonah cast up by the whale (*tall window above the ambulatory, to the left of the chancel*).

More recent stained-glass windows which date from the Protestant period were added between 1594 and 1603 on the western side. Donated by the free towns of Holland, they depict armorial bearings, historical events, allegories and a few biblical scenes. They include:

25: the raising of the siege of Leiden (in 1547) in the middle of floods; portrait of William the Silent; silhouette of Delft (✆*Illustration: see Introduction, Time Line*)

27: the Pharisee in the temple

28: the adulteress

28A (*right aisle*): Stained-glass window by Charles Eyck placed in 1947 and evoking the Liberation of the Netherlands.

The seven stained-glass windows in the **chapel** (*door under window 14 in the chancel*) depict the Arrest of Jesus, Christ Mocked, the Scourging, the Ecce Homo at Pontius Pilate's House, the Bearing of the Cross, the Resurrection, Ascension and the feast of Pentecost; they come from a nearby convent.

The organ at the end of the church (*west side*) dates from 1736. The new organ in the chancel dates from 1974. Interesting tombstones are strewn over the floor of the building.

▸ *Walk round the church to the right, to the north entrance of the Museum Het Catharina Gasthuis.*

Museum Het Catharina Gasthuis★

🕐*Open Wed–Fri 10am-5pm, Sat–Sun noon–5pm.* 🕐*Closed 1 Jan and 25 Dec.* ✆*4€ (ticket also valid for Museum De Moriaan).* ☎*0182 33 10 00. www.museum gouda.nl.*

Installed in the former St Catherine's Hospital (Gasthuis), this municipal museum has a varied collection of paintings, period rooms and items illustrating the history of the hospital and the town. To the north of the museum, there is a gateway dating from 1609, the **Lazaruspoortje**, leading to the garden and the museum entrance. It has a polychrome low relief depicting Lazarus the leper at the table of a rich man, and comes from the former lepers' home. The old part of the hospital (1542), where the wards once were, is now used for temporary exhibitions. A 19C municipal pharmacy is on display in an adjoining room.

Behind the 17C–19C period rooms is the **Great Hall** (Ruim) devoted to the Gouda civic guard; the schutterstukken, group portraits of companies of the civil guard, include one by Ferdinand Bol. Next-door are the boardrooms, the kitchen and pantry, and the chapel. The latter is devoted to **religious art**: 16C altarpieces, silver and a chalice given to the town by Jacoba of Bavaria in the 15C.

A small cellar contains old torture instruments and a "lunatics' cell", the only surviving one of its kind in the Netherlands.

On the upper floor there are collections of toys, the reconstruction of the surgeons' Guild Room, and paintings by the Barbizon School and The Hague School (Anton Mauve, Isaac Israëls, Jacob Maris) as well as Jan Toorop.

Museum De Moriaan

🕐*Open Wed–Fri 10am–5pm, Sat–Sun noon–5pm.* ✆*4€; children free (ticket also valid for Museum Het Catharina Gasthuis).* ☎*0182 33 10 00. www.museum gouda.nl.*

Under the sign of the Blackamoor (*moriaan*) evoking a tobacco shop, this Renaissance-style house built c. 1625 has a lovely façade overlooking the picturesque Gouda canal. The tobacco shop of 1680 has been reconstructed. Fine collections of clay pipes and decorated **Gouda pottery** (*Gouds plateel*) are displayed in elegant settings, bearing witness to the town's rich tradition as a centre of the pottery industry, which began producing the famous Gouda clay pipes in the 17C. In about 1900, it began making ornamental ceramics instead (*see Introduction, Decorative Arts*).

Jeruzalemstraat

At the corner of Patersteeg is the **Jeruzalemkapel**, a 15C chapel. Opposite, on the other corner is the former orphanage, **Weeshuis** of 1642, now a library, with a lovely façade with a voluted gable, and beside it, a doorway topped by a low relief depicting two orphans. On the opposite pavement at n° 2 an old people's home, **Oude Mannenhuis** opens by a door (1614), altered in the 18C.

At the far end of Spieringstraat is the **municipal park** with an 1832 windmill, **Walmolen 't Slot** which was formerly used for milling grain. In the park there is a tree which was planted when Queen Wilhelmina came of age in 1898.

Driving Tours

The Reeuwijkse Plassen and Woerden★

▶ *30km/19mi to the north. Leave Gouda by Karnemelksloot. After the canal, take the 2nd road on the left in the direction of Platteweg.*

Reeuwijkse Plassen★

The intensive use of these vast stretches of water by water sports enthusiasts has done nothing to spoil the captivating landscape through which the road passes, winding between the lakes.

▶ *After Sluipwijk, go in the direction of Bodegraven then Woerden.*

Woerden

Woerden was an important stronghold on the Oude Rijn and was for long considered "the key to Holland", as those who occupied Woerden had access to the rest of the country. In 1672 Louis XIV's armies, commanded by the Duke of Montmorency-Luxembourg, defeated William III's Dutch army.

The 15C **castle**, beside the town's southern gate, has served as a quartermaster's store since 1872. The old town hall is now occupied by the municipal museum, or

Stadsmuseum (*open Tue–Sun 1pm–5pm; closed Easter, Whitsun, 25 and 31 Dec; 2.50€; 0348 43 10 08; www.stadsmuseumwoerden.nl (in Dutch)*). This delightful small building dating from 1501 is flanked by a turret and has a lovely façade with voluted gables above. The windows along the entire width of the first floor provide the outlook for the 17C council chamber. An old pillory takes up the right part of the façade. Woerden also has a stage mill (1755), De Windhond (The Greyhound).

From Oudewater to Schoonhoven

▶ *34km/21mi. Leave Gouda by Nieuwe Veerstal and follow the very narrow dyke road; passing is difficult.*

This road, which follows the Hollandse IJssel, offers picturesque **views**★ of the river with its marshy banks and farmhouses.

Oudewater

Oudewater is one of the Netherlands' oldest small towns and was the birthplace of **Jacob Arminius** (c. 1560–1609) (*see DORDRECHT*), and the Primitive painter **Gerard David** (c. 1460–1523), who moved to Bruges in 1483.

Oudewater is famous for its witches' scales or **heksenwaag** (*open Apr–Oct, Tue–Sun and public holidays, 11am–5pm; 4.25€; 0348 56 34 00; www.heksenwaag.nl*), which can be seen in the Waag, or weigh-house; the small Witches Museum in the attic retraces the history of witchcraft with engravings, documents and a short film. This fine Renaissance building with crow-stepped gables is near Markt, which spans a canal. In the 16C women accused of witchcraft came from afar to be weighed at Oudewater in the presence of the burgomaster of the town. If the woman was not underweight for her size she was too heavy to ride a broomstick, so she was not a witch. She was then given a certificate of acquittal. All the people weighed in Oudewater were acquitted. The last certificate was issued in 1729.

Next to the weigh-house, at nº 14, note the Renaissance façade (1601) of Arminius' birthplace. Other attractive façades are to be admired in the surrounding streets of Oudewater (Wijdstraat). At nº 3 Donkere Gaard, near Markt, there is a fine house.

Near Markt, the Renaissance **stadhuis** (town hall, 1588) has a side façade preceded by a flight of steps and topped with a crow-stepped gable.

▸ *Take the Gouda road to Haasrecht, then follow the valley of the Vlist towards Schoonhoven.*

It is a picturesque **route**★. The road, shaded by willows, runs alongside the river banks with their abundant vegetation. Beautiful farmhouses with reed-covered roofs and conical haystacks topped with a small roof line the road.

Vlist

There is a lovely wooden windmill here.

▸ *On leaving Vlist, cross the river.*

Bracket clock (c. 1715) by A Witsen; Nederlands Goud-, Zilver- en Klokkenmuseum, Schoonhoven

Collectie Nederlands Goud-, Zilver- en Klokkenmuseum

Schoonhoven

This charming small town, with a population of around 12 000, is at the confluence of the Vlist, and the Lek is known for its traditional gold- and silverware; a few smiths continue the craft today. The town is traversed by an attractive canal and linked to Lek's south bank by a ferry. Close to the ferry terminal stands the town's south gate, **Veerpoort**, which was built in 1601. It is the only remaining medieval entrance gate of Schoonhoven and was built to protect the town from the floods of the river Rhine; it still constitutes a water barrier.

At the near end of the picturesque canal is the **Edelambachtshuys** (◷ *open Tue–Sat 10am–5pm;* ◷ *closed 1 Jan, 30 Apr, 25 and 26 Dec;* ▰*1.50€;* ☎*0182 38 26 14*), housing a large collection of antique silver and an old workshop. A little further along, the **Stadhuis**, dating from 1452, overlooks the canal. Although it has been modernised it retains a tall roof topped by a pinnacle (carillon). On the left is the **Grote Kerk**, with its characteristic leaning tower. On the Dam, in the centre of the canal, is the **Waag**, or weigh-house, a building from 1617 still in its original state with a hipped roof. Nearby is the **Nederlands Goud-Zilver- en Klokkenmuseum** (◷ *open Tue–Sun noon–5pm;* ◷ *closed 1 Jan and 25 Dec;* ▰*5€;* ♿☎*0182 38 56 12; www.ngzkm.nl (in Dutch)*), or Netherlands Gold, Silver and Clock Museum. This has a fine **collection**★ of wall clocks from Friesland and the Zaan, French dial cases, 18C timepieces, a large number of watches, a collection of silverware, an assay office for gold and silver testing, and a silversmith's workshop. Since 1996 the picturesque, 50m/164ft-high neo-Gothic **water tower** (1901) has been the centre of the Zilver in Beweging initiative. Some lovely houses can be seen in the town, notably no 37 Lopikerstraat; the 1642 façade is decorated with a double crow-stepped gable and red shutters.

GRONINGEN

GRONINGEN P
POPULATION 181 819
PLAN OF THE CONURBATION IN THE CURRENT RED-COVER MICHELIN GUIDE BENELUX

Groningen is the dynamic provincial capital and the main town in the north of the Netherlands. The town's university and various other colleges mean that it has a young population and is dominated by students, who fill the many outdoor cafés in summer. Groningen also has a remarkably large number of cyclists; over half the population travels to school and work by bike.

- **Information:** Grote Markt 25, 9712 HS. ☎ 0900 202 30 50. http://portal.groningen.nl.
- **Orient Yourself:** The town is located at the northern extremity of the Hondsrug with polderlands to the north and peat bogs to the southwest; accessible via the A 7.
- **Parking:** see Address Book.
- **Don't Miss:** From an architectural point of view, the Groninger Museum is well worth seeing.
- **Organizing Your Time:** The town has enough interest to warrant a whole day

A Bit of History

A settlement already existed by the year AD 1000. By the beginning of the 13C Groningen belonged to the Hanseatic League. A convention concluded in 1251 with the neighbouring cantonnes made Groningen the only grain market in the region, bringing it six centuries of prosperity.

Under the Bishop of Utrecht's authority the town passed into the hands of the Duke of Geldern in 1515. Then, having tried to escape from the Habsburg authority, it finally gave in to Charles V in 1536. It joined the Union of Utrecht in 1579 and was taken by the Spanish in 1580 and then by Maurice of Nassau in 1594. An era of prosperity followed with the construction of a new town rampart.

The university was founded in 1614; it very quickly acquired a great reputation and students came from all over Europe. Descartes chose it in 1645 to arbitrate in his conflicts with Dutch theologians. Today it still plays an important role in the life of the town.

The town of Groningen is the homeland of the painters **Jozef Israëls** (1827–1911), head of The Hague School, and **Hendrik Willem Mesdag** (1831–1915), who was one of its members.

A dynamic town – Groningen is an important communications junction and also has two harbours. It is linked to the sea by means of important canals. Groningen is a large industrial centre (high-technology, tobacco, asphalt and steel). The town is Western Europe's number-one sugar-beet centre.

Groningen Gas

Groningen has been the oil capital of the Netherlands and nerve centre of its power supply ever since oil was found in the Drenthe near Schoonebeek in 1945. In 1960 large deposits of natural gas were also discovered in the province of Groningen. The reserves are estimated at c. 1 800 billion cu m/over 63.5 billion cu ft, which makes it one of the largest deposits in the world. The region features 29 extraction centres which all have several winding shafts. One of these centres is located in Slochteren, east of Groningen. Nearly half the country's production of natural gas is channelled through pipelines towards Belgium, France, Germany and Italy.

Address Book

For coin ranges, see the Legend on the cover flap.

WHERE TO STAY

As well as Groningen's great museums, the town also has a number of attractive hotels in historic buildings.

Auberge Corps de Garde – *Oude Boteringestraat 74, 9712 GN,* ☎*050 314 54 37. Fax 050 313 63 20. www.corpsdegarde.nl. 24 rooms.* A 17C guardhouse and an adjoining building on the Boteringebrug are now a cosy hotel, with large, comfortable rooms and antique furniture.

Schimmelpenninck Huys – *Oosterstraat 53, 9711 NR.* ☎*050 318 95 02. Fax 050 318 31 64. www.schimmelpenninckhuys.nl (also in English). 38 rooms.* A pleasant hotel in an old mansion close to Grote Markt, with a choice of suites or rooms overlooking the courtyards. There are rooms of various sizes with modern décor; the main emphasis, as in the rest of the hotel, is on white. Breakfast is served in the Baroque Room, the conservatory or the garden.

Hotel De Ville – *Oude Boteringestraat 43, 9712 GD.* ☎*050 318 12 22. www.hotels.nl/groningen/deville. 66 rooms.* Behind the simple exterior of these restored mansions is a chic but charming hotel. Quietly located in the old town centre, it has a classically styled interior and spacious modern rooms. The bar in the conservatory looks out onto an attractive courtyard garden.

WHERE TO EAT

Ni Hao Chinatown – *Ged. Kattendiep 122.* ☎*0220 318 14 00.* Chinese restaurant near the station.

Bistro 't Gerecht – *Oude Boteringestraat 45.* ☎*050 589 18 59. www.www.bistrohetgerecht.nl (in Dutch).* French-inspired bistro next to (and part of) the Hotel De Ville. Long benches, wooden panelling and mirrored walls; traditional, mainly French, cuisine.

De Pauw – *Gelkingestraat 52.* ☎*050 318 13 32. www.depauw.nl.* This centrally located restaurant has an unusual formula: the main course consists of a trolley buffet placed beside your table, with starters and desserts to order.

Restaurant Grand Café Schimmelpenninck Huys – *Oosterstraat 53.* ☎*050 311 18 72. www.schimmelpenninckhuys.nl (also in English).* Enjoy a cup of coffee, a light meal or a full dinner, and rub shoulders with the great and good of Groningen. You can eat in the conservatory, the Jugendstil or Empire Rooms, or the pleasantly green courtyard. See also Hotel Schimmelpennick Huys above.

Muller – *Grote Kromme Elleboog 13.* ☎*050 318 32 08.* This restaurant in one of Groningen's busiest areas for nightlife serves excellent food to a smart clientele.

BRASSERIES, CAFÉS, BARS, COFFEE SHOPS...

De Apedans – *Verlengde Oosterstraat 1.* ☎*050 312 41 64. www.apedans.nl.* This trendy bodega restaurant has a tastefully designed interior and serves simple food.

Het Goudkantoor – *Waagplein 1.* ☎*050 312 41 64. www.apedans.nl (in Dutch).* An elegant building housing one of the town's busiest café-restaurants; a must if you're in the Waag area.

Newscafé – *Waagplein 5.* ☎*050 311 18 44.* Besides a cocktail bar and reading table, this café also has computers for anyone wanting to do some Internet-surfing. International dishes are served on the first floor.

't Feithhuis – *Martinikerkhof 10.* ☎*050 313 53 35. www.feithhuis.nl (in Dutch).* This trendy town-centre café provides day-long sustenance: breakfast, lunch, salads, afternoon tea and dinner.

PRACTICAL INFORMATION

General information – The tourist office, **VVV Groningen** (*Grote Markt,* ☎*0900 202 30 50. www.vvvgroningen. nl, also in English*), has information on

Groningen Municipal Theatre

sights, tours and accommodation. It also offers special accommodation packages and can book hotels and tickets for plays, concerts and other events.

TRANSPORT

If yours is a short visit, there are clearly **signposted car parks** in the centre of Groningen. If you are staying longer, park at a **Park and Ride sites** on the outskirts of town and take the Citybus to the centre, which is largely car-free and not accessible to through traffic. **Public transport timetables** and tickets are available from the VVV. Groningen is an ideal cycling town, with an extensive network of cycle paths. You can hire a **bicycle** in the Central Station or under the library.

WALKS AND TOURS

The VVV sells street maps and suggested **walking routes** and **guided walks** depart from here on Monday afternoons in summer.

BOAT TRIPS – CANAL TOURS

These leave from opposite Groningen's Central Station from May to September. Information: Rondvaartbedrijf Kool *050 312 83 79 or from the VVV. www. rondvaartbedrijfkool.nl (also in English).*

SHOPPING

Groningen's main shopping street is **Herestraat**, but there are other good areas for shopping. These include the historic **Korenbeurs** or corn exchange,

at A-Kerkhof 1, and the modern **Waagstraat complex** on Grote Markt.

Markets – On Good Friday, Vismarkt becomes a blaze of colour as the annual **flower market** takes over. There are also **weekly markets**: one on Tuesdays, Fridays and Saturdays selling **general** items on Grote Markt and Vismarkt; an **organic food market** and **small flea-market** on Vismarkt on Wednesdays, and a **non-food market** on Grote Markt on Thursdays. Various Sunday markets are also held.

THEATRE AND CONCERTS

The VVV publishes a newspaper (*Uitgaanskrant Groningen*) giving details of all the events, concerts and exhibitions taking place in Groningen; it also sells tickets. The main theatres are the **Stadsschouwburg** (municipal theatre) (*Turfsingel 86; *050 312 56 45) and **De Oosterpoort** (*Trompsingel 27; *050 313 10 44; www.de-oosterpoort.nl (in Dutch)*).

NIGHTLIFE

Groningen's nightlife centres on Grote Markt and the Waag, Gedempte Zuiderdiep and Kromme Ellebogen. Most of the discos are in Poelestraat and Peperstraat. Attractions include **Holland Casino** Gedempte Kattendiep 150 (*050 312 34 00; www.hollandcasino.nl*) and cinemas. The VVV publishes a film listing every Thursday.

Around Grote Markt

Grote Markt

Prolonged by Vismarkt, the fish market, this vast and busy square, lined by the town's main buildings, forms the city centre. Grote Markt gives onto the different pedestrian precincts; the main shopping street is Herestraat. Various markets take place here (&see Address Book).

Stadhuis

The Neoclassical town hall (1810) is linked by a glassed-in footbridge to a modern annexe.

Goudkantoor★

This gracious Renaissance Gold Office, built in 1635, has elegant façades with finely worked gables; the windows are topped by shell motifs. Originally the provincial tax collector's office, it is now a café and restaurant (&see Address Book).

Martinikerk

⏱Open Jun–Aug, Tue–Fri noon–5pm; Easter–mid Nov, Sat noon–5pm. ☎050 311 12 77. www.martinikerk.nl. This church, the second on this site, was rebuilt in the 15C. It is known for its **tower**★ (⏱open Jun–Aug, Tue–Fri noon–5pm, Easter–mid-Nov, Sat noon–5pm; ☎0900 202 30 50), which is the pride of Groningen. Measuring 96m/315ft high with six storeys, this bell-tower is topped

The tower of Martinikerk

Ben Deiman Fotografie/NBTC

by a weathervane in the shape of a horse depicting St Martin's mount. It has a carillon cast by the Hemony brothers and affords a fine view over the canals, the square, the roofs of Martinikerk, and the Prinsenhof and its gardens. Inside the church, the chancel is decorated with 16C frescoes depicting scenes in the life of Christ.

Additional Sights

Groninger Museum★

⏱Open Tue–Sun 10am–5pm (Fri 10pm). ⏱ Closed 1 Jan and 24–25, 31 Dec. ᐧ10€. ☎050 366 65 55. www.groninger museum.nl.
The highly original, almost futuristic, **polymorphous building**★★ (1992–94) housing the Groninger Museum lies opposite the station, on a small island in the Verbindingskanaal. Because the museum's collections were very diverse, different architects and designers were asked to work together on the design. Each of the three main buildings has its own distinctive character, and uses different materials, colours and forms. The museum is entered through a golden tower designed by Alessandro Mendini (b. 1931), which is used as a store. The lower part of the west pavilion is clad in red brick, and is the work of Michele De Lucchi (b. 1951); this houses the archaeological and historical collections, which are shown in rotation. The round room above it was designed by Philippe Starck (b. 1949); in the display case that follows the sloping wall and in the maze of curtains, there is a particularly fine **Oriental porcelain collection**★, including pieces from the wreck of the East India Company vessel De Geldermalsen. Mendini designed the first of the two pavilions one above the other on the east side, in which temporary exhibitions of contemporary art are held. The upper one, a superb example of Deconstructivism, was designed by Coop Himmelb(l)au. It houses the collection of visual art from 1500–1950, which includes works by the local artists' group "De Ploeg", or temporary exhibitions.

Peter Tahl/Groninger Museum

Exhibition Room designed by Alessandro Mendini, Groninger Museum

Noordelijk Scheepvaartmuseum en Niemeyer Tabaksmuseum★

Open Tue–Sat 10am–5pm, Sun, 1pm–5pm. Closed 1 Jan, 30 Apr, 28 Aug and 25 Dec. 3€. 050 312 22 02. www.noordelijkscheepvaartmuseum.nl.
These museums are located in two beautifully restored medieval merchants' houses: the Gotisch Huis (*on the left*) and the Canterhuis (*on the right*).

The **Noordelijk Scheepvaartmuseum**★ is devoted to inland water transport and coastal shipping in the northern part of the Netherlands since the 6C. The scale models of ships, navigational instruments, charts, paintings and ceramics are particularly well displayed and retrace the brilliant period of the Hanseatic League, the Dutch East and West India Companies, the activities relative to peat extraction and its transportation by boat, the coastal shipping of bricks, and schooners, which replaced the traditional galliots.

The **Niemeyer Tabaksmuseum** (tobacco museum) is located at the rear of the Gotisch Huis. A fine collection of pipes, snuffboxes and jars illustrates the use of tobacco over the centuries. A 19C tobacco merchant's shop has been reconstructed.

Martinikerkhof

This lovely square, laid out on the site of a 19C cemetery (*kerkhof*), is surrounded by houses which have been attractively restored.

To the northeast is the **Provinciehuis**, rebuilt in 1916 in neo-Renaissance style and flanked by an onion-shaped turret. On its left, Cardinaal house has a small Renaissance façade (1559), whose gable is decorated with three heads: Alexander the Great, King David and Charlemagne. This façade has been reconstructed from that of a house which no longer exists. To the north of the square, the Prinsenhof, originally built for the Brethren of the Common Life (*see DEVENTER*), became the Bishop of Groningen's residence in 1568. Preceded by a courtyard and a 17C portal, it is built onto the Gardepoort, a small gateway (1639).

Behind the **Prinsenhof** there is a small 18C garden, the **Prinsenhoftuin**, with hedges, roses and herbs. It opens on to the Turfsingel, a canal where peat (*turf*) was transported, via a gateway called the Zonnewijzerpoort which has an 18C **sundial** on the garden side.

Ossenmarkt

At n° 5 there is a fine 18C **patrician house**; it is a good example of the local architectural style, having a wide façade with rows of rather narrow windows.

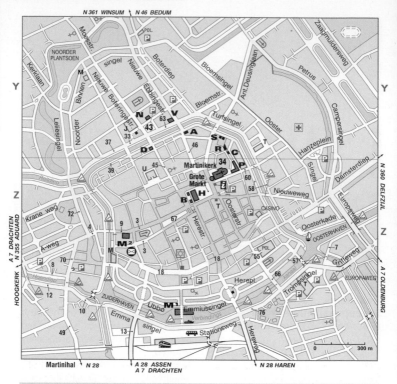

GRONINGEN			Grote Markt	Z		Rademarkt	Z	55
			Herestr.	Z		Radesingel	Z	57
A-Kerkhof	Z	3	Lopende Diep	Y	33	Schuitendiep	Z	58
A-Str.	Z	4	Martinikerkhof	YZ	34	St Jansstr.	Z	60
Brugstr.	Z	9	Noorderhaven N. Z.	Y	37	Spilsluizen	Y	63
de Brink	Z	7	Noorderhaven Z. Z.	Z	39	Verlengde Oosterstr.	Z	66
Eeldersingel	Z	10	Oosterstr.	Z		Vismarkt	Z	67
Eendrachtskade N. Z.	Z	8	Ossenmarkt	Y	43	Westerhaven	Z	70
Eendrachtskade Z. Z.	Z	12	Oude Boteringestr.	Z	45	Westersingel	Z	72
Emmaviaduct	Z	13	Oude Ebbingestr.	Y	46	Zuiderpark	Z	76
Gedempte Zuiderdiep	Z	18	Paterswoldseweg	Z	49			

17 de-eeuwse huizen	Y	V	Kortegaard	Y	D	Prinsenhof	Y	R
Gevelsteen met hert	Y	A	Noordelijk Scheepvaartmuseum			Provinciehuis	Z	P
Goudkantoor	Z	B	en Niemeyer			Stadhuis	Z	H
Groninger Museum	Z	M	Tabaksmuseum	Z	M²	Zonnewijzer	Y	S
Huis Cardinaal	Y	C	Patriciërshuis	Y	N			

Not far away, at the corner of Spilsluizen and Nieuwe Ebbingestraat, stand two 17C houses. The one on the left is also characteristic of the Groningen style. On the other side of the canal a sculptured stone depicting a stag juts out from the wall of a house.

At the corner of Spilsluizen and Oude Boteringestraat is the former guard room, **Kortegaard**, with a covered gallery (1634) where cannons once stood.

Excursions

Hortus Haren

6km/3.7mi south. Leave Groningen via Hereweg; Hortus Haren is south of Haren. ◐*Open Tue–Sun 9.30am–5pm.* ◐*Closed 1 Jan and 25 Dec.* ☞*5€.* ♿☎*050 537 00 53. www.hortusharen.nl.*

"Hortus" means garden, and this 21ha/52 acre area has various **themed gardens** such as sculpture and rose gardens, with others focusing on particular countries and regions such as Great Britain, France or Bengal. Exotic trees and plants grow in the greenhouses, while the denizens of the vivarium include grisly bird-eating spiders. Beside the Hortus is **Het Verborgen Rijk van Ming**, or The Hidden Empire of Ming. This recalls the time of the Ming Dynasty (1368–1644), and includes rocks, bridges, pagodas, hundreds of red carp and many flowering plants, all brought to the Netherlands from China. There are also demonstrations of calligraphy, tai chi and silk painting, and tea ceremonies are held in a traditional teahouse.

Northwest Groningen

27km/17mi northwest by motorway.

Aduard

Although the façade of **Nederlandse Hervormde Kerk** (☉*open Mon–Fri 9am–noon, 2pm–5pm;* ☎*050 403 17 24*) is sober, the interior has interesting decorative details: Gothic bays alternating with blind arches depicting geometric motifs, bays on the ground floor surrounded by ceramic cable moulding. The 18C furnishings are elegant: a decorated pulpit, pews with carved backs, the lords' pews topped by a canopy with heraldic motifs and copper lecterns.

Leens

Petruskerk a church built in the 12C and 13C, houses a lovely Baroque organa built by Hinsz in 1733.

Lauwersoog

&*Local map see DE WADDENEILANDEN. Departure point for ferries to Schiermonnikoog.*

The scale models, photographs and illuminated maps in the **Expozee exhibition** (☉*open Apr, May, Sept and Oct, Wed and Sat–Sun 11am–5pm; Jun, Wed–Sun 11am–5pm; Jul and Aug, Wed–Sun 10am–5pm.* ☎*0519 34 90 45*) give an interesting presentation on the Lauwersmeer

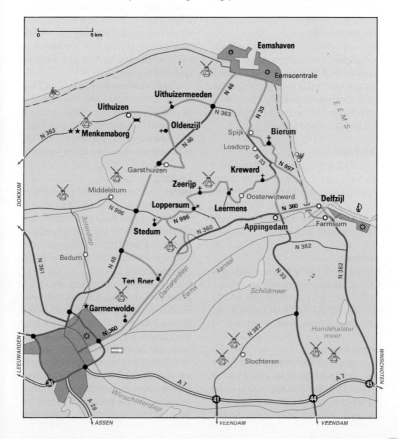

polders and the protection of the Wad-denzee. There is also a tank containing animals from the Waddenzee.

Rural Churches★

▷ *Round tour of 118km/73.3mi to the northeast. Leave Groningen by Damsterdiep.*

Every village in the province of Groningen has its brick church which dates from the 12C and 13C and is usually in the transitional Romanesque-Gothic style. Architecturally they are quite simple but they are often adorned with attractive decorative brickwork both inside and outside. Sometimes they are built on a terp, and the saddleback roof of the bell-tower often emerges from behind a screen of tall trees. Characteristic features of the interiors are the frescoes, lovely carved furnishings and hatchments. The farmhouses of the region are also quite imposing (❦ *see Introduction, Farmhouses*).

Garmerwolde

The nave of this 13C **village church** was demolished in the 19C, so it has a free-standing **bell-tower**★. The flat east end has bays outlined by recessed arches and a gable with blind arcading. The interior still has some 16C frescoes on the vaults and an 18C carved pulpit.

Ten Boer

On a terp, a 13C **church**, topped by a pinnacle, has some lovely decoration, especially on the north side: bays outlined by recessed arches, medallions, multifoil blind arcading and gables both with reticulate brickwork.

Stedum

Built on a terp surrounded by moats, this typical **church** with its tall saddleback-roofed bell-tower is picturesque. A frieze runs above the modillions sculptured with characters or heads of animals.

Loppersum

This large Gothic **church** has two transepts with blind arcading on the gables. The interior is interesting for its **frescoes**★, which decorate the chancel vaults and the Lady Chapel. In the

chapel south of the chancel there are many memorial slabs.

Zeerijp

Next to its free-standing bell-tower, the **church's** interior is remarkable for its **domes**★ with brick decoration which varies in each bay. Blind arcading decorates the end of the nave. The organ, the Renaissance pulpit, and hatchments are also worth seeing.

Leermens

This 13C **church** has a flat east end decorated with blind arcading and a background decorated with brick motifs.

Krewerd

This **church**, built on a terp, has vaults decorated with brick motifs. The organ dates from 1531.

Appingedam

This town is renowned for its twice-yearly agricultural market (April and October).
From the footbridge (Vrouwenbrug) over the canal there is a fine **view**★ of the overhanging kitchens and the town hall's pinnacle.
The **old raadhuis** flanked by a 19C bell-tower, dates from 1630. The façade is decorated with shell motifs, a facing brick with a pelican, a statue of Justice and a voluted pediment. The 13C **Nikolaikerk** has some lovely frescoes.

Delfzijl

Delfzijl is an industrial city and a busy shipping port on Dollard Gulf; it is linked to Groningen by Eemskanaal. Delfzijl also has a large pleasure boat harbour; **boat trips** (*By arrangement. Information from VVV; ☎0596 61 81 04*) are organised.
From the dyke on Dollard, there is a **view** over the harbour and the town, overlooked by a tall wall mill, called **Molen Adam** (1875). On a square near the station, a monument topped by a swan, **Het Zwaantje**, commemorates the Resistance. A small **statue of Maigret** on the lawns of the Damsterdiep (*600m/656yd from the pumping station to the west of Eemskanaal, opposite the RWR warehouses*) is a reminder that

Georges Simenon (1903–89) was a visitor in 1929. It is believed that he created his most famous character, police inspector Maigret, while in Delfzijl.

Bierum

On a terp there is a small 13C **church**, whose bell-tower was reinforced by a flying buttress. The semicircular east end of the chancel dates from the 14C.

Eemshaven

This port was built on reclaimed polderland of Emmapolder and Oostpolder. The port started trading in 1973 and has given rise to an important industrial zone. To the east the imposing **Eemscentrale** power station has been powered by natural gas since 1976.

Uithuizermeeden

The **church** with a 13C nave and a transept (1705) has a white tower rebuilt in 1896–97. The pulpit was sculptured in the 18C.

Uithuizen

To the east of Uithuizen, **Menkemaborg Castle**★★ (◷ open Mar–Sept, daily 10am–5pm; Oct–Dec, 10am–4pm; ⬡6€; ☎0595 43 19 70; www.menkemaborg.nl (in Dutch)) is surrounded by a moat and a typically Dutch garden laid out in Renaissance and Baroque tradition; the grounds also feature a maze,

Oldenzijl – Romanesque church

an orchard and a vegetable garden. The oldest part (14C) of the building, with only a few small windows, was extended by the addition of two wings in the 17C and 18C.

Oldenzijl

The small Romanesque **church** and its churchyard stand on a terp encircled by a moat and a screen of trees. Inside the plainness of the brick walls is broken by several small round windows trimmed with mouldings and the decorative effect of the blind arcading in the chancel.

▷ *Return to Groningen by Garsthuizen, the N 46, Ten Boer and the N 360.*

Menkemaborg Castle

DEN HAAG★★

THE HAGUE OR 'S-GRAVENHAGE – ZUID-HOLLAND P
POPULATION 474 244
PLAN OF THE CONURBATION IN THE CURRENT RED-COVER MICHELIN GUIDE BENELUX

Although The Hague, whose official name is 's-Gravenhage (generally shortened to Den Haag), is home to the Dutch government and Parliament, as well as many foreign embassies, it is only the provincial capital. Dutch monarchs have been enthroned in Amsterdam since 1813. This coastal town is a pleasant and quiet residential community, with a multitude of squares, parks (more than 700 public gardens) and several canals.

The Hague sprawls over a large area and has a relatively small population, earning itself the title of "the biggest village in Europe". It is marked by a certain aristocratic charm and is considered to be the most worldly and elegant town in the Netherlands; in fact, some of its 19C colonial atmosphere still remains.

However, the city also has some important modern architecture, such as Rem Koolhaas' Lucent Danstheater and H Hertzberger's transport and planning ministry building. The "De Resident" development between the Binnenhof and the station involved a large number of international architects, including Richard Meier, who designed the new city hall.

- **Information:** Kon. Julianaplein 30– 2595 AA. ☎0900 340 35 05. www.denhaag.com/tourism/nl.
- ▶ **Orient Yourself:** Den Haag is a sprawling metropolis, but its heart and its main attractions lie around Centraal Station, towards the south of the city.
- P **Parking:** There are numerous car parks around the city, like the one at Centraal Station, but they are expensive. Off-street parking is metered.
- ⊘ **Don't Miss:** Mauritshuis, home of the Royal painting collection, which is one of the finest in the world. Also visit nearby Scheveningen, an elegant seaside resort and a must for a leisurely lunch overlooking the long, wide beach.
- ◷ **Organizing Your Time:** Allow at least a half day to explore the centre of Den Haag, and another to see the sights beyond the city.
- Kids **Especially for Kids:** Madurodam, a miniature Dutch town of windmills and bulb fields.

A Bit of History

A meet – Up to the 13C, The Hague was just a hunting lodge built by Count Floris IV of Holland but about 1250 his son William II built a castle on the site of the present Binnenhof.

A village... – 's-Gravenhage, the Count's Hedge or Die Haghe, the hedge, rapidly developed without being more than a place of residence and rest. The cloth trade, which started in the 15C, was not enough to make it a mercantile town.

... which develops – Seat of the States General of the United Provinces, then the government, it became an impor- tant centre of diplomatic negotiations in 17C. Up to the end of the 18C substantial mansions in Renaissance and Baroque styles were built round the medieval centre of the Binnenhof.

The French entered The Hague in 1795. Eleven years later the town had to cede its rank of capital to Amsterdam where Louis Bonaparte had installed his government.

The 19C confirmed the residential character of the town, which had become the favourite residence of colonials returning from Indonesia. This period marked it so profoundly that it is sometimes referred to as "the widow of the Indies". Even today, The Hague has a sizeable Indonesian community.

©Arjan de Jager/Den Haag Marketing & Events

Binnenhof

The Hague School – Between 1870 and
1890 a group of painters in The Hague
tried to renew painting, and notably the
art of landscapes, in the manner of the
Barbizon School in France.
A group of artists gathered around the
leader, **Jozef Israëls**, a painter of fishing
scenes and portraits: **JH Weissenbruch**
(1824–1903), painter of landscapes,
noted for his sky and light paintings;
Jacob Maris (1837–99), painter of dunes
and beaches; **HW Mesdag**, painter of
numerous seascapes and the famous
Mesdag Panorama; **Anton Mauve**
(1838–88), painter of the Gooi heathland; **Albert Neuhuys** (1844–1914),
painter of household interiors; **Johannes Bosboom** (1817–91), painter of
church interiors; and **Blommers** (1845–
1914), painter of the life of fishermen.
Neuhuys and Mauve, having worked in
Laren, are sometimes attached to the
Laren School.
The diplomatic town – The Hague
was chosen several times as a centre
for international negotiations, including the peace conferences of 1899 and
1907. Finally the construction of the
Peace Palace (1913) established its vocation as a diplomatic town. It is the seat
of the International Court of Justice, an
organisation dependent on the UN, the
Permanent Court of Arbitration and the
Academy of International Law.

Centre

Stately mansions line the wide avenues
around the Binnenhof, the centre of the
country's political life. Nearby, shops are
grouped in the pedestrianised area: the
town has a great many antiques dealers
and luxury boutiques.

Buitenhof
This is the "outer courtyard" of the old
castle which once belonged to the
Counts of Holland. A statue of King
William II stands in the centre.

Binnenhof★
Enter by the Stadtholder doorway to
reach the inner courtyard (Binnenhof)
in the centre of which stands the Ridderzaal, or Knights' Hall. The buildings
all around date from different periods in
Dutch history. They now house the Upper
House of Parliament and the Ministry of
General Affairs (*north wing*), part of the
State Council (*west wing*) and the Lower
House (*south and east wing, as well as
the new extensions*). Van Oldenbarnevelt
(see AMERSFOORT) was executed in this
courtyard on 13 May 1619.

Binnenhof Visitor Centre
*Open Mon–Sat 10am–4pm. Closed
public holidays. No charge. 070
364 61 44.*

Benedictus de Spinoza

The great philosopher Spinoza spent the last seven years of his life in The Hague; he died here in 1677. Born in Amsterdam in 1632, this Jew of Portuguese origin was a brilliant scholar. In 1656 Spinoza was excommunicated and banished from Amsterdam by the synagogue authorities for questioning the orthodox Jewish doctrines and interpretations of scripture. He took refuge for a time in Ouderkerk aan de Amstel, then went to live in Rijnsburg near Leiden in 1660. For three years he devoted himself to philosophy and polishing lenses to earn a living. After a few years spent in Voorburg, a suburb of The Hague, in 1670 he moved into a modest residence in Paviljoensgracht.

It was only after his death that his *Posthumous Works*, published in 1677, appeared in Latin; it included **The Ethics**, which became universally famous.

Bildarchiv Pisarek/akg-images

This has a **model** of the Binnenhof and a historical timescale showing the political history of the Low Countries over the past twelve centuries. It is also the starting point of a tour, which begins with a video about the Binnenhof and continues through the Ridderzaal and the Upper and Lower Houses of Parliament.

Ridderzaal★

By guided tour only (45min): Mon–Sat 10am–4pm. ☎070 364 61 44.

An **exhibition** in the cellars of the Ridderzaal (*n° 8a*) explains the origin and workings of the two chambers and the roles of the head of state and the monarch.

The Ridderzaal, built as a banqueting hall for Count William II of Holland, was completed c. 1280 by his son Count Floris V. The building, which looks very much like a church, was located in the prolongation of the old castle. Its façade with a pointed and finely worked gable is flanked by two slender turrets. Inside, the great hall, restored c. 1900, has recovered its vault with open-work beams.

The back of the building, visible from the Binnenhof's second courtyard, consists of the old castle built c. 1250 by Count William II.

Eerste Kamer

By guided tour only (45min): Mon–Sat 10am–4pm. ☎070 364 61 44.

The First or Upper Chamber is situated in the north wing, in the **Stadtholders' Quarters**, bordered by a covered gallery. Since 1848 it has been used as a place of assembly for the Upper House or Senate, which consists of 75 members elected for four years by the twelve Provincial States. It has a wooden ceiling painted in the Baroque style by two of Rubens' pupils: A de Haan and N Wielingh.

Trêveszaal

🔒*Closed to the public.*

The Truce Hall, where in 1608 a 12-year truce with Spain was prepared, is now used by the Council of Ministers.

Tweede Kamer

By guided tour only (45min): Mon–Sat 10am–4pm. ☎070 364 61 44.

The Second or Lower Chamber is composed of 150 representatives, elected for four years by universal suffrage.

Decorated in the Louis XIV style, the ballroom has a balcony and several boxes. In 1992 the members of the Lower Chamber moved to **modern buildings** (*Entrance Plein 2A*) based on plans by the Dutch architect Pi de Bruijn and set up among the existing buildings

Address Book

For coin ranges, see the Legend on the cover flap.

WHERE TO STAY

As The Hague is the country's diplomatic, administrative and commercial centre, hotels are mostly modern business-orientated ones. However, it does have two unusually good 19C hotels.

YOUTH HOSTEL

Stayokay Den Haag – Scheepmakerstraat 27, 2515 VA Den Haag. ☎070 315 78 78. www.stayokay.com. 220 beds. Close to the station, and has its own brasserie.

HOTELS

Petit – Groot Hertoginnelaan 42, 2517 EH Den Haag. ☎070 346 55 00. www.hotelpetit.nl. 20 rooms. This hotel is located in an elegant mansion near the Haags Gemeentemuseum. It has comfortable rooms and its own car park.

Sebel – Zoutmanstraat 40, 2518 GR Den Haag. ☎070 345 92 00. www.hotelsebel.nl. 33 rooms. Simple family hotel in a row of terrace houses within walking distance from the city centre. Car-parking spaces available.

Corona – Buitenhof 42, 2513 AH Den Haag. ☎070 363 79 30. www.corona.nl. 36 rooms. Right in the heart of the city, close to the Binnenhof, and thus the ideal base for a visit to The Hague. The comfortable rooms are decorated in Louis XVI style or Art Deco.

Des Indes – Lange Voorhout 54, 2514 EG Den Haag. ☎070 361 23 45. www.intercontl.com. 92 rooms. This stately hotel, formerly the residence of a wealthy baron, is a journey back in time to the 19C. It has red carpets, high ceilings, grand staircases, marble and stucco, obviously in combination with every modern facility. For a taste of bygone days, there's none better, but be warned: it doesn't come cheap.

Kurhaus – Gevers Deynootplein 30, 2586 CK Scheveningen. ☎070 416 26 36. www.kurhaus.nl. 255 rooms. This imposing 19C Scheveningen beach hotel offers a choice of royal suites or luxury rooms. The hotel is full of character, with the huge domed Kurzaal (see below), the outside terrace overlooking the sea and, of course, the thermal baths which gave this stylish hotel its name.

Parkhotel – Molenstraat 53, 2513 BJ Den Haag. ☎070 362 43 71. www.parkhoteldenhaag.nl (also in English). 114 rooms. This modern business hotel borders the gardens of Paleis Noordeinde. The rooms are functional yet comfortable, some looking out over the park and others overlooking the beautiful inner courtyard. The hotel has a fine staircase in the style of the Amsterdam School.

Saur – Lange Voorhout 47. ☎070 346 25 65. www.saur.nl (Dutch only). A French restaurant in a beautiful location opposite the Paleis. Food is served at the bar downstairs.

WHERE TO EAT

Kurzaal – Gevers Deynootplein 30. ☎070 416 26 36. www.kurhaus.nl (also in English). Lunch or dine in style at this buffet restaurant in the imposing old concert hall of the Kurhaus.

Shirasagi – Spui 170. ☎070 346 47 00; www.shirasagi.nl (also in English). Japanese restaurant with food prepared at the table (teppan-yaki). Indonesian cuisine.

The Raffles – Javastraat 63, ☎070 345 85 87. http://theraffles.orientalrestaurants.nl (Dutch only).

Brasserie Buitenhof – Buitenhof 39. ☎070 363 79 30. Atmospheric brasserie restaurant of the Corona hotel. A good place for a genteel cup of coffee; covered terrace.

It Rains Fishes – Noordeinde 123. ☎070 365 25 98. www.itrainsfishes.nl (dutch only). Trendy fish restaurant offering "fusion cuisine": Western produce prepared in eastern style, with sometimes surprising but always delicious results.

SCHEVENINGEN

Westbroekpark – Kapelweg 35. ☎070 354 60 72. Once you've had enough of the sea, sample the delicious cuisine of this restaurant in the park, overlooking the famous rose garden.

Seinpost – *Zekant 60.* ☎*070 355 52 50. www.seinpost.nl (also in English).* A circular restaurant offering excellent fish dishes and a wonderful view of the North Sea.

BRASSERIES, CAFÉS, BARS, COFFEE SHOPS...

't Goude Hooft – *Dag. Groenmarkt 13, Den Haag.* ☎*070 346 97 13. www. tgoudehooft.nl (also in English).* International cuisine in one of The Hague's best-known brasseries, with its own sun terrace.

Zeldenrust – *Bankastraat 32, Den Haag.* ☎*070 350 38 16.* Brasserie with a café and terrace located between Madurodam and Panorama Mesdag. Tasty sandwiches and salads and a pleasant atmosphere.

Deining Brasserie de la mer – *Stevinstraat 80 (at the corner of Badhuisweg), Scheveningen.* ☎*070 358 92 92.* Quiet brasserie away from the buzz of the boulevard; particularly ideal if you get peckish late at night, as the kitchen is open till midnight. Meals are served in the garden on warm summer nights.

Museumcafé Het Paleis – *Lange Voorhout 74, Den Haag.* ☎*070 427 77 30.* This café in the basement of the Museum Het Paleis has the original Art Deco interior of the Krul coffee house in The Hague, and is a good place for a drink before or after a visit to the museum.

Slagerij PG Dungelman – *Hoogstraat 34, Den Haag.* ☎*070 346 23 00. www. dungelmann.nl (Dutch only).* Neither a bar nor a café, but a butcher's serving wonderful hot croquettes.

PRACTICAL INFORMATION

GENERAL INFORMATION

The **VVV tourist offices** in **The Hague** (*Hofweg 1, Den Haag, next to Grand Café Dudok, other office opposite the Parliament buildings and Wagenstraat 193*) and **Scheveningen** (*Gevers Deynootweg 1134, Palace Promenade shopping centre, 2586 BX Scheveningen*); all have the same telephone number: ☎*070 338 58 00. www.denhaag. com.* They can provide information on sights, events, cultural activities and accommodation packages, and publish an annual information guide including a list of bars, restaurants, hotels, youth hostels, apartments and campsites. Hotel rooms can be booked through the tourist office by ringing ☎*0800 849 6372 (in the UK)* or visiting *www.hotels.nl/the-hague.*

EMERGENCIES

The Hague's **Tourist Assistance Service (TAS)** offers help to foreign tourists who are victims of crime or road or other accidents. ☎*070 424 40 00 (Open Apr–Sept, 9am–9pm; Oct–Mar, 9am–5pm).* Outside these hours, only in emergencies, the Emergency Helpline can be called ☎*070 379 51 72.*

Passage

TRANSPORT

Parking in the centre of The Hague or Scheveningen is difficult and expensive. Most **parking is metered** and if you don't put enough into the meter or park illegally you are likely to be clamped. If this happens, go to the payment office in the multi-storey car park behind the Centraal Station. Alternatively, use one of the many well-signposted **car parks**. The main sights in the city centre are within walking distance of one another, but you can also take a **bus** or **tram**. You can buy individual tickets from the driver, but it is cheaper to buy a **strip-penkaart** (strip of tickets) beforehand. These are available from VVV offices, post offices, nearly all tobacconists and newsagents, and in many hotels. If you plan to be in The Hague for several days, a **meerdagenkaart** (multi-day travelcard) is a good idea.

TOURS AND WALKS

In summer, the VVV organises two **guided bus tours** of the town: a royal tour of the palaces of The Hague and Scheveningen, and an architectural tour of the city's buildings, both ancient and modern. For bookings, ☎*0900 340 35 05*. The VVV also sells booklets giving details of **self-guided walking tours** on various themes.

BOAT AND FISHING TRIPS

Boat trips depart from **Scheveningen harbour:** *www.godenhaag.nl/uk/ sports_&_recreation; City Mondial, Wagenstraat 193. 070 402 33 36; Ooievaart, Bierkade. 099 340 35 05;* **Fishing trips:** *Rederij Vrolijk, Dr. Lelykade 22a, Scheveningen. www. rederijvrolijk.nl/nl.htm.*

SHOPPING

The Hague is a great place to shop. In addition to the big **city-centre department stores** and chain stores there are lots of excellent small shops in the streets and squares around the palaces. Indoor shopping is available at the stylish Passage (*Hofweg 5–7/Buitenhof 4–5*) and at the Babylon shopping centre next to the Centraal Station. But The Hague is best known for its countless **antique shops** and **commercial art galleries**; the VVV publishes brochures full of useful shopping suggestions.

Antique shop

Late-night shopping is on Thursdays, when the shops are open until 9pm. The best places to shop in **Scheveningen** are Palace Promenade, Gevers Deynootplein and the boulevard. Late-night shopping day is Friday, except in Palace Promenade, where the shops are open every day from 10am–10pm.

Markets – The Hague has excellent markets several days a week. There are **general goods markets** in Herman Costerstraat (Monday, Wednesday, Friday and Saturday) and on Markthof (Mon–Sat). A **farmers' market** takes place by the Grote Kerk on Wednesdays. A lively **art and antiques market** is held on Lange Voorhout on Thu and Sun from May to Sept, and on Thu on the Plein during the rest of the year.

THEATRES AND CONCERTS

Classical music: Dr. Anton Philipszaal, *Spuiplein 150.* ☎*070 360 98 10. www. dapz.ldt.nl.* Sunday morning concerts in the Circustheater, *Circusstraat 4, Scheveningen.* ☎*070 416 76 00. www.circustheater.nl.*

Pop rock blues: 't Paard, *Prinsegracht 12.* ☎*070 360 18 38. www.paard nl*

Theatre and dance: Koninklijke Schouwburg, *Korte Voorhout 3.* ☎*0900 345 67 89. www.koninklijke-schouwburg.nl.* Lucent Danstheater, *Spuiplein 152,* ☎*070 360 49 30. www. ldt.nl;* World Forum Convention Centre, *Churchillplein 10,* ☎*070 306 63 66. www. congresscentre.com.*

to the south of the Binnenhof. The central hall, whose glass roofing lets in the daylight, houses an original work of art by Lex Wegchelaar, made with marble elements taken from a low relief (1938) by RN Roland Holst. The plenary sessions are held in the semicircular chamber. Behind the speaker's chair are painted panels by R van de Wint.

Plein

The Ministry of Defence overlooks this square; in the centre stands the statue of William the Silent (1848). Number 23 is a splendid 18C building designed by Daniël Marot. In winter a market selling art and antiques is held on the square every Thursday.

Mauritshuis★★★

🕐 *Open Tue–Sat 10am–5pm, Sun and public holidays 11am–5pm. Also open Apr–Aug, Mon 10am–5pm.* 🕐 *Closed 25 Dec and 1 Jan.* ∞9.50€. *(including Galerij Prins Willem V).* ♿✉070 302 34 56. *www.mauritshuis.nl.*

This museum is named after Count Johan Maurits of Nassau-Siegen, who in around 1640 commissioned **Pieter Post** to build this elegant residence to plans by Jacob van Campen. It was built in a strictly Classical style, with its height, width and depth all approximately the same (c. 25m/80ft). Since 1822 it has been the home of the royal painting collection, one of the finest in the world; the relatively small number of paintings makes for a most agreeable visit.

The collection is still expanding, and is displayed in the form of temporary exhibitions, each highlighting a particular aspect of this rich assemblage of artworks. The permanent collection as described below is therefore rarely all on show at the same time.

Ground floor

This is devoted to foreign schools and the Flemish School. The first room of the **Flemish School** is remarkable with the moving *Lamentation of Christ* (c. 1450) by Rogier van der Weyden, the penetrating *Portrait of a Man* by Memling, and *Christ Carrying the Cross* by Quentin Metsys. There are lovely portraits by Holbein the Younger (16C), one of a young woman by the German Bartholomeus Bruyn; two portraits by Antonio Moro, including one of a goldsmith.

DEN HAAG

Street	Code	No.	Street	Code	No.	Street	Code	No.
Alexanderstr.	HX		Dr. de Visserpl.	DS	21	Houtzagerssingel	FV	
Amaliastr.	HX	3	Dr. Lelykade	DT		Hubertusviaduct	FT	
Amsterdamse Veerkade	JZ	4	Drie Hoekjes	HY	22	Huijgenspark	JZ	
Anna Paulownastr.	FU	6	Duinstr.	DT		Jacob Catslaan	EU	
Annastr.	HY	7	Duinweg	ET		Jacob Catsstr.	FV	
Ary van der Spuyweg	EU	9	Dunne Bierkade	JZ		Jacob Pronkstr.	DS	36
Badhuiskade	DS	10	Eisenhowerlaan	DET		Jan Hendrikstr.	HZ	
Badhuisweg	ES		Elandstr.	EFU		Jan van Nassaustr.	FU	
Bankastr.	FTU		Fahrenheitstr.	DUV		Javastr.	FU	
Beeklaan	DUEV		Fluwelen Burgwal	JY	24	Johan de Wittlaan	ETU	40
Belgischepl.	ES		Frankenslag	DT		Jozef Israëlslaan	GU	
Benoordenhoutseweg	GTU		Fred. Hendriklaan	DT		Juliana van Stolberglaan	GU	42
Bezuidenhoutseweg	GU		Geest	HY		Jurriaan Kokstr.	DS	
Binckhorstlaan	GV		Gentsestr.	ES		Kalvermarkt	JY	
Bleijenburg	JY	12	Gevers Deynootpl.	ES	27	Kanaalweg	ET	
Boekhorststr.	HZ		Gevers Deynootweg	DES		Kazernestr.	HJ	
Breedstr.	HY		Goudenregenstr.	DV		Keizerstr.	DS	
Buitenhof	HY		Groene Wegje	JZ	31	Kerkhoflaan	ET	
Buitenom	FV		Groenmarkt	HZ		Kneuterdijk	HY	45
Burg. de Monchypl.	FU	15	Groot Hertoginnelaan	DEU		Koningin Emmakade	EUV	
Burg. Patijnlaan	FU		Grote Marktstr.	HJZ		Koningin Julianapl.	GU	48
Carnegielaan	EU	18	Haringkade	EST		Koningin Marialaan	GU	51
Conradkade	DEU		Harstenhoekweg	ES		Koninginnegracht	FTU	
de la Reyweg	EV	96	Herengracht	JY		Koningskade	FU	
de Passage	HY	85	Heulstr.	HY	32	Koningspl.	EU	
Delftselaan	EV		Hobbemastr.	FV		Koningstr.	FV	
Denneweg	JX		Hoefkade	FV		Korte Molenstr.	HY	52
Doornisestr.	FS		Hofweg	HJY		Korte Poten	JY	54
Doornstr.	DT		Hogewal	HX		Korte Vijverberg	JY	55
Dr. Aletta Jacobsweg	FT	19	Hoogstr.	HY		Korte Voorhout	JX	
			Hooikade	JX	33	Kranenburgweg	DU	
			Houtrustweg	DU				

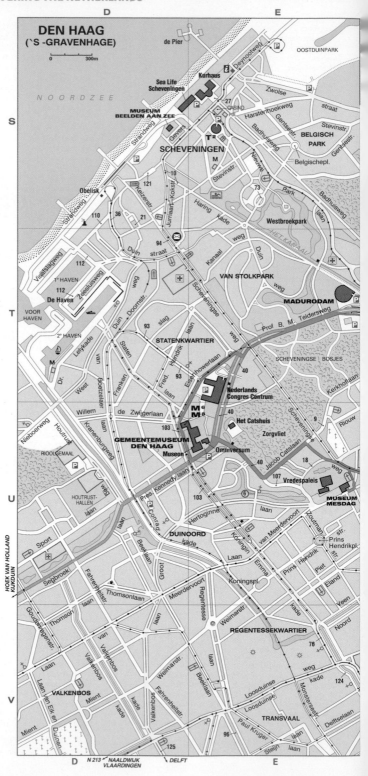

DEN HAAG
(`S -GRAVENHAGE)

0   300m

NOORDZEE

de Pier

OOSTDUINPARK

Sea Life
Scheveningen

Kurhaus

MUSEUM
BEELDEN AAN ZEE

27 CASINO
Pl.

Zwolse   straat

Harstenhoekweg Gentsestr.

BELGISCH
PARK

Stevinstr.

S

SCHEVENINGEN

Gevers

T²

M

Stevinstr.

Nieuwe

Belgischepl.

10

121

Keizerstr.

73

Park

Badhuisweg

Obelisk

110   36   21

Haring   kade

Westbroekpark

Straatweg

Visafslagweg

Strandweg

94

Duin   straat

Kanaal   weg

Duin   weg

VAN STOLKPARK

HET KANAAL

112

1° HAVEN

112

Zeesluisweg

De Haven

VOOR
HAVEN

2° HAVEN

M

Dr.   West

Boerzelaer

Franken

Fred   laan

93   slag

93

Scheveningse   weg

Eisenhowerlaan

Fred Hendrik   laan

Staten

van

Duin - Doornstr.

STATENKWARTIER

MADURODAM

Prof. B. M. Teldersweg

SCHEVENINGSE BOSJES

Kerkhoflaan

40

Nederlands
Congres Centrum

M⁶
M⁸

40

Het Catshuis

Scheveningse

9

Rouw

Willem   de   Zwijgerlaan

103

GEMEENTEMUSEUM
DEN HAAG

Museon

Omniversum

Zorgvliet

40   Jacob Catslaan

18   weg

Nieboerweg

RIOOLGEMAAL

Houtrust

Kranenburgweg

laan

107

Vredespaleis

MUSEUM
MESDAG

HOUTRUST-
HALLEN

weg

Pres. Kennedylaan

103

6

laan

Pres.   Conrad

HOEK VAN HOLLAND
KIJKDUIN

Sport

laan

laan

Hertoginne

DUINOORD
kade

Koningin   Emma

van Meerdervoort

Routman

Prins Hendrik

str.

Prins
Hendrikpl.

Piet   Eland

Beeklaan

Laan

Koningspl.

Weimarstr.

Piet

Veen

Noord

Segbroek

laan

Thomsonlaan

Meerdervoort

Regentesse

REGENTESSEKWARTIER

78

Gouderegenstr.

Thomson

laan

van

Valkenbos

Fahrenheitstr.

Beeklaan

laan

weg

kade

124

VALKENBOS

Mient

Valkenbos kade

Fahrenheitstr.

Loosduinse

Loosduinse

Monsterse

V

Mient

Laan en Elk en

Duinen

125

Paul Kruger   laan

96   Stein   laan

TRANSVAAL

Delftselaan

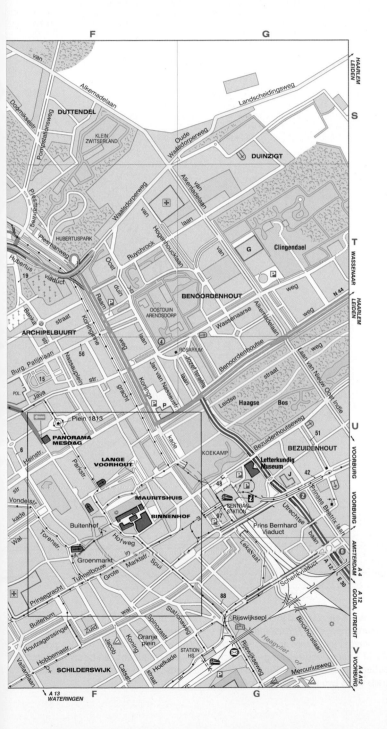

DEN HAAG

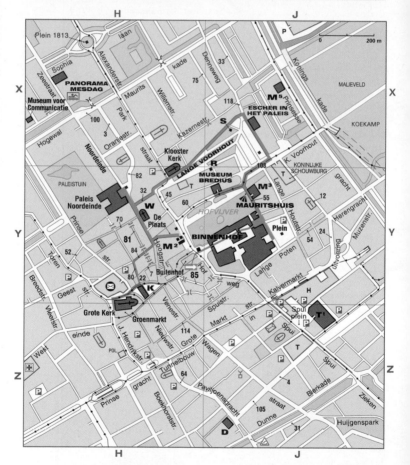

Two rooms are reserved for **Rubens** and his contemporaries. *The Adoration of the Shepherds* by Jordaens and canvases by David Teniers feature alongside a rich collection of works by Rubens: portraits of his two wives; *Michel Ophovius,* bishop of 's-Hertogenbosch; and finally the famous *Garden of Eden with the Fall of Man* (c. 1615), where the two people painted by Rubens can be seen against a landscape executed with charming meticulousness by Jan Brueghel the Elder. The two worked in collaboration.

First floor

Among the Dutch painters of the **Golden Age, Rembrandt** is the reigning master here. Between the portrait of the artist when he was 23 (1629; *Illustration:* (👁️ *see LEIDEN*), which holds one's attention by its meticulous precision of detail and its taste for scrupulous observation, and the portrait of 1669, one of his last works, with an overwhelming depth, one can see the whole evolution of the painter.

The Anatomy Lesson of Doctor Nicolaes Tulp (1632), his first group portrait painted when he was 26, brought him glory; the research in composition, the contrasts of light give the scene a dramatic intensity already characteristic.

The same emotion appears in *Susanna* of 1637, one of the rare nudes by Rembrandt, the *Simeon in the Temple* (1631) with its subdued muted light, or in the more fiery works like the pathetic *Saul and David* (1658) and *The Two Negroes* (1661).

The museum also has two admirable paintings by **Johannes Vermeer**, the *View of Delft* and the *Girl with a Pearl Earring* both c. 1660.

The museum has a number of genre paintings: some Jan Steens, where the verve, malice, and delicacy bring charming anecdotes to life (*Merry Company, Girl Eating Oysters*), some Van Ostades

Girl with a Pearl Earring (c. 1655) by Johannes Vermeer

with scenes of country life (*The Violinist*), portraits by Frans Hals (*Head of a Child*), some Ter Borchs and *The Young Mother* by Gerrit Dou. There are also landscape painters; painters of rivers (Van Goyen and Van de Velde), of the countryside (Salomon van Ruysdael and his nephew Jacob van Ruisdael), of skaters (Avercamp) and of domestic animals (Paulus Potter, *Young Bull*). There are also some small gems: the famous *Goldfinch* (1654) which Carel Fabritius, Rembrandt's pupil, painted in the year of his death at the age of 32.

Hofvijver

From Korte Vijverberg, there is a lovely **view**★ over this artificial lake in which are reflected the Mauritshuis, the

Hofvijver

octagonal tower of the Prime Minister's quarters, the windows of the Truce Hall and the Upper Chamber. In the middle of the lake, which has a fountain, there is an island planted with trees. Storks have nested here for many years, and the stork appears in the city's coat of arms.

Haags Historisch Museum
Open Tue–Fri 10am–5pm, Sat–Sun and public holidays noon–5pm. 4€. 070 364 69 40. www.haags historischmuseum.nl.
The collections of the Hague Historical Museum, installed in the former premises of the Archers' Company of St Sebastian (1636), illustrate the history of the town and the life of its townspeople: furniture, eggshell porcelain, church silver, views of the city, a doll's house and other items.

▶ *Follow Lange Vijverberg.*

Museum Bredius★
Open Tue–Sun and public holidays, 11am–5pm. Closed 25 Dec–1 Jan. 4.50€. 070 362 07 29. www.museum bredius.nl.
This museum has a privileged setting: a fine mansion built in 1757. The painting collection features many of the works left to the town by Abraham Bredius (1855–1946), an art historian and former director of the Mauritshuis. In the remarkable section on 17C art, you can admire the famous *Satyr among the Peasants* by Jan Steen, a fine *Christ's Head* by Rembrandt, *Festivities on the Ice* by A van der Neer, along with canvases by Albert Cuyp, Adriaen van Ostade, Willem Pieter Buytewech and JJ van de Velde. On the floor above, note the drawings by Rembrandt and Jacob van Ruysdael.

Lange Voorhout★
Along the tree-lined avenues of Lange Voorhout there are some of the most beautiful patrician residences in The Hague. Most of them are occupied by embassies. There is a large **art and antiques market** on Lange Voorhout in the summer and from the end of June to the beginning of September a large

open-air exhibition of modern sculpture is also held here every year.

Museum Het Paleis
Open Tue–Sun 11am–5pm. Closed between exhibitions, 1 Jan, and 25 Dec. 4.50€. 070 338 11 11.
The former palace of Queen Emma (1858–1934), wife of William III and mother to Wilhelmina, stands at the far end of the main avenue. Its elegant 18C façade was the work of Pieter de Swart. The municipal museum organises temporary exhibitions here.

Noordeinde
This busy street, lined with antique shops, crosses the square where the **Paleis Noordeinde** stands. Also called Het Oude Hof, this 16C–17C building is where Queen Beatrix has installed her offices. Opposite there is an equestrian statue of William the Silent.

▶ *Return via Noordeinde, past Heulstraat.*

Museum de Gevangenpoort
By guided tour only, on the hour, Tue–Fri 10am–5pm, Sat–Sun and public holidays noon–5pm. Closed 25 Dec and 1 Jan. 4€. 070 346 08 61. www. gevangenpoort.nl.
This 13C gatehouse was part of the ducal castle on the Binnenhof. In the 15C it became a prison, where a number of famous figures including Cornelis de Witt (see DORDRECHT) were incarcerated. It is now a museum, housing a collection of medieval instruments of torture and punishment.

Galerij Prins Willem V★
Open same times as Mauritshuis. 3€ (free for visitors with a Mauritshuis ticket). 070 302 34 35.
Although it only features a few works belonging to an original royal collection, the present display of 17C paintings is very interesting. It includes landscapes by Philips Wouwerman, a number of works by Jan Steen, *The Bear Hunt* by Paulus Potter, *Girl with a lamp* by Gerard Dou, and a picture by Van de Velde the Younger: *The War Ship at Sunset.*

Groenmarkt

This is the central square of The Hague, home to both the town hall and the Grote Kerk. Numerous pedestrian precincts start from here, notably **Paleispromenade** to the north, and **De Passage**, the large covered passage built in 1880, to the south.

Grote Kerk or St Jacobskerk

🕐*Open Jul and Aug, Mon–Fri, 11am–4pm; rest of the year by appointment.* ☎ *070 302 86 30. www.grotekerkdenhaag.nl (in Dutch).*
This great brick hall-type church (c. 1450) is roofed with a wooden vault. Several stained-glass windows are worth seeing in the ambulatory; on one, Charles V is shown kneeling at the Virgin's feet. The pulpit of 1550 is beautifully sculpted. The church is now used for cultural and commercial events.

Oude Raadhuis

The old town hall has a lovely 16C façade with crow-stepped gables. The 18C side façade is elegantly decorated. At the top of the richly ornamented front is the motto Ne Jupiter Quidem Omnibus (Even Jupiter cannot please everyone). The statues above the centre section depict Justice and Prudence with the coat of arms of The Hague and a Latin inscription which, loosely translated, means "Wise men learn by other men's mistakes, fools by their own."

Beyond the City Centre

Panorama Mesdag★

🕐*Open Mon–Sat 10am–5pm, Sun and public holidays noon–5pm.* 🕐*Closed 25 Dec, Jan 1.* ⊜*5€.* ☎ *070 364 45 44. www.panorama-mesdag.nl.*
Installed in a rotunda on piles, this extraordinary landscape, 120m/394ft in circumference and 14m/46ft in height, shows Scheveningen as it was in 1880, and is the work of artist **Hendrik Willem Mesdag**
Since the spectator is 14m/46ft away from this painting and standing on flotsam-strewn sand, the effect is that of looking down on the panorama from the top of a high dune. In the entrance halls, paintings and watercolours by Mesdag and his wife are exhibited.

Museum Mesdag★

🕐*Open Tue–Sun noon–5pm.* 🕐*Closed 25 Dec and 1 Jan.* ⊜*5€.* ☎*070 362 14 34. www.museummesdag.nl.*
Using the fortune he inherited from his father, Mesdag constructed this building beside his house in 1887 to house his growing collection of arts and crafts. He bequeathed everything to the State in 1903. The original house is now part of the museum. On the ground floor, in the studio where his wife Sientje formerly painted, authentic objects recreate the atmosphere of Mesdag's former studio. The museum allows an interesting comparison to be made between the Barbizon School with Millet, Daubigny, Corot, Théodore Rousseau, Courbet, and The Hague School with Bosboom, Mauve, the Maris brothers, Jozef Israëls and obviously Mesdag, the painter of seascapes. In the paintings of the two schools one finds fairly sombre tones, often greys, and a distinct preference for nature and landscapes.

Vredespaleis

➣*Guided tours Mon–Fri 10am, 11am, 2pm, 3pm and 4pm (by advanced booking). Museum only open for visitors in the guided tour at 11am and 3pm.* ⊜*5€.* ☎*070 302 42 42. www.vredespaleis.nl.*
The Peace Palace was inaugurated a year before the start of World War I, on 28 August 1913. On the initiative of Czar Nicholas II the first **Peace Conference** took place in The Hague (at Huis Ten Bosch) in 1899. It was decided at that time to create a Permanent Court of Arbitration whose functions were defined in 1907 during the Second Peace Conference which took place in the Riderzaal. In the meantime the American industrialist and philanthropist, Andrew Carnegie, donated the funds to house this Court, the Netherlands government donated the land and the French architect Cordonnier was put in charge of the construction. In 1922 the palace became, in addition, the seat of the Permanent Court of International Justice, which in 1946 became the **International Court**

of Justice (the United Nation's main judicial organ). It also houses the Academy of International Law of The Hague, founded in 1923.

Each nation has contributed to the furnishings and decoration of the palace. The Japanese room, hung with sumptuous tapestries, is where the Administrative Council meets, and where French is the official language; the members sit round an immense table with seats decorated with the various countries' coat of arms.

Walk alongside **Zorgvliet Park** to see **Het Catshuis** the Dutch Prime Minister's house which belonged to **Jacob Cats**.

Gemeentemuseum Den Haag★★

🕙Open Tue–Sun 11am–5pm. 🕙Closed Dec 25, Jan 1. ⊜8.50€. ☎070 338 11 11. www.gemeentemuseum.nl.

The Hague's municipal museum is a masterpiece of 20C museum architecture. Designed by **HP Berlage** and built in 1935, it consists of a reinforced concrete skeleton with a brick facing. A gallery leads to the different exhibition rooms, designed to gain the maximum advantage from natural light. A major refurbishment completed in October 1998 has restored this, Berlage's last design, to its former glory; it also included the addition of a fashion gallery.

The rich and very varied collections consist of decorative arts, 19C and 20C

Mill in Sunlight (1908) by Piet Mondriaan

Collectie Gemeentemuseum Den Haag/The Hague VCB

visual arts, costumes, musical instruments, drawings and prints.

Decorative arts

This section includes ceramics from Italy and Spain, Venetian glassware, blue and polychrome delftware and glassware manufactured in the Netherlands (17C and 18C). The collections of local silverware (15C–19C) and porcelain and ceramics (1776–1790; 1885–1914) give a picture of the items made in The Hague. Other objects are on display in 17C and 18C period interiors. Decorative arts from c. 1900 (including major examples of Dutch Art Nouveau) and modern design are well represented. The 15 new rooms around the fashion gallery feature masterpieces of decorative art from the Islamic world and the Far East.

Modern art

The museum houses works by great masters of the 19C and 20C. The **French School** is well represented, with paintings by Courbet, Sisley, Monet, Signac and Van Gogh (including *Garden at Arles* and *Poppy Field*). The museum also has three paintings by Picasso (*Woman With a Pot of Mustard, Harlequin, Sibyl*), and single works by Braque, Léger and Marquet. Like Van Gogh and Van Dongen, Jongkind worked in France for much of his life. The work of this artist, regarded as a precursor of French Impressionism, is well represented.

The collection of mainly German Expressionists includes works by Kirchner, Schmidt-Rottluff, Jawlensky and Kandinsky.

The museum offers an excellent overview of **Dutch painting** from the 19C to the present; the Romantics with W Nuyen, The Hague School (the Maris brothers, Jozef Israëls, Weissenbruch, Anton Mauve and Isaac Israëls), and Breitner, Verster and Toorop. However, the Gemeentemuseum is best known for its large collection of paintings and drawings by **Piet Mondrian**, including his last, uncompleted painting *Victory Boogie-Woogie* (1943–44, 🕭 *see AMERSFOORT*). It also owns important works by other pioneers of abstract art, such as the **De Stijl** group (🕭 *see AMERSFOORT*).

Among the post-war Dutch artists represented are Appel, Corneille, Constant, Schoonhoven, Van der Heyden and the sculptor Carel Visser. There is also work by foreign artists such as Vasarely, Arp, Ernst, Henry Moore and Francis Bacon.

Music
In addition to an extensive collection of musical instruments from all over the world, there is an exceptional display of European instruments from the 16C to the electronic age. Exhibitions are held in the music print section.

Fashion gallery
This new gallery has temporary exhibitions on historic and contemporary clothing and the work of specific designers.

Print collection
This has an impressive selection of works by 19C French artists including Daumier, Bresdin, Redon and Toulouse-Lautrec. Works by modern Dutch artists include watercolours and drawings by the Hague School, prints by Werkman and a significant proportion of the work of **MC Escher** (*Illustration: see LEEUWARDEN*). Temporary exhibitions are held.

Museon
Open Tue–Sun and daily during school holidays, 11am–5pm. Closed 25 Dec and 1 Jan. 7.50€. 070 338 13 38. www.museon.nl.

This broad-based science museum presents collections related to the history of the Earth, dealing with subjects such as geology, human evolution, the cultures of the world, science and technology. Photographs, film, sound and computers are used in both the permanent displays and temporary exhibitions, and visitors are invited to take an active part.

Omniversum
Open Mon 10am–5pm(Tue–Wed 7pm, Thu and Sun 9pm, Fri–Sat 10pm).For the film programme, see website. 9.50€. 0900 666 48 37. www.omniversum.nl.

The films and other presentations shown on this huge screen (840sq m/9 042 sq ft), which also serves as a planetarium,

are aimed at familiarising the viewer with the world of science, nature and culture. Two projection systems, around 40 loudspeakers and a great many projectors for special effects make for a breathtaking visual experience.

Nederlands Congres Centrum
The Netherlands Conference Centre was built to plans of the architect JJP Oud by his son between 1964 and 1968. The conference centre is a vast building with walls of sky-blue tiles and yellow bricks, overlooked by a triangular 17-storey tower. The entrance, on the north side, is highlighted by a large composition by Karel Appel in red and blue mosaic. Among the many meeting rooms, the large conference centre (seating capacity 2 000) is three storeys high. In the basement the festival hall, which can hold 4 000 people, is used for banquets and exhibitions.

Madurodam★★
Open Mar–Jun, daily 9am–8pm; Jul and Aug, daily 9am–11pm; Sept–Feb, daily 9am–5pm. 13.75€. 070 416 24 00. www.madurodam.nl.

This miniature town was built in 1952, and was originally intended for children, but adults will also enjoy the superb 1:25-scale models. It is essentially a microcosm of the Netherlands, with buildings, monuments and typical scenes from all around the country, including bulb fields, windmills, and

© Madurodam/The Hague VCB

Madurodam

farmhouses from the different provinces. The miniature town was completely renovated during the 1990s. In addition to the old favourites such as the Sint-Janskathedraal in 's Hertogenbosch, the Domtoren in Utrecht, Anne Frank's house and the Muiderslot, new buildings have been added, including the ING Bank in southeast Amsterdam, the "De Maas" office building and the Erasmus Bridge in Rotterdam, the environment ministry in The Hague, and the new Groninger Museum. Working trains, cars, buses and boats and night-time lighting add to the fascination of this living town.

Additional Sights

Heilige Geesthofje
Built in 1616, this almshouse is a charming enclosure with small low houses with crow-stepped dormer windows. Opposite, near the house (n° 74) where Spinoza ended his days, stands the statue of this illustrious philosopher.

Museum van Het Boek/Museum Meermanno-Westreenianum
Open Tue–Fri 11am–5pm, Sat–Sun and public holidays, noon–5pm. Closed 25 Dec and 1 Jan. 4€. 070 346 27 00. www.meermanno.nl.
On Prinsessegracht, lined with 18C mansions, this museum houses the Baron van Westreenen's collections. The ground floor is usually devoted to exhibitions about modern and antique books. On the 1st floor, in the library, there are **manuscripts and incunabula** from the medieval period. The museum also contains Greek, Roman and Egyptian antiquities.

Letterkundig Museum   Kids
Access via the library (Koninklijke Bibliotheek). Open Tue–Fri, 10am–5pm, Sat–Sun and public holidays, noon–5pm. Closed 30 Apr, Easter and 1 Jan. Sunday, 5 May, Whitsun and 25 Dec. 3.50€; children 2€. 070 333 96 66. www.letmus.nl.
This museum of literature uses manuscripts, letters, curios, portraits and audio-visual material to give an overview

of Dutch literature from 1750 onwards. There is also a **museum of children's books** and temporary exhibitions are also held.

Haagse Bos
Crossed by Leidsestraatweg, these woods surround the royal palace, **Huis ten Bosch**, where the first Peace Conference was held in 1899. This edifice was built in the 17C by Pieter Post for Amalia Van Solms, the widow of Stadtholder Frederick Henry. It is Queen Beatrix's official residence.

Clingendael
This extensive park, with its meadows shaded by majestic trees and strewn with lakes, was once private property; there is a splendid Japanese garden.

Westbroekpark
This park surrounded by lakes (rowing) is famous for its **rose garden** (*early July–late September*) where an international exhibition is held annually.

Scheveningen

G. Deynootweg 1134 – 2586 BX. 0900 340 35 05. www.scheveningen.nl.
Scheveningen is an elegant seaside resort with a very large and busy beach. It has often been devastated by storms; the storm of 1570 submerged part of the village. The church, originally located in the town centre, is now near the beach. Today Scheveningen is protected by many breakwaters and a high dyke.

The beach
This long and wide stretch of fine sand is lined for 3km/1.8mi by a boulevard, Strandweg, which is the continuation to the east of a promenade where many café terraces are opened up during the summer months. Overlooking the beach, the imposing restored **Kurhaus** (1885; *see Address Book*) is now home to a casino; special events are also held here.
The **Pier**, with its long promenade, leads to four constructions built on piles offering entertainment. An observation tower 45m/147.6ft high offers a

NBTC

Kurhaus, Scheveningen

panoramic view of Scheveningen, The Hague, the dunes towards Wassenaar and out to sea.

The port

Beyond the lighthouse, towards the west, the fishing port remains very busy. Two inner docks have coasting vessels, pleasure boats and a fleet of trawlers. The **obelisk** commemorates the place where William I landed from England to take possession of his throne in November 1813.

Museum Beelden aan Zee★★

Open Tue–Sun, 11am–5pm. Closed 25, 26 Dec and 1 Jan. 7€. 070 358 58 57. www.beeldenaanzee.nl

This seaside sculpture museum was designed by the Dutch architect **Wim Quist** and opened in 1994. On display is the exceptionally varied collection of Mr and Mrs Scholten-Miltenburg. It consists of works by contemporary artists from all over the world, such as Karel Appel, Fritz Koenig, Francisca Zijlstra, Shinkichi Tajiri, Waldermar Otto, Man Ray and Igor Mitoraj. The theme of the collection is the **universality of the human figure** with all its different experiences, feel-

ings and moods. On the **south patio** there is a magnificent bronze sculpture of the royal family by Arthur Spronken. There is a fine view of the North Sea from the **sea room**

Sea Life Scheveningen

Open daily 10am–7pm (Aug until 8pm). Closed 25 Dec. 070 354 21 00. www.sealife.nl.

This aquarium features life forms from the beach to the deepest depths of the sea, and includes sharks, rays, crabs, conger eels and jellyfish. There is also an underwater observatory, a tropical reef adventure and an underwater tunnel.

Excursions

Voorburg

3km/1.5mi to the east via the A 12 exit 4. **Hofwijck Manor** stands quite near Voorburg station, and today it houses the **Huygensmuseum Hofwijck** (open Tue, Wed, Thu and Sat–Sun, 1pm–5pm; closed public holidays. 6€; 070 387 23 11; www.hofwijck.nl). This small manor, surrounded by water, was designed by **Constantijn Huygens**

(1596–1687) and built by the architect **Pieter Post** in the years 1641–43. Part of the symmetrical garden still exists today. Constantijn Huygens, who acted as first secretary to the stadtholders Frederick Henry, William II and William III, was also a poet and a composer. He decided to have Hofwijck built as a refuge from his busy life in The Hague; "hof wijk" means "refuge from the court." His son **Christiaan Huygens** (1629–95), inventor of the pendulum clock and a great astronomer and physicist, returned to the Netherlands here after a long stay in London and Paris. He settled in Hofwijck, where he lived until his death. The collections in the museum retrace the history of the family: portraits, original editions of works by Constantijn Huygens and a replica made in Leiden of Christiaan Huygens' world-famous pendulum clock.

Wassenaar

12km/7.4mi to the north; leave The Hague via Benoordenhoutseweg.
Wassenaar is one of the most attractive residential suburbs of the Randstad conurbation, and large numbers of people commute from here to The Hague. It has many substantial villas hidden among trees. The **Duinrell theme park** (*open early Apr–Oct, daily 10am–5pm (6pm Jul and Aug); 16€; 070 515 52 58; www.duinrell.nl*) is hidden amid the woods and dunes, and includes a large recreation area, roller coasters, numerous water attractions and a large tropical swimming-pool complex, the **Tikibad**.

Naaldwijk

16km/10mi to the south via Oude Haagweg. In the heart of Westland, Naaldwijk (sometimes called the Glass Town) is a large horticultural centre and has a major **auction** (*open Fri–Wed 8am–10am. Closed public holidays. 6€. 0174 63 21 58. www.bvh.nl*) of cut flowers and potted plants (*Dijkweg 66, Honselersdijk*). On Wilhelminaplein, the old 17C **town hall** has a Baroque voluted gable.

HAARLEM★★

NOORD-HOLLAND P
POPULATION 147 020
LOCAL MAP SEE KEUKENHOF
PLAN OF THE CONURBATION IN THE CURRENT RED-COVER MICHELIN GUIDE BENELUX

The town played an important role in the history of the earldom of Holland, and, being the birthplace of Dirk Bouts and Adriaen van Ostade as well as the residence of Frans Hals, it was also of great significance in the history of Dutch art. Today the town is the centre of a large bulb-growing region (*see Keukenhof*). In spring, the Bloemencorso or flower parade starts in Noordwijk and ends in Haarlem. Although Haarlem is not situated very far inland, it is well protected from the North Sea winds by the dunes. And although it lies only about twenty kilometres from Amsterdam, it still has the typical atmosphere, tranquility and elegance of the towns in Holland's hinterland.

- **Information:** Stationsplein 1 – 2011 LR. 0900 616 16 00. www.vvvzk.nl.
- **Orient Yourself:** Situated on the Spaarne, Haarlem is the capital of the province of Noord-Holland.
- **Parking:** There are not many car parks in the heart of the city centre but there are more within walking distance.
- **Don't Miss:** The paintings of Frans Hals are one good reason for spending time in Haarlem.
- **Organizing Your Time:** Give yourself a day to fully enjoy the city.

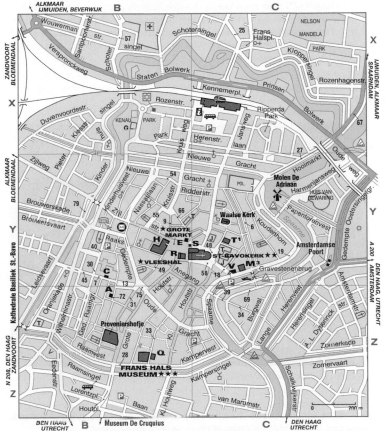

HAARLEM						
		Ged. Voldersgracht	BY 30	Nieuwe Groenmarkt	BY	55
		Gierstr.	BZ 31	Ostadestr.	BX	57
Anegang	BCY	Groot Heiligland	BZ 33	Oude Groenmarkt	BCY	58
Bakenessergracht	CY 6	Grote Houtstr.	BYZ	Smedestr.	BY	66
Barrevoetestr.	BY 7	Hagestr.	CZ 34	Spaardamseweg	CX	67
Barteljorisstr.	BY 9	Hoogstr.	CZ 39	Spaarnwouderstr.	CZ	69
Botermarkt	BYZ 13	Jacobstr.	BY 40	Tuchthuisstr.	BZ	72
Damstr.	CY 18	Keizerstr.	BY 45	Verwulft	BYZ	75
Donkere Spaarne	CY 19	Klokhuispl.	CY 48	Zijlsingel	BY	79
Frans Halsstr.	CX 25	Koningstr.	BY 49	Zijlstr.	BY	
Friese Varkenmarkt	CXY 27	Kruisstr.	BY			
Gasthuisvest	BZ 28	Nassaustr.	BY 54			

Brouwershofje	BZ A	Teylers Museum	CY M³	Voormalig Sint-Elisabeths		
Hofje van Loo	BY C	Toneelschuur	CY T¹	Gasthuis	BZ	Q
Hoofdwacht	BY E	Verweyhal	BY R	Waag	CY	V
Stadhuis	BY H	Vishal	BCY S			

A Bit of History

Haarlem was founded in the 10C and is therefore older than Amsterdam. It was the residence of the Counts of Holland and was fortified in the 12C. It obtained its city charter in 1245. In the 13C some of the townspeople took part in the Fifth Crusade and the capture of Damietta in Egypt in 1219. The bells of the Grote Kerk are still called *damiaatjes* in memory of this great deed.

A bloody siege – During the uprising against the Spanish, Haarlem was besieged for seven months (1572–3).

Frans Hals

This painter was born in Antwerp c. 1582, but his family moved to Haarlem around 1591. Frans Hals became the portrait painter of the town's bourgeois at a time when the portrait and particularly group portraits (guilds, brotherhoods) were in fashion. Of the 240 works ascribed to Hals, no fewer than 195 are portraits.

Hals abandoned the tradition of rigid poses and stilted compositions and introduced, especially in his commissioned works, a certain vitality and more natural attitudes for his subjects. In some cases he went so far as to catch them unawares. His bold and fluent brushwork was considered sloppy at the time. He enlivened his canvases with bright splashes of colour on scarves and flags. His rapid but expressive brush strokes, which foreshadowed modern art and especially Impressionism, gave his models a life, a mobility which made his portraits real snapshots.

For a long time a frank cheerfulness radiated from his paintings, but after 1640 there was no longer the verve and fantasy in his works. In the famous group of regents and regentesses the return to black and white, verticality, expressionless faces, even disenchantment, left a sinister impression, almost a forewarning of his death two years later (1666) at the age of 84.

Frans Hals' many pupils included **Judith Leyster** (1609–60), the Fleming **Adriaen Brouwer** and **Adriaen van Ostade** (1610–85), painter of village scenes. The latter's pupils were his brother Isaack, as well as Jan Steen.

Frans Halsmuseum

The Banquet of the Officers of the Civic Guard of St Adrian by Frans Hals

During the winter, William the Silent managed to provide the town with supplies through the Beggars, who came on skates over Haarlemmermeer, but despite the heroic defence by the whole population, the town capitulated in June 1573.

The 17C marks the peak of Haarlem; the town took advantage of the fall of Flemish cities by developing the linen industry and made a fabric sold all over Europe under the name of 'holland' (a plain weave linen).

Haarlemmermeer – Formed by peat exploitation, this great lake of about 18 000ha/44 479 acres was a threat to Amsterdam and Leyden due to storms. As early as 1641, the famous hydraulic engineer, **Jan Adriaenszoon Leeghwater**, had suggested draining it by using windmills and making polders. The work was not undertaken until two centuries later, when steam-powered **pumps** took the place of windmills. Three pumping stations were installed, one being the one invented by Cruquius.

The present territory of Haarlemmermeer, which has become a district borough, is an average 4m/13ft below sea level, and Schiphol Airport, which is located there is 4.5m/14.7ft below. The silty marine deposits found under the peat bogs are very fertile.

A hot-bed of artistic genius – Haarlem is probably the birthplace of **Claus Sluter** (c. 1345–1406), a sculptor who produced works of great realism, working for the Dukes of Burgundy in the Charterhouse of Champmol near Dijon. The painters Dirk Bouts, who went to live in Leuven (Belgium), and Jan Mostaert, who painted religious scenes and was painter to Margaret of Austria, were both born in Haarlem during the 15C, while **Geertgen tot Sint Jans** lived here for a time (⚲ see LEIDEN).

In the 16C **Maarten van Heemskerck** (1498–1574) was the pupil of **Jan van Scorel** during his stay in Haarlem from 1527–29. **Cornelis van Haarlem**, Mannerist painter (1562–1638), and **Willem Claeszoon Heda** (1594–1680), famous for his still-life paintings, were born in this town. The engraver **Hendrick Goltzius** (1558–1617), **Pieter Claeszoon** (1597–1661), another still-life painter, and **Pieter Saenredam** (1597–1665), painter of serene church interiors, all ended their days here. **Hercules Seghers** (1589/90–1638), a remarkable landscape painter, was probably born here. **Lieven de Key** (c. 1560–1627), who was part of the 'brain drain' from Flanders to the Netherlands and who became the town's architect in 1593, was one of the great Renaissance architects. ⚲ For information about Frans Hals, see text box above.

Portrait painter **Bartholomeus van der Helst** (1613–70), **Philips Wouwerman** (1619–68), a painter of horses, imitated by his brother Pieter, and **Nicolaes Berchem** (1620–83) who, unlike his father Pieter Claeszoon, painted landscapes, were also born in Haarlem. Another native of Haarlem, **Adriaen**

van Ostade (1610–84), was principally a genre painter whose work is characterised by extreme realism. **Salomon van Ruysdael**, who was born in Naarden (c. 1600–70) but settled in Haarlem, was one of the foremost pioneers of Dutch landscape painting together with Jan van Goyen. His nephew and pupil **Jacob van Ruysdael** (1628/9–82) was born in Haarlem. He painted more tormented landscapes, already romantic with dark cliffs, waterfalls, trees menaced by storm, and disquieting chiaroscuros.

Around Grote Markt

Grote Markt★

This great square is bordered by the Grote Kerk, the Stadhuis and the former meat market. In the square there is a statue of **Laurens Coster** (1405–84) (his real name was Laurens Janszoon) considered in the Netherlands to be the inventor of printing in 1423, that is to say about ten years before Gutenberg.

Grote Kerk or St Bavokerk★★

Entrance: Oude Groenmarkt 23. ⊙*Open Mon–Sat 10am–4pm, Sun in summer 10am–7pm.* ☎ *023 553 20 40. www. bavo.nl (in Dutch).*

This large 15C church, which should not be confused with the Catholic St Bavo's (*Leidsevaart*), has an elegant wooden lantern tower covered with lead sheeting, 80m/262.4ft high over the **transept crossing**★. The entrance to the church is surrounded by booths, erected against the southern façade. These booths were rented out by the clergy to pay for the maintenance of the sacrarium.

Inside, admire the short nave and, in the long chancel, a lovely cedar-wood stellar **vault**★. The gravestones on the floor include that of **Pieter Saenredam**, and **Frans Hals** is also buried here (*in the chancel*). Note also a 17C pulpit with a Gothic sounding board, choir stalls (1512) carved with amusing subjects, the copper lectern in the shape of a pelican (1499), and above all the lovely early 16C **chancel screen**★, backed by finely worked brass. The great **organ**★ (*illustration:* ⚲ *see Introduction, Music*) built by Christiaen Müller in 1738 was decorated according to the drawings of Daniël Marot. It has long been considered one of the best organs in the world, and it is said that Handel and Mozart (as a child) came to play this instrument. An international organ festival is organised every two years in Haarlem (&see Calendar of events).

Vishal

&Same opening times as Frans Halsmuseum. ✆5€. & ✆023 532 68 56. www.devishal.nl (in Dutch).

The fish market was built in 1769, up against the northern façade of St Bavokerk; like the meat market, it is an annexe of the Frans Hals museum.

Vleeshal★

&Same opening times as Frans Halsmuseum. ✆5€. & ✆023 511 57 75.

The Meat Hall is an ornamental building in the Mannerist style, built by Lieven de Key between 1602 and 1604. It has richly decorated dormer windows and a façade decorated with the heads of oxen and sheep. The building is part of the Frans Halsmuseum, and is used for temporary exhibitions. The basement houses the **Archeologisch Museum Haarlem** (&open Wed–Sun 1pm–5pm. &closed 25, 26 Dec and 1 Jan; ✆no charge; ✆023 531 31 35).

Verweyhal

&Same opening times as Frans Halsmuseum. ✆5€. ✆023 511 57 75. www.franshalsmuseum.nl

This hall, also part of the Frans Halsmuseum, is named after the Haarlem-born Impressionist painter Kees Verwey; some of his work is on display in the museum.

Stadhuis★

✆Guided tours by appointment only. ✆023 511 31 58.

The town hall, with its slim tower, is a 14C Gothic building to which numerous alterations have been made; the protruding section on the right has a gallery on the ground floor and a 15C and 17C voluted façade, while on the left there is a Renaissance-style loggia above the flight of steps. The **Gravenzaal** or

Counts' Hall on the 1st floor has kept its original appearance; the paintings which hang here are copies of old murals from the Carmelite convent and depict the Counts of Holland.

Frans Hals Museum
★★★ 1hr 30min

&Open Tue–Sat 11am–5pm, Sun and public holidays, noon–5pm. &Closed 25 Dec and 1 Jan. ✆7.50€. ✆023 511 57 75. www.franshalsmuseum.nl.

Since 1913, this museum has occupied a **former almshouse for old men** built between 1607 and 1610. Prior to being used as a museum the building was an orphanage (1810–1908).

The façade is characteristic of this type of institution with a row of low houses on either side of the entrance, topped with a crow-stepped gable and window. Behind this façade is an inner courtyard around which the rooms are arranged. The group of houses with crow-stepped gables opposite the museum used to be part of the **St Elisabeths Gasthuis**, whose regents were the subject of portraits painted by Frans Hals.

Works by Frans Hals

The eight paintings of civic guards (room 21) and regents by Frans Hals constitute a remarkable collection making it possible to follow the evolution of the master's style.

The first painting which marks the already brilliant beginnings of the painter dates from 1616, when Hals was about 34 years old. It is the **The Banquet of the Officers of the Civic Guard of St George** The mobility of the characters and their personalities are shown in an extraordinary way. The atmosphere is less restrained in the The Banquet of the Officers of the Civic Guard of St George and The Officers of the Civic Guard of St Adrian, both painted in 1627 and rich in spontaneity and colour. In **The Officers of the Civic Guard of St Adrian** of 1633, Frans Hals displays the height of his virtuosity. **The Officers of the Civic Guard of St George** of 1639, with a self-portrait of the artist (figure n° 19 in the top left-hand corner) is the last of this genre.

In 1641 a tendency for restraint and solemnity appears in Frans Hals' work and predominates in the Regents of *St Elizabeth's Hospital* (*room 25*). The sombre colour of the garments underlines the expression on the faces and the very studied attitude of the hands. In 1664, Hals was over eighty when he produced *Regents of the Old Men's Home* (*room 28*); in this daring, somewhat cynical study of six characters, Hals had the cheek to portray one of them as being quite tipsy with his hat perched on the back of his head. Painted the same year, the painting of the **Regentesses of the Old Men's Home** (*room 28*) with furrowed hands, bony faces, and severe looks, communicates a sentiment of anguish and discomfort.

The Haarlem School

A distinction is usually made between the first and the second Haarlem School. The **first Haarlem School** (15C and first half of the 16C) is particularly associated with religious art, characterised by strong realism. The Mannerist works of Jan van Scorel (*Baptism of Christ in the River Jordan*), Maarten van Heemskerck, Karel van Mander and Cornelis Corneliszoon van Haarlem (*Baptism of Christ*) are perfect examples of this movement. The **second Haarlem School**, which flourished in the second half of the 17C, saw the development of the various types of subject into separate genres. Frans Hals was the master of the group portrait; Esaias van de Velde, Salomon and Jacob van Ruysdael, and Van Goyen specialised in landscapes; Terborch, Van Ostade and Judith Leyster painted mainly genre scenes; Verspronck produced very fine portraits; Wouwerman and Cuyp specialised in painting animals; Pieter Saenredam and Jacob Berckheyde painted mainly church interiors; and Floris van Dijck and Willem Claeszoon Heda founded a distinguished tradition of still-life painting.

Crafts

Apart from paintings, the museum contains collections of furniture, Haarlem silverware (in the former ward); a **book of tulip drawings** by Judith Leyster, the reconstruction of an **apothecary** with delftware jars and, in a room with Dutch gilded leather, an 18C **doll's house**.

Modern art

In a new wing there are **modern and contemporary Dutch paintings**, notably by Isaac Israëls, Jan Sluyters, Piet Mondrian (figurative period) and members of the Cobra Group.

Additional Sights

Teylers Museum★

🕐*Open Tue–Sat 10am–5pm, Sun and public holidays noon–5pm.* 🕐*Closed 25 Dec and 1 Jan.* ✆*7€.* ☎*023 516 09 60. www.teylersmuseum.nl (in Dutch).*
The first museum to open in the Netherlands (1784), this is now the oldest public museum in the Netherlands, built after the Haarlem banker and wool and silk merchant, Pieter Teyler van der Hulst (1702–78). He wrote a will leaving all his money to the furtherance of the arts and sciences and construction began in 1779.
The old rooms, and particularly the beautiful stucco-decorated **Ovale Zaal** (1784), have kept their attractively antiquated appearance. They contain displays of early fossil finds, minerals and scientific instruments, including the largest electrostatic generator ever built, dating from 1791.
The Aquarellenzaal, or **Watercolour Room**, was converted in 1996 to house a changing selection from the superb **collection of drawings★★**. This consists of around 2 500 works by Dutch masters such as Goltzius, Rembrandt and

The Ovale Zaal (1784), Teylers Museum

Schelfhout, some 1 500 Italian works by artists including Michelangelo, Raphael, Pietro Testa and Annibale Carracci, many of which formerly belonged to Queen Christina of Sweden, and drawings by Dürer, Watteau, Boucher and others.

The two rooms of paintings contain interesting examples from the Romantic era, and works from the Hague School and the Amsterdam School, including *Summer Landscape* by Barend Cornelis Koekkoek, *The River Lek at Elshout* by J Weissenbruch, *Evening at Sea* by Hendrik Willem Mesdag, and *Children in the Dunes* by George Hendrik Breitner.

The **numismatic collection** contains examples of Dutch medals from the 16C to the 20C, and coins from Gelderland and West Friesland.

The most recent wing (1996) is used for temporary exhibitions.

Waag

At the corner of Damstraat and Spaarne stands the **Waag**, or weigh-house, built in 1598 in the Mannerist style and attributed to Lieven de Key. This is where the ships' cargo used to be weighed.

Waalse Kerk

The Walloon Church is Haarlem's oldest place of worship, and was the chapel of the Beguine convent until 1586.

Amsterdamse Poort

This late 15C gateway, preceded on the town side by two turrets, was also a water-gate commanding the Spaarne.

Haarlem Station

The Netherlands' first railway line, between Amsterdam and Haarlem, was built in 1839 (see *Introduction, Industrial heritage*). The elegant Art Nouveau station, dating from 1908, is still in use.

Former Sint-Elisabeths Gasthuis

Groot Heiligland 47, diagonally opposite the Frans Hals Museum.

This former hospital now houses the following:

Historisch museum Haarlem

Open Tue–Sat noon–5pm, Sun 1pm–5pm. Closed 25, 26, 31 Dec and 1 Jan. 2€. 023 542 24 27. www.historisch museumhaarlem.nl (in Dutch). This small museum tracing the town's history includes a model of Haarlem in 1822. The story of the town is told by Laurens Janszoon Coster in an audio-visual presentation.

ABC Architectuurcentrum

Open Tue–Sat noon–5pm, Sun 1pm–5pm. Closed public holidays. No charge. 023 534 05 84. www.architect uurhaarlem.nl (in Dutch).

This centre of architecture holds temporary exhibitions on historic and modern architecture.

Spaarnestad Fotoarchief

First floor. Open Tue–Sun noon–5pm. Closed 5 May, Easter, 26 Dec and 1 Jan. 023 551 84 32. www.spaarnefoto.nl.

These photo archives, the largest in the Netherlands, contain more than three million press photographs, spanning the period from 1870 right up to the end of the 20C. The temporary exhibitions provide a good insight into the archives' full collection.

Oude hofjes (Almshouses)

Among the numerous charitable institutions which the people of the wealthy town of Haarlem had from the 15C on are the **Proveniershof** of 1592 which has a large doorway opening on Grote Houtstraat, the **Brouwershofje** (1472) in Tuchthuisstraat and the charming **Hofje van Loo** of 1489, visible from Barrevoetestraat.

Kathedrale Basiliek

Leidsevaart 146. Open Apr–Sept and during school holidays, Mon–Sat 10am–4pm, Sun 1pm–4pm. 023 553 33 77.

The sacristy of this very large neo-Gothic basilica, built between 1895 and 1906 by JT Cuypers, son of PJH Cuypers (see *Introduction, Industrial heritage*), contains the **treasury**: a large collection of liturgical objects, mainly gold and silverware (15C–20C). Note the early 16C robes which come from an old Beguine convent in the town.

Outskirts

Museum De Cruquius★

7km/4.3mi to the southeast via the Dreef, northeast of a large bridge on the road to Vijfhuizen. Local map see KEUKENHOF. Open Mar–Oct, Mon–Fri 10am–5pm, Sat–Sun and public holidays 11am–5pm; Nov–Feb, Sat–Sun 11am–5pm. 5€. ☎023 528 57 04. www.museumde cruquius.nl.

This museum, on the edge of the old Haarlemmermeer, is installed in one of the three pumping stations, which were used between 1849 and 1852 to drain it. The station bears the name of the hydraulic engineer Nicolaas de Kruik, alias **Nicolaas Cruquius** (1678–1754), instigator of a project (1750) to drain the lake. The museum presents interesting material on the technical developments in the history of man's fight against the sea, and on the creation of polders, including a scale model illustrating the theory of a polder and an animated scale model showing the part of the Netherlands which would be flooded by the sea in the absence of dykes and dams.

Visitors may also admire the station's original **steam engine★**, fitted with eight beam engines and eight pumps, in the neo-Gothic engine room. Built in Cornwall, this unique machine was inaugurated in 1849.

Stoomgemaal Halfweg

8km/5mi east via the A 5 towards Amsterdam (Zwanenburg exit). Open Apr–Sept, Wed and Thu 1pm–4pm, Sat 10am–4pm. 2.50€. ☎020 497 43 96. www.stoomgemaalhalfweg.nl.

This is the world's oldest working steam-driven pumping station, built in 1853. It originally had a capacity of 25 000l/5 499gal of water a second. One of the two steam boilers has been dismantled to show the mechanism of the pumping station.

Spaarndam

8km/5mi to the northeast via Spaarn-damseweg, which becomes Vondelweg, then after a bend take Vergierdeweg on the right.

The houses of this picturesque village – a wonderful place to enjoy some smoked eel and a glass of beer – huddle up along both sides of the dyke. This is interspersed with several locks and on one of them there is a statue of **Hans Brinker**. According to legend, the young boy plugged a hole he had discovered in a protecting dyke with his finger for a whole night and thus saved the town from being flooded. The origin of this anecdote is a children's book written in 1873 by the American novelist, Mary Mapes Dodge, *Hans Brinker or the Silver Skates*. Beyond this small monument is the marina; a path makes it possible to walk alongside the water to reach the Oost- and Westkolk docks to see some beautifully restored houses.

Zandvoort⌂⌂⌂

11km/6.8mi west via Leidsevaart. Town plan in the current red-cover Michelin Guide Benelux.

This is one of the busiest seaside resorts in the Netherlands. A large avenue runs along the dunes which overlook the beach. Since 1976 Zandvoort has had a **casino** The **Circus Zandvoort** (*Gasthu-isplein 5*) is a fine example of modern architecture by Sjoerd Soeters, built in 1991 and including a cinema and a theatre. The famous Zandvoort **racing circuit** lies to the north of the town. The Dutch Formula 1 Grand Prix was held here until 1985, and today it is the Formula 3 racing circuit.

Excursions

Bulb fields★★★ –

See KEUKENHOF, Bulb fields.

From Bloemendaal aan Zee to Beverwijk

35km/21.7mi to the north via Verspronckweg.

Bloemendaal aan Zee

This is Haarlem's family beach.

Nationaal Park Zuid-Kennemerland

Visitor centre at the southeast entrance to the park in Overveen. Open Tue–Sun 10am–5pm. Closed Easter, Whitsun, 25 Dec and 1 Jan. No charge. ☎023 541 11 23.

This national park, 3 800ha/9 390acres in area, is situated on the long line of dunes edging the North Sea, and criss-crossed by foot- and cycle paths. Large numbers of migratory birds pass through here.

Bloemendaal

Behind the chain of dunes, this is an elegant residential centre where the villas stretch over wooded hills. In the open-air theatre, or Openluchttheater (*Hoge Duin en Daalseweg 2*), theatrical performances are given in summer. Nearby is the highest dune in the country, **Het Kopje** (50m/164ft). Further to the north are the ruins of **Kasteel Brederode**, destroyed by the Spanish in 1573.

IJmuiden

IJmuiden, at the far end of the North Sea canal, is famous for its locks, but it is also a seaside resort and ranks as the country's biggest fishing port. Three sea **locks**★ make it possible for seagoing ships of up to 80 000 tonnes to sail up to Amsterdam. The north lock, the most recent, was inaugurated on 29 April 1930. It is 400m/1 312ft long, 40m/131ft wide and 15m/49ft deep.
The local beach is somewhat marred by chimney stacks and plumes of smoke.

Beverwijk

Together with Heemskerk, this community forms the residential area of the **IJmond**, one of the country's leading industrial zones. The **Beverwijkse Bazaar** a large covered market (*weekends only*), has some 3 000 stalls. The blast furnaces between Beverwijk and the seaside resort **Wijk aan Zee** are hidden from view by a green belt.

HARDERWIJK

GELDERLAND
POPULATION 42 057

Harderwijk was another of the Hanseatic League ports on the old Zuiderzee. It has retained a few picturesque lanes, the remains of its brick ramparts and its port, where you can eat excellent smoked eel. The hinterland, which is part of the Veluwe with great stretches of dunes, forests and heathland, is very attractive and includes several nature reserves. **Carolus Linnaeus** (Carl von Linné, 1707–78), the famous Swedish botanist and pioneer of scientific classification, is closely associated with Harderwijk, having attended the university here. Founded in 1647, this institution was abolished by Napoleon in 1811.

- **Information:** ANWB Harderwijk Bleek 102 3841GC. ☎0341 42 66 66. www.vvvharderwijk.nl (in Dutch).
- **Orient Yourself:** Situated on the edge of Veluwemeer, Harderwijk has two pleasure boat harbours and a beach, and attracts many tourists.
- **Especially for Kids:** Seeing the dolphins and a boat trip on the lakes at Elburg.
- **Also See:** FLEVOLAND.

Boat tours (*Operate July and Aug. Information from Rederij Flevo.* ☎0341 41 25 98. (*in Dutch*) www.red erijflevo.nl*) of the Flevoland polders depart from Harderwijk.

Sights

Dolfinarium★
Open mid-Feb–late Oct, daily 10am–5pm (Jul–Aug 6pm). Closed 25, 31 Dec and 1 Jan. 21€; children 17.50€. ☎0341 46 74 00. www.dolfinarium.nl (*in Dutch*).

This very popular attraction is the largest marine mammal park in Europe, with dolphins, sea lions and walruses, all of which take part in the performances. Other highlights include the touch-tank, Roggenrif; the Laguna, where visitors can wonder at life above and below the surface of the water; the three-dimensional Pirate film; and the exciting SOS *Barracuda*. Fort Heerewich is a sanctuary for stranded dolphins.

Old town

A number of well-restored Renaissance houses and 18C patrician residences are the heritage of a prosperous past.

Enter the old town through the charming 14C–16C **Vischpoort** (near Strandboulevard) which leads to the old fish market (Vischmarkt).

▶ *The Kleine Marktstraat on the right and the Hondegatstraat lead to the main square, Markt.*

Markt

In the main square stands the old town hall, or **stadhuis**, which dates from 1837. The stadhuis is recognisable by its portico crowned with a pinnacle.

Donkerstraat is a pedestrian street lined with numerous grand 18C mansions with Rococo doorways. Looking up Academiestraat on the left, note the 16C tower, **Linnaeustorentje**, which marks the site of the university's botanical gardens. At the far end of Donkerstraat (*no 4*), an 18C mansion is now home to the **Museum Nairac** (○*open Tue–Fri 10am–5pm, Sat 1pm–5pm;* ○*closed public holidays;* ≈*2.50€;* ☎*0342 415 666; www.nairac.nl*), which is devoted to the history of the Veluwe (coins, costumes, model ships) and to the old college of Harderwijk. The rostrum of the former Nassau-Veluws Gymnasium illustrates the importance of education in the town's past; the low seat was occupied by examination candidates, while the upper seat was reserved for the rector. Apart from Carolus Linnaeus, both Herman Boerhaave (⑤*see LEIDEN*) and Constantijn Huygens (⑤*see Den HAAG, Excursions*) received doctorates in Harderwijk.

Taking Smeepoortstraat on the right, pass in front of the **Grote Kerk** (○*open mid-May–mid-Sept, Mon–Fri;* ☎*0341 41 23 95; www.grotekerk.fol.nl*), a tall 14C church. At the far end of the street, Bruggestraat returns to Markt.

Excursion

Elburg

20km/12mi to the northeast.

In the 14C, Elburg was a busy mainland port looking out on the Zuiderzee. Today this small town, encircled by its square walls (14C) and canals, retains its medieval character, but now looks out across the polders of Flevoland. The streets are laid out in a regular grid pattern and are often fronted by attractive houses, such as the row alongside the Beekstraat Canal. The only town gate to remain is the one that faced northwards onto the sea, the 14C **Vischpoort** (○*open mid-Jun–Aug, Tue–Fri 10am–noon, 1pm–4.30pm;* ○*closed public holidays and Sept–May.* ≈*3€;* ☎*0525 68 13 41; www.museumelburg.nl (in Dutch)*). At the other end of the street the former convent (Agnietenklooster) dates from 1418. The collections of the **Gemeentemuseum** (○*open Tue–Fri 10am–5pm; Jul–mid-Aug, Tue–Sat 11am–4pm;* ○*closed public holidays; also Oct–Mar, Mon.* ≈*3€;* ☎*0525 68 13 41; www.museumelburg.nl (in Dutch)*), or Municipal Museum, are displayed in the Gothic chapel and other conventual buildings. The 14C **St Nicolaaskerk** (○*open Jun, Mon–Fri 1.30pm–4.30pm; Jul and Aug, Mon 1.30pm–4.30pm, Tue–Fri 10am–noon, 1.30pm–4.30pm;* ☎*0525 68 15 20 (VVV)*) has a massive square tower. **Boat trips** (&*depart May–Sept, Tue–Sat, every 1hr from 10am–5pm;* ☎*0341 41 41 59*) are organised on the lakes (Veluwemeer and Drontermeer).

HARLINGEN

FRYSLÂN

POPULATION 15 450

LOCAL MAP SEE WADDENEILANDEN

Harlingen (Harns in Frisian) was formerly a great whaling port, with its boats sailing as far as Greenland until c. 1850. Today this town at the mouth of Harinxma Canal is a centre of shrimp and prawn fishing, and exports dairy products to Britain. Harlingen has a school of fluvial navigation and a college for shipbuilding. The town now also has two pleasure boat harbours.

It is also the departure point for boats to the islands of Terschelling and Vlieland (*see WADDENEILANDEN*).

- ▣ **Information:** Noorderhaven 50, 8861 AP, Harlingen. ☎0900 919 19 99. www.harlingen.nl.
- ▶ **Orient Yourself:** The best place to start a tour of Harlingen is Noorderhaven and take a leisurely stroll along the side of its canal.
- ℗ **Parking:** Harlingen is about 26km/16mi west of Leeuwarden on the coast. The town offers a few car parking areas, which are clearly signposted, along with free off-street parking.
- ⊚ **Don't Miss:** The Gemeentemuseum Het Hannemahuis, which is the best possible introduction to the town.
- ⊙ **Organizing Your Time:** A compact town, Harlingen can be explored in a day, which allows time for lunch beside the canal.
- ⚘ **Also See:** LEEUWARDEN, DE WADDENEILANDEN.

Sights

The charm of Harlingen's old streets makes it an attractive town. It is pleasant to stroll along the main street, Voorstraat, and along the quays of the two old ports, the Noorderhaven and the Zuiderhaven. There are some interesting 16C to 18C façades.

Noorderhaven★

This dock, which has become a marina, is lined with picturesque houses and warehouses. On the north quay there are some lovely façade stones. On the south side stands the 18C **stadhuis**, topped by a low relief depicting the archangel St Michael; the rear of the building giving on to Voorstraat is flanked by a tower with a carillon.

Gemeentemuseum Het Hannemahuis

Voorstraat 56. ⊙Open from Sept 2008: phone or check website for opening hours and admission rates. ☎0517 41 36 58. www.hannemahuis.nl.

Installed in the Hannemahuis, an 18C residence, this museum is devoted to the history of Harlingen and its maritime past. The furniture, the seascapes by Nicolaas Baur, a painter born in Harlingen (1767–1820), engravings, collections of Chinese porcelain, Frisian silverware and scale models of ships, are all beautiful. A room overlooking the garden has a lovely collection of earthenware tiles. At the far end of the street, near the canal, there is a statue of a schoolboy, Anton Wachter, hero of a series of novels by **Simon Vestdijk** (1898–1971), a famous writer born in Harlingen; his works describe middle-class provincial life.

De Stenen Man (Stone Man)

At the top of a dyke to the south of the port, there is a monument crowned with two bronze heads, erected in 1774 in memory of the Governor Caspar de Robles who had the dyke rebuilt in 1573. Behind the dyke is Harlingen's beach, with a beautiful view of the harbour.

HEERLEN

LIMBURG
POPULATION 90 125

This town was the main centre of the Netherlands' coalfields which cross Limburg, continue into Belgium in the Maaseik region, and the Aachen basin in Germany. Mining started in 1896 and was abandoned in 1975. However, a number of industries have been established in the region and Heerlen is becoming an important commercial centre. The city possesses a modern quarter built round a vast pedestrian precinct, **Promenade**. The Romanesque St Pancratiuskerk has for a tower the old castle keep built in 1389 by the Duke of Burgundy, Philip the Bold.

- **Information:** Bongerd 22 – 6411 JM. ☎045 571 62 00. www.vvvzuidlimburg.nl.
- **Orient Yourself:** Head for Bongera as this is central to all Heerlen has to offer the visitor.
- **Parking:** Heerlen is about 25km/15.5mi east of Maastricht. The city has plenty of car parking areas, most are inexpensive, and some even free.
- **Don't Miss:** The Kasteel Hoensbroek, a moated castle and one of the finest in the area.
- **Organizing Your Time:** Allow at least a half day to really appreciate Heerlen's character and sample one of its eateries. Make time to visit Abdij Rolduc, a fine cultural centre housed in a former abbey.

A Bit of History

Coriovallum – Heerlen, ancient Coriovallum, was a Roman camp on the great route going from Boulogne-sur-Mer to Cologne via Maastricht. In 1C AD another route (Xanthus-Trier) passed this Roman camp. Important Roman baths (2C to 4C) were found in Heerlen.

Sight

Thermenmuseum

○Open Tue–Fri 10am–5pm, Sat–Sun and public holidays noon–5pm. ○Closed 1 Jan, Carnival, 30 Apr, 24, 25, 31 Dec. ☜5€. ☎045 560 45 81. www.thermen museum.nl.

This museum houses the remains of the Roman baths, which can be seen from an elevated walkway. It also contains objects found during excavations: coins, bronze statuettes, pottery. Models, reconstructions and a light show give an impression of the building as it once was.

Excursions

Kasteel Hoensbroek★

5km/3mi in a northerly direction. ○Open daily 10am–5.30pm. ○Closed Carnival, 24, 25, 31 Dec and 1 Jan. ☜6.25€. ☎ 045 522 72 72. www.kasteelhoens broek.nl.

This impressive moated castle in Maasland Renaissance style is made up of a 14C round tower and 17C and 18C living quarters built round three inner courtyards. The bedrooms, workrooms and tower-rooms are open to visitors, as are the kitchen and cellars. The medieval tower affords a fine view of the surrounding area.

Kerkrade

10km/6.2mi east of Heerlen.

This border town has been a centre of mining activity since the Middle Ages. Since mining ceased, Kerkrade has diversified its industrial sector. Every four years (☜see Calendar of events) an International Music Competiton (**Wereld Muziek Concours**) is held here, attracting groups of amateur musicians.

Industrion★

Open Tue–Sun 11am–5pm (10am Jul–Aug). *Closed Carnival, 25 Dec and 1 Jan.* 12.50€. 045 567 08 09. *www.industrion.nl (in Dutch).*

This modern museum traces the development of industry and the way in which it has influenced society. In the past, Limburg was particularly important for its minerals: marl for making cement; clay as a raw material for the ceramics industry (particularly in Maastricht); and, of course, gravel and coal. Life was tough for workers in these industries, as the reconstruction of a street and a single-room home shows, and a miner describes his work underground. This interactive, hands-on display gives a vivid picture of life in the past, and there is also a working metal factory.

Abdij Rolduc★

Go towards Herzogenrath and turn left before the railway. *Open daily 10am–5pm.* 045 546 68 88.

This former abbey, in the grounds of a hotel, stands to the east of the town high on the valley slope overlooking the River Wurm, which marks the frontier. The **abbey church** (*abdijkerk*) is surrounded by 17C and 18C buildings. Started in the early 12C, it has been restored several times, in particular in the 19C by Cuypers, who replaced the Gothic chancel with a Romanesque one. On the west side, it has a façade with a massive porch tower flanked by two square towers. Inside, level with the first and third bays of the nave, pseudo-transepts have been built in the side aisles. The **capitals**★ in the nave are very varied. Note also the bases of certain engaged columns in the side aisles. The heightened apse is trefoil in shape and built above a Romanesque crypt (remarkable capitals).

DEN HELDER

NOORD-HOLLAND

POPULATION 60 000

LOCAL MAP SEE WADDENEILANDEN

Den Helder owes its importance to its position on the Marsdiep Channel, which separates it from Texel Island. It grew from the small fishing village **Huisduinen**, which expanded eastwards. In 1500 the new town took the name of Den Helder.

Information: Bernhardplein 18 – 1781 HH. 0223 62 55 44. www.vvvkopvannoordholland.nl.

▶ **Orient Yourself:** Bernhardplein, the location of the tourist information centre, is an ideal place to start to orient yourself in Den Helder. It has few sights, but all are around this area.

P **Parking:** Inexpensive parking is signposted.

Don't Miss: The Marinemuseum and the Nationaal Reddingmuseum Dorus Rijkers are both fascinating. Also not to be missed is the abundance of wildlife at Callantsoog.

Especially for Kids: The acquarium at Fort Kijkduin and the Dutch Navy Museum.

Organizing Your Time: Allow two or three hours to see Den Helder.

A Bit of History

In 1811 Napoleon made Den Helder a stronghold. He called it the Gibraltar of the North, and visited it in October of that year. Today it is the **Netherlands' chief naval base**, and also the departure point for boats to Texel. **Navy Days** are held here in July of each year.

Sights

Marinemuseum   Kids
🕐 *Open Tue–Fri 10am–5pm, Sat–Sun and public holidays noon–5pm, also open Mon from May–Oct.* 🕐 *Closed 25 Dec and 1 Jan.* ✆ *5.50€; children 4.50€.* ☎ *0223 65 75 34. www.marine museum.nl (in Dutch). Daily boat trips with the historical lifeboat Johan de Witt mid-Mar–early Nov, 1pm–4pm.*
The Dutch Naval Museum evokes the history of the Dutch navy from the 17C onwards with a selection of scale models, instruments, photos, uniforms, emblems, maps, paintings and films. The collection includes a submarine, a minesweeper from World War II and a 19C ram-type vessel, the "Schorpioen", The Maintenance and Technical Department is located on the site of the former Rijkswerf Willemsoord, within walking distance of the museum.

Nationaal Reddingmuseum Dorus Rijkers
🕐 *Open Mon–Sat 10am–5pm, Sun and public holidays 1pm–5pm.* 🕐 *Closed 25 Dec.* ✆ *5€, children 4€.* �& ☎ *0223 61 83 20. www.reddingmuseum.nl.*
The national maritime rescue museum includes lifeboats, equipment, prints and models, as well as a ship's bridge and numerous hands-on exhibits which are ideal for children.

Fort Kijkduin   Kids
🕐 *Open daily 10am–6pm.* ☞ *Guided tours at 11am, 1pm and 3pm.* ✆ *7€ ☎0223 61 23 66. www.fortkijkduin.nl.*
This is one of Den Helder's six forts, built on the orders of Napoleon to house 700 soldiers. It has been extensively restored, and now contains a **museum** and a marine aquarium. The tour of the underground passageways and vaults brings the fort's history to life and in clear weather, the fort has a fine **view** of the De Razende Bol sand flats, the North Sea and the island of Texel.
The **North Sea Aquarium** in the former bunkers has a particularly interesting glass tunnel which you walk through surrounded by fish (including sharks) on all sides. Of special interest also is a section of the acquarium that recreates the environment under the North Sea, one filled with wrecks that are covered in algae, anaemones, mussels, oysters and conger eels, and which attract lobsters sea bass, turbot and wrasses. There is also a stroking tank where children can stroke different types of sealife like anemones, turbot and starfish.
Of equal educational value is the tidal tank where a simulated tide changes occurs every five minutes, showing how the sealife – mussels, periwinkles, Sea Dahlias, hermit crabs and plaice – react to the change.
Children will also enjoy seeing the ray tank where sometimes it is possible to stroke these relatively affectionate fish.

Excursion to Callantsoog and Schagen
27km/17mi to the south

The road runs along a dyke behind which there are several beaches.

Callantsoog
To the south there is a nature reserve, **Het Zwanenwater** (🕐 *open Apr–Jul, daily 7am–9pm; rest of the year, dawn–dusk.* ☎ *0224 58 15 41 (VVV)).* The reserve stretches over 573ha/1 415 acres among coastal dunes and the moors round two lakes which attract many birds. The best time to visit is around mid-May during nesting time. The breeding grounds can be seen from a distance, generally among the reeds. Spoonbills (*illustration, ☞ see WADDENEILANDEN*) arrive from West Africa at the end of February and leave again in July and August.

Schagen
11.8km/7.3mi to the southeast.
On Thursdays in summer (☞ *see Calendar of events*) a colourful **market** (West-Friese markt) is held in this town where the costumes of West Friesland are worn.

'S-HERTOGENBOSCH

DEN BOSCH – NOORD-BRABANT P
POPULATION 133 500
PLAN OF THE CONURBATION IN THE CURRENT RED-COVER MICHELIN GUIDE BENELUX

Capital of the Noord-Brabant province, 's-Hertogenbosch is also the seat of a Catholic bishopric. It differs from other towns in the country in its almost Mediterranean character, which can be seen in its noisy carnival (*see Calendar of events*). An annual art and antiques market is held here at Easter.

- **Information:** Markt 77 – 5211 JX. ☎0900 11 22 33 4. www.vvvdenbosch.nl.
- ▶ **Orient Yourself:** The Markt is situated centrally to the town, and most of its attractions are in the roads that radiate from it.
- P **Parking:** Car parks are plentiful, and most within easy walking distance of the Markt.
- **Don't Miss:** The quite beautiful Sint-Janskathedraal (St John's Cathedral).
- **Organizing Your Time:** Whatever you do, don't hurry your visit to the cathedral. Allow at least an hour to really study its beauty. The rest of 's-Hertogenbosch can be explored in a couple of hours. Motoring enthusiasts might fit in some time to admire early models of cars such as a Benz and a Ford Model T at the Autotron Rosmalen, around 6km/3.7mi from 's-Hertogenbosch.

A Bit of History

The great forests of the area were the hunting grounds of Duke Godefroy of Brabant, hence the name 's-Hertogen Bosch, the Duke's Wood. Today the town is usually called **Den Bosch** the Woods, and numerous commercial and industrial establishments have developed in the area. The weekly cattle market, which takes place on Wednesdays in the **Brabanthallen** is a particularly important one. There is a horse market on Thursdays.

The town has two lakes (the **Zuiderplas** and **Oosterplas**) and the **Prins Hendrik Park** where there is a deer park and another large lake.

Sint-Janskathedraal★★

Open daily 10am–4.30pm.
St John's Cathedral, one of the most beautiful churches in the Netherlands, was assigned to the Protestant faith from 1629–1810, after which Napoleon returned it to the Catholic faith. It was built between 1380 and 1530 in the Brabant Gothic style. It has a 13C belfry porch whose **carillon**, placed in 1925, has become famous.

The cathedral (*plan: see Architecture*) seen from **Parade**, the square to the south, has impressive proportions and a wealth of ornamentation. The fantastic world of grotesque personages astride the **flying buttresses**★ may have inspired Hieronymus Bosch. Other amusing figures decorate the side chapels' gable spandrels. The apse is superb with its numerous radiating chapels round the ambulatory. A squat tower with five lantern turrets rises above the transept crossing.

Sint-Jansmuseum De Bouwloods

Open May–Sept, Tue–Sun 1pm–4.30pm. 2€. ☎073 612 68 79.
The site next to the cathedral has been turned into a museum containing some of the original sculptures that have been replaced during successive periods of restoration work.

Interior

The very luminous interior has a grandiose appearance with its five naves and 150 columns which, in the characteristic style of Brabant Late Gothic, are a cluster of slender pillars without capitals. The last restoration, completed in 1985, brought to light the vault fres-

A Magician's Art

's-Hertogenbosch was the birthplace of **Hieronymus Bosch** (c. 1450–1516), whose real name was Jeroen van Aeken. The life of this painter is not well known, except that he lived a comfortable life in this town.

A solitary genius, Hieronymus Bosch did not belong to any school. Flemish influence is discernible only in his landscapes with distant perspectives, the naturalistic tone given to the scenes he paints and in the somewhat archaic outline drawings of his characters.

The Prodigal Son, Hieronymus Bosch

But with this visionary painter, reality is placed at the disposal of a prodigious imagination. Objects and animals take strange shapes, men and beasts fill fantastic scenes of a dream-like, even nightmarish, universe where it is often difficult to distinguish hell from paradise. Condemning evil, denouncing the ravages of sin was probably the intention of this mysterious artist, who was as passionately interested in alchemy as ethics, judging by the presence of numerous symbols in his works.

His early works were mostly simple and sober, then later the compositions became more complex and the subjects more and more strange, as in the most extraordinary of his works, the *Garden of Earthly Delights,* where the painter would have had no cause to envy the Surrealists. This last painting is in the Prado Museum in Madrid, but one can see several fascinating works by Hieronymus Bosch in the Museum Boijmans Van Beuningen in Rotterdam.

---

coes, which are very varied. The oldest, in the chancel, date from the first half of the 15C.

Note the canopy, slightly turned and finely worked, above a statue leaning against a pillar of the transept crossing.

The pulpit with its 16C Renaissance low reliefs, the restored 15C stalls and the 17C Renaissance-style organ case by Florens Hocque are worth seeing. The copper baptismal font (1492), in the chapel on the left of the great organ, is a masterpiece by a Maastricht coppersmith.

In 1629 when Frederick Henry, Prince of Orange, seized 's-Hertogenbosch, the canons left the town for Brussels, taking with them the altarpieces which Hieronymus Bosch had painted for the cathedral. The rood screen (1610) is now in the Victoria and Albert Museum in London. The stained-glass windows were all made after 1850.

St Anthony's Chapel in the south arm of the transept has a fine **15C altarpiece**★ by the Antwerp School which came from a local village. The six small

Sint-Janskathedraal

scenes of the lower part depict in rather naïve fashion the birth and childhood of Jesus, but the main theme of the altarpiece is the Passion of Christ, with Calvary in the centre. The figures carved in wood are particularly remarkable for their expressions.

Additional Sights

Markt

This very busy triangular market square is in the heart of the city, where one of the main shopping pedestrian precincts, **Hinthamerstraat**, starts. A general market is held on the square on Wednesdays and Saturdays. In front of the Stadhuis stands a statue (1929) of Hieronymus Bosch.

Stadhuis

Open Mon 11am–5.30pm, Tue–Fri 9am–5.30pm, Sat 9am–4pm; May–Sept also open Sun 11am–3pm. Guided tours, Thu at 7pm, Sat at 2.30pm. Closed public holidays. 073 613 50 98.

Dating from the 15C , the town hall was given a classical façade in 1670. Part of its **carillon** was cast by the Hemony brothers. On the ground floor, the Trouwkamer (marriage room) has lovely Cordoba leather hangings. The Gothic cellar has been transformed into a café and restaurant.

De Moriaan

This building, which houses the tourist information centre (VVV), has, to the north of the Markt, a brick façade with a 13C crow-stepped gable.

Noordbrabants Museum★

Open Tue–Fri 10am–5pm, Sat–Sun noon–5pm. Closed 25 Dec and 1 Jan. 7€. 073 687 78 77. www.noordbrabantsmuseum.nl (in Dutch).

The museum sheds light on various aspects of the history, art and culture of the North Brabant province, focusing on several themes: the medieval town, the guilds, the Eighty Years' War, the Church, popular art and archaeology. The highly interesting collection features objects excavated from various sites, including an **amber statue of Bacchus** (c. AD 200). The painting collection includes the admirable *Study of a Brabant Peasant* by Van Gogh and *The Four Seasons* by David Teniers the Younger. One can also see sculptures, costumes and ornamental *objets d'art* (guild silverware and rustic jewellery).

The museum also holds temporary exhibitions on contemporary art.

Museum Slager

Open Tue–Sun 2pm–5pm. Closed public holidays. 3€. 073 6133 216. www.museum-slager.nl.

This houses works by a family of painters, from Petrus Marinus Slager (1841–1912) to Tom Slager, born in 1918.

Museum Het Kruithuis

Magistratenlaan 100, 5223 MB, 's-Hertogenbosch. Open Tue and Thu 1pm–9pm, Wed, Fri, Sat and Sun 1pm–5pm. 4€. 073 627 36 80. www.museumhetkruithuis.nl.

This hexagonal brick edifice, built 1617–1621, is located in the northern part of town. It is built around a courtyard and was once circled by a moat. Today the rooms on the ground floor are the setting for exhibitions on design and contemporary art. The first floor presents collections of modern jewellery and ceramics, from 1950 up to the present day.

Boat trip on the Binnendieze

Open May–late Oct, Tue–Sun 11am–5pm, Wed 2pm–5pm. 073 612 23 34.

A trip along this river, which in places flows under the houses and streets, is a pleasant introduction to the different facets of the city.

Excursions

Autotron Rosmalen

Open Apr–Jun, Sept, daily 10am–5pm (Jul–Aug 6pm). 073 523 33 00. www.autotron.nl (in Dutch).

This automobile theme park has a wide variety of attractions for young and old. The collection on the first floor of the **AutoDome**★ automobile museum retraces over 115 years of motor car history. The ground floor features the magnificent products of the Dutch man-

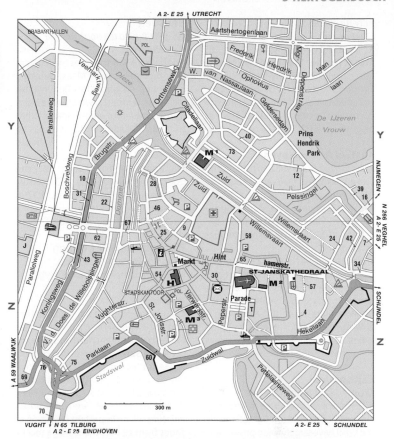

ufacturer Spijker (1899–1925), a number of dream cars and limousines, and a selection of sports and racing cars.

Heeswijk-Dinther

14km/8mi to the southeast via Maastrichtseweg.
Northwest of this village stands the 14C **Kasteel Heeswijk** (guided tours only: May–Sept, Sun tours noon, 1pm, 2pm, 3pm and 4pm), Tue–Wed 11am, noon, 1pm, 2pm, 3pm and 3.30pm, Thu 11am, noon, 1pm and 2pm; Oct–Apr every first and third Sun of the month, noon, 1pm, 2pm, 3pm and 4pm; closed Carnival, Easter, Whitsun, 25, 26 Dec and 1 Jan; 11.50€; 0413 29 23 52; www.kasteelheeswijk.nl), set in the woods and surrounded by moats. It contains beauti-

fully furnished rooms and interesting objets d'art.

At Heeswijk, a farmhouse museum, **Meierijsche Museumboerderij** (*Meerstraat 28;* ⏱*open May–Sept, Wed, Sat–Sun and public holidays 2pm–5pm;* ✉*2.50€;* ☎*0413 29 15 46; www.museum boerderij.nl*) recreates the life of Brabant peasants in 1900.

Kasteel Ammersoyen

In Ammerzoden. 11km/6.8mi to the north. Leave 's-Hertogenbosch via Orthenseweg. 👁*By guided tour only: mid-Apr–Oct, Tue–Sat and public holidays, 10am–5pm, Sun, 1pm–5pm.* ⏱*Closed 30 Apr.* ☎ *0413 36 66 33. www.kasteel-ammer soyen.nl.*

This imposing 14C moated castle is built up in a square around an inner courtyard with vast towers in each of the four corners. Formerly (1876–1945) a convent of the Poor Clares, part of the building is now the town hall. The great hall, the ladies' apartments and the tower rooms are all open to the public.

Zaltbommel

15km/9.3mi to the north. Leave 's-Hertogenbosch via Orthenseweg.
The walls of this old stronghold beside the Waal have largely been preserved. On Markt, the **stadhuis** dates from 1763. At n° 18 Boschstraat, next to a pharmacy, there is a Renaissance house with caryatids. This, the main street, leads to the 14C water gate, **Waterpoort**
In Nonnenstraat, the **Huis van Maarten van Rossum** (⏱*open Tue–Fri 10am–12.30pm, 1.30pm–4.30pm; Sat (except Oct–Mar) and Sun 2pm–4.30pm;* ⏱*closed Easter, Whitsun, 25 Dec and 1 Jan;* ✉*2.50€;* ☎*0418 51 26 17*) has been converted into a regional museum, the Maarten van Rossummuseum.
At the far end of Nieuwstraat is the 14C **Grote- of St Maartenskerk**, abundantly decorated, where the imposing 15C belfry porch is 63m/206.7ft high.

Heusden

19km/11.8mi to the northwest via Vlijmenseweg.
On the banks of the Maas, which here becomes the Bergse Maas, Heusden is an old stronghold fortified in 1581. Inside its ramparts, which have been transformed into an esplanade, it has some fine façades. Worth seeing is no 4 Hoogstraat (main street), a 17C house with very elaborate scrolls.
The **Vismarkt** (fish market) near the dock is surrounded by 17C houses. A covered market (Visbank) of 1796 still stands.
Heusden has three **post mills**.

Waalwijk and De Efteling

25km/15.5mi to the west. Leave 's-Hertogenbosch by Vlijmenseweg.

Waalwijk

Main centre of the Netherlands' leather and shoe industry, Waalwijk has an interesting leather and shoe museum, the **Nederlands Leder- en Schoenenmuseum** (⏱*open Tue–Fri 10am–5pm, Sat–Sun noon–4pm;* ⏱*closed Easter, Whitsun, 25 Dec and 1 Jan;* ✉*3.50€;* ♿ ☎ *0416 33 27 38; www.schoenen museum.nl*). An important collection of shoes from all over the world; a reconstruction of a c. 1930 shoe factory and a 1870 tannery. Other display cases show the evolution of the European shoe.

De Efteling★★ 　　　　　　　　　Kids

South of Kaatsheuvel. ⏱*Open late Mar–late Oct, daily 10am–6pm; Jul and Aug, daily 10am–9pm (Sat midnight).* ✉*27€ (summer 29€).* ♿ ☎ *0416 27 35 35. www.efteling.nl.*
A theme park with the Fairy Tale Wood (Sprookjesbos), Dream Flight (Droomvlucht), Fairy Tale Show (Sprookjesshow) and the House of the Five Senses (Huis van de Vijf Zintuigen); excitement in Pegasus, Python, Piraña and the Half Moon; spine-chilling encounters in Villa Volta and the Haunted Castle (Spookslot); and a voyage to exotic places in Fata Morgana and Carnival Festival.

HILVERSUM

NOORD-HOLLAND
POPULATION 83 500
TOWN PLAN IN THE CURRENT RED-COVER MICHELIN GUIDE BENELUX

Hilversum in the picturesque moors and woods of the Gooi is, in a way, a large residential suburb of Amsterdam: it is an extensive residential area with villas scattered among the trees. Because Hilversum is relatively high, it has long been the country's main centre of broadcasting.

- **Information:** Kerkbrink 6, 1211 BX Hilversum. ☎035 629 28 10. www.vvvhilversum.nl.
- **Orient Yourself:** Hilversum is a compact town with all the main attractions for the visitor in or around Kerkbrink. The train station is a stone's throw from here.
- **Parking:** Inexpensive car parking is provided outside of the central pedestrianised areas.
- **Don't Miss:** The outstanding architecture of the Raadhuis (town hall), and in particular its elegant interior. Also don't miss Soestdijk, the location of the Royal Palace where the former Queen of the Netherlands, Juliana, lived before her death in 2004.
- **Organizing Your Time:** Hilversum can be seen in two hours or so, and then allow a little time to visit nearby villages, such as Baarn.

Sights

Raadhuis★

To the north of town. Illustration: 🖙 see Architecture. Built between 1927 and 1931, the town hall is the work of **WM Dudok** (the Netherlands' main exponent of Cubic Expressionist architecture) and is considered to be his magnum opus. For the most part it is a harmonious juxtaposition of cubic masses in which the different volumes create a play of horizontal and vertical lines and give the building a different appearance from every side. The horizontal lines of the brickwork are emphasised by putting the mortar bed of the bed joints further back from the brick face, producing an effect of rows of horizontal stripes. Inside all is functional and rational. The furniture, clocks, lighting – even the burgomaster's gavel – were designed by Dudok. The **Dudok Centrum** in the basement documents Dudok's life and work.

The Muiderslot

Eduard Bergman/NBTC

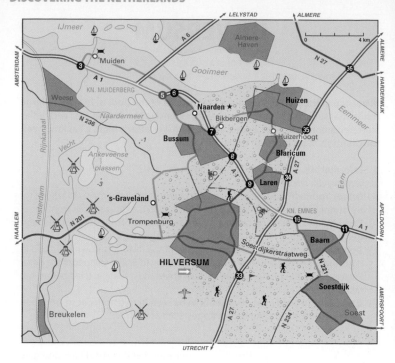

Museum Hilversum

Kerkbrink 6. ◑*Open Tue–Sat 11am–5pm, Sun noon–5pm.* ◑*Closed 25 Dec, 1 Jan and 30 Apr.* ◉*4€.* ♿ ☏ *035 629 28 26. www.museumhilversum.nl.*

This museum in the old town hall uses archaeological finds, objects and photographs to chronicle the history of Hilversum and the Gooi region.

Driving Tour

The Gooi★

Round tour of 62km/38.5mi – allow one day.

▶ *Leave Hilversum via Soestdijkerstraatweg.*

Soestdijk

To the north of town is the Royal Palace, **Koninklijk Paleis** residence of the late former Queen of the Netherlands, Juliana. This former hunting lodge was used in the summer by the Dutch sovereigns.

Baarn

A pleasant, leafy residential area. **Kasteel Groeneveld** (◑ *open Tue–Sun 11am–5pm;* ◑*closed 30 Apr, 25, 31 Dec and 1 Jan;* ◉*4€;* ☏*035 542 04 46; www. kasteelgroeneveld.nl*) (c. 1710) is now home to the nature conservation centre, Nationaal centrum voor Bos, Natuur en Landschap. The landscaped park is also open to visitors.

Near Laren lies the **Gooi** This densely wooded region of Noord-Holland is in fact an immense residential suburb with many substantial houses tucked away in lovely parks where Amsterdamers have chosen to live.

Laren

A picturesque village, Laren is a painter's haven. At the end of the 19C the **Laren School** gathered together several painters under the guidance of Neuhuys and Anton Mauve. Several of the artists were also members of The Hague School.

In the centre of the village, around the villa of the American painter William Henry Singer (186–1943), stands the **Singer Museum** (◑*open Tue–Sat 11am–5pm, Sun and public holidays* noon–5pm; ⊙closed 30 Apr, 25 Dec and 1 Jan; ♿☎035 539 39 39; www.singerlaren.nl), built in 1956 by Singer's widow. The museum holds temporary exhibitions on modern art as well as showing its permanent collection on a rotational basis. This collection includes works by Singer himself, 19C and 20C French painters, the Amsterdam and Hague Schools, the Laren School and Modernists.

Blaricum
Lovely residential town in the heart of the Gooi.

Naarden★ – *See NAARDEN.*

Muiden
Near this small harbour used frequently by pleasure boats is a castle, the **Muiderslot★** (by guided tour only (50min) Apr–Oct, Mon–Fri 10am–5pm, Sat, Sun and public holidays noon–6pm; Nov–Mar, Sat–Sun noon–5pm; ⊙closed 25 Dec and 1 Jan. ⇒8.75€; ☎0294 25 62 62; www.muiderslot.nl), standing on the banks of the IJmeer and at the mouth of the Vecht. Built c. 1204 to defend the mouth of the Vecht, it was rebuilt by Floris V, Count of Holland. As of 1621 the castle became the meeting place for the **Muiderkring** (Muiden Circle), an intellectual and literary circle which gathered around the then owner of the premises, the historian and poet **PC Hooft** (158–1647). When Hooft died, the castle fell into neglect, but today the rooms have been refurbished to show their former 17C glory.

Bussum
An important residential town on the edge of the Gooi.

▶ *On leaving Bussum, turn right towards 's-Graveland.*

's-Graveland
In the vicinity of this town, there are a number of fine manor houses. **Trompenburg** (closed to the public) is probably the most elegant with its gracious silhouette reflected in the waters of the lake.

▶ *Return to Hilversum continuing on the same road.*

HINDELOOPEN
FRYSLÂN
LOCAL MAP SEE SNEEK

This small town (Hylpen in Frisian), on the banks of the IJsselmeer, is one of the 11 towns of Friesland. It was once very prosperous due to its trade with Norway, and was a member of the Hanseatic League. The main road bypasses Hindeloopen, a quiet and peaceful town with lanes winding between houses and gardens, its footbridges spanning small canals; the presence of many pleasure boats in summer tends to disturb the calm.

- **Information:** www.hindeloopen.com.
- ▶ **Orient Yourself:** From the A 7, take the exit for Bolsward (17) and follow the signs for Workum / Balk on the N 359; after Workum follow the signs to Hindeloopen. From the A 6, take exit Lemmer (17), follow the signs for Balk / Bolsward on the N359 and after Koudum follow the signs to Hindeloopen.
- **Also See:** SNEEK.

Hindeloopen's Crafts

Furniture and costumes – Since the 18C, Hindeloopen has specialised in hand-painted furniture, where red and dark green prevail. The colours as well as the motifs and shapes are inspired by Scandinavian styles seen by sailors during their long journeys (see Introduction, Traditions and Folklore).

NBTC

Making bobbin lace in Hindeloopen

Museum Hidde Nijland Stichting★

🕐 *Open Mar–Oct, Mon–Fri 11am–5pm, Sat–Sun and public holidays 1.30pm– 5pm. ⊛3€. ☎0514 52 14 20. www.museumhindeloopen.nl.*

Located near the church, this museum (formerly the town hall [1683]) captivates by its reconstructed interiors, collections of fine traditional costumes, the series of tiles or earthenware pictures and its images of the great sailing ships of the past.

NATIONAAL PARK DE HOGE VELUWE★★★

GELDERLAND

The Hoge Veluwe National Park, which covers 5 500ha/13 585 acres, is the Netherlands' largest nature reserve. It contains the famous Kröller-Müller Museum, the St Hubertus hunting lodge, the Museonder underground museum, and countless sculptures and monuments. The park is a unique combination of nature and culture.

- ℹ **Information:** Arnhemseweg 14, 6731 BS, Otterlo. ☎0318 59 12 14. www.vvvotterlo.nl (in Dutch).
- ▶ **Orient Yourself:** Between Arnhem and Apeldoorn, the park is reached by the A 12 and there are entrances at Schaarsbergen in the south, Otterlo in the northwest and Hoenderloo to the northeast.
- 🅿 **Parking:** Parking space is available at the three entrances.
- ⊛ **Don't Miss:** The birdlife in winter and the native animals in the summer.
- Kids **Especially for Kids:** The sight of animals in the wild.

Park★★★   Kids

Allow half a day

🕐 *Open daily: Apr, 8am–8pm; May, 8am–9pm; Jun and Jul, 8am–10pm; Aug, 8am–9pm; Sept, 9am–8pm;*

Oct, 9am–7pm; Nov–Mar, 9am–6pm. ⊛Including/not including the museum 14/7€; children 7/3.50€; May–Sept, 50% reduction for park entrance after 5pm. ☎0900 464 38 35. www.hogeveluwe.nl.

A Day in the Hoge Veluwe

- The park is served by **public transport** from Arnhem, Ede and Apeldoorn. Bus route 12 (from Arnhem) runs through the park from late March to late October; the driver provides a commentary.

- The park has three **entrances** at Otterlo, Hoenderloo and Schaarsbergen.

- There are large car parks at the three entrances: the Kröller-Müller Museum, the St Hubertus hunting lodge and the visitor centre. The maximum speed in the park is 50kph/31mph. Only the surfaced roads (marked in white on the plan) may be used by cars.

- The **white bicycles** at the entrances to the park, the Kröller-Müller Museum and the visitor centre may be used free of charge and ridden anywhere on the paths. They should be returned to the place where they were issued at the end of the day.

- There are 42km/26mi of **signposted cycle paths** including three routes (10, 18 and 26km/6, 11 and 16mi). Brochures detailing routes taking in most of the park's monuments and works of art are on sale in the visitor centre.

- Apart from certain areas reserved for game, visitors are free to walk anywhere in the park, and walking tours of various lengths are marked by **wooden poles** with coloured tops. Information and maps are available in the visitor centre.

- The park also has **five game observatories** The most accessible of these are De Klep and the Vogelvijvers (bird lakes). The visitor centre has information on where and when to see specific animals.

- **Restaurants and toilets** are located at the visitor centre, the Kröller-Müller Museum and at the Schaarsbergen entrance. **Picnicking** is allowed anywhere, and there is a picnic area at the visitor centre. Cooking and fires are not allowed.

- **Dogs** and other animals are not allowed inside the buildings, and must be kept on a lead in the park.

- **Camping** in the park is permitted only on the campsite at the Hoenderloo entrance. There are also various campsites outside the park.

- **Tickets** on sale at the entrances to the park provide entry to all sights except the Kröller-Müller Museum, entrance to which costs an extra 12€.

History – This site was purchased in 1914 by an industrialist couple, Mr and Mrs Kröller-Müller, as a country residence. Mr Kröller wanted a place to hunt, and his wife wanted a culture park. The St Hubertus hunting lodge was designed by **HP Berlage**, who had already designed office buildings for the couple, and was built between 1914 and 1920. Under Mrs Kröller-Müller's influence, sculptures and monuments were added to the northern part of the park. In 1938, the couple decided to donate the site and their valuable art collection to the state, on condition that the state built a museum, the Kröller-Müller Museum. These two great patrons of the arts lived in the park until they died, and were buried on the Franse Berg, the area of high dunes behind the museum.

Landscapes – A desolate landscape of heathlands, grass, sand dunes and lakes is interspersed with clusters of tall oak and beech trees, pine and birch woods. These are the many faces of the Hoge Veluwe, and it is worth a visit at any time of year. The rhododendrons flower in May and June, while in August there are great expanses of purple heather. In autumn, the deciduous trees are brilliantly coloured, and the park looks magical under a coating of snow.

Fauna – The park has a rich wildlife ranging from red deer, moufflons, wild boar and roe deer to a wide variety of birdlife. Mid-September to mid-October, during the **rutting season** of the red deer, is a particularly interesting time to visit. The best time to observe the animals is in the late afternoon when

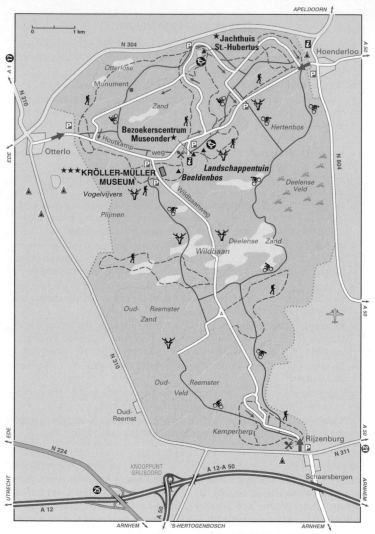

APELDOORN

★ **Jachthuis St.-Hubertus**

Hoenderloo

N 304

Otterlose Monument

Zand

Bezoekerscentrum Museonder ★

Hertenbos

Houtkamp

weg

Otterlo

Landschappentuin Beeldenbos

★★★ KRÖLLER-MÜLLER MUSEUM

Deelense Veld

Vogelvijvers

Plijmen

Wildbaanweg

Deelense Zand

Wildbaan

Oud-Reemster Zand

Oud-Veld

Reemster Veld

Oud-Reemst

Kemperberg

Rijzenburg

N 311

Schaarsbergen

N 224

KNOOPPUNT GRIJSOORD

A 12-A 50

A 12

ARNHEM   'S-HERTOGENBOSCH   ARNHEM

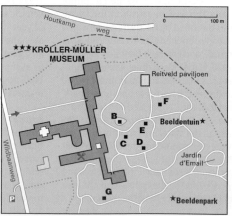

NATIONAAL PARK DE HOGE VELUWE

🛈	Information
🐦	Birds
	Game observation hide
🚲	Cycling track
	Waymarked trail
▲	Campsite
✕	Restaurant
P	Car park
→	One way
	Quicksand
	Heathland
	Woodland

Houtkamp weg

0   100 m

★★★ KRÖLLER-MÜLLER MUSEUM

Reitveld paviljoen

Wildbaanweg

B

F

Beeldentuin ★

C   D   E

Jardin d'Email

G

★**Beeldenpark**

they are searching for food, in winter and spring (*until the end of May*).

Visitor Centre

🕐 *Open daily, 9.30am–5pm (6pm Apr–Oct).* ☎*0900 464 38 35. www.hoge veluwe.nl.*

This snail-shaped building is linked to the Museonder and offers detailed information about the park and its sights and recreation facilities. It also sells details of cycling and walking paths, and has an excellent display, including films, on the history, landscapes, flora and fauna of the park. ♿The centre makes an ideal starting point for a visit to the park.

Kröller-Müller Museum★★★ *3hr*

🕐*Open Tue–Sun 10am–5pm; also Mon during public holidays.* 🕐*Closed 1 Jan.* 💶*7€.* ♿☎*0318 59 12 41. www.kmm.nl.*

The Kröller-Müller Museum was built to the designs of **Henry van de Velde** and is named after its founder, Helene Kröller-Müller. The museum was inaugurated in 1938, and in 1961 a Sculpture Garden was created. In 1977 **Wim Quist** was commissioned to build a new wing. The museum houses an important collection of paintings, sculptures and drawings, including works by Van Gogh.

To the right of the main entrance is the **Beeldenzaal**, or sculpture room, displaying *The Rider and Horse* by Marini (1952) and works by Zadkine. Early 20C paintings are hung in the six rooms that follow. There are a number of canvases by **Mondrian** showing his diversity of style. The paintings by **Van der Leck** are followed by works of the **Constructivists** (Strzeminski, Schlemmer) and **Futurists** (Ballà, Severini and Boccioni). **Cubism** is represented by Picasso, Braque, Gris and Léger (*Soldiers Playing Cards*, 1917). Another room is dedicated to the work of **Charley Toorop**. One of the most important works in this section is *The Beginning of the World,* a bronze sculpture (1924) by Brancusi, regarded as marking the beginning of modern sculpture. Further on there are works by James Ensor and Pointillist canvases by Seurat (*Le Chahut*), Van Rijsselberghe and Signac.

A selection of works by **Van Gogh** is arranged in chronological order from right to left around a patio. Looking at them in this order brings out the contrast between the sombre early works (*The Potato Eaters, Weavers*) and the later, more brightly coloured and dynamic paintings. The latter include *The Olive Grove, Road with Cypress and Star, Evening Café, The Bridge at Arles, Old Man in Sorrow, The Good Samaritan* (after Delacroix) and superb portraits such as *Postman Roulin, L'Arlésienne* (after a drawing by his friend, Gauguin) and the *Self-Portrait*. There are also works of 1887 like the *Faded Sunflowers,* which was Mrs Kröller-Müller's first acquisition, and *Still-life with Plaster Statue*.

In the rooms behind the patio, along with **French Impressionists** (Cézanne, Renoir and Monet), there are landscapes by Jongkind, Millet and Corot. **Symbolism** is represented by the work of artists such as Jan Toorop and Johannes Thorn Prikker. Other 19C paintings include works by Israëls and Breitner. Then come the **Dutch painters** of the Golden Age (Avercamp, Van Goyen and Van de Velde the Younger) and masters of the 16C such as Bruyn the Elder (*Portrait of a Woman with a Carnation,* with a vanitas on the reverse side), a *Venus and Cupid* (1525) by Hans Baldung Grien and a *Venus and Cupid as a Honey Thief* by Cranach. There are also works from 15C Italy and France.

Kröller-Müller Museum

The Cat (1914) by Bart van der Leck

271

Also on display are Greek ceramics, Chinese and Japanese porcelain, Mexican and African sculpture and 20C ceramics (Csàsky).

The **new wing** is used for displaying the collection of **contemporary sculpture** (Minimal Art, Zero Group and Arte Povera) in the form of temporary exhibitions. Giacometti's *Striding Man* (1960) is in the passage leading to one of the rooms.

Sculpture Garden and Sculpture Park★★

Go through the museum to reach the sculpture garden.

This pleasant tree-shaded garden is the setting for some 20 sculptures by contemporary artists.

On leaving the museum note the floating polyester sculpture by Marta Pan (1961) (B), *Reclining Niobe* by Permeke (1951) (C), *The Great Penelope* by Bourdelle (1912) (D) and *The Air* by Maillol (1939) (E). Further on is a **pavilion** designed by Rietveld in 1953. The park contains many other works, including Dubuffet's **Jardin d'émail** (1975), a white construction so large that it is possible to walk around inside it; *Concetto Spaziale Nature,* five spheres by Lucio Fontana (1965) (F); the gigantic *Trowel* (1971) by Claes Oldenburg, *Igloo* by Mario Mertz and *Construction of 56 Barrels* by Christo. Finally, there is a very fine example of land art: *Spin Out* by Richard Serra (G),

consisting of three steel discs in the hollow of a dune.

The **sculpture park** on the steep slope of the Franse Berg, has another 10 sculptures.

Sculpture Wood

Enter via the road to the visitor centre.

This small site is dotted with contemporary sculptures: *Herbaceous Border* (1987) by F Morellet, the surprising *Otterlo Beech Tree* (1988) by Penone, André Volten's quadruple composition *1: 4 = 1 x 4* (1986) and *One* (1988), a bronze by Serra.

Additional Sights

Museonder★

Same opening times as visitor centre. *0900 464 38 35. www.hogeveluwe.nl.* The "museum underneath" is located underground next to the visitor centre, and is a very original display of the world beneath the surface of the soil. It includes the underground lives of plants and animals, the role of ground water, the effects of climatic change on the soil and the history of the Veluwe landscape, in a fascinating presentation which uses a wide variety of media.

Landschappentuin

This garden is actually a miniature version of the whole park, showing the

Spin Out (1972–1973) by Richard Serra in the Sculpture Garden

many different landscapes of the Hoge Veluwe within the space of a short walk. There is a hut made of turf at the beginning of the route.

Jachthuis St Hubertus★

By guided tour only. Apr–Oct, daily every 30min between 11am and 12.30pm and 2pm and 4.30pm; Nov–Mar (except Jan), daily 2pm and 3pm. ⚲2€. ☎0900 464 38 35. www.hogeveluwe.nl. This hunting lodge is actually a large castle, the plan of which is in the shape of a pair of antlers. It was built by Berlage between 1914 and 1920, and is regarded as one of his masterpieces. Both the building, with its 31m/102ft tower, and the two lakes and surrounding gardens are highly geometric. The interior and furnishings were also designed by Berlage. As in the rest of the building, every shape, colour and detail has symbolic significance, referring to the legend of St Hubert, the patron saint of hunters. This ingenious aspect of the building is described in detail on the tour (*free;*

booking at visitor centre compulsory). Helene Kröller-Müller died here in 1939, and her husband two years later. Today, the hunting lodge is used as a residence for guests of the government.

Excursion

Otterlo

1km/0.6mi from the west entrance to Hoge Veluwe National Park.
Otterlo is the home of the **Nederlands Tegelmuseum** (◐*open Tue–Fri 10am–5pm, Sat–Sun and public holidays 1pm–5pm;* ◑*closed 25 Dec and 1 Jan.* ⚲4€; ♿☎0318 59 15 19; www. nederlandstegelmuseum.nl), or Dutch Tile Museum, which gives a history of Dutch wall and floor tiles from 1510 to the present day. Tile production was introduced to the northern Netherlands from Italy and Antwerp in the early 16C. By the 18C Dutch tiles were highly popular and were exported all over the world.

HOORN★
NOORD-HOLLAND
POPULATION 68 150
PLAN OF THE CONURBATION IN THE CURRENT RED-COVER MICHELIN GUIDE BENELUX

On the banks of the IJsselmeer, Hoorn is one of the most typical of the old Zuiderzee ports. The town played a part in the foundation of the East India Company and today remains a thriving commercial centre. Hoorn has a busy marina and, with its period buildings and winding streets, is a pleasant place for visitors to walk round.

- ℹ **Information:** Veemarkt 4 – 1621 JC. ☎0900 403 10 55. www.vvvhoorn.nl.
- ▶ **Orient Yourself:** One of the best ways to get to know Hoorn is on foot. From the rail station, head south through the Veemarkt, one of the oldest areas of Hoorn, and follow the signs to the harbour. The route takes you through the modern pedestrianised area.
- 🅿 **Parking:** There is plenty of free parking around the Veemarkt area.
- 🧒 **Especially for Kids:** A ride on the steam tram.
- 👁 **Don't Miss:** The harbour with its gabled houses and fine restaurants, and be sure to visit the Westfries Museum. It tells the story of Hoorn through paintings.
- 🕐 **Organizing Your Time:** Hoorn can be explored in a day, but to really take in its atmosphere, stay overnight and spend an evening in the Old Town. Allow at least three hours to explore the Old Town. Take a ride on the old-fashioned steam tram (*www.museumstoomtram.nl*) runs from Hoorn to Medemblik, where the journey can be continued by boat to Enkhuizen. *Further information is available from the tourist information office (VVV).*

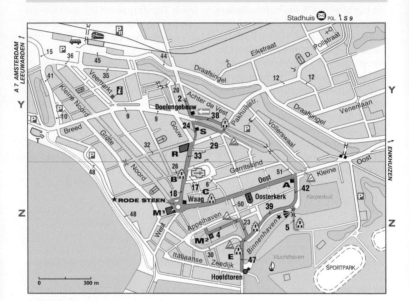

A Bit of History

Hoorn was founded c. 1357 on the shores of the natural haven and it grew rapidly to become the main settlement of Western Friesland. Overseas trade and fishing brought great prosperity to the town. It was also an important base for the Dutch East India Company (VOC) during Holland's 'Golden Age' (& see Introduction, The East India Company). It was in Hoorn that the first large herring-net was made in 1416, marking the beginning of what was to become a flourishing industry.

To the north of the town centre, gardens mark the course of the moats of the early 16C fortifications.

In October 1573 the famous naval engagement, the Battle of the Zuiderzee, took place just outside the harbour; the combined fleets of the towns of Hoorn, Enkhuizen, Edam and Monikendam – all towns already in the hands of the Sea Beggars – defeated the Spanish under Admiral **Bossu**. However, Hoorn's hour of glory came in the 17C when it served as the administrative and commercial centre of all Holland north of Amsterdam.

The town had one of the six "chambers" which comprised the federal organisation of the Dutch East India Company (& see Introduction, Time line).

In 1616 **Willem Schouten** (1580–1625) was the first to round the southernmost tip of South America, 96 years after

Magellan had discovered the Magellan Strait. Schouten named the southern-most rocky headland of Tierra del Fuego Cape Horn, after his native town.

Jan Pieterszoon Coen (1587–1629), also a native of Hoorn, was the enterprising Governor General of the Dutch East Indies from 1617 to 1623 and again from 1627 to his death in 1629. He founded Batavia, today Jakarta, and is generally considered to be the founder of the Dutch commercial empire in the Dutch East Indies (Indonesia).

Like the rest of the country, Hoorn declined in the 18C, and it was two centuries later before it was to experience a recovery.

Old Town★

This was the original site of Hoorn and today a succession of old façades, many with lovely sculptured stones with a seafaring theme, can still be seen.

Achterstraat

The **Doelengebouw** (target building) at n° 2 was formerly used for practice by the town's company of archers. The scene above the doorway (1615) shows the martyrdom of St Sebastian, the patron saint of archers.

Onder de Boompjes

On the corner of this canal and Pakhuisstraat an old storehouse of 1606 is decorated with a sculptured **façade stone** depicting two sailing ships of the United East India Company. To protect spices and other costly goods from enemy attack, these storehouses were usually located on the far side of town from the harbour.

Korte Achterstraat

At n° 4 in this street is the old orphanage or **Weeshuis** (1620). A commemorative plaque recalls that Admiral Bossu was imprisoned in Hoorn for three years after his naval defeat (*see opposite left*).

Nieuwstraat

In this shopping street stands the old **stadhuis** with its double crow-stepped gabled façade (1613).

The house at **n° 17** has a façade with Poseidon and his wife Amphitrite accompanied by dolphins; along with Poseidon's trident, these animals symbolised free trade and sea power.

Kerkplein

At n° 39, opposite a church (secularised), is **De Boterhal** (the butter market), formerly St John's almshouse (St Jans Gasthuis). The building, which dates from 1563, is a fine residence with a gable decorated with sculptures.

Kerkstraat

At n° 1 there is an attractive 1660 façade.

Rode Steen★

This picturesque square is overlooked by the Westfries Museum and by the Waag, or weigh-house. The name Rode Steen, red stone, refers to the blood that was shed here during public executions. In the centre stands a 19C statue of Jan Pieterszoon Coen (⚫ *see above left*).

The house at n° 2 has a façade stone depicting a blacksmith, hence its name: *In Dyser Man* (The Iron Man).

Westfries Museum

Rode Steen 1. ⏱ *Open Mon–Fri 11am–5pm, Sat–Sun and public holidays, 1pm–5pm.* ⏱ *Closed third Mon in Aug, 25 Dec and 1 Jan.* ⊛*5€.* ☎*0229 28 00 28. www.wfm.nl (in Dutch).*

The West Friesland Museum is an elegant Baroque edifice dating from 1632. Its tall **façade**★ is imposing with its large windows, very colourful coats of arms (House of Orange and West Friesland) and cornices topped by lions bearing

Westfries Museum

Willem Ysbrantszoon Bontekoe – the Hero of Hoorn

Willem Bontekoe (1587–1657) published his *Journael* in 1646. It was a great success, and was translated into a number of other languages. The book describes his adventures as the master of a United East India Company vessel from 1618 to 1625. The first part, describing his journey from Hoorn to Batavia (now Jakarta), became particularly famous. The voyage was a nightmare for the crew of 206; the mainmast broke not long after they set sail, there was an epidemic of scurvy on board, and the ship finally blew up not far from Batavia. Bontekoe describes how he and 54 other crew members survived this disaster and finally reached their destination.

The second part of Bontekoe's book is devoted to his years of sailing in Asian waters and fighting the Portuguese and Chinese, and the third section recounts his stay in Madagascar.

Bontekoe remains a source of inspiration even in the 20C: he was the subject of Johan Fabricius' 1924 bestseller, *De scheepsjongens van Bontekoe* (Bontekoe's Cabin Boys), though his role is not the heroic one portrayed in his own journal.

the coats of arms of seven local towns: Alkmaar, Edam, Enkhuizen, Hoorn, Medemblik, Monnickendam and Purmerend. It was the seat of the States' College consisting of delegates from seven important towns, which governed West Friesland and the Noorderkwartier (Northern Quarter). In the entrance note a lovely gate (1729).

Worthy of note on the ground floor are the ceiling in the Louis XVI drawing room, and the fine hall (Grote Voorzaal) decorated with a lovely chimney and group portraits of marksmen's guilds. On the upper floors, the rooms decorated with lovely furniture and *objets d'art* reproduce the refined interiors of the 17C and 18C. The Admiralty Room contains scale models and weaponry and a portrait of Admiral Bossu. Also the painting by Hendrik Corneliszoon Vroom **View of Hoorn**★ (1622) is interesting; remarkably the view of the old harbour depicted in this painting shows that today the harbour has remained almost intact. The attic still contains two cells dating from the time of the French occupation, when the building served as a court of law. In the basement there is an exhibition of finds from local excavation sites.

Waag
Rode Steen 8, near the Westfries Museum.
Probably the work of Hendrick de Keyser, the weigh-house is a fine building in blue stone, built in 1609. Today it houses

a restaurant. In a niche, a unicorn (the symbol of the town) holds a shield depicting a cornucopia.

Grote Oost
In this street the houses near the square are very steeply inclined and topped with imposing sculptured balustrades in the Rococo style.
Number 43, the imposing **Foreestenhuis**, is named after Nanning van Foreest, one of the town's best-known governors. The elegant Louis XIV-style façade dates from 1724, and the balcony is supported by Atlas figures.

Oosterkerk
This recently restored church was founded in 1453; a Renaissance façade, added in 1616, is topped with a charming wooden pinnacle. The church is now used mainly as a venue for cultural events.

Bossuhuizen
Slapershaven 1–2.
The frontage of these houses has a frieze in relief depicting the sea battle of 1573, in which Admiral Bossu was defeated. The left façade is very typical of the old shops on the quayside, with a ground floor topped by tall narrow windows separated by carved wood pilasters.

Oude Doelenkade
On the picturesque **Binnenhaven**★ quay, or inner harbour, there is a row of old warehouses; note nºs 21 and 1–19

with their façade stones depicting navigational scenes. In fine weather the harbour is often busy with elegant sailing ships and crowds of onlookers.

Veermanskade★

This quay is lined with a series of fine restored houses. Most of them are old merchants' residences, some with the typical Hoorn façade, with carved wood pilasters. Others have lovely façade stones and are topped by crow-stepped or bell gables.

Note the birthplace of the navigator **Willem Bontekoe** (1587–1630); the façade displays a spotted cow (*koe:* cow; *bonte:* spotted).

Hoofdtoren

Built in 1532 to keep watch over the port's main (*hoofd*) entrance; in 1651 it was topped by a wooden pinnacle. On the other side of the tower a sculpture depicts a unicorn, the symbol of the town. Since 1968 a trio of ship's boys – bronze sculpture by Jan van Druten – contemplate the port from the foot of the tower. They are the heroes of a children's novel by Johan Fabricius, dedicated to Bontekoe.

Bierkade

This is the quay where beer brought by ship from Hamburg and Bremen was unloaded.

At n° 4, two cheese warehouses from 1903 now house the **Museum van de Twintigste Eeuw** (*open Tue–Fri 10am–5pm, Sat–Sun noon–5pm; closed 25 Dec, 1 Jan, 30 Apr; 4€; 0229 21 40 01; www.museumhoorn.nl*), or Museum of the Twentieth Century. This gives an overview of the rapid pace of technological change and the many discoveries made during the past hundred years.

HULST

ZEELAND
POPULATION 28 021

At the frontier with Belgium, Hulst is a small town with cheerful, colourful houses and streets paved with pink brick. It is an old fortified town which was built in accordance with the Old Dutch system (*see Introduction, Military Architecture*).

- **Information:** Grote Markt 19 – 4561 EA. 0114 38 92 99. www.vestingstad.nl (in Dutch).
- ▶ **Orient Yourself:** Head for the Grote Markt and you will not go far wrong – it's central, and as Hulst is so small you will find your way around in minutes.
- **Parking:** There are plenty of places to park in the centre, some free.
- **Don't Miss:** The view from the top of the ramparts near the Keldermanspoort gate.
- **Organizing Your Time:** Hulst is a pretty little town with some interesting architecture, but you will probably be able to see it all in less than two hours.
- **Also See:** The impressive locks at Terneuzen.

A Bit of History

Hulst was once the capital of the Vier Ambachten, or Four Shires, comprising Hulst, Axel, Assenede and Boechout (these last two towns became Belgian in 1830). The 17C ramparts with their nine **bastions** and five ravelins, or triangular outworks, have been preserved. They are planted with fine trees and are still encircled by moats.

Reynard's city – The surroundings of Hulst are evoked in the Dutch version of the 13C epic, *Van den vos Reinaerde* (*Reynard the Fox*). Near Gentsepoort is a monument (Reinaertmonument) in honour of Reynard, a legendary trickster about whom tales have been told throughout Europe since the 12C.

Sights

Grote Markt

The **stadhuis**, with a perron flanked by a square tower, dates from the 16C. The **St Willibrordusbasiliek** is a fine building in the Brabant Gothic style. Its modern tower has an excellent carillon. For more than a century (1807–1931), the church was used by both Catholics and Protestants: the chancel and ambulatory being reserved for the former, the nave for the latter.

Keldermanspoort

This 16C gateway and water-gate were uncovered during excavations in 1952. The latter gave access to a military port. The top of the nearby ramparts affords a view of the crow-stepped gable and octagonal turret of the **hostel** which belonged to Dunes Abbey, near Koksijde in Belgium. This hostel houses the **Streekmuseum De Vier Ambachten** (⏱ *open Easter Day–Oct, daily 2pm–5pm;* ✉ *1.50€;* ☎ *0114 32 06 92*), or Four Shires Local History Museum.

Excursion

Terneuzen

24km/15mi to the northwest.
This port at the mouth of the Scheldt commands the entrance to the Gent-Terneuzen canal. There are three **locks**, the largest being 290m/951.4ft long and 40m/131ft wide.

HUNEBEDDEN ★

DRENTHE AND GRONINGEN

A *hunebed* is a prehistoric funerary monument, with a side entrance usually orientated to the south. Megaliths of this type are found in the Netherlands, concentrated in the Drenthe where 53 have been registered and numbered. Only one is not included, that of Noordlaren, which is in the province of Groningen.

- **Information:** www.missgien.net/stone-age/hunebedden.html.
- ▶ **Orient Yourself:** The Drenthe is accessed via the A 28.
- ⏱ **Organizing Your Time:** The length of your visit will be largely determined by the degree of interest generated by the remains of the stone monuments.
- **Also See:** ASSEN.

A Bit of History

Dutch dolmens – During the Neolithic period (between ca. 5 000 and 2 000 BC) the people who lived in what is now the north of the Netherlands are known as the Funnel Beaker People, named after their claywork. Their culture was expressed in stone and, while not on so great a scale as did their contempories at Stonehenge, or Newgrange or Skara Brae, the remains of their achievements are equally significant and inspiring. Fewer than 50 of their monuments survive, most of them in the province of Drenthe. These monuments were built as gravestones, using huge granite stones weighing up to 25 000 kg/55 155.5lb, which were carried to a selected site and and set in a geometric shape, topped by a covering stone, to form a rectangular gravestone.

Imposing dimensions – The smallest *hunebedden* are no less than 7m/23ft long, and a length of 25m/82ft is not unusual. The biggest is near Borger: the slabs which form it weigh more than 20 tonnes. The megaliths used to build *hunebedden* are erratic boulders from the **Hondsrug** (Dog's back), an end moraine deposited by a Scandinavian glacier, which extended from Groningen to Emmen. The *hunebedden* we can see today have lost their original appearance. When first built, the *hunebed* was hidden under a small burial mound, the earth being held up by a ring of upright stones; the space between these uprights was filled in with rubble. In Emmen, and especially south of Schoonoord, one can see reconstructed *hunebedden*.

A funerary monument – Hunebedden prove that prehistoric man lived in the Drenthe from 3 000 or 2 000 BC. They were used as collective burial chambers. Dishes, plates, tools and even jewellery were placed next to the bodies. Consequently, excavations in the vicinity of the *hunebedden* have been very fruitful. The objects discovered, notably pottery, have made it possible to connect *hunebedden* with the civilisation known as the Bell-Beaker culture.

The mystery remains – as to why these people dragged these great boulder stones and organised their energies in so collective a spirit. Similiar questions have been asked regarding the pyramids, Stonehenge and the dolmens of Ireland.

Hunebed Trail★
52km/32.3mi from Emmen to Noordlaren – allow 1 day

Emmen – *See EMMEN.*

Klijndijk
Go towards Valthe on the right. On leaving the village, turn right on to a sandy path, then left. Skirting the woods one reaches a long *hunebed* where two capstones remain.

Valthe
On leaving the village towards the northeast, on the right before a petrol station, a lane marked *hunebed* (*about 400m/437.4yd*) leads to a pair of *hunebeds*, D 35 and D 37, surrounded by oaks and lying to the south of Valthe. They are in fact two covered alley-

ways, one of which has been knocked down by three large oaks.

▶ *Going towards Odoorn, on the left after a wood, there is a small lane marked* hunebed *which leads to* hunebed *D 34.*

Set among heather, it is a small covered alleyway with two leaning slabs.

Odoorn
The town of Odoorn, at the heart of sheep-rearing country, organises an important annual sheep market. At **Exloo** (*4km/2.5mi north of Odoorn*) a sheep-shearing festival and a traditional handicraft festival are held each year (for these two events see Calendar of events).

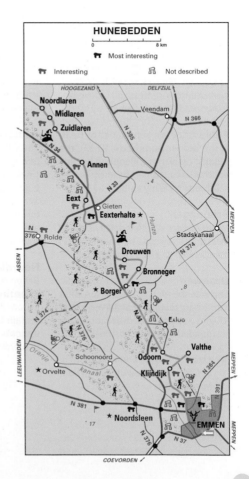

Hunebed in Eexterhalte

P. Gajic/MICHELIN

On leaving Odoorn, *hunebed* D 32, reached by a small path marked "hunebed", is hidden behind a curtain of trees. It is topped by four capstones.

Borger

In the main street, take the road to Bronneger.

The **Nationaal Hunebedden Infocentrum** (*open Feb–Dec, Mon–Fri 10am–5pm, Sat–Sun and public holidays 11am–5pm;* ⊘ *closed Jan and 25 Dec;* ≈5.75€ ⊠☎*0599 23 63 74;* www.hunebedcentrum.nl) is devoted to *hunebedden* and life during prehistoric times.

A little further on, surrounded by trees, is the Borger **hunebed**★ (D 27), the biggest of all. It is still topped by nine enormous capstones. Its entry on the south side is clearly visible.

Bronneger

In this hamlet, a path marked hunebed leads to an oak wood. There are five small hunebedden (D 23/25 and D 21/22).

Drouwen

The *hunebedden* (D 19/20) are on a rather bare mound, near the main road (they are visible from the road). One is surrounded by a circle of stones.

▸ *6km/3.7mi to the north of Drouwen, go left towards Assen, then turn right towards Eext.*

Eexterhalte

Shortly after the fork, on the right there is a **hunebed**★ (D 14) topped by six capstones. One can still see some of the stones encircling it.

Eext

In this village, in line with a bend, a path on the left leads to a hunebed (D 13), which has kept its original appearance; set in a cavity at the top of a mound, it consists of a square of uprights pressed closely together, and still has one of the capstones which served as the roof. Two stones set further apart mark the entrance, located, exceptionally, on the east side.

Annen

Small *hunebed* (D 9) on the left of the road.

Zuidlaren

This small town (around 10 000 inhabitants) in the province of Drenthe is an important tourist centre, due to its many cultural attractions and statues. The annual Zuidlaardermarkt (cattle market, country market and fair) is a highlight.

Midlaren

The village has two *hunebedden. Turn left, between two houses, on to a dirt track called* Hunebedpad. A further 200m/656ft away, after having crossed a road, and behind two houses shaded by large trees, there are two covered alleyways (D 3/D 4) each one made of several enormous slabs.

Noordlaren

Before reaching the mill, take a lane on the left marked "hunebed" which leads to a grove. This *hunebed* (G 1), where there remain two capstones resting on five uprights, is the only one in the Groningen province.

IJSSELMEER

FLEVOLAND – FRYSLÂN – GELDERLAND – NOORD – HOLLAND – OVERIJSSEL

IJsselmeer is the name that has been given to the Zuiderzee since it was cut off from the sea by the construction of a Barrier Dam in 1932.

▷ **Orient Yourself:** Take a look at a map of the Netherlands, find Amsterdam and the area immediately above it beyond the Markermeer is the IJsselmeer.

◎ **Don't Miss:** Taking the barrier dam road from Den Oever to Sneek and see the large stretch of the IJsselmeer's water to your right. To the left will be the Waddenzee.

◷ **Organizing Your Time:** A tour by car could occupy half a day or stretch into two days. Try and make sure you get to see the mighty structure of the Stevin Lock.

◔ **Also See:** DE WADDENEILANDEN.

A Bit of History and Geography

The old Zuiderzee – The IJssel river formerly flowed into a series of small lakes. Enlarged progressively, they developed into a large lake, called **Lake Flevo** by the Romans and known in the Middle Ages as **Almere** or Almari. In 1287 a tidal wave destroyed part of the north coast, enlarged the mouth of the lake and invaded the low-lying regions which surrounded it, turning it into a large gulf open to the North Sea.

Creation of the IJsselmeer – The idea of closing the Zuiderzee by a dyke was first proposed in the 17C as a means of

combating the devastation caused by the North Sea. In 1825 a violent storm ravaged the coasts of the Zuiderzee. In 1891 a project was presented by the engineer **Dr C Lely** (1854–1929). It was only adopted by Parliament in 1918, following the terrible floods of 1916 and when Lely had become Minister of Public Works for the third time. The aim envisaged was triple: by the construction of a dyke to put an end to the floods which menaced the banks of the Zuiderzee, create a reserve of fresh water to stop the increasing salinity of the soil, and with the formation of polders to gain 225 000ha/555 987 acres of fertile land. The work on the IJsselmeer started in 1919; in 1924 the small Amsteldiep dyke

The barrier dam

Place Names In Frisian

You may encounter both Dutch and Frisian place names on maps and road signs. The following are the names of some of the places described in this book:

Dutch	Frisian	Dutch	Frisian
Grou	Grouw	Rinsumageest	Rinsumageast
Harlingen	Harns	Sloten	Sleat
Hinderloopen	Hylpen	Sneek	Snits
Hoorn	Hoarne	Twijzel	Twizel
Leeuwarden	Ljouwert	West-Terschelling	West-Skylge
Oudkerk	Aldtsjerk	Workum	Warkum

linking **Wieringen Island** to the mainland was completed.

Wieringermeer Polder – From 1927 to 1930 this polder was reclaimed. It stretches over 20 000ha/49 421 acres in a former gulf of the Zuiderzee between Medemblik and Wieringen Island. Immediately after the drainage (700 million cu m/24 720 million cu ft of water), the polder presented a surface of muddy clay. In 1945, two weeks before their surrender, the Germans blew up the Wieringermeer Polder dyke and flooding ensued. The surging water created two funnel-shaped holes of more than 30m/98ft deep. These 'gaping' holes could not be repaired and the dyke had to be re-routed round what is now called **De Gaper**. Again drained and returned to its former state, the polder is now a flourishing agricultural region.

Construction of the dyke – The barrier dam, or Afsluitdijk, was built in 1927 between the Frisian coast and the former Wieringen Island, by creating an artificial island (Breezand) between the two points. With clay dredged from the bottom of the Zuiderzee, a dyke was built, against which sand was deposited; the sand doubled by a layer of clay was collected on the spot by pumping. As the work advanced the current grew stronger and the remaining channel was sealed off with great difficulty.

The barrier dam was completed on 28 May 1932; 30km/18.6mi long and 90m/295.3ft wide at sea level, it is more than 7m/23ft above sea level and formed a new lake, the IJsselmeer.

Three large polders – Once the barrier dam was completed, the creation of the second IJsselmeer polder was undertaken, the **Noordoostpolder** (*see NOORDOOSTPOLDER*) and then the two **Flevoland**★ (*see Flevoland*) polders.

The project concerning the development of the very last IJsselmeer polder (**Markerwaard**) has been abandoned. Only the northern part of the surrounding dyke has been completed: a road, the N 302, now links Enkhuizen to Lelystad.

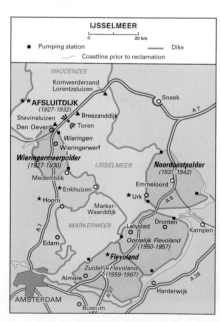

Afsluitdijk★★
(Barrier Dam) *30km/18.6mi*

On the **Den Oever** side, at the dam's entrance, stands a **statue** of the engineer Lely on the left. On the seaward side the barrier dam has a breakwater which protects a bicycle path and a dual carriageway. Below the barrier dam on the IJsselmeer side, fishermen come to place their nets on the bottom of the lake, mainly to catch eels.

Stevin Lock

This lock, which bears the name of the engineer Stevin who first proposed the idea in the 17C, forms the first group of locks for ships to pass through.

At the point where the two sections of the barrier dam joined in 1932 there is now a **tower** with the inscription "A living nation builds for its future". From the top of this monument there is a **panorama** over Waddenzee and IJsselmeer. Near this edifice a footbridge spans the road. Further on, a viaduct built in 1979 enables traffic to cross between the two ports of **Breezanddijk** and gives drivers the possibility of turning back.

The **Kazemattenmuseum Kornwerderzand** (*open May–Sept, Wed and Sat 10am–5pm; Jul and Aug also open Sun 1pm–5pm; ⊚3€; ☎0517 57 94 53 or 05 15 23 14 22; www.kazemattenmuseum.nl (VVV Makkum)*), or Kornwerderzand Bunkers Museum, is by the **Lorentzsluizen** (*access via Kornwerderzand turnoff*). Some of the 17 wartime bunkers have been restored to their original condition (May 1940) and opened to the public. The museum also has displays on the period from 1932 to 1965, including the building of the Afsluitdijk, the German invasion in 1940, resistance and liberation, and the Cold War.

KAMPEN★

OVERIJSSEL
POPULATION 50 000
TOWN PLAN IN THE CURRENT RED-COVER MICHELIN GUIDE BENELUX

Kampen extends along the IJssel's west bank, near the mouth of the river. In the Middle Ages it was a very prosperous port due to the herring trade. It was a Hanseatic League city, an association of towns in Northern Europe which had the monopoly of traffic in the Scandinavian countries. One of Kampen's most renowned inhabitants is the painter **Hendrick Avercamp** (158–1634), also called the Mute of Kampen, who settled in the town in the early 17C.

- 🛈 **Information:** Oudestraat 151, 8261 CL, Kampen. ☎0900 112 23 75. www.vvvkampen.nl (in Dutch).
- ▶ **Orient Yourself:** Make your way to Oudestraat where most of the major sights in Kampen can be seen, in particular the leaning square tower of the Niewue Toren.
- 🅿 **Parking:** Plenty of inexpensive car parking is provided.
- ⊛ **Don't Miss:** The iron cage at the Oude Raadhuis.
- 🕒 **Organizing Your Time:** Small and compact, Kampen makes a good destination for an afternoon or day's excursion. Make sure you're there to witness the view of the town from the east bank of the IJssel; it is particularly beautiful at sunset. In the centre, the onion-shaped turret of the Oude Raadhuis and the Nieuwe Toren stand out. To the right the 14C **Buitenkerk** (**1**), and to the left St Nicolaas and the large towers of the Koornmarktspoort. This is arguably the most attractive river bank in the Netherlands.

A Bit of History

In the 16C there was a very rapid decline in the town brought about by the wars, which ruined the hinterland, and by the silting up of the IJssel. In the 19C a channel was made leading to the Zuiderzee, but the closing of this sea reduced

Gregory Wrona/Apa

Kampen, boats in harbour

Kampen to the state of a river port. This barrier to its development resulted in many of the town's old buildings being preserved, and the town centre is surprisingly attractive, with nearly 500 historic monuments.

Sights

Oude Raadhuis★ (2)
🕐*Open by appointment only.* ⊚*1€.*
☎*038 331 73 61.*
A little dwarfed by the new 18C town hall, the old town hall is a small brick edifice dating from 1543, crowned with galleries and flanked at the back by a slightly leaning tower with an open-work onion-shaped dome. Its gable, with a helical **chimney**★, is surrounded by bartizans. Note the iron cage by the façade, in which offenders used to be locked up and exposed to the public as a punishment. The **Magistrates' Hall**★ (Schepenzaal), with sombre 16C oak wainscoting forming the seats, has a **bench** richly decorated with

Renaissance-style reliefs, next to a monumental **chimneypiece**★ by Colijn de Nole (1545).

Oude Vleeshuys
Oudestraat 119.
The town's coat of arms is engraved on the Renaissance stone façade (1596) of the old butcher's shop; it portrays two lions framing a fortified gateway.

Nieuwe Toren
🕐*Open May–mid-Sept, Wed and Sat 2pm–5pm; Jul and Aug also open Fri 2pm–5pm.* 🕐*Closed public holidays.*
☎*038 331 73 61.*
This tall square tower, erected in the 17C, has an octagonal bell-tower with a carillon cast by François Hemony. Next door, a fine Art Nouveau building houses a bakery.

Gotische Huis
On the right of the Nieuwe Toren.
This elegant residence, with a tall façade, crowned with pinnacles and pierced with numerous windows, has

been thoroughly restored and contains the municipal museum, the **Stedelijk Museum** (🕐*open Tue–Sat 11am–5pm and by appointment;* 🕐 *closed Jan, Easter, Whitsun 25,26, 31 Dec;* ⊜*3€;* ☎ *038 331 22 94; www.stedelijkemuseakampen.nl*). The museum houses a fine collection of silverware of the boatmen's guild, including a fine 1369 **goblet**★, and chronicles Kampen's past. At the rear, the remnants of a horse mill are on display.

▶ *Pass under the Nieuwe Toren and follow Nieuwe Markt to Burgwal, a quay running alongside Burgel Canal, which crosses the town. Turn left.*

Broederkerk (3)

This is the 15C former church of the Minorites (Franciscans).

Broederweg

On the right side of this street, there is a Gothic chapel, a former Walloon church which in 1823 became a **Mennonite church** (**4**).

Broederpoort (5)

This is a lovely gateway with a voluted gable (1465) flanked by graceful turrets.

▶ *After the gateway, turn left.*

Plantsoen

This is the name of the pleasant park which follows the old ramparts: the moats form the Singelgracht.

Cellebroederspoort★ (6)

An elegant building flanked by steeply-pitched roofed towers, this gateway, which was part of the 15C walls, was altered in 1617 in the Renaissance style.

▶ *Go through the gateway and follow Cellebroedersweg then Geerstraat. By Boven Nieuwstraat, on the right, you reach Muntplein.*

St Nicolaaskerk or Bovenkerk (7)

🕐*Open Easter Sun–early Sept, Mon and Tue 1pm–4pm, Wed–Fri 10am–4pm; mid-Sept–autumn half-term, Mon–Fri 1pm–4pm.* ☎*038 331 36 08. www.debovenkerk.nl* (*in Dutch*).

This imposing Gothic edifice (14C) is overlooked by a tower 70m/229.6ft high. The interior consists of a nave and four aisles, a wide transept and a large ambulatory with radiating chapels. Note the 16C chancel screen and a Late Gothic stone pulpit. The **organ** has 3 200 pipes and was built in 1741 by Hinsz.

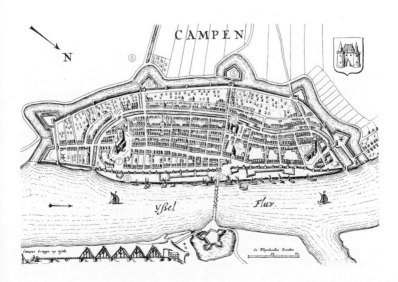

Kampen and the Tobacco Industry

In 1813 two small tobacco factories were set up in Kampen, followed by the first major cigar manufacturer in 1826. By 1880 almost 40% of Kampen's labour force worked in the cigar industry, with the town's 1 400 cigar makers producing 1.5 million cigars a week in their heyday. But the 1930s economic crisis, World War I and the increasing popularity of cigarettes brought this thriving industry to its knees. Some of the buildings that evoke the town's involvement with tobacco include the **Kamper Tabaksmuseum** (*by appointment only;* ☎*038 331 58 68*), featuring tools used in the tobacco industry and smokers' implements; the tobacco factory (**tabaksfabriek**) in Voorstraat 102–106; and the tobacconist's shop "**De Olifant**" at n° 101 Oudestraat.

Koornmarktspoort (8)

This is the oldest gateway to the town. Dating from the 14C and situated on the old corn market, Koornmarkt, near St Nicolaas, the gateway has retained its defensive character with a massive central keep flanked, since the late 14C, by two squat towers.

KEUKENHOF AND BULB FIELDS ★★★

ZUID-HOLLAND AND NOORD-HOLLAND

Bulbs have been grown in the region around the Keukenhof for hundreds of years. In spring, the fields between Leiden and Haarlem resemble a vividly coloured chessboard.

- **Information:** www.keukenhof.nl.
- ▶ **Orient Yourself:** From the Apeldoorn direction take the A 1 to Amsterdam and follow signs for the Schiphol before taking the A 4 for The Hague. At exit 4 follow the N 207 towards Lisse and follow the signs to Keukenhof. If coming from The Hague, use the A 44, take exit 3 to Noordwijkerhout/Lisse. and the N 208 to Lisse.
- **Parking:** Parking fees apply in Keukenhof.

A Bit of History

An original speculation – The tulip is said to have been brought from Turkey by Augier Ghislain de Busbecq (1522–92), the Imperial envoy. The bulbs were given by Busbecq to Charles de l'Ecluse (1526–1609), a scientist better known as **Carolus Clusius**, who at the time was in charge of the Emperor's garden of medicinal plants in Vienna. Professor at the University of Leiden in 1593, Clusius started to cultivate tulips on the sandy and humid soil which stretched along the North Sea between Leiden and Haarlem. This experiment was a great success.

Other flowers such as hyacinths and gladioli had also been introduced, but it was the tulip which attained the highest prices. Between 1634 and 1636 speculation was rife and "tulip mania" ("tulipomania") reached insane proportions. A rare tulip bulb was sold for 6 000 florins. Buyers even went so far as to exchange one bulb for a coach and two horses, for acres of land or for a house. The Dutch States put an end to this speculation in 1636 and the flower industry was regulated. At the end of the 17C the tulip craze gave way to that of the hyacinth.

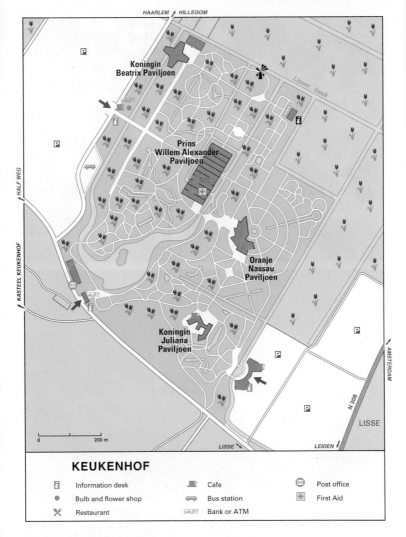

KEUKENHOF

🛈	Information desk	🍴	Cafe	✉	Post office
●	Bulb and flower shop	🚌	Bus station	✚	First Aid
✕	Restaurant	🏧	Bank or ATM		

The Keukenhof★★

The **Keukenhof National Flower Exhibition** (🕙 *open late Mar–late May, daily 8am–7.30pm*; ∞ *13.50€*; ♿ ☎ *0252 46 55 55*) has been held every spring since 1949.

When a group of bulb-growers was looking for an exhibition site, Keukenhof was chosen as the ideal location and has ever since served as the showcase for Dutch growers. Each year this extraordinary garden attracts nearly 900 000 visitors.

In the 15C the site was Jacoba van Beieren's (♿ *see GOES*) kitchen garden

(*keuken:* kitchen and *hof:* garden); the countess used the castle, which still stands nearby, as her hunting lodge. The castle grounds are landscaped in the English style, contrasting with the geometric shapes of the surrounding bulb fields, and include fountains, water features, lakes with swans, themed gardens and works of art. The layout is changed each year, so there is always something new to see, and the brilliant colours of the tulips, hyacinths and narcissi form a striking contrast with the cool greens of the grass and trees. Three layers of bulbs are planted one on top of the other, providing new

www.keukenhof.nl

www.keukenhof.nl

Flower display at Keukenhof

blooms throughout the entire season. The less hardy plants are displayed in large greenhouses, and changing flower shows are held in the various pavilions. There is a permanent **orchid display** in the Koningin Beatrix Paviljoen. Flowering shrubs, themed gardens (including a wild garden, a music garden and a historical garden), fountains and water features all add to the splendour of the park. The **beeldenroute** is a trail that takes in some 50 art works. The Groningen windmill on the north side of the park has a splendid **view**★ of the surrounding bulb fields.

Since 1999 a summer exhibition has been held on the newly acquired site, the **Zomerhof** (7ha/17.3 acres; ⏱*open Aug–mid-Sept, daily 9am–6pm;* ♿☎*0252 46 55 55; www.keukenhof.nl*),

which comprises a dune landscape and a terp planted with summer blooms, as well as themed gardens, water features and a Japanese garden. The annual bulb market (Bloembollenmarkt) takes place in October.

Bulb Fields★★★

Today in the Netherlands, bulbs cover an area of 14 400ha/35 583 acres across the country. The main production areas are in the south of Haarlem and to the north of the line formed between Alkmaar and Hoorn. Flevoland is also a bulb-growing area.

More than a half billion euros' worth of bulbs are exported all over the world each year.

The Tulip Vase

The tulip vase was a 17C Dutch invention. It was usually spherical or fan-shaped, and sometimes took the form of a pagoda. There were holes or tubes around the outside, each holding a single flower. Despite their name, the vases were not just used for tulips. Whole vases full of one type of flower were not fashionable in the 17C, particularly as tulips were so expensive. Instead, people preferred to show off a selection of different flowers. The vases were often made as pairs, so that they could be placed at either end of a table or shelf in a similar way to candlesticks.

Bulb-growing – The most widespread species in the Netherlands are the tulip, narcissus, hyacinth, iris and crocus, but numerous other flowers are cultivated such as the gladiolus, lily, grape hyacinth, dahlia, anemone and freesia.

Towards mid-March the bulb fields take on their first colour with the blossoming of orange and violet **crocuses**, which are followed by white and yellow narcissi (end March). In mid-April the **hyacinths** flower, along with the early **tulips**. A few days later, the most beautiful tulips open out. It is, therefore, at the end of April that the fields are usually at their most beautiful. Divided into multicoloured strips separated by small irrigation canals, they look like an immense patchwork. It is the time of the Bloemencorso, the flower parade from Haarlem to Noordwijk (*see Calendar of events*). The fields are then covered by **irises**, and **gladioli** in August. Another floral float procession takes place in September between Aalsmeer and Amsterdam (*see Calendar of events*).

Shortly after blossoming the stems are cut off by mechanical means, in order to strengthen the bulb. Once harvested, the large bulbs are sold. The bulbules are replanted in autumn.

Crossing the bulb fields by railway from Leiden to Haarlem offers lovely views; flying over them in an **aeroplane** (*Information: Kroonduif Air B.V., Heathrowbaan 4, 3045 AG Rotterdam; 010 415 78 55. www.kroonduif-air.nl*) is even better.

Excursion through the Bulb Fields★★

Circular tour from Haarlem – allow one day

Haarlem★★ – *See HAARLEM.*

▶ *Leave Haarlem to the south via Van Eedenstraat.*

Going through the outskirts of Haarlem there is a succession of fine houses in spacious grounds, before the first bulb fields appear. On the right is a 17C–18C mansion, **Huis de Manpad**.

▶ *Take the first road on the right and once over the level crossing turn left.*

Vogelenzang

The village is set in a pleasant location, amid woods not far from the coastal dunes. Once again there are some prestigious villas in well-tended grounds. To the south of De Zilk the pale tints of the sand dunes contrast with the brightly coloured carpet of flowers. Beyond Noordwijkerhout the road starts climbing to the junction with the road to Sassenheim, which offers splendid **views**★ of the bulb fields.

Noordwijk aan Zee – *See LEIDEN, Excursions.*

▶ *Continue towards Lisse/Sassenheim. Just past the Voorhout sign on the right, turn left into Loosterweg.*

Keukenhof★★ – *See above.*

Lisse

One of the main villages in the bulb-growing area. The **Museum de Zwarte Tulp** (Black Tulip Museum; *open Tue–Sun 1pm–5pm; Closed 25, 26, 31 Dec and 1 Jan; 3€; 0252 41 79 00; www.museumdezwartetulp.nl*), located in an old house in the centre, offers information about the bulb-growing industry and has a collection of preserved tulips. There are photographs and videos on the preparation of the soil for bulbiculture. A bulb shed is part of the display, showing how the storage racks were

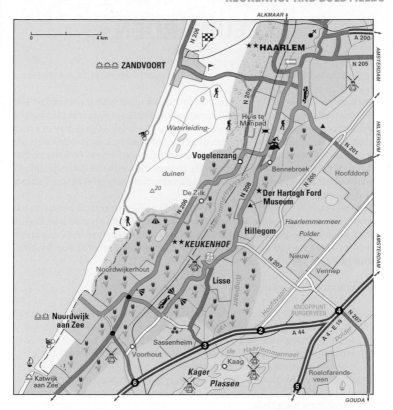

used to organise the work of preparing bulbs. Hyacinth bulbs were laid out to dry before they were graded by size, while ones earmarked for the Christmas trade were kept on the racks for up to nearly two months at a constant temperature.

The two rooms serving tea, coffee and snacks are noteworthy for their impressive proto-Renaissance style of design. Tours of the **Kagerplassen** lakes and the picturesque island village of **Kaagdorp** depart from Lisse.

Nearby, close to the important bulb-growing centre of **Sassenheim**, are the ruins of **Kasteel Teylingen**, where Jacoba or Jacqueline of Hainaut spent the last years of her life.

Hillegom

The **Den Hartogh Ford Museum**★ (*Haarlemmerstraat 36;* open Wed–Sun 10am–5pm; closed 30 Apr, 25, 26, 31 Dec and 1 Jan; 7.50€; 0252 51 81 18; www.fordmuseum.nl) has a display of 185 cars made by the Detroit manufacturer. They date from the period 1903–48, and form the world's largest private collection of Fords. They include the popular Model T, a Lincoln 160 from 1929 and a 1936 Ford 720 coupé. The last room contains lorries, buses and some fire engines, all made by Ford.

▶ *Continue towards Haarlem and follow the signs to Cruquius.*

Museum De Cruquius★ –
See HAARLEM, Outskirts.

LEEUWARDEN★

FRYSLÂN **P**

POPULATION 92 203

PLAN OF THE CONURBATION IN THE CURRENTRED-COVER MICHELIN GUIDE BENELUX

Leeuwarden (Ljouwert in Frisian) is an attractive town with scenic canals and historic buildings. The former residence of the Frisian stadholders is now the dynamic capital and cultural centre of Fryslân. The town is the centre of a thriving dairy farming industry and herds of the famous black and white cattle are a regular feature of the surrounding countryside. The famous Frisian cow has been immortalised by a larger-than-life bronze statue on the Harlingersingel-Harlingerstraatweg roundabout. The locals affectionately refer to it as Us Mem Our Mother.

The Friday cattle markets in the huge Frisian Expo Centre and the annual cattle inspection reflect the importance of this industry. Fryslân is also well known for its beautiful black horses. Famous figures who have lived in Leeuwarden include **Mata Hari**, **JJ Slauerhoff** and **MC Escher**. The writer **Simon Vestdijk** also spent his youth here.

- **Information:** Stationsplein 1 – 8901 AC. ☎0900 202 40 60. www.vvvleeuwarden.nl (in Dutch).
- ▶ **Orient Yourself:** The tourist information centre is in Stationsplein, which is an ideal starting place for a tour of Leeuwarden. It is central in the town and all the sights are within easy walking distance from it.
- **Parking:** There are several small car parks, although the main ones are located next to the station (fees apply).
- **Don't Miss:** The glorious façade of the Kanselarij, a former courthouse at Turfmarkt.
- **Organizing Your Time:** Leeuwarden has much to offer the visitor, and to see all the sights you could easily spend a day or two here.
- **Especially for Kids:** Feeding time at Aquazoo Friesland.

A Bit of History

Founded from the linking of three mounds located on the edge of the old **Middelzee**, a sort of gulf, drained between the 14C and 18C, Leeuwarden gained some importance in the 12C when it was fortified.

Capital of Friesland – Friesland was a bone of contention between the Counts of Holland and the Dukes of Saxony, whose feudal lord was the German emperor. In 1499 the Emperor Maximilian gave the fief to **Duke Albert of Saxony**, who elected to reside in Leeuwarden, which had become the provincial capital. In 1516 the Emperor Charles V gave the town a new set of fortifications.

After the independence of the United Provinces, Leeuwarden became the resi-

dence of the **stadholders** of Friesland and Groningen in 1584. The first was **William Louis** of Nassau (1560–1620), son of John of Nassau (brother of William the Silent). In 1675, under Henry Casimir II (1657–96), the Frisian stadholdership became hereditary.

John William Friso (1648–1711) received the title of Prince of Orange as a legacy from the Holland stadholder (and King of England), William III. Friso's son, **William IV** (1711–51), stadholder of Friesland, was chosen as the first hereditary stadholder of the whole country in 1747. The present dynasty in the Netherlands stems from him, the first king being his grandson, William I.

In 1580, Leeuwarden received its new curtain wall and, at the beginning of the 17C, a few bastions to the north and west. These were razed in the 18C and today have been converted into

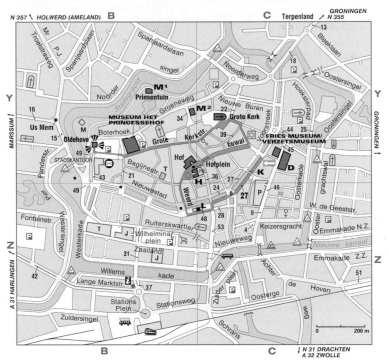

the Prinsentuin, or Princes' Garden, bordered by the Stadsgracht.
Since 1909, Leeuwarden has been the departure point of the famous **Eleven Towns Race** (Elfstedentocht).

Mata Hari – In 1876, Margarethe Geertruida Zelle was born in Leeuwarden. Having learnt to dance in the Dutch Indies (Indonesia), she went to Paris in 1903 and became famous as an exotic dancer under the name of **Mata Hari** (In Malayan: Eye of the Day). She was shot in 1917 for allegedly spying for the Germans.

Sights

Fries Museum/ Verzetsmuseum★★

Open Tue–Sun 11am–5pm. Closed 25 Dec and 1 Jan. 6€. 058 212 01 11. www.friesmuseum.nl (in Dutch) and www.verzetsmuseum.nl.

The Frisian Museum and Resistance Museum is housed in two historic buildings on Turfmarkt, linked by an underground tunnel. The Frisian museum has a very varied collection of items relating to Frisian culture. The Resistance museum tells the story behind – and

Address Book

For coin ranges, see the Legend on the cover flap.

WHERE TO STAY

Although Leeuwarden has only a few hotels, some are particularly characteristic.

Wyswert – *Rengerslaan 8, 8917 DD. ☎058 244 11 88. www.hotelwyswert. nl. 28 rooms.* This hotel school to the north of the centre offers inexpensive rooms. Service is provided by students under professional supervision.

het Stadhouderlijk Hof – *Hofplein 29, 8911 HJ. ☎058 216 21 80. www.stadhouderlijkhof.nl. 25 rooms.* This town-centre hotel is the former residence of the Frisian stadholders. The only room where there are still traces of this aristocratic past is the Nassau-Zaal, where portraits of princes and counts from the Van Nassau-Dietz dynasty hang on the walls; it is now used for weddings. The rest of the hotel, including the large bedrooms, is decorated in a tasteful and very modern style.

Van den Berg State – *Verlengde Schrans 87, 8932 NL. ☎058 280 05 84. Fax 058 288 34 22. 6 rooms.* This small hotel and restaurant (*see below*) is located in a 19C country house in a quiet residential area south of the centre. The rooms are very spacious, with their own lobbies and luxurious bathrooms. The suite has a waterbed and jacuzzi.

WHERE TO EAT

Kota Radja – *Groot Schavernek 5. ☎058 213 35 64.* Asian cuisine served in agreeable surroundings.

Van den Berg State – *Verlengde Schrans 87. ☎058 280 05 84.* This hotel and restaurant outside the centre offers excellent food, classic décor and a view of the garden; meals are served outdoors in clement weather.

BRASSERIES, CAFÉS, BARS, COFFEE SHOPS...

Het Haersma Huis – *Tweebaksmarkt 49. ☎058 213 18 28.* This grand café lies a stone's throw from the Fries Museum and is an ideal venue for a snack before or after a visit to the museum. It has classic modern décor in a historic building, and there is also a terrace.

De Koperen Tuin – *Prinsentuin 1. ☎058 213 11 00. www.dekoperentuin. nl. Closed Oct–Mar.* From the terrace of this garden tearoom enjoy lunch or just a drink or ice cream. There are free concerts on Sundays, and much of Simon Vestdijk's book, *De Koperen Tuin,* was set in the garden.

't Pannekoekschip – *Willemskade 69. ☎058 212 09 03.* This delightful ship moored on Willemskade, between the station and the old town, offers a choice of 90 kinds of pancake.

PRACTICAL INFORMATION

The **VVV tourist office** has information on sights, tours, excursions or accommodation and publishes an annual tourist guide to Leeuwarden.

TRANSPORT

There are two indoor **car parks** De Klanderij and Zaailand, and a park and ride point next to the station. **Bicycles** are available for hire from the Zaailand car park.

SHOPPING

Leeuwarden is a pleasant place to shop, and has an extensive **pedestrian area** Late-night opening is on Thursdays, and shops also open on the first Sunday of the month. The VVV sells a booklet on interesting places to shop in Leeuwarden.

Apart from all these modern shops, Nieuwesteeg, in the heart of town between Nieuwestad and Bagijnestraat, has authentic old shops practising traditional crafts. These include a 19C corn chandler's, a barber's, a coppersmith's, a wine cellar and a coffee room; we defy you to leave empty-handed.

NIGHTLIFE

The theatre in modern glass is **Stadsschouwburg De Harmonie** *Ruiterskwartier 4, ☎058 233 02 33. www.deharmonie.nl* (in Dutch) Cinemas, and lively bars in the town centre.

Events – Variations on the famous Elfstedentocht in summer, and the annual **cattle stud inspections** at the Frisian Expo Centre.

The Elfstedentocht

In winters when it is cold enough for the Frisian canals to freeze over, the whole country is gripped by Elfstedentocht fever. Once the ice reaches an average thickness of 15cm/6in, the green light is given for the preparations to begin. The organisers then have only 48hrs to get the course ready and make arrangements for thousands of participants and tens of thousands of spectators from the Netherlands and abroad. At 5.30am on the third day, the starting signal is given and this 200km/125mi tour of 11 towns begins. It starts and finishes in Leeuwarden, passing through Sneek, IJlst, Sloten, Stavoren, Hindeloopen, Workum, Bolsward, Harlingen, Franeker and Dokkum. All entrants completing the course within the regulation time receive a small silver cross. The current record, set in 1985, is 6hrs 47min. The last Elfstedentocht took place on 4 January 1997, for only the 15th time since the first official race on 2 January 1909, though the tradition is believed to date from the 18C.

A visit to Het Eerste Friese Schaatsmuseum (The First Frisian Skating Museum) in Hindeloopen (*see HINDELOOPEN*) is a must for anyone interested in the history of the Elfstedentocht.

The Elfstedentocht

Lee/EUREKA SLIDE

all the names of – the 290 people who died in the cause of the Frisian resistance and the 600 Jews who were expelled from Friesland and murdered.

Kanselarij

This former courthouse in the Renaissance style (1566), on Turfmarkt, has a wide, heavily decorated façade with a flight of steps, and a statue of Charles V at the top of the façade.

On the second floor there is a selection of the **top items** from each collection, including archaeological finds, Frisian silver, Indian chintz, a chest from Hindeloopen, and portraits. Objects from 16C Friesland are displayed in the adjoining rooms.

The first floor is mainly devoted to **17C painting**: still-life paintings, historical paintings, landscapes and, most importantly, portraits. This genre was particularly popular during the Golden Age; the wealthy middle classes liked to immortalise themselves and their families for posterity. The best-known Frisian portrait painter of this period was Wijbrand de Geest. There is also a portrait from the studio of Rembrandt depicting Saskia van Uilenberg, the daughter of Leeuwarden's mayor and later Rembrandt's wife.

The **silverware**★★★ department in the vaulted cellars is one of the biggest and finest in the country. It includes a superb collection of 16C drinking horns and goblets, and the 17C and 18C Frisian ornamental silver is also particularly fine: the Baroque Popta treasure, the finely engraved boxes with knots symbolising the marriage vows, and oval brandy bowls with ornamental handles.

The top floor houses the **Frisian Resistance Museum**, with photographs and other objects evoking the atmosphere of World War II. It follows four families, illustrating the different attitudes to occupation: collaboration, adaptation, resistance and persecution.

The tunnel and the modern section of the museum are used for temporary exhibitions of **modern Frisian art**.

Eysingahuis

This late 18C house is the former residence of the aristocratic Eysinga family. Its **period rooms** give a fascinating picture of life at the time, and include Louis XVI- and Empire-style furniture and Chinese porcelain. On the lower floor, there is a room devoted to the life of **Mata Hari**.

The room of paintings on the first floor contains portraits, landscapes, seascapes and still-life paintings giving an overview of 19C **Frisian painting**. Well-known artists from that time include Laurens Alma Tadema and Christoffel Bisschop, who was also a collector of silver, porcelain, furniture, costume and paintings. His collection is on display in the **Bisschop rooms**. There are also two **Hindeloopen rooms** with furniture decorated with the typically colourful motifs of the region (see Introduction, Furniture). Samplers and 18C and 19C Frisian clothing are exhibited in the **costume and textile room**.

The **archaeology department** on the second floor focuses on three periods: the Stone Age, the terp period and the late Middle Ages.

Over de Kelders

One of the quays on this canal is dug out of cellars (kelders). From the bridge to the north there is a fine view over the quays of Voorstreek and the bell-tower of St Boniface. The small **statue of Mata Hari** was erected in 1976 for the 100th anniversary of her birth.

Waag

On Waagplein, in the centre of the town, this weigh-house is a 1598 building of red brick, the first floor decorated with heraldic lions. Above them is a frieze sculptured with various motifs. The weighing of butter and cheese took place here up to 1880. The large awning was to protect the goods from sunlight. The building is now home to a small museum displaying material related to the cheese-making process. There is also information on other local crafts, including pottery and tile painting. A small shop retails several varieties of cheese but, best of all, try to be here on a Thursday morning when a traditional cheese market takes place outside the Waag.

Weerd

This narrow street plunges into Leeuwarden's old quarter.

Hofplein

The **stadhuis** (town hall) is on this square: a sober, classical building (1715) topped by a 17C carillon. At n° 34, note a fine façade stone (1666) depicting Fortune. In the stadhuis annexe, added in 1760, the *Raadzaal* (Council Room) has a side façade with Rococo decoration topped by the lion which appears on the town's coat of arms.

Opposite this is the **Stadhouderlijk Hof** (see Address Book) or former residence of the Frisian stadtholders. The building itself dates from 1881, and has medieval remains underneath. In the centre of the square there is a statue of William Louis, first hereditary stadtholder, called by the Frisians **"Us heit"** (Our Father). Nearby, at n° 35, a façade stone depicts a stork.

Eewal

This wide, main road is lined with elegant 18C residences. Some still have lovely façade stones (n°s 52 and 58).

Grote Kerk or Jacobijnerkerk

Open Jun–Aug, Tue–Fri 2pm–4.30pm. ☎ 058 212 83 13. www.grotekerkleeuwarden.nl (in Dutch).

Dating from the 13C, the Jacobin Church was reconstructed in the 15C and 16C and devastated by the revolutionaries in 1795.

Since 1588 it has been the Nassau Frisian mausoleum. The great **organ** was built in 1724–7 by Christian Müller. The Oranjepoortje (1663) on the south side of the church was the entrance for the stadtholder's family, and the copper orange tree above it refers to this fact.

Fries Natuurmuseum

🕐*Open Tue–Sun 11am–5pm.* 🕐*Closed 25 Dec and 1 Jan.* 👓*5€.* ♿☎*058 233 22 44. www.natuurmuseumfryslan.nl (in Dutch).*
The former 17C municipal orphanage is now the home of the Frisian Natural History Museum, which has displays on the soil and the various landscapes of the region and the plants and animals that live there. The basement has an excellent exhibition, **Friesland onder Water** in which visitors can explore the bottom of a drainage ditch. The whales and dolphins exhibition on the first floor includes the skeleton of a 15m/50ft **sperm whale** beached near Ameland in 1994.

Grote Kerkstraat

The tall house where Mata Hari is believed to have lived has been converted into the **Frysk Letterkundich Museum en Dokumintaasjesintrum**, or Frisian literary museum and documentation centre. Further on at n° 43 there is a fine façade stone depicting a lion and a fortified castle, then near the corner of Doelestraat, at n° 17, a lovely Baroque portal is decorated with garlands in the Frisian style.

Museum Het Princessehof, Nederlands Keramiek Museum★★

🕐*Open Tue–Sun 11am–5pm.* 🕐*Closed 25 Dec and 1 Jan.* 👓*8€.* ☎*058 294 89 58. www.princessehof.nl.*
During the 18C, this 17C palace (hof) was the official residence of Princess Marie-Louise of Hessen-Kassel (known familiarly as Maaike-Meu), widow of the Frisian stadtholder, John William Friso, Prince of Orange. Her dining and music room on the ground floor is richly decorated with a stucco ceiling, gold curtains, portraits and Chinese porcelain.
This palace and adjoining buildings are now home to the Netherlands Ceramics

Iranian tile (Lagwardina, c. 1300)

Museum Het Princessehof – Nationaal Keramiek Museum Leeuwarden

Museum, containing collections of porcelain, pottery and stoneware pieces from many different countries (*illustrations: see Introduction, Decorative Arts*).
The exhibits from **Asia** are displayed in chronological order (five rooms).
Some samples of the **Japanese production** are on show but the most splendid of all are the **Chinese porcelain**★★. They illustrate the development of the industry from the terracotta pieces made in the 3rd millennium BC up to the objects manufactured under the Ching dynasty (1644–1912), renowned for its *famille verte, famille noire* and *famille rose,* much sought after by European collectors. There is also a room devoted to "chine de commande", earthenware commissioned from China by Europeans.

European ceramics are the subject of a beautiful display: majolica from Italy, Delftware, Wedgwood, porcelain, Art Nouveau and Art Deco ceramics (1900–1930).
The museum also presents an extensive collection of **earthenware tiles**★★, mainly from Spain, France, Portugal and the Netherlands. The colourful tile pictures used on floors, walls and fireplaces are particularly interesting. There is also an Islamic collection with tiles from Turkey, Iran and elsewhere.
Two rooms are devoted to the JWN van Achterbergh collection, giving an overview of Dutch ceramics between 1950 and 1985. The De Prins van Leeuwarden gallery shows contemporary **European ceramics**.

Oldehove

🕐Open May–Sept, Tue–Sat 2pm–5pm. ☎0900 02 40 60 (VVV).

This massive Gothic tower in brick was never completed due to the instability of the ground, which explains why it leans sharply. The plan of the adjacent church, which was destroyed in 1595, is indicated on the square by coloured paving. From the top of the tower (40m/131ft), there is an overall **view** of the town and the surrounding area; the Waddeneilanden (🔵see DE WADDENEILANDEN) are visible in fine weather.

Prinsentuin

Near the tower, a footpath leads across the old, tree-covered quays of Stadsgracht, a wide canal which follows the outline of the fortifications. The garden contains the **Pier Pander Museum** (🕐open Sat–Sun 1pm–5pm; 🔵3€; ☎058 233 83 99), mainly devoted to the work of this Frisian sculptor (1864–1919).

Additional Sights

Aquazoo Friesland   Kids

7km/4.3mi northeast via the N 355 towards Groningen. 🕐Open daily, May –Jun 9.30am–6pm; Jul–Aug, 9am–6pm; Sept 9.30am–6pm; Oct–Apr, 10am–5pm. 🔵14.50€; children 12.50€. ☎0511 43 12 14. www.frieslandzoo.nl (in Dutch).

In 1988, when the last otter in the Netherlands died after being run over, the Netherlands Otter Station Foundation decided to set up a breeding centre (🔑 closed to the public) and a nature park. This now provides an opportunity to encounter a wealth of freshwater fauna, centring on the otter which, because it is at the top of the food chain, is a good way of gauging water quality. Otters are mainly active at night, so the best time to see them is at **feeding time** The park also contains mink, polecats, beavers, deer, storks and waterfowl, while the central exhibition building has aquariums, vivariums, exhibitions and films. As well as getting close to the otters, children will also enjoy seeing seals, pelicans, flamingos, beavers and penguins.

Marssum

5km/3mi to the west via Harlingerstraatweg. The **Poptaslot** (📷🔵guided tours Jul–Aug, hourly 11am–5pm; Apr–May, Jun and Sept–Oct, Tue–Sat, by appointment only; 🔵4€; ☎058 254 12 31; www.poptaslot.nl), or Heringa State, preceded by a gatehouse with voluted gables, is a 16C–17C manor house containing 17C and 18C furnishings. Nearby, the old almshouse, **Popta-Gasthuis** founded in 1712 is a picturesque group of low buildings with a monumental portal.

Drachten

27km/16.7mi to the southeast via Oostergoweg.

The great apartment complexes and brick houses of Drachten extend over the Frisian countryside with rich meadows bordered by poplar trees. This town is a commercial and industrial centre with busy streets and pedestrian precincts, adorned with statues.

Driving Tour

Terp Region

▶ Round tour of 118km/73.3mi. Leave by Groningerstraatweg. Turn left after 9km/6mi.

From the beginning of the 5C BC and up to the 12C AD in the low regions liable to sea or river flooding, the Frisians established their farmhouses and later their churches on manmade mounds called **terps**.

About a thousand of these terps still exist today, two-thirds of which are in the province of Friesland and the rest in the province of Groningen, where they are called wierden. Their average height is between 2 and 6m/6.5 and 19.6ft, and their area between 1 and 12ha/2.5 to 29.5 acres. The excavations have been very successful.

The tour covers a region where most of the villages have a terp with a church of tufa and brick with rustic charm, whose tower with a saddleback roof rises from a curtain of trees indicating its presence. The typical Frisian countryside is scattered with lovely farmhouses with

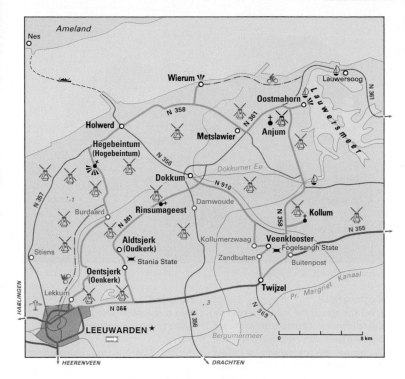

gables decorated with an *"uilebord"*. Windmills and beautiful black Frisian horses are also a common sight.

Oentsjerk (Oenkerk)

This lovely forest-like castle park, **Stania State**, is open to the public.

Aldtsjerk (Oudkerk)

This village, known as **Oudkerk** in Dutch, has a castle and a church on a terp.

Rinsumageest

The **church**, built on a terp, has a Romanesque crypt with two elegantly sculptured capitals. The interior is typical of Frisian churches.

Dokkum – &See DOKKUM.

▶ *Follow the canal to the southeast.*

The road soon climbs.

▶ *Turn right towards Kollumerzwaag.*

Veenklooster

A charming village with thatched cottages round a brink. A leafy avenue leads to **Fogelsangh State** (&open by appointment only; ☎0511 44 19 70), built on the site where an abbey once stood; there is a **museum** in the garden.

Twijzel

All along the main road, which passes through this town for a couple of miles, stand a row of magnificent **farmhouses**★. Behind the pleasant façades stand enormous barns, often with thatched roofs (*illustration: &see Introduction, Traditional Structures*).

▶ *At Buitenpost, turn left.*

Kollum

This town has a 15C Gothic **church** with a 13C tower. The nave is separated from the side aisles by stocky columns. The vaults with painted ribs are decorated with naive frescoes, as is the north wall where one can see a St Christopher.

Farmhouse and Frisian horses

Oostmahorn

From the top of the dyke, there is an overall view of **Lauwersmeer** (&see *GRONINGEN, Excursions*). Like the Zuiderzee, this low-lying region was flooded by the sea in the 13C. To avoid floods and create new polders, a barrier dam has been built, creating the lake, a popular centre for water sports.

Anjum

This village has retained an 1889 windmill. On a small terp there is a Romanesque church, enlarged in the Gothic style.

▶ *Take the road to Dokkum, then turn right towards Metslawier.*

Metslawier

Grouped round the Gothic church, the old, remarkably well-restored houses form a harmonious whole.

Wierum

This is a small harbour with modest homes; its church is built on an oval *terp* and surrounded by a cemetery. The top of the dyke affords a fine **view** over the Waddenzee, which at low tide forms an immense beach. The islands of Ameland and Schiermonnikoog are visible on the horizon.

Holwerd

This is the departure point for boats going to Ameland Island.

▶ *After Blija, turn left to Hogebeintum.*

Hogebeintum

This village on the highest terp in Friesland (nearly 9m/29.5ft above sea level) has a **church** (&open Apr–Oct, Tue–Sat 10am–5pm; Sun noon–5pm; ☎0518 41 17 83) with a bell-tower with a saddleback roof and surrounded by a cemetery. The interior is interesting for the series of **16 hatchments**★ (from the 17C to the early 20C) which decorate the walls. On each carved wood panel, there is a coat of arms adorned with Baroque motifs, symbols of death and heads of cherubs in naïve and rustic styles. There are also some lovely seignorial pews in wood.

▶ *Reach Birdaard to the south and follow the Dokkumer Ee Canal towards the south. Via the village of Lekkum, Prof. Mr PS Gerbrandyweg and Groningerstraatweg, one returns to Leeuwarden.*

LEIDEN★★

LEYDEN – ZUID-HOLLAND
POPULATION 117 530
PLAN OF THE CONURBATION IN THE CURRENT RED-COVER MICHELIN GUIDE BENELUX

Built on the Oude Rijn, Leiden is an agreeable, lively town criss-crossed by canals. It is famous mainly for its university, the oldest in the country, but also for being the place where the first Dutch tulips (&*see KEUKENHOF AND BULBFIELDS*) were grown. It is also the birthplace of Rembrandt. Leiden has a number of exceptional museums and many idyllic "hofjes" or almshouses.

- **Information:** Stationsweg 2d – 2312 AV. ☎0900 222 23 33. www.hollandrijnland.nl/ leiden.
- ▶ **Orient Yourself:** Head for Breestraat and Haarlemmerstraat that lie opposite each other across a canal. From here all the main sights of Leiden are within easy reach.
- **Parking:** Car parks are plentiful around the town; see Address Book for more details.
- **Don't Miss:** The Old Town: it oozes history at every turn.
- **Especially for Kids:** Naturalis, Vogelpark Avifauna, Archeon and the Space Expo will also engage the interest of children.
- ◐ **Organizing Your Time:** Leiden is a sprawling place, but the Old Town itself is compact and easily explored in a day or two. Stay overnight to sample at least one of its fine evening dining restaurants (&*see Address Book*).
- **Also See:** KEUKENHOF AND BULBFIELDS.

A Bit of History

In Roman times Leiden was called Lugdunum Batavorum. The medieval town grew at the foot of a fortified castle, the Burcht, erected in the 9C on an artificial mound. It owed its prosperity to its location on the Oude Rijn, which was then the main branch of the river, but the displacement of the mouth of the estuary towards Rotterdam reduced the town's role to that of an inland market. In the 14C Leiden regained a certain prosperity with the linen industry introduced by weavers from Ieper (Belgium) taking refuge from the Black Death.

John of Leiden was born here in 1509. He was the leader of the Anabaptists, members of a religious sect, who took refuge in Münster, Germany, in 1534. The town was seized in 1535 and John of Leiden died the following year.

A heroic siege – In the 16C the town was besieged twice by the Spanish. The first siege (end 1573 to March 1574) failed. The second, started a month later,

was terrible. The population, reduced to half due to plague and starvation, revolted against the burgomaster Van der Werff, who offered his body to the famished. Revived by the courage of their leader, the inhabitants continued their resistance.

Finally, William the Silent had the idea of breaching the dykes to flood the surrounding countryside. On 3 October the Spanish were attacked by the Sea Beggars, who had sailed in over the flooded land on flat-bottomed boats; the Spaniards raised the siege, abandoning, at the foot of the ramparts, a big pot of beef stew (*hutspot*). The inhabitants of Leiden were then supplied with bread and herring. Since that time a commemorative feast, **Leidens Ontzet** has taken place annually with a historical procession, distribution of herring and white bread and eating of beef stew (*hutspot*) in memory of the pot left by the Spanish. To reward the town, William the Silent founded a university here in 1575.

Address Book

For coin ranges, see the Legend on the cover flap.

WHERE TO STAY

As a student town, Leiden has few really special hotels, but here are some suggestions.

Hotel Leiden – *Haagse Schouw- weg 14, 2332 KG. ☎071 573 17 31. www. valk.com. 62 rooms.* This modern hotel, part of the Van der Valk chain, is outside the centre near the A 44 motorway. It is linked by a covered footbridge to a 17C inn, Het Haagsche Schouw, where the restaurant and dining rooms are located.

De Doelen – *Rapenburg 2, 2311 EV; ☎071 512 05 27. www.dedoelen.com. 16 rooms.* This small hotel is located in a historic building a stone's throw from many of the main sights, and thus an ideal base for a visit to the town. Start your day in style in the beautiful breakfast room.

Nieuw Minerva – *Boommarkt 23, 2311 EA. ☎071 512 63 58. www.nieu- wminerva.nl. 40 rooms.* Fourteen of the 40 rooms in this centrally located hotel have their own names and individual style. There is for instance the Angel's Paradise (Engelenbak) with a canopy bed; the Keukenhof Room, named after the famous bulb fields and decorated with tulip motifs; the Safari Room with a mosquito net and the Posh Room with a wooden bedstead. There is also an unusual bridal suite.

WHERE TO EAT

Oudt Leyden 't Pannekoeken- huysje – *Steenstraat 49. ☎071 513 31 44. www.oudtleyden.nl.* Here delicious pancakes are served on delft plates.

Anak Bandung – *Garenmarkt 24a. ☎071 512 53 03.* Indonesian cuisine, including rijsttafel. Meals served on the terrace in summer. Open evenings only.

De Poort van Leyden – *Haven 100. ☎071 524 09 33. www.poort.nl.* This brasserie, located in the Zijlpoort (1667), one of two remaining town gates of Leiden, has a good atmos- phere, and a fine view of the town ramparts from the conservatory. In the summer months the terrace by the water's edge is opened up. Good for a quick lunch, an extensive evening meal, or just a drink.

Stadscafé/Restaurant Van der Werff – *Steenstraat 2. ☎071 513 03 35. www.stadscafevanderwerff.nl (in Dutch).* A stylish place for a drink or snack when visiting the Rijksmuseum voor Volkenkunde.

De Knip – *In Voorschoten, 5km/3mi from the centre of Leiden, Kniplaan 22 (4km/2.5mi via Veurseweg); ☎071 561 25 73.* Wonderful meals served on a shaded waterside terrace. Closed Mondays.

PRACTICAL INFORMATION

The **VVV tourist information** office (*Stationsweg 2d, 2312 AV Leiden. ☎0900 222 23 33. www.hollandrijnland. nl/leiden*) has information on sights, tours, cultural events, excursions, etc. The staff can also help with finding accommodation. The VVV publishes an annual brochure listing hotels, pensions and camp sites in and around Leiden.

TRANSPORT

Be aware that some car park ticket- machines only accept payment by cards. **Bicycles** can be hired at the Rijwielshop (bicycle shop) behind the station, ☎071 512 00 68. **Buses** One- day travel pass for Connexxion-busses are available from the VVV office, costing 10€.

TOURS AND WALKS

The VVV sells leaflets detailing two walking tours: one of Leiden's alm- shouses and the other following in the footsteps of Rembrandt.

BOAT TOURS

Canal tours of the town centre depart from Beestenmarkt (operated by *Rederij Rembrandt, ☎071 513 49 38. www.red- erij-rembrandt.nl.* Trips along the **Oude Rijn** to Avifauna leave from Oude Singel (*see Excursions*); there are also **tours to Braassem** and the **polders** and **windmills** leaving from the harbour opposite no 14 (*Rederij Slingerland; ☎071 541 31 83; www.partyboot.nl*).

Leiden University – It was the first in the Low Countries liberated from Spain, and for a long time rivalled that of Leuven, which had remained Catholic; it very quickly acquired a European reputation due to its relatively tolerant spirit and the great minds it drew there: the Flemish humanist, Justus Lipsius (1547–1606); the philologist Daniël Heinsius (1580–1655); the famous theologians, Gomarus, Arminius and Episcopius (&see DORDRECHT); the French philologists, Saumaise (1588–1653) and Joseph Scaliger (1540–1609); the physician and botanist, **Boerhaave**, master of clinical education (1668–1738); and **Van Musschenbroek** (1692–1761), inventor in 1746 of the Leiden jar, the first electrical condenser. In 1637 **René Descartes** (1596–1650) published anonymously in Leiden his *Discourse on Method*, written in Utrecht, where he had formerly lived. The influence of the university was increased by the fact that Leiden had become a great centre of printing in the 17C due to the illustrious **Elzevier** family; the first member of the family to settle here was Louis, who came from Leuven (Belgium) and moved to Leiden in 1580.

The Protestant refuge – In the 16C and 17C Leiden welcomed numerous Flemish and French Protestants (who fled in 1685 because of the Revocation of the Edict of Nantes) as well as English. In 1609 a hundred or so English Puritans arrived via Amsterdam, led by their spiritual leader, **John Robinson** (c. 1575–1625). They had left their country under the threat of persecution. Former farmers, they had to adapt themselves to their new urban conditions and applied themselves to various handicraft trades. A printing press published religious works which were exported to England and Scotland. Their stay became difficult and the Puritans decided to leave Leiden and go to America. Sailing from Delfshaven on the *Speedwell* they reached England and embarked on the *Mayflower* in Plymouth. The 102 emigrants among which there were 41 Puritans or **Pilgrim Fathers** landed in December 1620 on the coast southeast of present-day Boston and founded Plymouth Colony, the first permanent settlement established in New England.

Leiden School

From the 15C to the 17C a great number of painters were born in Leiden, including the illustrious Rembrandt.

Geertgen tot Sint Jans (c. 1465–1495), who died in Haarlem, is heralded as the most gifted painter of the late 15C. Although still turned towards the Middle Ages, he showed virtuosity in the treatment of fabrics (*illustration: &see Introduction, Painting*). **Cornelis Engebrechtszoon** (1468–1533) also retained a Gothic style, with crowded compositions and rather tormented linear painting. His pupil, **Lucas van Leyden** (1489 or 1494–1533), is the great Renaissance painter. Influenced by Italian art, his *Last Judgement,* which can be seen in the Lakenhal, is a very fine work, with its balance of composition, sense of depth, elegant draughtsmanship and fine colours.

At the beginning of the 17C a few artists of the Leiden School painted **vanitas**, still life paintings where certain specific objects representing the arts and sciences (books, maps, etc.), wealth (jewellery), earthly pleasures (goblets, playing cards) or death (skulls) are depicted with great precision, often with a moralistic message. These subjects were much used by Jan Davidszoon de Heem (☝see UTRECHT) when he stayed here before going to Antwerp.

Jan van Goyen, born in Leiden in 1596, went to live in Haarlem in 1631 where he died (1656). He was a great painter of pale, monochromatic landscapes with immense skies covered with clouds. Son of **Willem van de Velde the Elder** (c. 1611–93), **Willem van de Velde the Younger** (1633–1707), specialised like his father in painting pictures of naval battles, in which the light formed an integral part of the composition. The Van de Veldes ended their lives in London, where they became court painters to Charles II.

Gerrit Dou (1613–75) is perhaps the most conscientious of all the intimate genre painters of Leiden. He took to chiaroscuro when a pupil of the master, Rembrandt, but he produced mainly scenes of bourgeois life (*Young Woman Dressing,* Museum Boijmans Van Beuningen in Rotterdam). His pupil **Frans van Mieris the Elder** (1635–81) depicted smiling people in refined interiors. **Gabriel Metsu** (1629–67) was a genre painter and a master in his manner of treating fabrics and the substance of objects; he treated with great sensitivity slightly sentimental subjects .

Unlike his contemporaries, **Jan Steen** (1626–79) depicts very busy scenes with humour. His paintings display the whole human comedy where somewhat dishevelled people indulge in various pleasures; they play music, drink, eat and play in a very unruly atmosphere (*illustration:* ☝*see AMSTERDAM*).

The Old Town and its Museums★★

Rijksmuseum voor Volkenkunde★★

🕒*Open Tue–Sun and public holidays, 10am–5pm.* 🕒*Closed 3 Oct, 25 Dec and 1 Jan.* ✆7.50€. ☎ 071 516 88 00. *www.rmv.nl.*

This ethnology museum is famous for its collections of non-Western civilisations. These ethnographic collections were started by King William I (1772–1843), who sent scholars all over the world to build a collection of rarities. Later, three significant Japanese collections were acquired (including the PF von Siebold collection), and the Indonesian collection also grew. Today the museum collection covers the entire world and is divided into ten areas: **Africa** (bronze from Benin, masks, sculptures), the **Arctic regions** (ivory, leather coats), **China** (earthenware, wooden Bodhisattva sculptures, roller paintings), **Indonesia** (gamelans, wajang marionettes, basalt Hindu figures, Kris daggers, textiles), **Japan and Korea** (bronze Buddha figures, lacquerware, prints, porcelain), **Latin America** (mummies from Peru, Mexican earthenware, headdresses), **North America** (fighting implements, Kachina masks), **Oceania** (tree-bark paintings, women's figures), **Southern and Southeast Asia** (Indian prints, Nepalese spinning wheel) and **Southwest and Central Asia** (objects used in Tibetan worship, Turcoman amulets). The museum was extensively renovated and extended between 1997 and 2001 and is now beautifully presented. Visitors can either walk from one continent to another or choose to follow an itinerary taking in all the major exhibits. The park in which the museum is set contains sculptures by contemporary non-Western artists.

Molenmuseum De Valk

🕒*Open Tue–Sat 10am–5pm, Sun and public holidays, 1pm–5pm.* 🕒*Closed 3 Oct, 25 Dec and 1 Jan.* ✆2.50€; ☎071 516 53 53.

This tower mill, the last in Leiden and built in 1743, bears the name of a bird of prey (*valk:* falcon). It has seven floors and the first ones were the living quarters. The mill was in operation until 1964. Today the repair workshop, the forge and the drawing room (*zondagskamer*) are all open to visitors. There is also an exhibition retracing the history of Dutch windmills.

Stedlijk Museum De Lakenhal★★

🕒*Open Tue–Fri 10am–5pm, Sat–Sun and public holidays noon–5pm and 3 Oct, 10am–noon.* 🕒*Closed 25 Dec and 1 Jan.* ✆4€. ♿ ☎071 516 53 60. *www.lakenhal.nl.*

Installed in the old cloth merchants' hall (*lakenhal*) of 1640, this is a museum of decorative arts (furniture, silverware, pewterware), which also contains a fine selection of paintings.

The 1st floor focuses on the **textile industry** that has been so important to Leiden. The various stages of wool production are shown in a 16C series of paintings by Isaac van Swanenburgh. On the 2nd floor the town's history is evoked, including the raising of the **siege of Leiden** on 3 October 1574. Its religious past is also chronicled; there is a chapel from the old Catholic church (💧 *see UTRECHT*) and a display on the persecution and execution of the Remonstrants (💧 *see DORDRECHT*) in 1623. All over the museum are objects from the collections of glassware, silver, tin and tiles, as well as **paintings and decorative arts** from the 16C to the 20C, including numerous Leiden masters.

By Cornelis Engebrechtszoon (*room 16*) there are two admirably detailed triptychs: *Crucifixion* and *Descent from the Cross,* as well as a small *Carrying of the Cross.* But the works of **Lucas van Leyden** dominate. In his luminous triptych of the **Last Judgement** (1527) painted with assurance of draughtsmanship, the painter knew how to free the figures from constraint and rigidity. The central panel shows the Son of Man enthroned in thick clouds for the Supreme Judgement. On the panels heaven and hell are painted, and on the back, St Peter and St Paul, the town's patron saints. Among the 17C Leiden painters exhibited are Gerrit Dou, Jan Steen and some of the highly polished works of Mieris the Elder as well as an early work by Rembrandt. The museum also possesses some fine 17C paintings: a still-life by J Davidszoon de Heem, *Horse Market at Valkenburg* by Salomon van Ruysdael and landscapes by Van Goyen. The period from the 18C to the early 20C is also represented. The collection of contemporary art is shown in temporary exhibitions.

To the south of **Turfmarkt** there is a lovely **view** over the harbour and the mill. Further on, on **Prinssesekade** an old warehouse has been restored, which looks on to Galgewater harbour.

Rapenburg★

This is the most beautiful canal in Leiden, spanned by triple-arched bridges and lined with trees. On the west side there are some fine houses dating from the town's golden era.

Rijksmuseum van Oudheden★★

🕐 *Open Tue–Fri 10am–5pm, Sat–Sun and public holidays noon–5pm.* 🕐 *Closed 3 Oct, 25 Dec and 1 Jan.* 🎫 *8.50€.* ♿ 🕿 *0900 660 06 00. www.rmo.nl.*

The national museum of antiquities has important collections of items from Egypt, the Middle East, Greece and Rome, as well as a Dutch archaeology section. The museum boasts a covered inner courtyard and air-conditioned rooms. The **Egyptian collection**★★, including sarcophagi, mummies, funerary amphora and other funerary objects, is particularly interesting. The sculpture collection includes two burial chapels, reliefs, the splendid stele from Hoey and the famous figures of Maya and Merit. Bronze figurines, jewellery, amulets, earthenware, etc. are brought together to give a good overall picture of ancient Egyptian handicrafts. Egyptian art from the time of the Roman emperors and Coptic art also feature. The **Classical Antiquity** section includes glassware and ceramics, but is primarily known for its sculptures and its amphorae decorated with mythological figures. The rooms devoted to the **Middle East** contain archaeological finds from Mesopotamia, Syria-Palestine,

National Museum of Antiquities/V Leiden/ The Netherlands

The pair statue of Maya and Merit, 1300BC

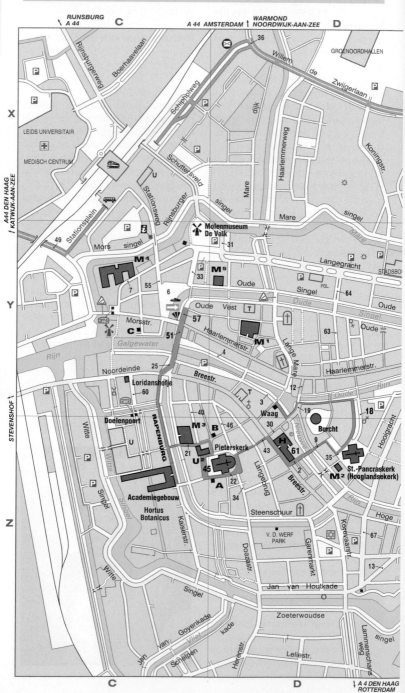

Turkey and Iran, and include examples of cuneiform script and utensils and decorative objects made of stone, ivory, bronze, gold and silver. The **Dutch archaeology section** provides detailed coverage of the Netherlands' early history from 250 000 years ago to the early Middle Ages and includes the gold brooch from Dorestad and the silver Viking treasure from Wieringen.

In the Taffeh hall is the **Temple of Isis from Taffeh** in Nubia, dating from the Augustan age (27 BC to AD 14). It was given to the Netherlands in 1969 by the Egyptian government as a gesture of thanks for its contribution to UNESCO's international campaign in connection with the Aswan dam. The building of the dam involved flooding a large part of Nubia, and various monuments had to be dug up and moved.

Academiegebouw

Since the 16C the administrative offices of the university have been housed in the chapel of a former convent. Upstairs on the first floor there is a "sweating room" where the nervous students waited to take their exams. The **Academisch Historisch Museum** (*o–̱ closed for renovation until spring 2009; ☎ 071 527 72 42; www.ahm.leidenuniv.nl*), housed in the vaulted room, retraces the history of the university since 1575.

Hortus Botanicus

Open Apr–Oct, daily 10am–6pm; Nov–Mar, Sun–Fri 10am–4pm. Closed 8 Feb, 3 Oct and 25 Dec–2 Jan. ⊜5€. ☎ 071 527 72 49. www.hortus.leidenuniv.nl.

The botanical garden was founded by the university in 1590 for the purpose of cultivating and studying plants from all over the world, but more particularly from Asia. In 1593, Clusius brought the first Dutch tulips into flower here. The Clusiustuin (Clusius garden) is a reconstruction of the original garden. The orangery and greenhouses contain tropical and subtropical plants, such

Clusius garden, Leiden

NBTC

Rembrandt

Rembrandt Harmenszoon van Rijn was born in Leiden in 1606. Son of a miller, he lived near the Rhine, hence his name Van Rijn. His childhood remains mysterious. In 1620 he enrolled at Leiden University, but attracted by painting he soon became an apprentice to Jacob van Swanenburgh, then in 1623 in Amsterdam to **Pieter Lastman** (1583–1633), a great admirer of Italy and Caravaggio. Although he painted numerous portraits and even self-portraits, Rembrandt right from the start showed a penchant for biblical history, which he first painted with minute detail typical of the Leiden School.

Unlike other great painters of his time the artist never studied in Italy, and adopted a very personal style. His chiaroscuro was not that of Caravaggio, where strong contrasts between light and shade existed, but showed an imperceptible change from shadow to people suffused with a warm light who occupied the centre of the painting. His works are steeped in a mysterious atmosphere from which an intense emotion and profound spirituality emanate. Beginning in 1628 he took up etching and drawing, sometimes seeking inspiration from ordinary people, such as beggars.

Self-portrait, 1669 by Rembrandt van Rijn Mauritshuis, The Hague

At the end of 1631 he settled in Amsterdam; it was then that he painted the famous **The Anatomy Lesson of Doctor Tulp** (1632). This group portrait brought glory to the young painter of 26. Orders started flowing in. Rembrandt met Saskia whom he married in 1634. Several children were born, one of whom, Titus, was born in 1641. In 1639 he moved to a house in the Jewish quarter, the present Rembrandthuis. In 1642 he painted his greatest work, the **Night Watch**, a group portrait of members of the civic guard. This genre, which had already been revived by Frans Hals (see HAARLEM), is treated by Rembrandt with daring and complexity of technique up to then unequalled. However, not much interest was shown in this painting at the time, although it was to become his most famous. In addition, 1642 marked the beginning of the painter's misfortune: he lost his wife Saskia, having already seen his parents die in 1630 and 1640. He painted numerous portraits including that of the young Titus (1655) and a solemn *Self-Portrait* (1652), but the wealthy art patrons began to abandon him with the exception of the burgomaster, Jan Six. In 1657 and 1658 he was unable to pay his debts and had to sell his house and goods. In 1661 his *Conspiracy of Julius Civilis*, commissioned for the town hall, was rejected (National Museum in Stockholm).

In 1662 he lost his mistress Hendrickje Stoffels. The **Sampling Officials of the Drapers Guild** (1662) was his last group painting, but he still did some marvellous paintings such as the *Jewish Bride* before passing away, forgotten, a year after his son, Titus, in 1669. He had just completed his last self-portrait.

The Rijksmuseum in Amsterdam has a large and exceptional collection of Rebrandt's works.

Among Rembrandt's numerous pupils in Amsterdam, were the landscape painter **Philips Koninck** (1619–88) and several painters who came from Dordrecht (see DORDRECHT) or Leiden, such as Gerrit Dou.

Leiden's "hofjes"

Hofjes are almshouses built round a central courtyard or garden; Leiden has 35 of them, and they are primarily a Dutch phenomenon. They were originally intended as homes for the elderly poor, and were mostly set up by wealthy church elders hoping to gain a place in heaven through the prayers of the occupants, who received free accommodation and sometimes food, drink and clothing. In return, they had to comply with a strict set of rules laid down by the regents, or governors, who were usually descendants of the dead founder. Sometimes the regents had a separate meeting room (*regentenkamer*) in the almshouses.

Most hofjes have only one entrance from the street, consisting of a passageway (sometimes with a gatehouse) or entrance hall. In the past, the gate would be opened and closed by a porter at fixed times of day.

Today, the hofjes are oases of tranquillity amid the hubbub of the city, and are therefore very popular places to live. When you visit, please respect the peace and privacy of the people who live there.

as Victoria Amazonica, the giant water-lily that flowers at night. The garden also contains centuries-old trees and a Japanese garden. There is a beautiful Winter garden, too, where a footbridge affords a fine view over the trees and plants below.

Latijnse School
The Latin School was founded in 1324, and in 1599 it was given a Renaissance frontage.

▶ *Continue to Breestrat via Pieterskerkkoorsteeg.*

Gravensteen
This former prison is now home to the Law Faculty and has a lovely classical front on the church side.

Pieterskerk
Open daily 1.30pm–4pm. Closed during services. ☎ *071 512 43 19. www. pieterskerk.com.*
St Peter's, a large and heavily built Gothic church with a nave and four aisles, stands in the middle of the churchyard (Pieterskerkhof). There are memorial slabs to the painter Jan Steen and Professor Boerhaave as well as the Puritan leader, John Robinson. The church is now a multi-purpose centre.

Jean Pesijnhofje
Built in 1683 on the site of John Robinson's house and intended for the

members of the Walloon church, this almshouse took the name of its founder, Jean Pesijn, a French merchant of Huguenot origin. There is a memorial slab to John Robinson here.

Breestraat
This, the town's main shopping street, is typically very busy. At the point where the itinerary crosses it, there is a **blue stone** where executions took place.

Stadhuis
Built in 1600 and damaged by a fire in 1929, the town hall was rebuilt in its original style. It has a perron in front and is topped with a very decorative gable.

Burcht
At the beginning of Nieuwstraat one can see the 17C entrance doorway of the **Burcht** topped by a lion with the town's coat of arms (two keys). This fortress was built on an artificial mound at the confluence of the Oude Rijn and the Nieuwe Rijn. There remains a stout curtain wall with crenellations and loopholes. Its watchpath offers a panorama over the town.

St Pancraskerk or Hooglandsekerk
This 15C church has interesting Flamboyant sculptured portals at the transepts.

Leiden American Pilgrim Museum

🕐 *Open Wed–Fri 1pm–5pm, Sat 10am–5pm.* 👝*2€.* ☎*071 512 24 13.*
In this small 16C house is a collection of objects and documents associated with the Pilgrim Fathers during their time in Leiden (1608–1620).

Hooglandse Kerkgracht

Alongside this filled-in canal is the old orphanage, **Weeshuis**, with a decorative panel above the doorway depicting foundlings. At nºs 19–21 is the centre for visual arts, the **CBK** (Centrum Beeldende Kunst Leiden), where exhibitions and other activities are held.

Waag

The weigh-house was built in 1657–59 by Pieter Post.

Additional Sights

Museum Boerhaave★

🕐 *Open Tue–Sat 10am–5pm, Sun and public holidays noon–5pm.* 🕐*Closed 1 3 Oct and 1 Jan.* 👝*6€.* ☎*071 521 42 24. www.museumboerhaave.nl.*
This well-appointed museum is located in the former hospital Caeciliagasthuis (1596), where the famous scientist and doctor Herman Boerhaave taught his medical students from his sickbed. Its very varied collection of instruments and documents is one of the most important in the world, giving an overview of five centuries of natural sciences and medicine. It includes the collection of astronomical and surgical instruments formerly owned by Christiaan Huygens, inventor of the pendulum clock, and the microscopes of the naturalist, Antonie van Leeuwenhoek. The reconstructed Anatomy Theatre (1596) contains a collection of human and animal skeletons.

Loridanshofje

The 1656 **almshouse** at nº 1 Oude Varkenmarkt has a simple inner courtyard. At the far end of Oude Varkenmarkt is the 1645 gateway, **Doelenpoort**, crowned with an equestrian statue of St George, the patron saint of the archers' guild.

Naturalis★★ 🔲Kids

Follow Plesmanlaan towards The Hague; turn right into Darwinweg after the Academisch Ziekenhuis (Leiden teaching hospital). 🕐*Open Tue–Fri 10am–5pm, Sat–Sun and public holidays 10am–6pm.* 🕐*Closed 25 Dec and 1 Jan.* 👝*9€; children 6€.* ♿☎*071 568 76 00. www.naturalis.nl.*
The entrance to this natural history museum is located in the 17C pest-house, which was built outside the centre because of its function. The buildings around the attractive courtyard include a **Nature Information Centre**. The glass **zebra bridge** leads to the modern part of the museum, which contains seven permanent exhibitions. These bring the complexity and richness of the natural world to life in an exciting and interactive way.

The **Oerparade** (prehistoric parade) exhibition includes hundreds of fossils, dinosaur skeletonnes and a mosasaur, an extinct aquatic lizard. Don't miss the million-year-old remains of Java Man, discovered in 1891 by the Dutch anthropologist, Eugène Dubois. The lights in the central tree trunk trace the 3.8-billion-year evolution from the first life forms to the animals of today. The top of the tree is in the floor of the **Natuurtheater**, where hundreds of (stuffed) animals run, fly, swim and crawl. The rich variety of plants, fungi, algae and bacteria are displayed in an original way, followed by stones and minerals. **Aarde**, or Earth, shows how earthquakes and volcanoes occur, why the Earth's crust and the weather and the atmosphere are in a constant state of change, and what happens at the centre of the planet. **Leven** (life) explores how humans and animals obtain food, protect themselves and reproduce. On the walls of the **Ecosystemen** room, videos show the different types of ecosystems. The history of how different periods and cultures (Islam, 18C Enlightenment, Tao culture, ancient Egypt) have viewed life and nature is explored in **Visies op natuur**. Another unmissable attraction is the **Schatkamer** (treasury), which includes King William I's collection of precious stones, as well as unusual minerals and extinct animals such as the Cape lion and the Tasmanian wolf. In view of the fragility of the objects, the Treasury is open only from 1.30pm to 4.30pm. **Kijkje Aarde**, a look at the Earth, is ideal for children, with stones, trees and animals talking about the various cycles that exist in nature.

Excursions

Keukenhof★★ –
See KEUKENHOF and BULB FIELDS.

Alphen aan den Rijn
17km/10.5mi to the east via the Hoge Rijndijk.
Can be reached by boat. Alphen aan den Rijn is a small industrial town on the banks of the Oude Rijn.

Vogelpark Avifauna   Kids
Open daily 9am–6pm. 11€; children 10.50€. 0172 48 75 75. www.avifauna.nl.
This substantial bird park has over 3 000 birds, with large cages for rare birds, a tropical aviary with waterfall, a pool complete with penguins, and ponds with pink flamingos. It also has a large playground and is the departure point for **boat trips** to the Braassemermeer, the lake to the north of Alphen.

Archeon★   Kids
On the south side of Alphen. Open Easter–Jul and Sept–Oct, Tue–Sun 10am–5pm. 13.90€; children 11.90€ (includes meal). Opening times may vary, check latest details on 0172 44 77 44. www.archeon.nl
This archaeological theme park is divided into three areas showing what life in the Netherlands was like during the prehistoric, Roman and medieval periods, with people dressed in authentic costumes bringing the past to life. In the park, where the planting is designed to be appropriate to each particular historical era, there are excellent

reconstructions of settlements, camps and homes. The Roman section includes a bath-house where visitors can obtain a massage, while gladiator fights are held in the arena. The medieval section is bustling with people: the civic guard keeps an eye on visitors as they enter, and the basket-maker, baker and shoemaker give demonstrations of their work. The monastery of Gravendam has been reconstructed based on excavations in Dordrecht, and here you can obtain a medieval meal prepared by the Friars Minor.

Katwijk aan Zee and Noordwijk aan Zee
18km/11mi to the northwest; leave Leiden by Oegstgeesterweg. Local map see KEUKENHOF, Bulb fields.

Katwijk aan Zee
This is a popular resort not far from the bulb fields. The long sandy beach is backed by lines of dunes.

Noordwijk aan Zee
A fashionable seaside resort with a wide sandy beach. Several flower parades (Bloemencorso) pass through Noordwijk (*see Calendar of events*).
Behind the dunes of Noordwijk is ESTEC, the technical branch of the European Space Agency, where satellites are tested and European space projects are managed. A little further on is **Noordwijk Space Expo** (Kids *Keplerlaan 3; open Tue–Sun 10am–5pm; also open Mon during school holidays 10am–5pm; closed 25 Dec and 1 Jan; 9€ (children 6€); 071 364 64 46; www.spaceexpo.nl*), where model rockets, real satellites, space suits, photographs, a slide show and other items tell the story of mainly European space flight. There is also a discovery trail for children, the reward for which is an astronaut's diploma signed by Wubbo Ockels, the first Dutchman into space.

NATIONAAL MUSEUM PALEIS HET LOO ★★★

GELDERLAND

Het Loo Palace and its gardens were opened to the public in 1984 following an extensive restoration programme. The palace and gardens are surrounded by a 650-ha/1 626-acre **park** (in the heart of the Veluwe, which abounds in game.

- **Information:** ☎055 577 24 00. www.paleishetloo.nl and www.hetloo.nl.
- ▶ **Orient Yourself:** From A 1 and A 50 take the Paleis Het Loo turning and follow the signs. By public transport, bus N° 102 from Apeldoorn Bus Station (by the railway station) stops at Paleis Het Loo; the park is 40 minutes on foot from the station.
- 🅿 **Parking:** There is a charge of 3€ at the car park.
- **Don't Miss:** The gardens will compete for your attention with the apartments.

A Bit of History

When **William III** (1650–1702), Prince of Orange and Stadtholder of the United Provinces, bought the 14C–15C castle, Het Oude Loo in 1684, this ardent huntsman was fulfilling a lifetime's dream. In 1685 the first stone of Het Loo Palace was laid, about 275m/300yd from the site of the old castle, by William's wife, Princess **Mary II**, daughter of James II. Het Loo Palace was intended for the princely couple with their court and guests, as well as their large hunt.

The palace was built by **Jacob Roman** (1640–1716), pupil of Pieter Post. The interior decoration and the design of the gardens were commissioned by **Daniël Marot** (1661–1752), a Parisian Huguenot, who probably arrived in the Netherlands shortly after the Revocation of the Edict of Nantes (1685).

In 1689, William III was proclaimed King of England after his father-in-law and uncle, James II, had fled the country. Het Loo Palace was to become a royal palace, and had to be enlarged: the colonnades which linked the main part of the building to the wings were replaced by four pavilions and the gardens were further embellished.

1684	**William III** Prince of Orange and Stadtholder of the United Provinces, buys Het Oude Loo.
1685	Building starts at Het Loo. Revocation of the Edict of Nantes.
1688-97	War of the League of Augsburg.
1689	William and Princess Mary crowned King and Queen of England.
1692	An extension is made to the palace.
1694	Queen Mary dies in England.
1702	The King-Stadtholder William III dies without a successor.
1747-51	**William IV** son of John William Friso, hereditary Stadtholder of the United Provinces.
1751-95	**William V** son of the precedent stadtholder.
1795	Conquest of the country by the French army. William V flees to England. Het Loo seized by the French, suffers from the destructive rage of the soldiers.
1795-1806	The Batavian Republic.
1806-10	Louis Bonaparte, King of Holland, puts rough-cast on the palace façade and commissions an English-style park.
1810	The Kingdom of Holland becomes part of the French Empire.

Oct 1811	Emperor Napoleon stays briefly at Het Loo Palace.
1815	Het Loo, now State property, is offered to **King William I** as a summer residence.
1840	At Het Loo Palace, William I abdicates in favour of his son, William II.
1849-90	Reign of **William III**
1890-98	Regency of **Queen Emma**
1898	Reign of **Wilhelmina** only daughter of William III and Emma.
1901	Marriage of Queen Wilhelmina to Duke Henry of Mecklenburg-Schwerin.
1904-14	The State decides to extend and refurbish the palace.
1948	Abdication of Queen Wilhelmina, who retires to Het Loo Palace.
1962	Death of Queen Wilhelmina.
1967-75	Princess Margriet, daughter of Queen Juliana, and her family are the last members of the royal family to live at Het Loo.
1969	Queen Juliana donates the palace to the nation and it is decided to create a museum.
1977-84	Restoration of the palace and gardens.
June 1984	
	Opening of the **National Museum**

Tour *about 3hr*

🕐 *Open 10am–5pm.* 🕐 *Closed 1 Jan.* 💶*10€.* ♿☎*055 577 24 00. www.hetloo.nl.* 👁*Since the rooms are lit as they were in days gone by, some of the rooms can be fairly dark. It is, therefore, advisable to choose a sunny day on which to visit the palace.*

After having walked alongside the **royal stables** (fine series of vintage cars and sleighs, late 19C–early 20C), the visitor comes to a wide avenue, where the beech trees form a magnificent vault. Beyond this is a vast brick building flanked with long wings which surrounds the main courtyard.

The finely proportioned building, built on a north-south axis, is impressive for its severe sobriety, characteristic of the Dutch Baroque style. The only decorative elements are the tympana (sandstone) of hunting scenes, and the window sills. The sash windows of the main part of the building and the pavilions were a novelty often believed to be a Dutch invention and characteristic of English Georgian style.

East Wing

The east wing contains a collection of historic documents, ceramics, paintings and prints as well as *objets d'art* regarding the most illustrious members of the House of Orange. Many of the documents were written in French, the language used by the Dutch court until the regency of Queen Emma (1890).

West Wing

On the ground floor there is a video film show on the history of the palace and its restoration. On the first floor the **Museum of the Chancery of the Netherlands Orders of Knighthood** (Museum van de Kanselarij der Nederlandse Orden) exhibits insignia, uniforms, Dutch and foreign Orders.

Apartments★★★

Access by a staircase on the side of the steps leading to the main building.

From the vaulted cellars a staircase leads up to the **great hall** (**1**) where two 17C garden vases, after drawings by Daniel Marot, are exhibited.

The **old dining room** (**2**) is hung with 17C Antwerp tapestries. Note the cabinet (Antwerp, 1630), with biblical scenes painted by Frans Francken the Younger.

The remarkable **new dining room**★★★ (**3**) (c. 1692) is a very good example of Marot's contribution to the palace's interior decoration. The white columns and pilasters, decorated with gold bands, combine with the coffered ceiling to give this room, hardly bigger than the old dining room, a majestic character. At the end of the **white hall** (**4**), which has portraits of members of the Nassau family who lived in Friesland, a staircase leads up to the **chapel** (**5**) where **organ**

concerts (*Last Friday of every month at 8.15pm. Reservations:* ☎ *055 578 71 98; www.paleisconcerten.nl*) are held. The coffered stucco ceiling is by Marot. The Bible exhibited is a gift from the Dutch people to their King, William III, who had shown generosity during the 1861 floods. It was in this chapel that many Dutch filed past to bid farewell to Queen Wilhelmina (her funeral took place in Delft).

▷ *Go back down the stairs and take the left corridor.*

At the end of the corridor on the left, **Prince William IV's Chamber** (**6**), a luminous room due to the yellow silk damask, has, apart from portraits of the stadtholder and his wife Anne of Hanover, Princess of England, daughter of George II, a crystal chandelier (c. 1747) and a ceiling decorated with Chinese motifs. The walls of the **Frisian Cabinet** (**7**), opposite, are covered with gilded leather (18C). Note also the portraits of the Frisian Nassaus.

The **library**★ (**9**), on the first floor, was laid out after Marot's drawings and decorated with a stucco ceiling inlaid with mirrors. Beyond the library, the **gallery** (**10**), decorated with panelling and green damask, has some magnificent chandeliers and contains a fine collection of paintings. Next to the window giving on to the main courtyard, there are portraits of René de Chalon and his wife, Anne of Lotharingia (1542); William the Silent (two first portraits on the left) inherited the Principality of Orange from René de Chalon. Adriaen van de Venne (1589–1662) has depicted the sons and nephews of William the Silent on horseback. On either side of the chimney there are William III and Mary, King and Queen of England, Ireland and Scotland, by G Kneller, a German artist working at the English court. The portrait above the chimney showing the King-Stadtholder on horseback, is a study for a large painting exhibited in Hampton Court in London.

After crossing the **drawing room** of e **Stadtholder William V** (**11**) where orcelain chandelier from Berlin hangs the stucco ceiling – note also por-

traits (1795) of William V and his v Princess Wilhelmina by John Hoppne the visitor reaches the drawing room o the first Dutch King, **William I** (**12**). The Empire chairs, covered in blue and gold cloth, were made in the Dutch workshop of A Eeltjes (1751–1836) for Het Loo Palace at the request of Louis Napoleon. On the walls there are portraits of the king and his daughter, Marianne.

▷ *Move on to visit the apartments of Queen Mary and the King-Stadtholder William III, reconstructed in their 17C layout.*

In **Mary Stuart's Bedroom** (**13**) the sumptuous canopied four-poster bed (c. 1685) is covered in Genova velvet; it comes from Kensington Palace in London, where Mary lived. The table, the two pedestal tables and the mirrors in silver and gilt silver (c. 1700) are the work of an Augsburg gold and silversmith, J Bartermann. The decoration on the ceiling, where the four elements and the four cardinal virtues are depicted, is by the painter Gerard de Lairesse (1641–1721).

Mary Stuart's Dressing Room (**14**), the walls of which are covered with 17C Dutch tapestries, adjoins the **Queen's Antechamber**★★★ (**15**), which is decorated mainly in red and green. This lovely little room, where Mary had a splendid view over the gardens, has a lacquer cabinet (1690) made in England, as well as Delft and Chinese porcelain.

The **great staircase** (**17**), designed by Marot, was reconstructed by W Fabri at the request of Queen Wilhelmina.

The landscapes on the walls of the **great hall**★ (**18**) were painted by J Glauber (1646–1726); this room with lovely grisailles on a golden background is where King William I abdicated in 1840. At certain times visitors have access to the roof (entrance located between rooms 18 and 19) which affords a splendid **view**★★★ of the gardens

A **passage** with gilt leather hangings (**19**) leads to the **King-Stadtholder William III's Closet** (**20**). There is a fine Dutch writing-desk (late 17C). In

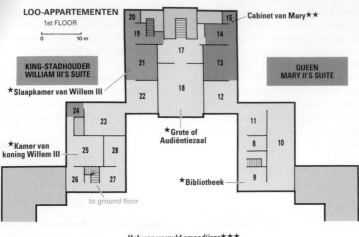

LOO-APPARTEMENTEN
1st FLOOR

Cabinet van Mary★★

KING-STADHOUDER WILLIAM III'S SUITE

QUEEN MARY II'S SUITE

★Slaapkamer van Willem III

★Kamer van koning Willem III

★Grote of Audiëntiezaal

★Bibliotheek

to ground floor

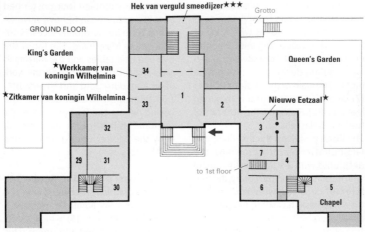

Hek van verguld smeedijzer★★★   Grotto

GROUND FLOOR

King's Garden

★Werkkamer van koningin Wilhelmina

★Zitkamer van koningin Wilhelmina

Queen's Garden

Nieuwe Eetzaal★

to 1st floor

Chapel

William III's Bedroom★ (**21**) the wall hangings are carmine red.

The next room (**22**) was laid out according to the taste of **King William II** with neo-Gothic rosewood furniture (c. 1845).

When reconstructing **Sophia's Drawing Room** (**23**) the watercolours painted at the queen's request, which depict the rooms she occupied, were an excellent reference. The 19C German artist, Franz Xaver Winterhalter, painted the portrait of Queen Sophia in a dark green dress. The small room (**24**) which gives on to the King's Garden was the **King-Stadtholder William III's Closet**. At the request of the sovereign, Melchior d'Hondecoeter (1639–c. 1695), painter of still-life paintings and animals, decorated the mantelpiece. The furnishings in **King William III's Bedroom★** (1817–90) (**25**) are in walnut and ebony, inlaid with ivory, brass, mother-of-pearl and semi-precious stones.

The following three small rooms contain, respectively: objects relating to **Prince Henry** (1820–79) (**26**), brother of William III; a **collection of 19C watercolours** (**27**); toys and furniture which had belonged to **Queen Wilhelmina** as a child (**28**).

On the ground floor, **Queen Sophia's Closet** (**29**) has been fitted out in Moorish style. There is also the **trophy room** (**30**) of Prince Henry, husband of Queen Wilhelmina. On the left of the windows is the prince in hunting costume (1917) by J Kleintjes.

Queen Emma's Drawing Room (**31**) – Emma was second wife of William III – and that of **Prince Henry** (**32**) are furnished according to the tastes of the time (1900). The palace visit ends with Queen Wilhelmina's Drawing Room and Officea (**33** and **34**) arranged as they were when she was alive.

▸ *Go down to the vaulted cellars, then pass between the two staircases and turn right, then left to reach the gardens.*

On the way, do not miss the **small kitchen** covered in Delft tiles. Queen Mary used this kitchen when she prepared jam, with fruit from her garden. The small grotto has shells, fine stones and marble decoration.

Gardens★★
Go up to the terrace.
The superb **garden gate**★★★ in gilded wrought iron at the rear of the palace used to provide access to the terrace. It took one year for a Dutch craftsman to recreate this masterpiece (designed by D Marot) by resorting to the techniques used at the time of its original making. Under the crown the initials of William and Mary (W and M) are visible, and in the lower part, orange trees and acanthus leaves.
The terrace, flanked by two statues in sandstone symbolising the rivers which edge the Veluwe, affords a fine **view**★ over the gardens (6.5ha/16 acres). Documents of the time, as well as traces discovered under the layers of sand in the 19C English garden, have made it possible to reconstitute the 17C gardens. In addition the choice of plants decorating the flower beds has been limited to species known at the time.
There are four gardens: the **lower garden** surrounded on three sides by terraces, consists of four *parterres de broderie* (embroidery-like pattern) and four English-style *parterres* decorated with statues representing Flora and Bacchus

Statue of Venus, central fountain

C. Bastin, J. Ervard/ MICHELIN

(*east side*) and Apollo and Venus receiving a golden apple from Paris (*west side*). The Venus adorning the central fountain is the replica of a statue by Gaspar Marsy (1625–81), which is in Versailles. Note the terrestrial and celestial globes; the first (*on the left*) reflects the world as it was known in Europe at the end of the 17C, whereas the positioning of the second (*on the right*) corresponds to that of the sky above Het Loo at the birth of Princess Mary Stuart. Beyond the path lined with a double row of oak trees which led to Het Oude Loo (a few turrets can be seen) extends the **upper garden**. This is delimited by colonnades – go up the staircase to see the view – and among the large trees in the English-style garden, there is a tulip tree, recognisable by its leaves ending not in a point but in a V-shaped notch. The king's fountain symbolises the power of the sovereign, William III, who wished to shoot water higher into the air than the fountains of his rival, Louis XIV, could.
The **King's Garden** (*to the west of the palace*), where blue and orange are the dominant colours, has a lawn which was once a bowling-green.
Flowers in pastel shades and fruit trees were chosen for the **Queen's Garden** (*to the east of the palace*).

MAASTRICHT★★

LIMBURG
POPULATION 118 378
PLAN OF THE CONURBATION IN THE CURRENT RED-COVER MICHELIN GUIDE BENELUX

Once prized for its strategic location on the borders of Belgium and Germany, Maastricht is now the bustling cosmopolitan provincial capital of Limburg. The city has developed on the banks of the great Maas river from which it takes its name. The town is quite distinct from the rest of the country. Its houses built of Namur limestone are more typical of the Maasland than of Limburg, and its hilly hinterland is equally atypical of the Netherlands.

A university town since 1976, Maastricht has seven faculties. Its student population gives this historic town a vibrant feel, and its somewhat exuberant character reveals itself in the many restaurants, cafés and annual carnival festivities.

- **Information:** Kleine Staat 1 – 6211 ED. ☎043 325 21 21. www.vvvmaastricht.nl.
- ▶ **Orient Yourself:** Maastricht is a large city, but its heart – and most of the tourist attractions – are situated in the area around Ceramique-Wijk. On the opposite side of the Maas river that runs through the city is the area of Wyck.
- **Parking:** Parking is not allowed in the centre of Maastricht itself, but there are areas clearly marked around its perimeter (fees apply).
- **Don't Miss:** The lively street café atmosphere of the Vrijthof in the Old Town or the caves at Grotten Noord – they are fascinating and worth a visit.
- **Organizing Your Time:** Allow at least a half day to explore the Old Town, and try to schedule in an overnight stay so you can enjoy Maastricht by night.

A Bit of History

The original settlement grew around a fortified bridge built by the Romans on the Roman road from Bavay (in northern France) to Cologne, hence its name which means the Maas crossing (Mosae Trajectum).

St Servatius, finding it safer than Tongeren (Belgium), transferred his bishopric here in 382 AD. In 722 St Hubert moved it to Liège. The town already belonged to the Frankish kings. In 1204 it passed into the trusteeship of the Duke of Brabant who, in 1283, shared his power with the Prince-Bishop of Liège. It was given its first defensive walls in 1229.

The sieges of Maastricht – Maastricht having rallied to the Revolt of the Netherlands, the Spanish besieged the town in 1579, took it by surprise, devastated it and left only 4 000 people alive. The United Provinces annexed the town in 1632.

In 1673, 40 000 French, commanded by Louis XVI, appeared before the walls of Maastricht. The siege was terrible, the Dutch defence fierce. England contributed some 6 000 troops under the command of the Duke of Monmouth. But Vauban, who was directing the operations, won a victory for the French who lost 8 000 men on the battlefield, among them **D'Artagnan**, officer of the musketeers.

The French captured Maastricht again in 1748, due to a clever move by Maurice de Saxe, Marshal of Saxony. Taken by Kleber in 1794, Maastricht was annexed to France, as was Breda.

In 1814 the town became part of the Netherlands kingdom. In 1830 the garrison resisted against the Belgians, thus obtaining the right to remain part of the Netherlands, but this was only confirmed by the Treaty of London in 1839. The fortifications were partly demolished in 1867.

During the occupation, Maastricht was one of the first towns liberated, in September 1944; only its bridges were damaged.

The Maastricht Treaty – On 10 December 1991, the governments of the 12 EC members reached agreement in Maastricht on political, monetary and economic union. The Treaty on European Union was signed by the heads of government involved in February 1992, again in Maastricht.

Maastricht today – Continuing its tradition as a busy medieval centre on an important trading route, Maastricht is an active industrial centre specialising in ceramics, papermaking and cement. The annual **carnival**★ (*see Calendar of events*) is a highly popular event which draws large crowds of townspeople and visitors to the general merry-making. The town is also known for its male voice choir, the **Mastreechter Staar**, founded in 1883.

Old Town★

Vrijthof
This square is the heart of the town, with a large number of pedestrianised shopping streets radiating out from it. It has many outdoor cafés and restaurants, and is overlooked by two churches.

Museum Spaans Gouvernement
By guided tour only (1hr): Wed–Sun 1pm–5pm. Closed Carnival, Easter, 30 Apr, Whitsun, 25 Dec and 1 Jan. *3.50€.* ☎ 043 321 13 27. www.museumspaans gouvernement.nl.
To the south there is the Gothic façade of the 16C Spanish Government House, where William the Silent was declared an outlaw by Philip II of Spain. This former chapter-house has a number of period rooms around an attractive courtyard, with furniture, silverware, porcelain, glass and ceramics dating from the 17C and 18C.

St Servaasbasiliek★★
Enter via Vrijthof. Open daily 10am–5pm (6pm Jul and Aug). Closed Carnival, 25 Dec and 1 Jan. ☎043 321 04 90.

St Servatius with a model of the basilica

This imposing monument, one of the oldest in the Netherlands, although often altered, was begun c. 1000 on the site of a 6C sanctuary. It then had one nave and side aisles, a transept and a flat east end. In the 12C it was enlarged on the one hand by the present chancel, flanked by two square towers and an apse, and, on the other hand, by a monumental **westwork**. The westwork is characteristic of the Rhenish-Mosan style (*see Introduction: Architecture and Sculpture*); the basilica is one of the first examples of this style. Topped by two towers, it is decorated with Lombard arcading. There is a carillon in the south tower of the westwork.

The lovely south portal, or **royal portal**★, (Bergportaal) was built in the 13C and is now painted with vivid colours; the tympanum illustrates the death, ascension and crowning of the Virgin.

In the 15C the side chapels and the north portal were added. The north portal gives on to cloisters also built in the 15C.

Interior
On the basilica's entrance portal there is a 15C statue of St Peter.
The **chancel**★ vaults (restored) have recovered their 16C paintings. With its tall pillars and the gallery above the ambulatory, the chancel forms a harmonious whole.

Address Book

For coin ranges, see the Legend on the cover flap.

WHERE TO STAY

Maastricht is known as the most 'Burgundian' town in the Netherlands, the term Burgundian evoking the times of Burgundian dominion when life, food and wine were enjoyed at their fullest. Maastricht's exuberant character reveals itself in its array of places to stay and eat.

Botticelli – *Papenstraat 11, 6211 LG.* ☎*043 352 63 00. www. botticellihotel.nl. 18 rooms.* As its name suggests, the atmosphere in this quiet hotel a stone's throw from the Vrijthof is very much an Italian one. The panelled walls of this 18C house are decorated with *trompe-l'oeil* paintings, and some of the rooms have fresco-style wall decorations. The furnishings are modern, and the spacious rooms are tastefully decorated. There is a beautiful courtyard garden between the front and back of the building.

De Dousberg – *Dousbergweg 4, 6216 GC.* ☎*043 346 67 77. 32 rooms.* Budget hotel with simple rooms. On bus routes 55 and 56. Has its own café.

Dis – *Tafelstraat 28, 6211 JD.* ☎*043 321 54 79. www.hoteldis.nl. 6 rooms.* This small hotel enjoys a central position and occupies the upper floor of a historic building. The rooms are spacious, tastefully decorated (contemporary art and modern furniture) and adequately appointed. Breakfast is served downstairs in the vaulted room, which also functions as an art gallery.

Les Charmes – *Lenculenstraat 18, 6211 KR.* ☎*043 321 74 00. www. hotellescharmes.nl. 15 rooms.* This delightful small hotel is housed in an inconspicuous patrician's house dating from 1725. The informal atmosphere of the bedrooms, each one with its own individual character, echoes the relaxed personal welcome on arrival. The breakfast room has a conservatory overlooking the garden.

d'Orangerie – *Kleine Gracht 4, 6211 CB.* ☎*043 326 11 11. www.hotel-orangerie.nl. 33 rooms.* This charming hotel is located in two historic buildings near the Maas. The rooms of various sizes still bear traces of the original interior, such as stucco ceilings, marble fireplaces and thick beams. The rest of the decor is in classic English and French style, and there is an enclosed garden at the back.

Derlon – *O.L.-Vrouweplein 6, 6211 HD.* ☎*043 321 67 70. www.derlon. com. 42 rooms.* This modern hotel near the Onze Lieve Vrouwebasiliek has a unique feature: Roman remains in the cellar. Important relics of a town square, a well and a road from ancient Maastricht were found here during rebuilding. This hotel is literally full of history.

WHERE TO EAT

TOWN CENTRE

Sukhotai – *Tongersestraat 54.* ☎*043 321 79 46. www.sukhothai.nl.* Excellent Thai dishes served in suitably oriental surroundings. The patio terrace is used in summer.

Le Petit Bonheur – *Achter de Molens 2.* ☎*043 321 51 09. www.petit-bonheur.nl.* This restaurant lies hidden in the heart of the town, and has a rural French feel to it. In summer, you can dine at the little tables in the courtyard.

Au Coin des Bons Enfants – *Ezelmarkt 4.* ☎*043 321 23 59. www. aucoindesbonsenfants.nl.* Housed in a 16C building, this restaurant serves culinary delights inspired by French cuisine. Meals are served on the terrace in fine weather.

Beluga – *Centre Céramique, Plein 1992 – Nº 12.* ☎*043 321 33 64. www.rest-beluga.com.* This small restaurant in the Stokstraat quarter serves fine French cuisine. The quiet terrace overlooks a small square, Op de Thermen.

Toine Hermsen – *St Bernardusstraat 2.* ☎*043 325 84 00. www.toinehermsen.com.* The culinary high point of this 'Burgundian' town; a truly excellent restaurant near the Onze Lieve Vrouwebasiliek.

RIGHT BANK (Wyck)

⊜⊜**Gadjah Mas** – *Rechtstraat 42.* ☎*043 321 15 68. www.gadjahmas.nl.* Affordable, high-quality Indonesian cuisine.

⊜⊜⊜**Mediterraneo** – *Rechtstraat 73.* ☎*043 325 50 37. www.ristorante-mediterraneo.nl.* An Italian restaurant further along this busy street.

⊜⊜⊜**'t Pakhoes** – *Waterpoort 4–6.* ☎*043 325 70 00. www.pakhoes.nl.* As the name suggests, this restaurant was once a warehouse (*pakhuis*). It serves Belgian-French cuisine and has a downstairs bar and its own terrace in the summer.

OUTSIDE MAASTRICHT

⊜⊜⊜⊜**Château Neercanne** – *5km/3mi south of Maastricht along Bieslanderweg. Cannerweg 800.* ☎*043 325 13 59. www.chateauhotels.nl.* Unique in the Netherlands as the country's only terrace-castle, the restaurant here serves delicious French cuisine. The view over the Jeker valley, the Baroque gardens and the marl caves (where you can visit the wine cellars) make dining at this 17C castle an experience to remember. The 1611 chapel now houses l'Auberge, a lunchtime restaurant. Overnight accommodation is also available.

BRASSERIES, CAFÉS, BARS, COFFEE SHOPS...

Eetcafé Rilette – *St Pietersstraat 54.* ☎*043 325 52 84.* A welcoming café with art on the walls and a French and Italian menu.

Café Sjiek – *St Pietersstraat 13.* ☎*043 321 01 58. www.maastricht restaurants.nl.* Despite its trendy-sounding name, a relaxed kind of place serving food *like grandmother used to make*. The terrace in the municipal park is a great place to sit in summer.

Café Bistro 't Liewke – *Grote Gracht 62.* ☎*043 321 04 59.* This attractive old house near the Vrijthoftheater makes an excellent venue for an evening out, with its intimate décor and Italian food.

PRACTICAL INFORMATION

General information – The **VVV** at *Het Dinghuis, Kleine Staat 1, 6211 ED Maastricht;* ☎*043 325 21 21; www.vvv-maastricht.eu;* offers details of local sights, events, cultural activities, concert and theatre tickets and bargain accommodation packages.

Transport – Parking is not allowed in the centre of town except where expressly stated. All **parking spaces** are either metered or **pay-and-display**, and if you do not pay the right amount you risk being clamped. Alternatively, use one of the many well-signposted **multi-storey car parks**. The main town-centre sights are within walking distance of one another; another option is to hire a **bicycle** from Rijwielshop "Aon de Stasie" on Stationsplein.

Tours and walks – The VVV organises walks in the historic town centre during the summer months. Leaflets with details of **self-guided walks** covering particular themes and areas are also available.

Boat trips – From April to early December, **Rederij Stiphout** (☎*043 351 53 00; www.stiphout.nl*) organises various trips on the Maas, including day trips to Liège and dinner cruises.

SHOPPING

The best area is between Vrijthof and the station, where late-night shopping is on Thursdays. The best-known (and most expensive) shopping street is **Stokstraat**. There are also a large number of art galleries and antique shops.

Markets – There's a **small market** in Marktplein on Wed and Fri.

THEATRE AND CONCERTS

Uit in Maastricht includes detailed listings of all plays, concerts and other events, and is available from the VVV.

Theater aan het Vrijthof (*Vrijthof 47.* ☎*043 350 55 55. www.theateraanhetvrijthof.nl* (in Dutch)), is the home of the Limburg Symphony Orchestra. The **Mastreechter Staar** (*www.mastreechterstaar.nl*) the town's well-known male-voice choir, usually rehearses in the Staargebouw (the former Augustinian church) on Monday and Thursday evenings.

NIGHTLIFE

Maastricht has various districts, each with its own distinct atmosphere, and

NBTC

Maastricht Carnival

all with plenty of bars and restaurants. **Rechtstraat**, on the right bank, is Maastricht's answer to the Rue des Bouchers in Brussels; the **Jekerk-wartier** (around the stream called the Jeker) is the town's "Latin Quarter", while the **historic old town** between Markt, Vrijthof and O.L.-Vrouweplein has numerous places to eat.

EVENTS

There is always something going on in Maastricht. It all starts with the **Grand Carnival**, followed by **Easter**, featuring international big bands and choirs. Early May is the time of the **St Servaas-feest**, and the year ends with the **Festival Musica Sacra** (September) and the town-centre **Christmas market**.

Inside the westwork, on the first floor, is the Emperor's Room (Keizerszaal), topped by a dome. The **capitals**★ of the westwork are interesting for their rich decoration.

The last chapel on the north aisle, towards the transept, has a Sedes Sapientiae (Seat of Wisdom) and a seated Virgin and Child, of 13C Mosan type. Nearby is a doorway, formerly the main access to the church, opening onto cloisters. Outside, it is topped by a lovely tympanum depicting Christ in Majesty.

The **crypt**, which is under the nave, contains the tomb of St Servatius behind a grille, the sarcophagus of Charles the Simple and the sarcophagus of the Bishops Monulfus and Gondulfus, founders of the primitive church in the 6C, as well as two other bishops, Candidus and Valentinus. The neighbouring crypt with square pillars, under the chancel, belonged to the 6C primitive church.

Treasury★★ (Kerkschat)

The collegiate chapel (12C) houses the treasury: a rich collection of liturgical objects, mainly gold and silversmiths' work, ivory, sacerdotal ornaments, paintings, altarpieces and statues. There is notably a bust of St Servatius, a symbolic silver key decorated with foliated scrolls which would have been given to him by St Peter, the pectoral cross, said to have belonged to St Servatius (late 10C), pieces of oriental cloth, as well as a great number of reliquaries and shrines of the late 12C. The most remarkable object is **St Servatius' shrine** called Noodkist. In oak, covered with gilded copper, enamelled, chased and decorated with precious stones, it is an important work of the Mosan School (c. 1160); at each end Christ and St Servatius are depicted, with the apostles at the sides.

St Janskerk

This Gothic church, Protestant since 1632, was built by the canons of St Servatius to be used as a parish church. Since 1987, it has been used by the Reformist community. Dating from the 12C, it was enlarged in the 15C with a chancel and a tower 70m/230ft high, decorated in the Utrecht style.

▷ *Take a few steps along Bonnefantenstraat.*

From this street there is a fine view looking over a **17C house** with crow-stepped gables and the gardens of the Natural History Museum, located on the other side of the canal.

▷ *Turn back and take Looiersgracht.*

Grote Looiersstraat

On this charming shaded square surrounded by old houses, a sculptured group depicts children listening to the popular Maastricht storyteller, Fons Olterdissen.

Natuurhistorisch Museum★

🕓*Open Mon–Fri 10am–5pm, Sat–Sun and public holidays 2pm–5pm.* 🕓*Closed Carnival, Good Friday, Easter Day, Ascension Day, Whitsun, 25 Dec and 1 Jan.* ✆*4.50€.* ☎*043 350 54 90. www.nhm maastricht.nl (in Dutch).*

This natural history museum focuses on the region of Zuid-Limburg. In the **geology** section visitors are taken on a journey of discovery going back 350 million years, starting with the Carboniferous period and ending with the arrival of the first Romans. Particular attention is given to the **fossils** which were found in the Maastricht limestone beds. Many date from the Upper Cretaceous (74–65 million years ago), a period which is also referred to as the Maestrichtian. Note also the remains of the enormous Mosasauri and giant tortoises, found in Sint-Pietersberg. In the **biology** section, **dioramas** give explanations about the flora and fauna that thrive in the area today and the aquariums give visitors an insight into life under water. In the basement are reconstructions of a flint mine and a marlpit. Also worthy of note are the fine collection of precious stones, the Kabinet and the period room. There is also a botanical garden, which features wild plants specific to the local area.

Walmuur★

The defensive walls still preserved to the south of town, are dominated by numerous towers. Shaded by beautiful trees they are surrounded by pleasant gardens. On the two sections which survive one can follow the rampart walk from where there are fine views.

▷ *Follow the rampart walk, then leave it to take a footbridge crossing the small river.*

Monseigneur Nolenspark

A lovely park laid out at the foot of the ramparts. Animals such as deer are kept in enclosures.

▷ *Take the rampart walk again.*

From the top of the first tower one overlooks the lakes where swans and ducks swim. On the north side of the ramparts one can see the **Bejaardencentrum Molenhof** building. Beside it, near the Jeker, hides an old watermill. Continuing, one reaches the semicircular tower, **De Vijf Koppen** where one overlooks a large lake.

Helpoort

This gate, flanked by two round towers, was part of the 13C curtain wall. It is the oldest town gate in the country.

Onze Lieve Vrouwebasiliek★

🕓*Open daily 8am–5pm.* ☎*043 325 18 51.*

This is the oldest building in town. It is thought to lie on the site of an old Roman temple where a cathedral was built at the time when Maastricht was the episcopal see. The edifice already existed in the year 1000. The very tall **westwork** in front of the church, as at St Servaasbasiliek, dates from this period. It is flanked by two round turrets; its upper part, added c. 1200, is decorated with Romanesque blind arcading. The nave and the beautiful apse date from the 12C.

Among interesting sculptures grouped under the left porch of the westwork,

Westwork of Onze Lieve Vrouwebasiliek

P. Gajic/MICHELIN

note the effigy of a bishop (c. 1200). Inside, the **chancel**★★ with an ambulatory topped by a gallery, thus forming two rows of superimposed columns, like that at St Servaasbasiliek, is remarkable. Furthermore, the richly decorated capitals are very varied. The nave, like that of Rolduc Abbey near Kerkrade, has alternating thick and thin pillars supporting the vault, restored in the 18C. The transept was given pointed vaulting in the 15C. The organ case dates from 1652. The church has two Romanesque crypts, one under the transept crossing (1018), the other under the westwork, and 16C cloisters.

Treasury (Kerkschat)

🕐 *Open Easter Day–autumn half-term, Mon–Sat 11am–5pm, Sun 1pm–5pm.* ☎ *043 325 18 51.*

MAASTRICHT

Abtstr.	CZ	
Achter de Molens	CZ	3
Akersteenweg	BX	
Ambyerstr. Noord	BV	
Ambyerstr. Zuid	BV	
Ambyerweg	BV	5
Begijnenstr.	DZ	6
Bergestr.	BVX	
Bieslanderweg	AX	
Bonnefantenstr.	CZ	8
Boschstr.	CY	
Bouillonstr.	CZ	10
Bredestr.	CYZ	
Brusselsestr.	CY	
Brusselseweg	AV	
Burg. Cortenstr.	BX	9
Burg. Kessensingel	BX	
Cabergerweg	AV	
Cannerweg	AX	
Capucijnenstr.	CY	
Carl Smulderssingel	AV	12
Cortenstr.	DZ	13
Dorpstr.	BX	
Dr van Kleefstr.	AV	14
Europapl.	BX	
Ezelmarkt	CZ	
Franciscus Romanusweg	ABV	17
Fregatweg	BV DY	
Grote Gracht	CY	
Grote Looiersstr.	CY	
Grote Staat	CY	
Heksenstr.	CZ	15

Helmstr.	CY	23
Hertogsingel	AX	24
Hoenderstr.	DY	27
Hondstr.	CZ	
Hoogbrugstr.	DZ	
John Kennedysingel	BX	29
Kapoenstr.	CZ	32
Keizer Karelpl.	CY	33
Kesselkade	DY	35
Kleine Gracht	CDY	
Kleine Staat	DY	37
Kleine Stokstr.	DY	41
Koningin Emmapl.	AX	38
Koningspl.	BX	39
Lenculenstr.	CZ	
Limburglaan	BX	
Looiersgracht	CZ	16
Luikerweg	AX	40
Maasboulevard	DYZ AX	
Maaspuntweg	DZ	
Maastr. Brugstr.	DY	42
Maastr. Heidenstr.	CDZ	44
Maastr. Smedenstr.	DY	47
Mariënwaard	BV	
Meerssenerweg	BV	
Mergelweg	AX	49
Minckelerstr.	CY	50
Molenweg	BV	
Muntstr.	DY	
Nassaulaan	BX	52
Nieuwenhofstr.	CZ	
Nooderbrug	AV	54
Oeslingerbaan	BX	
Onze Lieve Vrouwepl.	DZ	55

Oranjepl.	BX	56
Oude Molenweg	BX	
Oude Tweebergenpoort	CY	57
Papenstr.	CZ	59
Platielstr.	CY	
President Rooseveltlaan	BV	60
Rechtstr.	DY	
Rijksweg	BX	
Scharnerweg	BX	61
St Annadal	AX	
St Annalaan	AX	62
St Bernardusstr.	DZ	63
St Hubertuslaan	CZ	64
St Jacobstr.	CZ	65
St Maartenslaan	DY	66
St Pieterstr.	DZ	68
St Servaasbrug	DY	
St Servaasklooster	CYZ	
Statensingel	AV	73
Stenenwal	DZ	
Stokstr.	DYZ	74
Terblijterweg	BV	
Tongersestr.	CZ	
Tongerseweg	AX	
Veldstr.	BX	
Via Regia	AVX	
Viaductweg	BV	
Vijverdalseweg	BX	78
Wilhelminabrug	DY	
Wilhelminasingel	DY	
Willem Alexanderweg	BV	
Witmakersstr.	CZ	80
Wycker Brugstr.	DY	
Wyckergrachtstr.	DYZ	

17 de-eeuws huis	CZ	E
Bonnefantenmuseum	BX	M¹
Centre Céramique	DZ	
Dinghuis	DY	
Fort St Pieter	AX	
Gouvernement	BX	P
Grotten Noord	AX	
Grotten Zonneberg	AX	
Helpoort	DZ	

Kazematten	AX	N
MECC	BX	
Markt	CY	
Monseigneur Nolenspark	DZ	
Museum Spaans Gouvernement	CY	A
Natuurhistorisch Museum	CZ	M²
Onze Lieve Vrouwebasiliek	DZ	

St Janskerk	CY	D
St Pietersberg	AX	
St Servaasbasiliek	CY	
Stadhuis	CY	H
Vrijthof	CY	
Walmuur	CDZ	
de Vijf Koppen	DZ	K

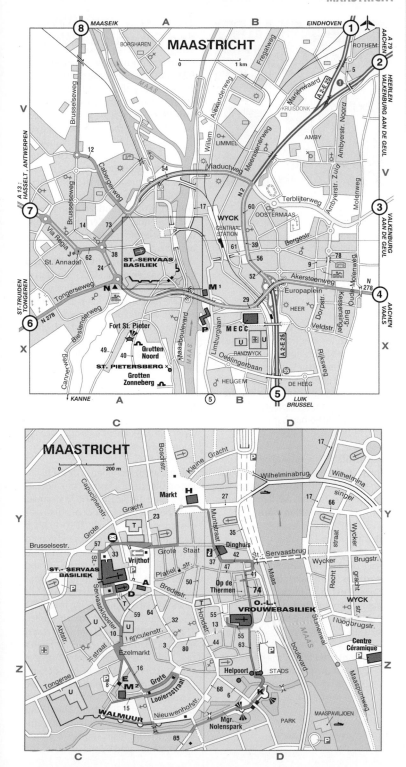

Kouprianoff/ MICHELIN

A flower shop on Stokstraat

The treasury has precious reliquaries and shrines, ivory, and liturgical ornaments including Bishop Lambert's early 8C dalmatic.

Stokstraat

This is a pleasant pedestrian precinct where the lovely 17C and 18C restored houses, decorated with pediments, façade stones and signs, are now art, antique and print shops.

At n° 28 there is a façade decorated with sculptured friezes. To the west, on a small square called **Op de Thermen**, paving stones indicate the site of remains of old Roman baths discovered here in 1840.

Dinghuis

This picturesque narrow-fronted building in the Mosan Renaissance style was formerly the courthouse. It now houses the tourist information office.

Markt

On this busy main square a market takes place on Wednesdays and Fridays. The **Stadhuis** (town hall), built 1659–65 by **Pieter Post**, is an imposing quadrilateral building preceded by a large perron and topped by a bell-tower with a **carillon**.

▶ *Return to Vrijthof by the pedestrian precinct crossing the shopping quarter.*

The Right Bank (Wyck and Céramique-Wijk)

The monumental **St Servaasbrug** (1280–1298) is one of the oldest bridges in the country. It crosses to the "other" Maastricht: the narrow streets of the **historic Wyck district** were once the commercial centre of the town. There are still many elegant 17C and 18C mansions, particularly on the long Rechtstraat; most of these are now bars and restaurants. There are also many commercial art galleries and antique shops here.

Further on is a modern commercial and residential area, **Céramique-Wijk**, which shows no traces of the area's rich past. It is home to the Bonnefantenmuseum, the **Maastricht Exhibition and Congress Centre** or MECC, the **Centre Céramique** (town hall, library, city archive, the European Journalism Centre) and the **Gouvernment** or government building, built partly on an island, where the European Council met in December 1991. This meeting led to the signing of the Maastricht Treaty on 7 February 1992 in the Statenzaal of the building.

Bonnefantenmuseum★★

Open Tue–Sun and public holidays, 11am–5pm. Closed Carnival, 25 Dec and 1 Jan. 8€. 043 329 01 90. www.bonnefanten.nl.

This museum reopened in a new building on the site of a former ceramics factory beside the Maas in 1995. The simple, E-shaped stone and brick building was designed by Aldo Rossi (1931–1977). It has a prominent silver-coloured domed tower, 28m/91.8ft high. The museum has very varied collections of pre-20C and modern art. The **Wiebengahal** opposite the museum is all that remains of an industrial complex dating from 1912 (*see Introduction, Industrial heritage*). The **pre-20C art section** (*first floor*) includes Southern Flemish works by studios and masters such as Pieter Brueghel the Younger (*Census at Bethlehem*) and Harry Met de Bles (*Landscape with the Repudiation of Hagar*), and Italian panel paintings from 1300–1600. There is an important collection of medieval sculpture from the Maas region (c. 1400–1550), dominated by the works of the

Bonnefantenmuseum

Master of Elsloo and of the early 16C Maastricht sculptor Jan van Steffeswert. Also worthy of particular attention is the superb **Neutelings**★★★ collection. The collection of medieval art amassed by Willem Neutelings (1916–1986) is of exceptionally high quality, consisting of complete domestic altars, wood and alabaster altar fragments, delicate ivory diptychs, sculpture groups and free-standing copper and bronze figurines. There is a beautifully expressive late 15C alabaster "St John's charger" from Nottingham (the name refers to the beheading of St John the Baptist) and a statue of the Assumption and Coronation of the Virgin Mary, which still bears traces of red and blue paint; also a bishop's crozier (c. 1240) from Limoges, ornamented with enamel, and a 16C Antwerp domestic altar with a centre panel showing Mary and Joseph with the infant Christ in a setting of Gothic architecture, and wings painted by Jan van Dornicke. The collection also includes a movingly simple 12C bronze of Christ Crucified, probably from near Mechelen in Belgium. There is also a collection of 18C Maastricht silverware.

Selections from the museum's **modern art collection** are displayed in rotation on the second floor. This includes works by artists who made a name for themselves in the 1960s and 70s, such

as Luciano Fabro, Bruce Nauman, Marcel Broodthaers, Robert Mangold, Mario Merz and Sol Le Witt, as well as contemporary artists such as Imi Knoebel, Jan Dibbets, René Daniëls, Didier Vermeiren and Marien Schouten. The museum also organises modern art exhibitions with an international flavour and aimed more specifically at the young viewer.

Additional Sight

Kazematten

✆⌖*By guided tour only (1hr): Jan–Apr and Nov–Dec, Sun at 2pm; May, Jun, Sept and Oct, Sat–Sun at 2pm; Jul and Aug, daily at 12.30pm and 2pm; during school holidays, daily at 2pm.* ✆3.95€. ☎043 325 21 21 (VVV).

The casemates are to be found in Waldeckpark. They belonged to a system of fortifications which was built between 1575 and 1825. Most of the fortifications above ground were razed in 1867, but the network (10km/6.2mi) of underground galleries remains. Some of these galleries are open to the public, and visitors who are able to tackle the labyrinth of corridors and stairs can visit the **Waldeck Bastion** with its domed vaults, gunpowder stores and lookout posts.

Not far away, near the fortified walls there is a bronze statue of D'Artagnan.

Pietersberg★

2km/1.2mi to the south via Sint-Huber-tuslaan and Luikerweg.

Between the valleys of the Maas and the Jeker, St Peter's Mount rises to more than 100m/328ft high. It is above all famous for its **caves**, old quarries which have been worked since Roman times (⭖see VALKENBURG). The stone, a sort of marl that hardens on exposure to the air, was used for numerous buildings in Maastricht.

Today the galleries extend for more than 200km/124mi with a height of up to 12m/39ft high, and are decorated with charcoal drawings. They were excavated by lowering the floor level so that now the oldest drawings covering the walls are near the roof. The sedimentary rock contains a large number of fossils. In 1780 the head of a Prehistoric animal was found; it was called Mosasaurus (*Mosa:* the Maas). This was confiscated by the French in 1795 and is now on display in the Musée d'Histoire Naturelle in Paris. A second head was found in 1998 and can be seen in the Natural History Museum

During troubled times the caves were used to shelter the people of Maastricht; they retain traces of these periods of refuge. This was not always a pleasant experience, since the temperature is about 10°C/50°F and it is very damp.

Fort St Pieter

By guided tour only (1hr): Jun–Oct, Sun at 3.30pm; Jul and Aug and school holidays, daily at 3.30pm. ☎ 043 321 71 32(VVV). www.fortsintpieter.nl.
Now an attractive restaurant, from the fort's (1701) terrace, there is an overall view of the town. The innermost part of the fort is linked to the system of tunnels inside the hill.

Marl caves (Grotten Noord)

By guided tour only (1hr): Jan–mid-Mar, Wed–Fri at 2pm, Sat–Sun at 12.30pm and 2pm; mid-Mar–late Apr and Nov–Dec, Wed, Fri and Sat–Sun at 12.30pm and 2pm; late Apr–Jun and Sept–Oct, daily at 12.30pm, 2pm and 3.30pm; Jul and Aug, daily 10.45am–3.45pm; during school holidays, daily at 12.30pm and 2pm. ⊜3.95€. ☎043 325 21 21 (VVV).

During World War II these caves sheltered **Rembrandt's** painting *The Night Watch*. There are graffiti here and a bas-relief of the Mosasaurus.

▷ *Continue along the road then take the second on the left to reach other caves.*

Grotten Zonneberg

By guided tour only (1hr): Apr, Mon–Sat at 12.45pm, 1.45pm and 2.45pm; May–mid-Sept, Mon–Sat 10.45am–3.45pm (departing hourly), Sun 1.45pm–3.45pm (hourly); autumn half-term, daily at 1.45pm (2.45pm on Sun); Nov–mid-Dec, Sat–Sun at 2.45pm. ⊜3.95€. ☎ 043 325 21 21 (VVV).

These caves are very similar to the preceding ones, steeped in history and a maze of corridors covered with graffiti.

Outskirts

Cadier and Keer

5km/3mi to the east via ④ on the town plan.

The **Afrikacentrum** (⭖open Tue–Sun 1.30pm–5pm; ⭖closed Carnival, Easter, Whitsun, 25 Dec and 1 Jan; ⊜ 5€; ☎043 407 73 83; www.afrikacentrum. nl) exhibits interesting collections of art (figures, sculptures, gold weights and masks) and utensils from Africa. There is also a section focusing on daily life in Africa and, around three times a year, different temporary exhibition are mounted. These temporary shows, often bringing in contemporary art from different regions of Africa, can be worth a visit in their own right.

From Meerssen to Susteren

35km/22mi. Leave via ① on the town plan.

Meerssen

Former residence of the Frankish kings. In 870 a treaty was signed sharing Lotharingia, the domain of King Lothair II (855–869) between the two brothers Louis the German and Charles the Bald, the King of France. In the 13C Meerssen attracted the monks from the Abbey of St Rémi in Reims. They built the fine **basilica** of the Blessed Sacrament (13C–14C). The chancel has a richly decorated stone tabernacle in the Flamboyant Gothic style (early 16C).

Elsloo

This small village, with its rich history of lords, and Goat Riders has retained much of its old charm. The former **Schippersbeurs** (◐*open Tue–Thu 1pm–4pm, Sun 2pm–5pm;* ◑*closed Fri, Sat, 1 Jan, Easter Day, Whitsun and 25 Dec;* ☜*1.50€;* ☎*046 437 60 52*) houses a small regional museum. The **castle gardens** and the nearby wood **Bunderbos** make for a pleasant walk. The old watermill near **Kasteel Elsloo** dates from 1552.

Stein

Stein is the home of the small **Natuurhistorisch Museum** (◐*open Mon–Fri 10am–5pm, Sat–Sun and public holidays 2pm–5pm;* ◑*closed Carnival, Easter, Whitsun, 25 Dec and 1 Jan;* ☜*3.50;* ☎*043 350 54 90*). Built around a megalithic communal grave, the museum also has collections associated with Prehistoric, Roman and Merovingian sites in the region. A little further on stands the **Witte Toren** or white tower, a remnant of Kasteel Stein.

Sittard

Sittard, which obtained its charter in 1243, was a much disputed stronghold. A large part of the town is still surrounded by ramparts (**Fort Sanderbout**). It is a busy commercial and industrial town, known in particular for.

On the **Markt**, the main square, there stands St Michielskerk in the 17C Baroque style, and a picturesque half-timbered house with a corbelled gable, built c. 1500. In Rosmolenstraat, **Kritzraedthuis** is a lovely bourgeois house which dates from 1620. The 14C **Grote Kerk or St Petruskerk** (◐*open Jun–Aug, Mon–Fri 2pm–4pm;* ☎ *046 452 41 44* (*VVV*)) has carved wooden Gothic stalls, which are probably the oldest in the country.

Stedelijk Museum Het Domein (*Kapittelstraat 6;* ◐*open Tue–Sun 11am–5pm, and Easter Monday, Whit Monday, 26 and 31 Dec;* ◑*closed Carnival, Easter Sunday, Whitsun, 25 Dec and 1 Jan;* ☜*4€;* ☎*046 451 34 60; www.hetdomein.nl*), occupying a former 19C municipal school in the historic centre of town, is a museum of local history and archaeology as well as a contemporary art museum. The Contemporary Art Department on the ground floor focuses mainly on work by young artists and includes photography and new media. Exhibits in the history section, The Urban History & Archaeology Department on the top floor, relate to prehistoric times, Limburg and multimedia.

Susteren

St Amelbergakerk (◐*open May–Oct, Tue and Sun 2pm–5pm;* ☎*046 449 46 15* (*VVV*)), an old abbey church, was built in the Romanesque style probably during the first half of the 11C. The nave, very simple and covered with a flat ceiling, leans on square pillars alternating with squat columns. The crypt outside the apse was probably inspired by that of Essen Cathedral in Germany. It contains an 8C sarcophagus and a 13C calvary. The **treasury** (◐*open Jun–Sept, Sun 2pm–5pm;* ☎*046 449 46 15* (*VVV*)) next door to the church houses an evangelistary, the Amelberga shrine from 1100 and silverware.

MARKEN ★

NOORD-HOLLAND

Marken, whose population is Protestant, has from the beginning formed a close community. It has kept its atmosphere of days past with its wooden houses and townspeople who, in season, wear the traditional costume.

Before the IJsselmeer was created, the population earned its living from fishing; today tourism is a major source of income, although Marken has not made as many concessions as Volendam in this respect.

▶ **Orient Yourself:** Separated from the continent in the 13C during the formation of the Zuiderzee, Marken was an island 2.5km/1.5mi from the shore until 1957. Now connected to the mainland, it is on the edge of the Gouwzee, a sort of inland sea.

▣ **Parking:** There should be no problem finding parking space.

◉ **Don't Miss:** A walk through the village to appreciate the traditional style of building.

◕ **Organizing Your Time:** An hour should provide plenty of time for your visit, unless you take the walk which will add two hours to your time.

◔ **Also See:** VOLENDAM.

Marken architecture

The village★

The village consists of two quarters: Havenbuurt, near the port and Kerkbuurt, around the church. In the past, it was subject to regular flooding, so the houses were grouped on small mounds and built on piles. When there was a threat of flood, the openings under the houses were closed. Most of the houses are painted dark green, with slightly corbelled side gables; some are tarred and have roof tiles.

The **interiors**, painted and polished, are richly decorated with ceramics and ornaments. The box beds have a drawer which was used as a cradle.

The **village church** dates back to the first decade of the 20C. It has some attractive stained glass windows and inside there is a collection of old photographs of Marken.

Traditional costume, Marken

From the village marina there is a **walk** that follows the dyke and which takes less than two hours. The route is a circular one and returns you to your starting point. Wear sensible shoes because the ground is not always level.

Costumes★

The women wear a wide skirt and a black apron over a striped petticoat. The striped blouse, worn in summer, is covered with a corselet and a printed front. The headdress is just a brightly coloured lace and cotton skullcap, from which a fringe of starched hair sometimes sticks out like a peak. The men wear a short waistcoat, baggy trousers tightened at the knees, and black socks. The children wear a costume more rarely; boys and girls wear a skirt and bonnet, only the shapes and colours differ. The costume worn on feast days, and particularly at Whitsun, is more elaborate (*see Introduction, Traditions and Folklore*).

Sight

Marker Museum

Kerkbuurt 44. Open Easter Day –Oct, daily 10am–5pm (11am–4pm Oct). 2.50€. 0299 60 19 04. www.marker museum.nl (in Dutch).
This small exhibition on the history of Marken is located in four smoke-houses, once used for smoking herrings and eels.

Lighthouse

The Paard (Dutch for 'horse') lighthouse is supposed to resemble the shape of a horse, although this may not be obvious to everyone. The original lighthouse was built early in the 18C but what you see today was built on its foundations in 1839. it gives six seconds of light at two-second intervals. *www.thijsvan detoren.nl (in Dutch).*

MEDEMBLIK

NOORD-HOLLAND

Medemblik received its charter in 1289, when it became the capital of West Friesland. It was then part of the Hanseatic League. Today it is one of the "ghost towns" of the former Zuiderzee region. The dyke that marks the eastern end of the Wieringermeer Polder starts at Medemblik. To the north of the town, the **Ir Lely** pumping station is the most important one used to dry out the polder.

- **Information:** Dam 2 – 1671 AW. 0227 54 28 52. www.vvvmedemblik.nl.
- ▶ **Orient Yourself:** An old steam tram links the town to Hoorn and a boat service operates between Medemblik and Enkhuizen.
- **Parking:** Follow the signs for P-centre and park at the Old Harbour.
- **Don't Miss:** A stroll down Nieuwstraat, noting N° 26 and the weigh-house at the end of the street.
- **Organizing Your Time:** A couple of hours, perhaps around a lunch break, will be sufficient.
- **Also See:** HOORN.

Sights

Nieuwstraat

The main street, Nieuwstraat, has several old houses with pretty stone façades. No 8 is the **Bakkerijmuseum** (open Apr–Oct, Tue–Sun (daily during school holidays) noon–5pm; mid-Feb–Mar and –Dec, Sat–Sun noon–5pm; 4€;

0227 54 50 14; www.deoudebakkerij. nl), a bakery museum.

Westerhaven

This quay, stretching along one of the port's two main basins (Westerhaven means western basin) retains several fine houses: nºs 9 to 14, with crow-stepped gables, and nºs 16 to 20.

...erhaven★

...g the quay skirting this basin ...Oosterhaven means eastern basin ...stand a great many old façades: nos 22, 43 and 44 have carved stones. The far end of the quay affords a pleasant **view** of IJsselmeer.

Kasteel Radboud

On the opposite side of Oosterhaven. Open mid-May–mid-Sept, daily 10am–5pm; rest of the year, Sun and public holidays 2pm–5pm. 4€. Closed 25 Dec and 1 Jan. 0227 54 19 60. www.kasteel radboud.nl.

Around 1288 the Count of Holland, Floris V, fortified and altered this castle to keep the newly subjugated Frisians in check. Only two wings have been preserved, surrounded by moats, the rest having been destroyed in the 17C and 18C. In the attic above the great hall an exhibition retraces the history of the castle and the surrounding area.

Nederlands Stoommachinemuseum

Oosterdijk 4. Open Tue–Sun, 10am–5pm. The machines operate Sat–Sun. 5€. 0227 54 47 32. www.stoom machinemuseum.nl.

Housed in what was the steam pumping station for draining the nearby polder, the museum has an interesting collection of steam-operated machinery which can be seen working one weekend a month from April to October. (see Introduction, Industrial heritage).

MIDDELBURG★

ZEELAND P
POPULATION 47 300
LOCAL MAP SEE DELTA

Middelburg, the capital of the province of Zeeland, is an old fortified town, with canals marking what used to be its outer limits. Two 18C wall mills still stand.

▸ **Information:** Nieuwe Burg 40– 4331 AH. 0118 65 99 00. www.middelburg.nl.
▸ **Orient Yourself:** Middelburg is 26km/16mi east of Goes on the A 58. The mighty abbey complex is the heart of Middelburg.
P **Parking:** Inexpensive car parks are plentiful on the outskirts of the centre, with off-street parking further afield.
Don't Miss: The Abbey – the medieval complex houses the seat of the government of Zeeland. Also interesting to see is the Miniatuur Walcheren, a scale model of the peninsula.
Organizing Your Time: If you like history and churches Middelburg will prove a great day out. It has some good hotels and eateries if you are planning a longer stay.

A Bit of History

Formerly, Middelburg was a prosperous commercial city, with its cloth trade and its imports of French wine from Argenteuil and Suresnes shipped from the port of Rouen to Rouaansekaai.

The Sea Beggars captured it in 1574. In 1595 and 1692 the town was given its first line of fortifications with bastions. These have remained more or less intact up to the present, but the only old gate which remains is **Koepoort** (1735) to the north. It is said that a spectacle manufacturer of Middelburg, Zacharias Jansen, invented the microscope in 1590 and the telescope in 1604. However, some people prefer to attribute the invention of the microscope to Van Leeuwenhoek.

In 1940 heavy German bombing destroyed the historic centre of the town. Its old buildings have been rebuil... and it remains the great market of t...

Walcheren peninsula. In July and August, on the Molenwater, visitors can watch a **ringrijderij**, a sort of tournament where the aim is to unhook a ring.

The Heart of Town

Stadhuis★

By guided tour only: Apr–Oct, Mon–Sat 11am–5pm, Sun noon–5pm; Nov–Mar, Sat–Sun at 1.30pm and 2.45pm. ☎0118 67 54 50.

Overlooking the **Markt** or main square (*market every Thursday*), this imposing building is inspired by the Hôtel de Ville in Brussels. Almost wholly destroyed by fire in May 1940, it has been rebuilt in the Late Gothic style.

The main façade is remarkable with its ten first-floor Gothic windows. Between each window double niches have statues, remade in the 19C, depicting the Counts and Countesses of Zeeland back to back. The roof is decorated with 24 dormer windows. The finely decorated octagonal turret on the right dates from the 17C.

A highly distinctive belfry, 55m/180ft high, has a pinnacle at each corner and dominates the whole. The interior contains antique furnishings, in particular the immense **Burgerzaal**, the former cloth hall. On the left is the **Vleeshal** (*open Tue–Sun 1pm–5pm;* ☎0118 67 55 23; *www.vleeshal.nl*), the former meat hall which is now used as exhibition space.

In front of the town hall in the Balans square stands a bronze **fountain** by Ilya and Emilia Kabakov. The fountain is near the Zeeland Museum (Zeeuws Museum).

Behind the town hall there is a lovely restored chapel called the English Church, **Engelse Kerk**

Abbey★

Today the seat of the provincial government of Zeeland, this vast monastic building was a Premonstrant abbey, built in the 12C on the site of a Carolingian castle; the circular shape of this castle is still visible on the town map. The abbey was secularised after the capture of the town by the Sea Beggars.

To the east, one of the defen‑ the **Gistpoort** on Damplein, ha. Late Gothic façade.

▶ *Head in the direction of Abdijplein.*

Provinciehuis

On the east side of the main square, where the old hostelry once stood, is the new provincial government building.

Zeeuws Museum★

Open Mar–Oct, Tue–Sun 10am–5pm (9pm on Fri); Nov–Feb, Wed–Sun 10am–5pm. ⊜8€. ☎0118 62 30 00. *www.zeeuwsmuseum.nl.*

The Zeeland Museum, on the site of the former clergy houses and the Gravenhof, has very varied collections relating to the history of the province of Zeeland. The Celtic goddess **Mehallenia** features prominently with several votive steles dating from Roman times, which were found in Domburg and in Noord-Beveland. The goddess is usually shown sitting, wearing a long dress and a pelerine, accompanied by a dog and carrying a basket of fruit. There is also an 18C collection of rarities where notably an orrery can be seen. Several of the fine series of local 16C **tapestries** illustrate Zeeland's naval victories over the Spanish. There are also collections of decorative art, including antique furniture, Zeeland silverware, Chinese porcelain and delftware, and of local **costumes**. There is a painting collection, comprising work by old masters and by artists who found inspiration in Zeeland, including Jan and Charley Toorop and Jacoba van Heemskerck.

Kloostergang

On the south side of the monastery, the cloisters enclose a **herb garden**. In the Medieval crypts, the **Historama Abdij Middelburg** (☎0118 62 30 00) shows the history of the abbey and its inhabitants with a 20-minute video and pictures, and the bones of a **mammoth** that lived in Zeeland 10 000 years ago are displayed in a corner section of the cloisters. The adjoining former chapter-room is now part of the **Roosevelt Studiecentrum**. This famous American family is said to have its roots in Zeeland.

MIDDELBURG

...e Houttuinen	AZ	3	Korte Delft	BYZ	18	Pottenmarkt	AZ	2

Abbey churches

Adjacent to the cloisters, standing side by side, are three churches. The **Koorkerk** (*left*), with a 14C nave and apse, has a 15C organ whose case was renovated in the 16C. The 16C **Nieuwe Kerk** (*right*) holds organ concerts in the summer. In between these two churches is the *Wandelkerk*, against which Middelburg's landmark tower, known as **Lange Jan** (Tall John), leans. ○*Open Apr–Oct, Mon–Sat 11am–5pm, Sun noon–5pm;*

∞3€ (including entry to Historama Abdij Middelburg); ☎*0118 62 66 55 (Zeeuws Museum); www.langejanmiddelburg.nl.* This octagonal stone construction dates from the 14C, crowned with a small 18C onion-shaped dome, is 85m/278.8ft high. Lange Jan has been destroyed several times over the years by fire: notably in 1568, 1712 and 1940. From the top of it there is a fine view over the abbey, the town and its canals.

Domburg beach

Additional Sights

Miniatuur Walcheren★

Open mid-Mar–Nov, daily 10am–7pm. 8€. 0118 61 25 25.|www.miniatuur walcheren.nl.

This is an open-air scale model of Walcheren Peninsula with its dykes, ports and main buildings, made to a scale of 1:20. A little further on stands the **Koepoort**, built in 1735.

The quays

The **Rotterdamsekaai**, **Rouaansekaai** and **Londensekaai** are lined with fine rows of 18C merchants' houses and storehouses, witness to the prosperity of that time.

Kloveniersdoelen

This is the former arquebusiers' mansion (17C), built in the Flemish Renaissance style. Since 1795 it has been used as a military hospital. It has a very wide brick façade streaked with white stone and brightened by painted shutters. The central voluted gable bears a sculptured low relief of arquebuses and cannon balls, topped by an eagle. An arquebus (*haarkbus* in Dutch, meaning 'hook gun') was an early muzzle-loaded gun.

Driving Tour

Walcheren Peninsula

49km/30.4mi – allow 2hr – local map see DELTA.

▶ *Leave by ③ on the town plan.*

Domburg⚜⚜

This seaside resort with a large beach situated at the foot of high dunes is very popular. Just outside Domburg (on the road to Oostkapelle) is **Kasteel Westhove**, a 13C moated castle which is now a youth hostel

The route follows the dunes which isolate Walcheren Peninsula from the sea.

Westkapelle

This town is on the western point of Walcheren, where the dunes are not strong enough to hold out against currents and are reinforced by a dyke. This extends over 4km/2.5mi and its highest crest is 7m/23ft above sea level. Westkapelle, a family seaside resort, has a beach facing south.

Zoutelande

This is a small seaside resort.

Vlissingen – *See VLISSINGEN.*

▶ *Return to Middelburg by ② on the town plan.*

NAARDEN ★

NOORD-HOLLAND
POPULATION 18 000
LOCAL MAP SEE HILVERSUM

Naarden used to be the capital of the Gooi (*see HILVERSUM*). It was formerly situated about 3km/1.8mi to the northeast of its present position, but was burned down in the civil war between the Cods and the Hooks in 1350. As it had been prone to flooding, it was rebuilt further inland. Naarden became an important stronghold, taken by the Spanish in 1572, then by the French in 1673. Today it is a small, peaceful town, still circled by its extensive 17C **fortifications**★, shaped as a 12-pointed star with six bastions surrounded by a double ring of walls and canals. The educational reformer, Jan Amos Komensky, better known as **Comenius** (1592–1670), was buried in Naarden. The town is also the birthplace of **Salomon van Ruysdael**, the famous 17C landscape painter.

- **Information:** Adr. Dorstmanplein 1b, 1411 RC. ☎035 694 28 36. www.vvvnaarden.nl.
- ▶ **Orient Yourself:** To the southeast of the capital, Naarden is in a region that the Dutch sometimes refer to as the Garden of Amsterdam.
- **Don't Miss:** Shopping opportunities at Het Arsenal and along Markstraat and Cattenhagestraat.
- **Also See:** HILVERSUM

Sights

Stadhuis★

Open Apr–Sept, Mon–Sat 1.30pm–4.30pm. *Closed public holidays.* ☎035 695 78 11.

The fine Renaissance-style town hall with crow-stepped gables dates from 1601. The interior is embellished with old furniture; it contains 17C paintings and a scale model of the 17C fortifications.

Grote Kerk

Open mid-May–mid-Sept, Tue–Sat 10.30am–4.30pm, Sun–Mon 1.30pm–4.30pm; other times by appointment. ☎035 694 98 73. www.grotekerknaarden.nl (in Dutch).

This Gothic church is dedicated to St Vitus. Inside, the wooden barrel vaulting is decorated with beautiful 16C **paintings**★. From the top of the 45m/150ft tower (235 steps) there is an impressive **view**★ of the fortifications and, in fine weather, of Amersfoort, Amsterdam and Hilversum in the distance.

Comenius Museum

Kloosterstraat 33. *Open Wed–Sun noon–5pm.* *Closed 25 Dec, 31 Dec, 1 Jan.* 3.50€. ☎035 694 30 45. www.comenius museum.nl.

The collections displayed here illustrate the life and work of the Czech humanist. Born in Moravia, Comenius belonged to the Bohemian Brotherhood (*see UTRECHT, Excursions*). He was persecuted and in 1628 he fled to Poland. He spent the last 14 years of his life in Amsterdam. He devoted himself primarily to educational research and was a strong advocate of the theory that education should seek to develop the child's individual powers of observation through teaching by illustration. Comenius was also one of the first to advocate education for all. His tomb can be seen in the former Walloon chapel, which has been turned into a mausoleum.

Het Spaanse Huis

Turfpoortstraat 27.

The façade stone of this building (1615) depicts the Spaniards' massacre of the townspeople in 1572, hence its name The Spanish House.

Nederlands Vestigingmuseum★

Westwalstraat 6. Open mid-Mar–Oct, Tue–Fri 10.30am–5pm, Sat–Sun noon–5pm; Nov–Mar, Sun noon–5pm; Christmas period, Tue–Fri 10.30am–5pm, Sat–Sun and public holidays, noon–5pm. Closed 25, 31 Dec and 1 Jan. 5.50€; boat trip round the fortress walls 3€. 035 694 54 59. www.vesting museum.nl.

At the end of the 17C, Baron van Coehoorn successfully proposed a new system for defending towns from attack. A large area from the Zuiderzee in the north to the rivers Maas and Rhine in the south could be flooded to hold back an invading army. To cover the few roads that would remain accessible, fortresses like the one at Naarden were built and walled. This worked well until the development of aircraft and aerial bombing, as happened in 1940. During the German occupation many bunkers were built by the Germans to counter the threat of an Allied invasion from the sea, and remains of these can still be seen in the area.

Exclusive Shopping in a Military Arsenal

If you're interested in art, design and/or fine food, don't miss Het Arsenaal (*Kooltjesbuurt 1*). This 17C complex, formerly used to store weapons and ammunition, was converted into a design centre by the furniture designer Jan des Bouvrie in 1993. An elegant courtyard garden is surrounded by exclusive shops, a restaurant and a gallery of modern art. Elsewhere, there are many interesting small shops in Marktstraat and Cattenhagestraat.

The five pillboxes of one of Naarden's original bastions (*Turfpoort*) have been transformed into a fortress museum. Cannons and other weapons, uniforms, engravings and an audiovisual presentation retrace the eventful history of Naarden. One of the highlights of the visit is the 61m/200ft long passageway intended to be used to listen to the enemy at night.

NIJMEGEN★

GELDERLAND

POPULATION 160 681

PLAN OF THE CONURBATION IN THE CURRENT EDITION OF THE RED-COVER MICHELIN GUIDE BENELUX

The only town in the Netherlands built on several hills, Nijmegen is the gateway to the delta region, due to its location on the Waal, main branch of the Rhine, and near the canal, the Maas-Waalkanaal. **Boat trips** (*operate July and August only. Information: Rederij Tonissen, 024 323 32 85.*) **are organised on the Waal.**
Nijmegen is a lively university town with a booming nightlife. On the sports front, Nijmegen is involved in the **Wandelvierdaagse**, the four-day walking event which starts and finishes in the town.

- **Information:** Keizer Karelplein 2 – 6511 NC. 0900 112 23 44. www.vvvnijmegen.nl.
- **Orient Yourself:** The Keizer Karelplein, home of the tourist information office, is a large square in the centre of Nijmegen and a good place from which to orient yourself.
- **Parking:** There are several car parks dotted around the town, the largest near the station.
- **Don't Miss:** Several hundred bikes of all shapes and sizes gathered together at the National Fietsmuseum Velorama.
- **Organizing Your Time:** Nijmegen is a compact town and you should be able to see most of what it has to offer in a day. Allow time for a cruise on the Waal – some boats will even take you as far as Rotterdam.

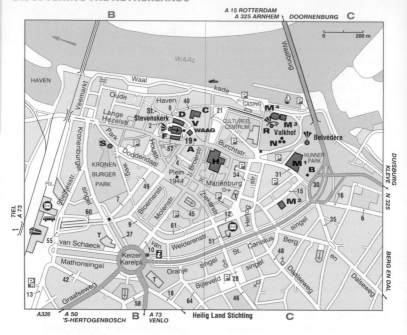

A Bit of History

An old Batavian oppidum, Nijmegen was conquered by the Romans and became a prosperous city called Ulpia Noviomagus.

Nijmegen was one of Charlemagne's favourite places to stay, and he built himself a castle on the present Valkhof. In the Middles Ages the town expanded west of this castle. In the 14C it became a member of the Hanseatic League. In 1585 it was taken by Alessandro Far-nese, Duke of Parma, but recaptured in 1591 by Maurice of Nassau. Nijmegen is the birthplace of **St Peter Canisius** (1521–97); he was named doctor of the church when he was canonised in 1925.

The peace of Nijmegen – After the French, under the leadership of Turenne, captured it without difficulty in 1672, Nijmegen gave its name to three treaties which were signed there between France, the United Provinces, Spain (1678) and the German Empire (1679). They mark the peak of Louis XIV's reign who, at the outcome of the war against the United Provinces, which had started in June 1672, annexed to France the Franche-Comté and a part of Flanders. The United Provinces remained intact. It was during the preliminary conferences for these treaties that the French language began to impose itself as the diplomatic language (despite this, the treaties were written in Latin as was customary).

Nijmegen in the 20C – In February 1944 the town was bombarded by the Americans. At the time of the Battle of Arnhem in September, Nijmegen was in the midst of heavy fighting. The bridge over the Waal, Waalbrug, built in 1936, which the Germans were threatening to destroy, was saved by a young inhabitant of the town, Jan van Hoof. A tablet to his memory has been put up in the centre of the bridge, on the east side. A **monument** at the southern end of the bridge commemorates the liberation of the town.

Sights

Grote Markt

In the centre of the square the **Waag**★ (weigh-house), built in 1612 in the Renaissance style, has a lovely façade with a perron where the red and black colouring of the shutters and the sombre red brick make an attractive combination. The ground floor is now a restaurant. There is also a bronze statue of **Mariken van Nieumeghen**, heroine of a late 15C religious drama in which, seduced by the devil, she followed him for seven years before repenting. The hands of the statue have three iron rings with which the Pope had ordered Mariken to chain her neck and arms. They loosened themselves when she had atoned for her sin. Near the weigh-house there is a group of four **17C houses** One, the **Kerkboog** is identifiable by its decorated gable (1605) above a vaulted passage; the passage leads to St Stevenskerk.
Near the east end of the church, the old **Latijnse School** is a fine building ˄ 1554.

St Stevenskerk

⏱ *Open early Mar–late Mar and Nov–mid-Dec, Sat 10.30am–5pm, Sun noon–5pm; late Mar–Oct, daily varying hours; call ahead for other times of year.* ☎024 360 47 10. www.stevenskerk.nl.
This large 13C Gothic church, enlarged in the 15C, is flanked by a massive square tower with an octagonal onion-shaped domed pinnacle (1604) which has an 18C **carillon**. The interior contains some lovely **furnishings**: the back of the door of the south arm of the transept (1632), the local gentry's pews in the Renaissance style by Cornelis Hermanszoon Schaeff of Nijmegen, and the Renaissance pulpit by Joost Jacobs. Note also the 18C princes' pew decorated with the armorial bearings of the town (eagles) and the province (lions), the **organ** built in the 18C by König and the copper chandeliers. From the **tower** (*access by the west façade, 183 steps*) there is a panorama over the town and the Waal.
The church's precinct has been restored; a large market takes place here on Monday mornings. To the north are lovely houses with gabled **Kannunikenhuizen**, or canons' houses.

Commanderie van St Jan

This 15C and 16C brick building (restored) overlooking the Waal, is an old hospital. Founded in the 13C to shelter pilgrims going to the Holy Land, it came into the possession of the Order of the Hospital of St John of Jerusalem in the following century. Today it houses the **Museumbrouwerij De Hemel** (⏱*open Tue–Sun from 12.20pm;* ⟵*guided tours (45min) at 2pm and 4pm;* ⟵*no charge for entry; guided tour 6.50€;* ☎024 360 61 67; www. brouwerijdehemel.nl) where the brewing and distilling processes are explained and visitors are shown how vinegar and mustard are made.

Stadhuis

⟵*Guided tours by prior arrangement (two weeks prior to visit) only, Mon–Sat.* ☎024 329 23 72.
This fine 16C and 17C town hall, partly destroyed by the bombardments, was restored in 1953. It is flanked by an onion-shaped turret. The exterior is decorated with statues carved by Albert

Termote depicting the emperors who were Nijmegen's benefactors or who had played a part in its history. On the corner is a statue of the Virgin.

Inside there are lovely rooms decorated in the old style, the Aldermen's Room (*Schepenhal*) and the Marriage Room (*Trouwzaal*). In the Truce Hall, **Trêves-zaal**, where the walls are covered with verdure tapestries, the treaties of 1678 and 1679 were signed. In the Council Room (*Raadzaal*) and the Great Hall (*Burgerzaal*) hang other tapestries.

Valkhof

This park has been laid out on the site of a castle built by Charlemagne. It took the name of "falcon's court" because Louis the Pious, son of Charlemagne and heir to his father's empire, bred falcons here for hunting. The castle, rebuilt by Frederick Barbarossa in the 12C, was destroyed in the 18C.

St Maartenskapel

In the centre of the park are the remains of the Romanesque chapel of Frederick Barbarossa's castle. Only a finely decorated apse, two columns with foliated capitals at the chancel's entrance, and blind arcades outside remain.

St Nicolaaskapel★

Near a terrace from where there is an interesting **view** over the Waal, this old chapel of the Carolingian castle stands

Emblem of the bargemen's guild, Museum Het Valkhof

hidden behind trees. It was probably modified in the 11C. It has 16 sides and is topped by an octagonal turret. Inside, one can see the pillars which encircle a central octagonal-shaped space. Upstairs there is a gallery with twin bays.

Belvedere Tower

Previously a watch tower (1640) in the old curtain wall, this is now a restaurant whose terrace offers a fine **view** over the Waal.

Museum Het Valkhof★

Open Tue–Fri 10am–5pm, Sat–Sun and public holidays, noon–5pm. *Closed 25 Dec.* *6€.* *024 360 88 05. www.museumhetvalkhof.nl (in Dutch).*

This modern, glass-clad museum, designed by Ben van Berkel, deals with the history, art and culture of Nijmegen and Gelderland. In addition to one of the country's largest collections of **Roman artefacts and works of art** it also has a fine collection of prehistoric and early medieval antiquities, mostly found during excavations in Nijmegen and the surrounding area. They include a bronze head of Emperor Trajan, silverware, jewellery, coins, glassware, bronze and all kinds of everyday objects. Prints, drawings and paintings help to bring the history of the town to life. There is an interesting triptych by an unknown master showing Christ on the cross with the parents of St Peter Canisius, Jan Van Goyen's *View of the Valkhof at Nijmegen*, and *The peace of Nijmegen,* painted in 1678 for Louis XIV. The museum also has an interesting collection of **modern and contemporary art** (Pop-Art, Expressionism) and holds temporary exhibitions.

Nationaal Fietsmuseum Velorama★

Open Mon–Sat 10am–5pm, Sun and public holidays 11am–5pm. *Closed 25 Dec and 1 Jan.* *5€.* *024 322 58 51. www.velorama.nl.*

The national bicycle museum has more than 250 examples from Britain, France, Germany and the United States, illustrating the progress made from the first dandy-horse to today's mountain bike.

and reclining bicycles. Velocipedes with wooden wheels, penny-farthings and the American Star with its small front wheel were followed by the British "Rover", an ordinary-sized bike with two wheels of the same size. Bicycles became much more comfortable to ride after pneumatic tyres were introduced in the late 19C, and shortly afterwards the bicycle began to enjoy unprecedented and growing popularity. On the second floor, there is a small room devoted to old and new Dutch bicycles.

Museum De Stratemakerstoren

Open Tue–Fri noon–5pm, Sat–Sun 1pm–5pm. Guided tours also. Closed 30 Apr, 25, 26 Dec and 1 Jan. 3.90€. 024 323 86 90. www.stratemakerstoren.nl.

In the underground passageways of this 16C curtain wall tower, temporary exhibitions are held which recount the town's rich past.

Natuurmuseum Nijmegen

Open Mon–Fri 10am–5pm, Sun 1pm–5pm. Closed Easter, 30 Apr, the Friday of the Vierdaagse, 25 Dec and 1 Jan. 3€. 024 329 70 70. www.natuurmuseum.nl.

This museum is housed in a former synagogue dating from 1912. The permanent exhibition, entitled 'Het Rijk te Kijk', invites visitors to take a closer look at the natural riches of Nijmegen and the surrounding area. Temporary exhibitions are also organised.

Kronenburgerpark

The **15C ammunition tower** in this park is all that remains of the old town walls. In the basement of the nearby **Paddestoelentoren Het Rondeel**, or mushroom tower, mushrooms are grown.

Excursions

Heilig Land Stichting (Holy Land Foundation)

4km/2.5mi to the southeast via Groesbeekseweg.

The **Museum Orientalis** (*open mid-Mar–Oct, daily 10am–5pm, mid-Dec–Jan,* *daily 10am–5pm, 1 Jan, noon–5pm; 9.50€; 024 382 31 10; www.museumparkorientalis.nl*) takes you back to the Palestine of biblical times. In the main building, the origin of the Bible and the Koran (Qu'oran) is recounted and the history of Judaism, Christianity and Islam is retraced. The open-air section contains reconstructions of a Palestinian village with its synagogue, a fishing village, an inn and the Via Orientalis, a depiction of Jerusalem with its Jewish, Roman, Greek and Egyptian houses.

Berg en Dal

6km/3.7mi to the east via Berg en Dalseweg.

This village (whose name means Hill and Valley) is located in a region appreciated for its woodlands and undulating countryside. The **Afrika Museum** (*open Mon–Fri 10am–5pm, Sat–Sun and public holidays 11am–5pm; closed Mon Nov–March, 25 Dec and 1 Jan; 8.50€; 024 684 72 72. www.afrikamuseum.nl*) is installed to the south (*Postweg 6*). It contains a collection of sculpture including masks and everyday objects, laid out in a modern building, and reconstructions in the open-air (Ghana and Mali dwellings, houses on piles).

Groesbeek

Nationaal Bevrijdingsmuseum 1944–1945 (*Wijlerbaan 4; open Mon–Sat 10am–5pm, Sun and public holidays noon–5pm; closed 25 Dec and 1 Jan; 9.50€; 024 397 44 04; www.bevrijdingsmuseum.nl*). The Liberation Museum, located in the place where Major-General James M Gavin landed with the 82nd Airborne Division on 17 September 1944, focuses on Operation **Market Garden** (*see ARNHEM*).

Doornenburg

10km/11mi to the northeast. Leave by Waalbrug and turn towards Bemmel and Gendt.

This village has a 14C **castle** which was rebuilt after World War II. It is a tall square fortress surrounded by water and is linked by a footbridge to a fortified courtyard where there is a chapel and a farmhouse.

NOORDOOSTPOLDER

FLEVOLAND
POPULATION 45 781
LOCAL MAP SEE IJSSELMEER

The Noordoostpolder was the second area to be reclaimed in the process of draining the Zuiderzee, but only once the sea had become a freshwater lake.

- ▣ **Information:** Postbus 155 – 8300 ED – Emmeloord. ☎527 63 39 11 www.noordoostpolder.nl (in Dutch).
- ▶ **Orient Yourself:** Follow the A 7 then A 6 south is coming from the north, or take the N 50 or A 6 northeast, if coming from the south.
- ⊙ **Organizing Your Time:** An hour will cover the main sights.
- Kids **Especially for Kids:** A boat trip to Urk.
- ◔ **Also See:** IJSSELMEER.

A Bit of History

Drainage – The polder covers more than 48 000ha/118 560 acres. The 55km/34mi long enclosing dyke was built between 1937 and 1940. From 1941 on three pumping stations at Vollenhove, Urk and Lemmer evacuated 1.5 billion cu m/52 971 billion cu ft of water. Collection and drainage ditches completed the draining process.

Development – Once the land had been drained, 500km/310.6mi of roads were built, and the future capital, **Emmeloord**, was built in the middle of the polder. After years (1942–62) of improving and fertilising the soil, the Noordoostpolder is now mainly devoted to agriculture and over 1 650 farmhouses have been built.

Sights

Emmeloord

The capital of the polder was laid out according to town planning concepts of the time. Right in the centre of the town the **water tower** (*information from Emmeloord tourist office* ☎*0527 61 20 00*), built in 1957, provides water for the whole polder and, true to Dutch traditions, has a carillon of 48 bells. The **view** from the top stretches north to the Frisian coast, southwest to Urk and the power station on the Oostelijk Flevoland Polder.

Schokland

This former island in the Zuiderzee was low-lying and difficult to protect from the sea. Its three villages were finally abandoned in 1859 – forced by royal decree. The former church (1834) and a modern building have been converted into the **Museum Schokland** (*between Ens and Nagele*; ⊙*open Apr–Oct, Tue–Sun 11am–5pm (also Mon Jul and Aug); Nov–Mar, Sat–Sun 11am–5pm;*⊙*closed 25 Dec and 1 Jan;* ⊚*3.50€;* ♿ ☎*0527 25 13 96; www.schokland.nl*) which relates the island's past: geology, prehistory and more recent times. Items on display include archaeological finds made during reclamation work on the polder.

Behind the presbytery there are remains of the stockade which protected the island from the onslaught of the sea. Steles set into the walls of the church and the presbytery indicate the levels of past floods.

Urk ★

The former island of Urk has been joined to the mainland since the creation of the polder, though it still forms a distinctive community with an island feel. Its traditions have been retained, including strict Calvinism and keeping Sunday as a day of rest. A few of the older people still wear the traditional costume: for the men, a black suit with a striped shirt; for the women, a black skirt with a floral or embroidered panel on the front of the blouse and a head brooch.

NBTC

Schokland Museum

Urk's fishing activities once centred around eel-fishing, but today sole and plaice are also fished. Its fish auction has become one of the largest on the European mainland, dealing in fish from the IJsselmeer and the North Sea. The busy **harbour** makes an attractive picture with the gaily painted eel-fishing **boats**.

Urk is also popular with water sports enthusiasts and tourists, the latter often crossing by **boat** (*operates late Jun–early Sept, Mon–Sat three times a day; crossing takes 105min; Information ☏ 0527 68 34 07*) from Enkhuizen.

From beside the church (1786) on its mound there is a **view** of the enclosing dyke and IJsselmeer beyond. In the maze of narrow streets that make up the old village centre many typical fishermen's cottages can still be seen.

Schokland and UNESCO

Since the end of 1995, the former island of Schokland has been a UNESCO World Heritage Site. It was chosen as an international symbol of the centuries of struggle between man and the sea.

Schokland, now part of an artificial polder and previously surrounded by the Zuiderzee, has not always been an island: in prehistory, it was an area of dry land, and the small lake did not appear until Roman times. This gradually expanded into a sea, and ensured that the subsoil remained untouched for centuries until the polderisation process began in 1941 and archaeologists made excavations. They found the remains of ancient houses built on piles and artificial mounds, and dozens of shipwrecks. Ceramics, stone tools, furrows and even a burial site containing 20 skeletonnes, all dating from the period between 4500 and 1800 BC, were unearthed. But the really important feature of this area is the large quantity of prehistoric remains such as fossils and bones of mammoth, aurochs and woolly rhinoceros, as well as large quantities of geological material. The huge and rare erratic boulders deposited here by glaciers during the ice ages are internationally renowned.

ROERMOND

LIMBURG
POPULATION 54 211
TOWN PLAN IN THE CURRENT EDITION OF THE MICHELIN GUIDE BENELUX

Roermond, the most important city of central Limburg, was founded as a bisphoric in 1559. It is the religious capital of this very Catholic province. It includes two marinas and vast stretches of water between the Maas and a side canal.

- **Information:** Kraanpoort 1 – 6041 EG. ☎0475-335 847. www.vvvroermond.nl.
- ▶ **Orient Yourself:** Roermond is an industrial town at the confluence of the Maas and the Roer, near the German and Dutch frontier.
- **Don't Miss:** The Brabant alterpiece in the town's old church.
- **Organizing Your Time:** Give yourself half a day to inlcude a visit to Thorn and a break for coffee or lunch.
- **Also See:** VENLO

A Bit of History

There was a settlement by the Roer river in Roman times and it developed over the centuries that followed. Roermond was granted its city rights in 1232, and was soon given a fortified wall of which only the 14C **Rattentoren** on the Buitenop remains. Roermond was one of the first towns captured in 1572 by William the Silent coming from Dillenburg, but was recaptured by the Spanish in October of the same year. Roermond then passed to first Austria, then France, and was only returned to the Kingdom of the Netherlands in 1815. The town, which suffered greatly in the Second World War, has been partly rebuilt.

Sights

Onze Lieve Vrouwe Munsterkerk

In the town centre. ⏰*Open Apr–Oct, 2pm–5pm.* ☎*0900 202 55 88 (VVV).*
This is the old church of a Cistercian abbey. It was started in 1218 in Rhenish style, and shows the transition between Romanesque and Gothic style; the church was restored at the end of the 19C by **Cuypers** (who was born here in 1827). To the west it has a massive porch framed by two towers with spires, and

it is topped by a dome flanked by two turrets at the transept crossing. The trefoil plan of the western part with the transept arms ending in apsidals, the apse's outside gallery, the roofs of the towers and turrets in the shape of bishops' mitres, and the decoration of Lombard arcading are typical features of Rhenish buildings.

The church has a Brabant altarpiece (c. 1530) in carved and painted wood, and at the transept crossing there is the tomb of the abbey's founders, the Count of Gelderland Gerald IV and his wife, Margaret of Brabant.

Near the church, at the corner of Pollartstraat, the Prinsenhof, built 1660–70, was once the palace of the stadtholders of Upper Gelderland during Spanish rule.

▶ *Take Steenweg, the main shopping street and a pedestrian precinct.*

Kathedrale Kerk

⏰*Open Apr–Oct, 2pm–5pm.* ☎*0900 202 55 88 (VVV). www.kathedraal-roermond.nl.*
Dedicated to St Christopher, it stands near Markt. Built in 1410 in the local Gothic style, it was damaged during the last war, but since restored.
Opposite the cathedral there is a 1764 **Baroque house**.

Ben Deiman Fotografie/NBTC

Thorn

Thorn, the White Village

*14km/8.7mi southwest of Roermond.
Leave Roermond via the A 68.*

Not far from the Belgian frontier, this large village built of pink brick, often painted white, has a certain charm. In the last quarter of the 10C an abbey was established here and this was the beginning of the village you see today. The abbey's founders were Count Ansfried and his wife Hereswint and between them they made the abbey a prosperous secular cloister for females of the aristocracy, with strong support from clerics.

Abdijkerk

⏰*Open Apr–Oct, Mon–Fri 10am–5pm, Sat 10am–4pm, Sun 11.30am–5pm; Nov–Mar, Sat–Sun 1pm–4pm.* ⊜*2€.* ☏*0475 56 19 62.*

Near Plein de Wijngaard, its paving decorated with geometric motifs, stands the abbey church fronted by a high brick tower striped with white stone. This is the old church of a women's abbey founded at the end of the 10C by Ansfried (who became Bishop of Utrecht in 995) and his wife Hilsondis. Rebuilt at the end of the 13C in the Gothic style, it has preserved from Romanesque times two staircase turrets and a crypt on the west side.

It was enlarged in the 15C, and remodelled in the Baroque style at the end of the 18C. It was restored by Cuypers at the end of the 19C. The interior is surprisingly white. The eastern chancel, raised and adorned by a Baroque altarpiece stands over a Gothic crypt which comprises the treasury (reliquaries, crowns). The chapels in the aisles have interesting low reliefs. In the south aisle there are charming 17C and 18C statues of saints in the folk art tradition. At the end of the nave, a double flight of stairs leads to the canonesses' chancel. From here one reaches a small **museum** installed in the old chapter-house containing the archives both of the 14C and 15C: engravings, portraits and scale models of the abbey. In the western crypt, which is Romanesque, there is a sculptured stone baptismal font (15C).

▷ *Take the main street (Akkerwal, Akker, Boekenderweg). At the second chapel (St Antoniuskapel) turn left.*

On a small shady square, the 1673 **Chapel Under the Lime Trees** (Kapel onder de Linden), was enlarged in 1811. Inside, the oldest part on the east side has fine Baroque decoration (stucco work, paintings), while the 19C part was decorated in the Empire style.

ROTTERDAM★★

ZUID-HOLLAND
POPULATION 584 046
LOCAL MAPS SEE DELTA AND ROTTERDAM
PLAN OF THE CONURBATION IN THE CURRENT EDITION OF THE MICHELIN GUIDE BENELUX

The Netherlands' second most populated city, Rotterdam is one of the world's largest ports, located on the **Nieuwe Maas**, 30km/19mi from the North Sea. It is near the mouth of two important waterways – the Rhine and the Maas – leading into the industrial heartland, and is thus the meeting point of sea and river traffic. The city of Rotterdam sprawls over both banks of the river and is linked by tunnels, bridges and the underground. It is part of the **Rijnmond**, a group of 23 municipalities forming part of **Randstad Holland**.

Almost completely destroyed during the Second World War, Rotterdam has been entirely rebuilt. During the 1980s and nineties, radical changes have been made to the city's skyline, and Rotterdam's many new buildings have earned it the nickname of Manhattan on the Maas; it also has a great deal of important modern architecture. The latest challenge is the development of the **Kop van Zuid** on the other side of the Maas, where the city council intends to create a second centre for Rotterdam by around 2010. The Erasmus Bridge (Erasmusbrug), completed in 1996, links the two halves.

- 🛈 **Orient Yourself:** Coolsingel 67 – 3012 AC. ☎0900 403 40 65. www.vvvrotterdam.nl.
- ▶ **Orient Yourself:** Rotterdam is a sprawling city and you will probably need to head for a district, explore that and then head for another. Start with Coolsingel, which is a long street close to Centraal Station and home to the tourist information office.
- 🅿 **Parking:** Parking areas are abundant in Rotterdam; most are inexpensive multi-storey car parks or free park-and-ride spaces on the outskirts. Payment is by chip-card, which can be purchased across the city from tobacconists and multi-storey car parks.
- ⊘ **Don't Miss:** The view of the city and port from the Euromast and Space Tower.
- 🕓 **Organizing Your Time:** Allow at least two hours to explore the centre, another two or three hours for the museums and then take a long, leisurely walk around the waterside areas of the city. Nightlife is lively, so an overnight stay is a must. Enjoy Rotterdam from the water: long or short cruises leave the harbourside platforms and include a tour of the massive Europoort and storm barrier.

A Bit of History

Rotterdam was originally a small village built on the dyke on the small river Rotte. The town was still of little importance when Erasmus was born there.

Expansion – In 1572 the Spaniards pursued by the Sea Beggars who had just captured Brielle, pleaded with the inhabitants of Rotterdam to be allowed to enter. Once inside, Admiral Bossu allowed his troops to pillage the town. After this betrayal, Rotterdam joined the revolt.

From 1576 to 1602 ports were constructed which were used by the Sea Beggars' fleet; the town rapidly surpassed its rival, Dordrecht, and became the second-largest in Holland. Nevertheless, when Rotterdam was captured by the French in 1794, its trade suffered severely.

Major dock work – It was only after Belgium and the Netherlands separated in 1830 that Rotterdam once again became a transit port for the Rhine. As the depth of the river in the estuary (Brielse Maas) had become inadequate

Address Book

For coin ranges, see the Legend on the cover flap.

WHERE TO STAY

Rotterdam is a city of modern architecture, so this is not the place to go looking for quaint old hotels.

YOUTH HOSTEL

Stayokay Rotterdam – *Rochussenstraat 107-109, 3015 EH. 010 436 57 63. www.stayokay.com. 22 rooms. Near the Museumpark.*

HOTELS

Breitner – *Breitnerstraat 23, 3015 XA. 010 436 02 62. www.hotelbreitner. nl. 32 rooms.* Small, central hotel in a quiet street. The simple rooms of different sizes all have shower/bath and toilet.

Inntel – *Leuvehaven 80, 3011 EA. 010 413 41 39. www.hotelinntel. com. 263 rooms.* This business hotel is next to the IMAX cinema, at the foot of the Erasmus bridge, and has a view over the Nieuwe Maas, the Erasmusbrug and Leuvehaven. It has a pool, sauna and gymnasium, and an underground car park.

New York – *Koninginnehoofd 1, 3072 AD. 010 439 05 00. www. hotelnewyork.nl. 72 rooms.* Once the former headquarters of the Holland-Amerika shipping line, this is one of the few Rotterdam hotels to be located in a historic building. It is on the other side of the Maas, and therefore not particularly central, but highly recommended nevertheless.

Parkhotel – *Westersingel 70, 3015 LB. 010 436 36 11. www. bilderberg.nl. 189 rooms.* The rooms in the modern, silver-coloured tower of this hotel have a magnificent view of the city. It is within walking distance of the shopping and entertainment areas, and has its own garden, sauna, solarium, fitness and massage room, and parking.

WHERE TO EAT

De Tijdgeest – *Oost-Wijnstraat 14–16. 010 233 13 11.* Trendy brasserie in a set of old merchants' houses and warehouses near the old port (Oude Haven). Good value for money. Terrace.

Brasserie La Vilette – *Westblaak 160. 010 414 86 92.* Chic but lively brasserie offering good food that won't break the bank.

Café Rotterdam – *Wilhelminakade 699. 010 290 84 42. www.caferotterdam.nl.* This café-restaurant is right by the Hotel New York and located in the magnificent departure lounge of the Holland-Amerika Line. The glass wall on the Nieuwe Maas side provides a wonderful view of the city and the Erasmusbrug, which is lit at night.

Chalet Suisse – *Kievitslaan 31. 010 436 77 77.* Besides fondue and raclette, this Swiss chalet-style restaurant near Museumpark serves ordinary dishes as well. A large terrace looks out over the park.

De Engel – *Eendrachtsweg 19. 010 413 82 56. www.engelgroep. com (in Dutch).* One of the places to be in Rotterdam, serving good food in an informal setting; evenings only.

Kip – *Van Vollenhovenstraat 25. 010 436 99 23. www.kip-rotterdam. nl 9in Dutch).* A pleasant brasserie near Museumpark. Its name means "chicken", but it serves lots of other things, too. There is a small garden at the back.

Zeezout – *Westerkade 11. 010 436 50 49.* This modern seafood restaurant is very popular, so booking is advisable.

Parkheuvel – *Heuvellaan 21. 010 436 07 66.www.parkheuvel.nl.* This top-class restaurant is one of the city's finest, with a view of the ships on the Nieuwe Maas thrown in for good measure.

PRACTICAL INFORMATION

General information – The tourist office, **VVV Rotterdam** (*Coolsingel 67, 3012 AC; 0900 403 40 65; www.vvv.rotterdam.nl*) can help with just about anything you need to know, including sights, tours, cultural events, excursions, and bookings for hotels,

Old Port

theatres and concerts. It also publishes a handy guide to Rotterdam.

TRANSPORT

Park in one of the **multi-storey car parks** in the centre (charge payable) or the free **Park & Ride** sites on the edge of the city. **RET**, the city's public transport company, has an extensive network of metro, bus and train lines. Most of the main sights are easy to reach from Rotterdam Central Station. In summer the tourist tram, **route no 10**, crosses the whole of the city. RET's service point in front of the train station or at *Coolsingel 141* (☎0900 92 92) sells tickets valid for one, two or three days. **Bicycles** are available for rent in the cycle shop in the station, ☎010 412 62 20.

WALKS AND TOURS

The **VVV** organises a wide variety of guided and unguided bus tours, walks and cycle tours, as well as taxi tours of the city or port. If you have a specific interest in architecture, contact **Archi-Center** on ☎010 436 99 09.
The organisation **Gilde Rotterdam** offers walking tours of specific parts of the city and on particular themes such as architecture. ☎010 436 28 44. *www.gilderotterdam.nl*.

BOAT TRIPS

Flying Dutchman: harbour tours by hydrofoil, departing from Parkkade opposite the Euromast, ☎010 436 12

22. **Spido Havenrondvaarten**: tours of the port and the Delta project, departing from Leuvehoofd, ☎010 275 99 88. www.spido.nl. **Stichting De Croosboot**: trips to the Rottemeren lakes and Delfshaven leaving from Zaagmolenbrug, ☎010 414 97 51.

ROTTERDAM FROM THE AIR

Get a bird's-eye view of the city from the **Euromast**, or do it in style with an air tour operated by **Kroonduif Air**, ☎010 415 78 55. www.kroonduif-air.nl.

SHOPPING

Rotterdam has many shopping centres, including the **Lijnbaan**, Europe's first pedestrian area; the **Beurstraverse**, one of the city's architectural highlights; the Plaza, opposite the station (Centraal Station); and the 2km/1.2mi

Beurstraverse

long **Zuiderboulevard**. The **Vrij Entrepot** is a new shopping area in the Kop van Zuid district. The area in and around the former warehouse, De Vijf Werelddelen, has all kinds of shops and numerous restaurants and bars. There is late-night shopping on Fridays, when most shops stay open until 9pm. Shops in the town centre also open on Sundays from noon–5pm. The many commercial art galleries are centred around **Witte de Withstraat**, the cultural hub of Rotterdam. The VVV sells a guide to some of the more interesting places in which you can be parted from your money.

MARKETS

The **Centrummarkt**, one of the biggest markets in the country, takes place on the Binnenrotteterrein on Tuesdays and Saturdays. On Fridays there is a market here from noon–9pm and from April–December a **Sunday market** is held. An **antiques market** is held on Sundays during the summer on Schiedamsdijk. Other large markets include **Markt Zuid** on Wednesdays and Saturdays on the Afrikaanderplein, and **Markt West**, with a wide variety of exotic foreign products, on Grote Visserijplein on Thursdays and Saturdays.

THEATRES AND CONCERTS

R'Uit Magazine gives a full monthly summary of all exhibitions, dance and theatre performances, concerts and other events. It is available free from the VVV and elsewhere. The easiest way to book tickets is at the **VVV**'s **art and culture counter**. Leading venues include the Doelen concert and conference building, *Schouwburgplein 50, ☎010 217 17 00*; **Rotterdamse Schouwburg**, *Schouwburgplein 25, ☎010 404 41 11. www.schouwburg.rotterdam.nl*; **Theater Zuidplein**, *Zuidplein 60, ☎010 20 30 203. www.theaterzuidplein.nl*; **Lantaren/Venster**, *Gouvernestraat 133, ☎010 277 22 77. www.lantaren-venster.nl*; and **Luxor Theater**, Posthumalaan 29, *☎010 484 33 33, www.luxortheater.nl* (in Dutch).

NIGHTLIFE

Cinemas include the **IMAX** screen at Leuvehaven, **Cinema Pathé** on Schouwburgplein, and **Lantaren/Venster** (Gouvernestraat) for cinephiles. There are plenty of nightclubs and bars to choose from in Rotterdam. Try Delftshaven, Veerhaven and Westelijk Handelsterrein harbour areas for restaurants and bars.

for the increasingly large ships, an access canal had to be built across the island of Voorne in 1830, the Voornsekanaal. The Voornsekanaal also became insufficient, and in 1863 the Minister Jan R Thorbecke approved the plans drawn up by the young hydraulic engineer, **Pieter Caland**, for the construction of a waterway crossing the sandy plains separating Rotterdam from the North Sea. The **Nieuwe Waterweg**, a waterway 18km/11mi long and 11m/36ft deep at low tide, was dug between 1866 and 1872, and is comparable with Amsterdam's Noordzeekanaal, without locks. The port of **Hoek van Holland** was built at the sea end for passenger traffic. In 1997, the final project of the Delta Plan was completed: the gigantic storm surge barrier near Europoort (*see DELTA*). New docks started to be built on the south bank of the river towards 1870

(Binnen Dock, Entrepot Dock, Spoorweg Dock) which were bigger than the old ones and linked to the railway. Between 1876 and 1878 two bridges were built across the Maas (Willemsbrug and Koninginnebrug) as well as a railway viaduct 1 400m/4 593ft wide spanning the river. Three docks were built, the Rijn Dock (1887–94), the Maas Dock (1988–1909) and the Waal Dock (1907–31), which together formed the largest artificial harbour in the world. Subsequently the port was extended to the west along the north bank of the Nieuwe Maas (Merwe Dock, 1923–1932).

Delfshaven, the small outer harbour that had been part of Delft since 1400, was incorporated into Rotterdam in 1886.

A martyred city – On 14 May 1940, Rotterdam suffered German bombing

Erasmus Roterodamus

This was the way the great humanist Geert Geertsz signed his name throughout his life. Erasmus was born in Rotterdam in 1469. As a child, he lived in Gouda, Utrecht and Deventer, where he attended the school of the Brethren of Common Life. Both his parents died c. 1484. At his guardians' insistence, Erasmus became a monk in 1488 at the convent of Steyn, near Gouda, where he was able to continue his studies.

In 1493, having left the convent, he became secretary to the Bishop of Cambrai, whom he accompanied on his travels. He was, however, attracted by learning, and succeeded in getting a scholarship to study Theology at the Sorbonne. During a stay in England in 1499 he met Sir Thomas More, the author of *Utopia*, who was to become a close friend. In 1502, fleeing the plague which had spread throughout France, he arrived at the University of Leuven and soon became a professor there.

A tireless traveller, Erasmus was in Italy in 1506, where his **Adagia**, the commentary on quotations and proverbs from Antiquity he wrote in Paris in 1500, was reprinted. He was then in London in 1509 where he wrote and published his *In Praise of Folly* two years later. In Basle in 1514, Erasmus met Holbein who in 1515 illustrated an edition of *In Praise of Folly* and made several portraits of the humanist.

When, in 1517, Martin Luther put up the 95 Theses triggering the Reformation, Erasmus was in Leuven. He at first refused to take part in religious quarrels, but when the Faculty of Theology condemned Luther's Theses, his neutrality created problems. After spending some months at Anderlecht near Brussels in 1521, he left for Switzerland and published, in 1526, an enlarged edition of his satirical dialogues, **Colloquia Familaria**, which was very successful. The 'Prince of Humanists', as he was known, died in Basle in 1536.

Rotterdam University was named after him in 1973.

BridgemanGiraudon

that destroyed almost all of the old town. Only the town hall, the central post office, the stock exchange and Erasmus' statue were spared. In March 1943, Allied bombing completed the destruction. 280ha/692 acres were razed, 30 000 houses and buildings set on fire. The port was also very badly bombed during the last war, and was then sabotaged in 1944 by the Germans who destroyed 7km/4.3mi of docks and 20 per cent of the warehouses.

The New City

Reconstruction of the city – Immediately after the war, Rotterdam began rebuilding. Rational urban planning was adopted, which allowed for more open spaces and a cultural and commercial city centre.

Large numbers of people moved to the suburbs, which led to the spectacular development of the built-up area. Many communities were set up almost overnight, such as **Hoogvliet** in the south and **Alexanderpolder** in the east, and Prins Alexanderpolder (1971). The quarter south of the Maas was given a shopping centre, the **Zuidplein**; a theatre and a vast sports complex, the **Ahoy** (concerts, exhibitions). Numerous recreational areas were created on the city outskirts to meet the needs of the ever-growing suburban population. The most important are located to the west on the island of Voorne, not far from Brielle, and to the northeast along the Rotte.

The new port – In 1945 the reconstruction of the port began. It was decided that national industry should be developed. A new port, **Botlek**, was built in 1954 on the island of Rozenburg, where refineries and petrochemical plants were subsequently set up. When these facilities became inadequate, the new **Europoort** was added. Finally, to accommodate the giant tankers, open-sea docks were built to the south of the Nieuwe Waterweg, in the **Maasvlakte** region, where an industrial zone was created around the port and its installations. Due to the continued growth of the port, plans for a **second Maasvlakte** are currently underway.

Port activity – With a total goods traffic of 377 million tonnes in 2006, Rotterdam is one of the world's largest ports. This gigantic concern employs 60 130 people in total.

Petroleum and its by-products account for 114.5 million tonnes, or around 35% of the total activity. Four important refineries (Shell, Esso, Kuwait Petroleum and Nerefco) have been set up between Rotterdam and the sea. They have led to the creation of a powerful chemical industry (ICI, AZCO, DSM, ARCO, Shell®, etc.).

The port of Rotterdam enjoys a privileged situation at the mouth of two big European rivers and within easy reach of major road and railway networks, not to mention having Rotterdam BV airport just 7.8km/4.8mi northeast of town.

Both a home port and a port of transit, Rotterdam is used by over 300 regular international shipping lines; it receives an enormous number of deep-sea ships annually.

The port facilities have had to adapt to the remarkable increase in **container traffic** (which exceeds 10 million TEU a year). Transhipment centres (*distriparken*) have been set up, offering storage, distribution and reassembling services; they are located near the huge shipping terminals designed to receive the container vessels.

Bridges and tunnels – There are a number of tunnels and bridges spanning the Nieuwe Maas.

Maastunnel

Opened in 1942, the Maas Tunnel is 1 070m/3 510ft long, of which 550m/ 1 804ft are under the river. It has four separate galleries: two one-way roads for cars placed side by side, and two upper levels for cyclists and pedestrians with eight escalators.

Beneluxtunnel

This was built in 1967 to relieve some of the traffic from the Maastunnel and to allow a crossing between the two banks while avoiding the city centre. It is 1 300m/4 265ft long and the river bed was dredged 22.5m/74ft deep.

Willemsbrug★★

This cable-stayed bridge, recognisable by its red gateway-shaped pylons, was designed by C Veerling and opened in 1981. The dual carriageway across this bridge forms an important traffic artery.

Van Brienenoordbrug

This bridge to the east was inaugurated in 1965. It has a single span 297m/974ft long, rising 25m/82ft above the water. It ends in a bascule bridge on the north side. Since 1992 the 12-lane Tweede Brienenoordbrug (Second Bridge) has regulated traffic flow in the area.

Erasmusbrug★★

Illustration: see Architecture.

Ben van Berkel designed this bracket-constructed single-pylon bridge, which is 800m/2 600ft long. It was officially opened in 1996, and has become known among local people as "The Swan". The bridge consists of two approach ramps with a fixed steel cable bridge and a movable steel bascule bridge between them. The bridge links the city centre with the

Erasmusbrug

Kop van Zuid, where 125ha/300 acres of former port area has been redeveloped for residential and business use. There are also plans for recreational and other facilities by 2010.

1 The Centre

The centre of Rotterdam is a mass of high-rise office blocks, shops and banks.

Stationsplein
If you turn your back to **Centraal Station** (1957), the **Delftse Poort**★ office building (1986–91) is on your left. This was designed by A Bonnema, and houses the Nationale Nederlanden insurance company. The two mirror-glazed towers are 93m/305ft and 150m/492ft high. On the right, the **Groot Handelsgebouw** or Wholesale Building (1949–51), built by architect H Maaskant and covering an area of 2ha/5 acres, symbolises the reconstruction of the city of Rotterdam.

Kruisplein
To the right is the former **Bouwcentrum**, or **Building Centre** (today the Weena Point office building). On the corner of Weena is an enormous reproduction of Picasso's **Sylvette**. On the left, the elegant **Millennium Tower**★ was completed in the year 2000. This glass tower, reminiscent of the Empire

State Building, is 149m/489ft high and houses a luxury hotel and offices.

De Doelen★
This immense concert hall and conference centre is home to the Rotterdam Philharmonic Orchestra. The original building dates from 1966; the recent conference wing was built on in 2000. To the north of Westersingel stands a deeply moving statue symbolising the Rotterdam Resistance.

Schouwburgplein
This square has been completely redesigned by Adriaan Geuze. The esplanade has been clad in metal plates, some of which can be raised to serve as a podium. The four huge desk lamps that light the area can be controlled by members of the public. The **Cinema** Pathé on the western side, clad in corrugated metal, was designed by K van Velsen. The Schouwburg, or theatre, was designed by **W Quist** and opened in 1988.

Lijnbaan★
This shopping promenade may not look particularly modern now, but it was ahead of its time in the 1950s.
The architects, Van den Broek and Bakema, designed adjoining low-rise shops with tall flats behind them. The idea of a traffic-free, pedestrianised

shopping centre provided inspiration for cities all over the world.

▷ *Cross Lijnbaan to reach the town hall.*

Opposite the town hall is the **War Memorial**. It was designed by Mari Andriessen in 1957; three generations are depicted.

Coolsingel

This is the city's main thoroughfare, and the town hall, the post office and the stock exchange are situated here.

Built between 1914–20, the **town hall** is one of the few buildings to have survived the bombings. It has an excellent **carillon**. Among other statues in front of the building is one of the great jurist, Grotius (1970).

Inside the **post office**, dating from the same period as the town hall, the remarkable concrete framework of the building is visible. Facing the Stock Exchange, in front of the department store, De Bijenkorf (The Beehive), stands a gigantic metal **"Construction"**; it is the work of Naum Gabo (1957) and illustrates the reconstruction of the town. The **Beurs** (Stock Exchange) was built in 1936–1940 and designed by JF Staal. The **World Trade Center**★ (1983–86), a 23-storey block built through the roof of the Stock Exchange hall, is a distinctive landmark. Designed by the architect RB van Erk, it has the shape of a flattened ellipse with green glass façades.

Beursplein

The rebuilding of this square to the designs of Pi de Bruyn was carried out in 1994. The plan includes the **Beurstraverse** (an underground shopping mall below Coolsingel), department stores, an apartment block and a car park.

▷ *Behind the Stock Exchange (Beurs), turn left and walk across the pedestrian bridge spanning the Rotte Canal.*

The **Statue of Erasmus** on Grotekerkplein is the work of Hendrick de Keyser and was finished in 1622.

Grote Kerk or St Laurenskerk

🕐 *Open summer, Tue–Sat 10am–4pm; winter, Thu noon–2pm.* 🚫 *No charge.* ☎ *010 413 19 89.*

Completed in 1646, with its truncated tower built into the transept, this Late Gothic church was destroyed in 1940, then restored. It now has, once more, a fine façade with a new bronze door (1968) by Giacomo Manzù.

The **interior**★ consists of a wide nave, the severity of which is attenuated by the warm colours of the panelled vaults, the copper chandeliers, the great red and gold organ (1973) and the 18C gilded ironwork of the sanctuary. The slightly protruding transept contains 17C admirals' tombs and a fine 16C organ. The bronze baptismal font (1959) is by Han Petri.

▷ *Go back to Beursplein and follow Korte Hoogstraat.*

Historisch Museum Het Schielandhuis★

🕐 *Open Tue–Fri 10am–5pm, Sat–Sun and public holidays 11am–5pm.* 🕐 *Closed 30 Apr, 25 Dec and 1 Jan.* 🚫 *3€.* ☎ *010 217 67 67. www.hmr.rotterdam.nl.*

Built from 1662–65 to house the administrative centre of the Schieland dykes, the carefully balanced Classical façade is richly decorated with sculpture.

The three period rooms on the first floor contain paintings by local artists and other items made in Rotterdam, including silver, glass and furniture. The Regency room is devoted to the works of Adriaen van der Werff (1659–1722); his fine technique and the quality of his works brought this painter international recognition.

This floor is also used for temporary exhibitions, including a display of prints and drawings from the **Atlas Van Stolk collection**, covering the history of the Netherlands.

In addition, there is a section on the history of Rotterdam showing its growth from a small 13C settlement to a major international port. It includes items such as medieval pilgrims' insignia, the oldest surviving Dutch clog, portraits of directors of the Dutch East India Company,

ROTTERDAM

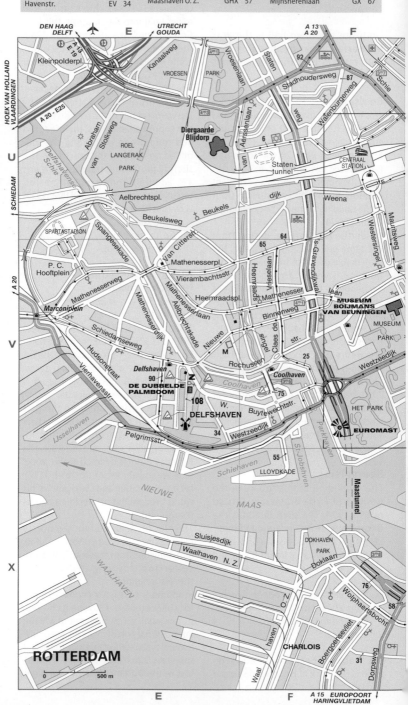

Pieter de Hoochweg	FV	75	Stadhouderspl.	FU	92	Informatiecentrum Kop		
Pleinweg	FGX	76	Utenhagestr.	GX	99	van Zuid	HV	K
Pretorialaan	HX	81	van der Takstr.	HV	94	Zakkendragershuisje	EV	Z
Schepenstr.	FU	87	Voorhaven	EV	108			
Spanjaardstr.	EV	90	Voorschoterlaan	HU	109			

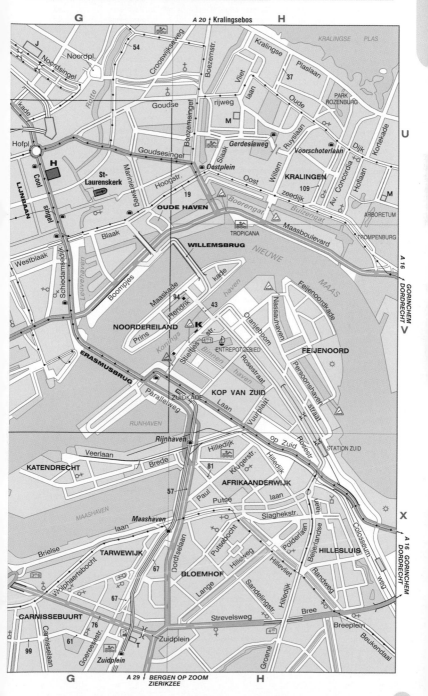

355

ROTTERDAM

Belasting & Douane Museum	JZ M6	Informatiecentrum Kop van Zuid	HV K	Natuurmuseum	JZ M4
Boompjestorens	KZ A	Kubuswoningen	KY	Nederlands Architectuurinstituut	JZ W
Café De Unie	JY N	Kunsthal	JZ M3	Nederlands Foto Instituut	JZ D
Chabot Museum	JZ M1	Mariniersmuseum	KY M9	Openlucht Binnenvaart Museum	KY M5
Constructie van Naum Gabo	JY B	Maritiem Buitenmuseum	KZ M7	Oude Haven	KY
De Doelen	JY	Maritiem Museum Rotterdam	KY	Schouwburg	JY T1
Delftse Poort	JY C	Millennium Toren	JY F	Stadhuis	KY H
Diergaarde Blijdorp	EU	Monument van Zadkine	KY S	Weena Point	JY
Euromast	JZ	Museum Boijmans Van Beuningen	JZ	Wereldmuseum	KZ
Groot Handelsgebouw	JY	Museum De Dubbelde Palmboom	EV	Willemswerf	KY
Grote of St Laurenskerk	KY	Museumpark	JZ	Witte Huis	KY X
Historisch Museum Het Schielandshuis	KY M2	Nationaal Schoolmuseum	KY M6	Witte de With	JZ E
Huis Sonneveld	JZ L			World Trade Center	KY Y
				Zakkendragershuisje	EV Z

and the white flag with which Rotterdam capitulated in 1940.

The top floor contains items from **everyday life** in times gone by (a doll's house, a reconstruction of a dairy, a toy kitchen from 1853) and a collection of clothes dating from 1900 to the present day.

The Schielandhuis is surrounded by three towers: on the right is the Schielandtoren (Schieland Tower), one of Europe's tallest residential buildings; on the left W Quist's **Robecotoren**; and opposite the museum the modern glass tower of the Fortis Bank head-office.

▶ *Cross Coolsingel and turn left into Binnenwegplein.*

Binnenwegplein

Upon entering the square one finds the **City Informatiecentrum** (○open *Mon 1pm–5.30pm, Tue–Fri 9am–5.30pm, Sat 11am–5pm;* ○*closed public holidays;* ⊜*no charge;* ☎*0800 15 45; www.cic.rotterdam.nl*), which provides information about the new developments in the city centre. **Het Ding** (The Thing; 1969) is a giant kinetic sculpture by the American artist George Rickey. Turn left by Doormanstraat, cross Westblaak and turn right into Witte de Withstraat.

Witte de Withstraat

This street is often referred to as the cultural district of the city because it has many art galleries and is close to the Museumpark. Places of interest include the **Witte de With Centrum** (○open *Tue–Sun 11am–6pm;* ○*closed Easter, Whitsun, 30 Apr, 25 Dec and 1 Jan;* ⊜*3.50€;* ☎*010 411 01 44*), which focuses on contemporary art – in particular experimental art and new art movements – with exhibitions dedicated to fine art, architecture, design and theatre. The **Nederlands Foto Instituut** (**NFI**) (*Wilhelminakade 66;* ○*open Tue–Sun 11am–5pm.* ○*closed 30 Apr, 25 Dec and 1 Jan;* ⊜*6€;* ☎*010 213 20 11; www.nederlandsfotomuseum.nl*) is dedicated to photography and new media. In addition to an archive, a restoration workshop and a school for photography and video, there are exhibition halls where temporary exhibitions are held.

Westersingel

The public garden in front of the Parkhotel contains a headless statue by Rodin, **Man Walking**. On the other side of Westersingel, at n° 22 on Mauritsweg, the façade of the reconstructed **Café de Unie** was designed by JJP Oud in 1925. Its lines and colours recall compositions by members of the abstract movement, De Stijl.

② The Museumpark★★

In the space of only a few years, the area around the **Museumpark** became the cultural heart of Rotterdam.

The park (1988–93) was designed by French landscape architect Yves Brunier and architect **Rem Koolhaas**, who was born in Rotterdam in 1944. They created three areas, each with its own distinct character; one paved with white shell grit and small apple trees, one consisting of a black asphalt podium, and one with a lake and a winding path, creating a romantic effect.

A number of important museums adjoin the park.

Boijmansmuseum Van Beuningen★★★

🕐Open Tue–Sun 11am–5pm. 🕐Closed 30 Apr, 25 Dec and 1 Jan. ✑9€. ☎010 441 94 00. www.boijmans.nl.

Located on the edge of the park, this fine art museum is in a building inaugurated in 1935, to which a wing was added in 1972. Besides an excellent collection of Old Masters, the museum contains a large number of modern and contemporary works of art, engravings and drawings and a decorative arts section.

Old Masters

This includes a remarkable collection of pre-Renaissance art. The *Three Marys at the Open Sepulchre* is a major work by the **Van Eycks**. There are admirable paintings by **Hieronymus Bosch**: *The Marriage at Cana*; *St Christopher;* and, in particular, *The Prodigal Son* where one can appreciate the painter's poetic humour, his flights of imagination and his mastery of colour. Note a *Virgin and Child* surrounded by angel musicians, *The Glorification of the Virgin*, a masterpiece by **Geertgen tot Sint Jans**. The Prophet Isaiah is shown on the left panel of the famous altarpiece by the **Master of the Annunciation of Aix**. *The Tower of Babel* by **Bruegel the Elder**, the delightful *Portrait of a Young Scholar in a red beret* (1531) by **Jan van Scorel**, and works by **Pieter Aertsen**, etc. represent the 16C. The 17C paint- ing collection is particularly interesting. There are two portraits by **Frans Hals**; church interiors by **Pieter Saenredam** and **Emmanuel de Witte**; two portraits and an oil sketching by **Rembrandt** of his young son Titus; landscapes by **Hercules Seghers**, **Van Goyen**, **Hobbema** and **Jacob van Ruisdael** and also interior scenes by **Jan Steen** and **Gerrit Dou**. The **Rubens** collection has, among other sketches, a remarkable series on the theme of Achilles' life. In the fine group of Italian paintings from the 15C to 17C, there are works by the Venetians: Titian, Tintoretto and Veronese.

Prints and Drawings

This important collection, a part of which is exhibited during temporary exhibitions, covers the 15C to the present day. It includes works by **Albrecht Dürer**, **Leonardo da Vinci**, Rembrandt, Watteau, **Cézanne** and **Picasso**.

Modern and Contemporary Art

It covers the period from 1850 to the present. The Impressionist artists **Monet**, Sisley and Pissaro are represented as well as Signac, Van Gogh, Mondrian and Kandinsky. Note the small 14-year-old ballet dancer, a graceful statuette by **Degas**.

Among the Surrealist works there are paintings by Salvador Dali and René Magritte. The collection also includes works by Kees van Dongen, who was born in Delfshaven.

The contemporary art collection is exhibited by rotation; it includes sculptures by Richard Serra, Oldenburg, Joseph Beuys, Bruce Nauman and Walter De Maria, and Donald Judd, and paintings by the Germans Kiefer and Penck, the Italians Cucchi, Clemente and Chia.

Dutch contemporary art is represented by Van Elk, Carel Visser, Rob van Koningsbruggen and René Daniels.

Among the contemporary trends are works by Milan Kunc and Salvo as well as sculptures by Thomas Schütte, Bazilebustamente and Niek Kamp.

Applied Art and Design

The museum also has a very rich collection of objects spanning many centuries; from 18C glass- and silverware to medi-

Finger on cheek, Kees van Dongen

Museum Boijmans Van Beuningen, Rotterdam

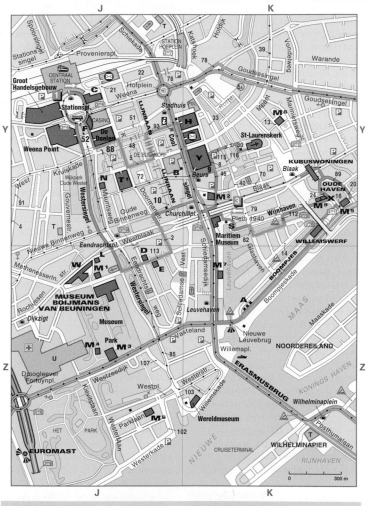

eval cooking pots. In recent years the museum has extended its design collection from early 20th century items like chairs by Rietveld and Gispen to objects by hip designers like Marcel Wanders and Dick van Hoff, thus providing an overview of Dutch Design.

Nederlands Architectuurinstituut★

🕐Open Tue–Sat 10am–5pm, Sun and holidays 11am–5pm, 24 and 31 Dec, 10am–4pm. 🕐Closed 30 Apr, 25 Dec and 1 Jan. ⬡8€. ☎010 440 12 00. www.nai.nl.

The Dutch architect Jo Coenen designed this complex, known as NAi, which opened in 1993. A number of other architects, including the Czech, Borek Sipek, were involved in designing the interior of the complex, which consists of four buildings, each serving a different function and with its own style.

As you enter from the Museumpark side, you will see a sculpture by Auke de Vries in the pond on the left. The tall, transparent section of the institute houses the offices and a library of some 35 000 books and journals on Dutch and foreign architecture and related subjects, which is open to museum visitors. Underneath the transparent section, level with the pond, are an auditorium and the foyer. After the reception desk, a ramp leads to the different levels of the exhibition

Nederlands Architectuurinstituut, Jo Coenen

wing, recognisable from the outside by its purplish-brown brick walls. This wing is used to stage temporary exhibitions on various aspects of architecture, urban planning, landscape architecture and related disciplines.

The curved wing on concrete pillars on Rochussenstraat is known as the collection wing (*accessible only on group tours*). This houses archives of items relating to Dutch architecture from 1800 to the present day, including working drawings and models by leading architects such as Cuypers, Berlage, Rietveld, Coenen, Koolhaas and Weeber. The outer walls have no windows, and are clad in red-painted corrugated steel. At night, the colonnade is lit in changing colour combinations in a light installation designed by Peter Struycken.

See also the later entry under Additional Sights for Huis Sonneveld, the house next to NAI.

Chabot Museum

🕐Open Tue–Fri 11am–4.30pm, Sat 11am–5pm, Sun noon–5pm. 🕐Closed public holidays. ⬡5€. ☎010 436 37 13. www.chabotmuseum.nl.

The Chabot Museum building dates from 1938; the architects GW Baas and L Stokla created a functional-looking villa of glass, steel frames, a flat roof and whitewashed walls in the spartan Nieuwe Bouwen style of the 1920s, 30s and 40s. Since 1993, the **villa**★ has been an appropriate home for the drawings and paintings of the local expressionist artist Hendrik Chabot (1894–1949). Chabot was also a graphic artist and sculptor.

Kunsthal

🕐Open Tue–Sat 10am–5pm, Sun and public holidays 11am–5pm. 🕐Closed 30 Apr, 25 Dec and 1 Jan. ⬡8.50€. ☎010 440 03 01. www.kunsthal.nl.

This building beside the Westzeedijk holds important temporary exhibitions of the visual arts, architecture, design, photography and non-Western cultures.

The architect, **Rem Koolhaas**, has made ingenious use of the difference in level between the Museumpark and the dyke. A series of exhibition spaces are grouped around a slope linking the two areas. The fa çade on the park side is made of travertine and glass; on the dyke side, a service road runs underneath the building. The figures of the camel driver and his camel on the roof by the artist Henk Visch are a reminder of the temporary, nomadic nature of the exhibitions.

Natuurmuseum

Open Tue–Sat 10am–5pm, Sun 11am–5pm. Closed 30 Apr, 25 Dec and 1 Jan. 4€. 010 436 42 22. www.nmr.nl.
This monumental villa dating from 1852 features stuffed mammals and birds, insects and shells. The new glass pavilion houses a 15m/50ft whale skeleton. A permanent exhibition entitled RegioNatuur looks at the flora and fauna of the Rijnmond area.

3 City of Water★

A walk through this part of the city gives a good overview of the city's links with the sea.

Maritiem Museum Rotterdam★

Open Tue–Sat 10am–5pm, Sun and public holidays 11am–5pm. Jul and Aug also Mon 10am–5pm. Closed 30 Apr, 25 Dec and 1 Jan. 5€. 010 413 26 80. www.mmph.nl
This museum is located on Leuvehaven, Rotterdam's first artificial sea harbour. An interactive exhibition entitled *WereldHaven/HavenWereld* chronicles the history of the port of Rotterdam through film, time navigators and large scale-models. The exhibition *I name you... – Shipbuilding in the Netherlands* covers the rich history of this industry in the Netherlands since the 17C. The *Mens aan boord* exhibition illustrates the hard lives of seafarers on board ship during the 17C and 18C. *De Collectie* gives an insight into the riches contained in the museum collection, with ship models, navigation instruments, maps, globes and other objects. *Professor Plons* is an interactive exhibition for children.
Leuvehaven is also the home of an old armoured vessel, the **Buffel** (1868), which belongs to the museum. Cabins belonging to the different crew members are on

view, as well as the prison cells and the well-appointed captain's cabin.

Het Havenmuseum

Open Tue–Fri 10am–5pm, Sat–Sun and public holidays 11am–5pm; also Mon in school holidays. Closed 30 Apr, 25 Dec and 1 Jan. No charge. 010 404 80 72. www.havenmuseum.nl.
The historical ships and cranes in this outdoor maritime museum illustrate how the port operated in earlier times. The pavilions contain workshops and two exhibitions.

IMAX

From the comfort of your seat, enjoy the 70mm/2.75in images projected by the IMAX system onto a screen measuring 23m/75ft high and 17m/56ft across. Combined with six-channel sound, the effect is sensational.

▷ *At the end of Schiedamsedijk, turn left across the Nieuwe Leuvebrug.*

The Nieuwe Leuvebrug offers an excellent view of the **Erasmusbrug**★★ (*see above*). Harbour tours depart from Leuvehoofd, which is dominated by the 50m/115ft high **Nationaal Monument voor de Koopvaardij**, a monument dedicated to merchant shipping.

Boompjes★

In the 17C, this was an elegant promenade with a double row of lime trees; hence its name, which means "little trees." Now, it is a modern boulevard with a variety of places to eat and drink, and residential and office buildings. The three towers, the **Boompjestorens**, were designed by the architect Henk Klunder and are lit in red, blue and yellow at night.

▷ *Continue along Boompjeskade until it widens out; turn left into Scheepmakershaven and follow he quay to the right.*

The 92m/300ft-high white office block, **Willemswerf**★, is the headquarters of the shipping company Nedlloyd. The architect, **Wim Quist**, built it in two sections; the other, beside the Nieuwe Maas, is wedge-shaped.

Follow the Boompjes under the Willemsbrug approach road.

Oude Haven★

The old port was Rotterdam's first harbour, built in 1325. It is now a pleasant place for a stroll, and visitors can sit out on one of the busy terraces in fine weather. The **Witte Huis**, or White House, on the southwest side, is the only remnant of the pre-war period. This 11-storey office block dates from 1897–1898, and was the Netherlands' first high-rise building. The old Dutch commercial sailing ships of the Inland Waterways Museum, **Openlucht Binnenvaart Museum**, can be seen moored in Oude Haven. Nearby the impressive form of the cable-stayed **Willemsbrug**★★ spans the Nieuwe Maas.

Overblaak

The architect **Piet Blom** built his **kubuswoningen**★★★ (cube-shaped apartments) over a pedestrian bridge between 1978 and 1984. One **apartment** (○open 11am–5pm (Jan, Fri only); ○closed 25 Dec and 1 Jan; ≈2€; ☎010 414 22 85; www.kubuswoning.nl), no 70, is open to the public. The so-called "Pencil" or Het Potlood apartment block towers above the area.

Behind the cube apartments is the entrance to the **Blaak metro** and railway station (1983–93). The architect, H Reijnders, placed a huge canopy of coloured tubes over the street-level part of the station.

▶ *Go back to the Oude Haven and follow Gelderskade to the Wijnhaven.*

Mariniersmuseum

○Open Tue–Fri 10am–5pm, Sat–Sun 11am–5pm. ○Closed public holidays. ≈2.80€. ☎010 412 96 00. www.mariniersmuseum.nl.

This museum, next door to the Witte Huis, chronicles the history and work of the Marine Corps. Opposite is the Houtepen, a shallow-water mine sweeper dating from 1961.

▶ *Follow Wijnhaven and then turn right to reach Plein 1940.*

A sculpture by the Franco-Russian artist Zadkine, **Monument to a Devastated City** (1953) is located to the north of the Leuvehaven; the man's heart has been torn out, and he gestures in despair, symbolising Rotterdam's suffering during the war.

4 Delfshaven★

From Delfshaven, Delft's old port, the Pilgrim Fathers embarked in 1620 for England from where they sailed for the New World.

Piet Hein was born here in 1577, the Admiral who distinguished himself in Mexico in 1628 against the Spanish. The painter **Kees Van Dongen** was born here in 1877 (d 1968). He portrayed violently coloured female figures.

Zakkendragershuisje★

○Open Tue–Fri 10am–5pm, Sat 11am–5pm. ○Closed public holidays. ≈No charge. ☎010 477 70 77. www.hmr.rotterdam.nl.

To the north of Voorhaven, beside the lock, this renovated 17C building is where porters used to gather when ships had to be loaded or unloaded. It contains a tin smelting workshop where traditional methods are still used.

Voorhaven★

By the lever bridge at the front end of this picturesque quay stands a 15C chapel with a pinnacle known as the Pilgrim Fathers' Church.

Museum De Dubbelde Palmboom★

○Open Tue–Fri 10am–5pm, Sat–Sun and public holidays 11am–5pm. ○Closed 30 Apr, 25 Dec and 1 Jan. ≈3€. ☎010 476 15 33. www.hmr.rotterdam.nl (in Dutch).

The "Double Palm Tree" Museum is attractively installed in a converted warehouse dating from 1825. It chronicles the long history of Rotterdam as a place where people meet, ideas are exchanged and goods are traded. On the first floor, archaeological finds show

Bongers/NBTC

Delftshaven

that goods were being imported here as early as 2400 BC. Goods that were being traded in the port of Rotterdam included tiles, majolica, tinware and luxury items imported by the United East India Company. Industrialisation and the history of the port from 1870 to 1970 is the theme of the second floor, which focuses on the first steam engines and the storage of goods. The third floor contains reconstructions of Rotterdam shops and other interiors from the 1930s to the 1950s. Finally, the top floor is devoted to the history of Delfshaven, including the Pilgrim Fathers and the sea hero Piet Hein, of whom there is a statue (1870) not far from the museum, opposite Coolhaven.

Molen De Distilleerketel

This tower mill dates from 1727 and is still operational.

5 Kop Van Zuid★

This former dockland area (125ha/300 acres) south of the Maas has become a permanent building site over the past few years. The local authorities plan to create a second city centre here, with 5 300 new homes and 435 000sq m/525 000 sq yd of office space and industrial units. Some of the projects already completed are the **Wilhelminahof** (lawcourt, offices, underground, etc.) opposite Erasmusbrug, the **Belvédère**

(KPN Telecom), the new **Luxor Theater** and the **World Port Center** on Wilhelminapier and the **Ichthus Hogeschool** in Posthumalaan. New buildings will stand alongside renovated and converted dockland buildings. Some splendid examples include the **Vrij Entrepot** (shopping and entertainment), the **Hotel New York** (once the head-office of the transatlantic shipping company Holland-Amerika Lijn) and the **Café Rotterdam** (the former departure hall of Holland-Amerika Lijn). Further information about this gargantuan project (scale models, film, walks) is available from the **Kop van Zuid Information Centre** (○ *open Mon–Fri 10am–5pm, Sat noon–5pm;* ○ *closed public holidays;* ○ *no charge;* ☎ *010 213 01 01; www.kopvanzuid.rotterdam. nl*). Nearby, the former railway bridge **De Hef**★, which dates from 1927, is left permanently open.

Additional Sights

Het Park

This park is an oasis of peace and tranquillity amid the hustle and bustle of Rotterdam. It comprises the small wooden church **Noorse Zeemanskerkje** (Westzeedijk) and **Euromast**.

Euromast★

○ *Open Apr–Sept, 9.30am–11pm, Oct–Mar, 10am–11pm. Opening times Christ-*

Euromast

mas and New Year, see website. ∞8.30€.
☎010 436 48 11. www.euromast.nl.
This tower was built in 1960 and is situated close to Parkhaven. From the viewing platform, which is 100m/328ft up, there is a remarkable **view**★ of the city and the port.
The Space Tower was added in 1970, bringing the total height of Euromast to 185m/607ft. The **panorama**★★ stretches 30km/19mi in all directions and includes the Europoort.

Wereldmuseum

🕒*Open Tue–Sun 10am–5pm.* 🕒*Closed 5 Dec, 25 Dec, 1 Jan, 30 Apr.* ∞*exhibitions 8€; museum free.* ☎*010 270 71 72. www. wereldmuseum.rotterdam.nl.*
This Ethnography Museum is housed in the old Royal Yacht Club building. In Hotel Het Reispaleis, where guests from all over the world stay, children are given an insight into multicultural society in an interactive way. The *Rotterdammers* exhibition tells the stories of 10 families in an attempt to give visitors an insight into migration patterns in the 20C and the effects on society in Rotterdam today. In the treasury some splendid items of the museum's rich collections are on display, including objects from Africa, America, the Islamic world, Indonesia, Oceania and Asia. There is also a collection of textiles and some contemporary art from foreign cultures.
Opposite the museum is the **Clubgebouw van de Koninklijke Roei- en Zeilvereniging De Maas** (1908–09), a fine building which is home to the Royal rowing and sailing club De Maas.

Belasting & Douane Museum

🕒*Open Tue–Sun 11am–5pm.* 🕒*Closed Easter, 30 Apr, Whitsun, 25 Dec and 1 Jan.* ∞*No charge.* ♿ ☎*010 436 56 29. www.belastingsdienst.nl/bdmuseum.*
This museum uses prints, paintings and other objects to chronicle the history of tax levying in the Netherlands since the Middle Ages. The examples of the ingenuity of smugglers illustrates how unpopular taxation has always been.

Nationaal Schoolmuseum

🕒 *Open Tue–Sat 10am–5pm, Sun 1pm–5pm.* 🕒*Closed public holidays.* ∞*4€.* ☎ *010 404 54 25. www.school museum.nl.*
The national school museum is a small but interesting museum housed in the **former town library**★, dating from 1923. Half a dozen classrooms retrace the history of education since the Middle Ages. Exhibits include some fine hornbooks, pencil boxes and other school requisites. Opposite the museum, the fountain **De Maagd van Holland** dates from 1874.

Diergaarde Blijdorp★

🕒 *Open summer, 9am–6pm, winter 9am–5pm.* ∞*17.50€.* ☎*010 443 14 95. www.diergaardeblijdorp.nl.*
In a floral park, this zoo contains an interesting collection of over 2 000 animals. The large Riviera Hall includes aquariums, terrariums containing reptiles and amphibians, a tropical hothouse and aviaries. **Taman Indah** is a reconstructed rainforest, with its own hot, wet climate, and is home to elephants, rhinoceroses and tapirs. The new **Oceanium** houses sea-lions, sharks, turtles, penguins, jelly-fish and thousands of tropical fish. The zoo also has a bat cave, a nocturnal animal house and a monkey island (**Gorilla-eiland**).

Arboretum Trompenburg

🕒 *Open Apr–Oct, Mon–Fri 9am–5pm, Sat–Sun 10am–4pm; Nov–Mar, Mon–Fri 9am–5pm, Sat 10am–4pm.* ∞*3.75€.* ♿ ☎*010 233 01 66. www.trompenburg.nl.*

The oldest part of this botanical garden (6ha/15 acres) is an English landscaped garden dating from 1820. Other features include a rose garden, hothouses with cacti and succulents and a nursery.

Kralingsebos
This wood surrounds a big lake (Kralingseplas) and has two windmills on the east side. One of them, the **Ster** (Star), is an old spice mill dating from 1740 and rebuilt in 1969.

Van Nelle Factory
Van Nelleweg 1, 3044 BC.
Construction work on this building, one of the most innovative of all 20C industrial buildings, began in 1929. The system of cladding is regarded as a superb example of a fully developed curtain-wall and the employment of light, air and space is hugely admired by architects. A great view of the building can be had from the train window as you are leaving or entering the city's central station on the main line between Rotterdam and Amsterdam.

Huis Sonneveld
Ned. Architectuurinstituut Museumpark 25, 3015 CB. Open Mon–Fri 10am–5pm, Sun 11am–5pm. ☎010 440 12 00. *www.nai.nl.*
Huis Sonneveld (the 'white villa') is next to the NAi and it has been completely restored to show what a truly hyper-modern house looked like in 1933. Brinkman and Van der Vlugt, the architects also responsible for the Van Nelle factory, designed the house for one of the directors, Mr. A.H. Sonneveld, and his family. The interior, complete with furnishings of the period, has also been meticulously restored.

The Port★★

Boat tours *departing from Leuvehoofd (see Address Book).*

Short harbour tour
Tours Jun–Sept, 10.15am–5pm (Oct until 4pm); mid–Mar–May, 9.15am–5pm; Nov–Feb, 11am–3.30pm. 9.25€. ☎010 275 99 88. www.spido.nl.

The boat sails west, down the Nieuwe Maas to Eemhaven. It follows the north bank, past Het Park and Euromast on the right (below the ventilation towers lies the Maastunnel) and then **Delfshaven Merwehaven** (specialising in fruit), **Schiedam** (see SCHIEDAM), **Wilhelminahaven** (naval repairs on a floating dock) and Wiltonhaven. The boat then turns round and crosses the river to sail back up the opposite bank towards Rotterdam, past **Eemhaven** (specialising in container traffic and transhipment of goods), **Waalhaven Maashaven** (previously mainly grain but now handling miscellaneous goods) and **Rijnhaven**. This dock is lined by quays, where in the past the great transatlantic liners of the **Holland-Amerika Line** moored. Elegant cruise ships still dock here.

Longer tour of the port
Tours Jun–Aug, at 11am and 2pm. 15€. ☎010 275 99 88. www.spido.nl. This tour goes all the way to Botlek.

Europoort tour
Tours July and Aug, Tue at 10.30am. 45€. ☎010 275 99 88. www.spido.nl. The tour allows one to grasp the sheer size of the port installations and takes in the Nieuwe Waterweg storm surge barrier (Stormvloedkering in de Nieuwe Waterweg) (see DELTA).

Driving Tours

To Europoort and Maasvlakte

▶ *79km/49mi to Maasvlakte. Leave Rotterdam towards Schiedam and take the Beneluxtunnel on the left.*

At the south exit there is a fine view of the Pernis oil terminal.

▶ *Take the motorway on the right, running alongside a railway line.*

Botlektunnel
Opened in 1980 under the Oude Maas which comes from Dordrecht, this tunnel has a single carriageway 500m/1 640ft long and 21m/69ft below sea level. It

was built to relieve the traffic congestion on the old bridge.

Botlek

Botlek is a grain port and oil terminal. Moreover, it has installations for chemical products, bulk transport and naval repairs.

▶ *Leave the Europoort road opposite, and continue right to rejoin the river.*

Rozenburg

On Het Scheur, the river's opposite bank, is the Maassluis (🔵*see below*) industrial sector. Near the Rozenburg church there is a windmill called "De Hoop" (Hope).

▶ *Shortly afterwards leave the Europoort road on the left to take Noordzeeweg which runs between the Nieuwe Waterweg and the Calandkanaal.*

On the left unloading facilities for oil tankers of different companies can be seen. The end of the road goes around an old radar station, where there is a **view** of the Hoek van Holland, Europoort and the estuary which is divided by a dyke; towards the north, there is the entrance to the Nieuwe Waterweg leading to Rotterdam, and to the south, the entrance to Europoort – 30 000 ships pass through the estuary every year.

▶ *Return by the same route and take the Calandbrug, then go under Brielsebrug to reach Europoort.*

Europoort

The vast installations of Europoort, built between 1958 and 1975, cover 3 600ha/8 892 acres on the south bank of Nieuwe Waterweg. To the right one passes the oil terminals which have already been seen, and to the left the **Hartelkanaal**, which has recreational areas on either side of it; and then along the edge of **Brielse Meer**, an artificial lake for pleasure boats that was once a branch of the Maas, the Brielse Maas.

Dintelhavenbrug

A bridge over an access canal to Dintelhaven, the mineral port. From this bridge one can occasionally see a ferry in **Beneluxhaven**, which like Hoek van Holland is a port for ferries between England (Kingston upon Hull) and the Netherlands.

Once over the Suurhoffbrug, turn right towards Maasvlakte.

Oostvoornse Meer

This lake was created by the closing of the Brielse Gat in 1965; swimming, surfing and sailing facilities have been provided.

Maasvlakte (Maas Plain)

A stretch of sandy land reclaimed from the North Sea in 1965–1971 to accommodate the inevitable extension (around 1 200ha/3 000 acres) of Rotterdam's port. At present it houses an oil terminal (Maasvlakte Olie Terminal), a container terminal (Europe Container Terminus BV), an electric power station (EZF), facilities for the storage and transhipment of minerals (EMO) and a branch of Holland's national gas board (Nederlandse Gasunie).

A new lighthouse has replaced that of Hoek van Holland as the Maasvlakte development had left it stranded inland. Due to the continuing expansion of the port of Rotterdam, plans are under discussion for a second Maasvlakte, which would lie in front of the current Maasvlakte and would also be reclaimed from the sea.

From Schiedam to Hoek van Holland

31km/19mi by the A 20 motorway going west.

Schiedam – 🔵*See SCHIEDAM.*

Vlaardingen

This major river and sea port used to specialise in herring fishing. Today it is also an important industrial and commercial centre. From the banks of the Nieuwe Maas one can look at the unending traf fic of ocean-going ships toing and froing from Rotterdam. Downstream along the south bank is the Botlek oil terminal.

Maassluis

This port is on the Scheur, between the Nieuwe Maas and the Nieuwe Waterweg. To protect Rotterdam from flooding, a **storm surge barrier**★ has been built in the Nieuwe Waterweg between Maassluis and Hoek van Holland. This opened in May 1997, and consists of two immense white gates that are able to close off the 360m/1 200ft Nieuwe Waterweg completely. Both gates have steel trusses resembling horizontal versions of the Eiffel Tower. Control of the whole complex is largely automatic, and is the only one of its kind in the world. The **Keringhuis** (open Mon–Fri 10am–4pm, Sat–Sun and public holidays from 11am–5pm; no charge; 0174 51 12 22; www.keringhuis.nl) information centre has a permanent exhibition about the barrier.

Hoek van Holland

At the mouth of the Nieuwe Waterweg, the Hook of Holland is the passenger port for Rotterdam and for ferries going to England (Harwich). It is an impressive sight to see the ships heading for Rotterdam or the North Sea. Opposite are the Europoort installations. An artificial beach was created north of Hoek van Holland in 1971.

Brielle and Oostvoorne

▶ *41km/26mi to the southwest. Leave Rotterdam via Dorpsweg.*

Brielle – See BRIELLE.

Oostvoorne

This is a seaside resort situated near a chain of dunes. A 311-ha/768-acre nature reserve, the **Duinen van Voorne**, has been laid out in the dunes; the reserve is criss-crossed by paths. A visitor centre provides information about the reserve's flora and fauna.

Windmills and polders

▶ *Round tour of 81km/50mi – about 3hr - leave Rotterdam via Maasboulevard, go towards Gorinchem and turn off towards Alblasserdam.*

The narrow dyke road follows the Noord, a stretch of water frequently used. Between the Noord and the Lek lies the **Alblasserwaard**. This old **waard** (low land surrounded by rivers) has a ring of dykes around it and has been made into a polder.

Alblasserdam

This town on the Noord has naval shipyards.

Kinderdijk

Kinderdijk means children's dyke, for it is said that during the great floods which occurred on St Elisabeth's feast day in 1421, the sea washed up on the dyke a crib with a crying baby and a cat.
Towards the end of the village an opening between houses on the right gives a pretty view of the windmills which dot the plain.

Kinderdijk windmills★★

 Open Apr–Sept, 9.30am–5.30pm. No charge. 078 691 51 79. www.kinderdijk.nl.
Near the Nederwaard pumping station, along the "boezems" or drainage pools for the polderland, stand 19 windmills. Their exceptional number, their size and the beauty of the marshy plain have made them famous, and they were designated as a UNESCO World Heritage Site in 1997. Up to 1950 they helped drain the Alblasserwaard, which is below sea level; today, their sails turn for tourists only on Windmill Days (*see Calendar of events*).
One can walk along the dykes or take a **boat tour** (*Operates May–Sept, 10am–5pm. 2.50€. Information from Rederij J.C. Vos & Zoon, 0180 51 21 74*).
The eight windmills of the Nederwaard are round stone polder mills (*see Introduction, Windmills*) dating from 1738 (1 to 8). The interior of the second mill can be visited. A little further on there is a smaller hollow post mill

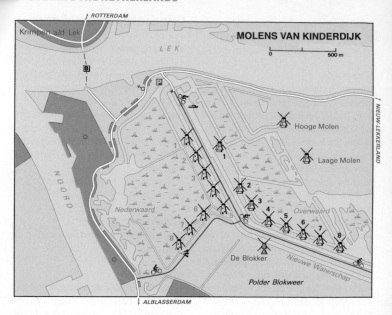

(*see Introduction, windmills*) called De Blokker or Blokweerse Wip. There are also eight windmills dating from 1740 with rotating caps along the other canal, but which are octagonal in shape and thatched (1 to 8). Hidden behind them are two other windmills built in 1761.

▶ *Continue by car along the dyke road which follows the Lek.*

From Nieuw-Lekkerland on, just down to the right of the dyke, large T-shaped farmhouses can be seen; they are thatched and have haystacks beside them protected by a little roof (*illustration: ⚭ see Introduction, Farmhouses*). Orchards surround these farmhouses. Other windmills can soon be seen.

▶ *At Groot-Ammers take the Molenaarsgraaf road.*

Soon four **windmills** appear in a single row along the canal. Three are hollow post mills, the fourth is an octagonal polder mill.

▶ *Further on rejoin the large canal which crosses the Alblasserwaard and follow the south bank until you come to Alblasserdam.*

The **road** ★ which is almost at water level is picturesque. There are large hall-farm-houses (⚭ *see Introduction, Farmhouses*) and windmills along the way. Some of these farmhouses have a safety exit a little above ground level, which led into the living room and which was used during floods.

▶ *Return to Rotterdam via Maasboulevard.*

SCHIEDAM

ZUID-HOLLAND
POPULATION 76 000

Although it is part of the Rotterdam conurbation, Schiedam (pronounced Sreedam) is a typical small town whose centre is surrounded by canals, lined with several windmills. Shipbuilding yards and numerous industries make it a busy town but its main claim to fame is its genever industry (genever is similar to gin).

🛈 **Information:** Buitenhavenweg 9 – 3113 BC. ☎0900 119 21 92.
www.vvvschiedam.nl.

▸ **Orient Yourself:** You would be highly unlikely to lose yourself in Schiedam. It has few roads, and the centre around Bultenhavenweg is surrounded by a canal.

🅿 **Parking:** There is an inexpensive car park and off-street parking.

☺ **Don't Miss:** The fascinating collection of old advertisements and bottle labels in the National Distillery Museum.

Walking Tour

Stedelijk Museum
Hoogstraat 112. ◔*Open Tue–Sun 10am–5pm.* ◔*Closed 25 Dec and 1 Jan.* ⊜*5€.* ♿☎*010 246 36 6. www.stedelijkmuseum schiedam.nl.*
Located in the town's pedestrianised area, the museum is housed in the former hospital, St Jacobs Gasthuis, an impressive 18C building with a portico. Its collections relate to the history of the town, and (mainly Dutch) contemporary art such as the CoBrA group, systematic painting, Pop Art and New Figurative Art.
In the basement, there is the National Distillery Museum, **Nederlands Gedistilleerd Museum De Gekroonde Branderketel** (◔ *open Tue–Sat 11am–5pm, Sun and public holidays 12.30pm–5pm;* ◔*closed 25 Dec and 1 Jan;* ⊜*4.40€;* ☎*010 246 96 76; www.het gedistilleerdmuseum.nl*). Old labels, advertisements, miniatures and stills illustrate the making of genever in the 18C, and a wide variety of genever, liqueurs and bitters can be sampled.

Windmills
The town was formerly surrounded by 19 huge mills, mainly used for milling grain intended for the distilleries. Five stage mills stand along Noordvest, the canal marking the course of the old ramparts; these are among the tallest ☐urope.

De Walvisch (The Whale)
This is the southernmost of the five mills, and dates from 1794.

▸ *Continuing along the quay towards the north, one can see the four other mills.*

De Vrijheid (Freedom)
Started in 1785, it still mills grain.

De Noord (The North)
This mill of 1803 is 33.33m/109ft tall including the cap, maximum height of sails 44.56m/146ft. Its premises are used for tasting sessions by an important distillery, whose buildings are opposite.

Windmills in Schiedam

The Home of Genever

The Dutch started to distil grain c. 1600. As time went on, they narrowed their production down to malt spirit, finally specialising in making genever, using the juice of juniper berries to give the 'gin' its particular flavour. At one time Schiedam had 400 distilleries, and the monumental 18C and 19C mansions, warehouses, windmills and former distilleries along the canals bear witness to the industry's importance. Today, only about five remain, producing young genever (*jonge jenever*) and old genever (*oude jenever*), the latter having a fuller flavour. Each distillery has its own recipe, which is kept a closely-guarded secret. The locals have a variety of ways of ordering a genever: a *'hassebassie'*, a *'neut'*, a *'pikketanissie'* or a *'schiedammertje'*, but whatever it is called, it is always genever and it always tastes good.

De Nieuwe Palmboom (The New Palm Tree)

The **Nederlands Malend Korenmolenmuseum** (◔ *open Tue–Sat 11am–5pm, Sun and public holidays 12.30pm–5pm;* ◔ *closed 25 Dec and 1 Jan;* ⊜*2.50€;* ☎ *010 426 76 75; www.schiedamse molens.nl*), or Netherlands Corn-Milling Museum, has a working windmill which is used for milling rye and malt for the De Gekroonde Brandersketel distillery.

▶ *Take the road opposite the Stedelijk Museum and cross the Lange Haven, the town's central canal. Then follow the quay (Oude Sluis) on the right.*

Behind the old Korenbeurs (Corn Exchange) there is the gracious 1725 guildhouse of the Porters' Guild, the **Zakkendragershuisje**.

Maasboulevard

From this boulevard near the pleasure boat harbour, there is an interesting **view** of the heavy maritime traffic between Rotterdam and the sea. The port of Pernis is on the opposite bank.

SLUIS

ZEELAND

POPULATION 7 000 (SLUIS-AARDENBURG)

This small town, situated near the Belgian border, was together with Damme an outer harbour of Bruges in the 14C when it was at the mouth of the Zwin, which is now silted up. Today it is a pleasant and busy tourist town, owing part of its appeal to its numerous sex shops. The grassy mounds visible on entering the town are remains of the old ramparts. Sluis is also the birthplace of **Johan Hendrik van Dale** (1828–72), the founder of the great Dutch monolingual dictionary *Van Dale Groot Woordenboek der Nederlandse Taal.*

- 🛈 **Information:** St-Annastraat 15 – 4524 JB. ☎0117 46 17 00. www.sluisonline.nl.
- ▶ **Orient Yourself:** Sluis revolves around one main street that runs alongside a canal and is full of specialist shops and eateries. Smaller streets are worth exploring.
- 🅿 **Parking:** There's limited off-street parking, but an inexpensive car park is situated at one end of the main street.
- ◉ **Don't Miss:** The view of the network of canals from the Molen de Brak.
- ◔ **Organizing Your Time:** Two or three hours will be ample time to explore Sluis.
- ◔ **Also See:** BELGIUM.

Sights

Stadhuis

🕐Open May–Oct, Sun 2pm–5pm, also Whitsun and Ascension Day 2pm–5pm; Jul and Aug, 1pm–5pm. ☎0117 46 17 00.

The town hall is overlooked by a tall 14C **belfry**, the only one existing in the Netherlands. It is decorated with turrets and a jack-o'-the-clock.

Molen de Brak

This wall mill, destroyed in 1944, was rebuilt in 1951. From the gallery the view extends over the surrounding countryside and the Het Zwin nature reserve (👆see the Green Guide Belgium Luxembourg).

Outskirts

St Anna ter Muiden

2km/1.2mi to the northwest, near the frontier.

At the foot of the church's imposing 14C brick tower, the small triangular **square**, the rustic houses and the water pump form a charming picture. Note a thatched wooden barn at the far end of the square.

Aardenburg

8km/5mi to the southeast.

The fine Gothic church, **St-Bavokerk**, with characteristics of the Scheldt Gothic style (which developed in Belgium), contains 14C and 15C sarcoph-agi with interesting paintings on the inside panels.

Excursions

IJzendijke

22km/14mi to the east.

This old stronghold only has a small halfmoon-shaped bastion or ravelin remaining from its ramparts, covered with earth and surrounded by water. Nearby there is a lovely windmill. The spire topped with a golden cock belongs to the oldest Protestant church (1612) in Zeeland.

At n° 28 Markt is the Regional Museum **Streekmuseum WestZeeuws-Vlaanderen** (🕐open Tue–Sat 1pm–5pm; mid-May–early Oct, also open Sun 1pm–5pm; 🕐 closed public holidays; ☎0117 30 12 00). Apart from a rustic interior typical of Cadzand around 1850, there are implements used in the cultivation of flax and madder and a section devoted to the Zeeland plough horses.

Breskens

29km/18mi to the north.

A fishing port at the mouth of the Westerschelde, Breskens is the departure point for the **ferry** (*Leaves daily every 30min, Sun every 1hr. Only for pedestrians and cyclists.* ☎0118 46 59 05; www.bba.nl) to Vlissingen. It also has a pleasure boat harbour.

©Mikhail Lavrenov/Bigstockphoto.com

...skens Lighthouse

SNEEK

FRYSLÂN
POPULATION 33 115
TOWN PLAN IN THE CURRENT RED-COVER MICHELIN GUIDE BENELUX

Sneek (Snits in Frisian) is a small, active and very popular tourist centre. In the Middle Ages it was a port on the Middelzee, an inland sea, which has since disappeared. Sneek is situated in the centre of a region much admired for its lakes, in particular Sneekermeer which is used for various water sports. Sneek has a marina and several sailing schools. One can hire motor boats, sail boats, or take boat trips in season (apply to the VVV).

Every year regattas are organised during the great **Sneekweek**. In addition, every summer for a fortnight the *skûtsjesilen* are held on the Frisian Lakes and IJsselmeer. These are regattas with **skûtsjes**, old trading boats with brown sails and a wide, flat hull flanked by two leeboards, still found in several Frisian towns.

- **Information:** Marktstraat 18 – 8601 CV . ☎0515 41 40 96. www.sluisonline.nl.
- ▶ **Orient Yourself:** Sneek centres on its port and waterfront, but has some interesting buildings and museums around the area of the tourist information office and town hall in Markstraat.
- **Parking:** Parking is not a problem in Sneek, where provision has been made for visitors, complemented by areas to park free of charge along the waterfront.
- **Don't Miss:** The chance to enjoy a boat cruise on the Sneekermeer waters.
- **Organizing Your Time:** You could easily spend a leisurely day in Sneek. Enjoy a day in Heerenveen, which offers areas ideal for walkers and ramblers.

Sights

Waterpoort★

This elegant 1613 gateway in brick decorated with sandstone protected the entrance to the port. Its central part pierced with arcades and forming a bridge over the Geeuw is flanked by two turrets.

Fries Scheepvaart Museum/ Sneker Oudheidkamer

Kleinzand 14. ◷*Open Mon–Sat 10am–5pm, Sun noon–5pm.* ◷*Closed public holidays.* ☜*3€.* ☎*0515 41 40 57. www.friesscheepvaartmuseum.nl (in Dutch).* This maritime museum is devoted to Frisian navigation, both fluvial and maritime, with a large collection of models of ships used in the 18C and 19C, reconstructed pleasure-boat interiors, paintings, sail and mast workshops, and navigational instruments. Nine interiors have been recreated, including the delightful room from a neighbouring farm, decorated with naive 18C Frisian landscape paintings.

Excursion

Heerenveen

23km/14mi to the southeast.
Heerenveen was founded in the 16C by Frisian lords, hence its name which means the Lords' Peat or Fen. About 4km/2.5mi to the south, the flower-covered houses of **Oranjewoud** are hidden among the hundred-year-old trees of a 17C Nassau Frisian property, crossed by small canals. Two manor houses, **Oranjewoud** and **Oranjestein** (*Oranjewoud and Oranjestein;* ◷*open occasional Sat–Sun in Jul and Aug; information from the tourist office ☎0513 62 55 55),* adorn this magnificent landscape (access by Prins Bernhardlaan). The lovely municipal park, De Overtuin, and paths in the woods make it a pleasant place for walks.

Driving Tour

Friese Meren★ (Frisian Lakes)

▶ *Round tour of 134km/83mi – about 1 day – leave Sneek in the direction of Bolsward.*

The most attractive part of Friesland is without doubt this area of broads and canals with picturesque and historic villages.

Bolsward★ – *See BOLSWARD.*

▶ *Near the Workum crossroads, take a minor road towards Exmorra.*

Exmorra, Allingawier and Ferwoude are situated on the tourist route (**Aldfaers Erf**).

Exmorra

This **Fries Landbouwmuseum** (Frisian agricultural museum; ◷*open Apr–Oct, daily 10am–5pm;* ≈*2€.* ☎*0511 44 54 21; www.landbouwmuseum.nl*) uses machinery, tools and photographs to illustrate the development of agriculture in Friesland. A grocer's shop from 1885 and a village school can also be viewed. Further on, the charming 13C church on a terp, surrounded by a cemetery, has been restored.

Allingawier

Near the church with a saddleback-roofed bell-tower is a typical old **Friesland farmhouse** (◷*open Apr–Oct, daily 10am–5pm;* ☎*0515 23 16 31; www. aldfaerserf.nl*): a large building contains the huge barn and the stable, while the living quarters are on the first floor of the annexe to leave room underneath for the dairy.

Makkum

This is a picturesque fishing port on the edge of the IJsselmeer and on a canal. On the main square, the **Waag** (weigh-house) houses the Museum of Frisian Ceramics, **Fries Aardewerkmuseum DeWaag** (◷*open Apr–Oct, Mon–Sat 10am–5pm, Sun 1.30pm–5pm; Nov–Mar, Mon–Fri 10am–noon, 1pm–4pm; closed public holidays;* ≈*2€;*

☎*0515 23 14 22*), in the attic and in the adjacent house. The museum displays objects used daily or for decorative purposes (plates, platters, hot plates) from 1600–1880.

In Tichelaar's Royal Pottery and Tile Factory, **Tichelaars Aardewerk- en Tegelfabriek** (◷*open Mon–Fri 9am–5.30pm, Sat 10am–5pm;* ⋯*guided tours Mon–Fri at 11am, 1.30pm and 3pm;* ◷*closed 25, 26 Dec and 1 Jan;* ☎*0515 23 13 41; www. tichelaar.nl*), founded in 1594, one can see an exhibition of earthenware and visit the workshops to see the different stages in pottery-making.

Take the narrow road in the direction of Workum. The road runs parallel to the dyke on one side and the canal on the other. Keep your eyes open for herons.

▶ *In Gaast, turn left to reach Ferwoude.*

Ferwoude

In this locality an old farmhouse and its carpentry **workshop** (◷*open Apr–Oct, daily 10am–5pm;* ≈*4.25€;* ☎*0515 23 16 31; www.aldfaerserf.nl*) is open to the public.

Workum – *See WORKUM.*

Hindeloopen – *See HINDELOOPEN.*

Stavoren

8.5km/5.2mi from Koudum.
A fishing village, Stavoren (Starum in Frisian) has two pleasure boat harbours. It is linked to Enkhuizen by a boat service (*see ENKHUIZEN*).

Balk

Near Slotermeer, this town is on a canal bordered with several lovely 18C houses, witness to its former prosperity due to the butter trade, for which Balk was the centre.

Sloten★

Near Slotermeer and on the fringe of the wooded Gaasterland region, Sloten seems to have been built on a reduced scale, which accentuates its charm; narrow streets with tiny 17C and 18C houses run alongside the small canal lined with the trees. Following the quays, one reaches **Lemsterpoort**, an old water-gate and its **mill** of 1755 with a lovely view over the canal and the lakes.

Joure

Since the 17C this town has special-ised in clock-making. Joure is also the birthplace of Egbert Douwes, founder of the well-known brand of coffee. The **Museum Joure** (housed in the first Douwe Egberts factory; ⏱ *open Tue–Fri 10am–5pm, Sat–Mon 2pm–5pm. ⏱ Closed Easter Day, Whitsun, last Thu in Sept, 25, 31 Dec and 1 Jan; ☜3.50€; ☎0513 41 22 83; www.museumjoure.nl*) deals with the old trades of the town: coffee, tea and tobacco trade, clock-making, gold and silversmithing, cop-per casting, and the baking and printing trade, as well as the local wildlife and countryside. In the garden is a recon-struction of the labourer's cottage where Egbert Douwes was born in 1723.

Slightly north of Joure, the road runs along a narrow strip of land between two lakes; there are some fine **views**. On the left, **Sneekermeer** is one of the most frequented Frisian lakes.

Grou

Near a lake, Grou is a very popular water sports centre.

Wieuwerd

The village has a crypt with strange powers. Built in the 14C on a small terp surrounded by a cemetery and altered in the 19C, this small **church** was used as a tomb in the 17C and 18C for 11 people. The corpses were protected from decom-position by an antimonious gas which rose from the ground; four of the mum-mies are exhibited under a sheet of glass. To illustrate this phenomenon, several birds, one of which was a parrot (1879), were suspended from the vault.

Bozum

This charming village has a restored 12C and 13C **Romanesque church** built of tufa and brick in front of a tower with a saddleback roof. To the west is a semi-circle of lovely low houses. The church interior is rustic and the paintings in the chancel (c. 1300) are very faded.

▷ *Return to Sneek via ① on the town plan.*

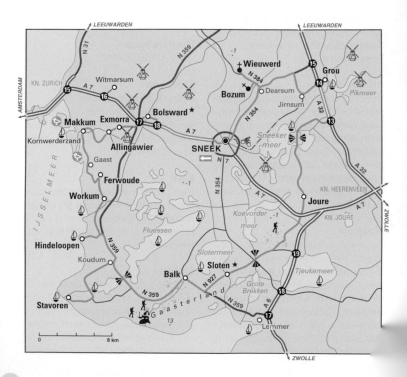

STADSKANAAL

GRONINGEN
POPULATION 34 117

In this former fenland area, which has been reclaimed as agricultural land, the villages are linear settlements strung out along the main canals, giving the impression of being one long village. Stadskanaal (canal town) is one of these, as are Veendam and Musselkanaal.

🛈 **Information:** Hoofdstraat 28, 9501 CM. ☎0599 65 06 71.

▶ **Orient Yourself:** Stadskanaal is in the northeast of the Netherlands, not far from the border with Germany.

🅿 **Parking:** Finding somewhere to park is never a problem here.

☺ **Don't Miss:** The photogenic little village of Nieuweschans.

👣 **Also See:** BOURTANGE.

Excursions

Ter Apel

20km/12.4mi to the southeast.

Ter Apel's **former convent, Museum-Klooster Ter Apel** (🕐*open Tue–Sat 10am–5pm, Sun and public holidays 1pm–5pm, 31 Dec 10am–3pm;* 🕐*closed 1 Jan;* ✆*4.50€;* ☎*0599 58 13 70; www.kloosterterapel.nl*), is pleasantly situated in a park which boasts some splendid oak trees.

The convent was originally a monastery that dated back to the middle of the 15C. The building, one of the few church structures in the region that survived the Reformation with its physical integrity reasonably intact, was restored in 1933 and now serves as a museum. Occasionally in the summer months there are special reconstruction events with historical themes and participants dressed in period costumes.

The church and two ranges of the cloisters are all that remain, and the visitor can visit the cloisters, the refectory and the cellar, where the sarcophagi that were found during excavations in the cloister garth are now on show. The chapel has been lovingly restored, and includes a number of interesting features, such as the tripartite sedila, where the priest and his assistants would sit during church rituals, and a rood screen (the screen crossing the nave of a church beneath the chancel-arch and separating the nave from the choir). What

remains of the wings of the church are a mixture of Gothic and Rococo styles.

A herb garden has been planted in the inner courtyard. The **church** has a Gothic rood screen of carved wood (1501), and stalls of the same period which are quite plain but have misericords carved with quaint figures.

Bourtange

25km/15.5mi in an easterly direction.
👣*See BOURTANGE.*

Nieuweschans

35km/21.7mi to the northeast.

This small, quiet village, with a population of around 2 000, lies in the eastern part of the province of Groningen quite near to the German border and the most easternmost point of the Netherlands. The low houses have been tastefully restored. Nieuweschans was purchased in 1628 from the Count of Oost-Friesland (now a part of Germany) and a fortress was built here. There is no trace of the castle today, but to symbolise its prior existence, a cannon has been placed on the arms of Nieuweschans, and a spear and habard appear in a cross formation on the village's flag.

Veenpark

A short walk from the village of Borger is an open-air museum spread across several old canals, consisting of a series of reconstructed villages.

STAPHORST★

OVERIJSSEL
POPULATION 15 903

The neighbouring villages of **Staphorst** and Rouveen form a world of their own. The townspeople adhere to a strict form of Protestantism and Calvinism, a bastion against the innovations of modern life: even now no cars are allowed to drive through the village while Sunday services are in progress. Some of the women, both young and old, wear the traditional costume but categorically refuse to be photographed. No visits to the village are allowed on Sundays.

- **Information:** Binnenweg 26, 7951. 0522 46 74 00. www.vvvstaphorst.nl (in Dutch and German).
- **Don't Miss:** The characteristic of local farmhouses: a line of doors along one of the side walls. The racks for the empty milk churns are often finely carved and painted.
- **Especially for Kids:** The farm museum will interest younger children.
- **Also See:** ZWOLLE.

Farmhouses★

The two villages stretch out along the road for over 8km/5mi. The thatched hall-type farmhouses (*see Introduction, Traditional Structures*) are all identical, with neatly painted green shutters and doors, blue window frames and milk churn racks, and a tree of life in the window of the front door. Two **working farm museums** (*open Apr–Oct, Mon–Sat 10am–5pm; closed public holidays; admission fee;* 0522 46 25 26; *open Jun–Sept, Mon–Fri 10am–5pm, Sat 10am–noon; closed public holidays;* 0522 46 10 87) are open to visitors.

Costumes★

The attractive woman's costume is worn quite often. Although rather sombre (black shoes, stockings and pleated skirt with a blue or black apron), it is brightened up by a floral bodice-front (*kraplap*) with a matching bonnet. A red (blue if in mourning) tartan fichu is sometimes worn over the shoulders.

Staphorst local costume

TIEL
GELDERLAND
POPULATION 41 184

Tiel is well situated on the banks of the Waal in the centre of the fruit-growing region of the **Betuwe**; the orchards make a magnificent sight when the trees are blossoming. Tiel was another of the Dutch towns that belonged to the Hanseatic League back in the 15C. Every second Saturday in September a procession, the **Fruitcorso**, celebrates the end of the **fruit-picking season**.

- **Information:** Achterweg 24001 MV Tiel. ☎0344 63 71 11. www.tiel.nl (in Dutch).
- **Orient Yourself:** Tiel, in the middle of the Netherlands, lies at the centre of the river plain situated between the Lek, Nederrijn (Lower Rhine), Waal and Maas rivers.
- **Organizing Your Time:** Half a day will give you time to walk around the town and take in the excursions.

Excursions
19km/11.8mi to the northwest

Buren

The earliest reference to any settlement here was in the late 8C. The castle, built by the lords of Buren, was first referenced at the end of the 13C.

This small town, hemmed in by its castle walls, became the seat of an earldom in 1492, which passed to the House of Orange when Anne of Buren married William the Silent.

The **old orphanage**, founded by Maria of Nassau in 1613, is a well preserved Renaissance building and has a porch with heavy ornamentation. It contains the **Museum der Koninlijke Marechaussee** (*open Apr–Oct, Mon–Fri 12.30pm–4.30pm, Sat–Sun and public holidays 1.30pm–4.30pm; otherwise by appointment only; ⊕4€; ☎0344 57 12 56; www.marechausseemuseum.nl*), which tells the story of the Dutch police. Not far away, part of the curtain wall bordering the river has been turned into a promenade and affords lovely **views** over the river and the Betuwe orchards. In the main street, Voorstraat, is a church with a 15C bell-tower crowned by an octagonal Renaissance upper section, itself topped out with a pinnacle turret. The **stadhuis**, recognisable by its

Rococo doorway, was rebuilt in the 18C. At the end of Voorstraat is a brick town **gateway** and a 1716 **wall mill**.

Culemborg

This historic village received its charter in 1318 and became the seat of an earldom in 1555. Some sections of its old walls still stand along with parts of the foundations of the castle that was built in the early 14C (it was demolished in the 18C). Culemborg was the birthplace of **Jan van Riebeeck** (1619–77), who in 1652 founded the Cape Colony (now Cape Town, South Africa) for the Dutch East India Company as a stopping place on the way to the East Indies. In **Marktplein** stands the **stadhuis**, built in the Flamboyant Gothic style. The only gateway to remain of Culemborg's old walls is the **Binnenpoort**. This gate dates from the 14C but only the lower part is that old; in the mid-16C it was topped with a tower and belfry. Entering Culemborg through Binnenpoort, with canals on either side, is a pleasant experience. The **Museum Elisabeth Weeshuis** is housed in a 16C orphanage and relates the history of Culemborg and the building. A number of original rooms (kitchen and trustees' room) have been preserved, and in the cellar a fine silver collection is on display.

TILBURG

NOORD-BRABANT

POPULATION 201 087

Tilburg is one of the Netherlands' largest towns in terms of population. Tilburg has a student population of over 25 000, with educational institutions including the Catholic University of Brabant and the Tilburg Theological Faculty. The country's first and only rock academy opened here in September 1998.

- **Information:** Spoorlaan 364 – 5038 TC. ☎0900 202 08 15. www.vvvtilburg.nl.
- ▶ **Orient Yourself:** Located on the Wilhelminakanaal, it is known as the "Modern Industrial Town" and is a flourishing business and retailing community.
- **Parking:** Parking space is tight; use the official car parks.
- **Don't Miss:** The De Pont art collection is the highlight of a visit to Tilburg.
- **Organizing Your Time:** Allow half a day at the least.
- **Especially for Kids:** The safari park beckons children of all ages.
- **Also See:** BREDA.

Fairs and Festivals

Tilburg is proud of its annual two-week July **fair**. It is also the venue for the **Festival Mundial**, focusing on the Third World, which is held in Leijpark every year in June and is the largest of its kind in the Netherlands.

A Bit of History

The town was also the birthplace of the artist **Cornelis van Spaendonck** (1756–1840) and his brother Gerardus (1746–1822), both of whom specialised in flower paintings and worked in Paris. King William II regularly stayed in Tilburg, and the distinctive neo-Gothic palace he had built on Willemsplein now houses the tourist office. The king died in Tilburg in 1849.

The economy of the town was long dominated by the **textile industry**. In 1871 there were 125 woollen mills employing 4 600 people. These were mainly family businesses with a low degree of specialisation, but they failed to keep abreast of change and were therefore unable to keep pace with increasing competition from the rest of Europe in the 1960s. The main industries now are chemicals, photographic products, paper and printing.

The industrial development of Tilburg has not been at the expense of green places where visitors can enjoy a picnic and take a walk. The main woods and parks are the Wandelbos, Oude Warande, Leypark and Wilhelminapark.

Sights

Stadhuisplein

There are quite a number of recently constructed buildings in Tilburg's main square. The shopping streets leading off to the north are now pedestrian zones.

Stadsschouwburg

The 1961 municipal theatre was the work of the architects Bejvoet and Holt. Glass curtain walls adjoin curved surfaces of bare brick.

Stadhuis

The sober lines of the black granite-clad town hall (1971) were the work of Kraayvanger. The town hall adjoins the neo-Gothic palace of King William II.

Natuurmuseum Brabant and Scryption

Open Tue–Fri 10am–5pm, Sat–Sun 1pm–5pm. Closed Easter Day, 30 Apr, 25 Dec and 1 Jan. 6€. ☎013 535 39 35. www.natuurmuseumbrabant.nl. **Scryption**: 4.50€. www.scryption.nl.

The natural history museum is located diagonally opposite the station and deals with the flora and fauna of North Brabant and the relationship between nature and man. Next door is the Scryption, a museum of written communication. Its collection includes typewriters, calculators, office machines, inkstands and pens.

De Pont ★★ (Stichting voor Hedendaagse Kunst)

🕐 *Open Tue–Sun 11am–5pm.* 💶 *6€.*
♿🚊 *013 543 83 00. www.depont.nl.*

Jan de Pont (1915–87) was a local businessman who asked that part of his estate should be used to promote modern art. A foundation was therefore set up, and at the beginning of the 1990s a former woollen mill was converted into a 4 200sq m/45 000sq ft exhibition space. This magnificent space is flooded with natural light, and is used to display a selection of the foundation's very varied art collection. This includes works by Richard Serra, Marlene Dumas, Thierry De Cordier, Gerhard Merz, Anish Kapoor, James Turrell, Jan Dibbets, Marien Schouten, Rob Birza, Guido Geelen and Richard Long. Alongside the large central hall are the former wool sheds, which are ideally suited to works requiring a more intimate display area. The museum holds temporary exhibitions, and makes its garden available to an artist in the summer.

Nederlands Textielmuseum★

Open Tue–Fri 10am–5pm, Sat–Sun noon–5pm. Closed public holidays. 6€. 013 536 74 75. www.textiel museum.nl

This museum is very appropriately housed in one of the last textile factories to survive in Tilburg. The main hall, built for large, heavy machinery, has a distinctive saw-toothed roof to maximise the amount of natural light.

The central focus of this working museum is a permanent exhibition on the textile industry in the Netherlands, which shows the technological and social changes wrought upon the industry by the advent of the steam engine. The museum's impressive working steam engine dates from 1906. There are a number of other machines of the kind used by the Tilburg wool industry. The wool arrived in the factory in large sacks, and first had to be washed. The fibres were then mechanically untangled, blended, and carded to make the fibres lie parallel; the wool could then be taken to the spinning machine. Demonstrations of some of the textile machines are given, and the museum presents various aspects of the industry: knitting, dyeing, linen manufacture and fabric-printing. The four-storey building that used to house the spinning machines is now a braid-weaving mill. There is also a visual arts section with works in which textiles play an important part, a tufting workshop and an interesting display of Dutch household textiles since 1890.

Excursions

Safari Beekse Bergen★   Kids

4km/2..5mi to the southeast via ② on the town plan. North of Hilvarenbeek. Open Jan and Dec, daily 10am–4pm; Feb, Oct and Nov, daily 10am–4.30pm; Mar–Jun and Sept, daily 10am–5pm; Jul and Aug, daily 10am–6pm. 17.50€; children 15.50€. 0900 233 57 32. www.safari park.nl (in Dutch and German).

The **safari park** (110ha/272 acres) is home to over 1 000 animals. Lions, rhinoceroses, cheetahs, giraffes, antelopes, zebras and baboons are just some of the residents of the drive-through area, which can be toured by bus or boat, or in the visitor's own car. The section with the penguins, flamingoes, squirrel monkeys and other rare species can be visited **on foot**. There is also an African village and, for children, there is an adventure **safari trail** as well as demonstrations with birds of prey, given from May to October.

Adjacent to the safari park is **Speelland Beekse Bergen**, an amusement park offering a variety of pursuits including sailing, rowing, swimming, crazy golf, trampolining and more. There is a cable car to take visitors over to the other side of the water.

Oisterwijk★

10km/6.2mi to the east via ① the town plan.

This pleasant holiday centre offers a choice of excursions in its immediate vicinity, where wooded dunes, heather-clad moors and numerous lakes are to be found. There are a number of possibilities for outdoor activity by way of cycling or walking and for further information on routes and where bicycles can be rented, contact the Oisterwijk Visitor Centre at Tienhovenlaan 5 in Oisterwijk (www.oisterwijk.nl).

In the town itself the **house** at nos 88–90 Kerkstraat, dating from 1633, has an elegant gable. De Lind, the charming square in front of the town hall, is planted with lime trees to form an avenue traditionally followed by wedding processions.

UTRECHT★★

Utrecht is a lively but intimate town with a maze of streets and numerous old buildings testifying to its long and rich history. Its picturesque canals, wharves and terraces give it a unique character; it is also a university town and a commercial centre well known for its trade fair, which was first held in 1917. The Catholic church also plays an important role. Every year a **Festival of Ancient Music**★ is held here. And during the annual **Dutch Film Festival**, the Gouden Kalf (golden calf) awards are held (see Calendar of events).

- **Information:** Vredenburg 90 – 3511 BD. ☎0900 414 14 14. www.utrechtyourway.nl.
- ▶ **Orient Yourself:** A city of two halves with a canal running through its middle, Utrecht is a sprawling city that is surprising easy to find your way around. Head for the Vredenburg square and from here most of the city's main tourist sights are within easy walking distance.
- **Parking:** Utrecht is well supplied when it comes to car parks, but they are expensive. You can park overnight free of charge after 11pm.
- **Don't Miss:** The Old Town, where beautiful period buildings house sophisicated restaurants and shops, and Kasteel De Haar, the largest castle in the Netherlands.
- **Organizing Your Time:** Allow at least a half day to really explore the Old Town of Utrecht, and another to see the museums. Try to stay overnight to enjoy its lively evening atmosphere.

A Bit of History

Utrecht was founded at the beginning of our era on the Rhine, which passed through the town at that time. Under the Roman Empire the town was called Trajectum (ford) from which it gets its present name. In the 7C it was chosen as the seat of Friesland missions. **St Willibrord** (658–739) was made Bishop of the Frisians in 695 but settled in Utrecht, Friesland then being considered a dangerous place.

At the time of Charlemagne, who extended his empire northwards, the area became part of the Carolingian Empire. After the Treaty of Meerssen, Utrecht became a fief of the German emperors. Under their domination, Bishop Balderik (918–976) succeeded in enlarging the bishopric's jurisdiction. Having become very powerful, the bishops extended their sovereignty over the present-day provinces of Utrecht, Overijssel, Drenthe and Groningen: their territory was called the **Sticht**. Born in Utrecht in 1459, **Adrian VI**, tutor to Charles V and then a professor in Leuven (Belgium), was the only Dutch pope (1522–23). Charles V took possession of the Sticht in 1528. Made an archbishopric by Philip II of Spain in 1559, the bishopric of Utrecht from that time covered all the main towns of the area, except 's-Hertogenbosch. However, the town's prosperity was coming to an end as the commercial centre of the Low Countries had moved towards the coast. In 1577 the inhabitants expelled the Spanish garrison.

The Union of Utrecht – In January 1579 the representatives of the states of Holland and Zeeland and the territories of Groningen and Utrecht, and the stadtholder of Gelderland united to sign the **Union of Utrecht**; they decided that no separate agreement would be made with Philip II, and that the Protestant religion would be the only one authorised in Holland and Zeeland, but in the other regions, practice of the Catholic religion would not lead to prosecution. In the same year, signatures were added by representatives from Overijssel, Friesland and Drenthe and some southern towns, such as Antwerp.

This treaty, following the Union of Arras by which the Duke of Parma had forced the southern states to submit to Spain, was the cause of the split between South and North Low Countries (which later became the United Provinces).

In 1635, **René Descartes** stayed in Utrecht and wrote the *Discourse on Method*, which was published in Leiden. The year 1636 was marked by the founding of Utrecht University, the second in the country after the one in Leiden.

The schism of the Old Catholics – In the 15C a first schism shook the bishopric of Utrecht, where the chapter had retained the privilege of electing its bishops. In 1423, opposition to a pontifical candidate caused a bitter conflict between the partisans of the two opposing bishops. In 1702 the Archbishop of Utrecht, Petrus Codde was accused of Jansenism and dismissed from his duties by the pope. In 1723 the Chapter of Utrecht elected a successor without pontifical agreement. Thus, in 1724, the Old Catholics Church was formed in Utrecht. A large number of French Jansenists, fleeing to the Netherlands after the condemnation of their religion by the papal bull Unigenitus in 1717, became members of this independent church with Jansenist tendencies. In 1870 a group of Germans, refusing the dogma of pontifical infallibility, joined the Church of Old Catholics in Utrecht. In 1889 a great meeting of members of this Church, coming from several countries, took place in Utrecht. This religion is still practised in the Netherlands where it has about 7 000 followers.

The Utrecht School of painting – In the 16C a school of painting with a strong Italian influence developed in Utrecht. **Jan van Scorel** (1495–1562) was born near Alkmaar, but lived in Utrecht apart from a visit to Italy and a stay in Haarlem. He helped spread the Italian influence in the Netherlands; *The Baptism of Christ* (in the Frans Halsmuseum in Haarlem) is one of his best works. His pupil, **Maarten van Heemskerck**, was also a Romanist painter (a 16C

Northern pean artist greatly influenced by the Italian Renaissance). An excellent portrait painter, Jan van Scorel also had as a pupil **Anthonis Mor** (1517–76) who made his career under the name of Antonio Moro, particularly in Spain, where he showed his talent painting the court of Philip II. At the beginning of the 17C, **Abraham Bloemaert** (1564–1651), born in Gorinchem, passed on his admiration for Italian painting to many of his pupils, including **Hendrick Terbrugghen** (1588–1629) who, born in Deventer, worked mostly in Utrecht and who, on his return from Italy, was one of the first to take his inspiration from Caravaggism (those artists greatly influenced by Caravaggio's chiaroscuro); **Gerard van Honthorst** (1590–1656), born in Utrecht and who also became a faithful imitator of Caravaggio after a visit to Italy; and **Cornelis van Poelenburgh** (c. 1586–1667), who painted with precision luminous landscapes. One who remained uninfluenced by the problems of chiaroscuro was **Jan Davidszoon de Heem** (1606–c. 83). He was born in Utrecht and lived in Leiden and then in Antwerp, and specialised in the vanitas still-life paintings.

From the 17C to the 19C – In the 17C Utrecht was a very important fortified town; today a ring of canals marks the course of the fortifications. The town was occupied by the armies of Louis XIV from 1672–74 and in 1712. Prepared in Utrecht's town hall in January 1712, the **Treaty of Utrecht** was signed in 1713 in Het Slot van Zeist (🔾 *see Excursions*) and brought an end to the Spanish War of Succession which had broken out in 1701, caused by the accession to the throne of Philip V, Louis XIV's grandson. In 1806 the King of Holland, Louis Bonaparte, stayed with his court in a private mansion in Utrecht (at nº 31 *Drift*). Utrecht was once famous for **Utrecht velvet**, which was used for covering walls and furniture.

Modern Utrecht – Utrecht has been expanding since the mid-20C and has many new quarters and buildings. Among many achievements there is a very large indoor shopping mall

Address Book

For coin ranges, see the Legend on the cover flap.

WHERE TO STAY

Utrecht is primarily a university and business town, and there are few hotels with much in the way of old-world charm.

YOUTH HOSTEL

Stayokay Utrecht-Bunnik – *Rhijnauwenselaan 14, 3981 HH Bunnik. ☎030 656 12 77. www.stayokay.com. 127 beds. 6km/4mi east of the centre by n° 40/41 bus towards Rhijnauwen.*

HOTELS

Ouwi – *F.C. Dondersstraat 12, 3572 JH. ☎030 271 63 03.www.hotel-ouwi.nl. 34 rooms and 4 studios.* This small hotel consists of a row of houses in a quiet street on the edge of town. The rooms are small and clean, with en-suite bathrooms. Good value for money.

Malie – *Maliestraat 2, 3581 SL. ☎030 231 64 24. www.maliehotel.nl. 45 rooms.* This hotel is located in a 19C building near the centre. The rooms are comfortable, with modern furnishings, and there is a terrace in the large garden.

Mitland – *Ariënslaan 1, 3573 PT. ☎030 271 58 24. www.mitland.nl. 118 rooms, 15 apartments and 2 suites.* Modern hotel in a leafy location on the outskirts, with a waterside restaurant and leisure facilities including a pool, sauna, tennis and bowling.

WHERE TO EAT

Bistro Chez Jacqueline – *Korte Koestraat 4. ☎030 231 10 89.* Friendly bistro near the tourist office.

Wilhelminapark – *Wilhelmina-park 65. ☎030 251 06 93. www.wilhelminapark.nl.* This pavilion in the park is an ideal way of escaping the hustle and bustle of Utrecht. The food is excellent, there is a view of the lake, and you can eat outside in summer.

BRASSERIES, CAFÉS, BARS, COFFEE SHOPS...

Toque toque – *Oudegracht 138. ☎030 231 87 87. www.toque.nl.* Pleasant corner café serving delicious international cuisine.

Stadskasteel Oudaen – *Oudegracht 99. ☎030 231 18 64. www.oudaen.nl.* This medieval castle is now home to a brewery, complete with copper brew-kettles, a tasting room, a waterside terrace, a restaurant, and theatre performances too.

Winkel van Sinkel – *Oudegracht 158. ☎030 230 30 36. www.dewinkel vansinkel.nl.* A meal or drink in this old warehouse provides an opportunity to admire the attractive central atrium with its glass roof and balustraded gallery.

Film-theatercafé 't Hoogt – *Slachtstraat 5. ☎030 232 83 88. www. hoogt.nl.* Busy arts café where you can watch a play or film and then have a drink afterwards.

Stairway to Heaven – *Mariaplaats 11-12. ☎030 234 03 38. www.stairway. nl.* A rock café with a restaurant. Live concerts on Wednesdays, and dancing on Thursdays, Fridays and Saturdays.

PRACTICAL INFORMATION

General information – The **VVV tourist office** is in the same complex as the Muziekcentrum Vredenburg (*Domplein 9, 3512 J, Utrecht; ☎0900 128 87 32; www.12utrecht.nl*). It offers information on sights, cultural and other events, accommodation packages, and tickets for theatre and other performances. For hotel bookings, contact **Utrecht Hotel Service** (*Vinkenburgstraat 19, 3512 AA, Utrecht. ☎030 236 00 25. www.vvvutrecht.nl*).

TRANSPORT

Parking in the streets of Utrecht is difficult and expensive; it is free only after 11pm. If you want to avoid getting ticketed or clamped, use one of the many **multi-storey car parks**, which are signposted. It is actually not possible to drive across the centre of town; instead, use the ring road. There is a park and ride site at the Galgenward stadium east of the centre. All the main sights are within walking distance of one another.

TOURS AND WALKS

The VVV sells brochures giving details of **walking routes** on various themes.

Canal running through the City

It also offers a **guided walk around town** on Sundays from mid-May to mid-September. Tours by **horse-drawn carriage** leave from Domplein.

BOAT TOURS

Tours of the canals, and further afield on the **Vecht**, the **Kromme Rijn** and to the **Loosdrechtse Plassen**: *Rederij Schuttevaer, Oudegracht opposite n° 85, ☎030 272 01 11. www.schuttevaer.com; Rederij Lovers, Nieuwekade opposite n° 269, ☎030 231 64 68. www.lovers utrecht.nl.*

SHOPPING

Hoog Catharijne is the Netherlands' largest indoor shopping precinct; another is **Shoppingcenter La Vie**, though shopping is much more interesting in the large pedestrian area in the old town. Late-night shopping is on Thursdays. For a truly authentic shopping experience, try the **Museum voor het Kruideniersbedrijf** (Grocer's Shop Museum. *Closed Sun, Mon and public holidays. Free admission. ☎030 231 66 28.*) in a small street behind the Statenkamer. This attractive shop dating from 1873 sells all kinds of old-fashioned delicacies, such as sweets, liquorice and peppermint, all measured out using copper weights. For antiques lovers the Oudegracht is the place to be.

Markets – There is a **general market** on Vredenburg every Wednesday and Saturday, and a **farmers' market** on Fridays. On Saturdays, one **flower market** takes place on the Bakker-brug and part of the Oudegracht, and another on Janskerkhof. Finally, a **fabrics market** is held in Breedstraat on Saturday mornings.

Specialities – **Boterspritsjes**, delicious butter shortbread biscuits, are a local delicacy.

THEATRES AND CONCERTS

Uitloper, a free weekly publication available in many cafés, restaurants and theatres, lists all the films, theatres and exhibitions on offer. **Vredenburg**, *Vredenburgpassage 77. ☎030 231 45 44. www.vredenburg.nl (in Dutch);* **Stadsschouwburg** (municipal theatre), Lucas Bolwerk 24. *☎030 230 20 23. www.utrecht.nl/stadsschouwburg (in Dutch);* **'t Werftheater**, *Oudegracht aan de werf 60. ☎030 231 54 40. www. werftheater.nl (in Dutch);* **Huis aan de Werf**, *Boorstraat 107. ☎030 231 53 55. www.huisaandewerf.nl (in Dutch).*

Nightlife – Utrecht is a university town, and has countless bars and cafés. There are large numbers on Janskerkhof, Neude and of course the canalside cellars where you can eat and drink outdoors in summer.

EVENTS

Bluesroute, held on the third weekend in April, offers free concerts.

©Jurjen Drenth/NBTC

the **Hoog Catharijne**, a municipal theatre (1941) by Dudok, the **Rietveld-Schröderhuis** (1924) by Rietveld and the **Kanaleneiland** (or island of canals) quarter (1962) to the west near the Amsterdam-Rijnkanaal and the **Muziekcentrum** (1979) on the Vredenburg, designed by the architect Hertzberger. The University of Utrecht has a new campus to the east, **De Uithof**. Its **Educatorium**, or educational centre, was designed by the leading Dutch architect, **Rem Koolhaas**.

Old Town★★

The tree-lined **canals**★★ (Oudegracht and Nieuwe Gracht) of Utrecht's city centre are edged by canalside quays which are much lower than the street and on to which open vaulted cellars.

Vredenburg
This large square, which links the old town with the new quarters, is the heart of Utrecht. The old fortress of Charles V stood here; the foundations were discovered during the laying out of the square. A Music Centre (**Muziekcentrum**) with an original design by the architect Herzberger was built here in 1979. The main auditorium seats 1 700 people. The VVV tourist office is also located in this complex.

To the west, the new **Hoog Catharijne** shopping mall extends to the station. This vast urban complex includes shopping galleries with air-conditioning in the basement, a large hotel, and the **Beatrixgebouw**, the main building of the Exhibition Palace (Jaarbeurs) where there are international fairs and a permanent commercial exhibition.

From Oudegracht bridge, there is a fine **view** over the canal (reach via Lange Viestraat). On the left is the open dome of the Neoclassical **Augustinuskerk** (1839).

Oudegracht★
Narrow and spanned by numerous bridges, this old canal passes through the town from one side to the other, originally linking the Rhine to the Vecht. It includes some of the city's liveliest areas, both on the upper and the lower quays, which are lined with shops and restaurants.

At the point where it forms a bend one can see the **Drakenborch**, a house rebuilt in 1968 in the old style. Opposite at n° 99, the 14C **Huis Oudaen** (*see Address Book*) has a tall façade topped by crenellations.

▶ *Cross the first bridge (Jansbrug).*

The quay on the opposite side is reserved for pedestrians. Walking along, one soon has a lovely **view**★ of the cathedral's tall tower (Domtoren).

▶ *Return to the other quay.*

On this bridge and along Oudegracht there is a flower market on Saturdays. The **Winkel van Sinkel** (1839) at the end of Oudegracht is one of the country's oldest warehouses. Both the large caryatids in the portico and the four white sculptures at the top are made of cast iron.

Pass in front of the **stadhuis** with its Neoclassical façade (1826) which conceals ruins dating from the Middle Ages. From here, there is a fine **view**★ of the continuation of the Oudegracht and of the Domtoren.

Vismarkt
In the days when this was still a fish market, fish was kept in large baskets in the canal to keep it fresh. Numerous antique shops line the canal further along from Vismarkt.

Domtoren★★
By guided tour only (1hr): Mon–Sat 10am–4pm, Sun noon–4pm. Tickets from RonDom, Domplein 9. 7.50€. Closed 25, 26, 30 and 31 Dec. 030 233 30 36. www.domtoren.nl.

This bell-tower was formerly linked by an arch to the nave of the cathedral, which was destroyed shortly after a church service in 1674 by a hurricane which also devastated the town. Built between 1321–82 in the Gothic style, restored at the beginning of the 20C, it influenced many other bell-towers in the country, of which it is the highest. Its

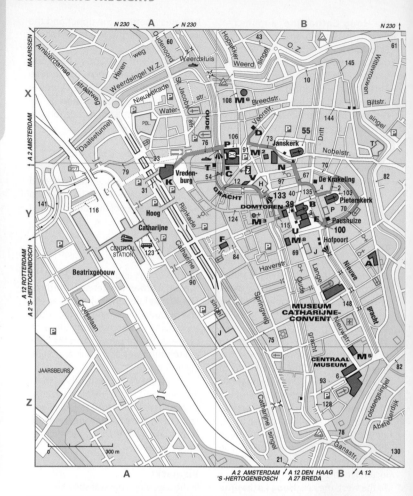

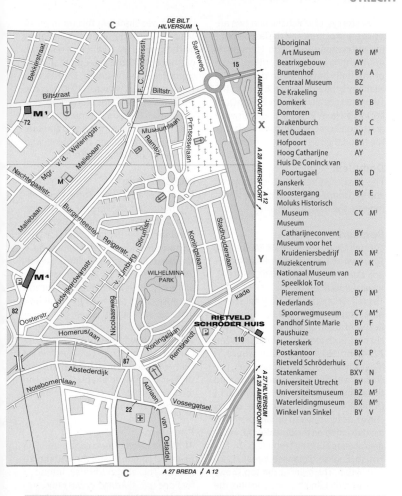

Aboriginal		
Art Museum	BY	M[8]
Beatrixgebouw	AY	
Bruntenhof	BY	A
Centraal Museum	BZ	
De Krakeling	BY	
Domkerk	BY	B
Domtoren	BY	
Drakenburch	BY	C
Het Oudaen	AY	T
Hofpoort	BY	
Hoog Catharijne	AY	
Huis De Coninck van		
Poortugael	BX	D
Janskerk	BX	
Kloostergang	BY	E
Moluks Historisch		
Museum	CX	M[1]
Museum		
Catharijneconvent	BY	
Museum voor het		
Kruideniersbedrijf	BX	M[2]
Muziekcentrum	AY	K
Nationaal Museum van		
Speelklok Tot		
Pierement	BY	M[3]
Nederlands		
Spoorwegmuseum	CY	M[4]
Pandhof Sinte Marie	BY	F
Paushuize	BY	
Pieterskerk	BY	
Postkantoor	BX	P
Rietveld Schröderhuis	CY	
Statenkamer	BXY	N
Universiteit Utrecht	BY	U
Universiteitsmuseum	BZ	M[5]
Waterleidingmuseum	BX	M[6]
Winkel van Sinkel	BY	V

three storeys, of which the first two are square and of brick and the last octagonal and of stone, soar up to 112m/367ft in height. It has a fine carillon, most of the bells having been cast by the Hemony brothers. From the tower (465 steps, tickets available from RonDom at Domplein n° 9), there is an immense and magnificent **panorama**★★ over the town and the surrounding area.

Domplein

This square lies between the Domtoren and the Domkerk. A line of paving stones indicate the nave's old layout.

Domkerk★

○*Open May–Sept, Mon–Fri 10am-5pm, Sat 10am–3.30pm, Sun 2pm–4pm; Oct–Apr, daily 11am–4pm.* ☎*030 231 04 03. www.domkerk.nl.*

The tall silhouette of its transept stands miraculously preserved from the hurricane of 1674; hidden behind it is the chancel. Both are Gothic, built between 1254 and 1517 on the site where St Maartenskathedraal once stood. The chancel with five chapels radiating round the ambulatory was inspired by that of Doornik Cathedral. The bronze **doors** (1996) are by Theo van de Vathorst; they are decorated on the outside with evangelical texts in seven languages: Dutch, Frisian, English, Japanese, Greek, Latin and Syrian. The relief at the top shows St Martin dividing his cloak. Inside, the doors depict the works of charity. Inside there are **funerary monuments**, in particular in the second chapel on the south side of the ambulatory, the tomb of Bishop Guy of Avesnes, who died in 1317. The neo-Gothic organ dates from 1831. The stained-glass windows (1926, 1936) are by Roland Holst. The Domkerk was formerly a cathedral, but this title is now held by the Catharijnekerk next to the Museum Catharijne Convent.

Utrecht University

Built at the end of the 19C in the neo-Renaissance style, the university incorporates the cathedral's old **chapter-house** (1409), now used as the main lecture hall or **Aula**. The Union of

Utrecht was signed in this room on 15 January 1579. The seven coats of arms on the stained glass windows recall the provinces and the regions that were signatories to the union. On the wall seven tapestries woven in 1936 bear the emblems of the various faculties.

The statue (1887) on the square outside the university depicts **Jan van Nassau**, the brother of William the Silent, who instigated the Union of Utrecht.

Kloostergang

A replica of a 10C runic stone from Jelling (Denmark), evoking the conversion of the Danes to Christianity, stands at the entrance to the 15C cathedral cloisters. Around the cloisters, the gables have low reliefs illustrating the life of St Martin, patron saint of the old cathedral and of the city. The **view** of the transept and the apse of the cathedral from this intimate cloister garden is very pretty. Go past a fountain with a statue of a canon writing to reach the south side of the cloisters. In the street called Achter de Dom (meaning behind the cathedral) is the back of the old chapterhouse. The medieval building beside it is a cloisterhouse where canons lived.

Pausdam

At the junction of two canals, this is a beautiful square where the **Paushuize** stands. This elegant house, intended for Pope (*paus*) Adrian VI was only completed in 1523, the year of his death. The stepped gable on the canal has a statue of the Saviour.

Nieuwegrach

This canal is similar to the Oudegracht, but is lined with elegant residences. One can see Hofpoort, a 17C Baroque doorway of the Law Courts, and n° 37, a lovely old house. Further on, at n° 63, is the Museum Catharijneconvent (see below). From the bridge, a fine **view** over the canal and Domtoren can be found.

▶ *Walk back to Pausdam and turn into the picturesque Kromme Nieuwegracht. The houses on the left side all have their own little bridges.*

Pieterskerk

🕐 *Open Tue–Sat 11am–4.30pm.*
☎ *030 231 14 85.*

This early-Romanesque church was built in 1048. Pieterskerk is one of the four churches Bishop **Bernulphus** had built to form the shape of a cross round what was then St Maartenskathedraal. Two of these churches have disappeared: abbey church of St Paulusabdij and St Mariakerk, where only the cloisters remain. The two others, Pieterskerk and Janskerk are all that remain of the famous **Bernulphus's Cross** of Churches. The vaults in the transept are Gothic, but the nave with its wooden barrel vault supported by ten red columns is Romanesque. Four **Mosan low reliefs**★ (c. 1170), found during the church's restoration, are embedded in the wall in front of the raised chancel. They show the Judgement of Christ by Pilate, the crucifixion, the angel outside the empty tomb and the three Marys with the herbs. The Romanesque baptismal font has corners decorated with heads. In the chapel to the left one can see the remains of Romanesque frescoes showing the Virgin on the moon's crescent. **Concerts** are given on the new organ at the far end of the church.

Crypt★

The groined vaulting is supported by stout fluted columns. In the apse there is a red sandstone sarcophagus which contains the remains of Bishop Bernulphus, founder of the church.

At n° 8, on the corner of Achter St Pieter and Keistraat, there is a lovely 17C house, **De Krakeling**; the front is decorated with festoons and the door with a palm tree.

Janskerkhof

On Saturdays, the beautiful 17C and 18C houses around this square provide a picturesque backdrop to the colourful flower market. In the middle of the square is the Romanesque-Gothic **Janskerk**, founded by Bishop Bernulphus as the northern end of the cross of churches. The building has undergone major restoration and houses, among other things, an early music performance centre. The small building (1683)

with a coat of arms opposite the church is the **main guardhouse** of the States of Utrecht, whose members met in the Statenkamer opposite. In front of it is a **statue of Anne Frank**, and to the right an equestrian statue of **St Willibrord**. To the south of the square is the old restored **Statenkamer**, where the States General of the province met. This building, which originally belonged to a monastery of Friars Minor, is now the law faculty of Utrecht University.

Post Office

Despite what its exterior might suggest, this building on Neude is pleasantly well lit inside. It was designed in the style of the Amsterdam School by J Crouwel and built between 1918 and 1924. The extraordinary **parabola vaulting**★ is made up of lines of glazed yellow brick and glass, and the imposing black statues symbolise the five continents, trade and prosperity. The statue in the vestibule represents mail sent by land (horses), sea (fish) and air (birds).

Huis De Coninck van Poortugael

Dating from 1619, the "House of the King of Portugal" has a charming Mannerist façade with a crow-stepped gable; above the ground-floor windows are the coats of arms of Nijmegen and Portugal. The man in the centre with a sceptre is King Philip III of Portugal and Spain. The heads of an ox and two rams on the façade on the other side of the street belong to the former **Grote Vleeshuis**, or meat market (1637).

The Museum District

The Utrecht Museum District, established in 1995 in the old town and comprising the following museums, forms the historic cultural heart of Utrecht.

Nationaal Museum van Speelklok tot Pierement★

🕐 *Open Tue–Sun and public holidays 10am–5pm.* 🕐 *Closed 30 Apr, 25 Dec and 1 Jan.* 🚫 *8€.* ♿ ☎ *030 231 27 89. www. museumspeelklok.nl.*

Located in an old five-aisled Gothic church, the Buurkerk, this museum has a magnificent collection of 18C to 20C **mechanical musical instruments**★★. The guide operates a number of these during the tour. Exhibited are old clocks and music boxes, pianolas and orchestrions made for cafés and dance halls, a Steinway player piano (1926) and a Hupfeld automatic violin (1910). The museum also houses a superb collection of barrel organs, small street organs and enormous fair or dance organs (*see Introduction, Music*).

Aboriginal Art Museum

🕐*Open Tue–Fri 10am–5pm, Sat–Sun 11am–5pm.* 🕐*Closed 30 Apr, 25 Dec and 1 Jan.* ✆*8€.* ✆*030 238 01 00. www. aamu.nl.*
This new museum contains collections of contemporary Aboriginal art, including paintings (some on bark), ceremonial sculptures, memorial stones, didgeridoos and utensils.

Museum Catharijneconvent★★

🕐*Open Tue–Fri 10am–5pm, Sat–Sun and public holidays 11am–5pm.* 🕐*Closed 1 Jan.* ✆*8.50€.* ♿✆*030 231 38 35. www. catharijneconvent.nl.*
This large museum of religious art is housed in the Late Gothic convent of St Catherine (originally a monastery belonging to the Knights of St John) and an 18C canalside house. It is devoted to the history of Christianity in the Neth-

Breviary belonging to Beatrijs of Assendelft, Delft, (c. 1485)

erlands, and has the country's largest collection of **medieval art**★★★. The very varied collections are beautifully displayed. They include magnificent liturgical robes (such as the 15C cope of David of Burgundy), manuscripts and miniatures (including the finely worked evangeliarum of Lebuinus, gold and silver objects, sculptures, altarpieces and paintings by such artists as Geertgen tot Sint Jans, Jan van Scorel, Rembrandt, Frans Hals, and Pieter Saenredam. The history of the Catholic and Protestant churches, and events such as the Iconoclasm and the Reformation, are inextricably tied up with that of the country as a whole. The differences between the two churches are explored in the canalside house, focusing on such themes as church interiors, the different church services, the role of religion in everyday life, and the relationship between church and state. The **St Catherinakerk** can also be visited from the museum (subject to certain conditions).

Universiteitmuseum★

🕐*Open Tue–Sun 11am–5pm.* 🕐*Closed 30 Apr, 24, 25, 31 Dec and 1 Jan.* ✆*7€.* ✆*030 53 80 28. www.museum.uu.nl.*
This museum is the home of the collections built up by Utrecht University since it was established in 1636. The visit begins with the **Bleulandkast**★, dating from 1816, which contains an impressive collection of medical preparations and wax models. A permanent exhibition, **Geleerd in Utrecht** (Learned in Utrecht), retraces 360 years of university education and includes the standard metre and kilogram, which the Netherlands received from France's Metre Committee in 1799 to bring an end to the differences between weights and measures in different countries. On the second floor are **collections**★ relating to dentistry and ophthalmology, with often bizarre instruments and models displayed in rotation. The **Rarities collection** between the two includes stuffed animals, skeletons and fossils. The museum also organises temporary exhibitions. **Jeugdlab** is a laboratory specifically designed for the younger visitors.

Behind the museum is the **Old Botanical Garden** (1724), with greenhouses, orangeries, a seed-house, a herb garden and ginkgo trees.

The **Beyerskameren**, a late 16C almshouse with a courtyard, is located at the end of Lange Nieuwstraat on the left. The impressive Baroque building in Agnietenstraat is the **Fundatie van Renswoude**, built in 1756 as a school for orphans. Around the corner to the left is a row of beautiful small almshouses, the **Kameren Maria van Pallaes**, founded in 1651.

Centraal Museum★★

Open Open Tue–Sun noon–5pm, Fri noon–9pm. Closed 30 Apr, 25 Dec and 1 Jan. 8€. 030 236 23 62. www.centraalmuseum.nl.

This museum is housed in the former monastery of St Agnes and contains rich collections relating mainly to Utrecht. The **pre-20C painting collection** (*main building, ground floor*) includes work by Jan van Scorel, Abraham Bloemaert and the Utrecht School, Pieter Saenredam, and the Utrecht Caravaggists Hendrick Terbrugghen and Gerard Honthorst. This section also includes a fine 17C **doll's house**. The **modern painting collection** (*main building, first floor*) is dominated by the Utrecht surrealist **Moesman** and the magic realists **Pyke Koch** and **Carel Willink**. The **Van Baaren collection** (*medieval wing, first floor*) contains work by late 19C and early 20C Dutch and French artists (Breitner, Van Gogh, Isaac Israëls, Daubigny, Maris and Verster). The **Kids Centraal** exhibitions (*medieval wing, top floor*) are specifically for children. The most important exhibit in the archaeology department (*medieval wing, basement*) is the **Utrecht Ship**, which is made from one single tree trunk. It dates from 997 and was excavated in Utrecht in 1930. The Chapel contains **medieval sculptures** from the time when Utrecht was the main religious centre in the Northern Netherlands. And finally, the Stables house a display devoted to the **topography of Utrecht** and contain a Louis XVI drawing-room and the 1926 Rietveld Harrenstein bedroom. The museum also holds major temporary exhibitions.

The wing on the opposite side of Agnietenstraat contains the **Rietveld collection**, which uses scale models and chairs (including the red and blue chair) to give an overview of the work of this famous architect. There is also a room dedicated to **Dick Bruna**, the creator of the popular picture books for toddlers.

Nederlands Spoorwegmuseum★

Open Tue–Sun 10am–5pm. Closed 30 Apr and 1 Jan. 12.50€. 030 230 62 06. www.spoorwegmuseum.nl.

The former Maliebaan Station is the setting for the Dutch Railway Museum, which illustrates the history of the Dutch railways, beginning with the evolution from horse-drawn carriages to the first steam train. The Netherlands' first railway was built between Amsterdam and Haarlem in 1839. Excellent scale models and films give an idea of the subsequent history of railways, from the steam locomotive to the high-speed train.

Outside on the tracks (no longer used) there are more than 60 locomotives, carriages and tramcars. One of the museum's highlights is a reconstruction of the engine *De Arend* (the eagle) which in 1839 with another engine (*De Snelheid*) drew the first train to run in the Netherlands. There is also a signal box, an evocative reconstruction of a station, a children's railway and an exciting multimedia display called **Holland-RailShow**.

Additional Sights

Bruntenhof

The main entrance to this picturesque 1621 **almshouse** has a Baroque portal. The Leeuwenberchkerk (1567) on the left was once part of a pest-house, used for victims of the Plague.

Kloostergang van St Marie

Only the Romanesque cloisters in brick remain of this church built in the 11C, one of the four churches of Bernulphus' Cross (see Pieterskerk).

P. Gajic/MICHELIN

Rietveld Schröderhuis

Waterleidingmuseum

🕐*Open Tue–Fri and Sun 1.30pm–5pm, Sat 11am–4pm.* 🚫*Closed public holidays.* ⏏*2€.* ☎*030 248 72 11. www.water leidingmuseum.nl (in Dutch).*
This fine water-tower, dating from 1895, chronicles the history of the mains water supply and of washing and ironing. It also offers a fine view of the town.

Moluks Historisch Museum

🕐*Open Tue–Sun 11am–5pm.* 🚫*Closed Easter Day, 25 Apr, 25 Dec and 1 Jan.* ⏏*4.50€.* ☎*030 236 71 16. www.museum -maluku.nl.*
This museum deals with the history and culture of the Moluccan people of Indonesia, from their war with Japan to the arrival of the first immigrants in the Netherlands in 1951. Temporary exhibitions are also held.

Rietveld Schröderhuis★★

🕐*Open Tue–Sun noon–5pm, Fri noon– 9pm.* 🚫*Closed 30 Apr, 25 Dec and 1 Jan.* ⏏*8€.* ☎*030 236 23 10 (Centraal Museum). www.centraalmuseum.nl.*
Restored after the owner's death (Mrs Schröder, in 1985), this world-famous house, built in 1924, illustrates perfectly the architectural theories of the **De Stijl** movement to which **Gerrit Rietveld** (1888–1964) belonged. In response to Mrs Schröder's demands (she attached

a great deal of importance to communicating with nature; every room has a door to the outside) Rietveld created an open plan where the different elements placed at right angles determined the space. Rietveld limited himself to neutral tones (white and grey) for the large surfaces, and primary colours for linear details. Visiting the interior enables one to appreciate the originality of the layout. On the ground floor the rooms are clearly divided, while the first floor is a large open space with sliding partitions to close off the living room and bedrooms.

Het Geldmuseum (Royal Coin Collection)

🕐*Open Tue–Fri 10am–5pm, Fri–Sat noon–5pm.* 🚫*Closed 30 Apr, 25 Dec and 1 Jan.* ⏏*7€.* ☎*071 516 09 99. www.geld museum.nl (in Dutch).*
A new museum that opened in 2007 with a large collection of coins relating to the Netherlands and its colonies.

Excursion

Zeist

10km/6.2mi. Leave Utrecht by Biltsestraatweg.
Zeist is a charming and elegant holiday resort nestling among lush woods. From

the centre of the town a path leads to the **stately home of Slot Zeist**, built between 1677 and 1686 by Willem van Nassau-Odijk with interiors designed by Daniël Marot. **The Treaty of Utrecht** was signed here in 1713. The building was originally surrounded by magnificent grounds. It is now used as a conference and exhibition centre. The 18C buildings on **Broeder- en Zusterplein**, on either side of the drive, belong to the **Moravian Brotherhood** community, refugees from Moravia and Bohemia and disciples of Jan Hus, who was burnt at the stake in 1415.

Driving Tour

Loosdrechtse Plassen★★

▶ *Round tour of 70km/44mi – allow 1 day. Leave Utrecht via Sartreweg.*

Set between lush green strips of land, these lakes cover about 3 600ha/8 900 acres producing an unspoilt landscape known as the Water Garden of the Netherlands. The **Loosdrechtse Plassen**★★ are flooded peat workings that go back to the 14C. Particularly favourable for water sports, they are served by numerous pleasure boat harbours. Authentic farmsteads and splendid villas line the road.

Westbroek

The picturesque route is edged by canals spanned by small bridges, each one leading to a house surrounded by a charming garden.
After **Breukeleveen** the road follows the lakeshore; there is a fine **view**.

Kasteel-Museum Sypesteyn

By guided tour only (1hr): Apr and Oct, Sat–Sun and public holidays noon–5pm; May–Sept, Tue–Fri 10am–5pm, Sat–Sun and public holidays noon–5pm. 7.50€. ☎035 582 32 08. www.sypesteyn.nl.
This castle is located just outside **Nieuw-Loosdrecht**; it was rebuilt based on old illustrations between 1912 and 1927, and was later turned into a museum. Displayed inside are furniture, portraits,

sculptures, weapons, silverware, clocks and especially Loosdrecht porcelain. The park has a rose garden, an orchard and a maze.

Oud-Loosdrecht

This is the main tourist centre in the region. It has a large pleasure boat harbour.

▶ *Turn right then left towards Vreeland.*

The road soon returns to the lake; it has lovely views.

Vreeland

An attractive **lever bridge** makes it possible to cross the Vecht, which is then rejoined at Loenen aan de Vecht. The **Vecht**, formerly a busy waterway, was replaced in 1952 as the main link from the Rhine to Amsterdam (Amsterdam-Rijnkanaal). The road runs along this peaceful and winding river, on whose banks are charming villas and small manor houses surrounded by magnificent parks.

Loenen

This small town with trim houses bedecked with flowers has a tall stage mill with a handrail called De Hoop (hope).

Breukelen

In the 17C this locality gave its name to a quarter in New York founded by Dutch settlers: Breukelen, pronounced in English as Brooklyn.
To the south of Breukelen, there is a pleasant **route**★ which offers views of lovely estates on the banks of the Vecht. To the right of the road the 17C castle **Kasteel Nijenrode** now houses Nijenrode University.

Kasteel De Haar★

Guided tours only (hourly): mid-Mar–May and mid-Oct –mid-Nov, Tue–Sun, 1pm–4pm; Jun–mid-Aug, Mon–Fri 11am–4pm, Sat–Sun 1pm–4pm; mid-end Nov and Jan–mid-Mar, Sun 1pm–4pm. Castle and Gardens 8€; gardens only 3€. ☎030 677 85 15. www.kasteelhaar zuilens.nl.

NBTC

Kasteel De Haar

Standing to the west of **Haarzuilens** in the middle of a large park, this moated castle is the largest in the Netherlands. It was built in 1892 by PJH Cuypers, the architect of the Rijksmuseum in Amsterdam, in neo-Gothic style. The enormous brick construction was erected on the site of the old medieval castle and on soil consisting partly of clay and partly of sand, and as a result is gradually being damaged by subsidence. It is hoped that extensive restoration work will remedy this problem.

The main building, with pepper-pot roof towers, is surrounded by wide moats and linked to a large fortified gateway by a covered bridge. The pentagonal inner courtyard has a steel roof, exacerbating the subsidence. The interior, which is still inhabited in summer, contains the

Belle, the Rebel of the Vecht

Isabella Agneta Elisabeth van Tuyll van Serooskerken, known for short as Madame de Charrière or Belle van Zuylen, still appeals to the modern imagination. This feminist before her time was born at Slot Zuylen on 20 October 1740, and spent her summers there and winters at the family's canalside house in Utrecht. She caused a great stir in the salons of Utrecht and The Hague with her interest in literature, science, philosophy and music, her unconventional attitudes and above all her satirical view of the aristocracy. When her first novel *Le Noble* was published in Paris and Amsterdam in 1763, her enraged father bought up all the copies and had them destroyed.

Belle van Zuylen's independent attitude was perhaps best illustrated when the famous Scottish writer, James Boswell, asked for her hand in marriage. Her reply was short and to the point: "I have no talent for subservience." At the age of 31, however, she escaped the stifling atmosphere of her parents' home by marrying a Swiss, Charles-Emmanuel de Charrière de Penthaz. She moved to Neuchâtel in Switzerland, where she died in 1805. Belle wrote of her marriage: "I still feel that my thoughts, words and deeds are unhindered. I have a different name and do not always sleep alone, but that is all that has changed."

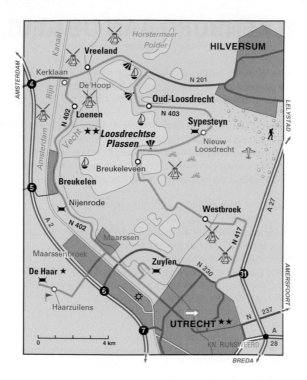

exceptional **collections**★ of Baron van Zuylen van Nijevelt, notably lovely old furnishings paintings and porcelain. The 19C bathroom, still in working order, is also worthy of note.

▶ *Return to Haarzuilens, cross over the motorway and the canal, then turn right, then left to reach Oud-Zuilen.*

Slot Zuylen

By guided tour only (1hr): mid-Mar–mid-May and mid-Sept–mid-Nov, Sat 2pm–4pm, Sun 1pm–4pm; mid-May–mid-Sept, Tue–Thu 11am–4pm, Sat 2pm–4pm, Sun 1pm–4pm. 7€. 030 244 02 55. www.slotzuylen.nl.

Situated near the Vecht at **Oud-Zuilen**, this castle is a solid medieval moated castle. It was originally built in the 13thC; it was rebuilt c. 1751, although parts of the castle dating to the 16C are still standing, and four octagonal towers were added.

Belle van Zuylen was born here in 1740 and a large part of her early life was spent in and around Slot Zuylen.

The castle houses ancient objects illustrating the daily life of the past, lovely furniture, a richly endowed library and a Chinese porcelain collection. One room is decorated with a large tapestry (1643) woven in Delft. In the modest rooms where Belle van Zuylen lived, a bust of her, a few books and some engravings evoke the life of the writer.

Belle's sophistication is reflected in her many letters, including her 11 years of passionate correspondence with the Baron d'Hermenches, and in her novels and plays. She was a friend of Benjamin Constant and Madame de Staël, and wrote in French, the international language of 18C culture.

The large gardens surrounding the castle are landscaped in a variety of styles and can be walked around freely until 5pm.

▶ *Return to Utrecht by Amsterdam-sestraatweg.*

VALKENBURG AAN DE GEUL★

LIMBURG – POPULATION 17 180

It is a bustling and fairly fashionable holiday resort with a casino and a health spa, the Thermae 2000. The town has preserved two fortified gateways: 14C **Grendelpoort** and 15C **Berkelpoort** with its footbridge.

Marl-stone, a sort of limestone, predominates in the surrounding hilly country-side as at St Pietersberg not far from Maastricht. Yellow marl-stone has been quarried locally for centuries as a building stone. A certain number of the caves and galleries (*70km/44mi*) can now be visited, and quite a number have been transformed into museums or other tourist attractions.

- **Information:** *Th.* Dorrenplein 5 – 6301 DV. ☎0900 97 98. www.vvvzuidlimburg.nl.
- ▶ **Orient Yourself:** Valkenburg is a small old town situated in the charming Geul Valley, between two branches of the river.
- **Don't Miss:** The charcoal drawings at Gemeentegrot.
- **Organizing Your Time:** There is plenty to see, and if the excursion is undertaken a whole day is needed; an overnight stay suggests itself.
- **Also See:** MAASTRICHT.

Sights

Castle ruins

Open Jan–Mar, Tue–Sun 10am–4.30pm, Mon 11am–1.45pm; Apr–Sept, daily 10am–5.30pm (6pm Jul–Sept); Oct–Dec daily 10am–4.30pm. *Closed Carnival, 25, 26 Dec and 1 Jan.* 3.25€. ☎043 609 01 10. www.kasteelvalkenburg.nl.

The ruins of the castle of the lords of Valkenburg dominate the town. Only parts of walls and broken arches still remain. The castle was built in c. 1115 and was subjected to a great number of sieges. In 1672 it was blown up by order of the King-Stadtholder, William III. From the top of the ruins there is a fine view of the town and the Geul valley.

Fluweelengrot

By guided tour only (1hr): Jan–Easter, Mon–Fri at noon, 1.30pm, Sat–Sun and during school holidays 11am–3pm; Easter–Jun, Sept and Oct, daily 11am–4pm; Jul and Aug, daily 11am–5pm; Nov and Dec, Sat–Sun 11am–3pm. *Closed Carnival, 25, 26 Dec and 1 Jan.* 4.95€; combination of Castle Ruins and Fluweelengrot 6.50€. ☎043 609 01 10. www.kasteelvalkenburg.nl.

This system of caves, which is connected to the castle by secret passages, is named after the former owner, Fluwijn. Like the Gemeentegrot (municipal cave), the Fluweelengrot (temperature inside: 10°C/50°F) is an old marl-stone quarry where refugees sought shelter, to which the many drawings and low reliefs bear witness.

Steenkolenmijn Valkenburg★

Guided tours (75 minutes including short film): Apr–Oct, daily hourly from 10am–5pm; Nov–Christmas, daily tours at noon, 1.30pm and 3pm; after Christmas–Mar, Mon–Fri at 2pm. *Closed Carnival, 25 Dec and 1 Jan.* 7.25€. ☎043 601 24 91. www.steenkolenmijn.nl.

A coal mine has been reconstructed in the galleries of an old quarry (*see Introduction, Industrial heritage*). The visit provides information on the methods of coal extraction as practised in Limburg before the last workings were closed. A film from 1966 provides a realistic picture of a coal mine, then walk along the galleries to see the trains used for the transportation of miners or coal, the water pumps, the shaft supports, the systems for evacuating the coal and the safety systems. A number of animal fossils are also on display.

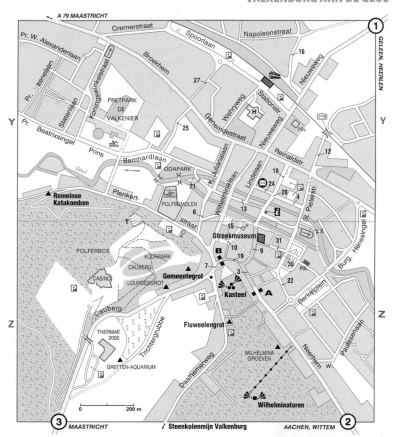

VALKENBURG			Hekerbeekstr.	Y	12	Plenkertstr.	YZ	
			Jan Dekkerstr.	Y	13	Poststr.	Y	24
Berkelstr.	Z	3	Kerkstr.	Z	15	Prinses Margrietlaan	Y	25
Dr Erensstr.	Y	4	Kloosterweg	Y	16	Sittarderweg	Y	27
Emmalaan	Y	6	Louis van der Maessenstr.	Y	18	Theodoor Dorrenpl.	Y	28
Grendelpl.	Z	7	Muntstr.	Z	19	Walrampl.	Z	30
Grotestr.	Z	9	Oranjelaan	Y	21	Walravenstr.	Z	31
Halderstr.	Z	10	Palankastr.	Z	22	Wilhelminalaan	YZ	

Berkelpoort	Z	A		Grendelpoort		Z	B

Gemeentegrot★

By guided tour only, on foot (1hr) or by miniature train (30min): daily from 10.15am–4pm in summer (see website for full schedule of tour times). ⊘*Closed 25, 26 Dec and 1 Jan.* ≤*5€.* ☎*043 601 22 71. www.gemeentegrot.nl.*

These are ancient marl quarries (14 °C/57°F) which were already known to the Romans. They sheltered the population in time of war, notably in September 1944 upon the town's liberation. The walls are covered with charcoal drawings and low reliefs, some repre-senting the animals whose fossils have been found in the sedimentary marl-stone, such as the Mosasaurus (*see MAASTRICHT: Excursions*); others rep-resent artistic (Mona Lisa) or religious subjects. The stone was gradually quar-ried downwards, leaving some drawings placed very high up.

Wilhelminatoren

Access either by car from Daalhemerweg, then turn left, or by chairlift.
From the top of the tower (160 steps), 30m/98ft high, there is a good view of

the town's wooded surroundings. There are also two toboggan runs.

Roman Catacombs
Open Apr–Aug and school holidays, daily 11am–4pm. Sept–Mar, Sat–Sun 2pm, or by appointment. 5.50€. 043 601 25 54.
In the old quarries 14 Roman catacombs have been reconstructed. They were designed by the architect of the Rijksmuseum PJH Cuypers, based on drawings by archaeologists.

Streekmuseum
Open Tue–Fri 10am–5pm, Sat–Sun 1pm–5pm. Closed 25, 26 Dec and 1 Jan. 2.70€. 043 601 63 94. www.streekmuseumvalkenburg.nl.
Objects found during excavations of the castle and reconstructed workshops and mementoes of marksmen's guilds are exhibited here.

Station
The oldest in the Netherlands, this neo-Gothic station dates from 1853.

Driving Tour

Zuid-Limburg★
Round tour of 58km/36mi – about half a day

Southern Limburg is a transitional region between the Dutch plains and the Ardennes hills jutting out between Belgium and Germany. It is a rural area whose appearance is not marred by the region's coal mines. Its fertile plateaux, lush valleys, its fields shaded by apple trees, its hilltops from which can be seen vast stretches of countryside, form a pleasant landscape dotted with fine manor houses and white half-timbered farms (see Introduction, Traditional Structures).

▶ *Leave Valkenburg by ② on the town plan, going eastwards in the direction of Gulpen.*

The road follows the verdant Geul Valley.

Oud-Valkenburg
On the left is the fine 17C **Kasteel Schaloen**, restored in the 19C by Cuypers. The park is watered by a branch of the Geul. A little further on, behind a chapel, is **Kasteel Genhoes**, built in the 16C and 18C and surrounded by moats.
After Wijlre, notice on the left **Huis Cartils**, in the middle of a fine park.

Wittem
On the right, the **Kasteel Wittem** is a 15C building, restored in the 19C in the neo-Gothic style. It is now a hotel and restaurant. A road over the plateau leads to Vaals.

Zuid-Limburg landscape

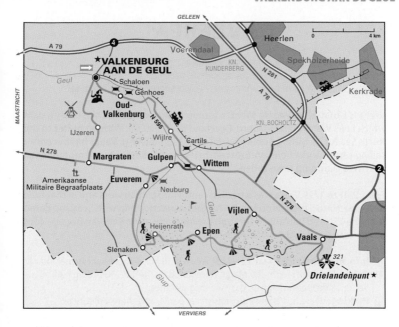

Vaals

This busy resort owes its lively atmosphere to the proximity of the German frontier and Drielandenpunt.

A winding road climbs through the woods to Drielandenpunt. 500m/546.8yd before the end of the road, on the left, there is a fine **view**★ of Aachen.

Drielandenpunt★

This site is the meeting point (*punt*) of three (*drie*) countries' (*landen*) frontiers: Germany, Belgium and the Netherlands. It is also the highest point in the Netherlands being at 321m/1 053ft. From the top of the **Boudewijntoren** there is a **panorama**★ over the region.

Vijlen

This village still has a few half-timbered houses to admire.

By a road through the woods one reaches the road from Vaals to Epen: pretty **view** over the hills to the south.

Epen

Resort where several houses still have half-timbered walls. On the edge of the village (*turn left before the church*) is a

fine half-timbered farmhouse The climb gives fine **views**★ over the frontier hills to the south.

After Heijenrath there is a fine **view** on the right over Gulp Valley which one crosses at **Slenaken**, a small frontier village. Then follow the river towards the resort of Gulpen.

Euverem

In pools near the Gulp, trout are farmed; some of them are sent to nearby fishing waters. At the junction of the N 278, on the right there is a **view** of **Kasteel Neuburg**, which is now a hotel.

Gulpen

A resort at the confluence of the Gulp and the Geul.

Margraten

To the west of this town lies the **Netherlands American Military Cemetery**. On the walls the names of the 1 722 missing are engraved. In the cemetery lie the graves of 8 301 soldiers marked out by crosses.

VEERE ★

ZEELAND
POPULATION 21 974
LOCAL MAP SEE DELTA
TOWN PLAN IN THE CURRENT RED-COVER MICHELIN GUIDE BENELUX

Veere is situated on **Veerse Meer**, a former branch of the sea closed by a dam which links Walcheren to Noord-Beveland (ℹ *see DELTA*). With no outlet to the North Sea for its fishing boats (the dam was built in 1961), Veere has become a sailing centre and a holiday resort. With its paved alleyways and monuments, Veere is a charming town full of character.

From 1541 to 1799 Veere was a trading centre for Scottish wool and in that time developed into a prosperous port. This special relationship with Scotland dated from the 15C and had arisen through the marriage of Wolfert van Borsele, lord of Veere, to the daughter of King James I of Scotland.

- **Information:** Oudestraat 28 – 4351 AV. ☎0118 50 13 65. www.vvvzeeland.nl.
- ▶ **Orient Yourself:** From the Markt, dominated by the 15C–16C town hall, all Veere's sights are within an easy walking distance.
- 🅿 **Parking:** Veere has a few inexpensive car parks, and there's plenty of off-street parking.
- 😊 **Don't Miss:** The courtroom at the Oude Stadhuis; it is elaborately decorated and one of the oldest in the Netherlands.
- 🕐 **Organizing Your Time:** Veere is compact and offers a wonderful way to spend a couple of hours leisurely walking among its fine buildings.
- ♿ **Also See:** MIDDDELBURG.

Sights

Campveerse Toren

This 15C tower is part of the town's old fortifications. It is built of brick and decorated with bands of white stone and has a crow-stepped gable. It has been a tavern for the past five centuries.

Schotse Huizen ★

Kade 25 and 27. 🕐*Open Apr–Oct, daily 1pm–5pm.* 🕐*Closed 30 Apr and Ascension Day.* ♿*3€.* ☎*0118 50 17 44. www. schotsehuizen.nl.*
Built in the 16C in the Flamboyant Gothic style, these two buildings were used as offices and warehouses by the

Campveerse Toren

©Wessel Cirkel/Dreamstime.com

Scottish-wool merchants who lived in Veere. At n° 25 the façade stone depicts a lamb, symbol of the wool trade, and at n° 27 an ostrich; both illustrate the name of the house. Inside there are Zeeland costumes and a reconstruction of a typical back room.

Oude Stadhuis★

🕑 *Open Jun–Aug, Mon–Sat 1pm–5pm.* 🕑 *Closed during weddings.* ☎*0118 50 60 64.*

This two-storey Gothic building, made of sandstone, was started in 1474. The windows on the first floor are separated by recesses surmounted by canopies, under which are the statues of the four lords and three ladies of Veere. These statues (1934) replace the original ones, which are now kept in the Schotse Huizen. The roof is dominated by a 1599 onion-shaped belfry with a **carillon** of 48 bells.

In the **courtroom** (*ground floor*), one of the oldest in the Netherlands, there is the silver gilt goblet which **Emperor Charles V** gave to Count Maximilian of Buren in 1548. The portraits displayed in the **council chamber** depict marquesses and marchionesses from Veere, members of the house of Orange-Nassau.

Grote Kerk or Onze Lieve Vrouwekerk

🕑*Open Apr–Oct, Mon–Sat 10am–5pm, Sun 1pm–5pm.* ☎*0118 50 18 29.*

A massive 15C structure in the Brabant Gothic style, with a large tower which was never completed. In the 19C it became a hospital and barracks; traces of that time are still visible in the windows. Today it houses a cultural centre.

VENLO

LIMBURG

POPULATION 92 080

PLAN OF THE CONURBATION IN THE CURRENT RED-COVER MICHELIN GUIDE BENELUX

In the northern part of the province of Limburg, near the German-Dutch frontier, Venlo is a small industrial town on the banks of the Maas.

- 🅸 **Information:** Koninginneplein 2 – 5911 KK. ☎077 354 38 00. www.vvvvenlo.nl (in Dutch).
- ▶ **Orient Yourself:** From the station head for Koninginneplein and from here it's a gentle walk to the main attractions of Venlo and the Maas river.
- 🅿 **Parking:** Venlo has a number of car parks dotted around the town, including by the riverside and the train station.
- 😒 **Don't Miss:** The richly carved Gothic stalls of St Martinuskerk that date from the 15C.
- 🕑 **Organizing Your Time:** Allow around two to three hours to explore Venlo, and more if you want to take a boat trip on the Maas.
- 👣 **Also See:** Arcen Castle gardens; situated around 9km/5.6mi from Venlo, they contain woodlands, lakes and outstanding shrub gardens.

A Bit of History

A legend of the Middle Ages gives AD 90 as the date of Venlo's foundation by Valuas, chief of a Germanic tribe, the Bructeri. In 1364, Venlo, by then a prosperous town, became a member of the Hanseatic League. Today it is the centre of a large market gardening area, which stretches north to the outskirts of Grubbenvorst. The town's immediate surroundings are covered with hothouses.

The **carnival** (👣*see Calendar of events*) is a very lively one.

Boat trips

Boat trips are organised on the Maas. Landing stage: Maaskade.

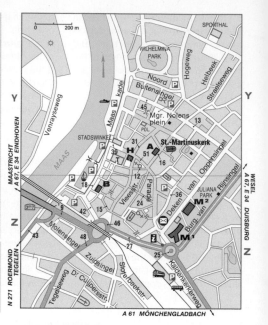

Sights

Stadhuis★

In the middle of Markt, the town hall is a fine quadrilateral Renaissance building (c. 1600). The façade is flanked by two octagonal corner towers topped with onion-shaped spires and has steps leading up to a perron at the centre.

St Martinuskerk

🕐 Open daily 9am–noon, 2pm–4pm. ☎077 351 24 39.

The tower of this church, which dates from the beginning of the 15C, has a carillon of 48 bells. The interior has interesting **furnishings**★ and *objets d'art*. The 15C Gothic **stalls** are carved to represent about 20 scenes of the Old and New Testaments. On the left of the triumphal arch, note a 16C *Virgin and Child*; on the right, a 17C Christ; in the chancel of Sacraments, north of the high altar, a carved 16C oak bench; in the chancel of Our Lady on the right of the high altar, a 15C limestone *Pietà* and an *Ecce Homo* painted by Jan van Cleef, a painter born in Venlo (1646–1716). A beautiful brass **baptismal font**, dating from 1621, stands at the back of the south side aisle.

In the same street (Grote Kerkstraat), at nᵒs 19–21, there is the interesting façade of the **Huize Schreurs** built in the Renaissance style (1588), topped by a voluted gable; on the 1st floor, blind arcades lean on two corbels carved with the head of a lion.

Limburgs Museum★

🕐 Open Tue–Sun 11am–5pm. 🕐 Closed Carnival, 25 Dec and 1 Jan. ⊚6€. ☎077 352 21 12. www.limburgsmuseum.nl (in Dutch and German).

A modern construction of glass, wood, concrete, steel and brick, this museum building was designed by Jeanne Dekkers. The brick wall, measuring over 100m/110yd in length, recalls the rampart that occupied this site until the 19C. The starting point is **Historoscoop**, a multimedia show giving information on the region and the River Maas in particular. The other 11 rooms take visitors on a voyage of discovery into the past, from prehistoric man mining flint to today's high-tech society. The museum also organises temporary exhibitions.

The museum's **information centre** is housed in a nearby 1930s petrol station.

Museum Van Bommel-Van Dam

Open Tue–Sun 11am–5pm. Closed Carnival, 25 Dec and 1 Jan. 2€. 077 351 34 57. www.vanbommelvandam.nl. This museum of 20C and contemporary Dutch art holds mainly temporary exhibitions.

Excursions

Tegelen en Steyl

4km/2.5mi to the southwest via Prof Gelissensingel.
Tegelen is a small industrial town well known for its **Passion Plays** (Passiespelen) enacted every five years at De Doolhof open-air theatre (*see Calendar of events*).
In Steyl there is a small museum contains artefacts collected from all over the world by Dutch missionaries. Not far from the museum, there is a botanical garden, **Jochum-Hof** (*open Easter–Oct, Tue–Sun 11am–5pm; 077 326 65 50*).

Arcen Castle gardens

9km/5.6mi north of Venlo via the N 271. Open Apr 10am–5pm; May–Sept 10am–6pm; Oct 10am–5pm. Winterwonderland, 11am–5pm. Closed Nov–Christmas period. 14.50€. 077 473 18 82. www. kasteeltuinen.nl (in Dutch and German).
The 32-ha/80-acre gardens of this castle dating from 1653 include a Rosarium, lakes, a wood containing deer, oriental gardens and the Casa Verde, a large subtropical glasshouse.

Venray

27.6km/17mi northwest of Venlo, along the A73.
Venray has a population of 39 078 The town became embroiled in a battle during World War II; as part of the Allied Offensive, Operation Market Garden, the town of Venray was captured. Venray suffered heavy losses in this battle, its being one of the bloodier battles fought on Dutch soil in World War II.
On Grote Markt in the town, **St-Petrus Bandenkerk** (*open Apr–Oct, Mon–Sat 2pm–4pm; 0478 51 05 05 (VVV)*), a large Gothic church, contains some interesting furnishings. Apart from the Baroque pulpit, note a fine late 15C brass lectern

and a remarkable series of wooden **statues** and the one of St Paul in stone; the oldest is of St James (15C). The Apostles, with their attributes, stand against the pillars of the nave. In the aisles there is a series of saints, including a beautiful St Lucy, which come from old altars no longer in existence. At the entrance there is a Baroque statue of St Peter, shown as pope.
A music festival with various types of music, V-Kick, takes place on Schouwburgplein every year. www.v-kick.nl (in Dutch).

Overloon

7km/4.3mi to the north.
For three weeks in the autumn of 1944 the British and Americans fought a battle round this village to support Operation Market Garden (*see ARNHEM*), one of the biggest tank battles of the war, often compared with that at Caen, because of the terrible artillery bombardment and the number of tanks involved. Overloon was completely destroyed in this ferocious battle and over 2 500 soldiers from in and around the village were killed.
The **Nationaal Oorlogs- en Verzetsmuseum** (*open Sept–Jun, 10am–5pm; Jul–Aug 10am–6pm; closed 24, 25, 31 Dec and 1 Jan; 11€; 0478 64 12 50. www.oorlogsmuseum-overloon.nl*), or National War and Resistance Museum (built in 1946), is to the east of Overloon in the woods where the fighting principally occurred.
A 15ha/37 acre enclosure and large exhibition hall contain an interesting collection of German and Allied equipment: tanks, planes, a one-man submarine, guns, bombs, torpedoes, etc. In the Documentation Centre the history of the Second World War is told by means of photographs, models, maps, weapons, uniforms, and so on. In a building devoted to concentration camps in Europe and Asia (Kampengebouw), a permanent exhibition illustrates the tragic plight of the victims through photographs, films, documents and various other objects.
An ANVT (mud-track race for 4 by 4s) is held in Overloon.

VLISSINGEN

FLUSHING – ZEELAND
POPULATION 46 00
LOCAL MAP SEE DELTA

Flushing is both a fishing port and an industrial centre with large naval shipyards. Flushing also has a Naval College and warships are moored here. From the ferry terminal there are car ferry services to England (Sheerness) and across the estuary to Breskens (⚓see SLUIS, Excursions).

- 🛈 **Information:** Oude Markt 3 – 4381 ER. ☎0118 42 21 90. www.vvvzeeland.nl.
- ▶ **Orient Yourself:** Flushing is on the Westerschelde estuary and commands entry to the Walcheren canal.
- 🅿 **Parking:** There are a number of car parks in the area.
- ⊘ **Don't Miss:** A bracing walk along the town's seafront, the so-called Boulevard.
- 🕐 **Organizing Your Time:** A couple of hours will cover most of the attractions.
- 🧒 **Especially for Kids:** Both maritime museums are well geared up for children and the reptile zoo will have an instant appeal.

A Bit of History

Flushing became important in the 14C on account of its commercial activities (mainly with England) and herring fishing industry. From 1585 to 1616 the town was pledged to the English as a guarantee of the costs incurred by the Earl of Leicester's army to uphold the United Provinces after the assassination of William the Silent.

Vlissingen Harbour

Boat trips

Operate Jul and Aug. Information from the tourist office, ☎0118 42 21 90. Flushing is the starting-point for boat trips along the coast of Walcheren Peninsula.

Sights

The Boulevard

The town's seafront is a long avenue known as the Boulevard, flanked by an esplanade.
The 15C **Gevangentoren** or Prison Tower stands here. Down below stretches a wide beach sheltered from northern winds. At the far end of the Boulevard, on an old bastion, note the little lighthouse and the statue of Admiral de Ruyter. From there you have a nice **view** of the port below and the **Old Exchange** (1635), a fine building with green shutters surmounted by a pinnacle.

Maritiem Attractiecentrum Het Arsenaal 🧒

Arsenaalplein 1. 🕐*Open Mar–May, Tue–Sun 10am–7pm; Jun–Sept and during school holidays, daily 10am–8pm; Oct–Dec, Tue–Sun 10am–7pm.* 🕐*Closed 25 and 31 Dec.* ⊜*12€; children* ⊜*10€.* ♿☎*011 41 54 00. www.arsenaal.com.* This former arsenal (1823) now provides an exciting introduction to the seafaring world for children in particular.

Zeeuws Maritiem MuZEEum `Kids`

Bellamypark 19. ◷ *Open Mon–Fri 10am–5pm, Sat–Sun 1pm–5pm, public holidays 1pm–5pm.* ◷ *Closed 1 Jan.* ⊸ *7€; children 4€.* ☎ *0118 41 24 98. www.muzeeum.nl.*

This museum tells the story of the town's rich maritime past. It focuses particularly on the famous admiral Michiel de Ruyter and the East India Company, and the local pilotage service. The display also includes items of cargo from ships that have run aground on the sandbanks.

Reptielenzoo Iguana `Kids`

Bellamypark 35. ◷ *Open Jun–Oct, Sun–Mon 1pm–5pm, Tue–Sat 10am–5.30pm; Oct–Jun, daily 1pm–5.30pm.* ◷ *Closed 25 Dec and 1 Jan.* ⊸ *8.50€; children (4–11 yrs) 7€.* ☎ *0118 41 72 19. www. iguana.nl (in Dutch).*

Over 500 living reptiles, amphibians and insects are on view here. There is also a "baby room" in which eggs are hatched and young animals are kept.

Excursion

Fort Rammekens

On Rammekensweg by Ritthem, east of Flushing. ◷ *Open Apr–Oct, Tue–Sun 1pm–5pm.* ⊸ *2€.* ☎ *0118 41 24 98 (Stedelijk Museum). www.muzeeum.nl.*

This sea fort is the oldest in Western Europe and was built in 1547 to defend the ports of Middelburg and Antwerp. The casemates added in 1809 by Napoleon now house exhibitions on the history of the fortress and on the surrounding countryside.

VOLENDAM★

NOORD-HOLLAND

POPULATION 22 000

Volendam, like Marken, stands on a small land-locked sea, Gouwzee. It is one of the best known ports of the old Zuiderzee. Its townspeople – who, unlike the people of Marken, are mostly Catholic – wear the traditional costume in summer, and it has become a symbol of the Netherlands for foreigners, though any sense of authenticity has long since been lost. Tourism is an important activity.

- **Information:** Zeestraat 37 – 1131 ZD. ☎ 0299 36 37 47. www.vvvvolendam.nl.
- ▶ **Orient Yourself:** Volendam is easy to navigate; head for Zeestraat, one of its few main streets and follow its path to the harbour area.
- **P** **Parking:** Car parks have sprung up in recent years to cater to the many tourists who visit Volendam constantly (fees apply).
- **Don't Miss:** The locals who dress in traditional Dutch costumes, albeit nowadays more for the tourists than for everyday dress.
- ◷ **Organizing Your Time:** There are a couple of fine museums and the harbourside to explore, so allow around three hours.

A Bit of History

The development of a community of farmers and fishermen was well underway by the middle of the 15C. By the 19C the villagers had built their own parish-church (1860) and in the 1890s their fleet of 258 fishing-boats had become the largest along the old Zuyderzee. The lively fishing community retained its centuries-old tradition of folk-dances and song , as well as its individual style of wood-built houses and colourful dress, and as a result of this began to attract artists as well as tourists. In 1884 steamboat companies opened a regular service from Amsterdam and the combined round trip, known as the Marken-Express, became very popular.

The Cartographers of 17C Europe

The daring and enterprise of Dutch merchant-seamen and navigators led to the rise of the United Netherlands as a maritime power. Amsterdam became not only the centre of international commerce, but also of commercial cartography. Indeed, the cartographers of the period were often equally at home as engravers and publishers

Great names in Dutch cartography included Petrus Plancius; Mercator (of the projection and Atlas 1606); Hondius, who revised Mercator's Atlas and mapped Sir Francis Drake's round-the-world voyage; Blaeu (Willem Jansz), publisher of the poet and dramatist Vondel and cartographer to the East India Company from 1634; his arch rival, Johannes Jansonius, son-in-law of Hondius and successor to the family firm; and Van Keulen, founder of a publishing house famous for its nautical charts.

Operates from Volendam mid-Feb–Oct, Sat and Sun 10.30am–5.30pm every 30/45min; from Marken Sat and Sun 11am–6pm every 30/45min; crossing takes 30min. www.markenexpress.nl (in Dutch).

Sights

Village

The long street, which runs along the top of the high dyke, is just a line of shops, but behind and below the dyke there are picturesque narrow alleyways winding between small brick houses with wooden gables.

Traditional costume★

The men wear black trousers with silver buttons, short black jackets over striped shirts, and round caps. The women's costume consists of a black skirt with a striped apron or a striped skirt with a black apron, a shirt with a flowered front under a black, short-sleeved blouse, and a necklace of large coral beads with a gold clasp, hidden in winter by a blue and white shawl. When they are not wearing a pointed black bonnet, they wear a lace cap for feast days that is very tall with turned-up wings, whose shape is famous. Visitors should watch the congregation leaving church when the couples cross the little wooden bridge in front of the Catholic church.

At *Fotoshop Volendam*, on the harbourfront and opposite the fish auction building (☎0299 36 98 33), you can have your photograph taken in one of the traditional costumes and have the picture printed on a T-shirt, wall plate, key holder, coffee mug or a greeting card. The shop is open from 10am to 6pm in the summer.

Volendams Museum

Zeestraat 37. Open Easter–autumn half-term, daily 10am–5pm. 2€. ☎0299 36 92 58. www.volendamsmuseum.nl.
This museum is located in a small shop and classroom and there is a lot to see. The exhibits include examples of national dress and ornaments as well as various works of art relating to the artists' colony that developed here at the end of the 19C.
Ethnographic exhibits also feature recreated domestic interiors, with original furniture dating from the period 1815 to 1920, and artefacts from the local fishery industry as well as home crafts. Each year a temporary exhibition, focusing on a particular theme of local interest, is mounted by the museum.
Visitors to the museum also experience the adjoining art deco picture-theatre with a selection of documentary films by Dutch directors, and video recordings. Perhaps the most original exhibit is to be found in the adjoining cigar bands-house, where some 11 million cigar-bands have been used to compose mosaics.

DE WADDENEILANDEN★★
WADDEN ISLANDS

The Wadden Islands are a unique nature reserve in the north of the country. There are five inhabited islands, extending between the North Sea and the Waddenzee. The largest, **Texel**, is part of the province of Noord-Holland; the others, **Vlieland**, **Terschelling**, **Ameland** and **Schiermonnikoog**, are part of Fryslân. There are also smaller islands and sandbanks, such as the bird island of **Griend**, and **Rottumeroog** and **Rottumerplaat**, both in Groningen province. The belt of islands continues northwards along the coasts of Germany and Denmark.

- **Information:** www.vvv-wadden.nl.
- ▶ **Orient Yourself:** De Waddeneilanden, or the Wadden Islands, lie to the north of the country, a short distance west of Groningen.
- 🅿 **Parking:** There are a few car parks and viewing areas dotted around the islands and some are free for the parking motorist; however, Vlieland and Schiermonnikoog don't allow cars at all and not all the ferries can accommodate vehicles. It is best to cycle or walk.
- 😊 **Don't Miss:** The chance to explore Schiermonnikoog, an island designated a national park.
- 🕒 **Organizing Your Time:** You could easily spend a week exploring this long string of islands.
- 🖢 **Also See:** The islands from the sea – be sure to take a boat trip from one of the Wadden islands.

A Bit of History and Geography

The formation of the islands and the Waddenzee – Along with the German and Danish islands, the islands are the remains of an ancient chain of dunes which stretched as far as Jutland in Denmark. As far back as the Roman period the sea had breached the chain of dunes and invaded the flat hinterland forming the **Waddenzee**. In the 13C this was connected to a vast gulf which had just been formed, the Zuiderzee (🖢see IJSSELMEER).

Tides and currents – The islands are still subject to the action of strong currents and the North Sea continues its insidious undermining process to the **west** of the islands. Kilometre posts are planted in lines along the beaches to record the movement of the sand, and the **breakwaters** are built to reduce this movement.
To the **east**, the strong currents displace the sand which then silts up the Waddenzee. At low tide, the sea leaves huge stretches of mudflats or sand called wadden (because they can be waded across). These are popular with birds, but cause ships to make large detours to follow the marked channels. At certain times of year and when weather permits, the Waddenzee can be walked with a guide (🖢see below).

The power of the wind – The constant strong west wind has always been the greatest enemy of the Wadden region. Over the course of time, it has gradually 'turned' the islands round to the east; villages on the islands' west sides, such as Westerburen on Schiermonnikoog and Westervlieland on Vlieland, have been swallowed up by the sea. Even today, huge areas of sand are forming on the southwest sides of the islands. Since 1900, large-scale conifer planting has been carried out in an attempt to prevent the spread of these areas, and this, combined with breakwaters, dykes and careful maintenance of the dunes, has kept the large islands more or less in place. Some of the sandbars, such as **Noorderhaaks** (better known as De Razende Bol, the fast-moving ball) are constantly on the move.

The strong wind does have one advantage: because it makes the clouds move faster, the Wadden Islands have less rain than other parts of the country.

Battling against the sea – Time and time again, the low-lying islands have been flooded by big storms as the dunes and dykes prove unable to resist the power of the sea. For example, the small island of **Griend**, between Vlieland and Harlingen, was a prosperous place in the 13C; little by little it was eroded by the high tides, and had to be abandoned in the 18C; what remains of it now is an important breeding ground for birds. Likewise the dyke built between Ameland and the Frisian coast in 1871 was destroyed by storms eleven years later, and Rottumerplaat was regularly under water until 1950.

Landscape – The northern and western sides of the islands have wonderful **beaches** of very white sand bordered by **dunes**. The dunes have been planted with marram grass to prevent them from being carried along by the wind. They are particularly high and wide on Texel, but the highest dunes are on Ameland and Terschelling, where they reach a height of over 30m/98.4ft.

The **coniferous forests** planted inland in the early 20C radically changed the appearance of the islands, which had hitherto been largely treeless.

The very flat south coasts of the islands are protected by **dykes**. The countryside is generally subdivided into several **polders** separated by small dykes, where numerous herds of cows and a few horses graze. Texel specialises mainly in sheep-raising.

There are also several small **harbours** on the Waddenzee. They were once the departure point for fishing and whaling; today they are mostly marinas.

Fauna – All these islands form a vast sanctuary for **seabirds**. Some come to lay their eggs, including gulls of all kinds, spoonbills, and Pintail ducks.

In the autumn, a great number of migratory birds from northern Europe (Scandinavia, Iceland) and from Siberia stop for a time on the Waddenzee, which is rich in food (fish and shellfish), then continue on their way to warmer climates (France, Spain, North Africa). This is the case with the Avocet; others spend winter on the Waddenzee. Among the waders are a large number of different types of Dunlin and oystercatchers.

Nature reserves have been designated on each island, and in some cases visitors can only visit when accompanied by a guide. The largest reserves are usually on Forestry Commission (Staatsbosbe-

Spoonbills

S. Dijksen/ECOMARE

NBTC

Cycling on Ameland

heer) land. Many areas are closed to the public during the nesting season, from mid-March to mid-August.

Seals used to come in great numbers to the sand banks on the north side of the islands, but their numbers were seriously depleted in the 1980s by a virus. Fortunately, there are now signs that the numbers are on the increase again, and you may be lucky enough to see them basking in the sun on one of the many sandbanks as you cross to the islands.

Flora – The **plant life** on the dunes, which are interspersed with small pools, is exceptionally varied. The most common species include the Sea Buckthorn with its edible orange berries, the Burnet Rose, and grasses such as scurvy grass, Parnassus grass with white flowers, and succulent plants such as Milkwort. Terschelling is also the only place in Europe where cranberries are cultivated.

Tourism on the islands – Even if you are not interested in ornithology or botany, you will enjoy the natural beauty of the islands, an unpolluted environment (clear seas, the wild open expanses of dunes and a healthy climate), and the peace and quiet, though they do get very busy in summer. The islands also have a great deal to offer in autumn and winter.

The drawbacks – Tourism has taken its toll, and the Wadden Islands are also used by the army; aircraft noise from the military bases on Texel and Vlieland has scared away some of the birdlife. In addition, rich reserves of natural gas have been found under the Waddenzee, and a drilling platform has been built between Den Helder and Texel.

Ameland
Fryslân – Population 4 500
This long island covering about 5 800ha/14 326 acres with its large stretches of dunes, fine sandy beaches on the North Sea, and woods, is very popular with tourists, including a large number of Germans who come here in the summer. Nearly 100km/62mi of bicycle tracks cross the island passing through woods and over dunes. Like the other Wadden Islands, Ameland has its **nature reserves** for birds, including **Het Oerd** at the far eastern end of the island.

The inhabitants of Ameland specialised in **whaling** in the 17C and 18C. This activity was discontinued in the mid-19C, but the captains' houses can still be seen here and there on the island, and in some places whale bones are still used as fences. The four picturesque villages are all conservation areas.

Redshank

S. de Wolf/
ECOMARE

O.Bos/ECOMARE

Lesser Black-backed Gull

Short-eared Owl

S. de Wolf/ECOMARE

Kestrel

S. de Wolf/ECOMARE

Address Book

THE WADDEN ISLANDS: PRACTICAL INFORMATION

Getting there by boat – The ferry situation varies from one island to another; some are high-speed and others are not; some allow cars and others do not. Ferries are quite frequent in the high season, but in the low season they may be limited to one a day, or even none in bad weather. It is therefore a good idea to check the appropriate ferry company's 24hr information line a few days before you go. Cars can be left in the large harbour car parks on the mainland.

Exploring the islands – The best way to get about is by **bicycle**, and on Vlieland and Schiermonnikoog, where cars are forbidden, it is the only way. Cycling or walking are also the best ways of seeing the nature reserves and dunes. Bikes can be hired on each island and in most villages. However, in the summer they can be hard to come by and it is highly advisable to bring a bicycle with you from the mainland. **Cycling and walking maps** are available from the VVV tourist office.

Most islands have **bus** services; another alternative is to travel by **taxi**, which is not only comfortable, but has the added bonus that the driver may tell you all about the area. Having your own car might be useful on Texel.

WHERE TO STAY

It is best to reserve rooms through the island's tourist information centre. There are a few hotels, but many islanders take in visitors. The VVV publishes an annual guide listing these, along with campsites and holiday cottages.

TOURS

The VVV can provide information on tours of the nature reserves or the mudflats, and birdwatching, seal-watching and beachcombing trips.

WALKING ACROSS THE MUDFLATS

Guided walks across the mudflats from early Apr–late Oct (weather permitting). Information and bookings: Stichting Wadloopcentrum Pieterburen (PB 1, 9968 ZG Pieterburen; ☎0595 52 83 00; www.wadlopen.com); or Dijkstra's Wadlooptochten (Hoofdstraat 118, 9968 AH Pieterburen; ☎0595 52 83 45; www.wadloop-dijkstra.nl). Most of these trips leave from Wierum (Fryslân) or Pieterburen (Groningen); for addresses. VVVs also organise shorter trips of this kind.

SPORTS

Sailing, surfing, fishing, parachuting, horse riding, golf, skating, cross-country skiing: the islands have them all, and the VVV can provide you with further information. **De Ronde om Texel**, the world's biggest catamaran race, is held in June.

Nes

This is the island's chief village, overlooked by an isolated **bell-tower** with a saddleback roof, dating from 1664. In Rixt van Doniastraat there are several old captains' houses, **Commandeurshuizen**, one-storey houses with a small lean-to on the side, and an entrance door that is slightly off-centre. A cordon of bricks or a geometric frieze outlines each floor, and there is often an iron anchor on the façade bearing the date when the house was built.

To the east on the road to Buren, past the new Catholic cemetery, the old **cemetery** is accessible by a small road on the left. It still has ancient tombstones, some decorated with a weeping willow, others very narrow and nearly 2m/6.5ft high. Several graves of British airmen whose planes crashed here during the war are to be found in this cemetery.

A visit to **Natuurcentrum Ameland** (🕑mid-Mar–Oct, Mon–Fri 10am–5pm, Sat–Sun 1pm–5pm; public holidays 1pm–5pm; 🕑 closed from Nov 2008 for renovation; ☜3.75€; ♿ ☎0519 54 27 37; www.amelandermusea.nl) will give you a much greater appreciation of the island's natural environment. Slides, photographs, sound recordings and models are used to give an impression of the different landscapes: mudflats, salt marshes, polders, woodland, dunes and beaches. There is an aquarium of North Sea fish, and the skeleton of one

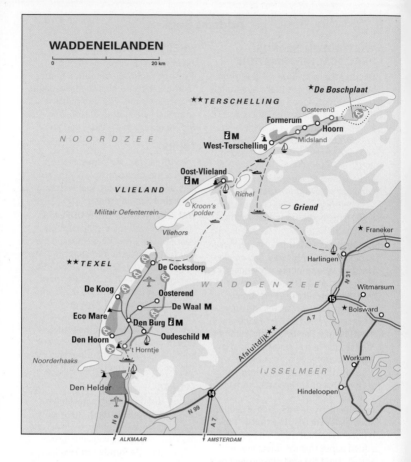

WADDENEILANDEN

0   20 km

NOORDZEE

★ *De Boschplaat*

★★ *TERSCHELLING*

Oosterend

Formerum   **Hoorn**

West-Terschelling ⓘ**M**   Midsland

Oost-Vlieland ⓘ**M**

VLIELAND

Militair Oefenterrein   Kroon's polder   Richel

Vliehors   ⌒ *Griend*

★ *Franeker*

Harlingen

★★ *TEXEL*

De Cocksdorp

WADDENZEE   N 31   Witmarsum

De Koog

Oosterend

De Waal M   15   ★ Bolsward

Eco Mare

Den Burg ⓘ**M**   A 7

Den Hoorn   Oudeschild **M**

't Horntje   Afsluitdijk ★★

Noorderhaaks   Workum

IJSSELMEER

Den Helder   14   Hindeloopen

N 9   N 99   A 7

↓ ALKMAAR   ↓ AMSTERDAM

of four whales which were stranded here in November 1997.

Buren

This is the island's easternmost village; further east is Het Oerd nature reserve. The village square has a bronze statuette of a hook-nosed woman with a storm lantern, **Rixt van het Oerd** (*see below*).

The **Landbouw en Juttersmuseum Swartwoude** (Swartwoude Agriculture and Beachcombing Museum; ◷*open mid-Mar–Oct, Mon–Fri 10am–12pm, 1.30pm–5pm, Sat–Sun 1.30pm–5pm; Nov– early Jan, Wed–Sat 1.30pm–5pm; ◷ closed 30 Apr, 6 Dec and 1 Jan; ⊜3€; ☎ 0519 54 28 45; www.ame landermusea.nl*) uses photographs and other items to bring to life the harsh existence led by people on Ameland as

recently as 1900. They eked out an existence from farming, fishing, poaching and beachcombing; the latter was made illegal in 1529, but was practised by poor coast-dwellers until late in the 18C. It was sometimes very lucrative when the cargoes of stranded ships were washed ashore, yielding such items as firewood, tins of food, alcohol and suitcases.

Ballum

The old tower amid the trees in the centre of this little village told the villagers the time and also sounded the alarm when danger threatened. Take Smitteweg, next to the new town hall, to the southeast to reach the **cemetery** where some of the beautiful old tombstones depict sailing ships or weeping willows.

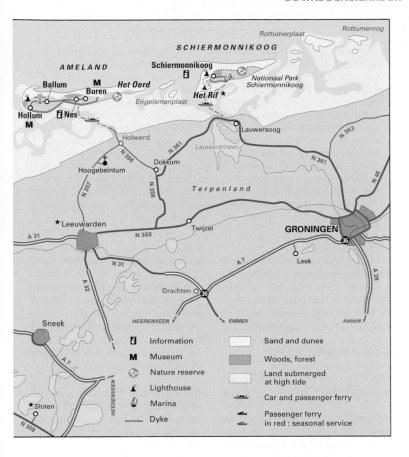

Hollum

To the south of the village stands a typically attractive church with a saddleback-roofed bell-tower. In the surrounding **cemetery** there are more 18C tombstones showing sailing ships.

Hollum was home to many of the captains of the whaling ships which operated out of Ameland, and one of their houses has been converted into a museum, the **Cultuur-Historisch Museum Sorgdrager** (🕐 open mid-Mar–Oct, Mon–Fri 10am–12pm, 1.30pm–5pm, Sat–Sun 1.30pm–5pm; Nov– early Jan, Wed–Sat 1.30pm–5pm; 🕐 closed 30 Apr, 6 Dec and 1 Jan; ⊚3€; ☎0519 55 44 77; www.amelandermusea.nl). Pieces of local furniture and tiled walls grace the interiors, which make an ideal setting for the collections of earthenware, pottery, costumes and other objects related to whaling, fishing and the dairy industry.

A lifeboat museum, **Reddingsmuseum Abraham Fock** (🕐 closed for renovation; ♿ ☎ 0519 55 42 43; www.amelandermusea.nl), is located in Oranjeweg. This is the home of the famous **Ameland lifeboat** (Demonstrations are given eight to ten times a year; contact the museum for information), which is drawn down to the

Ferry – Between Holwerd and Ameland. Departure times vary: call Wagenborg Passagiersdiensten on ☎0519 3 54 61 11 or 0900 455 4455. www.wpd.nl. Crossing lasts about 45min. Fares vary according to the time of the year: ⊚12.05€ return in the summer.
VVV (tourist office) – In Nes, ☎0519 546 546. www.ameland.nl.

How Het Oerd Got Its Name

Long ago, a widow called Rixt and her son Sjoerd lived at the eastern end of Ameland. They had virtually no contact with the other islanders, and lived off the land; the only thing of any worth that they possessed was a cow. Every day, Sjoerd would go poaching and Rixt would walk along the beach looking for useful objects that had been washed ashore. Everything went well until Sjoerd grow up and left home to become a seaman. At first Rixt managed on her own, but after a long period of finding nothing on the beach, she hatched a cunning plan. One dark and stormy night, she tied a storm lantern to the cow's head and led it up to the top of the highest dune. A ship in distress just off the coast of Ameland thought it had found a safe haven, and set a course towards the light. But it broke up on the rocks and all the crew drowned. Rixt hurried to the beach, full of expectation, but when she saw one of the bodies lying on the shore she screamed: it was her son, Sjoerd. Ever since then, if you listen carefully as the stormy winds blow across the island, you can still hear her heart-rending cry: 'Sjoooerd, Sjoooerd…'

water by a team of horses. The museum traces the evolution from beachcomber to lifeboat man, and a video describes how the latter have operated now and in the past. Ameland's red and white lighthouse is further to the northwest.

Schiermonnikoog
Fryslân – Population 1 500
This is the smallest of Waddenzee's inhabited islands: covering an area of 4 000ha/9 880 acres, it is 16km/10mi long and 4km/2.5mi wide, and has recently been designated a **national park**. The only village, Schiermonnikoog, has two large beaches and a small lake (pleasure boats), the Westerplas. To the east are the **Kobbeduinen** (dunes) and a nature reserve of 2 400ha/5 928

acres, **De Oosterkwelder**. With its wild scenery, its dunes, woods, beaches and its tranquillity, Schiermonnikoog is one of the most pleasant islands in the group.

The island became Frisian in 1580 before passing into the hands of several landowning families from 1639 to 1858 and finally becoming state property in 1945.

Schiermonnikoog
Schiermonnikoog has been a national park since 1987. The houses of this village are built among the trees. It developed after Cistercian monks from Friesland settled here c. 1400. The name of the island derives from *schier* meaning grey, *monnik* monk and *oog* island. A statue of

Overlooking the Waddenzee from Ameland

Leeden/NBTC

a monk on the green in the town centre is a reminder of its past.

Nearby, an arch made of two huge whale bones recalls the whaling of earlier times. The **visitor centre** (*www.nationaal park.nl/schiermonnikoog*) is housed in an old power station and contains an exhibition about the island's different landscapes. It also has information about excursions, walking and cycling routes in the area. The exhibition in the centre has the bones of one of four whales which were stranded on the island in 1997, as well as a small cultural and historical section.

In Middenstreek, a street which runs towards the west, and in the parallel Langestreek, there are interesting **old houses** with asymmetrical roofs.

The Rif★

Past the Westerplas, at the southwestern extremity of the island, lies a vast stretch of immaculate white sand reaching 1.5km/1mi in width. From Westerburenweg, a path which ends in the dunes, there is an excellent **view**★ of the Rif.

Terschelling★★

Fryslân – Population 5 500
This very long island (28km/17.5mi) covers 11 000ha/27 180 acres and is the second largest of the Wadden Islands, after Texel. Terschelling is an island with many faces: wide sandy beaches, tall dunes, salt marshes and mudflats with hundreds of birds, dense coniferous forests, broad polders and a few small villages. The ideal way to explore it is by the many cycle paths that criss-cross the island.

It welcomes many holidaymakers in summer, who enjoy its huge sandy beaches. Terschelling (pronounced Ter-srelling) still has a wild aspect. It is covered with vast areas of dunes where an abundant vegetation of grasses, flowers and moss grow. It also has several **nature reserves**, of which the largest is De Boschplaat.

Terschelling is the homeland of **Willem Barents** or Barentsz (c. 1555–97), the navigator who, while trying to find a northeast passage to India, discovered

Ferry – Between Laurwersoog and Schiermonnikoog. *Departure times vary: call Wagenborg Passagiersdiensten on ☎0519 34 90 50 or 0900 455 4455. www.wpd.nl. Crossing lasts about 45min.*

Bus – A direct bus transfer is available from Leeuwarden Railway station bus terminal: (ferry connection guaranteed). There is also abus departure from Groningen bus terminal (ferry connection also guarantted).

VVV (tourist office) – ☎*0519 53 12 33 or 0519 53 19 00. www.schiermonnikoog.net.*

Novaya Zemlya in 1594 and Spitsbergen in 1596 (᧞*see Introduction, Time line*). The portion of the Arctic Ocean which lies between these two archipelagos, the Barents Sea, bears his name. On his third expedition (1596–97), his boat was caught in the ice. He spent the winter in Novaya Zemlya in a hut made from boat planks, and died in an attempt to return to civilisation. In 1876 the ship's log was found.

The ten-day **Oerol festival** takes place every June, with events and performances being held all over the island, on beaches, in the dunes and in barns.

West-Terschelling

The capital of the island (known in Frisian as West-Skylge) is a small but lively port well situated in a large bay. It is overlooked by a square tower 54m/174ft high, the **Brandaris**, a lighthouse built in 1594 to replace the bell-tower of St Brandarius Chapel which had until then done sterling service as a lighthouse. The bell-tower was engulfed by the waves.

At the foot of the tower lies a large cemetery. The 19C and early 20C tombstones, engraved with naively depicted boats, recall the maritime past of its inhabitants. One of the stones, in the middle of the **cemetery**, recalls the episode during which five of the island's lifesavers tried to rescue the survivors from the wreck of the Queen of Mistley, on 3 January 1880.

West-Terschelling – The marina at the foot of the Brandaris

Terschelling Museum
't Behouden Huys [Kids]

Commandeurstraat 30. ◷Open Tue–Sat 10am–5pm, Sun noon–5pm. Jul–Aug, Mon–Sun 10am–5pm. ⊚5.50€; 3.50€. ☏0562 44 23 89. www.texelsmaritiem.nl.

This regional museum is housed in two dwellings belonging to captains (commandeurshuizen) (1668). It bears the name of the hut in which Willem Barents was forced to spend a winter on Novaya Zemlya. At the entrance, note the fine sculptured paving stones.

The top floor of the left-hand house tells the story of Terschelling; the rooms on the ground floor are furnished in 19C style. A new section of the museum contains a reconstruction of part of Willem Barents' ship, with a wide variety of objects and a panorama show recounting his voyages to the far north. The first floor is dedicated to pilotage and whaling. The other house contains model ships and related objects, together with a collection of flotsam and jetsam. Children's activities are also available at the museum (ages 3–9 years old).

Centrum voor natuur en landschap

Burg. Reedekkerstraat 11. ◷Open Apr–Oct, Mon–Fri 9am–5pm, Sat–Sun, public holidays and school holidays 2pm–5pm. ◷Closed Easter, Whitsun, 25 Dec and 1 Jan. ⊚5€. ♿☏0562 44 23 90. www.natuur museumterschelling.nl.

This centre is devoted to the island's rich plant and animal life, with films and other media being used to show how dunes form, how dykes are built, how water is managed, and the role of forestry. It places particular emphasis on the 'bird island' of Griend, and the De Boschplaat nature reserve. The centre also has large aquariums of fish, crabs and shellfish.

Terschelling and Its Cranberries

Cranberry wine is a speciality of Terschelling, and the damp valleys between the dunes are almost the only place in Europe where cranberries grow. According to tradition it all started in about 1840, when a beachcomber, Pieter-Sipkes Cupido, found a barrel full of cranberries that had washed ashore from a ship. He took it into the dunes, opened it, and then left it there, disappointed that the barrel did not contain anything more valuable. But Terschelling had gained a new crop as a result.

The centre of the industry is in Formerum, but all over the island you can taste tarts, ice creams, jam, liqueur, wine and meat dishes prepared using local cranberries.

Formerum

A small windmill, **De Koffiemolen** (the coffee mill) is worth seeing. It has a thatched roof and dates from 1876; it is now used to mill grain.

Hoorn

The Frisian name of this village is Hoarne. The 13C church built of brick in the Frisian style is surrounded by gravestones. The oldest date from the 19C and are topped by a low relief depicting a ship.

De Boschplaat★

⊙*Open (limited access) mid-Mar–mid-Aug. Motor vehicles not allowed. Haycart tours: contact the tourist office, Willem Barentszkade 19a ☎0562 44 30 00.*
No cars allowed; cycling paths in the western part. Haycart tours and guided walks are organised.

This nature reserve is the only **European natural monument** in the Netherlands, and a paradise for nature lovers. It covers 4 440ha/10 868 acres of the island's eastern end, which is uninhabited. Large numbers of birds come to nest on the dunes and estuaries. What makes it special is the large number of transitional zones between different ecosystems, for example between salt and fresh water, dry and wet, wind and shelter, and acid and alkaline soils. The vegetation is quite remarkable, as orchids and unique types of halophyte plants (those growing on salty soil) can be found. A large part of the Boschplaat is closed to visitors during the nesting season.

Texel★★

Noord-Holland – Population 15 500

Texel (pronounced Tessel) is 24km/15mi long and 9km/5.6mi wide, and is the largest of the Wadden Islands. If therefore has less of an island feel than its neighbours, but this "Netherlands in miniature" still has much to offer.

It is best to get around the island by car or bike; Texel has plenty of cycle paths. The capital, **Den Burg**, is roughly in the centre. **De Koog**, to the west, gives access to the main beach. **Oudeschild** is a small fishing and pleasure port. **Oosterend**, **De Waal** and **Den Hoorn** are small, picturesque villages; **De Cocksdorp** is the most northerly, and

Ferry – *From Harlingen. Departure times vary. Call the Rederij Doeksen on ☎0562 442 002. www.rederij-doeksen.nl. Tickets can be booked online and this saves what can be long queues at the terminal. The regular return fare is 20.86€ (5.60€ extra for the express service). The ferry crossing ( )takes about 2hr and the express service 45min.*
VVV (tourist office) – *In West-Terschelling, ☎0562 44 30 00. www.terschelling.net.*

its lighthouse has a view of Vlieland on a good day.

Bird Island

Birds are one of the most interesting features of Texel. Some 300 species nest and breed on the dunes or on the banks of the freshwater lakes. Texel has several state-owned **nature reserves**★ (*for guided tours, contact EcoMare or the tourist office. Boots and binoculars recommended; limited access during nesting season). The waymarked nature trails are for walkers only.*

De Eijerlandse duinen

These dunes belonged to an island, Eyerlandt, which has been joined to Texel since 1629 by a sand bar. Numerous birds nest here from the end of March to the end of July, especially eiders which provide the down to make eiderdowns.

De Slufter

This is a large area surrounded by dunes, linked to the sea by a gap. The vegetation growing here is impregnated with salt. About 40 different species of birds nest here. From the top of the dunes, at the end of the Slufterweg, which can be reached by a stairway, there is a **view**★ over this amazing wild landscape which is covered in July and August with a mauve flower called sea lavender.

De Muy

This is a partly marshy area in the hollow of the dunes, where nearly fifty species of birds nest, especially white spoonbills with their characteristic

Gregory Wrona / APA

Texel lighthouse

beak and the grey heron. There are also interesting plants (orchids, pyrola, and Parnassus grass).

De Westerduinen

Herring gulls nest on these dunes near the beach.

De Geul

This lake was formed in the dunes at the end of the 20C. Several other small lakes have formed since. In the reeds one can see the spoonbill, the Grey Heron and the Pintail Duck. Nearby, a wealth of interesting plants grow on the dunes and marshes. A fine viewpoint can be

---

Ferry – *From Den Helder. Departure times vary. For information call on ☎0222 36 96 00. www.teso.nl. The crossing takes about 20min; reservations are not accepted.*

VVV (tourist office) *Emmalaan 66, Den Burg, ☎0222 31 47 41 or www.texel.net.*

---

had over the reserve from the belvedere built on the **Mokweg**.

Eco Mare

Ruyslaan 92. Access by De Koog road and the road numbered 13. ⏱Open daily 9am–5pm. ⏱Closed 25 Dec and 1 Jan. ☞8.50€. ☎0222 31 77 41. www.ecomare.nl.

A building, set in the dunes to the north-west of Den Burg, houses this centre devoted to the Wadden Islands and the North Sea, as well as a small Natural History Museum, **Natuurhistorisch Museum**, with collections on Texel, the Waddenzee region and the North Sea. The first section is about the island's evolution, from its geological formation during the Ice Age up to its transformation into polders, and from its prehistoric inhabitants to the present-day tourist invasion. In another section, the nature reserves' flora and fauna can be studied with the help of dioramas, show cases with stuffed birds and photographs of plants. The underground **Waterzaal** (Water Hall) contains many aquariums, providing an interactive discovery tour

Texel and Its Sheep

The island's main activity, after agriculture and tourism, is sheep-breeding (there are about 16 000 sheep on the island, and some 20 000 lambs are born each spring). There are a particularly large number of sheep sheds around the ironically named Hoge Berg or "high hill" (15m/50ft) in the middle of the island. These are like small half-barns with thatched roofs, used to store hay and feed as well as to protect the sheep against the bitter west wind and the snow. They also take shelter behind the garden walls of the farmhouses, but Texel sheep always spend the winter outdoors.

Apart from their extremely fine meat, which has a natural salty taste from the grass they eat, the sheep also provide excellent wool and milk; it is said that the wool has a healing effect on muscle pain and rheumatism. The milk is also used to make cheese and even soap.

of the world above and below the surface of the sea. It covers such subjects as seals, the beach, the effects of tides, the fishing industry, and the Waddenzee. There is also a tank in which visitors can touch tame rays.

Young **seals**, and others recovering from illness and injury, cavort in the **salt water pools** outside; birds contaminated by pollution are also looked after here.

The **Duinpark** (dune park) contains three waymarked walks.

Oudheidkamer

In Den Burg, in Kogerstraat, on a small shady square called Stenenplaats. Open Apr–Oct and during Christmas holidays, Mon–Fri 10am–12.30pm, 1.30pm–3.30pm. 0222 31 31 35.

The "chamber of antiquities" is a former poorhouse, built in 1599; it is now a museum of paintings, costumes and everyday objects recalling local life. There is a tiny herb garden at the back.

Maritiem en Jutters Museum

In Oudeschild, southeast of Den Burg. Open Tue–Sat 10am–5pm, Sun noon–5pm. Jul–Aug, Mon–Sun 10am–5pm. Closed 25 Dec and 1 Jan. 5.50€. 0222 31 49 56. www.texelsmaritiem.nl.
The Maritime and Beachcombing Museum is located in the seaweed sheds around the De Traanroeier windmill. It contains lifeboats, a shipyard and a smithy. One of the sheds is fitted out as a beachcombers' store-room, full of hundreds of often bizarre finds from the beach. The various floors of the 19C grain

warehouses deal with the pilotage and rescue services, and the history of the roadsteads where East India Company ships had to await fair winds so that they could sail into the Zuiderzee; these brought great prosperity to the island in the 17C and 18C. Finally, a room on the ground floor explores the subject of underwater archaeology and the many shipwrecks in the Waddenzee.

Cultuurhistorisch Museum

At De Waal, north of Den Burg. Open Mon 1.30pm–5pm, Tue–Fri 10am–5pm, Sat 10am–4pm, Sun and public holidays 2pm–4pm. Closed after autumn half-term–Easter. 3.50€. 0222 31 29 51. www.cultuurmuseumtexel.nl.
The Agricultural and Cart Museum contains items formerly used on the island. On the top floor is a display showing the development of agriculture on Texel, and regular demonstrations are given in the smithy.

Oosterend

Oosterend is the second-largest of Texel's seven villages. Its green and white houses add to its picturesque beauty. Oosterend has four small churches, including **Maartenskerk**, dating from the 11C. This is the oldest church on the island. The village is a conservation area.

Vlieland

Fryslân – Population 2 000
This island, composed of dunes and woods, covering 5 100ha/12 597 acres is 20km/124.mi long with a maxi-

Cycling in Vlieland

mum width of 2.5km/1.5mi. There is only one small village, Oost-Vlieland. A single surfaced road crosses it from east to west. Only the army, at the western end, and tourists in season come and disturb the peace of this unspoilt countryside. The island is also beautifully quiet, because only the islanders are allowed to use cars.

There is a choice of accommodation on the island (see www.vlieland.nl for details).

Oost-Vlieland

Population 1 150

The earliest mention of Oost-Vlieland in the archives dates from the mid 13C. It was, however, until the 17C that the community began to flourish, mainly because of the island's location on the shipping route to the colonies.

Ferry – *From Harlingen or Terschelling (May–Sept only, 30min). Departure times vary; the ticket office opens one hour before departure time and reservations can be made online (and with a 5% discount). Call Rederij Doeksen recorded on ☎0562 44 20 02. www.rederij-doeksen.nl The ferry boat crossing takes about 1hr 30min, and the express service about 45min. Cars are not allowed on the island.*

VVV (Vlieland) – ☎0562 45 11 11 or www.vlieland.nl.

The village, protected by dykes and surrounded by trees and dunes, has a delightfully relaxed atmosphere and visitors enjoy just being here, taking a stroll between the shops and the places to serving food and drink. The only interruption to the peace and quiet comes from the village disco (☎0562 45 30 43 at Dorpsstraat 81).

In Dorpsstraat, the main street, there are a few old houses. On the south side of the street a house has been converted to create the **Museum Tromp's Huys** (⊙*open Apr and Oct, Tue–Sun 2pm–5pm; May–Sept, Tue–Sun 11am–5pm; Nov–Mar, Wed and Sat 2pm–5pm;* ⊙*closed 1 Easter, Whitsun, 25 Dec and 1 Jan;* ⊚*2.75€;* ☎*0562 45 16 00; www.vlieland.nl*). This is a typical island home, with fine furniture and collections of antiques and paintings, including works by the Norwegian artist Betzy Berg who lived here at the beginning of the 20C.

A small visitor centre, **De Noordwester** (⊙*open Apr–Sept, Mon–Sat 2pm–5pm; Jun, July and Aug, Mon–Sat 10am–noon, 2pm–5pm; Oct–Mar, Wed and Sat–Sun 2pm–5pm;* ⊙*closed 25 Dec and 1 Jan;* ⊚*3€;* &☎*0562 45 17 00; www.denoordwester.nl*), has been fitted out near the church. Photographs provide documentation on the island's flora and fauna; there are also some aquaria and a beachcombers' store-room. The 17C **church** on the other side of the square contains some whale jawbones from the adjoining **churchyard**. This has some interesting tombstones carved with hourglasses, anchors and ships, as well as the graves of soldiers from World War II.

To the left of the church is the beautiful 17C poorhouse or **deacons' house**, used to accommodate orphans, old people, and widows. There were quite a large number of these, despite the island's relatively small population, since the sea claimed many men's lives.

From the top of the **lighthouse** to the west of the village, there is a **view**⋆ over Oost-Vlieland, the dark green woods forming a contrast with the pale colour of the dunes, and the Waddenzee, where at each low tide vast stretches of mud flats appear, covered with flocks of birds.

WORKUM

FRYSLÂN

LOCAL MAP SEE SNEEK

This small town (Warkum in Frisian) was once a prosperous seaport where the eel trade flourished. Now it is a large holiday and water sports centre.
It is well known for its glazed pottery which is brown in colour and often decorated with a frieze of notched white scrolls. Workum still has several interesting houses with crow-stepped or bell-shaped gables (kolkgevel).

- **Information:** Noard 5 – 8711 AA. ☎0515 54 13 00. www.friesland-vvv.net.
- **Orient Yourself:** Workum is reached , from the north, by the A 7 or from the south by the A 50.
- **Parking:** You would be very unlucky not to find somewhere to park.
- **Don't Miss:** The Jople Hulsman museum is the main reason for coming here.
- **Organizing Your Time:** An hour or two will suffice.
- **Also See:** BOLSWARD.

Sights

Stadhuis
The town hall has a tall 18C façade. On the left is the old town hall, a small Renaissance-style building decorated with a carved stone.

St Gertrudiskerk
Open Apr–Oct, Mon–Sat 11am–5pm. ☎0515 54 19 76.
This large Gothic church was built in the 16C and 17C and has an imposing separate **bell-tower** crowned with a tiny onion-shaped dome. Inside the church there is a fine 18C pulpit and nine painted **biers** (*gildebaren*) illustrating the activities of the guilds. They were used during funerals to carry the bodies of guild members to the cemetery. The organ dates from 1697.

Waag
The former weigh-house is a fine 17C building with dormer windows. Inside is **Warkums Erfskip** (Workum's Heritage; *open Apr–Oct, Tue–Sun 1pm–5pm; 2€; ☎0515 54 31 55*), a museum of local history with the accent on shipping and the town's distinctive domestic ceramics.

Jopie Huisman Museum★
Opposite the VVV (tourist information office). Open Apr –Oct, Mon–Sat 10am–
5pm, Sun and public holidays 1pm–5pm. Mar and Nov, daily 1pm–5pm. 4€. ☎0515 54 31 31.
This attractive museum has a collection of paintings and drawings by the self-taught Frisian artist, Jopie Huisman, born in Workum in 1922. His often moving canvases show a warm interest in ordinary people and everyday objects; the impressive precision with which he painted shoes, dolls, household objects and clothes often makes them more tangible than the real objects in the display cases beside the pictures. The museum also includes some fine ink drawings.

Self-portrait, Jopie Huisman

Stichting Jopie Huisman Museum

ZAANSTREEK★

NOORD-HOLLAND

The Zaanstreek or Zaan Region is an area bordering the River Zaan to the north of Amsterdam. The succession of riverside towns were regrouped in 1974 to form the district of **Zaanstad** (population 5 126). This is now an important dormitory town for people working in Amsterdam.

- ▣ **Information:** Gedempte Gracht 76 – 1506 CJ. ☎075 616 22 21. www.zaanseschans.nl.
- ▶ **Orient Yourself:** Zaanstreek lies around 10km/6.2mi or so north of Amsterdam and hugs the shores of the river Zaan.
- ▣ **Parking:** An inexpensive car park provides ample parking for visiting motorists.
- ⊗ **Don't Miss:** The Zaanse Schans, a re-created open-air village.
- ◷ **Organizing Your Time:** Allow two or three hours to relax and explore this fascinating are, not forgetting a trip to see the pewtersmiths at work in the Tinkoepel.

A Bit of History

Originally the inhabitants gained a living from fishing. Then in 1592 Cornelius Corneliszoon built the first wind-powered saw-mill. Many other windmills were subsequently built for industrial purposes (*see Introduction, Industrial heritage*), and it is thought that c. 1760 there were some 600 in operation, making the Zaanstreek one of the first industrial regions in the world.

Saw mills made working the wood considerably easier, and as a result the shipbuilding industry started to flourish.

The shipyard's reputation was such that in 1697 the **Czar Peter the Great** paid a visit incognito to undergo a period of training with a local shipbuilder.

Many of the windmills still exist. These industrial mills are usually very tall as they were built over the workshop. They were used in the manufacture of mustard, paper, oil, paint and tobacco. Another feature typical of the region are the **wooden houses**; houses could not be built of stone because the ground was too soft. Most of these houses have now been reassembled in the Zaanse Schans (⊗*see opposite*).

Industrial windmills, Zaanse Schans

Zaanse Schans★

The museum-village takes its name from fortifications which were built in the late 16C against possible attacks from the Spanish. There is no longer any trace of the redoubt.

This living museum was established in the 1960s and 70s when structures from all parts of Zaanstreek and especially from the town of Zaandam were re-erected here. The buildings have all been restored and arranged to form a replica village where people live and work. The aim of the villagers is to give visitors an impression of the Dutch way of life in earlier centuries.

The village is laid out along a dyke, **Kalverringdijk**, alongside which runs a narrow canal spanned by several little humpbacked bridges. Some of the houses line secondary canals which are themselves followed by paths (such as Zeilenmakerspad). Most of the houses are timber-built and they display an amazing variety of gables. The houses are generally green in colour, or are tarred black, while the gables, window and doors are outlined in white. Each gable is topped out with a small wooden ornament (*makelaar*).

Several of the houses, shops and windmills are open to the public. There are demonstrations of the traditional crafts practised in Holland, and typical local products are on sale. Inevitably this has meant that the picturesque character of the Zaanse Schans has been somewhat overshadowed by commercial enterprise. **Boat trips** (*operate Apr Oct, daily 11am–4pm (every hour on the hour); Jul and Aug, daily 10am–5pm; ⊜5€; children 2.50€; ♿☎065 329 44 67*) on the River Zaan are also organised (*further information from the visitor centre*).

Zaans Museum

🕐*Open daily 9am–5pm, 26 Dec 10am–5pm, 31 Dec 9am–4pm.* 🕐*Closed 25 Dec and 1 Jan.* ⊜*4.50€.* ☎*075 616 28 62.*
This modern museum is devoted to the history of the Zaanstreek. The audio tour starts with a life-size model of the area and takes the visitor past several 'squares', where everyday objects such as clogs, horn-books, ploughs and signs are displayed. Each 'square' has a specific theme (wind, wood, industry, etc.) and films, computers and chat stations have been set up to give visitors more in-depth information. Z-watch on the top floor gives a good view of nearby factories, watercourses and windmills.

Ambachtenschuur

🕐*Open Nov–Feb, daily 8.30am–5pm, Mar–Oct, daily 8am–6pm; 25 Dec and 26 Dec 10am–4pm, 31 Dec 9am–4pm, 1 Jan 11am–4pm.* ☎*075 635 46 22.*
This crafts centre is housed in the old De Lelie warehouse from Westzaan and contains a glassworks and a delftware workshop.

Klompenmakerij

🕐*Open Nov–Feb, daily 8.30am–5pm; Mar–Oct, daily 8am–6pm; 25 Dec and 26 Dec 10am–4pm, 31 Dec 9am–4pm, 1 Jan 11am–4pm.* ♿☎*075 617 71 21. www.woodenshoeworkshop.nl.*
The clog-making workshop, located in the De Vrede warehouse (where grain and tobacco were stored and which dates from 1721), organises demonstrations of this traditional craft.

Scheepswerf

This late 18C barn is the boat-yard, where wooden boats are made and repaired.

Tinkoepel

Small pavilions like these, usually erected at the bottom of the garden, were used as a place in which to have tea. Today it houses a **pewter workshop** (🕐*open Nov–Mar, daily 11am–4pm; Apr–Oct, daily 10am–5pm; 26 and 31 Dec 10am–5pm;1 Jan noon–5pm;* 🕐*closed 25 Dec;* ☎*075 617 62 04; www.tinkoepel.nl*).

Museum van het Nederlandse Uurwerk

🕐 *Open Nov–Mar, Sat–Sun noon–4.30pm; Apr–Oct, Tue–Sun 10am–5pm, 26 Dec noon–4.30pm.* 🕐*Closed 25, 31 Dec and 1 Jan.* ⊜*4€.* ☎*075 617 97 69.*
The clock museum, housed in a 17C weaver's house, has a varied collection of timepieces made in the Netherlands between 1500 and 1850.

Museumwinkel Albert Heijn

🕐*Open Nov–Mar, Sat–Sun noon–4pm, Apr–Oct, Tue–Sun 10.30am–1pm, 1.30pm–4pm.* *No charge* ☎*075 659 28 08.*

This delightful old shop is a reconstruction of the very first **Albert Heijn** shop (today a large supermarket chain), which opened in Oostzaan in 1887, and sells old-fashioned items such as sugar candy, peppermint and liquorice.

De Hoop op d'Swarte Walvis

This reconstructed 18C orphanage from Westzaan is now a famous restaurant.

Het Noorderhuis

🕐*Open Mar–Oct, Tue–Sun 10am–5pm. Jul and Aug, daily 10am–5pm; Nov–Feb, Sat–Sun and public holidays 10am–5pm.* 🕐*Closed 25 Dec and 1 Jan.* ☎*075 617 32 37.*

The reception room of this merchant's house (1670) is open to the public, along with another room containing costumed figures and old dolls.

Mosterdmolen De Huisman

This octagonal smock windmill (1786) is used for making the much-sought-after local coarse-grain mustard.

Bakkerijmuseum In de Gecroonde Duyvekater

🕐*Open Nov–Feb, Sat–Sun 11am–5pm, Mar–Oct, Tue–Sun 10am–5pm, Jul–Aug, daily 10am–5pm; Christmas, 31 Dec and 1 Jan 11am–4pm.* ☎*075 617 35 22.*

This 17C house is named after a local speciality, *duivelskater*, a sweet loaf of bread. Note the marbled floor.

Weidemolen De Hadel

This small smock windmill stands at the far end of the Zeilenmakerspad (sailmakers' path).

Het Jagershuis

This merchant's house dating from 1623 is the oldest building in the Zaanse Schans. Today it is an antiques shop.

Kaasboerderij Catharina Hoeve

🕐*Open Nov–Feb, daily 8.30am–5pm; Mar–Oct, daily 8am–6pm, 25 Dec 8.30am–3pm, 26 Dec 8.30am–5pm, 1 Jan 9.30am–5pm.* ☎*075 621 58 20.*

Cheese is made in the traditional manner in this dairy, a 1988 replica of a farmhouse from the east of the Zaanstreek.

Houtzaagmolen De Gekroonde Poelenburg

This postmill used for sawing wood dates from 1869; it is built above the big workshop which turns with the mill when the sails are oriented to face the wind.

Verfmolen De Kat

🕐*Open Apr–Oct, daily 9am–5pm; Nov–Mar, Sat–Sun 9am–5pm.* *2.50€.* ☎*075 621 04 77, www.zaansemolen.nl.*

This mill, called The Cat, was used for grinding raw materials such as tropical woods into pigments for paints. In the 17C, there were 55 of these mills in the Zaanstreek.

Oliemolen De Zoeker

🕐*Open Mar–Sept, daily 9.30am–4.30pm.* *2.50€.* ☎*075 628 79 42. www.zaansemolen.nl.*

In this mill which dates from 1610, salad oil is made by grinding many types of seeds.

Oliemolen De Bonte Hen

This oil mill has been here since 1693.

Oliemolen De Ooievaar

This oil mill, to the south of the Zaanse Schans, is called The Stork.

Additional Sights

Zaandijk

The town of Zaandijk, on the opposite bank of the Zaan and forming part of the Zaanstad conurbation, has a local museum of antiquities, the **Honig Breet Huis** (🕐*open Tue–Sun 1pm–5pm;* 🕐*closed Easter, Whitsun, 25 Dec and 1 Jan;* *3€;* ☎*075 621 76 26*). The museum is housed in the brick-built home of a wealthy 18C merchant. The inside is lavishly decorated with woodcarvings, murals and tiled chimney pieces. The museum also has a fine collection of furniture and porcelain. The Zaankamer, a

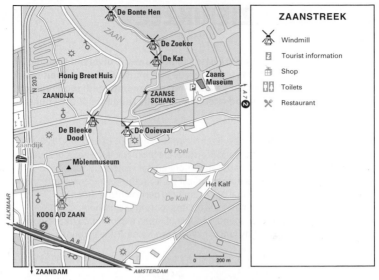

room added in the 19C, affords a lovely view over the River Zaan.

To the south is a 17C flour mill called **De Bleeke Dood** (Pale Death).

Koog aan de Zaan

In this small town there is an interesting Windmill Museum, the **Molenmuseum** (open Jun–Sept, Mon 1pm–5pm, Tue–Fri, 11am–5pm, Sat–Sun and public holidays 1pm–5pm; Oct–May, Tue–Fri, 10am–noon, 1pm–5pm Sat, 2pm–5pm, Sun and public holidays 1pm–5pm; 3€; 075 628 89 68). It is located in an attractive park, and shows different types of **scale models**★, ladders, tools, documents and engravings of the 17C to 19C.

ZIERIKZEE ★

ZEELAND

Zierikzee is the main town on the island of **Schouwen-Duiveland** (population 33 591) and in the past it was a prosperous port on the Gouwe, a strait which separated Schouwen from Duiveland. The town maintained good relations with the Hanseatic League and later it became the residence of the Counts of Holland and Zeeland.

- **Information:** VVV-kantoor Zierikzee Nieuw Haven 7 4301 DJ. ☎0900 20 20 233.
- ▶ **Orient Yourself:** Meelstraat and Poststraat are the roads at the heart of Zierikzee, and the area where most of the attractions are for visitors.
- **Parking:** Zierikzee has a number of car parks in the town centre and on the outskirts, plus the occasional opportunity to park off-street free.
- **Don't Miss:** The old ships that still occupy spots in the harbour.
- **Organizing Your Time:** Spend a couple of hours exploring Zierikzee, and be sure to make time to enjoy lunch in one of the harbourside eateries.

A Bit of History

The town is particularly remembered for an episode in its history when in 1576 the Spanish waded in water up to their shoulders across the Zijpe, separating Schouwen-Duiveland from the mainland, before taking the town. Decline set in from the 16C; however the town has been able to preserve its heritage of 16C to 18C houses.

Schouwen-Duiveland is linked to Goeree Overflakkee in the north by the Brouwersdam and the Grevelingendam, and to Noord-Beveland in the south by the Oosterschelde storm barrier and the Zeelandbrug (⏚ see DELTA).

When, in the early 1950s, Zierikzee was damaged by major flooding, the English town of Hatfield sent help and this was the beginning of a friendship that accounts for the twinning of the two towns.

Boat trips

Operate Jul and Aug, Mon–Thu. Information: Rederij Gebhard, ☎010 265 02 96. Zierikzee Harbour is the departure point for boat trips on the Oosterschelde.

Sights

Noordhavenpoort★

This double gateway presents two 16C Renaissance gables on the town side and an older crow-stepped gable on the outside.

The **Zuidhavenpoort** takes the form of a square tower with four 14C corner turrets and is linked to the previous gateway by a lever bridge.

Oude Haven

Rows of elegant 17C and 18C houses line the quaysides of the old harbour. There are still some old ships to be seen.

Havenpark

On the north side of this square the house called **De Witte Swaen** dating from 1658 has a lovely Baroque gable. The house itself was rebuilt after the 1953 floods.

Adjoining the Gasthuiskerk is a former market, the **Beurs**, consisting of a Renaissance-style arcaded gallery with Tuscan columns.

's-Gravensteen

This onetime prison has a 1524 crow-stepped gable with ornamental wrought-iron grilles on the first floor windows. It is now home to the **Maritiem Museum**

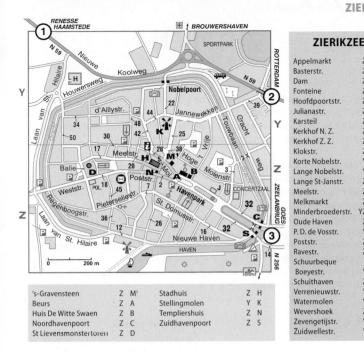

(⊙ *open Apr–Oct and during school holidays, Mon–Sat 10am–5pm, Sun and public holidays noon–5pm;* ⊙ *closed 25 Dec and 1 Jan;* ⊚*2€;* ☎*0111 45 44 64; www.museaschouwenduiveland.nl*).

Stadhuis

The town hall was formerly the meat market. The outstanding feature of the building, which has been altered several times, is the unusual wooden **tower** topped with an ornamental onion-shaped dome (1550) surmounted by a statue of Neptune. The tower has a **carillon**. Two decorative gables provide further ornamentation to the façade. The decorative pieces of wrought iron were for holding lighted torches.

The **Stadhuismuseum** (⊙ *open May–Oct, Mon–Sat 10am–5pm, Sun noon–5pm;* ⊙ *closed public holidays;* ☎*0111 45 44 64; www.museaschouwenduiveland.nl*) inside is a local history museum. Most of the exhibits are displayed in the Harquebusiers' Hall with its fine timber ceiling.

Across from the stadhuis the 14C Huis De Haene, often called the **Tempelier-shuis**, is the oldest building in town. The influence of Bruges (Belgium) architecture can be seen in the ogee-shaped mouldings of the windows.

St Lievensmonstertoren

Information from VVV ☎*0111 41 24 50.*
This is the clock tower of the old Gothic cathedral, which was destroyed by fire in 1832. Building work on the tower started in 1454 and was supervised by a member of the Keldermans family, who were also responsible for Middelburg town hall. The tower rises to a height of 56m/184ft, but it remains unfinished. Next door is a large Neoclassical church (1848) with a portico.

Nobelpoort

The outside of this 14C square town gate is flanked by two tall towers, both later additions, topped by tall tapering pepperpot roofs.
Further on is a tall 19C **tower mill** called De Hoop (Hope).

ZUTPHEN★

GELDERLAND

POPULATION 36 500

Zutphen lies at the confluence of the IJssel, Berkel and Twentekanaal, not far from the heathlands of Veluwe. This pleasant historic city is the capital of the beautiful wooded region **Achterhoek** (𝓒see below). It is an important commercial centre and its pedestrian precincts come alive on market days.

🛈 **Information:** Stationsplein 39 – 7201 MH. ☎0900 269 28 88. www.achterhoektoerisme.nl.

▶ **Orient Yourself:** Gravenhof square is the best place to orient yourself and from here it's an easy walk to see all the main sights of Zutphen.

🅿 **Parking:** Inexpensive car parking is provided on the periphery of the town centre and around the waterside areas.

⊗ **Don't Miss:** The art collection at the Museum Henriette Polak: it's impressive.

🕐 **Organizing Your Time:** The old town can be explored in about three hours.

🕐 **Also See:** Bronkhorst, a pretty town a short distance from Zutphen and the smallest in the Netherlands.

A Bit of History

In the 14C the town belonged to the Hanseatic League and built an enclosing wall which was extended the following century. Zutphen was then recognised as an important strategic point due to its easily defendable position in the surrounding marshland (the name Zutphen, sometimes spelt Zutfen, comes from Zuidveen, the southern peat bog). Zutphen became one of the richest towns in Gelderland and in the 16C it was given a second town wall of which several sections still remain.

The town was captured by the Spanish in 1572 and only retaken by Maurice of Nassau in 1591. In 1586 the English poet Sir Philip Sidney died of wounds received in an action to prevent the Spaniards from sending supplies into the town. The French occupied Zutphen from 1672 to 1674 and recaptured it again in 1795.

Old Town★

's-Gravenhof

Both St Walburgskerk and stadhuis are to be found in this square. During excavations on the site in 1946 remains of the Counts of Zutphen's castle were uncovered and today the outline of the castle is marked out on the surface of the square.

St Walburgskerk

🕐*Open May–Sept, Mon–Fri.* ☎*0575 51 41 78.* www.walburgiskerk.nl (*in Dutch*). This early 13C Romanesque church, dedicated to St Walburga, was given successive extensions in Gothic style up to the 16C. The church was damaged in 1945 and lost the upper storey of its tower three years later. The original tufa facing of the tower has been repaired with limestone. On the north side the 15C **Mariaportaal** has been recently restored. **Inside** the vaulting is covered with 14C and 15C frescoes. The chancel has an extremely elaborate 15C ironwork **chandelier**★. The plainer pulpit is 17C, like the organ case with its rich ornamentation. The **baptismal font** is a triumphant piece of copperwork cast in Mechelen, Belgium, in 1527. It is decorated with the figures of the evangelists and saints with a pelican at the summit. The **library**★ dates from 1564 when it was built onto the ambulatory. The original appearance of the interior remains unchanged with low pointed vaulting and supporting columns. The ribs descend to sculpted consoles, and below in place of capitals are numerous small figures. The library houses around 750 titles, including eight manuscripts and 80 incunabula. About 100 books are displayed on wooden stands: illuminated missals, anthologies of texts written by

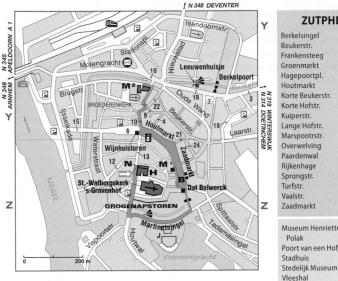

St Thomas Aquinas and Luther. It is one of the few libraries in Europe which has retained its original appearance and furnishings.

Stadhuis

This 15C town hall was considerably altered in 1716 and again in 1729. It adjoins the former **Vleeshal**, or meat hall. Inside, the great hall (*Burgerzaal*), has a lovely wooden ceiling.

▸ *Walk south along Lange Hofstraat.*

Martinetsinge

From here there is an attractive **view**★ of the town wall – with gardens sloping down to the green waters of the canal – and of the pointed towers of the Drogenapstoren away to the right and St Walburgskerk with its truncated tower in the background.

Drogenapstoren★

This splendid gateway dates from 1444–46. The change from square to octagonal is marked by crenellations and four octagonal turrets with pointed roofs. The tower itself is crowned by an even taller pointed roof.

Dat Bolwerck

This attractive Gothic house (1549) is surmounted by pinnacles.

Next door are the 1639 cavalry barracks, **Ruiter Kortegaard**, with an attractive scrolled gable.

Zaadmarkt

This was the site of the grain market, and is now a general market. On the right at n° 101 is the doorway of an **almshouse** dating from 1723.

Museum Henriette Polak

◷*Open Tue–Sun 11am–5pm.* ◯*Closed public holidays.* ◉*2.50€.* ☎*0575 51 68 78.*

The impressive **De Wildeman** mansion was altered in the 19C and today houses an interesting collection of paintings, sculptures and graphic arts by contemporary Dutch artists.

The secret chapel (1628) on the second floor was a refuge for Catholics.

Houtmarkt

The lovely 17C Renaissance tower, the **Wijndragerstoren**, stands on the site of the former timber market. It was made by the Hemony brothers. A market is held here every Thursday.

Stedelijk Museum

◷ *Open Tue–Fri 11am–5pm.* ☎ *0575 51 68 78. www.stedelijkmuseumzutphen paktuit.nl (in Dutch).*

The former Dominican convent is now the home of the municipal museum. The exhibits include sections featuring clocks and watches, glasswork, silver **Hannema-de Stuers Fundatie** work, as well as some paintings and medieval artefacts. There is also a local collection with costumes from between 1780 and 1950.

Additional Sight

Berkelpoort

This 14C brick-built water-gate spans the Berkel with three arches. The entrances are flanked by watch turrets. There is a good **view** of the gateway from the footbridge to the west.

Excursions

59km/36.6mi southeast by the Doetinchem road.

Known as the **Achterhoek**, the region from Zutphen to the German border is an area of woodland and pastures criss-crossed by quiet country roads and forest rides.

Bronkhorst

Bronkhorst is the smallest town in the Netherlands. At the intersection of the two main streets stand a 14C chapel, two taverns and an old Saxon farm.

Vorden

This town has two 19C **tower mills**. Vorden lies at the heart of a region where **eight castles** nestle in the surrounding woodlands: Vorden, Hackfort, Kiefskamp, Wildenborch, Bramel, Onstein, Medler and Wiersse. The nobility, attracted by the good hunting provided by the local forests, elected to build suitable residences locally. Some can only be reached on foot or by bicycle (*paths are signposted "opengesteld"*). The most impressive castle is **Kasteel Hackfort**, flanked by two great round towers.

Groenlo

The historic town of Groenlo stands on the banks of the Slinge and is still encircled by sections of its town walls. The town is famous for its beer, Grolsch, meaning "of Groenlo". The small **Brouwerij De Klok** (○*open Mon–Fri 9am–12.30pm, 1.30pm–5pm, Sat 9am–12.30pm, 1.30pm–4pm;* ○*closed public holidays;* ☎*0544 46 48 60; www.langegang.nl*) occupies a farmhouse dating from 1623.

Winterswijk

This town is also on the Slinge and is surrounded by tranquil forested areas dotted with impressive farmhouses.

©GOHV/Bigstockphoto.com

A farmhouse in Winterswijk

ZWOLLE

OVERIJSSEL P
POPULATION 114 554
PLAN OF THE CONURBATION IN THE CURRENT RED-COVER MICHELIN GUIDE BENELUX

Zwolle, capital of the province of Overijssel, has kept its special character in the historic centre within the ring of canals.

- **Information:** Grote Kerkplein 14 – 8011 PK. ☎0900 112 23 75. www.vvv-zwolle.nl.
- **Orient Yourself:** The Grote Kerkplein and Blijmarkt area is a good place to begin exploring Zwolle; it is central and contains most of the visitor attractions.
- **Parking:** Car parks are plentiful on either side of the waterway that encircles Zwolle.
- **Don't Miss:** Stedelijk Museum Zwolle; it's like stepping back in time as you wander around rooms presented in a bygone fashion.
- **Organizing Your Time:** Zwolle can be explored in just a few hours as it is compact, but it offers some rather fine restaurants so be sure to stay for a bite.
- **Also See:** Kasteel Het Nijenhuis, a medieval manor house around 15km/9.3mi from Zwolle, and home to an outstanding art collection.

A Bit of History

Zwolle was a member of the Hanseatic League in the 13C (*see IJSSELMEER*), and linked to the Zuiderzee by the Zwarte Water. After the Spaniards left in 1572, its 15C curtain wall was considerably strengthened but little remains, apart from the Sassenpoort in the south and, in the north, part of the late-medieval town wall. Today the ditches still surround the town and the pleasant gardens on the south and east sides mark the course of the ramparts and bastions.

Thomas à Kempis (1379/80–1471), who was a pupil at the School of the Brethren of the Common Life in Deventer and to whom is attributed the Imitatio Christi (The Imitation of Christ), entered the monastery of the order of Augustine monks near Zwolle, where he remained until his death.

Gerard Terborch (1617–81) was born in Zwolle. This painter, like his contemporary Gerrit Dou, is above all the meticulous painter of refined and peaceful interior scenes and excellent portraits and miniatures of the local notables.

Sights

Stedelijk Museum Zwolle★

Open Tue–Sat, 10am–5pm, Sun 1pm–5pm. Closed Easter Day, Whitsun, 25 Dec and 1 Jan. 4€. ☎038 421 46 50.
The municipal museum is located in an elegant 16C mansion, the Drostenhuis, and a new wing. The historic **Drostenhuis★★** contains a display of items relating to the town's rich past, including a number of splendid period rooms with

---

One of the town's specialities are **Zwolse balletjes**, sweets shaped like a small cushion with different flavours. One of the places you can buy them is the Zwolse Balletjeshuis opposite the VVV tourist office. Another of Zwolle's specialities is **blauwvingers**. If you want to find out how these shortbread biscuits, shaped like fingers and dipped in chocolate, got their name, then go to Banketbakkerij Van Orsouw, the bakery on *Grote Markt 6*, where the legend of these biscuits comes free of charge with your purchase.

Stedelijk Museum Zwolle – The kitchen of the Drostenhuis

Lescourret/ EXPLORER-HOA QUI

a fine collection of silverware from the Overijssel province and paintings by local artist Gerard Terborch. The new wing, devoted to contemporary art and cultural history, is used for temporary exhibitions.

Grote Kerk or St Michaëlskerk

🕐*Open Jul–Sept, Tue–Fri 11am–4.30pm, Sat 1.30pm–4.30pm.* ☎038 453 59 13.
St Michael's is a hall-church with three naves, dating from 1406–1446. Unlike the neighbouring church of Our Lady, with its distinctive tower usually referred to as the "**pepper mill**", it no longer has the traditional bell-tower, which did not survive the many disasters that befell the town. In 1690 an octagonal **vestry** was built on the site where the tower once stood. Inside, note a remarkable early 17C carved pulpit and an organ loft of 1721 comprising a splendid **organ**★ with 4 000 pipes, built by the Schnitger brothers. Attached to the left side of the fine 16C north portal there is a picturesque little building, the **Hoofdwacht** or guard room, dating from 1614 with a decorated pediment.

Stadhuis

🕐*Open Mon–Fri 9am–3pm.* 🎫*No charge.* ☎038 498 91 11.
Beside the old town hall (15C and 19C) which had become too small, a new one was built in 1976 by the architect JJ Konijnenburg. The old part on the left, covered with mustard-yellow roughcast, contains the **Aldermen's Hall** (*Schepen-zaal*) dating from 1448. This old courtroom has a ceiling whose beams are held by 14 corbels with **sculptures**★ depicting grotesque figures. Note the executioner's swords and the picture of the *Last Judgement*, a reminder of the room's original use.

Sassenpoort ★

Built in 1409, the Saxon Gateway is the only one which still exists from the fortified town wall. It has a machicolation and four octagonal corner towers. The pointed roofs were added in the 19C. The building was for a long time used as a prison, and now houses a **visitor centre** (🕐*open Wed–Fri 2pm–5pm, Sat–Sun noon–5pm;* ☎038 421 66 26) providing information about the history of the town.

Museum De Stadshof★

This museum of naïve and "outsider" art is an international collection of paintings, drawings and sculptures by people from outside traditional artistic circles. The pieces, such as Hans Langner's *Requiem for my Innocence,* are often highly imaginative and moving. In addition to the permanent collection, temporary exhibitions are also held.

Ecodrome

Willemsvaart 19, on the southern edge of Zwolle. 🕐*Open Apr–Oct and school holidays, daily 10am–5pm.* 🎫*9.95€; children 8.50€.* ☎*038 421 50 50. www.ecodrome.nl.*

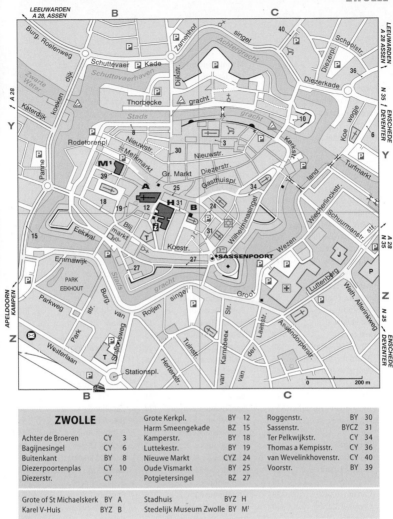

ZWOLLE			Grote Kerkpl.	BY	12	Roggenstr.		BY	30
			Harm Smeengekade	BZ	15	Sassenstr.		BYCZ	31
Achter de Broeren	CY	3	Kamperstr.	BY	18	Ter Pelkwijkstr.		CY	34
Bagijnesingel	CY	6	Luttekestr.	BY	19	Thomas a Kempisstr.		CY	36
Buitenkant	BY	8	Nieuwe Markt	CYZ	24	van Wevelinkhovenstr.		CY	40
Diezerpoortenplas	CY	10	Oude Vismarkt	BY	25	Voorstr.		BY	39
Diezerstr.	CY		Potgietersingel	BZ	27				

Grote of St Michaelskerk	BY	A	Stadhuis	BYZ	H
Karel V-Huis	BYZ	B	Stedelijk Museum Zwolle	BY	M¹

This theme park combines enjoyable displays on natural history, geology and the environment. The natural history museum contains skeletons of animals from the Ice Age and a colourful collection of birds, while the **Ecodrome pavilion** takes visitors through the story of the Earth's evolution. There are also plenty of attractions for children in the grounds.

Excursions

Kasteel Het Nijenhuis★
15km/9.3mi southeast of Zwolle. Take the **Heino** *turn-off, towards Wijhe.*

This medieval manor house is home to the international art collection of the foundation **Hannema-de Stuers Fundatie** (⏱ *open Tue–Fri 10am–5pm, Sat–Sun, 11am–5pm;* ⏱ *closed 25 Dec and 1 Jan;* ⊘ *3€; no charge for entry to garden and park.* ☎ *05/2 39 14 34; www. museumdefundatie.nl*). The house itself contains the collection of mainly 17C and 18C French and Italian art. The coach houses have been converted into exhibition space for a collection of 20C art. The park has been turned into a sculpture garden.

A

INDEX

INDEX

INDEX

INDEX

MAPS AND PLANS

LIST OF MAPS

THEMATIC MAPS

PLANS OF DISTRICTS

PLANS OF SITES AND MUSEUMS

LOCAL MAPS

COMPANION PUBLICATIONS

PLAN OF AMSTERDAM NO 36 AND SPIRAL-BOUND ATLAS OF AMSTERDAM NO 2036:

- a complete street map of the city (1cm = 150m) with all major thoroughfares, one-way streets, large car parks, major public buildings, cycle lanes, etc.
- a street index
- practical information

MAP OF THE NETHERLANDS NO 715

- 1:400 000 scale map:
- detailed information about the road network, intersections, border crossings, etc.
- indication of distances
- list of place names
- enlarged map of Amsterdam and Rotterdam

MAP OF THE NORTHERN NETHERLANDS NO 531

- 1:200 000 scale map:
- detailed information about the road network, intersections, border crossings, etc.
- indication of distances
- list of place names
- enlarged map of Amsterdam

MAP OF THE SOUTHERN NETHERLANDS NO 532

- 1:200 000 scale map:
- detailed information about the road network, intersections, border crossings, etc.
- indication of distances
- list of place names
- enlarged map of The Hague and Rotterdam

Special symbols

Landing stage

Outstanding frontage

Park and Ride

Abbreviations

G   Police station (Marechaussee)

H   Town Hall (Stadhuis)

J   Law courts (Gerechtshof)

M   Museum (Museum)

P   Provincial capital
(Hoofdplaats provincie)

P   Provincial council
(Provinciehuis)

POL.   Police (Politie)

T   Theatre (Schouwburg)

U   University (Universiteit)

Sports and recreation

Racecourse

Skating rink

Outdoor, indoor swimming pool

Multiplex Cinema

Marina, sailing centre

Trail refuge hut

Cable cars, gondolas

Funicular, rack railway

Tourist train

Recreation area, park

Theme, amusement park

Wildlife park, zoo

Gardens, park, arboretum

Bird sanctuary, aviary

Walking tour, footpath

Of special interest
to children

LEGEND

	Sight	Seaside resort	Winter sports resort	Spa
Highly recommended ★★★		≗≗≗	✳✳✳	⚑⚑⚑
Recommended ★★		≗≗	✳✳	⚑⚑
Interesting ★		≗	✳	⚑

Additional symbols

🛈	Tourist information
══ ══	Motorway or other primary route
❶ ❶	Junction: complete, limited
⊏⊐ ══	Pedestrian street
⊥≡≡≡⊥	Unsuitable for traffic, street subject to restrictions
⊥⊥⊥ ‒ ‒	Steps – Footpath
🚂 🚆	Train station – Auto-train station
🚌 🚌	Coach (bus) station
‒‒•‒‒	Tram
Ⓜ	Metro, underground
Ⓟ	Park-and-Ride
♿	Access for the disabled
✉	Post office
☏	Telephone
✉	Covered market
⚔	Barracks
△	Drawbridge
↻	Quarry
⚒	Mine
Ⓑ Ⓕ	Car ferry (river or lake)
🚢	Ferry service: cars and passengers
⛴	Foot passengers only
③	Access route number common to Michelin maps and town plans
Bert (R.)...	Main shopping street
AZ B	Map co-ordinates

Selected monuments and sights

⊙━━▭	Tour - Departure point
⛪ ✝	Catholic church
⛪ ✝	Protestant church, other temple
✡ ☪	Synagogue - Mosque
⌂	Building
■	Statue, small building
✝	Calvary, wayside cross
◎	Fountain
●━━◆	Rampart - Tower - Gate
⋈	Château, castle, historic house
⁖	Ruins
◡	Dam
✿	Factory, power plant
☆	Fort
∩	Cave
▣	Troglodyte dwelling
⊓	Prehistoric site
▼	Viewing table
�	Viewpoint
▲	Other place of interest

445

For the best little places, follow the leader.

MICHELIN

Great Britain & Ireland

lain Cities of Europe

Looking for the latest news on today's best hotels and restaurants? Pick up the Michelin Guide and look for the Bib Gourmand and Bib Hotel symbols. With 45,000 addresses in Europe, in every category and price range, the perfect place to dine or stay is never far away.

MICHELIN

A better way forward